Digital Trademarks and Brands

Digital Trademarks and Brands

Towards an Improved UDRP and Platform Policies

Raj Sachdev

Wolters Kluwer

Published by:
Kluwer Law International B.V.
PO Box 316
2400 AH Alphen aan den Rijn
The Netherlands
E-mail: lrs-sales@wolterskluwer.com
Website: www.wolterskluwer.com/en/solutions/kluwerlawinternational

Sold and distributed by:
Wolters Kluwer Legal & Regulatory U.S.
920 Links Avenue
Landisville, PA 17538
United States of America
E-mail: customer.service@wolterskluwer.com

ISBN 978-94-035-4169-3

e-Book: ISBN 978-94-035-4179-2
web-PDF: ISBN 978-94-035-4189-1

About the Author

Dr Raj Sachdev, MSc (Oxford), LLM, LLM(IP), MBA, DBA, PhD, PCM, CIPP/US, is an interdisciplinary scholar-practitioner, licensed attorney (California, USA), licensed solicitor (England/Wales), comparative researcher (Maastricht University Law), assistant facilitator (Cornell Law), associate professor (USNH-PSU), speaker (TEDx, AMA, major universities, and industry conferences/events), and consultant. He is the author of a leading textbook on Digital Marketing (McGraw-Hill) and the forthcoming author of Digital Marketing Law and Regulation: US, UK and EU (Edward Elgar). A graduate of Oxford University, he is a former visiting researcher at UC Berkeley, instructor at Stanford CSP, and lecturer at Oxford University. He has substantial professional experience, teaching and research and holds several degrees and certifications spanning law, business, and technology.

Table of Contents

List of Abbreviations

ACPA	Anti-cybersquatting Protection Act
ADR	Alternative Dispute Resolution
BCIP	Benelux Convention on Intellectual Property
ccTLD	Country Code Top-Level Domain
CJ	Court of Justice
CJEU	Court of Justice of the European Union
DMCA	Digital Millennium Copyright Act
DSA	Digital Services Act
ECHR	European Convention on Human Rights
EU	European Union
EUIPO	European Union Intellectual Property Office
EULA	End User License Agreement
EUTM	European Union Trademark
EUTMR	Regulation (EU) 2017/1001 of the European Parliament and of the Council of 14 June 2017 on the European Union Trademark
FAQs	Frequently Asked Questions
FTC	Federal Trade Commission
FTDA	Federal Trademark Dilution Act
GC	General Court
GNSO	Generic Names Supporting Organization
gTLD	Generic Top-Level Domain
IANA	Internet Assigned Numbers Authority
ICA	Internet Commerce Association
ICANN	Internet Corporation for Assigned Names and Numbers
IP	Intellectual Property
MPT	Meta Platforms Technologies

NFTs	Non-fungible Tokens
ODR	Online Dispute Resolution
RDNH	Reverse Domain Name Hijacking
TDRA	Trademark Dilution Revision Act
TMEP	Trademark Manual of Examining Procedure
TRIPS	Trade-Related Aspects of Intellectual Property Rights
TTAB	Trademark Trial and Appeal Board
UDNDRP	Uniform Domain Name Dispute Resolution Policy
UDRP	Uniform Dispute Resolution Policy
UEFN	Unreal Editor for Fortnite
UEMTDRP	Uniform E-Commerce Marketplace Trademark Dispute Resolution Policy
UGC	User Generated Content
UK	United Kingdom
UMATDRP	Uniform Mobile App Trademark Dispute Resolution Policy
UMTDRP	Uniform Metaverse Trademark Dispute Resolution Policy
URL	Uniform Resource Locator
URS	Uniform Rapid Suspension
US	United States
USATDRP	Uniform Search Ad Trademark Dispute Resolution Policy
USMTDRP	Uniform Social Media Trademark Dispute Resolution Policy
USMUDRP	Uniform Social Media Username Dispute Resolution Procedure
USPTO	United States Patent and Trademark Office
USRP	Uniform Social Media Intellectual Property Dispute Resolution Policy
USTLD	United States Top-Level Domain
VeRO	Verified Rights Owner
WIPO	World Intellectual Property Organization

Preface

The utilisation of digital trademarks (marks utilised on the Internet) in various platforms, including e-commerce marketplaces, search advertising, social media, mobile applications, and Metaverse platforms, is now not only commonplace but abundant. However, these raise several problems. This book analyses and makes recommendations for the UDRP and platform trademark policies. It introduces the Digital Trademark and Trade Practices Model, an adapted model developed from the problems identified for digital trademarks. It is informed by pertinent theories and concepts, select aspects of the EU and US and other legal frameworks, as well as existing policies, and forms the basis of the recommendations made. Ultimately, a uniform policy is recommended for each platform in line with a working approach, the UDRP, adapted based on the elements of the model and applied to platforms in a way that provides a comprehensive workable solution, fostering legal certainty. It provides the actual text for the proposed adapted UDRP as well as the uniform policies recommended for each type of platform and guidance for implementation. It is hoped that relevant bodies will take and implement recommendations for the UDRP and that platforms will implement proposed trademark policies. Beyond the specific platforms considered, other platforms and websites may model their trademark policies in line with the recommendations provided.

Acknowledgements

I am indebted to Maastricht University for allowing me the opportunity to pursue the underlying research for this book and to Kluwer International for publishing it. I would like to wholeheartedly thank the renowned Prof. Dr Anselm Kamperman Sanders for his great guidance and continued support of my research efforts, which have greatly informed this work and helped shape the trajectory of its contents. I also thank Dr Kalpana Tyagi for all her insightful suggestions, feedback, review of drafts, and the invitation to speak at the COMIPinDigiMarkets conference. Further, I thank Dr Anke Moerland for her comments on earlier drafts. Additionally, I thank committee assessors, Prof. Dr Dick van Engelen, Prof. Dr Meir Pugatch, Dr Peter Teunissen, and Dr Rogier de Vrey for their insights and comments. Moreover, I thank Prof. Lionel Bently for the opportunity to guest speak at CIPIL at the University of Cambridge Faculty of Law and Prof. Pamela Samuelson for the opportunity to conduct visiting research at Berkeley Law. I further thank intellectual property scholars, Prof. Eric Goldman, Prof. Lisa Ramsey, Prof. Jake Linford, Prof. Peter Karol, Prof. Rebecca Tushnet, and many others for great conversations at WIPIP and beyond. Additonally, I thank the project coordinators of the WIPO UDRP Review Team for their kind time in discussing my recommendations for the UDRP. I am indebted for having had the opportunity to interact with prominent, globally renowned academics, practitioners, and leaders throughout this journey. Any inadvertence is my own and opinions may not reflect those mentioned.

CHAPTER 1
Introduction

Trademarks are utilised in an increasing number of digital contexts. However, digital trademarks raise new issues not contemplated and often not or not adequately addressed by legal frameworks or platforms. If these are not addressed, the problems will only get worse as technology and innovation will continue at rates never seen before. Attempts at resolving these problems are not only far and few between, but do not adequately address the issues. Further, extensive costs, time, and litigation will continue to be expended to deal with the problem of trademarks in e-commerce marketplace, search advertising, social media, mobile app, and Metaverse platforms and as a matter of importance to brands, small businesses, sellers, consumers, and users alike, these should be reduced. Therefore, it is imperative to update the longstanding Uniform Dispute Resolution Policy (UDRP) and platform trademark policies based on the problems that digital trademarks raise using an adapted model that can be applied in the digital context.

1.1 INTRODUCTION

It has been said that 'the internet has done no more than to throw up existing, sometimes familiar, issues in a different guise'.[1] However, as Friedman says, 'it must be totally obvious to everybody how much a change in technology changes our world'.[2] 'And what changes our world, changes our law'.[3] Further, Landau noted that

1. James Mellor et al. (eds), *Kerley's Law of Trademarks and Trade Names* (15th edn, Sweet and Maxwell 2011) 858.
2. Lawrence M Friedman, 'The Eye That Never Sleeps: Privacy and Law in the Internet Era Legal Scholarship Symposium: The Scholarship of Lawrence M. Friedman' (2005) 40 Tulsa Law Review 561 https://digitalcommons.law.utulsa.edu/cgi/viewcontent.cgi?article=2488&context=tlr accessed 4 August 2025.
3. *Ibid.*

'[t]he internet was very, very different'[4] in the 1990s, and further that 'it is very, very different today'.[5] An evolving Internet will be a continuous theme as technical innovation changes the world.[6] Also, 'rapid expansion and commercialization of the Internet left courts facing novel legal disputes without the common law precedents that typically guide them'.[7] In fact, as Dinwoodie and Janis recognise, 'the rise of online commerce and media has highlighted the importance of branding to an extent not before seen in our lifetimes'.[8] However, the courts have applied 'offline precedent to Internet cases'[9] and 'these quick-fix doctrines were ill-advised at the time of their creation and soon became obsolete'.[10] As Reid, Tu and Port say, there is no doubt that '[t]rademark law encounters problems in cyberspace'[11] and this has been echoed by the courts. For example, a court indicated that it 'must be acutely aware of excessive rigidity when applying the law in the Internet context; emerging technologies require a flexible approach'.[12] In 1999, a judge commented, '[e]ntering the new millennium, our society is far more mobile than it was four decades ago'.[13] Fast forward to today, almost two and a half decades later, 'over half our time spent online is spent on mobile phones'.[14]

4. Michael Landau, 'Intermediary Liability in the Fourth Industrial Revolution', in Christopher Heath, Kamperman Sanders and Anke Moerland (eds) *Intellectual Property Law and the Fourth Industrial Revolution* (Kluwer Law International 2020) 221-224.
5. *Ibid.*
6. Lawrence M Friedman, 'The Eye That Never Sleeps: Privacy and Law in the Internet Era Legal Scholarship Symposium: The Scholarship of Lawrence M. Friedman' (2005) 40 Tulsa Law Review 561, 561 https://digitalcommons.law.utulsa.edu/cgi/viewcontent.cgi?article=2488&context=tlr accessed 4 August 2025.
7. Zachary J Zweihorn, 'Searching For Confusion: The Initial Interest Confusion Doctrine and Its Misapplication to Search Engine Sponsored Links' (September 2006) 91 Cornell Law Reveiw 1343 https://scholarship.law.cornell.edu/cgi/viewcontent.cgi?article=3041&context=clr accessed 4 August 2025; Amy Harmon, 'The Law Where There Is No Land: A Legal System Built on Precedents Has Few of Them in the Digital World' (*New York Times*, 16 March 1998) D1; Dominic Bencivenga, 'Cyberspace in Court: Arguments Are Part Tradition, Part Imagination' (1996) New York Law Journal, 5.
8. Graeme B Dinwoodie and Mark D Janis, 'The Drivers of Trademark Law Reform: Perspectives from the Academy' in Graeme B Dinwoodie and Mark D Janis (eds), *Research Handbook on Trademark Law Reform* (Edward Elgar 2021) 1.
9. Zachary J Zweihorn, 'Searching For Confusion: The Initial Interest Confusion Doctrine and Its Misapplication to Search Engine Sponsored Links' (September 2006) 91 Cornell Law Reveiw 1343, 1344 https://scholarship.law.cornell.edu/cgi/viewcontent.cgi?article=3041&context=clr accessed 4 August 2025; *Brookfield Commc'ns v. W. Coast Entm't Corp.*, 174 F.3d 1036 (9th Cir. 1999).
10. Zachary J Zweihorn, 'Searching for Confusion: The Initial Interest Confusion Doctrine and Its Misapplication to Search Engine Sponsored Links' (September 2006) 91 Cornell Law Reveiw 1343, 1344 https://scholarship.law.cornell.edu/cgi/viewcontent.cgi?article=3041&context=clr accessed 4 August 2025.
11. Amanda Reid, Sean Tu and Kenneth L Port, *Fundamentals of United States Intellectual Property Law: Copyright, Patent, and Trademark* (Wolters Kluwer 2018) 275.
12. *Multi Time Mach., Inc. v. Amazon.com, Inc.* 804 F.3d 930 (9th Cir. 2015).
13. *Circuit City Stores, Inc. v. Carmax, Inc.*, 165 F.3d 1047 (1999); Barton Beebe, 'Trademark Law: An Open-Source Casebook Version 7.0' (2020) 295 https://www.tmcasebook.org/wp-content/uploads/2020/08/BeebeTMLaw-v7-digital_edition.pdf accessed July 2024.
14. Laura Ceci, 'Mobile Internet Usage Worldwide: Statistics & Facts' (*Statista*, 16 May 2024) https://www.statista.com/topics/779/mobile-internet/#topicOverview accessed July 2024.

While trademarks[15] as a form of intellectual property (IP) have been in use for thousands of years,[16] with the advent of the Internet, the utilisation of trademarks has evolved and continues to further evolve today, not only with changes to the Internet but also changes and innovations in the technologies that are used with it. Digital trademarks, defined as those utilised on the Internet, may be utilised in different ways in what will be called platforms including select: (1) e-commerce marketplace platforms, (2) search advertising ('search ad') platforms, (3) social media platforms, (4) mobile application ('mobile app' or simply, 'app') platforms, and (5) Metaverse platforms. These platforms are especially crucial to businesses & consumers and are among the primary methods of conducting business and digital marketing in today's online world. This book is aimed at providing recommendations for trademark policies for each of the platforms listed above.

This book sheds new light on digital trademarks, especially those utilised within the above-mentioned platforms. Based on several key problems identified, it contributes an adapted model for digital trademarks informed by legal frameworks, platform policies, and theories and concepts adopted or elaborated by many great scholars in the international context. Further, it extends the recommendations for a uniform policy for social media[17] not only to this platform but also to many others by first reviewing and making recommendations for the existing uniform policy for domain names. It proposes the actual text of the uniform policies recommended based on grounding in the law, policies and relevant international academic literature.

1.2 DIGITAL TRADEMARK PROBLEMS AND WHAT THIS BOOK SEEKS TO ANSWER

While the regulation of trademarks, whether through legislation, arbitration, or self-regulation, developed over a long period of time, Peukert rightly notes that the Internet 'enables global communication'[18] and the 'use of a sign on the

15. It should also be noted that the spelling of trademark in this research will be in the form of *trademark* unless within a quote in which case the original form of the spelling was retained. Original spelling of terms within quotes were also retained.
16. WIPO, 'Trademarks Past and Present' (*WIPO*, March 2005) https://www.wipo.int/wipo_magazine/en/2005/02/article_0003.html accessed July 2024.
17. Rajeev Sachdev, 'Towards an Improved Framework for Trade-Mark Law and Regulation in Social Media Usernames: A Study of the Canadian, U.S., and U.K. Positions' (2016) 28 Intellectual Property Journal 379, 379-418; Daniel Doft, 'Facebook, Twitter, and the Wild West of IP Enforcement on Social Media: Weighing the Merits of a Uniform Dispute Resolution Policy' (2016) 49 The John Marshall Law Review 959; Thomas J Curtin, 'The Name Game: Cybersquatting and Trademark Infringement on Social Media Websites' (2010-2011) 19 Journal of Law and Policy 353; Erick J Heels, 'How to Twittersquat the Top 100 Brands' (*GiantPeople*, 8 January 2009) http://www.giantpeople.com/1298.html accessed 4 August 2025; Paul D McGrady, *McGrady on Social Media and the Metaverse* (Mathew Bender & Company, Inc. 2023) §12; John McElwaine and Christopher D Casavale, 'Tackling Bad Faith Registration of Domain Names in a Fast-Changing Landscape' (*WIPO Magazine*, December 2019) https://www.wipo.int/wipo_magazine/en/2019/06/article_0006.html accessed June 2025.
18. Alexander Peukert, 'The Coexistence of Trade Mark Laws and Rights on the Internet, and the Impact of Geolocation Technologies' (2016) 47 International Review of Intellectual Property and Competition Law 60, 70 https://doi.org/10.1007/s40319-015-0427-8.

Internet'[19] raises new issues. Likewise, Kamperman Sanders and Drexl recognise 'the need for established IP systems to cater appropriately for new innovation paradigms in a rapidly changing technological environment'.[20] Dinwoodie says that the Internet has altered the 'notion of the appropriate prescriptive authority of the state'[21] and due to 'the ubiquity of the Internet, all interests that were nationally-defined suddenly become global in nature'.[22] Not surprisingly, 'Internet trademark disputes appeared almost immediately after public access to the network became available, in the mid-1990s, even before other intellectual property disputes appeared.'[23] Also, '[t]rademark disputes have been a consistent feature of the Internet's legal landscape since then, appearing in connection with a range of successive technologies and platforms including domain names, e-commerce marketplaces, search engines, and keyword advertising',[24] in social media,[25] mobile apps, and Metaverse platforms.

This book seeks to make recommendations for the UDRP and platform policies relating to digital trademarks, specifically in the following platforms: (1) e-commerce marketplace, (2) search advertising, (3) social media, (4) mobile application, and (5) Metaverse.

This issue is important to look at because digital trademarks raise new issues not contemplated and often not or not adequately addressed by legal frameworks or platforms. If these are not addressed, the problems will only get worse as technology and innovation will continue at rates never seen before. Attempts at resolving these problems are not only far and few between, but do not adequately address the issues. Further, extensive costs, time, and litigation will continue to be expended to deal with the problem of trademarks in the above-mentioned platforms and as a matter of importance to brands, small businesses, sellers, consumers, and users alike, these should be reduced.

19. *Ibid.*
20. Josef Drexl and Anselm Kamperman Sanders (eds), *The Innovation Society and Intellectual Property* (Edward Elgar Publishing 2019) xiii.
21. Graeme B Dinwoodie, 'Remarks by Graeme Dinwoodie' (2005) 30 Brooklyn Journal of International Law 885, 887.
22. *Ibid.*
23. Dan L Burk, 'Trademark Doctrines for Global Electronic Commerce' (1998) 49 South Carolina Law Review 695, 696 in Dan L Burk, 'Cybermarks' (2010) 94 Minnesota Law Review 1375.
24. Dawn C Nunziato, 'Freedom of Expression, Democratic Norms, and Internet Governance' (2003) 52 Emory Law Journal 187, 193 in Dan L Burk, 'Cybermarks' (2010) 94 Minnesota Law Review 1375.
25. Rajeev Sachdev, 'Towards an Improved Framework for Trade-Mark Law and Regulation in Social Media Usernames: A Study of the Canadian, U.S., and U.K. Positions' (2016) 28 Intellectual Property Journal 379, 379-418; Thomas J Curtin, 'The Name Game: Cybersquatting and Trademark Infringement on Social Media Websites' (2010-2011) 19 Journal of Law and Policy 353; IPO, 'Domain Names & Social Media Committee' (*Intellectual Property Owners Association Internet Domain Names Committee*) ipo.org/index.php/about-ipo/committees/internet-domainnames-committee/ accessed 4 August 2025; Lisa P Ramsey, 'Brandjacking on Social Networks: Trademark Infringement by Impersonation of Markholders' (2010) 58 Buffalo Law Review 851 accessed July 2024; Danny Friedmann, *Trademarks and Social Media: Towards Algorithmic Justice* (Edward Elgar Publishing, 2015).

Some say that the current trademark policies and complaint procedures established for domain names, which are 'used as an internet address',[26] such as the Uniform Dispute Resolution Policy (UDRP),[27] are sufficient to deal with domain names, while others have sought change.[28] Additionally, individual trademark policies and complaint procedures have been established by e-commerce marketplaces, search advertising, social media, mobile apps, and Metaverse platforms for their own services. However, the question arises as to whether these are sufficient to address problems raised by trademarks in these platforms. This is especially important to consider because many seek legal certainty and the ability to resolve trademark disputes of various kinds and on various platforms in a cost-effective and timely manner as the Internet rapidly grows as a major place of commercial and digital marketing reliance.

While digital trademarks are very common, the focus on uniform policies has specifically been on addressing mainly covered domain names through the UDRP (and other domain-related policies).[29] Despite the UDRP being adopted in 1999, there is no specific uniform policy for trademarks in e-commerce marketplaces,[30] search advertising, social media,[31] mobile apps, or Metaverse platforms. As noted by De Werra, mechanisms of alternative dispute resolution (ADR) have special significance to trademarks because of their territorial nature.[32] Anderson and Cole discussed the

26. Dictonary.com, 'Domain Name' (*Dictionary.com*) dictionary.com/browse/domain-name accessed July 2024.
27. ICANN, 'Uniform Domain-Name Dispute-Resolution Policy' (UDRP) (*ICANN*, 25 February 2012) https://www.icann.org/resources/pages/policy-2012-02-25-en accessed June 2025.
28. Michael Geist, 'Fair.Com?: An Examination of the Allegations of Systemic Unfairness in the ICANN UDRP' (2001-2002) 27 Brooklyn Journal of International Law 903.
29. Regulation (EU) 2019/517 of the European Parliament and of the Council of 19 March 2019 on the implementation and functioning of the.eu top-level domain name and amending and repealing Regulation (EC) No. 733/2002 and repealing Commission Regulation (EC) No. 874/2004 with respect to.eu domains; 15 U.S. Code § 1125(d); ICANN, 'Uniform Domain-Name Dispute-Resolution Policy' (UDRP) (*ICANN*, 25 February 2012) https://www.icann.org/resources/pages/policy-2012-02-25-en accessed June 2025.
30. Edward C Anderson and Timothy S Cole, 'The UDRP: A Model for Dispute Resolution in E-Commerce' (2002) 6 Journal of Small & Emerging Business Law 235.
31. Rajeev Sachdev, 'Towards an Improved Framework for Trade-Mark Law and Regulation in Social Media Usernames: A Study of the Canadian, U.S., and U.K. Positions' (2016) 28 Intellectual Property Journal, 379, 379-418; Thomas J Curtin, 'The Name Game: Cybersquatting and Trademark Infringement on Social Media Websites' (2010-2011) 19 Journal of Law and Policy 353; IPO, 'Domain Names & Social Media Committee' (*Intellectual Property Owners Association Internet Domain Names Committee*) ipo.org/index.php/about-ipo/committees/internet-domainnames-committee/ accessed 4 August 2025; Lisa P Ramsey, 'Brandjacking on Social Networks: Trademark Infringement by Impersonation of Markholders' (2010) 58 Buffalo Law Review 851 accessed July 2024; Danny Friedmann, *Trademarks and Social Media: Towards Algorithmic Justice* (Edward Elgar Publishing, 2015).
32. Jacques de Warra, 'Alternative Dispute Resolution for Trademark Disputes' in Irene Calboli and Jane Ginsburg (eds) *The Cambridge Handbook of International and Comparative Trademark Law* (Cambridge University Press 2020) 142-158.

possibility of a UDRP-like procedure for e-commerce marketplaces.[33] Sachdev, McGrady, and others[34] have discussed the relevance of uniform policies for social media.[35] The lack of such uniform policies means that any trademark issues in these platforms are generally left to be regulated by the platforms themselves or, alternatively, through applicable legislation (whether or not geared towards digital trademarks) enforced by the courts or judicial processes. While trademark policies, terms, and complaint procedures by platforms address some of the considerations pertinent to trademarks in these platforms, it is argued in this book that these are insufficient to address existing trademark concerns and will only fall farther behind as technology permits the utilisation of marks in further novel ways. For example, individual platform enforcement can result in inconsistency within or among platforms in similar circumstances, differences in rules, unclear rules, lack of rules or coverage, unwarranted action or inaction, uncertainty, and other problems. Further, trademarks are utilised in different ways within the platforms listed above, and peculiarities within these platforms need to be specifically considered to avoid generalisations. Likewise, regulation through general trademark law, such as European Union (EU) and United States (US) law, can be uncertain as applied to Internet settings, may be insufficient, may be inconsistent among jurisdictions or even within jurisdictions, may result in costly litigation, and/or decisions may generally not be timely. At a minimum, uncertainty prevails in an international online environment, which begs for legal certainty that can promote commercial efficiency. This creates a much greater need for clear, efficient, and effective platform trademark policies, guidance, and complaint procedures.

The problems relating to digital trademarks, as identified and explained in detail in Chapter 2, include seven areas:[36] (1) use[37] and the place of use[38] of marks, (2) bad

33. Edward C Anderson & Timothy S Cole, 'The UDRP: A Model for Dispute Resolution in E-Commerce' (2002) 6 Journal of Small & Emerging Business Law 235.
34. Rajeev Sachdev, 'Towards an Improved Framework for Trade-Mark Law and Regulation in Social Media Usernames: A Study of the Canadian, U.S., and U.K. Positions' (2016) 28 Intellectual Property Journal 379, 379-418; Daniel Doft, 'Facebook, Twitter, and the Wild West of IP Enforcement on Social Media: Weighing the Merits of a Uniform Dispute Resolution Policy' (2016) 49 The John Marshall Law Review 959; Thomas J Curtin, 'The Name Game: Cybersquatting and Trademark Infringement on Social Media Websites' (2010-2011) 19 Journal of Law and Policy 353; Erick J Heels, 'How to Twittersquat the Top 100 Brands' (*GiantPeople*, 8 January 2009) http://www.giantpeople.com/1298.html accessed 4 August 2025; Paul D McGrady, *McGrady on Social Media and the Metaverse* (Mathew Bender & Company, Inc. 2023) §12; John McElwaine and Christopher D Casavale, 'Tackling Bad Faith Registration of Domain Names in a Fast-Changing Landscape' (*WIPO Magazine*, December 2019) https://www.wipo.int/wipo_magazine/en/2019/06/article_0006.html accessed June 2025.
35. *Ibid.*
36. 15 U.S. Code § 1127; EUTMR, Art. 18; WIPO 3rd.
37. The Agreement on Trade-Related Aspects of Intellectual Property Rights, 1995 (TRIPS), Art. 16; EUTMR, Art. 18; 15 U.S. Code § 1127; 15 U.S. Code § 1127.
38. EUIPO, '3 Place of Use' (*EUIPO Trade mark guidelines* 2024) https://guidelines.euipo.europa.eu/2214311/1982069/trade-mark-guidelines/3-place-of-use accessed January 2024.

faith[39] and abuse,[40] (3) confusion,[41] (4) unfair acts,[42] trade practices,[43] or competition,[44] (5) Terms, Policies, and Disclaimers,[45] (6) jurisdiction/territory,[46] and (7) justification. These were selected based on their recognition in the literature and/or legal frameworks considered. These need to be addressed or minimised; otherwise, it is argued that these problems will compound. To help address these, it is important to consider an adapted model based on these problems.

In order to arrive at the recommendations for the issues this book seeks to answer, it is necessary to consider the key problems pertaining to digital trademarks, specifically in e-commerce marketplaces, search advertising, social media, mobile apps, and Metaverse platforms and what adapted model can be developed to inform trademark issues in these platforms. These key problems are discussed in Chapter 2 and help to set the stage. From these, an adapted model naturally flows and is presented as a relevant approach to deal with these for Internet settings because of the importance of addressing the issues it raises. This adapted model, namely the Digital Trademark and Trade Practices Model, effectively extends existing research by summarising it, building upon it, applying it to areas of the Internet, and/or identifying areas where it can help to fill the problems in the context of the UDRP and platform trademark policies. This adapted model is needed to help assess and address these

39. The Paris Convention for the Protection of Industrial Property, 1883, amended 1967 (Paris Convention), Art. 6bis; EUTMR, Art. 59; TTAB, 'Fighting Bad Faith Trademark Filings in the United States' (*The Honorable Karen S. Kuhlke Administrative Trademark Judge*) https://www.jpo.go.jp/e/news/kokusai/tm5/document/bad_faith_seminar2/01.pdf accessed July 2024; UDRP, 4(a)(iii).
40. WIPO, 'WIPO Overview of WIPO Panel Views on Selected UDRP Questions, Third Edition' ('WIPO Jurisprudential Overview 3.0') (*WIPO*, 2017) https://www.wipo.int/amc/en/domains/search/overview3.0/ accessed June 2025.
41. Paris Convention, Art. 6bis; TRIPS, Art. 16(1); EUTMR, Art. 8(1)(b) and Art. 9(2)(b); 15 U.S. Code § 1114; 15 U.S. Code § 1125.
42. Anselm Kamperman Sanders, *Unfair Competition Law: The Protection of Intellectual and Industrial Creativity* (Oxford University Press, 1997) 8; Frauke Henning-Bodewig, *Unfair Competition Law European Union and Member States* (Kluwer Law International 2006) xv-xvi; Martin Senftleben, Michael Handler and Irene Calboli, 'Protection Against Unfair Competition Around the Globe' (2024) 19 Journal of Intellectual Property Law & Practice 79, 79-80 https://doi.org/10.1093/jiplp/jpad121; Paris Convention, Art. 10bis; EUTMR, Art. 9(2)(c); 15 U.S.C. § 1125(c)(2)(B).
43. *Ibid.*
44. *Ibid.*
45. WIPO, 'WIPO Overview of WIPO Panel Views on Selected UDRP Questions, Third Edition' ('WIPO Jurisprudential Overview 3.0') (*WIPO*, 2017) https://www.wipo.int/amc/en/domains/search/overview3.0/ accessed June 2025; Alexander Peukert, 'The Coexistence of Trade Mark Laws and Rights on the Internet, and the Impact of Geolocation Technologies' (2016) 47 International Review of Intellectual Property and Competition Law 60, 81 https://doi.org/10.1007/s40319-015-0427-8; Leslie Fair, 'Full Disclosure' (*FTC Business Blog*, 23 September 2014) https://www.ftc.gov/business-guidance/blog/2014/09/full-disclosure accessed June 2025.
46. Ansgar Ohly, 'Choice of Law in the Digital Environment: Problems and Possible Solutions' in Josef Drexl and Annette Kur (eds), *Intellectual Property and Private International Law: Heading for the Future* (Bloomsbury Publishing 2005) 241; Alexander Peukert, 'The Coexistence of Trade Mark Laws and Rights on the Internet, and the Impact of Geolocation Technologies' (2016) 47 International Review of Intellectual Property and Competition Law 60, 81 https://doi.org/10.1007/s40319-015-0427-8; *Gruma Corp. v. Mexican Rests., Inc.*, 2013 U.S. Dist. LEXIS 200183.

problems for digital trademarks and also provides an avenue and a lens through which to look at these problems.

How the above adapted model is informed by select theories and concepts, and select aspects of the EU and US (with some reference to others) legal frameworks, and what the resulting considerations for the UDRP and platform policies are is crucial and is discussed in Chapter 3. A review of relevant trademark and related theories and concepts as well as select aspects of the EU and US legal frameworks (with some reference to others such as the United Kingdom (UK), Canada, Australia, etc.) is conducted, including key treaties such as the Paris Convention for the Protection of Industrial Property, or simply, the Paris Convention, and the Agreement on Trade-Related Aspects of Intellectual Property Rights (TRIPS), which inform the Digital Trademark and Trade Practices Model. While the main focus will be on trademark law, it will cover select trade practices to the extent that they form part of, cover, address or relate to trademarks specifically.[47] The countries and regions (which will, for simplicity, be referred to as jurisdictions even though the EU has various jurisdictions/ countries/Member States within it) were selected because of extensive activity pertinent to the platforms under consideration, platform official presence within these, and arguably their major role in the applying trademark law to Internet situations. Nevertheless, some reference to illustrative cases from international jurisdictions will help to highlight specific issues. This approach helps to inform all of the elements of the adapted model, as these, in turn, help to provide considerations for the UDRP and/or the platforms of the study.

Then, in Chapter 4, recommendations are made for the UDRP in light of the above adapted model. A review of the UDRP is conducted in light of the Digital Trademark and Trade Practices Model and the considerations it raises. Key recommendations are made for a newly adapted UDRP while retaining what is considered a simplistic and successful uniform, international approach.

Recommendations are made for platform trademark policies in light of the UDRP, the recommendations for the UDRP, and the above adapted model in Chapter 5. Specifically, this is based on the newly adapted UDRP whose adaptations are based on the Digital Trademark and Trade Practices Model. In essence, informed by the model, uniform policies are recommended for each type of platform building on earlier research, some of which cites lack of or recommends uniform policies for e-commerce marketplace[48] and social media[49] platforms, and extends this to recommend and

47. Anselm Kamperman Sanders, *Unfair Competition Law: The Protection of Intellectual and Industrial Creativity* (Oxford University Press, 1997) 8; Frauke Henning-Bodewig, *Unfair Competition Law European Union and Member States* (Kluwer Law International 2006) xv-xvi; Martin Senftleben, Michael Handler and Irene Calboli, 'Protection Against Unfair Competition Around the Globe' (2024) 19 Journal of Intellectual Property Law & Practice 79, 79-80 https://doi.org/10.1093/jiplp/jpad121; Paris Convention, Art. 10bis; EUTMR, Art. 9(2)(c); 15 U.S.C. § 1125(c)(2)(B).
48. Edward C Anderson abd Timothy S Cole, 'The UDRP: A Model for Dispute Resolution in E-Commerce' (2002) 6 Journal of Small & Emerging Business Law 235.
49. Rajeev Sachdev, 'Towards an Improved Framework for Trade-Mark Law and Regulation in Social Media Usernames: A Study of the Canadian, U.S., and U.K. Positions' (2016) 28 Intellectual Property Journal 379, 379-418; Daniel Doft, 'Facebook, Twitter, and the Wild West

provide the text for an adapted UDRP and uniform platform policies designed to address key problems and gaps leading to better harmonization. Select platforms in this book include those discussed in the next section.

Beyond the scope of this book is a deep dive into detailed EU, Member State, US federal or state consumer protection level treatment.[50] It also does not purport to extensively cover certain areas such as dispute resolution provisions of the Digital Services Act (DSA), even though the contents herein become more relevant given the requirements of services acting as 'intermediaries'[51] to implement 'measures to counter illegal content online, including illegal goods and service'.[52] Further, the liability of platforms[53] or deep procedural aspects of digital trademark disputes, even if some reference may be made, are beyond the scope, as the focus will be more on recommendations for platform policies. Specifically, where platforms themselves are using trademarks and a user would like to file a dispute in this regard, a third party neutral panel approach* akin to the UDRP as outlined in Chapter 5 might be considered an option, although this book does not direclty analyse this issue. This book utilises select considerations from the legal frameworks of the EU (Union level only) and the US (federal level only) and references other legal frameworks. While the model developed and used in this book could be applied to the legal frameworks themselves, it does not purport to address improvement of the rules and legal frameworks themselves. As such, the development of the model is germane to this book and it is beyond the scope to include detailing the necessary steps for international harmonisation of digital trademark law at the judicial and legislative level of any legal framework.

1.3 THE UDRP AND PLATFORMS UNDER CONSIDERATION

The UDRP is first considered, based on its success as a simple and effective uniform approach to deal with digital trademark issues within domain names. Then, specific platforms are considered, shown in Table 1.1. Platforms have been selected based on

of IP Enforcement on Social Media: Weighing the Merits of a Uniform Dispute Resolution Policy' (2016) 49 The John Marshall Law Review 959; Thomas J Curtin, 'The Name Game: Cybersquatting and Trademark Infringement on Social Media Websites' (2010-2011) 19 Journal of Law and Policy 353; Erick J Heels, 'How to Twittersquat the Top 100 Brands' (*GiantPeople*, 8 January 2009) http://www.giantpeople.com/1298.html accessed 4 August 2025; Paul D McGrady, *McGrady on Social Media and the Metaverse* (Mathew Bender & Company, Inc. 2023) §12; John McElwaine and Christopher D Casavale, 'Tackling Bad Faith Registration of Domain Names in a Fast-Changing Landscape' (*WIPO Magazine*, December 2019) https://www.wipo.int/wipo_magazine/en/2019/06/article_0006.html accessed June 2025.

50. *Ibid.*
51. European Commission, 'Questions and Answers on the Digital Services Act' (*European Commission*, 2024) https://ec.europa.eu/commission/presscorner/detail/en/qanda_20_2348 accessed June 2025.
52. *Ibid.*
53. Christopher Heath and Anselm Kamperman Sanders, *Intellectual Property Liability of Consumers, Facilitators and Intermediaries* (1st edn, Kluwer Law International, 2012) §1:01.

* Amazon, 'Let's Protect the Brand You Built' (Amazon Brand Registry) https://sell.amazon.com/brand-registry accessed June 2025; Amazon.nl, 'Amazon Brand Registry' (Amazon.nl) https://sell.amazon.nl/brand-registry accessed June 2025.

their popularity, revenue, active users, international operation, and related considerations.

Table 1.1 Platforms to Be Considered

E-Commerce Marketplace Platforms	Amazon, eBay
Search Ad Platforms	Google, Yahoo, Bing
Social Media Platforms	Facebook, X (formerly, Twitter), Pinterest, LinkedIn, Snapchat
Mobile App Platforms	Apple App Store, Google Play Store
Metaverse Platforms	Roblox, Meta Horizon Worlds, Epic Games

By way of brief overview, E-Commerce marketplace platforms are considered, and the EU and the US are breeding grounds for e-commerce marketplace platform activity. Amazon was the number one online retailer in 2023, commanding 37.6% of the US market share, whereas eBay commanded 3%.[54] In 2023, Amazon 'was the most popular e-commerce and shopping website worldwide' and eBay placed second from the perspective of 'visit share'.[55] Many other e-commerce marketplace platforms exist and e-commerce revenue is set to be in the trillions annually worldwide over the coming years.[56] Both Amazon and eBay operate country-specific websites for several EU countries, the US, and several other countries worldwide.[57] Generally, consumers will use these e-commerce platforms for purposes of engaging in shopping for an increasing variety of options, large and small. However, their business models differ. Amazon offers facilities for third-party sellers to market their products on the platform, as does eBay; however, Amazon also markets its own products or sells under its own branding.[58] Search ad platforms, including three major platforms, Google, Yahoo! and Bing,[59] will also be considered. Google search engine is the most popular on a global level, in 2023 commanding more than 81% of the global market, with Bing serving just

54. Stephanie Chevalier, 'Market Share of Leading Retail E-Commerce Companies in the United States in 2023' (*Statista*, 22 May 2024) https://www.statista.com/statistics/274255/market-share-of-the-leading-retailers-in-us-e-commerce/ accessed July 2024.
55. Stephanie Chevalier, 'Most Popular E-Commerce and Shopping Websites Worldwide in December 2023, Based on Share of Visits' (*Statista*, 2 February 2024) https://www.statista.com/statistics/1198949/most-visited-websites-in-the-retail-sector-worldwide/ accessed July 2024.
56. *Ibid.*
57. Amazon, 'Website (Country/Region)' (*Amazon*, 2024) https://www.amazon.com/customer-preferences/country/?ref_=navm_em_locale_0_1_1_76 accessed July 2024; ebay, 'Homepage' (*eBay*, 2024) https://www.ebay.com/ accessed July 2024 (*See* eBay Sites on the bottom left of the homepage).
58. Gurufocus, 'Amazon vs. eBay: A Case Study in Business Models' (*Yahoo! Finance*, 16 June 2020) https://finance.yahoo.com/news/amazon-vs-ebay-case-study-200603093.html accessed July 2024.
59. Google, 'Google Search' (*Google*) https://www.google.com/ accessed July 2024; Yahoo, 'Yahoo' (*Yahoo! News*) https://www.yahoo.com/ accessed July 2024; Bing, 'Bing' (*Bing.com*) https://www.bing.com/ accessed July 2024.

over 10%, and Yahoo at just over 2%.[60] However, while relationships have changed over time, Bing still reports that Bing Ads may appear on Yahoo.[61] Social media platforms covered include Facebook (owned by Meta) with over 3 billion monthly active users in 2023, X (formerly, Twitter) with 666 million, Pinterest with 465 million, LinkedIn with 310 million, and Snapchat with 750 million.[62] Mobile app platforms covered include Google Play and the Apple App Store. The mobile app industry has grown rapidly and mobile apps are available on various platforms. Some examples of mobile apps are shopping, banking, gaming, music, calendar, picture, calculator, study apps, and many others.[63] By the end of 2023, Google Play offered more than 2.43 million Android (an operating system for devices) apps.[64] The Apple App Store offers 1.8 million iOS (Apple's operating system for devices such as the iPhone and others) apps.[65] Finally, the Metaverse, which is being called the 'next iteration of the internet',[66] while in its infancy in terms of widespread consumer adoption, may form a wave into the digital unknown. Metaverse platforms considered include Roblox, Meta Horizon Worlds, and Epic Games. These are among the various Metaverse platforms which are in operation and new ones regularly arrive.[67]

60. Tiago Bianchi, 'Market Share of Leading Desktop Search Engines Worldwide from January 2015 to January 2024' (*Statista*, 2024) https://www.statista.com/statistics/216573/worldwide-market-share-of-search-engines/ accessed July 2024.
61. Microsoft, 'Market Availability for Microsoft Advertising and Its Features' (*Microsoft*, 2024) https://help.ads.microsoft.com/apex/index/3/en-us/50873/ accessed July 2024.
62. Stacey Jo Dixon, 'Most Popular Social Networks Worldwide as of April 2024, by Number of Monthly Active Users (in Millions)' (*Statista*, 10 July 2024) https://www.statista.com/statistics/272014/global-social-networks-ranked-by-number-of-users/ accessed July 2024.
63. Google, 'Google Play' (*Google Play*) https://play.google.com/store?hl=en accessed January 2024; Apple, 'App Store' (*App Store – Apple*) https://www.apple.com/ios/app-store/ accessed July 2024.
64. Laura Ceci, 'Number of Available Applications in the Google Play Store from December 2009 to December 2023' (*Statista*, 2024) https://www.statista.com/statistics/266210/number-of-available-applications-in-the-google-play-store/ accessed July 2024.
65. Apple, 'App Store' (*Apple*, 2024) https://www.apple.com/app-store/ accessed July 2024.
66. Jessica Clement, 'Metaverse: Statistics & Facts' (*Statista*, 2024) https://www.statista.com/topics/8652/metaverse/#topicOverview accessed July 2024.
67. Isaiah Richard, 'Top Three Companies Creating the Metaverse Now: Meta, Epic Games, Roblox' (*TechTimes*, 2021) https://www.techtimes.com/articles/269701/20211223/top-three-companies-creating-metaverse-now-meta-epic-games-roblox.htm accessed July 2024.

CHAPTER 2

Overview of Digital Trademark Problems Leading to the Digital Trademark and Trade Practices Model

Digital trademarks raise problems in seven key areas, including: (1) use and the place of use of marks; (2) bad faith and abuse; (3) confusion; (4) unfair acts, trade practices, or competition; (5) terms, policies, and disclaimers; (6) jurisdiction/territory; and (7) justification as outlined in this chapter. These lead to the development of the Digital Trademark and Trade Practices Model presented in this chapter.

2.1 INTRODUCTION

As Reid, Tu and Port say, there is no doubt that '[t]rademark law encounters problems in cyberspace'[68] and this has been echoed by the courts. A court commented that it 'must be acutely aware of excessive rigidity when applying the law in the Internet context; emerging technologies require a flexible approach'.[69] Another court commented that '[e]ntering the new millennium, our society is far more mobile than it was four decades ago'.[70] Further, 'that recent technological innovations such as the Internet are increasingly deconstructing geographical barriers for marketing purposes, it appears to me that a re-examination of precedents would be timely ...'.[71] That was back in 1999, and with various platforms today, new challenges are raised. Bowden and

68. Amanda Reid, Sean Tu and Kenneth L Port, *Fundamentals of United States Intellectual Property Law: Copyright, Patent, and Trademark* (Wolters Kluwer 2018) 275.
69. *Multi Time Mach., Inc. v. Amazon.com, Inc.* 804 F.3d 930 (9th Cir. 2015).
70. *Circuit City Stores, Inc. v. Carmax, Inc.*, 165 F.3d 1047 (1999); Barton Beebe, 'Trademark Law: An Open-Source Casebook Version 7.0' (2020) 295 https://www.tmcasebook.org/wp-content/uploads/2020/08/BeebeTMLaw-v7-digital_edition.pdf accessed July 2024.
71. *Ibid.*

Chen have recognised that 'commercial trade in emerging technologies does not always fit easily'[72] which has implications for trademark use.[73] Janis and Dinwoodie recognise the impact that the Internet has on 'disputes about the use of trademarks in online advertising'.[74] Gerhart says that 'new ways to use brands in social media are pressuring traditional conceptions of trademark law'.[75] Today, we are also faced with consumer decisions about trademarks in non-fungible token (NFT) perfumes[76] and Metaverse avatars.[77] As time progresses, 'Metaverse environments will pose even greater challenges to IP rights.'[78]

Digital trademarks are utilised extensively on the Internet, including in the various platforms covered in this book and these raise several problems which are the subject matter of this chapter. The key problems pertaining to digital trademarks, specifically in e-commerce marketplaces, search advertising, social media, mobile apps, and Metaverse platforms, are outlined. Then, what adapted model can be developed to inform trademark issues in these platforms is uncovered.

2.2 OVERVIEW OF PROBLEMS RAISED BY DIGITAL TRADEMARKS

Several key problems exist with respect to digital trademarks as recognised in the literature and legal frameworks. These problems are summarised in Table 2.1 based on the discussion that follows, and importantly, a more detailed look at specific problems will be conducted in Chapters 4 and 5, which involve an analysis of the UDRP and each of the platform's policies. The result of these problems, as will be seen in this book, is legal uncertainty, increased costs, reduced trust, and confusion about the utilisation of digital trademarks. It should be noted that these key problems consist of different types or categories of problems. For example, some have to do with infringement-related criteria such as use[79] or confusion,[80] while others have to the way a mark is used, policy, place, justification or other category. These different types or categories are necessarily a part of the analysis since they consider different angles that are problematic from a digital perspective.

72. David Bowden and Junyi Chen, 'Canadian Trademark Law and "Use" in the Computer and Internet Age' 33 Canadian Intellectual Property Review 50, 50.
73. *Ibid.*
74. *Ibid.*
75. Deborah Gerhardt, 'Social Media Amplify Consumer Investments in Trademarks' (2011) 90 North Carolina Law Review 1491, abstract.
76. Sharono Edelson, 'Scents of Wood Travels to the Metaverse with First Fragrance NFT' (*Forbes*, 2022) https://www.forbes.com/sites/sharonedelson/2022/08/25/scents-of-wood-travels-to-the-metaverse-with-first-fragrance-nft/?sh = 19c37bef7079 accessed July 2024.
77. Meta, 'Express Yourself with Meta Avatars' (*Meta*, 2024) https://www.meta.com/avatars/ accessed July 2024.
78. César Ramírez-Montes, 'EU Trademarks in the Metaverse' 63 IDEA 557, 558.
79. EUTMR, Art. 18; 15 U.S. Code § 1127; WIPO, 'WIPO Overview of WIPO Panel Views on Selected UDRP Questions, Third Edition' ('WIPO Jurisprudential Overview 3.0') *(WIPO*, 2017) https://www.wipo.int/amc/en/domains/search/overview3.0/ accessed June 2025.
80. Paris Convention, Art. 6bis; TRIPS, Art. 16(1); EUTMR, Art. 8(1)(b) and Art. 9(2)(b); 15 U.S. Code § 1114; 15 U.S. Code § 1125.

Table 2.1 Summary of Digital Trademark Problems

Use[81] and specifically where digital trademarks are used[82] are not adequately dealt with by policies/platforms	- Assessing use[83] of trademarks and the place[84] where these are used[85] on the Internet is difficult. - Determining the 'nature of that use'[86] is problematic in different Internet environments. - There are many places where a digital mark may be utilised including but not limited to in domain names, in e-commerce marketplace, search advertising, social media, mobile app, and Metaverse platforms but also many different places within these platforms. The context of each of these may be different, and this may change the assessment of using[87] marks in these places.
Digital trademarks may easily and on large scale be utilised in bad faith[88] and abused[89] and this is not adequately addressed by policies/platforms	- Trademarks may be utilised in 'bad faith'[90] on the Internet and this is only somewhat addressed in a limited manner for domain names. - There is a 'bad faith'[91] requirement under 15 U.S. Code § 1125(d) for a domain name to be transferred to a complainant.[92] Likewise, it is one provision under the UDRP.[93] It is also an alternative

81. EUTMR, Art. 18; 15 U.S. Code § 1127; WIPO, 'WIPO Overview of WIPO Panel Views on Selected UDRP Questions, Third Edition' ('WIPO Jurisprudential Overview 3.0') *(WIPO*, 2017) https://www.wipo.int/amc/en/domains/search/overview3.0/ accessed June 2025.
82. WIPO, 'WIPO Overview of WIPO Panel Views on Selected UDRP Questions, Third Edition' ('WIPO Jurisprudential Overview 3.0') *(WIPO*, 2017) https://www.wipo.int/amc/en/domains/search/overview3.0/ accessed June 2025.
83. EUTMR, Art. 18; 15 U.S. Code § 1127.
84. *Ibid.*
85. *Ibid.*
86. Graeme B Dinwoodie and Mark D Janis, 'Confusion Over Use: Contextualism in Trademark Law' (2007) 92 Iowa Law Review 1597, 1599.
87. EUTMR, Art. 18; 15 U.S. Code § 1127; WIPO, 'WIPO Overview of WIPO Panel Views on Selected UDRP Questions, Third Edition' ('WIPO Jurisprudential Overview 3.0') *(WIPO*, 2017) https://www.wipo.int/amc/en/domains/search/overview3.0/ accessed June 2025.
88. ICANN, 'Uniform Domain-Name Dispute-Resolution Policy' (*ICANN*, 25 February 2012) https://www.icann.org/resources/pages/policy-2012-02-25-en accessed June 2025; 15 U.S. Code § 1125(d); WIPO, 'WIPO Overview of WIPO Panel Views on Selected UDRP Questions, Third Edition' ('WIPO Jurisprudential Overview 3.0') *(WIPO*, 2017) https://www.wipo.int/amc/en/domains/search/overview3.0/ accessed June 2025.
89. WIPO, 'WIPO Overview of WIPO Panel Views on Selected UDRP Questions, Third Edition' ('WIPO Jurisprudential Overview 3.0') *(WIPO*, 2017) https://www.wipo.int/amc/en/domains/search/overview3.0/ accessed June 2025.
90. ICANN, 'Uniform Domain-Name Dispute-Resolution Policy' (*ICANN*, 25 February 2012) https://www.icann.org/resources/pages/policy-2012-02-25-en accessed June 2025; 15 U.S. Code § 1125(d).
91. 15 U.S. Code § 1125(d).
92. *Ibid.*
93. ICANN, 'Uniform Domain-Name Dispute-Resolution Policy' (*ICANN*, 25 February 2012) https://www.icann.org/resources/pages/policy-2012-02-25-en accessed June 2025.

grounds[94] for.eu domains[95] and is a requirement in proceedings under various country level domains.[96] Although incorporated in various aspects relating to domain names, it is not adequately covered for other areas of the Internet.

- It is covered in the context of registration or cancellation in some jurisdictions[97] although this does not include registration of usernames and the like in the context of platforms.
- Where addressed, the extent to which the website associated with a domain name, the website associated with a search ad, the social media account or activity associated with a social media username, the mobile app icon or contents associated with a mobile app name, or specific aspects of Metaverse platforms will be considered in the analysis is not clear.
- There may also be persistent (or repeated)[98] 'bad faith'[99] of digital trademarks by some actors and such abuse[100] of marks is not adequately addressed, other than for domain names and within

94. WIPO, 'WIPO Domain Name Dispute Resolution Service for .EU (and.ею and.ευ)' (*WIPO*) https://www.wipo.int/amc/en/domains/cctld/eu/index.html accessed July 2024; Anne-Laure Covin and Edward J Fennesey, *Trademarks Throughout the World* (Thomson West 2007) §54:32.
95. Regulation (EU) 2019/517 of the European Parliament and of the Council of 19 March 2019 on the implementation and functioning of the .eu top-level domain name, Art. 4.
96. Registry Services, 'UsTLD Dispute Resolution Policy' (*Registry Services, LLC*, 2021) https://www.about.us/documents/policies/usTLD_Dispute_Resolution_Policy_(usDRP).pdf accessed July 2024; WIPO, 'WIPO Domain Name Dispute Resolution Service for .EU (and.ею and.ευ)' (*WIPO*) https://www.wipo.int/amc/en/domains/cctld/eu/index.html accessed July 2024.
97. Paris Convention, Art. 6bis; EUTMR, Art. 59; TTAB, 'Fighting Bad Faith Trademark Filings in the United States' (*The Honorable Karen S. Kuhlke Administrative Trademark Judge*) https://www.jpo.go.jp/e/news/kokusai/tm5/document/bad_faith_seminar2/01.pdf accessed July 2024; UDRP, 4(a)(iii).
98. WIPO, 'WIPO Overview of WIPO Panel Views on Selected UDRP Questions, Third Edition' ('WIPO Jurisprudential Overview 3.0') (*WIPO*, 2017) https://www.wipo.int/amc/en/domains/search/overview3.0/ accessed June 2025; Facebook, 'Facebook Terms of Service' (*Facebook*) https://www.facebook.com/legal/terms accessed January 2024; Instagram, 'Trademark' (*Instagram Help Center Trademark*) https://help.instagram.com/222826637847963 accessed January 2024.
99. ICANN, 'Uniform Domain-Name Dispute-Resolution Policy' (*ICANN*, 25 February 2012) https://www.icann.org/resources/pages/policy-2012-02-25-en accessed January 2024; 15 U.S. Code § 1125(d).
100. WIPO, 'WIPO Overview of WIPO Panel Views on Selected UDRP Questions, Third Edition' ('WIPO Jurisprudential Overview 3.0') (*WIPO*, 2017) https://www.wipo.int/amc/en/domains/search/overview3.0/ accessed January 2024; Facebook, 'Facebook Terms of Service' (*Facebook*) https://www.facebook.com/legal/terms accessed July 2024; Instagram, 'Trademark' (*Instagram Help Center Trademark*) https://help.instagram.com/222826637847963 accessed January 2024.

	some platforms.[101] However, abuse[102] may not consistently re-sultin enhanced sanctions.[103]
Utilising digital trademarks may cause confusion and this is not adequately addressed by policies/platforms	- The standards or factors for confusion[104] on the Internet are unclear. - While covered for domain names under the UDRP, no Internet specific factors to assess confusion[105] exists and it is difficult to apply existing factors in this context.[106] - Confusion may be applied in different ways resulting in the potential for inconsistent results even in similar situations across the Internet.
There may be unfair acts, trade practices,[107] or competition[108] involving digital trademarks[109] and this is not adequately addressed by policies/platforms	- Engaging in unfair acts, trade practices[110] or competition[111] and related concepts such as dilution,[112] unfair advantage,[113] passing off[114] etc. are unclear for digital trademarks.

101. Google, 'What Happens If You Violate Our Policies' (*Google*) https://support.google.com/adspolicy/answer/7187501?sjid=2768541143044478250-NA accessed July 2024; LinkedIn, 'How We Enforce Our Professional Community Policies' (*LinkedIn*) https://www.linkedin.com/help/linkedin/answer/a1342754 accessed July 2024.
102. WIPO, 'WIPO Overview of WIPO Panel Views on Selected UDRP Questions' (*WIPO Jurisprudential Overview 3.0*, 2017) https://www.wipo.int/amc/en/domains/search/overview3.0/ accessed 4 August 2025; Facebook, 'Facebook Terms of Service' (*Facebook*) https://www.facebook.com/legal/terms accessed July 2024; Instagram, 'Trademark' (*Instagram Help Center Trademark*) https://help.instagram.com/222826637847963 accessed January 2024.
103. *Ibid.*
104. *Ibid.*
105. *Ibid.*
106. *Ibid.*
107. *Ibid.*
108. *Ibid.*
109. Anselm Kamperman Sanders, *Unfair Competition Law: The Protection of Intellectual and Industrial Creativity* (Oxford University Press, 1997) 8; Frauke Henning-Bodewig, *Unfair Competition Law European Union and Member States* (Kluwer Law International 2006) xv-xvi; Martin Senftleben, Michael Handler and Irene Calboli, 'Protection Against Unfair Competition Around the Globe' (2024) 19 Journal of Intellectual Property Law & Practice 79, 79-80 https://doi.org/10.1093/jiplp/jpad121; Paris Convention, Art. 10bis; EUTMR, Art. 9(2)(c); 15 U.S.C. § 1125(c)(2)(B).
110. *Ibid.*
111. *Ibid.*
112. EUTMR, Art. 9(2)(c); 15 U.S.C. § 1125(c)(2)(B).
113. EUTMR, Art. 9(2)(c).
114. Ethan Horwitz and Benjamin Levi, 'Fifty Years of the Lanham Act: A Retrospective of Section 43(a)E' (1996) 7 Fordham Intellectual Property, Media and Entertainment Law Journal Article

	- Whether and the extent to which well-known,[115] famous,[116] strong,[117] reputable marks[118] will be afforded greater protectionon the Internet is unclear.
Terms, domain and platform policies, and uncertainty around disclaimers[119] inadequately address digital trademarks	- Uniform policies such as the UDRP focus on covered domain names and do not cover other areas of the Internet.[120] - Terms and policies of platforms are not consistent, often unclear, and are not adequate as will be seen in Chapter 5. - The effect and use of disclaimers is unclear and how these impact a trademark analysis is unclear.

6; David Bainbridge, *Intellectual Property* (Pearson Education Limited 2018) Chapter 30; EUTMR, Art. 17(2); 15 U.S.C. §1125.

115. Paris Convention, Art. 6bis; TRIPS, Art. 16(2); EUTMR, Art. 8(2)(c).
116. Stefan Martin, 'Well Known Marks and Parody: Dilution and Denigration? Unfair Advantage?' (*EUIPO*, 2017), https://euipo.europa.eu/knowledge/pluginfile.php/77920/mod_resource/content/8/Limits%20of%20trade%20marks%2C%20Parody%2018-5-2017.pdf accessed January 2024.
117. Timothy D Greene and Jeff Wilkerson, 'Understanding Trademark Strength' (2013) 16 Stanford Technology Law Review 535-582, abstract.
118. EUTMR, Arts 8(5) and 9(1)(c).
119. UDRP; Rajeev Sachdev, 'Towards an Improved Framework for Trade-Mark Law and Regulation in Social Media Usernames: A Study of the Canadian, U.S., and U.K. Positions' (2016) 28 Intellectual Property Journal 379, 379-418; Daniel Doft, 'Facebook, Twitter, and the Wild West of IP Enforcement on Social Media: Weighing the Merits of a Uniform Dispute Resolution Policy' (2016) 49 The John Marshall Law Review 959; Thomas J Curtin, 'The Name Game: Cybersquatting and Trademark Infringement on Social Media Websites' (2010-2011) 19 Journal of Law and Policy 353; Erick J Heels, 'How to Twittersquat the Top 100 Brands' (*GiantPeople*, 8 January 2009) http://www.giantpeople.com/1298.html accessed 4 August 2025; Paul D McGrady, *McGrady on Social Media and the Metaverse* (Mathew Bender & Company, Inc. 2023) §12; John McElwaine and Christopher D Casavale, 'Tackling Bad Faith Registration of Domain Names in a Fast-Changing Landscape' (*WIPO Magazine*, December 2019) https://www.wipo.int/wipo_magazine/en/2019/06/article_0006.html accessed June 2025; WIPO, 'WIPO Overview of WIPO Panel Views on Selected UDRP Questions, Third Edition' ('WIPO Jurisprudential Overview 3.0') (*WIPO*, 2017) https://www.wipo.int/amc/en/domains/search/overview3.0/ accessed June 2025; Alexander Peukert, 'The Coexistence of Trade Mark Laws and Rights on the Internet, and the Impact of Geolocation Technologies' (2016) 47 International Review of Intellectual Property and Competition Law 60, 81 https://doi.org/10.1007/s40319-015-0427-8; Leslie Fair, 'Full Disclosure' (*FTC Business Blog*, 23 September 2014) https://www.ftc.gov/business-guidance/blog/2014/09/full-disclosure accessed June 2025.
120. *Ibid.*

The Internet is global in nature and trade nark rules are mostly jurisdictional[121] and this is not adequately addressed by policies/platforms	- While treaties establish minimum standards, trademark rules are largely jurisdictional.[122] - International approaches do not extend to many digital trademarks. - The 'global nature of the Internet'[123] challenges the jurisdictional or 'territorial nature'[124] of trademark law and this is unclear for digital trademarks.[125] - A complicated patchwork of rules, terms, and policies may apply and this can cause serious legal uncertainty on a global level and global solutions are needed.[126]
How defences and justification may apply is unclear for digital trademarks[127] and this is not adequately addressed by policies/platforms	- Various justifications or defences may apply to trademarks. - The UDRP specifically identifies only some of these and provides some guidance as will be seen in Chapter 4.[128] - It is not always clear for digital trademarks, which specific defences and justifications may apply.

121. Roger E Schecter and John R Thomas, *Principles of Trademark Law* (West Academic Publishing 2021) 385; Alexander Peukert, 'The Coexistence of Trade Mark Laws and Rights on the Internet, and the Impact of Geolocation Technologies' (2016) 47 International Review of Intellectual Property and Competition Law 60, 81 https://doi.org/10.1007/s40319-015-0427-8.
122. Julien Chaisse, 'The Merging of Two Worlds: Cyber Law and Trade Law Normative Convergence on Internet Domain Names' (2019) 37 Boston University International Law Journal 281; Brendan J Witherell, 'Trademark Law: The Extraterritorial Application of the Lanham Act – The First Circuit Cuts the Fat from the Vanity Fair Test' (2006) 29 Western New England Law Review 193, 197.
123. WIPO, 'WIPO Overview of WIPO Panel Views on Selected UDRP Questions, Third Edition' ('WIPO Jurisprudential Overview 3.0') (*WIPO*, 2017) https://www.wipo.int/amc/en/domains/search/overview3.0/ accessed June 2025.
124. Graeme Dinwoodie, 'Trademarks and Territory: Detaching Trademark Law from the Nation-State' (2004-2005) 41 Houston Law Review 885, 890.
125. *Ibid.*
126. Frederick Mostert, 'The Internet: Regulators Struggle to Balance Freedom with Risk', (*Financial Times,* 2019) https://www.ft.com/content/e49c39e6-967d-11e9-8cfb-30c211dcd229 accessed December 2024.
127. The Constitution of the United States of America, the Charter of Fundamental Rights of the European Union; Constitution Act, 1982, Canadian Charter of Rights and Freedoms; TRIPS, Art. 16; Paris Convention, Art. 6bis; EUTMR, Art. 18; 15 U.S. Code § 1127.
128. ICANN, 'Uniform Domain-Name Dispute-Resolution Policy' (*ICANN*, 25 February 2012) https://www.icann.org/resources/pages/policy-2012-02-25-en accessed June 2025; WIPO, 'WIPO Overview of WIPO Panel Views on Selected UDRP Questions, Third Edition ('WIPO Jurisprudential Overview 3.0') (*WIPO*, 2017) https://www.wipo.int/amc/en/domains/search/overview3.0/ accessed June 2025.

2.2.1 Use and Specifically Where Digital Trademarks Are Used Are Not Adequately Dealt with by Policies/Platforms

There is no doubt that trademarks are heavily utilised in domain names and on all platforms in this study. However, it is important to consider how and specifically where within these places' marks are being utilised, as this has trademark implications. Under TRIPS, 'using in the course of trade'[129] is a necessary element; however, the utilisation of digital trademarks raises problems because determining the 'nature of that use'[130] is difficult in the various Internet environments. Further, the context of each utilisation may differ and how consumers interact with marks may differ. Below, utilisation of marks within various platforms is considered, including a related brief background for each platform.

The UDRP addresses trademarks utilised in covered domain names.[131] The policy covers any utilisation of marks which meets the requirements of the policy, regardless of whether these are used 'in the course of trade',[132] which is not generally a factor except in limited circumstances such as to establish standing to file a complaint under the policy.[133] If such 'use'[134] is not directly required, this creates the issue of differentiating trademarks in domain names from the most common and acceptable methods of using trademarks in accordance with TRIPS. As will be seen in Chapter 5, some platforms specifically require some form of commercial use in their policies, some mention it generally,[135] while the UDRP and other platforms do not (at least directly).[136]

In e-commerce marketplace platforms, trademarks may be used in individual listings, best seller results, banner ads, shopping ads and other places. For example, advertisers may promote a number of trademarked brands through images of such products. Alternatively, they may market trademarked products through listings where a mark may be incorporated or on the image of the product, within the listing description, within the seller's username, and in other places. Likewise, services may be advertised with service marks. These different places where the mark may be utilised may be authorised or may not be. In other cases, marks in e-commerce may not even be utilised in conjunction with the goods or services specifically for which they are registered[137] and it is unclear whether or when such utilisation may be acceptable.

129. TRIPS, Art. 16.
130. Graeme B Dinwoodie and Mark D Janis, 'Confusion Over Use: Contextualism in Trademark Law' (2007) 92 Iowa Law Review 1597, 1599.
131. ICANN, 'Uniform Domain-Name Dispute-Resolution Policy' (*ICANN*, 25 February 2012) https://www.icann.org/resources/pages/policy-2012-02-25-en accessed June 2025.
132. TRIPS, Art. 16.
133. WIPO, 'WIPO Overview of WIPO Panel Views on Selected UDRP Questions, Third Edition' ('WIPO Jurisprudential Overview 3.0') (*WIPO*, 2017) https://www.wipo.int/amc/en/domains/search/overview3.0/ accessed June 2025.
134. TRIPS, Art. 16.
135. Facebook, 'Trademark' (*Facebook Help*) https://www.facebook.com/help/507663689427413/?helpref=hc_fnav accessed January 2024.
136. Snap, 'Username Infringement' (*Snapchat Support*) https://help.snapchat.com/hc/en-us/articles/7047503878804 accessed January 2024.
137. EUTMR, Art. 18.

To understand where marks may be utilised in search advertising, a brief background is offered. Often, consumers will use an Internet search engine to find products or services, and many users conduct Internet searches using keywords[138] or keyphrases.[139] A keyword[140] may be one word and a keyphrase[141] may be a few words, a phrase or even sentences that form the basis of the search processed by a search engine's system and algorithms.[142] These keywords[143] or keyphrases[144] may be typed into search bars, and various results[145] are displayed with links to websites that may have information, goods or services related to the keywords searched.[146] These may include unpaid ('natural'[147] or 'organic search results')[148] or paid (sponsored) search ads by search advertisers.[149] The paid ads may be shown, for example, 'alongside or above search results';[150] however, this may differ depending on the search engine. Paid search ads may include or link to websites which may contain trademarks of others.

The name of a city or place may not always need to be a part of the search terms, depending on the search terms, device settings, the search engine company's protocols and/or other factors. This is because information about the location of the device from which the search is being conducted may automatically be picked up, although not always.[151] For example, when visiting a website such as Google.com, the site may pick up a user's location and produce localised results.[152] Sometimes, consumers are searching for information relating to products and services in other countries and relevant results may appear for those searches, such as when travelling to those

138. Google, 'Choose the Right Keywords' (*Google Keyword Planner*) https://ads.google.com/home/tools/keyword-planner/ accessed January 2024.
139. *Ibid.*
140. *Ibid.*
141. *Ibid.*
142. *Ibid.*
143. *Ibid.*
144. *Ibid.*
145. Google, 'Where Your Ads Can Appear' (*Google Ads Help*) https://support.google.com/google-ads/answer/1704373?hl=en#:~:text=Your%20text%2C%20image%2C%20and%20video,includes%20mobile%20sites%20and%20apps accessed January 2024; Google, 'Organic Search Result' (*Google*) https://support.google.com/google-ads/answer/6054492?hl=en accessed January 2024.
146. Google, 'How Search Algorithms Work (*Google Search Algorithm and Ranking System*) https://www.google.com/search/howsearchworks/algorithms/ accessed January 2024; Rolf Broer, 'Search Engine Algorithm Basics' (*Moz*, 8 December 2011) https://moz.com/blog/search-engine-algorithm-basics accessed January 2024.
147. Google, 'Organic Search Result' (*Google*) https://support.google.com/google-ads/answer/6054492?hl=en accessed January 2024.
148. *Ibid.*
149. Google, 'Where Your Ads Can Appear' (*Google Ads Help*) https://support.google.com/google-ads/answer/1704373 accessed January 2024.
150. *Ibid.*
151. Google, 'Understand & Manage Your Location When You Search on Google' (*Google*) https://support.google.com/websearch/answer/179386?hl=en&co=GENIE.Platform%3DAndroid accessed January 2024.
152. Search Engine Land, 'How to Localize Google Search Results' (*Search Engine Land*, 25 January 2016) https://searchengineland.com/localize-Google-search-results-239768 accessed January 2024.

countries and their location is picked up, or by using the name of the place within the keyphrase.

In addition, links that appear are normally based on a 'series of algorithms'[153] of the search engine. Therefore, results for different devices may depend on the search engine, keywords, location, search history and/or other factors.[154] Marks may be utilised in different places in the search ad, including the heading, display Uniform Resource Locator (URL), or description.[155] The display URL is the website domain name shown. However, the website address which is shown may or may not be the same as the actual website the search ad links to when clicked by a consumer (as designated by the advertiser).

Although much search advertising will undoubtedly include trademarks in 'use'[156] since they will often be promoting goods or services, this will not always be relevant 'use'[157] such as under TRIPS in the context of rights of mark holders to prevent the 'using in the course of trade'[158] of such marks, or 'genuine use in the Union in in connection with the goods or services in respect of which it is registered'[159] to avoid revocation in the EU,[160] or 'use in commerce'[161] in the US such as to avoid 'abandonment',[162] etc., where required.[163] Further, search advertisers may place ads using specific or multiple brands within different places in the ads, each may raise different considerations. For example, an ad showing trademarks of others in sitelinks which a consumer may recognise not to be that of the advertiser raises different issues than a heading clearly incorporating a trademark of another. Additionally, whether any or all such utilisations are 'using in the course of trade'[164] is not clear. For example, whether

153. Google, 'How Search Algorithms Work (*Google Search Algorithm and Ranking System*) https://www.google.com/search/howsearchworks/algorithms/ accessed January 2024.
154. Search Engine Land, 'How to Localize Google Search Results' (*Search Engine Land*, 25 January 2016) https://searchengineland.com/localize-Google-search-results-239768 accessed January 2024; Google, 'How Search Algorithms Work (*Google Search Algorithm and Ranking System*) https://www.google.com/search/howsearchworks/algorithms/ accessed January 2024; Rolf Broer, 'Search Engine Algorithm Basics' (*Moz*, 8 December 2011) https://moz.com/blog/search-engine-algorithm-basics accessed January 2024.
155. Google, 'About Text Ads' (*Google*) https://support.google.com/google-ads/answer/1704389?hl=en accessed January 2024.
156. TRIPS, Art. 16; EUTMR, Art. 18; 15 U.S. Code § 1127; 15 U.S. Code § 1127.
157. *Ibid.*
158. TRIPS, Art. 16.
159. EUTMR, Art. 18.
160. EUTMR, Art. 58(1)(a).
161. 15 U.S. Code § 1127.
162. *Ibid.*
163. It should be noted here that Art. 10(6) EU Trademark Directive 2015/2436 provides for protection 'against the use of a sign other than use for the purposes of distinguishing goods or services, where use of that sign without due cause takes unfair advantage of, or is detrimental to, the distinctive character or the repute of the trade mark'. Likewise, EUTMR, Art. 9(2)(c) states: 'irrespective of whether it is used in relation to goods or services which are identical with, similar to or not similar to those for which the EU trade mark is registered, where the latter has a reputation in the Union and where use of that sign without due cause takes unfair advantage of, or is detrimental to, the distinctive character or the repute of the EU trade mark'. The legal framework pertaining to both use and unfair competition (and related concepts) are discussed further in Chapter 3.
164. TRIPS, Art. 16.

or not a platform may take action on the mark based on the context in which a mark is being used[165] is not clear. As will be seen in Chapter 5, while the utilisation of a mark within an ad will be considered, Google does not restrict 'use of trademarks as keywords'.[166] Further, it may potentially consider the linked website or 'landing page',[167] although it is not always clear when this may be the case, and this is even more unclear for the other platforms considered, as will also be seen in Chapter 5.

In the context of social media, trademarks may be utilised in social media usernames,[168] social media advertising and social media activity, such as in social media posts[169] defined as where 'a single entry'[170] is published on a social media site. 'Use'[171] is especially a problem in the sense that much social media may not be used[172] in the trademark sense[173] and there is a lack of clarity around which uses[174] are infringing and which are not.[175] For example, 'use'[176] of marks in social media usernames poses special problems.[177] Likewise, from the perspective of mobile apps, when one tries to find and download a mobile app, a consumer may go to an 'app store'[178] such as those run by Google and Apple and search for apps[179] by name, which

165. *Ibid.*; EUTMR, Art. 18; 15 U.S. Code § 1127.
166. Google, 'Trademarks' (*Google*) https://support.google.com/adspolicy/answer/6118?visit_id=638419270508802311-4094647794&rd=1 accessed July 2024.
167. *Ibid.*
168. Daniel Chandler and Rod Munday, *A Dictionary of Social Media* (Oxford University Press, 2016) https://www.oxfordreference.com/view/10.1093/acref/9780191803093.001.0001/acref-9780191803093-e-1129; Lisa P Ramsey, 'Brandjacking on Social Networks: Trademark Infringement by Impersonation of Markholders' (2010) 58 Buffalo Law Review 851; Rajeev Sachdev, 'Towards an Improved Framework for Trade-Mark Law and Regulation in Social Media Usernames: A Study of the Canadian, U.S., and U.K. Positions' (2016) 28 Intellectual Property Journal 379, 379-418.
169. *Ibid.*
170. *Ibid.*
171. EUTMR, Art. 18; 15 U.S. Code § 1127.
172. *Ibid.*
173. *Ibid.*
174. *Ibid.*
175. *Ibid.*
176. *Ibid.*
177. Lisa P Ramsey, 'Brandjacking on Social Networks: Trademark Infringement by Impersonation of Markholders' (2010) 58 Buffalo Law Review 851; Danny Friedmann, *Trademarks and Social Media: Towards Algorithmic Justice* (Edward Elgar Publishing 2015) 3-15; Rajeev Sachdev, 'Towards an Improved Framework for Trade-Mark Law and Regulation in Social Media Usernames: A Study of the Canadian, U.S., and U.K. Positions' (2016) 28 Intellectual Property Journal 379, 379-418; Daniel Doft, 'Facebook, Twitter, and the Wild West of IP Enforcement on Social Media: Weighing the Merits of a Uniform Dispute Resolution Policy' (2016) 49 The John Marshall Law Review 959; Thomas J Curtin, 'The Name Game: Cybersquatting and Trademark Infringement on Social Media Websites' (2010-2011) 19 Journal of Law and Policy 353; Erick J Heels, 'How to Twittersquat the Top 100 Brands' (*GiantPeople,* 8 January 2009) http://www.giantpeople.com/1298.html accessed 4 August 2025; Paul D McGrady, *McGrady on Social Media and the Metaverse* (Mathew Bender & Company, Inc. 2023) §12.
178. Google, 'Google Play' (*Google Play*) https://play.google.com/store?hl=en accessed January 2024.
179. *Ibid.*

may result in a listing of apps and/or display of mobile app icons[180] containing trademarks. Such mobile app icons may consist of designs, colours, words and other aspects to form a representation of the app and may be displayed on the device of the consumer.[181] Asbell and Wernick summarise that an app '[n]ame,[182] [w]ord or [p]hrase',[183] '[l]ogo/[i]icon(s)/[g]raphic(s)',[184] '[s]logan or [t]agline',[185] '[c]olor(s)',[186] '[s]ound(s)'[187] and activity within the mobile app may include trademarks of others and raise various issues of potential infringement[188] Further, there are many apps that are free to download and are purely informational, and which may or may not be in some way related to or associated[189] with products and/or services. As will be seen in Chapter 5, Facebook and Snapchat specifically refer to commercial use[190] in their terms, although how this will be interpreted is not clear. On the other hand, other platforms considered generally do not make such direct reference and it is unclear what will be considered by these platforms, resulting in uncertainty.

In Metaverse platforms, marks may be utilised in NFTs, avatars, avatar names, usernames, stores, concerts and much more. Creators may utilise material which may incorporate the trademarks of others, such as the trademarks on products or buildings. Brands may create, or collaborate with, Metaverse platforms to create spaces within the platform to showcase their brand or provide an interactive experience. Within these spaces, trademarks may be utilised and it must be considered within these places whether these would be considered 'use',[191] such as alongside NFTs. Each of the number of ways within Metaverse platforms that trademarks may be utilised needs to be considered carefully from the angle of whether there is 'use'[192] of a mark, as this is often unclear.

180. Developers, 'Google Play Icon Design Specifications' (*Resources*, 16 April 2020) https://developer.android.com/google-play/resources/icon-design-specifications accessed January 2024.
181. *Ibid.*
182. Matthew D Asbell and Alan S Wernick, 'IP Protection for Mobile Apps: Navigating Name Selection, Trademark Clearance, Registration, Licensing and Infringement' (*Strafford*, 26 October 2016) http://media.straffordpub.com/products/ip-protection-for-mobile-apps-navigating-name-selection-trademark-clearance-registration-licensing-and-infringement-2016-10-26/presentation.pdf accessed January 2024.
183. *Ibid.*
184. *Ibid.*
185. *Ibid.*
186. *Ibid.*
187. *Ibid.*
188. *Ibid.*
189. EUTMR, Art. 9(2)(b); 15 U.S. Code §1125.
190. Facebook, 'Trademark' (*Facebook Help*) https://www.facebook.com/help/507663689427413/?helpref=hc_fnav accessed January 2024; Snap, 'Username Infringement' (*Snapchat Support*) https://help.snapchat.com/hc/en-us/articles/7047503878804 accessed January 2024.
191. TRIPS, Art. 16; EUTMR, Art. 18; 15 U.S. Code § 1127.
192. *Ibid.*

Determining whether the use is in 'the course of trade'[193] can be difficult and each 'place of use'[194] may raise different considerations and may or may not be authorised by mark holder or permitted under law. Utilisation of a mark may not always be with respect to goods or services or relevant goods or services. For example, the extent to which the website associated with a domain name, the website associated with a search ad, the social media account or activity associated with a social media username, or the mobile app icon or contents associated with a mobile app name, or Metaverse activity associated with a Metaverse platforms will be considered in the analysis by platforms is not clear.[195] Overall, if and how to assess 'use'[196] on the Internet, and to consider 'place of use',[197] is problematic and must be addressed in order for platforms to address the utilisation of marks for clarity and certainty, which is currently lacking.

2.2.2 Digital Trademarks May Easily and on Large Scale Be Utilised in Bad Faith and Abused and This Is Not Adequately Addressed by Policies/Platforms

Trademarks may be utilised in 'bad faith'[198] in platforms and this is only somewhat addressed in a limited manner, such as for domain names. Under the U.S. Anti-cybersquatting Protection Act (ACPA), there is a 'bad faith'[199] requirement where 'a domain name registrant's bad faith intent to profit must be shown'[200] for a domain name to be transferred to a complainant. It is also an alternative ground[201] for.eu domains under Article 4 of the Regulation (EU) 2019/517 of the European Parliament and of the Council of 19 March 2019 on the implementation and functioning of the .eu top-level domain name and a requirement in proceedings under various country-level

193. TRIPS, Art. 16.
194. EUIPO, '3 Place of Use' (*EUIPO Trade mark guidelines* 2024) https://guidelines.euipo.europa.eu/2214311/1982069/trade-mark-guidelines/3-place-of-use accessed January 2024.
195. Roblox, 'Terms of Use: Roblox Support' (*Roblox*) https://en.help.roblox.com/hc/en-us/articles/115004647846-Roblox-Terms-of-Use accessed January 2024; Facebook, 'Terms of Service' https://www.facebook.com/terms.php/ accessed July 2024; Meta, 'Supplemental Meta Platforms Technologies Terms of Service' (*Meta*) https://www.meta.com/legal/supplemental-terms-of-service/ accessed January 2024.
196. TRIPS, Art. 16; EUTMR, Art. 18; 15 U.S. Code § 1127.
197. EUIPO, '3 Place of Use' (*EUIPO Trade mark guidelines*, 2024) https://guidelines.euipo.europa.eu/2214311/1982069/trade-mark-guidelines/3-place-of-use accessed January 2024.
198. ICANN, 'Uniform Domain-Name Dispute-Resolution Policy' (*ICANN*, 25 February 2012) https://www.icann.org/resources/pages/policy-2012-02-25-en accessed January 2024; 15 U.S. Code § 1125(d).
199. 15 U.S. Code § 1125(d).
200. Deborah E Bouchoux, *Intellectual Property: The Law of Trademarks, Copyrights, Patents, and Trade Secrets* (Cengage Learning 2016) 152.
201. WIPO, 'WIPO Domain Name Dispute Resolution Service for .EU (and.ею and.ευ)' (*WIPO*) https://www.wipo.int/amc/en/domains/cctld/eu/index.html accessed July 2024; Anne-Laure Covin and Edward J Fennesey, *Trademarks Throughout the World* (Thomson West 2007) §54:32.

domains.[202] 'Bad faith'[203] is also one of the provisions under the UDRP.[204] Specifically, '[r]egistration and use of a domain name in bad faith' is required under the UDRP.[205] Although incorporated in various aspects relating to domain names, it is not covered by legislation specifically for e-commerce marketplaces, search ads, social media, mobile apps, or Metaverse platforms.

Generally, platforms do not have to consider 'bad faith'[206] for trademarks in their platforms. However, when and whether they do is rather uncertain. If considered, what aspects of a 'digital consumer interaction'[207] will be considered by platforms in a 'bad faith'[208] analysis is not clear. For example, a search ad, social media username,[209] mobile app name, metaverse avatar name may be 'registered'[210] or trademarks within these may be 'used'[211] in 'bad faith'[212] subject to the platform's policies, which may or may not directly cover this issue or explain how it will be applied, creating uncertainty.

202. CIRA, 'CIRA Domain Name Dispute Resolution Policy' (*CIRA*) https://www.cira.ca/policy/domain-name/cira-domain-name-dispute-resolution-policy accessed January 2024; Registry Services, 'UsTLD DisputeResolution Policy' (*Registry Services, LLC*, 2021) https://www.about.us/documents/policies/usTLD_Dispute_Resolution_Policy_(usDRP).pdf accessed January 2024; WIPO, 'WIPO Domain Name Dispute Resolution Service for .EU (and.ею and.ευ)' (*WIPO*) https://www.wipo.int/amc/en/domains/cctld/eu/index.html accessed January 2024.
203. Paris Convention 1967, Art. 6bis; ICANN, 'Uniform Domain-Name Dispute-Resolution Policy' (*ICANN*, 25 February 2012) https://www.icann.org/resources/pages/policy-2012-02-25-en accessed January 2024; 15 U.S. Code § 1125(d).
204. ICANN, 'Uniform Domain-Name Dispute-Resolution Policy' (*ICANN*, 25 February 2012) https://www.icann.org/resources/pages/policy-2012-02-25-en accessed January 2024.
205. *Ibid.*
206. *Ibid.*
207. Seung Ho Park and Maria Alejandra Gonzalez-Perez, *The Palgrave Handbook of Corporate Sustainability in the Digital Era* (Springer International Publishing 2020) 532.
208. ICANN, 'Uniform Domain-Name Dispute-Resolution Policy' (*ICANN*, 25 February 2012) https://www.icann.org/resources/pages/policy-2012-02-25-en accessed January 2024; 15 U.S. Code § 1125(d).
209. Rajeev Sachdev, 'Towards an Improved Framework for Trade-Mark Law and Regulation in Social Media Usernames: A Study of the Canadian, U.S., and U.K. Positions' (2016) 28 Intellectual Property Journal 379, 379-418; Thomas J Curtin, 'The Name Game: Cybersquatting and Trademark Infringement on Social Media Websites' (2010-2011) 19 Journal of Law and Policy 353; IPO, 'Domain Names & Social Media Committee', (*Intellectual Property Owners Association Internet Domain Names Committee*) ipo.org/index.php/about-ipo/committees/internet-domainnames-committee/ accessed 4 August 2025; Lisa P Ramsey, 'Brandjacking on Social Networks: Trademark Infringement by Impersonation of Markholders' (2010) 58 Buffalo Law Review 851; Danny Friedmann, *Trademarks and Social Media: Towards Algorithmic Justice* (Edward Elgar Publishing 2015) 3-15.
210. WIPO, 'Tackling Bad Faith Registration of Domain Names in a Fast-Changing Landscape' (*WIPO Magazine*, December 2019) https://www.wipo.int/wipo_magazine/en/2019/06/article_0006.html accessed January 2024.
211. *Ibid.*
212. Paris Convention, Art. 6bis; ICANN, 'Uniform Domain-Name Dispute-Resolution Policy' (*ICANN*, 25 February 2012) https://www.icann.org/resources/pages/policy-2012-02-25-en accessed January 2024; 15 U.S. Code § 1125(d).

In various platforms, there may also be persistent (or repeated)[213] 'bad faith'[214] of digital trademarks by some actors and such abuse[215] of marks is not squarely or adequately addressed, other than in a limited way for domain names and in limited and sometimes inconsistent ways by platforms. For example, abuse[216] may take place by engaging in 'bad faith'[217] on a large or repeated scale and, as will be seen in Chapter 4, this is addressed by the UDRP but only through a WIPO Overview to the UDRP and not directly in its policy. Specifically, the Overview states that, 'establishing a pattern of bad faith conduct requires more than one, but as few as two instances of abusive domain name registration'.[218] However, similar 'abuse'[219] may occur across many platforms. As will be seen in Chapter 5, some platforms consider various forms of repeat violations/infringement,[220] while others employ a '3 strikes'[221] maximum, and yet others reserve the right to take various actions, including suspension.[222] The nature and egregiousness of any action does not appear to fit well within a 'strikes'[223] approach, such that one very serious violation would still allow a bad actor to continue

213. WIPO, 'WIPO Overview of WIPO Panel Views on Selected UDRP Questions, Third Edition' ('WIPO Jurisprudential Overview 3.0') (*WIPO*, 2017) https://www.wipo.int/amc/en/domains/search/overview3.0/ accessed June 2025; Facebook, 'Facebook Terms of Service' (*Facebook*) https://www.facebook.com/legal/terms accessed January 2024; Instagram, 'Trademark' (*Instagram Help Center Trademark*) https://help.instagram.com/222826637847963 accessed January 2024.
214. ICANN, 'Uniform Domain-Name Dispute-Resolution Policy' (*ICANN*, 25 February 2012) https://www.icann.org/resources/pages/policy-2012-02-25-en accessed January 2024; 15 U.S. Code § 1125(d).
215. WIPO, 'WIPO Overview of WIPO Panel Views on Selected UDRP Questions, Third Edition, ('WIPO Jurisprudential Overview 3.0') (*WIPO*, 2017) https://www.wipo.int/amc/en/domains/search/overview3.0/ accessed June 2025; Facebook, 'Facebook Terms of Service' (*Facebook*) https://www.facebook.com/legal/terms accessed January 2024; Instagram, 'Trademark' (*Instagram Help Center Trademark*) https://help.instagram.com/222826637847963 accessed January 2024.
216. *Ibid.*
217. ICANN, 'Uniform Domain-Name Dispute-Resolution Policy' (*ICANN*, 25 February 2012) https://www.icann.org/resources/pages/policy-2012-02-25-en accessed January 2024; 15 U.S. Code § 1125(d).
218. WIPO, 'WIPO Overview of WIPO Panel Views on Selected UDRP Questions, Third Edition, ('WIPO Jurisprudential Overview 3.0') (*WIPO*, 2017) https://www.wipo.int/amc/en/domains/search/overview3.0/ accessed June 2025.
219. *Ibid.*
220. Amazon, 'Conditions of Use' (*Amazon*) https://www.amazon.com/gp/help/customer/display.html?nodeId = 508088&ref_ = footer_cou accessed January 2024; eBay, 'Verified Rights Owner (VeRO) Policy' (*eBay*) https://www.ebay.com/help/policies/listing-policies/selling-policies/intellectual-property-vero-program?id = 4349 accessed January 2024; Yahoo! 'Copyright and Intellectual Property Policy' (*Yahoo!*) https://legal.yahoo.com/us/en/yahoo/ip/index.html accessed January 2024.
221. Google, 'What Happens If You Violate Our Policies' (*Google*) https://support.google.com/adspolicy/answer/7187501?sjid = 2768541143044478250-NA accessed July 2024.
222. Amazon, 'Conditions of Use' (*Amazon*) https://www.amazon.com/gp/help/customer/display.html?nodeId = 508088&ref_ = footer_cou accessed January 2024 eBay, 'Verified Rights Owner (VeRO) Policy' (*eBay*) https://www.ebay.com/help/policies/listing-policies/selling-policies/intellectual-property-vero-program?id = 4349 accessed January 2024; Yahoo! 'Copyright and Intellectual Property Policy' (*Yahoo!*) https://legal.yahoo.com/us/en/yahoo/ip/index.html accessed January 2024.
223. Google, 'What Happens If You Violate Our Policies' (*Google*) https://support.google.com/adspolicy/answer/7187501?sjid = 2768541143044478250-NA accessed July 2024.

use of the platform. Largely, differences in treatment and interpretation result in uncertainty of whether and what type of 'abuse' activity will be considered, how it may be assessed, and if considered, whether this may consistently result in enhanced sanctions.[224]

Overall, it needs to be clear whether and specifically how platforms will consider 'bad faith'[225] with respect to trademarks in their platforms, and whether and how 'abuse'[226] will be considered, and if so, whether this results in specific further action by platforms.

2.2.3 Utilising Digital Trademarks May Result in Confusion and This Is Not Adequately Addressed by Policies/Platforms

Confusing[227] marks in e-commerce marketplace activity, search ads,[228] social media usernames,[229] social media activity,[230] mobile app names, mobile app content, and Metaverse activity, among other places, are problematic for platforms. Even in the context of offline consumer confusion,[231] the courts struggle with complicated and

224. WIPO, 'WIPO Overview of WIPO Panel Views on Selected UDRP Questions, Third Edition, ('WIPO Jurisprudential Overview 3.0') (*WIPO*, 2017) https://www.wipo.int/amc/en/domains/search/overview3.0/ accessed June 2025; Facebook, 'Facebook Terms of Service' (*Facebook*) https://www.facebook.com/legal/terms accessed January 2024; Instagram, 'Trademark' (*Instagram Help Center Trademark*) https://help.instagram.com/222826637847963 accessed January 2024.
225. UDRP, 4(a)(iii).
226. WIPO, 'WIPO Overview of WIPO Panel Views on Selected UDRP Questions, Third Edition' ('WIPO Jurisprudential Overview 3.0') (*WIPO*, 2017) https://www.wipo.int/amc/en/domains/search/overview3.0/ accessed June 2025.
227. TRIPS, Art. 16; Paris Convention, Art. 6bis; EUTMR, Art. 8(1)(b) and Art. 9(2)(c); 15 U.S. Code § 1114.
228. Maral Kilejian and Sally Dahlstrom, 'Trademark Infringement Claims in Keyword Advertising' (2016) 36 Franchise Law Journal 123; Derek R Lowrey, Caroline H Mead and Beth A Seals, 'Trademarks as Keywords in Internet Searches: What Brand Owners Can Do to Protect Their Rights' (*Lexology*, 30 July 2013) https://www.lexology.com/library/detail.aspx?g=e4c19b7e-e046-486b-8b49-d22e707b272f accessed January 2024; Findlaw, 'Court: Google's Use of Trademarks As Keywords Is Non-infringing' (*Findlaw*) https://technology.findlaw.com/legal-software/court-Google-s-use-of-trademarks-as-keywords-is-non-infringing.html accessed January 2024.
229. Rajeev Sachdev, 'Towards an Improved Framework for Trade-Mark Law and Regulation in Social Media Usernames: A Study of the Canadian, U.S., and U.K. Positions' (2016) 28 Intellectual Property Journal 379, 379-418; Thomas J Curtin, 'The Name Game: Cybersquatting and Trademark Infringement on Social Media Websites' (2010-2011) 19 Journal of Law and Policy 353; 'Domain Names & Social Media Committee' (*Intellectual Property Owners Association Internet Domain Names Committee*) ipo.org/index.php/about-ipo/committees/internet-domainnames-committee/ accessed 4 August 2025; Lisa P Ramsey, 'Brandjacking on Social Networks: Trademark Infringement by Impersonation of Markholders' (2010) 58 Buffalo Law Review 851; Danny Friedmann, *Trademarks and Social Media: Towards Algorithmic Justice* (Edward Elgar Publishing 2015) 3-15.
230. *Ibid.*
231. TRIPS, Art. 16; Paris Convention, Art. 6bis.

inconsistent rulings.[232] This causes confusion as to the standard for 'confusion',[233] especially for the Internet, and as a major basis of protection grounded in the Paris Convention and TRIPS,[234] this needs to be directly addressed by platforms. For example, utilising a mark may be done in many ways on the Internet when an e-commerce listing confusingly incorporates the mark of another, or a search advertiser wishes to direct traffic to their website using confusing[235] keywords.[236] Further, when a consumer is searching for a trademark name and the advertised results show some sort of product or service offering, such may be confused[237] with a trademarked brand.[238] However, the analysis may not always be clear-cut and this may result in elongated litigation, such as has been the case for alleged search-related confusing trademarks.[239]

Likewise, confusion[240] may result from using[241] the mark of another in social media and consumers become confused[242] about the source of the message. In social media, for example, there may be confusion[243] as to the source of a post, possibly

232. Barton Beebe, 'An Empirical Study of the Multifactor Tests for Trademark Infringement' (2006) 94 California Law Review 1581 https://doi.org/10.2307/20439078; Robert G Bone, 'Taking the Confusion out of "Likelihood of Confusion": Toward a More Sensible Approach to Trademark Infringement' (2012) 106 Northwestern University Law Review 1307.
233. Paris Convention, Art. 6bis; TRIPS, Art. 16; Robert G Bone, 'Taking the Confusion out of "Likelihood of Confusion": Toward a More Sensible Approach to Trademark Infringement' (2012) 106 Northwestern University Law Review 1307.
234. Paris Convention, Art. 6bis; TRIPS, Art. 16(1).
235. EUTMR, Art. 8(1)(b) & Art. 9(2)(c); 15 U.S. Code § 1125.
236. Maral Kilejian and Sally Dahlstrom, 'Trademark Infringement Claims in Keyword Advertising' (2016) 36 Franchise Law Journal 123; Derek R Lowrey, Caroline H Mead and Beth A Seals, 'Trademarks as Keywords in Internet Searches: What Brand Owners Can Do to Protect Their Rights' (*Lexology*, 30 July 2013) https://www.lexology.com/library/detail.aspx?g=e4c19b7e-e046-486b-8b49-d22e707b272f accessed January 2024; Findlaw, 'Court: Google's Use of Trademarks as Keywords Is Non-infringing' (*Findlaw*) https://technology.findlaw.com/legal-software/court-Google-s-use-of-trademarks-as-keywords-is-non-infringing.html accessed January 2024.
237. 15 U.S. Code § 1125; EUTMR, Art. 8(1)(b) and Art. 9(2)(c).
238. Maral Kilejian and Sally Dahlstrom, 'Trademark Infringement Claims in Keyword Advertising' (2016) 36 Franchise Law Journal 123.
239. *Interflora Inc & Anor v. Marks and Spencer Plc & Anor* [2013] EWHC 1291 (Ch) (21 May 2013); Bailii, 'England and Wales High Court (Chancery Division) Decisions' (*Interflora*, 21 May 2013) http://www.bailii.org/ew/cases/EWHC/Ch/2013/1291.html accessed January 2024; *Interflora Inc v. Marks and Spencer Plc* [2014] EWCA Civ 1403; Oeclaw, 'Approved Judgment' (*Final Judgment*, 5 November 2014) http://www.oeclaw.co.uk/images/uploads/documents/Interflora_v_Marks_and_Spencer_-_final_judgment_5_November_2014.pdf accessed January 2024; LexisNexis, 'Interflora v M&S: Adwords Are Ok Says Court of Appeal' (*Blogs*) https://blogs.lexisnexis.co.uk/wipit/interflora-v-ms-adwords-are-ok-says-court-of-appeal/ accessed January 2024.
240. EUTMR, Art. 8(1)(b) & Art. 9(2)(c); 15 U.S. Code § 1125.
241. EUTMR, Art. 18; 15 U.S. Code § 1127.
242. EUTMR, Art. 8(1)(b) & Art. 9(2)(c); 15 U.S. Code § 1125.
243. *Ibid.*

because of a 'username'[244] or account from which the message is coming.[245] Further, confusion[246] may occur when using a mark in or an altered or different spelling,[247] adding words to a trademark, capitalising on pronunciation,[248] in the context of social media usernames[249] or mobile app names. Additionally, using protected colours[250] for mobile app icons may cause 'confusion'.[251] During a search for apps, a consumer may be confused[252] in thinking they are downloading a mark-holders app when in fact they are not because a mark of another may be a part of the mobile app name or protected colours[253] in the mobile app icon. For example, when one searches for an app using a keyword,[254] it is likely that various search results will appear for different apps, and one may be confused[255] based on the names or appearance of the apps and may associate[256] one or more with a mark holder where they are not apps from those holders. Using trademarked logos or protected colours[257] in Metaverse platforms and

244. Lisa P Ramsey, 'Brandjacking on Social Networks: Trademark Infringement by Impersonation of Markholders' (2010) 58 Buffalo Law Review 851; Danny Friedmann, *Trademarks and Social Media: Towards Algorithmic Justice* (Edward Elgar Publishing 2015) 3-15; Rajeev Sachdev, 'Towards an Improved Framework for Trade-Mark Law and Regulation in Social Media Usernames: A Study of the Canadian, U.S., and U.K. Positions' (2016) 28 Intellectual Property Journal 379, 379-418.
245. *Ibid.*
246. EUTMR, Art. 8(1)(b) & Art. 9(2)(c); 15 U.S. Code § 1125.
247. USPTO, 'Possible Grounds for Refusal of a Mark' (*Process Overview*, 11 July 2016) https://www.uspto.gov/trademarks/additional-guidance-and-resources/possible-grounds-refusal-mark accessed January 2024.
248. *Ibid.*
249. Rajeev Sachdev, 'Towards an Improved Framework for Trade-Mark Law and Regulation in Social Media Usernames: A Study of the Canadian, U.S., and U.K. Positions' (2016) 28 Intellectual Property Journal 379, 379-418; Thomas J Curtin, 'The Name Game: Cybersquatting and Trademark Infringement on Social Media Websites' (2010-2011) 19 Journal of Law and Policy 353; IPO, 'Domain Names & Social Media Committee', (*Intellectual Property Owners Association Internet Domain Names Committee*) ipo.org/index.php/about-ipo/committees/internet-domainnames-committee/ accessed 4 August 2025; Lisa P Ramsey, 'Brandjacking on Social Networks: Trademark Infringement by Impersonation of Markholders' (2010) 58 Buffalo Law Review 851; Danny Friedmann, *Trademarks and Social Media: Towards Algorithmic Justice* (Edward Elgar Publishing 2015) 3-15.
250. Matthew D Asbell and Alan S Wernick, 'IP Protection for Mobile Apps: Navigating Name Selection, Trademark Clearance, Registration, Licensing and Infringement' (*Strafford*, 26 October 2016) http://media.straffordpub.com/products/ip-protection-for-mobile-apps-navigating-name-selection-trademark-clearance-registration-licensing-and-infringement-2016-10-26/presentation.pdf accessed January 2024.
251. Paris Convention, Art. 6bis; TRIPS, Art. 16(1); EUTMR, Art. 8(1)(b) and Art. 9(2)(b); 15 U.S. Code § 1114;15 U.S. Code § 1125.
252. EUTMR, Art. 8(1)(b) & Art. 9(2)(c); 15 U.S. Code § 1125.
253. Matthew D Asbell and Alan S Wernick, 'IP Protection for Mobile Apps: Navigating Name Selection, Trademark Clearance, Registration, Licensing and Infringement' (*Strafford*, 26 October 2016) http://media.straffordpub.com/products/ip-protection-for-mobile-apps-navigating-name-selection-trademark-clearance-registration-licensing-and-infringement-2016-10-26/presentation.pdf accessed January 2024.
254. EUTMR, Art. 8(1)(b) & Art. 9(2)(c); 15 U.S. Code § 1125.
255. *Ibid.*
256. *Ibid.*
257. Matthew D Asbell and Alan S Wernick, 'IP Protection for Mobile Apps: Navigating Name Selection, Trademark Clearance, Registration, Licensing and Infringement' (*Strafford*, 26 October 2016) http://media.straffordpub.com/products/ip-protection-for-mobile-apps-naviga

many other possibilities may cause 'confusion'.[258] While some Internet situations will clearly result in confusion,[259] there are a multitude of online scenarios for which it is unclear as to whether confusion[260] will be deemed by platforms to result and limited guidance is available. It should also be noted that 'distraction or diversion is not the same as confusion'.[261] What constitutes confusion[262] may depend on various aspects of digital marks, including where the mark was used[263] and the surrounding factors. Ohly asserts the need for consumers to be able to 'distinguish correctly'[264] and not be confused[265] by imitation products and services[266] and on the Internet, not only is this assessment strained, but the various areas where trademarks may be utilised complicate its assessment. In the context of the Metaverse, this is further exacerbated by the fact that '[t]here is currently no tool available to search for specific keywords across different metaverse platforms, nor can you easily locate items'.[267]

Despite this, and while forming a major basis under TRIPS[268] and the Paris Convention,[269] and while covered for domain names under the UDRP,[270] no broader Internet-specific factors to assess confusion[271] exist and it is difficult to apply existing factors in this context to platforms.[272] As will be seen in Chapter 4, the UDRP uses the terminology 'confusing similarity'[273] test, which may not necessarily be the same as 'likelihood of confusion',[274] although there is fairly clear guidance for what this constitutes under the UDRP.[275] As will be seen in Chapter 5, some platforms provide for

ting-name-selection-trademark-clearance-registration-licensing-and-infringement-2016-10-26/presentation.pdf accessed January 2024.

258. Paris Convention, Art. 6bis; TRIPS, Art. 16(1); EUTMR, Art. 8(1)(b) and Art. 9(2)(b); 15 U.S. Code § 1114;15 U.S. Code § 1125.
259. *Ibid.*
260. *Ibid.*
261. Christopher Heath and Anselm Kamperman Sanders, *Intellectual Property Liability of Consumers, Facilitators and Intermediaries* (1st edn, Kluwer Law International, 2012) §1:01.
262. EUTMR, Art. 8(1)(b) & Art. 9(2)(c); 15 U.S. Code § 1125.
263. EUTMR, Art. 18; 15 U.S. Code § 1127.
264. Angsar Ohly, '"Buy Me Because I'm Cool": The "Marketing Approach" and the Overlap Between Design, Trade Mark and Unfair Competition Law' in Annette Kur, Marianne Levin and Jens Schovsbo (eds), *The EU Design Approach: A Global Appraisal* (Edward Elgar 2018) 114.
265. *Ibid.*
266. *Ibid.*
267. Christian Tenkhoff, Philipp Grotkamp and Sylvia Burgess-Tate, 'Brands in the Metaverse: The Concept of "Interdimensional Confusion" Between the Physical and the Virtual Space under EU Trade Mark Law' (July 2023) 72 GRUR International 643-649, 648 https://doi.org/10.1093/grurint/ikad045.
268. TRIPS, Art. 16(1).
269. Paris Convention, Art. 6bis.
270. UDRP.
271. Paris Convention, Art. 6bis; TRIPS, Art. 16(1).
272. *Ibid.*
273. ICANN, 'Uniform Domain-Name Dispute-Resolution Policy' (*ICANN*, 25 February 2012) https://www.icann.org/resources/pages/policy-2012-02-25-en accessed June 2025.
274. David E Sorkin, 'Judicial Review of ICANN Domain Name Dispute Decisions' (2001) 18 Santa Clara Computer and High Technology Law Journal 35, 48.
275. WIPO, 'WIPO Overview of WIPO Panel Views on Selected UDRP Questions, Third Edition' ('WIPO Jurisprudential Overview 3.0') (*WIPO*, 2017) https://www.wipo.int/amc/en/domains/search/overview3.0/ accessed June 2025.

'confusion'[276] only through general means such as references in the form of a Frequently Asked Questions (FAQs),[277] others through general infringement-related prohibitions,[278] while others directly prohibit confusion.[279] Not only do these different possibilities create uncertainty, but platforms may apply 'confusion'[280] in their decision-making in different ways, resulting in the potential for inconsistent results even in similar situations across platforms.

2.2.4 There May Be Unfair Acts, Trade Practices[281] or Competition[282] Involving Digital Trademarks and This Is Not Adequately Addressed by Policies/Platforms

Although 'unfair competition'[283] is covered under Article 10bis of the Paris Convention, under 'civil liability and unfair competition'[284] provisions of EU Member State law, and under federal provisions in U.S. trademark legislation,[285] it is increasingly difficult to apply general provisions to digital trademarks. What may constitute an unfair[286] action on the Internet is also not clear, and while there may be disagreement about whether these be called unfair acts, 'unfair competition, unfair trade practices or unfair commercial practices',[287] and while this can differ in jurisdictions, there are a host of

276. Paris Convention, Art. 6bis; TRIPS, Art. 16(1).
277. Amazon, 'Intellectual Property Policy for Sellers: FAQ about Trademarks' (*Amazon*) https://sellercentral.amazon.com/help/hub/reference/external/GZUQ6GBBXQVHQKF2 accessed July 2024.
278. eBay, 'Verified Rights Owner Program' (*eBay*) https://www.ebay.com/sellercenter/ebay-for-business/verified-rights-owner-program#m17-1-tb2 accessed July 2024; Yahoo!, 'Yahoo Terms of Service' (*Yahoo!*) https://legal.yahoo.com/us/en/yahoo/terms/otos/index.html accessed July 2024.
279. Google, 'Trademarks' (*Google*) https://support.google.com/adspolicy/answer/6118?visit_id=638419270508802311-4094647794&rd=1 accessed July 2024; Microsoft, 'Intellectual Property Policies' (*Microsoft*) https://help.ads.microsoft.com/#apex/ads/en/ext60211 accessed July 2024; X, 'Trademark Policy' (*Trademark Policy*) https://help.x.com/en/rules-and-policies/x-trademark-policy accessed July 2024; LinkedIn, 'LinkedIn Advertising Policies' (*LinkedIn*) https://www.linkedin.com/legal/ads-policy accessed July 2024.
280. Paris Convention Art. 6bis; TRIPS, Art. 16(1).
281. *Ibid.*
282. *Ibid.*
283. Anselm Kamperman Sanders, *Unfair Competition Law: The Protection of Intellectual and Industrial Creativity* (Oxford University Press, 1997) 8; Frauke Henning-Bodewig, *Unfair Competition Law European Union and Member States* (Kluwer Law International 2006) xv-xvi; Martin Senftleben, Michael Handler and Irene Calboli, 'Protection Against Unfair Competition Around the Globe' (2024) 19 Journal of Intellectual Property Law & Practice 79, 79-80 https://doi.org/10.1093/jiplp/jpad121; Paris Convention, Art. 10bis; EUTMR, Art. 9(2)(c); 15 U.S.C. § 1125(c)(2)(B).
284. EUTMR, Art. 17.
285. 15 U.S. Code § 1125(a).
286. Anselm Kamperman Sanders, *Unfair Competition Law: The Protection of Intellectual and Industrial Creativity* (Oxford University Press 1997) 6-10.
287. Frauke Henning-Bodewig, *Unfair Competition Law European Union and Member States* (Kluwer Law International 2006) xv-xvi.

unfair actions which will collectively be termed as 'unfair competition'[288] in this book in line with the terminology used in the Paris Convention Article 10bis.

Kamperman Sanders notes that in cases '[w]here exploitation of another's achievements becomes inequitable, unfair competition law ... provides a remedy',[289] and tactics such as 'free riding'[290] and passing off[291] are prohibited. Riffel points out the flexibility of the doctrine of unfair competition[292] in the sense that it may be used to 'fill gaps in the intellectual property system due to the occurrence of new technology';[293] however, it does not appear that platforms are taking full advantage of this and a gap is left.

Further, while cybersquatting[294] is addressed through trademark infringement and 'unfair competition'[295] claims in the EU, through legislation[296] in the US, and through policies such as the UDRP, related issues including but not limited to impersonation[297] are also evident and sometimes rampant in e-commerce marketplace,[298] social media,[299] search ad, mobile app, and Metaverse platforms.

288. Anselm Kamperman Sanders, *Unfair Competition Law: The Protection of Intellectual and Industrial Creativity* (Oxford University Press 1997) 6-10; Frauke Henning-Bodewig, *Unfair Competition Law European Union and Member States* (Kluwer Law International 2006) xv-xvi.
289. Anselm Kamperman Sanders, *Unfair Competition Law: The Protection of Intellectual and Industrial Creativity* (Oxford University Press 1997) 6-10; Riffel, Christian Riffel, *Protection Against Unfair Competition in the WTO TRIPS Agreement: The Scope and Prospects of Article 10bis of the Paris Convention for the Protection of Industrial Property* (Brill 2016) 224.
290. Josef Drexl and Anselm Kamperman Sanders (eds), *The Innovation Society and Intellectual Property*, European Intellectual Property Institutes Network series (Edward Elgar Publishing 2019) 146-159.
291. Christopher Heath, Anselm Kamperman Sanders (eds), *Landmark Intellectual Property Cases and Their Legacy* (Kluwer Law International 2011) 56; Hossein Bidgoli, *The Internet Encyclopedia* (John Wiley & Sons, vol. 3, 2004) 452.
292. Christian Riffel, *Protection Against Unfair Competition in the WTO TRIPS Agreement: The Scope and Prospects of Article 10bis of the Paris Convention for the Protection of Industrial Property* (Brill 2016) 223-224.
293. *Ibid.*
294. 15 U.S. Code § 1125(d).
295. CMS, 'Protection of Trade Marks: Online Use and Anticybersquatting A European Perspective' (*CMS*, March 2007) https://www.cms-lawnow.com/~/media/lawnow/pdfs/cms%20publications/sector%20specific%20publications/tmc/ip/cmsanticybersquattingguide.pdf accessed January 2024.
296. 15 U.S. Code § 1125(d).
297. Lisa P Ramsey, 'Brandjacking on Social Networks: Trademark Infringement by Impersonation of Markholders' (2010) 58 Buffalo Law Review 851; Rajeev Sachdev, 'Towards an Improved Framework for Trade-Mark Law and Regulation in Social Media Usernames: A Study of the Canadian, U.S., and U.K. Positions' (2016) 28 Intellectual Property Journal 379, 379-418; Thomas J Curtin, 'The Name Game: Cybersquatting and Trademark Infringement on Social Media Websites' (2010-2011) 19 Journal of Law and Policy 353; IPO, 'Domain Names & Social Media Committee', (*Intellectual Property Owners Association Internet Domain Names Committee*) ipo.org/index.php/about-ipo/committees/internet-domainnames-committee/ accessed 4 August 2025; Danny Friedmann, *Trademarks and Social Media: Towards Algorithmic Justice* (Edward Elgar Publishing 2015) 3-15.
298. Edward C Anderson & Timothy S Cole, 'The UDRP: A Model for Dispute Resolution in E-Commerce' (2002) 6 Journal of Small & Emerging Business Law 235.
299. Lisa P Ramsey, 'Brandjacking on Social Networks: Trademark Infringement by Impersonation of Markholders' (2010) 58 Buffalo Law Review 851; Rajeev Sachdev, 'Towards an Improved Framework for Trade-Mark Law and Regulation in Social Media Usernames: A Study of the Canadian, U.S., and U.K. Positions' (2016) 28 Intellectual Property Journal 379, 379-418;

For example, trademarks may be utilised to 'pass off',[300] or alternatively to indicate that a seller is offering trademarked goods for sale, or merely to comment on the goods offered by a mark holder, although lines may be blurred as to when passing off[301] will be considered to be taking place on the Internet and whether or not a platform may consider it. Whether a social media post and/or chosen username would be considered engaging in 'unfair competition'[302] is unclear. For example, it is possible to impersonate[303] by creating false social media accounts[304] incorporating the marks of others. Moreover, where search, social media or Metaverse advertising is used to engage in 'comparative advertising',[305] it is difficult to assess whether infringement is taking place due to the often-limited space traditionally allocated to search ads and what role an associated website will take in the analysis, if any, and the fluid and changing nature of Metaverse ads at this time. Various platforms, including e-commerce marketplace platforms, face counterfeiting issues and efforts to mitigate such from happening in their platforms are an ongoing issue.[306]

As will be seen in Chapter 4, while the UDRP does not directly mention 'unfair competition',[307] or unfair acts or practices,[308] it does include some provisions that relate to these such as within the methods to provide 'rights and legitimate interests'[309]

Thomas J Curtin, 'The Name Game: Cybersquatting and Trademark Infringement on Social Media Websites' (2010-2011) 19 Journal of Law and Policy 353; IPO, 'Domain Names & Social Media Committee', (*Intellectual Property Owners Association Internet Domain Names Committee*) ipo.org/index.php/about-ipo/committees/internet-domainnames-committee/ accessed 4 August 2025; Danny Friedmann, *Trademarks and Social Media: Towards Algorithmic Justice* (Edward Elgar Publishing 2015) 3-15.

300. Lisa P Ramsey, 'Brandjacking on Social Networks: Trademark Infringement by Impersonation of Markholders' (2010) 58 Buffalo Law Review 851; Hossein Bidgoli, *The Internet Encyclopedia* (John Wiley & Sons, vol. 3, 2004) 452.
301. Lisa P Ramsey, 'Brandjacking on Social Networks: Trademark Infringement by Impersonation of Markholders' (2010) 58 Buffalo Law Review 851, Anselm Kamperman Sanders, *Unfair Competition Law: The Protection of Intellectual and Industrial Creativity* (Oxford University Press 1997) 6-10; Hossein Bidgoli, *The Internet Encyclopedia* (John Wiley & Sons, vol. 3, 2004) 452.
302. Anselm Kamperman Sanders, *Unfair Competition Law: The Protection of Intellectual and Industrial Creativity* (Oxford University Press 1997) 6-10.
303. Lisa P Ramsey, 'Brandjacking on Social Networks: Trademark Infringement by Impersonation of Markholders' (2010) 58 Buffalo Law Review 851; Google, 'Intellectual Property' (*Google*) https://play.google.com/about/ip-impersonation/ip/trademark/ accessed January 2024.
304. *Ibid.*
305. Louis S Ederer, 'Nominative Fair Use: Legitimate Advertising or Trademark Infringement?' (*Arnold & Porter LLP*) https://www.arnoldporter.com/~/media/files/perspectives/publications/2012/12/nominative-fair-use-legitimate-advertising-or-tr__/files/publication/fileattachment/nominative-fair-use.pdf accessed January 2024.
306. Elliot Champion, 'How to Identify and Subvert Counterfeiters in E-Commerce Marketplaces' (*World Trademark Review* 29 September 2023) https://www.worldtrademarkreview.com/guide/anti-counterfeiting-and-online-brand-enforcement/2023/article/how-identify-and-subvert-counterfeiters-in-e-commerce-marketplaces? accessed July 2024.
307. Anselm Kamperman Sanders, *Unfair Competition Law: The Protection of Intellectual and Industrial Creativity* (Oxford University Press 1997) 6-10; Frauke Henning-Bodewig, *Unfair Competition Law European Union and Member States* (Kluwer Law International 2006) xv-xvi 3.
308. *Ibid.*
309. ICANN, 'Uniform Domain-Name Dispute-Resolution Policy' (*ICANN*, 25 February 2012) https://www.icann.org/resources/pages/policy-2012-02-25-en accessed June 2025.

alongside a 'fair use'[310] justification (not as a specific ground of itself) where this must be not to 'misleadingly divert consumers or to tarnish'.[311] Registering a domain to sell, etc., to a competitor is prohibited, as is primarily to disrupt 'the business of a competitor'.[312] While not in the policy itself, the Overview states further that 'unfair competition or passing-off'[313] could help 'support standing'[314] in a UDRP matter.[315] Additionally, the Overview covers 'unfair practices',[316] 'unfairly passing itself off',[317] 'unfairly capitalize',[318] 'unfair advantage',[319] or 'abuse'[320] in the context of proving the 'bad faith'[321] element under the UDRP.[322] Lack of more direct mention of unfair acts,[323] trade practices[324] or competition[325] in the policy itself results in potential for these to not be considered or to not be adequately considered. Chapter 5 outlines the inconsistent and inadequate coverage of these by platforms, which results in inconsistency and unpredictability.[326] Some platforms cover this topic generally,[327] while others mention specific concepts such as 'unfair advantage',[328] 'unfair and/or parasitic competition',[329] 'deceptive or misleading',[330] 'impersonation',[331] etc., although this differs per

310. *Ibid.*
311. *Ibid.*
312. *Ibid.*
313. WIPO, 'WIPO Overview of WIPO Panel Views on Selected UDRP Questions, Third Edition' ('WIPO Jurisprudential Overview 3.0') (*WIPO*, 2017) https://www.wipo.int/amc/en/domains/search/overview3.0/ accessed June 2025.
314. *Ibid.*
315. *Ibid.*
316. *Ibid.*
317. *Ibid.*
318. *Ibid.*
319. *Ibid.*
320. *Ibid.*
321. *Ibid.*
322. *Ibid.*
323. Anselm Kamperman Sanders, *Unfair Competition Law: The Protection of Intellectual and Industrial Creativity* (Oxford University Press, 1997) 8; Frauke Henning-Bodewig, *Unfair Competition Law European Union and Member States* (Kluwer Law International 2006) xv-xvi; Martin Senftleben, Michael Handler and Irene Calboli, 'Protection Against Unfair Competition Around the Globe' (2024) 19 Journal of Intellectual Property Law & Practice 79, 79-80 https://doi.org/10.1093/jiplp/jpad121; Paris Convention, Art. 10bis; EUTMR, Art. 9(2)(c); 15 U.S.C. § 1125(c)(2)(B).
324. *Ibid.*
325. *Ibid.*
326. John McElwaine and Christopher D Casavale, 'Tackling Bad Faith Registration of Domain Names in a Fast-Changing Landscape' (*WIPO Magazine*, December 2019) https://www.wipo.int/wipo_magazine/en/2019/06/article_0006.html accessed June 2025.
327. ICANN, 'Uniform Domain-Name Dispute-Resolution Policy' (*ICANN*, 25 February 2012) https://www.icann.org/resources/pages/policy-2012-02-25-en accessed June 2025.
328. Amazon, 'Amazon Intellectual Property Policy' (*Amazon Seller Central*) https://sellercentral.amazon.nl/help/hub/reference/external/G201361070?locale=en-US accessed June 2025.
329. eBay, 'User Agreement' (*eBay Customer Service*) https://www.ebay.nl/help/policies/member-behaviour-policies/user-agreement?id=4259 accessed June 2025.
330. Google, 'Trademarks' (*Google*) https://support.google.com/adspolicy/answer/6118?visit_id=638419270508802311-4094647794&rd=1 accessed June 2025.
331. X, 'Misleading and Deceptive Identities Policy' (*X Help Center*) https://help.x.com/en/rules-and-policies/x-impersonation-and-deceptive-identities-policyaccessed June 2025; Snap, 'Community Guidelines' (*Snap Privacy, Safety, and Policy Hub*) https://values.snap.com/privacy/transparency/community-guidelines accessed June 2025.

platform. However, several platforms directly cover prohibition against 'counterfeiting'.[332] And while efforts to combat counterfeiting continue at law and through some platform programs,[333] it is rare for platform policies to adequately cover the trademark issues that arise in this context.

Further, in the EU, others are prevented from using reputable[334] marks 'without due cause'[335] where such will take 'unfair advantage of, or is detrimental to, the distinctive character or the repute of the EU trademark'[336] and the related problem of 'dilution'[337] is generally prohibited under 15 U.S. Code § 1125(c)(2)(B) and (C). Such activity is very difficult to assess in the Internet context and is not well defined. Although a 'well known'[338] mark will gain more protection,[339] the issue becomes what encompasses 'well known'[340] from the perspective of the Internet.[341] Marks that are 'well known'[342] offline may translate that to an online context. Alternatively, some marks are simply a product of their Internet savvy. Their reputation[343] may be a result of online activities and Internet sales and these marks may not have any significant, and in some cases, no offline presence. Some social media activity or some apps may go viral,[344] which may involve a mark spreading fast[345] and far,[346] and may result in fame[347] being gained very quickly.[348] However, in the offline context, it is not uncommon that such may take a considerably longer time. A mobile app name may

332. Amazon, 'Amazon Anti-Counterfeiting Policy' (*Amazon Seller Central*), https://sellercentral.amazon.com/help/hub/reference/external/G201165970 accessed June 2025; eBay, 'Counterfeits, Replicas and Unauthorized Copies Policy' (*eBay NL*) https://www.ebay.nl/help/policies/prohibited-restricted-items/fake-items-policy?id=4276 accessed June 2025; Yahoo! 'Counterfeit Policy' (*Yahoo!*) https://legal.yahoo.com/us/en/yahoo/ip/counterfeits/index.html accessed June 2025; Microsoft, 'Intellectual Property Policies' (*Microsoft*) https://help.ads.microsoft.com/#apex/ads/en/ext60211 accessed June 2025.
333. Regulation (EU) 2022/2065 of the European Parliament and of the Council of 19 October 2022 on a Single Market For Digital Services and amending Directive 2000/31/EC (Digital Services Act), US Shop Safe Act of 2021; Amazon, 'Let's Protect the Brand You Built' (*Amazon Brand Registry*) https://brandservices.amazon.com/ accessed July 2024.
334. EUTMR, Art. 9(2)(c).
335. *Ibid.*
336. *Ibid.*
337. Frank I Schechter, 'The Rational Basis of Trademark Protection' (1927) 40 Harvard Law Review 813 https://doi.org/10.2307/1330367;15 U.S. Code § 1125(c); Keola R Whitaker, 'Trademark Dilution in a Global Age' (2006) 27 University of Pennsylvania Journal of International Economic Law 907.
338. TRIPS, Art. 16; Paris Convention, Art. 6bis.
339. *Ibid.*
340. *Ibid.*
341. Haochen Sun, 'Anti-dilution Protection of Luxury Brands in the Global Economy' (2014) 45 Georgetown Journal of International Law 783.
342. TRIPS, Art. 16; Paris Convention, Art. 6bis.
343. TRIPS, Art. 16; Paris Convention, Art. 6bis; 15 U.S. Code § 1125(c).
344. Karine Nahon and Jeff Hemsley, *Going Viral* (Polity 2013) 2.
345. *Ibid.*
346. *Ibid.*
347. Stefan Martin, 'Well Known Marks and Parody: Dilution and Denigration? Unfair Advantage?' (*EUIPO*, 2017), https://euipo.europa.eu/knowledge/pluginfile.php/77920/mod_resource/content/8/Limits%20of%20trade%20marks%2C%20Parody%2018-5-2017.pdf accessed January 2024.
348. Karine Nahon and Jeff Hemsley, *Going Viral* (Polity 2013) 2.

also be created for the purpose of engaging in 'unfair competition'[349] or to dilute,[350] take 'unfair advantage'[351] of or be 'detrimental to'[352] the mark holder. Mobile apps may be dilutive[353] of mark holders' apps and marks within these may gain extreme fame[354] in a short time frame, such as if the apps go viral.[355] This impacts the analysis of 'reputation'[356] and traditional notions may not fit in a mobile app trademark analysis. As will be seen in Chapter 5, it is rare for platforms to incorporate these into their policies. Currently, there is no set Internet-specific criteria to assess online reputation[357] in platforms, or whether a mark is 'well known',[358] even though general rules and factors exist to draw from.[359] Whether clicks on a search ad or visits to the related website, or followers in social media accounts are impactful to clarify whether a mark is well-known[360] or reputable[361] is unclear.

Overall, inclusion or clarity regarding platform policies in the areas of unfair acts,[362] trade practices,[363] or competition[364] on the Internet is needed and how these will be assessed should be determined and made clear. Without inclusion or clarity relating to these, there will continue to be a reliance on potentially unclear individual platform policies and resulting decisions, or potentially expensive and timely litigation, which could be avoided.

349. Anselm Kamperman Sanders, *Unfair Competition Law: The Protection of Intellectual and Industrial Creativity* (Oxford University Press 1997) 6-10.
350. Keola R Whitaker, 'Trademark Dilution in a Global Age' (2006) 27 University of Pennsylvania Journal of International Economic Law 907, 909; 15 U.S. Code § 1125(c).
351. EUTMR, Arts 8 and 9(2)(c).
352. *Ibid.*
353. Keola R Whitaker, 'Trademark Dilution in a Global Age' (2006) 27 University of Pennsylvania Journal of International Economic Law 907, 909; 15 U.S. Code § 1125(c).
354. Stefan Martin, 'Well Known Marks and Parody: Dilution and Denigration? Unfair Advantage?' (*EUIPO*, 2017), https://euipo.europa.eu/knowledge/pluginfile.php/77920/mod_resource/content/8/Limits%20of%20trade%20marks%2C%20Parody%2018-5-2017.pdf accessed January 2024.
355. Karine Nahon and Jeff Hemsley, *Going Viral* (Polity 2013) 2.
356. EUTMR, Arts 8(5) and 9(1)(c).
357. *Ibid.*
358. Paris Convention, Art. 6bis; TRIPS, Art. 16.
359. *Ibid.*; 15 U.S. Code § 1125(c).
360. *Ibid.*
361. *Ibid.*
362. Anselm Kamperman Sanders, *Unfair Competition Law: The Protection of Intellectual and Industrial Creativity* (Oxford University Press, 1997) 8; Frauke Henning-Bodewig, *Unfair Competition Law European Union and Member States* (Kluwer Law International 2006) xv-xvi; Martin Senftleben, Michael Handler and Irene Calboli, 'Protection Against Unfair Competition Around the Globe' (2024) 19 Journal of Intellectual Property Law & Practice 79, 79-80 https://doi.org/10.1093/jiplp/jpad121; Paris Convention, Art. 10bis; EUTMR, Art. 9(2)(c); 15 U.S.C. § 1125(c)(2)(B).
363. *Ibid.*
364. *Ibid.*

2.2.5 Terms, Platform Policies, and the Status of Disclaimers Inadequately Address Digital Trademarks

While all platforms have terms of use or the equivalent and many have trademark rules or policies, there are no uniform terms or policies addressing trademarks for e-commerce marketplace,[365] search advertising, social media,[366] mobile app, or Metaverse platforms. However, the UDRP deals with domain name trademark disputes on an international level.[367] There are also some Country Code Top-Level Domain (ccTLD)[368] related policies[369] which apply to certain disputes relating to domain names. However, there are no such equivalent uniform policies for other platforms.[370] While individual platforms have their own policies and complaints may be lodged with

365. Edward C Anderson & Timothy S Cole, 'The UDRP: A Model for Dispute Resolution in E-Commerce' (2002) 6 Journal of Small & Emerging Business Law 235.
366. ICANN, 'Uniform Domain-Name Dispute-Resolution Policy' (*ICANN*, 25 February 2012) https://www.icann.org/resources/pages/policy-2012-02-25-en accessed June 2025; 15 U.S. Code § 1125(d);); Rajeev Sachdev, 'Towards an Improved Framework for Trade-Mark Law and Regulation in Social Media Usernames: A Study of the Canadian, U.S., and U.K. Positions' (2016) 28 Intellectual Property Journal 379, 379-418; Daniel Doft, 'Facebook, Twitter, and the Wild West of IP Enforcement on Social Media: Weighing the Merits of a Uniform Dispute Resolution Policy' (2016) 49 The John Marshall Law Review 959; Thomas J Curtin, 'The Name Game: Cybersquatting and Trademark Infringement on Social Media Websites' (2010-2011) 19 Journal of Law and Policy 353; Erick J Heels, 'How to Twittersquat the Top 100 Brands' (*GiantPeople*, 8 January 2009) http://www.giantpeople.com/1298.html accessed 4 August 2025; Paul D McGrady, *McGrady on Social Media and the Metaverse* (Mathew Bender & Company, Inc. 2023) §12; John McElwaine and Christopher D Casavale, 'Tackling Bad Faith Registration of Domain Names in a Fast-Changing Landscape' (*WIPO Magazine*, December 2019) https://www.wipo.int/wipo_magazine/en/2019/06/article_0006.html accessed June 2025.
367. ICANN, 'Uniform Domain-Name Dispute-Resolution Policy' (*ICANN*, 25 February 2012) https://www.icann.org/resources/pages/policy-2012-02-25-en accessed June 2025.
368. IANA, 'Root Zone Database' (*IANA*) https://www.iana.org/domains/root/db accessed January 2024.
369. US, 'Nexus Dispute Policy' (*AboutUS*) https://www.about.us/policies/ustld-nexus-dispute-policy accessed January 2024; WIPO, 'WIPO Domain Name Dispute Resolution Service for .EU (and.ею and.ευ)' (*WIPO*) https://www.wipo.int/amc/en/domains/cctld/eu/index.html accessed January 2024; CIRA, 'CIRA Domain Name Dispute Resolution Policy' (*CIRA*) https://www.cira.ca/policy/domain-name/cira-domain-name-dispute-resolution-policy accessed January 2024.
370. Rajeev Sachdev, 'Towards an Improved Framework for Trade-Mark Law and Regulation in Social Media Usernames: A Study of the Canadian, U.S., and U.K. Positions' (2016) 28 Intellectual Property Journal 379, 379-418; Thomas J Curtin, 'The Name Game: Cybersquatting and Trademark Infringement on Social Media Websites' (2010-2011) 19 Journal of Law and Policy 353; IPO, 'Domain Names & Social Media Committee', (*Intellectual Property Owners Association Internet Domain Names Committee*) ipo.org/index.php/about-ipo/committees/internet-domainnames-committee/ accessed 4 August 2025; Lisa P Ramsey, 'Brandjacking on Social Networks: Trademark Infringement by Impersonation of Markholders' (2010) 58 Buffalo Law Review 851; Danny Friedmann, *Trademarks and Social Media: Towards Algorithmic Justice* (Edward Elgar Publishing 2015) 3-15; Daniel Doft, 'Facebook, Twitter, and the Wild West of IP Enforcement on Social Media: Weighing the Merits of a Uniform Dispute Resolution Policy' (2016) 49 The John Marshall Law Review 959; Paul D McGrady, *McGrady on Social Media and the Metaverse* (Mathew Bender & Company, Inc. 2023) §12.

e-commerce marketplace, search ad, social media,[371] mobile app, or Metaverse platforms, it would be in the discretion of each platform to consider the matter and decide what action will be taken, if any.[372] This is also true of programmes such as Amazon's Brand Registry which, while welcome as a programme to combat trademark issues in its platforms, applies primarily to registered marks in select countries and is still based on Amazon's IP Policy, which, like all other platforms, lacks coverage of key concepts associated with the problems identified in this chapter, as will be seen in Chapter 5.[373] Inconsistency[374] results from having individual and separate terms and policies of various platforms, even if the same mark is being utilised across all of these.

The UDRP does not directly address disclaimers. However, the Overview states, 'where the respondent appears to otherwise have a right or legitimate interest in a disputed domain name, a clear and sufficiently prominent disclaimer would lend support to circumstances suggesting its good faith'.[375] Further, e-commerce listings, search ads, social media ads, mobile apps, and Metaverse sites may contain some sort of disclaimer relating to trademarks, whether formal disclaimers or simple words within a username or mobile app name itself. Peukert rightly recognises that disclaimers are important when technology cannot be used to avoid problems relating to marks

371. Facebook, 'Trademark' (*Facebook Help*) https://www.facebook.com/help/507663689427413/?helpref=hc_fnav accessed January 2024; Twitter, 'Trademark Policy' (*Twitter Trademark Policy*) https://help.x.com/en/rules-and-policies/x-trademark-policy accessed July 2024; Snapchat, 'Contact Us' (*Snapchat Support*) https://support.snapchat.com/en-US/i-need-help?start=5668251581284352 accessed January 2024; Rajeev Sachdev, 'Towards an Improved Framework for Trade-Mark Law and Regulation in Social Media Usernames: A Study of the Canadian, U.S., and U.K. Positions' (2016) 28 Intellectual Property Journal 379, 379-418; Thomas J Curtin, 'The Name Game: Cybersquatting and Trademark Infringement on Social Media Websites' (2010-2011) 19 Journal of Law and Policy 353; IPO, 'Domain Names & Social Media Committee', (*Intellectual Property Owners Association Internet Domain Names Committee*) ipo.org/index.php/about-ipo/committees/internet-domainnames-committee/ accessed 4 August 2025; Lisa P Ramsey, 'Brandjacking on Social Networks: Trademark Infringement by Impersonation of Markholders' (2010) 58 Buffalo Law Review 851; Danny Friedmann, *Trademarks and Social Media: Towards Algorithmic Justice* (Edward Elgar Publishing 2015) 3-15.

372. *Ibid.*

373. Amazon, 'Let's Protect the Brand You Built' (*Amazon Brand Registry*) https://brandservices.amazon.com/ accessed July 2024; Amazon, 'Brand Registry FAQ' (*Amazon*) https://brandservices.amazon.com/brandregistry/faq accessed July 2024.

374. ICANN, 'Uniform Domain-Name Dispute-Resolution Policy' (*ICANN*, 25 February 2012) https://www.icann.org/resources/pages/policy-2012-02-25-en; 15 U.S. Code § 1125(d); Rajeev Sachdev, 'Towards an Improved Framework for Trade-Mark Law and Regulation in Social Media Usernames: A Study of the Canadian, U.S., and U.K. Positions' (2016) 28 Intellectual Property Journal 379, 379-418; Daniel Doft, 'Facebook, Twitter, and the Wild West of IP Enforcement on Social Media: Weighing the Merits of a Uniform Dispute Resolution Policy' (2016) 49 The John Marshall Law Review 959; Thomas J Curtin, 'The Name Game: Cybersquatting and Trademark Infringement on Social Media Websites' (2010-2011) 19 Journal of Law and Policy 353; Erick J Heels, 'How to Twittersquat the Top 100 Brands' (*GiantPeople*, 8 January 2009) http://www.giantpeople.com/1298.html accessed 4 August 2025; Paul D McGrady, *McGrady on Social Media and the Metaverse* (Mathew Bender & Company, Inc. 2023) §12.

375. WIPO, 'WIPO Overview of WIPO Panel Views on Selected UDRP Questions, Third Edition, ('WIPO Jurisprudential Overview 3.0') (*WIPO*, 2017) https://www.wipo.int/amc/en/domains/search/overview3.0/ accessed June 2025.

on the Internet.[376] However, it is unclear how disclaimers may be utilised, what they need to say and whether they will be effective. Peukert further says these disclaimers should be 'sufficiently clear and prominent',[377] which may require a different placement for each of these different areas. As will be seen in Chapter 5, platforms do not generally reference the use of disclaimers in their terms or policies. Whether or not disclaimers will be considered by platforms, and if so, what these may need to include or where they need to be placed, is uncertain.

Overall, terms and policies with respect to trademarks in various platforms are different, may be missing key elements, may be inconsistent and often do not provide a clear understanding of how marks may be utilised within these. The effect and use of disclaimers are also unclear.

2.2.6 The Internet Is Global, yet Trademark Rules Are Mostly Jurisdictional and This Is Not Adequately Addressed by Policies/Platforms

The Internet is global in nature,[378] yet most rules are jurisdictional. The Internet is not confined to customary borders 'making the implementation of jurisdiction-specific laws difficult'.[379] George and Scerri say that content viewable on largely a global scale through the Internet raises 'legal issues regarding jurisdiction and applicable law'[380] and may be a source of uncertainty in relation to digital trademarks.[381]

The UDRP does not directly touch on this issue; although, as will be seen in Chapter 4, the Overview states that 'rules and principles of law'[382] may be considered and where 'the parties share a common nationality and the import of a specific national law concept is particularly germane to an issue',[383] local law may be considered although not usually required.[384] As will be seen in Chapter 5, while some platforms have terms and conditions which may be specific to regions, such as one for US customer, and one for EU and/or rest of world, they may only have slight differences

376. Alexander Peukert, 'The Coexistence of Trade Mark Laws and Rights on the Internet, and the Impact of Geolocation Technologies' (2016) 47 International Review of Intellectual Property and Competition Law 60, 81 https://doi.org/10.1007/s40319-015-0427-8.
377. *Ibid.*
378. Frederick Mostert, 'The Internet: Regulators Struggle to Balance Freedom with Risk', (*Financial Times*, 2019) https://www.ft.com/content/e49c39e6-967d-11e9-8cfb-30c211dcd229 accessed December 2024.
379. Carlisle George and Jackie Scerri, 'Web 2.0 and User-Generated Content: Legal Challenges in the New Frontier' 2007 (2) Journal of Information Law & Technology 5.2 http://www2.warwick.ac.uk/fac/soc/law/elj/jilt/2007_2/george_scerri accessed January 2024.
380. *Ibid.*
381. *Ibid.*
382. WIPO, 'WIPO Overview of WIPO Panel Views on Selected UDRP Questions, Third Edition' ('WIPO Jurisprudential Overview 3.0') (*WIPO*, 2017) https://www.wipo.int/amc/en/domains/search/overview3.0/ accessed June 2025.
383. *Ibid.*
384. *Ibid.*

in some cases.[385] However, these may not address the crux of the issue. For example, while e-commerce marketplace platforms often have a specific geographic target, this may not be for all countries,[386] and while search ads may be targeted geographically,[387] social media, mobile app and Metaverse platforms may, but do not necessarily have a geographic target. Social media advertising may be specifically targeted to geographic locations or regions; however, other social media or mobile app activity may not be, and it becomes unclear how to address jurisdiction-related matters in these contexts. Users may also register e-commerce accounts, social media usernames and mobile app names, usually with little registration difficulty.[388] If an e-commerce seller, search advertiser, social media account holder, mobile app operator, or Metaverse creator utilises a trademark in an unlawful manner (which itself is not well defined), issues of where to bring a legal action based on an alleged violation are raised often addressed by the terms in the context only of disputes between a user and the platform, not between users and other users.[389] This breeds inconsistency and prompts the possible need to comply with numerous, generally non-specific, regulations and laws of various jurisdictions. Also, where search ads are used to advertise goods and services globally, jurisdictional issues not clearly addressed by legal frameworks are raised, including which rules apply. Trademarks are very much jurisdiction-based, including the need to be used[390] in the jurisdictions (problem related to which were seen in section 2.2.1 above). Further, whether a mark may co-exist[391] online is problematic and, as is the case for domain names, social media usernames, mobile app names, etc., can generally

385. eBay, 'Intellectual Property Policy' (*eBay*) https://www.ebay.nl/help/policies/listing-policies/selling-policies/vero-policy?id=4349 accessed July 2024; Snap, 'Snap Inc. Terms of Service' (*Snap Inc.* 26 February 2024) https://www.snap.com/en-US/terms#sgl-terms accessed July 2024.
386. Amazon, 'Website (Country/Region)' (*Amazon*) https://www.amazon.com/customer-preferences/country? accessed July 2024; eBay, 'Homepage' (*eBay*) https://www.ebay.com/ accessed January 2024; *See* Amazon country dropdown list, and eBay Sites list, for example.
387. Google, 'Target Ads to Geographic Locations' (*Google Ads Help*) https://support.google.com/google-ads/answer/1722043?hl=en accessed January 2024; Microsoft, 'Audience Targeting' (*Microsoft Advertising*) https://about.ads.microsoft.com/en-us/solutions/audience-targeting/location-targeting accessed January 2024.
388. Google, 'Domains BETA' (*Google Domains*) https://domains.google/#/domains-header accessed January 2024; Twitter, 'Create Your Account' (*Twitter Signup*) https://twitter.com/i/flow/signup accessed January 2024; Google, 'Upload an App' (*Google Play Console Help*) https://support.google.com/googleplay/android-developer/answer/113469?hl=en accessed January 2024.
389. eBay, 'Intellectual Property Policy' (*eBay*) https://www.ebay.nl/help/policies/listing-policies/selling-policies/vero-policy?id=4349 accessed July 2024; Snap, 'Snap Inc. Terms of Service' (*Snap Inc.* 26 February 2024) https://www.snap.com/en-US/terms#sgl-terms accessed July 2024.
390. EUTMR, Art. 18; 15 U.S. Code § 1127.
391. EUIPO, '3.1 Coexistence Between the Marks Involved in the Opposition' (*EUIPO Trade mark Guidelines*) https://guidelines.euipo.europa.eu/2058843/2043906/trade-mark-guidelines/3-1-coexistence-between-the-marks-involved-in-the-opposition accessed January 2024; 15 U.S. Code § 1052(d); Alexander Peukert, 'The Coexistence of Trade Mark Laws and Rights on the Internet, and the Impact of Geolocation Technologies' (2016) 47 International Review of Intellectual Property and Competition Law 60, 81 https://doi.org/10.1007/s40319-015-0427-8; Tamara Nanayakkara, 'IP and Business: Trademark Coexistence' (*WIPO*, November 2006) https://www.wipo.int/wipo_magazine/en/2006/06/article_0007.html accessed June 2025.

only be registered once for each on a single platform. Also, there are differences among jurisdictions on how trademarks are registered, renewed, expunged or cancelled through trademark offices such as the European Union Intellectual Property Office (EUIPO) or the United States Patent and Trademark Office (USPTO).[392] Each has its own guidance or methods of determining or deciding on these, and even though a streamlined international registration process is available,[393] this does not alleviate jurisdiction-based actions and use[394] requirements.

Overall, the 'global nature of the Internet'[395] challenges the jurisdictional or 'territorial nature'[396] of trademark law.[397] This needs to be clarified in the context of platforms. Otherwise, a complicated patchwork of rules may apply and this causes serious legal uncertainty and potential for high costs.

2.2.7 How Defences and Justification May Apply Is Unclear for Digital Trademarks and This Is Not Adequately Addressed by Policies/Platforms

Defences, limitations and justifications to trademarks are not easily applied in an Internet context. There are conflicting considerations relating to 'Constitutional'[398] and 'human rights'[399] provisions, EU 'freedom of expression and information',[400] and US 'free speech'[401] and other areas must also be considered. The methods by which trademarks may be utilised without violating mark holder's rights must be clarified for platforms. Further, defences may differ amongst jurisdictions or may be applied differently in others and there is the problem between application of these in an offline context versus an online one. As will be seen in Chapter 4, the UDRP directly incorporates 'legitimate noncommercial or fair use'[402] as a way to demonstrate 'rights and legitimate interests'[403] and the Overview addresses fair use and freedom of

392. EUIPO, 'EUIPO' (*Homepage*) https://euipo.europa.eu/ accessed January 2024; USPTO Office of Public Affairs, 'United States Patent and Trademark Office' (*USPTO*) https://www.uspto.gov/ accessed January 2024.
393. WIPO, 'Madrid System: The International Trademark System' (*WIPO*) https://www.wipo.int/web/madrid-system accessed July 2024.
394. EUTMR, Art. 18; 15 U.S. Code § 1127.
395. WIPO, 'WIPO Overview of WIPO Panel Views on Selected UDRP Questions, Third Edition, ('WIPO Jurisprudential Overview 3.0') (*WIPO*, 2017) https://www.wipo.int/amc/en/domains/search/overview3.0/ accessed June 2025.
396. Graeme Dinwoodie, 'Trademarks and Territory: Detaching Trademark Law from the Nation-State' (2004-2005) 41 Houston Law Review 885, 890.
397. *Ibid.*
398. Lisa P Ramsey, 'Free Speech and International Obligations to Protect Trademarks' 35 The Yale Journal of International Law 405, 406.
399. *Ibid.*; Art. 10 of the European Convention on Human Rights (ECHR).
400. European Convention on Human Rights (ECHR), Art. 10; EU Charter of Fundamental Rights of the EU, Art. 11; Lisa P Ramsey, 'Free Speech and International Obligations to Protect Trademarks' 35 The Yale Journal of International Law 405, 406.
401. The Constitution of the United States of America, Amendment I.
402. ICANN, 'Uniform Domain-Name Dispute-Resolution Policy' (*ICANN*, 25 February 2012) https://www.icann.org/resources/pages/policy-2012-02-25-en accessed June 2025.
403. *Ibid.*

speech.[404] As will be seen in Chapter 5, platform policies significantly differ and are not consistent, causing confusion and uncertainty. Some platforms provide limited exceptions,[405] while others provide a detailed list of justifications and defences;[406] however, a consistent application of common justifications and defences is not present among platforms and interpretation can also be difficult. For example, users of trademarks in search advertising can raise the defence or justification of a 'fair'[407] type of use of the mark, or a 'bona fide use';[408] however, it is not always clear how to assess these. Applying defences and justifications to trademarks in search ads is difficult because of the lack of clarity as to how these apply. For example, when search ads are used to engage in parody,[409] it is unclear how that should be presented, to what may need to be included in the search ad to make that clear. Where and how trademarks of others may be permitted in social media pages and activity under a defence or justification is also unclear. For example, in LinkedIn, trademarks may be used to signify association[410] with certain organizations and in X (formerly, Twitter), reposting[411] (formerly, retweeting)[412] a message that includes a mark may not automatically trigger a violation such as when it is clear that it is being re-sent, forwarded, and this may be considered fair[413] if a trademark use[414] at all. As will be seen in Chapter 5, while some platforms have included some justifications in their policies, many instances are still not clear, and there is inconsistency among policies. Further clarity is required, such as when a user has a 'freedom of expression and information'[415] right or 'fair use defense, or a free speech interest in using the term in parody, satire, criticism, comparative advertising, news reporting, or other commentary'.[416]

404. WIPO, 'WIPO Overview of WIPO Panel Views on Selected UDRP Questions, Third Edition' ('WIPO Jurisprudential Overview 3.0') (*WIPO*, 2017) https://www.wipo.int/amc/en/domains/search/overview3.0/ accessed June 2025.
405. eBay, 'Intellectual Property Policy' (*eBay*) https://www.ebay.nl/help/policies/listing-policies/selling-policies/vero-policy?id=4349 accessed July 2024.
406. Amazon, 'Intellectual Property Policy for Sellers: FAQ about Trademarks' (*Amazon*) https://sellercentral.amazon.com/help/hub/reference/external/GZUQ6GBBXQVHQKF2 accessed July 2024.
407. Regulation (EU) 2017/1001 of the European Parliament and of the Council of 14 June 2017 on the European Union Trade Mark (EUTMR); 15 U.S. Code § 1115(b)(4).
408. Canadian Trademarks Act R.S.C., 1985, c. T-13, s. 22.
409. EUTMR, Art. 14.
410. 15 U.S. Code § 1127; EUTMR, Art. 18; Canadian Trademarks Act R.S.C., 1985, c. T-13, s. 2.
411. A, 'How to Repost' (*X*) https://help.x.com/en/using-x/how-to-repost accessed January 2024.
412. Twitter, 'How to Retweet' (*Twitter*) https://help.twitter.com/en/using-twitter/how-to-retweet; Oxford Dictionaries, 'Retweet | Definition of Retweet in English by Oxford Dictionaries' (*Oxford Dictionaries | English*) https://en.oxforddictionaries.com/definition/retweet accessed January 2024.
413. EUTMR, Recital 21; 15 U.S. Code § 1115(b)(4).
414. TRIPS, Art. 16; EUTMR, Art. 18; 15 U.S. Code § 1127.
415. European Convention on Human Rights (ECHR), Art. 10; EU Charter of Fundamental Rights of the EU, Art. 11; Lisa P Ramsey, 'Free Speech and International Obligations to Protect Trademarks' 35 The Yale Journal of International Law 405, 406.
416. Lisa P Ramsey, 'Brandjacking on Social Networks: Trademark Infringement by Impersonation of Markholders' (2010) 58 Buffalo Law Review 851; Lisa P Ramsey, 'Increasing First Amendment Scrutiny of Trademark Law' (2008) 61 SMU Law Review 381, 404-447.

2.2.8 Summary

Based on all of the above problems for digital trademarks, it is clear that platforms are impacted. In various cases, what rules or factors may apply are unclear. First, there is great legal uncertainty in terms of how these various issues will be dealt with respect to and by the Internet platforms. This results in confusion with respect to how marks can be utilised within these platforms. Parties may expend unnecessary time and cost to deal with the various issues that may result. If litigated, there may be great costs and lengthy litigation. In some cases, parties may forego litigation or give up despite having legitimate rights due to the time, effort, and/or cost issues. Solutions to these problems need to be identified and implemented urgently.

2.3 THE DIGITAL TRADEMARK AND TRADE PRACTICES MODEL BASED ON PROBLEMS IDENTIFIED

The themes that emerge from the problems identified above are important because they shed light on the areas where digital trademarks create serious issues. Drawing from these, an adapted model can be developed to dig deeper and form the basis of analysis. The adapted model is necessary to address or mitigate these problems, and it serves as a framework to recommend solutions to the problems identified for the UDRP and the platforms considered in this study.

Based on the above, there are problems in seven key areas. These include: (a) 'use' and[417]/'place of use',[418] (b) 'bad faith'[419] and 'abuse',[420] (c) 'confusion',[421] (d) unfair acts, practices, or competition,[422] (e) terms, policies, and disclaimers,[423]

---

417. 15 U.S. Code § 1127; EUTMR, Art. 18; Canadian Trademarks Act R.S.C., 1985, c. T-13, s. 2; ICANN, 'Uniform Domain-Name Dispute-Resolution Policy' (*ICANN*, 25 February 2012) https://www.icann.org/resources/pages/policy-2012-02-25-en accessed June 2025.
418. EUIPO, '3 Place of Use' (*EUIPO Trade mark guidelines* 2024) https://guidelines.euipo.europa.eu/2214311/1982069/trade-mark-guidelines/3-place-of-use accessed January 2024.
419. Paris Convention, Art. 6bis; 'Uniform Domain-Name Dispute-Resolution Policy' (*ICANN*, 25 February 2012) https://www.icann.org/resources/pages/policy-2012-02-25-en accessed June 2025.
    ICANN, 'Uniform Domain-Name Dispute-Resolution Policy' (*ICANN*, 25 February 2012) https://www.icann.org/resources/pages/policy-2012-02-25-en accessed June 2025; 15 U.S. Code § 1125(d).
420. WIPO, 'WIPO Overview of WIPO Panel Views on Selected UDRP Questions, Third Edition' ('WIPO Jurisprudential Overview 3.0') (*WIPO*, 2017) https://www.wipo.int/amc/en/domains/search/overview3.0/ accessed June 2025.
421. Paris Convention, Art. 6bis; TRIPS, Art. 16.
422. Anselm Kamperman Sanders, *Unfair Competition Law: The Protection of Intellectual and Industrial Creativity* (Oxford University Press 1997) 6-10; Paris Convention, Art. 6bis; TRIPS, Art. 16.
423. WIPO, 'WIPO Overview of WIPO Panel Views on Selected UDRP Questions, Third Edition' ('WIPO Jurisprudential Overview 3.0') (*WIPO*, 2017) https://www.wipo.int/amc/en/domains/search/overview3.0/ accessed June 2025; Alexander Peukert, 'The Coexistence of Trade Mark Laws and Rights on the Internet, and the Impact of Geolocation Technologies' (2016) 47 International Review of Intellectual Property and Competition Law 60, 81 https://doi.org/10.1007/s40319-015-0427-8; Leslie Fair, 'Full Disclosure' (*FTC Business Blog*, 23 September 2014) https://www.ftc.gov/business-guidance/blog/2014/09/full-disclosure accessed June 2025.

(f) jurisdictional/territorial issues,[424] and (g) justification/defences.[425] These seven key areas form the basis for an adapted model, referred to as the Digital Trademark and Trade Practices Model or simply, *the model*. Thus, the seven key areas of the model are formulated as individual *elements* of the model that need to be considered in an Internet trademark analysis for the UDRP and the platforms. The model is shown in *Figure 2.4* below, followed by a brief description.

Figure 2.4 Digital Trademark and Trade Practices Model[426]

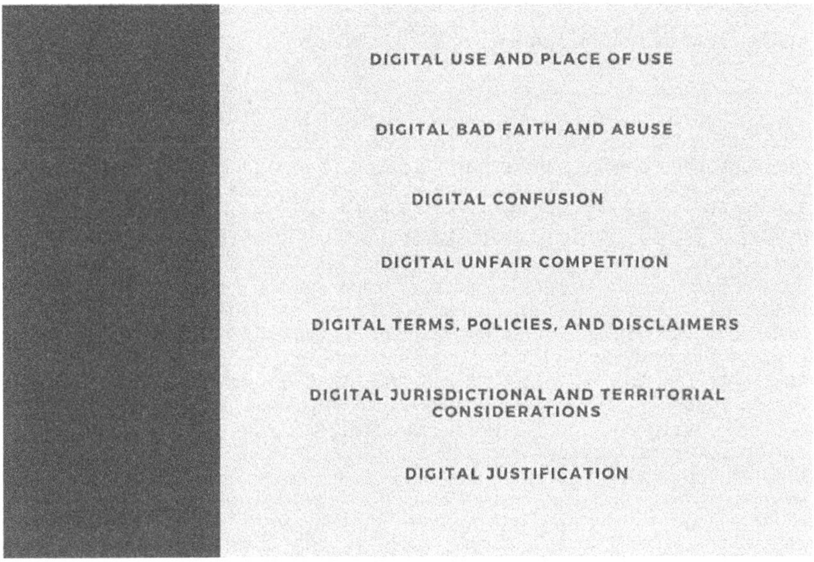

424. Julien Chaisse, 'The Merging of Two Worlds: Cyber Law and Trade Law Normative Convergence on Internet Domain Names' (2019) 37 Boston University International Law Journal 281; Brendan J Witherell, 'Trademark Law: The Extraterritorial Application of the Lanham Act – The First Circuit Cuts the Fat from the Vanity Fair Test' (2006) 29 Western New England Law Review 193, 197; Ansgar Ohly, 'Choice of Law in the Digital Environment: Problems and Possible Solutions' in Josef Drexl and Annette Kur (eds), *Intellectual Property and Private International Law: Heading for the Future* (Bloomsbury Publishing 2005) 241; Irene Calboli and Jane Ginsburg, 'Preface', in Irene Calboli and Jane Gindburg JC (eds), *The Cambridge Handbook of International and Comparative Trademark Law* (Cambridge University Press 2020) XXI.
425. ICANN, 'Uniform Domain-Name Dispute-Resolution Policy' (*ICANN*, 25 February 2012) https://www.icann.org/resources/pages/policy-2012-02-25-en accessed June 2025.
426. Adapted from/informed by 15 U.S. Code § 1127; EUTMR, Art. 18; Canadian Trademarks Act R.S.C., 1985, c. T-13, s. 2; ICANN, 'Uniform Domain-Name Dispute-Resolution Policy' (*ICANN*, 25 February 2012) https://www.icann.org/resources/pages/policy-2012-02-25-en accessed June 2025; EUIPO, '3 Place of use' (*EUIPO Trade mark guidelines* 2024) https://guidelines.euipo.europa.eu/2214311/1982069/trade-mark-guidelines/3-place-of-use accessed January 2024; Paris Convention, Art. 6bis; 'Uniform Domain-Name Dispute-Resolution Policy' (*ICANN*, 25 February 2012) https://www.icann.org/resources/pages/policy-2012-02-25-en accessed June 2025; ICANN, 'Uniform Domain-Name Dispute-Resolution Policy' (*ICANN*, 25 February

Digital Use and Place of Use[427] includes how a mark is used[428] and when this will be in the 'course of trade'[429] or like provision considered for policies/platforms. Also, the place of use,[430] or where specifically the mark is used, must be considered for policies/platforms as there is an ever-increasing number of specific places where marks may be used,[431] each of which may raise different considerations.

Digital Bad Faith and Abuse[432] includes the increasing ways in which marks may be utilised in 'bad faith'[433] and how this may be considered for policies/platforms. Further, 'abuse'[434] on the Internet is also considered, from the perspective of repeated 'bad faith'.[435]

Digital Confusion[436] includes, as a major infringement standard, how this may be considered for policies/platforms.

2012) https://www.icann.org/resources/pages/policy-2012-02-25-en accessed June 2025; 15 U.S. Code § 1125(d); WIPO, 'WIPO Overview of WIPO Panel Views on Selected UDRP Questions, Third Edition' ('WIPO Jurisprudential Overview 3.0') (*WIPO*, 2017) https://www.wipo.int/amc/en/domains/search/overview3.0/ accessed June 2025; Paris Convention, Art. 6bis; TRIPS, Art. 16; Anselm Kamperman Sanders, *Unfair Competition Law: The Protection of Intellectual and Industrial Creativity* (Oxford University Press 1997) 6-10; Paris Convention, Art. 6bis; TRIPS, Art. 16; Alexander Peukert, 'The Coexistence of Trade Mark Laws and Rights on the Internet, and the Impact of Geolocation Technologies' (2016) 47 International Review of Intellectual Property and Competition Law 60, 81 https://doi.org/10.1007/s40319-015-0427-8; Leslie Fair, 'Full Disclosure' (*FTC Business Blog*, 23 September 2014) https://www.ftc.gov/business-guidance/blog/2014/09/full-disclosure accessed June 2025; Julien Chaisse, 'The Merging of Two Worlds: Cyber Law and Trade Law Normative Convergence on Internet Domain Names' (2019) 37 Boston University International Law Journal 281; Brendan J Witherell, 'Trademark Law: The Extraterritorial Application of the Lanham Act – The First Circuit Cuts the Fat from the Vanity Fair Test' (2006) 29 Western New England Law Review 193, 197; Ansgar Ohly, 'Choice of Law in the Digital Environment: Problems and Possible Solutions' in Josef Drexl and Annette Kur (eds), *Intellectual Property and Private International Law: Heading for the Future* (Bloomsbury Publishing 2005) 241; Irene Calboli and Jane Ginsburg, 'Preface', in Irene Calboli and Jane Gindburg JC (eds), *The Cambridge Handbook of International and Comparative Trademark Law* (Cambridge University Press 2020) XXI.

427. EUTMR, Art. 18; 15 U.S. Code § 1127; Canadian Trademarks Act R.S.C., 1985, c. T-13, s. 2; ICANN, 'Uniform Domain-Name Dispute-Resolution Policy' (*ICANN*, 25 February 2012) https://www.icann.org/resources/pages/policy-2012-02-25-en accessed June 2025.
428. TRIPS, Art. 16; EUTMR, Art. 18; 15 U.S. Code § 1127.
429. TRIPS, Art. 16.
430. EUIPO, '3 Place of Use' (*EUIPO Trade mark guidelines* 2024) https://guidelines.euipo.europa.eu/2214311/1982069/trade-mark-guidelines/3-place-of-use accessed January 2024.
431. TRIPS, Art. 16; EUTMR, Art. 18; 15 U.S. Code § 1127.
432. Paris Convention, Art. 6bis; ICANN, 'Uniform Domain-Name Dispute-Resolution Policy' (*ICANN*, 25 February 2012) https://www.icann.org/resources/pages/policy-2012-02-25-en accessed June 2025; 15 U.S. Code § 1125(d).
433. Paris Convention, Art. 6bis; EUTMR, Art. 59; TTAB, 'Fighting Bad Faith Trademark Filings in the United States' (*The Honorable Karen S. Kuhlke Administrative Trademark Judge*) https://www.jpo.go.jp/e/news/kokusai/tm5/document/bad_faith_seminar2/01.pdf accessed July 2024; UDRP, 4(a)(iii).
434. WIPO, 'WIPO Overview of WIPO Panel Views on Selected UDRP Questions, Third Edition' ('WIPO Jurisprudential Overview 3.0') (*WIPO*, 2017) https://www.wipo.int/amc/en/domains/search/overview3.0/ accessed June 2025.
435. Paris Convention, 1967, Art. 6bis; 'Fighting Bad Faith Trademark Filings in the United States' (The Honorable Karen S. Kuhlke Administrative Trademark Judge Trademark Trial and Appeal Board United States Patent and Trademark Office) https://www.jpo.go.jp/e/news/kokusai/tm5/document/bad_faith_seminar2/01.pdf accessed 4 August 2025; EUTMR, Art. 59.
436. Paris Convention, Art. 6bis; TRIPS, Art. 16.

Digital Unfair Competition[437] includes the importance of considering how unfairness, including various unfair acts,[438] trade practices[439] and unfair competition[440] with several associated concepts, may be considered for policies/platforms. While many jurisdictions have some form of unfair competition law(s),[441] these are clearly not harmonised even on an EU level, and certainly not on a global level. However, the Paris Convention 1967 Article 10bis includes 'unfair competition', Article 6bis provides protection for 'well known' marks, TRIPS Article 16(2) also refers to 'well-known' marks and Article 16(3) provides for those which are 'not similar ... would indicate a connection ... and ... likely to be damaged by such use'. These support a legal basis to firmly consider key facets of unfair competition[442] as broadly defined to include unfair acts,[443] trade practices[444] and unfair competition[445] within an analysis of digital trademarks.

Digital Terms, Policies, and Disclaimers[446] include terms and policies such as the UDRP and those of various platforms. Further, this includes consideration of disclaimers for policies/platforms.

437. Anselm Kamperman Sanders, *Unfair Competition Law: The Protection of Intellectual and Industrial Creativity* (Oxford University Press 1997) 6-10; Paris Convention, Art. 6bis; TRIPS, Art. 16.
438. Anselm Kamperman Sanders, *Unfair Competition Law: The Protection of Intellectual and Industrial Creativity* (Oxford University Press, 1997) 8; Frauke Henning-Bodewig, *Unfair Competition Law European Union and Member States* (Kluwer Law International 2006) xv-xvi; Martin Senftleben, Michael Handler and Irene Calboli, 'Protection Against Unfair Competition Around the Globe' (2024) 19 Journal of Intellectual Property Law & Practice 79, 79-80 https://doi.org/10.1093/jiplp/jpad121; Paris Convention, Art. 10bis; EUTMR, Art. 9(2)(c); 15 U.S.C. § 1125(c)(2)(B).
439. *Ibid.*
440. *Ibid.*
441. INTA, 'Unfair Competition Survey Report' (*INTA*, 2018) https://www.inta.org/wp-content/uploads/public-files/advocacy/committee-reports/Unfair-Competition-Survey-Report.pdf accessed June 2025.
442. Anselm Kamperman Sanders, *Unfair Competition Law: The Protection of Intellectual and Industrial Creativity* (Oxford University Press, 1997) 8; Frauke Henning-Bodewig, *Unfair Competition Law European Union and Member States* (Kluwer Law International 2006) xv-xvi; Martin Senftleben, Michael Handler and Irene Calboli, 'Protection Against Unfair Competition Around the Globe' (2024) 19 Journal of Intellectual Property Law & Practice 79, 79-80 https://doi.org/10.1093/jiplp/jpad121; Paris Convention, Art. 10bis; EUTMR, Art. 9(2)(c); 15 U.S.C. § 1125(c)(2)(B).
443. *Ibid.*
444. *Ibid.*
445. Anselm Kamperman Sanders, *Unfair Competition Law: The Protection of Intellectual and Industrial Creativity* (Oxford University Press 1997) 6-10; Paris Convention, Art. 6bis; TRIPS, Art. 16.
446. WIPO, 'WIPO Overview of WIPO Panel Views on Selected UDRP Questions, Third Edition' ('WIPO Jurisprudential Overview 3.0') (*WIPO*, 2017) https://www.wipo.int/amc/en/domains/search/overview3.0/ accessed June 2025; Alexander Peukert, 'The Coexistence of Trade Mark Laws and Rights on the Internet, and the Impact of Geolocation Technologies' (2016) 47 International Review of Intellectual Property and Competition Law 60, 81 https://doi.org/10.1007/s40319-015-0427-8; Leslie Fair, 'Full Disclosure' (*FTC Business Blog*, 23 September 2014) https://www.ftc.gov/business-guidance/blog/2014/09/full-disclosure accessed June 2025.

Digital Jurisdictional and Territorial Considerations[447] includes the 'global nature of the Internet',[448] jurisdictional/territorial rules, and considerations for policies/platforms.

Digital Justification[449] includes the various justifications and defences for policies/platforms.

The benefit of this adapted model is that it will help illuminate the problems that digital trademarks raise for various platforms. The model will also be used to help solve or mitigate these problems for policies/platforms. To do this, each element of the model above is informed by theories/concepts and select aspects of legal frameworks of the EU and US (with reference to others), as will be seen next in Chapter 3 (hence, the name, adapted model). This adapted model will help to raise considerations for the UDRP and platforms, as also seen next in Chapter 3. These considerations are then applied to the UDRP in Chapter 4 and to platforms in Chapter 5 to help identify the problems and then provide solutions to the identified problems. In this way, the adapted model will be a guide not only to determine the specific problems, but also to help guide solutions.

The drawbacks of the model include that it cannot identify all possibilities that might relate to digital trademarks, considering that the Internet is ever evolving. The model is not designed to address trademarks on every possible place on the Internet; however, it provides coverage for all key aspects of the areas covered while retaining a simplistic model that can work in practice. Although it may integrate a few additional aspects beyond the UDRP model and in relation to platform policies, these are necessary to address based on Internet trademark peculiarities. It is also envisioned that the model might work across many jurisdictions, although it has not been applied beyond the jurisdictions covered in this book. These drawbacks are overshadowed by the usefulness of this model in that it is based on problems identified, general trademark principles which are widely applicable, and provides an Internet trademark-specific approach rather than continuing to force general trademark rules and policies to fit. The fact that it can even be used as a formal tool for a decision maker in an Internet infringement dispute provides added value on a practical level, especially for platforms.

---

447. Julien Chaisse, 'The Merging of Two Worlds: Cyber Law and Trade Law Normative Convergence on Internet Domain Names' (2019) 37 Boston University International Law Journal 281; Brendan J Witherell, 'Trademark Law: The Extraterritorial Application of the Lanham Act – The First Circuit Cuts the Fat from the Vanity Fair Test' (2006) 29 Western New England Law Review 193, 197; Ansgar Ohly, 'Choice of Law in the Digital Environment: Problems and Possible Solutions' in Josef Drexl and Annette Kur (eds), *Intellectual Property and Private International Law: Heading for the Future* (Bloomsbury Publishing 2005) 241; Irene Calboli and Jane Ginsburg, 'Preface', in Irene Calboli and Jane Gindburg JC (eds), *The Cambridge Handbook of International and Comparative Trademark Law* (Cambridge University Press 2020) XXI.
448. WIPO, 'WIPO Overview of WIPO Panel Views on Selected UDRP Questions, Third Edition' ('WIPO Jurisprudential Overview 3.0') (*WIPO*, 2017) https://www.wipo.int/amc/en/domains/search/overview3.0/ accessed June 2025.
449. ICANN, 'Uniform Domain-Name Dispute-Resolution Policy' (*ICANN*, 25 February 2012) https://www.icann.org/resources/pages/policy-2012-02-25-en accessed June 2025.

2.4 CONCLUSION

In conclusion, this chapter was intended to identify the key problems pertaining to digital trademarks, specifically in e-commerce marketplace, search advertising, social media, mobile app, and Metaverse platforms. It was also to determine which adapted model can be developed to inform trademark issues in these platforms.

This chapter showed problems in several areas for digital trademarks pertinent to each of the platforms under consideration. Together, these formed the basis of the adapted model, the Digital Trademark and Trade Practices Model, developed to inform the policies/platforms under consideration. As mentioned in the outset of this chapter, a more detailed analysis of the problems and gaps identified for the UDRP and platform policies is presented in Chapters 4 and 5.

In the next chapter, the model will be further explored to show how it is informed by various theories and concepts, as well as select aspects of legal frameworks (EU and US, with reference to others). This will be used to determine the resulting considerations for the UDRP and platforms. These will then be used to consider solutions for the UDRP (Chapter 4) and the platforms (Chapter 5) before offering a conclusion (Chapter 6).

CHAPTER 3

The Digital Trademark and Trade Practices Model Informed by Theories, Concepts and Select Aspects of the EU and U.S. (With Reference to Others) Legal Frameworks and Resulting Considerations for the UDRP and Platforms

The Digital Trademark and Trade Practices Model is informed by a number of theories and concepts, as well as select aspects of the EU and US legal frameworks (with reference to others), as analysed in this chapter. These help not only to illuminate key theoretical and conceptual basis, which are very important to understand not only digital trademarks and their context but also legislation, case law, treaties, agreements, and binding policies that impact their treatment. These, in turn, result in key considerations for the UDRP and platforms as outlined.

3.1 INTRODUCTION

This chapter mainly addresses how the Digital Trademark and Trade Practices Model is informed by select theories and concepts, and select aspects of the US and EU (with reference to other) legal frameworks, and what the resulting considerations are for the UDRP and platform policies.

Over many years, various trademark theories and concepts[450] have developed, some of which were coined when trademark law was still a new phenomenon, and

450. Oxford Dictionaries, 'Theory | Definition of Theory in English by Oxford Dictionaries' (*Oxford Dictionaries | English*) https://en.oxforddictionaries.com/definition/theory accessed January

others which are more recent. These theories and concepts look at trademarks from different perspectives, useful for an analysis of marks from various angles. At the same time, because platforms generally operate globally or in numerous jurisdictions, it is important to look at what aspects of the legal framework inform the model, including legislation, case law, treaties, agreements, and binding policies. As it is beyond the scope of this book to cover all global jurisdictions, select aspects of the EU and US are covered with limited reference to other jurisdictions, where relevant, such as where there have been relevant recent cases. The purpose of looking at the theories, concepts, and legal frameworks that inform the model is to help determine what the resulting considerations are for the UDRP and the platforms, and these considerations will be outlined to assist in providing recommendations for policies/platforms in the following chapters.

3.2 TRADEMARK THEORIES, CONCEPTS AND ASPECTS OF THE LEGAL FRAMEWORK THAT INFORM THE DIGITAL TRADEMARK AND TRADE PRACTICES MODEL AND RESULTING CONSIDERATIONS FOR PLATFORMS

The following Table 3.1 summarises the various theories, models, and aspects of the legal frameworks that inform the model, and the resulting considerations for the UDRP and platforms. This table is based on the analysis that follows throughout the chapter.

2024; Oxford Dictionaries 'Concept | Definition of Concept in English by Oxford Dictionaries' (*Oxford Dictionaries | English*) https://en.oxforddictionaries.com/definition/concept accessed January 2024. For purposes of this research, 'theory' is defined by the Oxford Dictionaries as '[a] set of principles on which the practice of an activity is based'. Also, a 'concept' is defined is defined by the Oxford Dictionaries as '[a]n abstract idea'. Thus, a trademark theory in this research will illustrate certain trademark 'principles' while a concept, on the other hand, is an 'idea' that may play a role in understanding important ideas related to trademarks. These terms are not used as a definitive assignment to or implications intended for the various theories and concepts mentioned and are simply for illustrative purposes. Theories and concepts utilised by courts are also be referenced.

Table 3.1 Digital Trademark and Trade Practices Model informed by Theories/Concepts & Select Aspects of Legal Frameworks, and Resulting Consideration for the UDRP and Platforms

Digital Trademark and Trade Practices Model	*Select Theories/Concepts That Inform Model*	*Select Aspects of the Legal Frameworks of the U.S. and EU (Legislation, Case Law, Treaties, Agreements, Policies) That Inform Model*	*Resulting Considerations for the UDRP and Platforms (If Not Already/Adequately Considered)*
Digital Use and Place of Use	Use Theory[451] Place of Use Concept[452] Property Theory[453]	TRIPS, Article 16 'using in the course of trade' UDRP, 4(c)(i) 'your use of, or demonstrable preparations to use, the domain name or a name corresponding to the domain name in connection with a bona fide offering of goods or services' EU: Article 18 EUTMR 'genuine use in the Union in connection with the goods or services' US: 15 U.S. Code § 1127 'use in commerce'	Whether the mark is being used as a mark. Where specifically the mark is being used (place of use). Whether the user of the trademark has property ownership of a mark or authorization to use it on the Internet.

451. Graeme B Dinwoodie and Mark D Janis, 'Confusion Over Use: Contextualism in Trademark Law' (2007) 92 Iowa Law Review 1597.
452. EUIPO, '3 Place of Use' (*EUIPO Trade mark guidelines* 2024) https://guidelines.euipo.europa.eu/2214311/1982069/trade-mark-guidelines/3-place-of-use accessed January 2024.
453. J Thomas McCarthy, *McCarthy on trademarks and unfair competition* (4th edn, vol. 69, Thomson Reuters, 2014) in Lisa L Ouellette, 'The Google Shortcut to Trademark Law' (2014) 102 California Law Review 351, 358; Lionel Bently, 'From Communication to Thing: Historical Aspects of the Conceptualisation of Trade Marks as Property' in Graeme B Dinwoodie and Mark D Janis (eds), *Trademark Law and Theory: A Handbook of Contemporary Research* (Edward Elgar, 2008) 3-41; Anselm Kamperman Sanders, *Unfair Competition Law: The Protection of Intellectual and Industrial Creativity* (Oxford University Press 1997) 109.

Digital Trademark and Trade Practices Model	*Select Theories/Concepts That Inform Model*	*Select Aspects of the Legal Frameworks of the U.S. and EU (Legislation, Case Law, Treaties, Agreements, Policies) That Inform Model*	*Resulting Considerations for the UDRP and Platforms (If Not Already/Adequately Considered)*
Digital Bad Faith and Abuse	Bad Faith Concept[454] Abuse Concept[455]	Paris Convention, 1967, Article 6bis 'cancellation or the prohibition of the use of marks registered or used in bad faith' UDRP 4(a)(iii) 'your domain name has been registered and is being used in bad faith' 'A pattern of abuse ... multiple trademark-abusive domain names ...'[456] EU: Article 59(1)(b) EUTMR 'applicant was acting in bad faith when he filed the application' WIPO Domain Name Dispute Resolution Service for.EU[457] 'or that are used in bad faith'	Whether bad faith is present. Whether abuse, in the form of repeated bad faith, is present.

454. Paris Convention, Art. 6bis; EUTMR, Art. 59; TTAB, 'Fighting Bad Faith Trademark Filings in the United States' (*The Honorable Karen S. Kuhlke Administrative Trademark Judge*) https://www.jpo.go.jp/e/news/kokusai/tm5/document/bad_faith_seminar2/01.pdf accessed July 2024; UDRP, 4(a)(iii).
455. WIPO, 'WIPO Overview of WIPO Panel Views on Selected UDRP Questions, Third Edition ('WIPO Jurisprudential Overview 3.0') (*WIPO*, 2017) https://www.wipo.int/amc/en/domains/search/overview3.0/ accessed June 2025.
456. *Ibid.*
457. WIPO, 'WIPO Domain Name Dispute Resolution Service for .EU (and.ею and.ευ)' (*WIPO*) https://www.wipo.int/amc/en/domains/cctld/eu/index.html accessed July 2024; Commission Implementing Regulation (EU) 2020/857 of 17 June 2020 laying down the principles to be included in the contract between the European Commission and the.eu top-level domain Registry in accordance with Regulation (EU) 2019/517 of the European Parliament and of the Council.

Digital Trademark and Trade Practices Model	*Select Theories/Concepts That Inform Model*	*Select Aspects of the Legal Frameworks of the U.S. and EU (Legislation, Case Law, Treaties, Agreements, Policies) That Inform Model*	*Resulting Considerations for the UDRP and Platforms (If Not Already/Adequately Considered)*
		U.S.: bad faith filing[458] ACPA 15 U.S. Code § 1125(d)(1)(A) 'has a bad faith intent to profit from that mark' usTLD Dispute Resolution Policy (applicable to.us domains)[459] 'registered in bad faith or is being used in bad faith'	
Digital Confusion	Confusion Theory and Concepts[460] Confusion Prohibition[461]	Paris Convention 1967, Article 6bis 'liable to create confusion' TRIPS, Article 16(1) 'likelihood of confusion' UDRP, 4(a)(i) 'confusingly similar'	Whether confusion is present or likely.

458. TTAB, 'Fighting Bad Faith Trademark Filings in the United States' (*The Honorable Karen S. Kuhlke Administrative Trademark Judge*) https://www.jpo.go.jp/e/news/kokusai/tm5/document/bad_faith_seminar2/01.pdf accessed July 2024.
459. Registry Services, 'UsTLD Dispute Resolution Policy' (*Registry Services, LLC*, 2021) https://www.about.us/documents/policies/usTLD_Dispute_Resolution_Policy_(usDRP).pdf accessed July 2024.
460. Ilanah Fhima and Dev S Gangjee, 'Assessing Likelihood of Confusion', *The Confusion Test in European Trade Mark Law* (New York, 2019; online edn, Oxford Academic) 160-203 https://doi.org/10.1093/oso/9780199674336.003.0006; Graeme B Dinwoodie and Mark D Janis, 'Confusion Over Use: Contextualism in Trademark Law' (2007) 92 Iowa Law Review 1597; Mark P McKenna, 'A Consumer Decision-Making Theory of Trademark Law' 98 Virginia Law Review 67; William M Landes and Richard A Posner, 'Trademark Law: An Economic Perspective' (1987) 30 The Journal of Law and Economics 265 https://doi.org/10.1086/467138; Lisa L Ouellette, 'The Google Shortcut to Trademark Law' (2014) 102 California Law Review 351, 358.
461. Paris Convention, Art. 6bis; TRIPS, Art. 16(1); EUTMR, Art. 8(1)(b) and Art. 9(2)(b); 15 U.S. Code § 1114;15 U.S. Code § 1125.

Digital Trademark and Trade Practices Model	*Select Theories/Concepts That Inform Model*	*Select Aspects of the Legal Frameworks of the U.S. and EU (Legislation, Case Law, Treaties, Agreements, Policies) That Inform Model*	*Resulting Considerations for the UDRP and Platforms (If Not Already/Adequately Considered)*
		EU: Article 9(2)(b) EUTMR 'exists a likelihood of confusion on the part of the public; the likelihood of confusion includes the likelihood of association between the sign and the trademark' U.S.: 15 U.S. Code § 1114 'likely to cause confusion' ACPA 15 U.S. Code § 1125(a)(1)(A) 'likely to cause confusion'	
Digital Unfair Competition	Unfair Competition Theory[462] Unfair Competition Prohibition[463] Unfair Trade Practices[464]	Paris Convention 1967 Article 10bis 'unfair competition' Article 6bis 'well known' TRIPS	Whether unfair acts, practices, or competition are present.

462. Anselm Kamperman Sanders, *Unfair Competition Law: The Protection of Intellectual and Industrial Creativity* (Oxford University Press, 1997); Christian Riffel, *Protection Against Unfair Competition in the WTO TRIPS Agreement: The Scope and Prospects of Article 10bis of the Paris Convention for the Protection of Industrial Property* (Brill 2016) 223-224.
463. Paris Convention, Art. 10bis; 15 U.S.C. § 1125(c)(2)(B); Anselm Kamperman Sanders, *Unfair Competition Law: The Protection of Intellectual and Industrial Creativity* (Oxford University Press, 1997).
464. Anselm Kamperman Sanders, *Unfair Competition Law: The Protection of Intellectual and Industrial Creativity* (Oxford University Press 1997) 6-10; Frauke Henning-Bodewig, *Unfair Competition Law European Union and Member States* (Kluwer Law International 2006) xv-xvi.

Digital Trademark and Trade Practices Model	*Select Theories/Concepts That Inform Model*	*Select Aspects of the Legal Frameworks of the U.S. and EU (Legislation, Case Law, Treaties, Agreements, Policies) That Inform Model*	*Resulting Considerations for the UDRP and Platforms (If Not Already/Adequately Considered)*
	Passing Off Concept[465] Comparative Advertising Concept[466] Marketing & Branding Theories[467] Symbols & Signs Concepts[468] Famous, Well Known, Reputable, Strong, Marks with Goodwill Concepts[469] Distinctiveness Concept[470]	Article 16(2) 'well-known' Article 16(3) 'not similar ... would indicate a connection ... and ... likely to be damaged by such use' EU: Article 9(2)(c) EUTMR 'unfair advantage, or is detrimental to' EU Member State law 'unfair competition' Article 8 EUTMR 'well known', 'repute', 'reputation' Article 7(1)(b) EUTMR 'devoid of any distinctive character'	Whether there is passing off. Whether there is legitimate use in comparative advertising. Whether and how a symbol or sign is being utilised. Whether the mark is famous, well known, reputable, strong, or has goodwill. Whether the mark is distinctive. Whether a mark is being diluted, taken unfair advantage of, is the subject of free riding, or is being misappropriated.

465. Ethan Horwitz and Benjamin Levi, 'Fifty Years of the Lanham Act: A Retrospective of Section 43(a)E' (1996) 7 Fordham Intellectual Property, Media and Entertainment Law Journal Article 6; David Bainbridge, *Intellectual Property* (Pearson Education Limited 2018) Chapter 30.
466. C-324/09 *L'Oreal SA v. eBay International AG* [2012] Bus. L.R. 1369 (ECLI:EU:C:2011:474).
467. Angsar Ohly, '"Buy Me Because I'm Cool": The "Marketing Approach" and the Overlap Between Design, Trade Mark and Unfair Competition Law' in Annette Kur, Marianne Levin and Jens Schovsbo (eds), *The EU Design Approach: A Global Appraisal* (Edward Elgar 2018) 108-141; Lisa P Ramsey, 'Brandjacking on Social Networks: Trademark Infringement by Impersonation of Markholders' (2010) 58 Buffalo Law Review 851, 856.
468. Mooij MKde, *Global Marketing and Advertising: Understanding Cultural Paradoxes* (SAGE 2010) 54.
469. Paris Convention, Art. 6bis; TRIPS, Art. 16(2); EUTMR, Arts 8(5) and 9(2)(c); 15 U.S. Code § 1125; Timothy D Greene and Jeff Wilkerson, 'Understanding Trademark Strength' (2013) 16 Stanford Technology Law Review 535.
470. Mark P McKenna, 'Teaching Trademark Theory Through the Lens of Distinctiveness' (2008) 52 St Louis University Law Journal 843, 847; Timothy D Greene and Jeff Wilkerson, 'Understanding Trademark Strength' (2013) 16 Stanford Technology Law Review 535; Lisa L Ouellette, 'The Google Shortcut to Trademark Law' (2014) 102 California Law Review 351, 352.

Digital Trademark and Trade Practices Model	*Select Theories/Concepts That Inform Model*	*Select Aspects of the Legal Frameworks of the U.S. and EU (Legislation, Case Law, Treaties, Agreements, Policies) That Inform Model*	*Resulting Considerations for the UDRP and Platforms (If Not Already/Adequately Considered)*
	Dilution Theory, Unfair Advantage, Free Riding, Misappropriation Concepts[471]	U.S.: 15 U.S. Code § 1125(c) 'any false designation of origin, false or misleading description of fact, or false or misleading representation of fact ...' 15 U.S. Code § 1125(c) 'famous mark' 15 U.S. Code § 1125(c) 'distinctive, inherently or through acquired distinctiveness' TDRA 15 U.S. Code § 1125(c)(2)(B), 'dilution by blurring' 15 U.S. Code § 1125(c)(2)(C) 'dilution by tarnishment' ACPA 15 U.S. Code § 1125(d) 'or dilutive of that mark'	

471. Anselm Kamperman Sanders, 'Odol: The Introduction of a Watery Concept with Steeled Resilience' in Christopher Heath and Anselm Kamperman Sanders (eds), *Landmark Intellectual Property Cases and Their Legacy* (Wolters Kluwer 2011) 51-56; Graeme B Dinwoodie, 'Dilution as Unfair Competition: European Echoes' in Rochelle C Dreyfuss and Jane C Ginsburg (eds) *Intellectual Property at the Edge: The Contested Contours of IP* (Cambridge University Press 2014) 100; Frank I Schechter, 'The Rational Basis of Trademark Protection' (1927) 40 Harvard Law Review 813 https://doi.org/10.2307/1330367;15 U.S. Code § 1125(c); Keola R Whitaker, 'Trademark Dilution in a Global Age' (2006) 27 University of Pennsylvania Journal of International Economic Law 907.

Digital Trademark and Trade Practices Model	*Select Theories/Concepts That Inform Model*	*Select Aspects of the Legal Frameworks of the U.S. and EU (Legislation, Case Law, Treaties, Agreements, Policies) That Inform Model*	*Resulting Considerations for the UDRP and Platforms (If Not Already/Adequately Considered)*
Digital Terms, Policies, and Disclaimers	Terms and Conditions, Terms of Use Uniform Policies[472] Disclaimers[473]	Contract law Platform terms and conditions/policies UDRP	Whether terms are adequate to address marks in their services. Whether uniform policies can be implemented. Whether disclaimers are used, and if they are effective.
Digital Jurisdictional and Territorial Considerations	Jurisdictional and Territorial Concepts Co-existence Concept[474]	UDRP EU: Article 18 EUTMR 'in the Union'	Whether there is relevant online targeting.

472. ICANN, 'Uniform Domain-Name Dispute-Resolution Policy' (*ICANN*, 25 February 2012) https://www.icann.org/resources/pages/policy-2012-02-25-en accessed June 2025; 15 U.S. Code § 1125(d);); Rajeev Sachdev, 'Towards an Improved Framework for Trade-Mark Law and Regulation in Social Media Usernames: A Study of the Canadian, U.S., and U.K. Positions' (2016) 28 Intellectual Property Journal 379, 379-418; Daniel Doft, 'Facebook, Twitter, and the Wild West of IP Enforcement on Social Media: Weighing the Merits of a Uniform Dispute Resolution Policy' (2016) 49 The John Marshall Law Review 959; Thomas J Curtin, 'The Name Game: Cybersquatting and Trademark Infringement on Social Media Websites' (2010-2011) 19 Journal of Law and Policy 353; Erick J Heels, 'How to Twittersquat the Top 100 Brands' (*GiantPeople*, 8 January 2009) http://www.giantpeople.com/1298.html accessed 4 August 2025; Paul D McGrady, *McGrady on Social Media and the Metaverse* (Mathew Bender & Company, Inc. 2023) §12.
473. Alexander Peukert, 'The Coexistence of Trade Mark Laws and Rights on the Internet, and the Impact of Geolocation Technologies' (2016) 47 International Review of Intellectual Property and Competition Law 60, 81 https://doi.org/10.1007/s40319-015-0427-8.
474. EUIPO, '3.1 Coexistence Between the Marks Involved in the Opposition' (*EUIPO Trade mark Guidelines*) https://guidelines.euipo.europa.eu/2058843/2043906/trade-mark-guidelines/3-1-coexistence-between-the-marks-involved-in-the-opposition accessed January 2024;15 U.S. Code § 1052(d); Alexander Peukert, 'The Coexistence of Trade Mark Laws and Rights on the Internet, and the Impact of Geolocation Technologies' (2016) 47 International Review of Intellectual Property and Competition Law 60, 81 https://doi.org/10.1007/s40319-015-0427-8; Tamara Nanayakkara, 'IP and Business: Trademark Coexistence' (*WIPO*, November 2006) https://www.wipo.int/wipo_magazine/en/2006/06/article_0007.html accessed June 2025.

Digital Trademark and Trade Practices Model	*Select Theories/Concepts That Inform Model*	*Select Aspects of the Legal Frameworks of the U.S. and EU (Legislation, Case Law, Treaties, Agreements, Policies) That Inform Model*	*Resulting Considerations for the UDRP and Platforms (If Not Already/Adequately Considered)*
		Articles 122-136 EUTMR Jurisdiction provisions US: 15 U.S. Code § 1127 'all commerce which may lawfully be regulated by Congress' (including interstate, territorial, and between the United States and a foreign country)' under TMEP[475]	Whether the activity involves any limits on geographic reach. Whether the marks can co-exist online.
Digital Justification	Fair Use, Freedom of Expression, Freedom of Artistic Expression or Use, Free Speech, and Parody Concepts[476]	TRIPS, Article 17 'limited exceptions ... such as fair use ... take account of the legitimate interests' UDRP 'fair use' guidance EU: Recital 21 EUTMR 'used fairly' 'full respect for fundamental rights and freedoms' 'accessories or spare parts'	Whether a justification or defence may apply.

475. USPTO, 'Trademark Manual of Examining Procedure (TMEP)' (*TMEP*) https://tmep.uspto.gov/RDMS/TMEP/current#/current/TMEP-900d1e98.html accessed January 2024.

476. The Constitution of the United States of America, the Charter of Fundamental Rights of the European Union; Constitution Act, 1982, Paris Convention, Art. 6bis; TRIPS, Art. 16; EUTMR, Art. 18; 15 U.S. Code § 1127; Canadian Charter of Rights and Freedoms.

Digital Trademark and Trade Practices Model	*Select Theories/Concepts That Inform Model*	*Select Aspects of the Legal Frameworks of the U.S. and EU (Legislation, Case Law, Treaties, Agreements, Policies) That Inform Model*	*Resulting Considerations for the UDRP and Platforms (If Not Already/Adequately Considered)*
		Article 10 ECHR; Article 11 Charter of Fundamental Rights 'Right to freedom of expression and information' U.S.: 15 U.S. Code § 1115(b)(4) 'fair use' The Constitution of the United States of America, Amendment I; 15 U.S. Code § 1125(c)(3)(A) 'free speech' 15 U.S. Code § 1125(c)(3)(B) News reporting and commentary 15 U.S. Code § 1125(c)(3)(C) Non-commercial use ACPA 15 U.S. Code § 1125(d)(1)(B)(IV) 'bona fide noncommercial or fair use'	

3.2.1 Digital Use and Place of Use

This section covers use related theories and concepts and select use[477] requirements that inform the model. Resulting considerations for the UDRP and platforms are summarised.

477. EUTMR, Art. 18; 15 U.S. Code § 1127; Canadian Trademarks Act R.S.C., 1985, c. T-13, s. 2.

3.2.1.1 *Use Theory and Use Requirements*

Under the trademark use theory,[478] 'a number of scholars have argued that an unauthorized user of a mark is only liable, and should only be liable'[479] when a mark is used[480] 'as a mark'.[481] In other words, the way in which an unauthorised user is using[482] a mark needs to be assessed, and courts need to initially determine the 'nature of that use'.[483] Essentially, if there is no trademark use,[484] no liability exists.[485] In the mid/late 2000s, there began to develop much academic debate around the use theory.[486] Janis and Dinwoodie argued against the theory by opining that it does not provide the 'certainty'[487] sought, and 'a firm foundation' in law[488] and prefer a focus on the 'confusion factor'.[489] Dogan replied that '[t]he court – like most scholars who oppose a trademark use requirement – worried that a trademark use requirement would give search engines carte blanche to adopt advertising practices that purposefully deceive consumers'.[490] She argued '[t]his assumption, however, is mistaken'[491] and that 'use requirement would not provide complete immunity from trademark liability for search engines or anyone else ... [b]ut it would treat them differently than run-of-the-mill infringers based on their status as intermediaries'.[492] Lemley and Dogan

478. Graeme B Dinwoodie and Mark D Janis, 'Confusion Over Use: Contextualism in Trademark Law' (2007) 92 Iowa Law Review 1597 *Articles by Maurer Faculty.* Paper 361; Stephen L Carter, 'Does It Matter Whether Intellectual Property Is Property?' https://digitalcommons.law.yale.edu/fss_papers/2259/ accessed 4 August 2025; William Fisher, 'Theories of Intellectual Property' (*Harvard Law*) https://cyber.harvard.edu/people/tfisher/iptheory.pdf accessed 4 August 2025; Shontavia J Johnson, 'Memetic Theory, Trademarks & the Viral Meme Mark' (2013) 13 The John Marshall Law School Review of Intellectual Property Law 96; EUIPO, '3 Place of Use' (*EUIPO Trade mark guidelines* 2024) https://guidelines.euipo.europa.eu/2214311/1982069/trade-mark-guidelines/3-place-of-use accessed January 2024; EUTMR, Art. 7.
479. Graeme B Dinwoodie and Mark D Janis, 'Confusion Over Use: Contextualism in Trademark Law' (2007) 92 Iowa Law Review 1597.
480. EUTMR, Art. 18; 15 U.S. Code § 1127; Canadian Trademarks Act R.S.C., 1985, c. T-13, s. 2.
481. Graeme B Dinwoodie and Mark D Janis, 'Confusion Over Use: Contextualism in Trademark Law' (2007) 92 Iowa Law Review 1597.
482. EUTMR, Art. 18; 15 U.S. Code § 1127; Canadian Trademarks Act R.S.C., 1985, c. T-13, s. 2.
483. Graeme B Dinwoodie and Mark D Janis, 'Confusion Over Use: Contextualism in Trademark Law' (2007) 92 Iowa Law Review 1597, 1599.
484. *Ibid.*
485. Graeme B Dinwoodie and Mark D Janis, 'Confusion Over Use: Contextualism in Trademark Law' (2007) 92 Iowa Law Review 1597, 1599; Margreth Barrett, 'Internet Trademark Suits and the Demise of "Trademark Use"' (2006) 39 University of California, Davis Law Review 371; Stacey L Dogan and Mark A Lemley, 'Trademark and Consumer Search Costs on the Internet' (2004) 41 Houston Law Review 777; Uli Widmaier, 'Use, Liability, and the Structure of Trademark Law' (2004) 33 Hofstra Law Review 603; Eric Goldman, 'Deregulating Relevancy in Internet Trademark Law' (2005) 54 Emory Law Journal 507.
486. Eric Goldman, 'Academic Debate over Trademark Use in Commerce' (*Technology & Marketing Law Blog*) https://blog.ericgoldman.org/archives/2007/04/academic_debate.htm accessed January 2024.
487. *Ibid.*
488. *Ibid.*
489. *Ibid.*
490. Stacey Dogan, 'Beyond Trademark Use' (2009) 8 Journal on Telecommunications and High Technology Law 135, abstract.
491. *Ibid.*
492. *Ibid.*

further discuss use in the context of marks on the Internet and say that '[i]t is no accident that the rise of these Internet-based trademark claims has occasioned a re-examination of the core principles of trademark law'.[493] They surmise that this limitation has its own place in the realm of trademark rights and that 'confusion' alone cannot address the areas 'use' is intended to.[494] Goldman, favouring the use theory, says that the 'use in commerce requirement' serves to keep 'commercial referential uses'[495] from falling within trademark law.[496] McKenna mediates the debate by concluding that '[t]rademark law is in desperate need of a reliable limiting principle … [and] … [u]nfortunately, trademark use is not capable of filling that role'.[497] In later accounts, Roberts argues that 'use' along with 'distinctiveness' can work to achieve intended results.[498] Ragavan reminds us that 'the use theory enjoyed immediate judicial acceptance and soon became foundational in American trademark law even as the concept of use lost its central position in the rest of the world'.[499] While it is beyond the scope of this book to further or attempt to mediate this debate, this book highlights the importance for platforms to consider a number of trademark areas as outlined by the model, including 'use'[500] as one element stemming from the TRIPS Agreement.

Under the TRIPS Agreement Article 16, '[t]he owner of a registered trademark shall have the exclusive right to prevent all third parties not having the owner's consent from *using in the course of trade* identical or similar signs for goods or services which are identical or similar to those in respect of which the trademark is registered where such use would result in a likelihood of confusion'[501] (*italics added*). Platforms should consider adopting TRIPS language with respect to the use requirement, specifically 'using in the course of trade',[502] as it forms the basis of use across many jurisdictions. In line with this, many jurisdictions have a use[503] requirement and those in the EU and US will now be discussed in turn. Before this, it should be noted that under the UDRP 4(c)(i): 'legitimate interests' of the complainant may be proven, *inter alia*, by 'use of, or demonstrable preparations to use, the domain name or a name corresponding to the domain name in connection with a bona fide offering of goods or services …'.

In the EU, 'genuine use in the Union in connection with the goods or services in respect of which it is registered'[504] is required under Article 18(1) of the Regulation

493. Mark A Lemley and Stacey L Dogan, 'Grounding Trademark Law Through Trademark Use' (2007) 92 Iowa Law Review 1669.
494. *Ibid.*
495. Eric Goldman, 'Academic Debate over Trademark Use in Commerce' (*Technology & Marketing Law Blog*) https://blog.ericgoldman.org/archives/2007/04/academic_debate.htm accessed January 2024.
496. *Ibid.*
497. Mark P McKenna, 'Trademark Use and the Problem of Source' (2009) University of Illinois Law Review 773.
498. Alexandra Roberts, 'Trademark Failure to Function' (2019) 104 Iowa Law Review 1977.
499. Srividhya Ragavan, 'The Use Doctrine in the Use Doctrine in Trademark Law: Issues from Trade and Transborder Reputation' (2021) 43 Cardozo Law Review 443, 446.
500. TRIPS, Art. 16; EUTMR, Art. 18; 15 U.S. Code § 1127; 15 U.S. Code § 1127.
501. TRIPS, Art. 16.
502. *Ibid.*
503. TRIPS, Art. 16; EUTMR, Art. 18; 15 U.S. Code § 1127; 15 U.S. Code § 1127.
504. EUTMR, Art. 18.

(EU) 2017/1001 of the European Parliament and of the Council of 14 June 2017 on the European Union trademark (EUTMR), although a grace period of five years is established.[505] Kur and Senftleben note that 'the requirement of use in connection with goods or services is a flexible concept that includes references to goods or services in advertising'[506] and opine that the test 'establishes a low threshold'.[507] In the context of the Internet, of course, 'it does not seem necessary that the mark be used directly on the product or its container',[508] even though 'the use must relate to those goods or services in respect of which the trademark is registered'.[509] It would appear that adequate advertising-oriented[510] references[511] on the Internet would suffice. Senftelben also notes[512] that 'use'[513] would be relevant only if there is a 'commercial effect in the EU Member State where protection is sought'.[514] This is important in the Internet context because it provides an avenue to assess whether 'use'[515] is being made of the trademark in a particular jurisdiction.[516] Further, under Article 9 EUTMR, a mark holder may prevent a non mark holder from 'using in the course of trade, in relation to goods or services ...'[517] its mark in outlined circumstances,[518] such as 'using the sign on business papers and in advertising'[519] or 'stocking'[520] the goods to 'offer' or put 'them on the market' without legal excuse. At the same time, Article 8(4) EUTMR clarifies that, where an opposition is initiated by a 'proprietor of a non-registered trademark or of another sign used in the course of trade of more than mere local significance', a mark will not be registered where '(a) rights to that sign were acquired prior to the date of application for registration of the EU trademark, or the date of the priority claimed for

505. *Ibid.*
506. Annette Kur and Martin Senftleben, 'Limitations, Defences, and Genuine Use' in Annette Kur and Martin Senftleben (eds), *European Trade Mark Law* (Oxford University Press 2017) 458.
507. *Ibid.*
508. *Ibid.*
509. Annette Kur and Martin Senftleben, 'Limitations, Defences, and Genuine Use' in Annette Kur and Martin Senftleben (eds), *European Trade Mark Law* (Oxford University Press 2017) 459.
510. *Ibid.*
511. Annette Kur and Martin Senftleben, 'Limitations, Defences, and Genuine Use' in Annette Kur and Martin Senftleben (eds), *European Trade Mark Law* (Oxford University Press 2017) 458.
512. In relation to WIPO, 'WIPOs Joint Recommendation Concerning Provisions on the Protection of Marks, and Other Industrial Property Rights in Signs, on the Internet' (*Article 2 WIPO publication No. 845, Geneva* 3 October 2001) https://www.wipo.int/edocs/pubdocs/en/wipo_pub_845.pdf accessed January 2024.
513. Annette Kur and Martin Senftleben, 'Limitations, Defences, and Genuine Use' in Annette Kur and Martin Senftleben (eds), *European Trade Mark Law* (Oxford University Press 2017) 281.
514. *Ibid.*; WIPO, 'WIPOs Joint Recommendation Concerning Provisions on the Protection of Marks, and Other Industrial Property Rights in Signs, on the Internet' (*Article 2 WIPO publication No. 845, Geneva* 3 October 2001) https://www.wipo.int/edocs/pubdocs/en/wipo_pub_845.pdf accessed January 2024.
515. EUTMR, Art. 18.
516. Martin Senftleben, 'Rights Conferred' in Annette Kur and Martin Senftleben (eds), *European Trade Mark Law* (Oxford University Press 2017) 281; WIPO, 'WIPOs Joint Recommendation Concerning Provisions on the Protection of Marks, and Other Industrial Property Rights in Signs, on the Internet' (*Article 2 WIPO publication No. 845, Geneva* 3 October 2001) https://www.wipo.int/edocs/pubdocs/en/wipo_pub_845.pdf accessed January 2024.
517. EUTMR, Art. 9.
518. *Ibid.*
519. EUTMR, Art. 9(3)(e).
520. EUTMR, Art. 9(3)(c).

the application for registration of the EU trademark; (b) that sign confers on its proprietor the right to prohibit the use of a subsequent trademark'.[521]

According to EUIPO guidelines, 'the presence of the trademark on websites can show inter alia the nature of its use or the fact that products or services bearing the mark have been offered to the public ... [h]owever, the mere presence of a trademark on a website is, of itself, not sufficient to prove genuine use unless the website also shows the place, time and extent of use or unless this information is otherwise provided'.[522] Also, according to EUIPO Guidelines, along with a way to tell when website evidence is from, it 'must show that the online transactions were connected with the goods or services designated by the mark'.[523] Further, '[u]se ... on YouTube can constitute use as a mark ... as can use in ... apps for mobile devices'.[524] While, in the recent case of *Mood Media,*[525] it was made clear that it is possible that 'websites fulfil a commercial and advertising function, because they present all the goods and services concerned and offer the possibility of obtaining them'.[526] In that case, in reference to 'videos presenting the goods and services sold by the applicant and ... videos of concerts organised by "Mood Media" in the context of entertainment services'[527] were considered 'documents [that] certainly prove use of the trademark as such ... and ... [t]he videos ... have a direct link with the goods and services sold under the contested mark, because they present those goods and services'.[528] Also in the recent 2022 decision in *Standard v. EUIPO,*[529] the General Court (GC) found in the context of 'advertisements and offers for sale'[530] in the EU for 'hotel and ancillary services'[531] in the US could constitute 'genuine use'[532] in the EU based on the fact that the mark was being 'used'[533] in the EU, citing 'by analogy'[534] *AMS Neve,*[535] and other cases.[536] Among the evidence before the Board of Appeals in its decision was 'advertisements, promotional campaigns aimed at customers located in the European Union ... a bookings portal accessible to European Union customers via the applicant's

521. EUTMR, Art. 8(4).
522. EUIPO, '6.1.2.6 Use on the Internet' (*EUIPO Trade mark guidelines*) https://guidelines.euipo.europa.eu/2214311/2215203/trade-mark-guidelines/6-1-2-6-use-on-the-internet accessed July 2024.
523. *Ibid.*
524. EUIPO, 'Overview of GC/CJ Case-Law Status: 01/01/2019: 30/09/2023' (*Board of Appeals Operations Area*) https://euipo.europa.eu/tunnel-web/secure/webdav/guest/document_library/contentPdfs/about_euipo/boards_of_appeal/case-law/case-law_overview_2019-2023_Q3_en.pdf accessed January 2024.
525. T-615/20, *Mood media*, EU:T:2022:109, § 62, 78, 82-86, 89-91.
526. *Ibid.*
527. *Ibid.*
528. *Ibid.*
529. Case T-768/20 *Standard International Management LLC v. EUIPO* ECLI:EU:T:2022:458.
530. *Ibid.*
531. *Ibid.*
532. *Ibid.*
533. *Ibid.*
534. *Ibid.*
535. C-172/18, *AMS Neve Ltd and Others v. Heritage Audio SL and Pedro Rodríguez Arribas* ECLI:EU:C:2019:674.
536. Case T-768/20 *Standard International Management LLC v. EUIPO* ECLI:EU:T:2022:458.

website, figures issued by Google Analytics software concerning traffic on the applicant's website, as well as printouts from such a website referring to various hotel services and equipment offered and used by customers, particularly in the European Union, or even articles focusing on awards and on prizes received'.[537] In fact, EUIPO Guidelines also state: 'where the goods or services are available abroad, such as holiday accommodation or particular products, advertising alone may be sufficient to amount to genuine use'.[538]

However, other Internet cases have not found 'use'.[539] For example, in *Leno Merken v. Hagelkruis Beheer*,[540] the 'genuine use'[541] condition 'requires that the mark must have been used to create or maintain market share for the goods and/or services protected by the registration'.[542] In other instances, proof of use was not established with marks on websites without 'actual use ... by potential and relevant consumers or complementary advertising and sales figures ... photos of the goods with the

537. *Ibid.*
538. EUIPO, '6.1.2.5 Use in Advertising' (*EUIPO Trade mark guidelines*) https://guidelines.euipo.europa.eu/2214311/1982061/trade-mark-guidelines/6-1-2-5-use-in-advertising accessed July 2024; *See* Fernando Do Blasi, 'Place of Use: Wrong Standard?' (*Kilburn & Strode* 1 November 2022) https://www.kilburnstrode.com/knowledge/european-ip/place-of-use-wrong-standard-hospitality-trade-mark accessed January 2024; Julia Stobbs, 'General Court Comes to a Decision About the Standard of Genuine Use' (*Kluwer Trademark Blog*, 22 February 2023) https://trademarkblog.kluweriplaw.com/2023/02/22/general-court-comes-to-a-decision-about-the-standard-of-genuine-use/ accessed January 2024; Similarly in Canada, under Canadian Trademarks Act R.S.C., 1985, c. T-13, s. 2 'use in association with goods or services' is required. In 2018, the court in *Hilton Worldwide Holdings LLP v. Miller Thomson*, 2018 FC 895 'found that Hilton had proven the requisite use of its trademark in Canada, notwithstanding the fact that it did not operate a physical hotel in Canada' in light of the fact that the category 'hotel services' did not necessarily require a physical hotel service. (*See* Athar K Malik, 'Trademark Interlocutory Injunctions: A Powerful Tool – When Available' (*TrademarkBlog*, 19 December 2019) http://trademarkblog.ca/trademark-interlocutory-injunctions-a-powerful-tool-when-available/ accessed January 2024). Importantly, the court decided that the 'scope of the registration ... must be considered in light of the development in online commerce'. Specifically, the court noted that 'In dismissing the appeal, the Federal Court of Appeals in *Miller Thomson LLP v. Hilton Worldwide Holding LLP* 2020 FCA 134, stated that 'website metrics', 'number of Canadians who have availed of the online services', 'sales figures', '[e]vidence showing that the content offered by the website' was 'stored on servers located in Canada may also be persuasive, as may evidence showing that consumers in Canada are targeted with advertising'. Likewise, listing prices 'in Canadian dollars' and any 'other indicators demonstrating that the website is directed to Canadian customers may also satisfy the requirements of sections 4 and 45 of the Act'. The court noted that '[u]ltimately, the question in each case will be whether the trademark owner has provided evidence that establishes that people in this country can derive a material benefit from services that are performed in this country'. *Hilton Worldwide Holdings LLP v. Miller Thomson*, 2018 FC 895.
539. TRIPS, Art. 16; EUTMR, Art. 18; 15 U.S. Code § 1127; 15 U.S. Code § 1127.
540. Case C-149/11 *Leno Merken BV v. Hagelkruis Beheer BV* EU:C:2012:816.
541. *Ibid.*
542. *Ibid.*

corresponding mark etc'.[543] In another instance, the 'connection to goods'[544] was not met because 'the goods could not be ordered online via the web page'[545] and 'a connection between the website and the number of items sold could not be established'.[546] *Fruit of the Loom v. EUIPO*[547] considered 'use'[548] for social media and it was held by the GC that employees using the term 'fruit'[549] in social media 'to refer to the applicant'[550] does not result in 'evidence capable of proving genuine use of the contested mark during the relevant period, since that evidence alludes to a solely internal use of the contested mark'.[551] For the same reason, the companies own use of the term to 'refer to its goods'[552] did not qualify. The court decided that 'it has not been established that goods bearing the contested mark might have been advertised ... on social media'.[553] The Court of Justice (CJ) considered search advertising relating to where one 'does not make use of that sign'[554] in *Mercedes-Benz Daimler AG v. Együd Garage.*[555] Specifically, a formerly authorised dealer of the Mercedes-Benz mark, when the contractual relation ended, sought to remove online advertising which indicated it as an 'authorised Mercedes-Benz dealer'[556] as well as ads 'published without its consent'.[557] Despite these efforts, some of these ads continued to appear. The CJ ruled based on the principle that 'no one can be legally obliged to do the impossible (impossibilium nulla obligatio est)',[558] especially because these were out of the control of the formerly authorised dealer.[559] Likewise, in the context of search ads, *DealDash Oyj,*[560] the plaintiffs sought to enjoin the defendant from using a mark 'or any other confusingly similar variation of the ... mark as a search keyword on the Internet'.[561] This remedy was denied because the 'wrongful behavior could not reasonably be expected to recur'[562] including but limited to the fact the contested mark was included

543. R 1809/2010-4, *SHARPMASTER/SHARP (fig.)*; EUIPO, '6.1.2.6 Use on the Internet' (*EUIPO Trade mark guidelines*) https://guidelines.euipo.europa.eu/2214311/2215203/trade-mark-guidelines/6-1-2-6-use-on-the-internet accessed July 2024.
544. T-355/09, *Walzer Traum*, EU:T:2013:22; C-141/13 P, *Reber Holding GmbH & Co. KG v. OHIM* EU:C:2014:2089; EUIPO, '6.1.2.6 Use on the Internet' (*EUIPO Trade mark guidelines*) https://guidelines.euipo.europa.eu/2214311/2215203/trade-mark-guidelines/6-1-2-6-use-on-the-internet accessed July 2024.
545. *Ibid.*
546. *Ibid.*
547. Case T-424/17 *FRUIT; Fruit of the Loom, Inc. v. EUIPO* EU:T:2018:824.
548. *Ibid.*
549. *Ibid.*
550. *Ibid.*
551. *Ibid.*
552. *Ibid.*
553. *Ibid.*
554. *Ibid.*
555. Case C-179/15 *Mercedes Benz Daimler AG v. Együd Garage Gépjárműjavító és Értékesítő Kft* EU:C:2016:134.
556. *Ibid.*
557. *Ibid.*
558. *Ibid.*
559. *Ibid.*
560. *DealDash Oyj v. Contextlogic Inc.*, 2018 U.S. Dist. LEXIS 135531.
561. *Ibid.*
562. *Ibid.*

as a 'negative keyword'[563] meaning their bids would not generally trigger an ad if that keyword was used by consumers,[564] thereby excluding it from its advertising bid and the keyword 'was not sought out'.[565] The defendant used[566] the plaintiff's mark within its mobile apps and later 'took a number of steps to cease its use'.[567] It replaced the plaintiff's marks within its mobile apps, which it 'could modify on users' devices by making changes through [defendant's] servers'.[568] It also 'released'[569] necessary 'updates, for all versions of the Wish and Sister apps'.[570] Platforms should consider whether the mark is being used, such as through some form of digital marketing that rises to such standard and consider relevant guidance from the cases above. The use of 'negative keywords'[571] should be informative to search ad platforms, provided that the inclusion as such is ongoing as part of the search ad campaign.

In relation to targeting, limited guidance from the CJ was provided in *L'Oreal SA v. eBay International.*[572] It was held 'that a trademark will be used in a particular Member State, only if the offer for sale of the relevant goods/services to which the trademark is affixed is targeted at consumers in that Member State, as opposed to the website merely being accessible in that jurisdiction'.[573] Therefore, 'including prices in Euros'[574] and 'different languages'[575] may help in 'targeting'[576] a specific Member State.[577] Senftleben notes in the context of the *Pammer and Hotel Alpenhof* cases[578] that '[f]actors that may also play a role in cases involving the use of digital trademarks include: the international nature of the activity that is advertised; use of a language or a currency other than the language or currency generally used in the Member State in which the trader is established; the possibility of making and confirming a reservation in another language; mention of telephone numbers with an international code; outlay of expenditure on an Internet referencing service in order to facilitate access to the website by consumers domiciled in another Member State; use of a top-level domain name other than that of the Member State in which the trader is established; and mention of an international clientele composed of customers domiciled in various

563. *Ibid.*; Google, 'Negative Keyword: Definition' (*Google*) https://support.google.com/google-ads/answer/105671 accessed January 2024.
564. Google, 'Negative Keyword: Definition' (*Google*) https://support.google.com/google-ads/answer/105671 accessed January 2024.
565. *DealDash Oyj v. Contextlogic Inc.*, 2018 U.S. Dist. LEXIS 135531.
566. *Ibid.*
567. *Ibid.*
568. *Ibid.*
569. *Ibid.*
570. *Ibid.*
571. *Ibid.*; Google, 'Negative Keyword: Definition' (*Google*) https://support.google.com/google-ads/answer/105671.
572. Case C-324/09 *L'Oreal SA v. eBay International AG* EU:C:2011:474.
573. *DealDash Oyj v. Contextlogic Inc.*, 2018 U.S. Dist. LEXIS 135531.
574. *Ibid.*
575. *Ibid.*
576. *Ibid.*
577. *Ibid.*
578. Joined Cases C-585/08 *Peter Pammer v. Reederei Karl Schlüter GmbH & Co. KG* and Case C-144/09 *Hotel Alpenhof GesmbH v. Oliver Heller* EU:C:2010:740.

Member States'.[579] Platforms should consider the specific types of targeting employed by the user of a mark and how that may impact the use requirement.[580]

Use[581] of trademarks in search advertising was also at issue in the EU Google France cases.[582] Whether Google itself was liable for any trademark-infringing activity was questioned.[583] In the joint cases involving Google and various parties, a reference for 'preliminary ruling'[584] was made to clarify liability of a 'search engine operator'.[585] For example, Louis Vuitton sought a declaration of trademark infringement against Google based on activity, *inter alia*, being able to bid on keywords 'which correspond to Vuitton's trademarks'[586] as well as keywords such as 'imitation'[587] and 'copy'.[588] The CJ found that Google was 'not using the mark within the meaning of the case law'.[589] The court decided that '[t]he function of indicating origin of the mark is adversely affected if the ad does not enable normally informed and reasonable attentive internet users, or enables them only with difficulty, to ascertain whether the goods or services referred to by the ad originate from the proprietor of the trademark or a third party'.[590] In this case, 'the Court may have felt that ... it was unnecessary to qualify keyword advertising services offered by search engines as relevant trademark use'.[591] In relation to an e-commerce marketplace platform itself 'stocking'[592] goods under Article 9(3)(b) EUTMR, in *Coty v. Amazon*,[593] the Court of Justice of the European Union (CJEU) decided that Amazon was not liable as having stocked[594] such goods.[595] The court decided that 'a person who, on behalf of a third party, stores goods which infringe trademark rights, without being aware of that infringement, must be regarded

579. Martin Senftleben, 'Rights Conferred' in Annette Kur and Martin Senftleben (eds), *European Trade Mark Law* (Oxford University Press 2017) 283.
580. TRIPS, Art. 16.
581. Case C-236/08 *Google France SARL and Google Inc. v. Louis Vuitton Malletier SA*, C-237/08 *Google France SARL v. Viaticum SA and Luteciel SARL* and C-238/08 *Google France SARL v. Centre national de recherche en relations humaines (CNRRH) SARL and Others* EU:C:2010:159.
582. *Ibid.*
583. *Ibid.*
584. *Ibid.*
585. *Ibid.*; Specifically, the reference concerned, as quoted from the case: 'interpretation of Article 5(1) and (2) of First Council Directive 89/104/EEC of 21 December 1988 to approximate the laws of the Member States relating to trade marks (OJ 1989 L 40, p. 1), Article 9(1) of Council Regulation (EC) No 40/94 of 20 December 1993 on the Community trade mark (OJ 1994 L 11, p. 1) and Article 14 of Directive 2000/31/EC of the European Parliament and of the Council of 8 June 2000 on certain legal aspects of information society services, in particular electronic commerce, in the Internal Market ("Directive on electronic commerce") (OJ 2000 L 178, p. 1).'
586. C-236/08 *Google France SARL and Google Inc. v. Louis Vuitton Malletier SA*, C-237/08 *Google France SARL v. Viaticum SA and Luteciel SARL* and C-238/08 *Google France SARL v. Centre national de recherche en relations humaines (CNRRH) SARL and Others* EU:C:2010:159.
587. *Ibid.*
588. *Ibid.*
589. *Ibid.*
590. *Ibid.*
591. Martin Senftleben, 'Adapting EU Trademark Law to New Technologies: Back to Basics?' in Christophe Geiger (ed.) *Constructing European Intellectual Property* (Edward Elgar 2013) 137.
592. T-615/20, *Mood media*, EU:T:2022:109.
593. Case *C-567/18 Coty Germany GmbH v. Amazon Services Europe Sàrl, Amazon Europe Core Sàrl, Amazon FC Graben GmbH, Amazon EU Sàrl* EU:C:2020:267.
594. *Ibid.*
595. *Ibid.*

as not stocking those goods in order to offer them or put them on the market for the purposes of those provisions, if that person does not itself pursue those aims'.[596] The utilisation of the mark on the Amazon website was not considered being used[597] in the way envisioned by Article 9(3)(b) EUTMR.

Ohly reminds us that '[i]t is clear from CJEU case law, in particular from L'Oréal v eBay, that operators of "pure" online marketplaces do not use the trademarks by providing third-party sellers with the opportunity to sell goods'.[598] However, he raises the question of whether 'an operator of a hybrid platform become[s] a user because its own sales and its activities as a marketplace provider are integrated ...?'[599] As Ramirez recently noted, '[i]n its much-awaited Louboutin v. Amazon ruling, the CJEU paved the way for a finding that not only thirdparty sellers, but also Amazon's activities as a platform operator, may result in "use" of the Louboutin trademark and therefore Amazon may be potentially directly liable for trademark infringement'.[600] In essence, a key question referred to the CJEU was whether an e-commerce marketplace platform operator (Amazon) may be considered using a mark under Article 9(2)(a) when a seller markets, without markholder permission, a good with the mark and 'a well-informed and reasonably observant user of that site establishes a link between the services of that operator and the sign at issue, which is in particular the case where, in view of all the circumstances of the situation in question, such a user may have the impression that that operator itself is marketing, in its own name and on its own account, the goods bearing that sign'.[601] The court added the relevant factors as being 'the fact that that operator uses a uniform method of presenting the offers published on its website, displaying both the advertisements relating to the goods which it sells in its own name and on its own behalf and those relating to goods offered by third-party sellers on that marketplace; the fact that it places its own logo as a renowned distributor on all those advertisements; and the fact that it offers third-party sellers, in connection with the marketing of goods bearing the sign at issue, additional services consisting inter alia in the storing and shipping of those goods'[602] (although the result may differ for different operators).[603]

596. *Ibid.*
597. EUTMR, Art. 18.
598. Angsar Ohly, 'Red Soles, a Marketplace and the Categories of Trade Mark Liability: Louboutin v Amazon Before the CJEU' (2022) 17 Journal of Intellectual Property Law & Practice 575, 583 https://doi.org/10.1093/jiplp/jpac047.
599. *Ibid.*
600. César Ramírez-Montes, 'EU Trademarks in the Metaverse' 63 IDEA 557, 685.
601. Joined Cases C-148/21 and C-184/21 *Christian Louboutin v. Amazon Europe Core Sàrl and Others* EU:C:2022:1016.
602. *Ibid.*
603. Allessandro Cerri, 'Hague Court Provides First Judgment on Online Marketplace IP Infringement Liability Following Louboutin v Amazon' (*The IPKat* 23 September 2023) https://ipkitten.blogspot.com/2023/09/hague-court-provides-first-judgment-on.html accessed July 2024; Mathijs Peijnenburg and Moïra Truijens, 'Louboutin v Amazon Does Not Apply to Ordinary Online Marketplaces, Says District Court' (*World Trademark Review 19 September 2023*) https://www.worldtrademarkreview.com/article/louboutin-v-amazon-does-not-apply-ordinary-online-marketplaces-says-district-court accessed July 2024.

A UK matter (based on activity pre-Brexit and applying EU law)[604] is informative, and is based on BEVERLEY HILLS POLO CLUB marks owned by Lifestyle in the UK and EU, whereas 'a commercially unrelated entity'[605] in the US owns the marks in the US.[606] Amazon advertised, offered and sold US goods to 'UK/EU customers on www.amazon .co.uk, www.amazon.de and www.amazon.com (as viewable in the UK/EU)'[607] and admitted to infringement for the UK/EU sites but not for amazon.com.[608] The Court of Appeal, based on 'targeting'[609] and UK/EU sales as 'use',[610] 'overturned' and 'granted an injunction'.[611] In Amazon's appeal to the UK Supreme Court, they argued against the finding of 'targeting at UK/EU consumers'[612] and misinterpretation of the case law as to 'whether sales on foreign websites could constitute infringement of the trade-marks in the UK/EU'.[613] The Supreme Court dismissed Amazon's appeal and held that 'Amazon targeted consumers in the UK by displaying the USA Branded Goods on its USA website and marking them available for shipment to the UK, which in turn infringed the UK/EU Marks'.[614] The above cases serve as warnings to platforms that platforms may be liable under certain models or approaches, and platforms that engage in such types of models should consider whether this has further implications for their own practices and policies.[615]

Turning now to US requirements, under 15 U.S. Code § 1127, a 'bona fide intention to use in commerce'[616] is required for registration. There must be 'bona fide use'[617] of a mark and it is clear that 'use made merely to reserve a right in a mark will not meet this standard'.[618] Specifically, under this section, 'use in commerce' is defined as 'the bona fide use of a mark in the ordinary course of trade, and ... shall be deemed to be in use in commerce – (1) on goods when – (A) it is placed in any manner on the goods or their containers or the displays associated therewith or on the tags or labels affixed thereto, or if the nature of the goods makes such placement impracticable, then on documents associated with the goods or their sale, and (B) the goods are sold or

604. *Lifestyle Equities CV and another v. Amazon UK Services Ltd and others* [2022] EWCA Civ 552; *Lifestyle Equities CV and another v. Amazon UK Services Ltd and others* [2024] UKSC 8.
605. *Lifestyle Equities CV and another v. Amazon UK Services Ltd and others* [2024] UKSC 8; the Supreme Court of the United Kingdom, 'Press Summary' https://supremecourt.uk/uploads/uksc_2022_0108_press_summary_8fe7a3aaad.pdf accessed July 2024.
606. *Ibid.*
607. UK Supreme Court, 'Lifestyle Equities CV and Another (Respondents) v Amazon UK Services Ltd and Others (Appellants)', 6 March 2024, https://www.youtube.com/watch?v=fixfCU6Msis.
608. *Ibid.*
609. *Ibid.*
610. *Ibid.*
611. *Ibid.*
612. *Ibid.*
613. *Ibid.*
614. *Lifestyle Equities CV and another v. Amazon UK Services Ltd and others* [2024] UKSC 8; the Supreme Court of the United Kingdom, 'Press Summary' https://supremecourt.uk/uploads/uksc_2022_0108_press_summary_8fe7a3aaad.pdf accessed July 2024.
615. César Ramírez-Montes, 'EU Trademarks in the Metaverse' 63 IDEA 557.
616. 15 U.S. Code § 1127.
617. *Ibid.*
618. USPTO, 'Trademark Manual of Examining Procedure (TMEP)' (*TMEP*) https://tmep.uspto.gov/RDMS/TMEP/current#/current/TMEP-900d1e72.html accessed January 2024.

transported in commerce, and (2) on services when it is used or displayed in the sale or advertising of services and the services are rendered in commerce, or the services are rendered in more than one State or in the United States and a foreign country and the person rendering the services is engaged in commerce in connection with the services'[619] (reformatted). Under *Automedx Inc. v. Artivent Corp.*[620] and *Clorox Co. v. Salazar*[621] and as outlined in the Trademark Manual of Examining Procedure (TMEP),[622] relevant factors may include '(1) the amount of use; (2) the nature or quality of the transaction; and (3) what is typical use within a particular industry'.[623] With respect to domain names, under the U.S. ACPA, 15 U.S. Code § 1125(d)(1)(B)(VI), a trademark domain name dealing for monetary benefit 'without having used, or having an intent to use, the domain name for a bona fide offering of any goods or services'[624] is considered a factor for 'bad faith'.[625] Also, under 15 U.S. Code § 1114, 'use in commerce any reproduction, counterfeit, copy, or colorable imitation of a registered mark in connection with the sale, offering for sale, distribution, or advertising of any goods or services on or in connection with which such use ...'[626] is prohibited. In line with this, Ramsey notes that '[c]ourts in some circuits will also require evidence of commercial use and/or trademark use of the mark for a prima facie trademark infringement claim'.[627]

As Goldman points out that two cases decided in 2023 in the U.S. Supreme Court, the *Jack Daniel's v. VIP Products*[628] and *Abitron v. Hetronic*[629] cases, stand 'for the proposition that trademark law only applies when parties are using a trademark *as a mark*, i.e., to identify and distinguish the source of marketplace goods'.[630] In the context of the Internet in the *Abitron* case, while the case itself did not pertain to marks on the Internet, Supreme Court Justice Jackson, concurred with the Court that sections '§1114(1)(a) and §1125(a)(1) are not extraterritorial and that the infringing "use in

619. 15 U.S. Code § 1127.
620. *Automedx Inc. v. Artivent Corp.*, 95 USPQ2d 1976 (TTAB 2010).
621. *Clorox Co. v. Salazar*, 108 USPQ2d 1083, 1086 (TTAB 2013).
622. USPTO, 'Trademark Manual of Examining Procedure (TMEP)' (*TMEP*) https://tmep.uspto.gov/RDMS/TMEP/current#/result/TMEP-900d1e72.html?q=amount%20of%20use&ccb=on&ncb=off&icb=off&fcb=off&ver=current&syn=adj&results=compact&sort=relevance&cnt=10&index=1 accessed January 2024; *Automedx Inc. v. Artivent Corp.*, 95 USPQ2d 1976 (TTAB 2010); *Clorox Co. v. Salazar*, 108 USPQ2d 1083, 1086 (TTAB 2013).
623. USPTO, 'Trademark Manual of Examining Procedure (TMEP)' (*TMEP*) https://tmep.uspto.gov/RDMS/TMEP/current#/current/TMEP-900d1e72.html accessed January 2024; *Automedx Inc. v. Artivent Corp.*, 95 USPQ2d 1976 (TTAB 2010); *Clorox Co. v. Salazar*, 108 USPQ2d 1083, 1086 (TTAB 2013).
624. CEB, *Internet Law Practice in California* (Continuing Education of the Bar, the Regents of the University of California 2015) §3.22.
625. *Ibid.*
626. 15 U.S. Code § 1114.
627. Lisa P Ramsey, 'Brandjacking on Social Networks: Trademark Infringement by Impersonation of Markholders' (2010) 58 Buffalo Law Review 851, 856.
628. *Jack Daniel's Properties, Inc. v. VIP Products LLC*, 599 U.S. 140 (2023).
629. *Abitron Austria GmbH v. Hetronic International, Inc.*, 600 U.S. 412.
630. Eric Goldman, 'In a SAD Scheme Case, Court Rejects Injunction over "Emoji" Trademark' (*Technology & Marketing Law Blog*, 5 October 2023) https://blog.ericgoldman.org/archives/2023/10/in-a-sad-scheme-case-court-rejects-injunction-over-emoji-trademark.htm accessed January 2024.

commerce" of a trademark provides the dividing line between foreign and domestic applications of these provisions'.[631] However, the Justice commented in a footnote that 'in the internet age, one could imagine a mark serving its critical source-identifying function in domestic commerce even absent the domestic physical presence of the items whose source it identifies'[632] and further citing (in accord) *In re Sones*[633] that 'with respect to the use in commerce requirement'[634] marks on the Internet (specifically on websites) can be a store or 'banner which encourages the consumer to buy the product'.[635] While the above cases focus on 'use in commerce'[636] with respect to particular goods, recently, in the 2022 decision in *LoanStreet, Inc. v. Troia,*[637] a District Court found 'use in commerce'[638] partially based on use within a search ad on Google, which labelled the advertisement as an 'Ad'.[639] Goldman finds the reasoning hard to grapple with because 'there should not be a "use in commerce" when the advertiser (here, Troia) doesn't actually offer any goods or services in the marketplace'.[640] In the earlier case of *Chobani, LLC v. Dannon Company, Inc.*,[641] the question of whether the use[642] was being made for an ad on Twitter (now, X) was 'in commerce'[643] was not directly addressed, although it was implied 'that use of an ad campaign on Twitter is a use in commerce'.[644] Essentially, there needs to be 'connection with any goods or services'.[645] In the context of hashtags, as Roberts mentions, unlike static websites, social media hashtags can be used collaboratively and dynamically.[646] Hashtags in social media will not always be considered trademarks, as was seen in the early case of *Eksouzian*,[647] especially where descriptive terms formed part of the hashtag, even

631. *Abitron Austria GmbH v. Hetronic International, Inc.*, 600 U.S. 412.
632. *Ibid.*
633. *In re Sones*, 590 F. 3d 1282, 1288 (CA Fed. 2009).
634. *Abitron Austria GmbH v. Hetronic International, Inc.*, 600 U.S. 412.
635. *Ibid.*
636. 15 U.S. Code § 1127.
637. *LoanStreet, Inc. v. Troia*, 2022 WL 3544170 (S.D.N.Y. 17 August 2022).
638. 15 U.S. Code § 1127.
639. *LoanStreet, Inc. v. Troia*, 2022 WL 3544170 (S.D.N.Y. 17 August 2022); Eric Goldman, 'Griper's Keyword Ads May Constitute False Advertising (Huh?)–LoanStreet v. Troia' (*Technology & Marketing Law Blog*, 9 September 2022) https://blog.ericgoldman.org/archives/2022/09/gripers-keyword-ads-may-constitute-false-advertising-huh-loanstreet-v-troia.htm accessed January 2024.
640. Eric Goldman, 'Griper's Keyword Ads May Constitute False Advertising (Huh?)–LoanStreet v. Troia' (*Technology & Marketing Law Blog*, 9 September 2022) https://blog.ericgoldman.org/archives/2022/09/gripers-keyword-ads-may-constitute-false-advertising-huh-loanstreet-v-troia.htm accessed January 2024.
641. *Chobani, LLC V. Dannon Company, Inc.* 157 F.Supp.3d 190 (2016).
642. 15 U.S. Code § 1127.
643. 15 U.S. Code § 1125(a)(1).
644. MTLR, '#Mark: Is a Hashtag a Use in Commerce?' (*Michigan Technology Law Review*) https://mttlr.org/2017/11/mark-is-a-hashtag-a-use-in-commerce/ accessed January 2024; *Chobani, LLC V. Dannon Company, Inc.* 157 F.Supp.3d 190 (2016).
645. 15 U.S. Code § 1127; 15 U.S. Code § 1114(1)(a); 15 U.S. Code § 1125(a)(1); Lisa P Ramsey, 'Brandjacking on Social Networks: Trademark Infringement by Impersonation of Markholders' (2010) 58 Buffalo Law Review 851, 876.
646. Alexandra J Roberts, 'Tagmarks' (2017) 105 California Law Review 634.
647. *Vahan Eksouzian et al v. Brett Albanese et al*, No. 2:2013cv00728 – Document 188 (C.D. Cal. 2015); Alexandra Roberts, 'Hashtags Are Not Trademarks: Eksouzian v. Albanese' (*Guest Blog*

though, as Goldman opines, the Court did not address descriptiveness for each term.[648] The TMEP 1301.04(h)(iv)(C) (in reference to SMs) specifically indicates that '[w]ebpages from social-networking websites should be scrutinized to ensure that the mark is properly directly associated with the identified services'.[649] Also, current practice shows that many hashtags have been granted registration, and as Roberts outlines, these should be looked at carefully in terms of their use and other factors to determine whether they should be afforded protection.[650] In *Yuga Labs Inc. v. Ripps*[651] (summary judgment granted in part in April 2023, and final judgment issued in October 2023),[652] the court considered and found that NFTs are goods and can be and were being 'used in commerce'[653] based on 10,000 NFT sales, customers having 'access to membership perks ... online games ... in person events',[654] and the seller entering into 'marketing partnerships and collaborations',[655] and having media coverage.[656] In 2025, the 9th Circuit confirmed that NFTs 'are not merely monkey business and can be trademarked'.[657] While proceedings are ongoing, Metaverse and other platforms should consider, with the rise of NFTs in Metaverse platforms, that these may be considered products and services, a number of brands are registering their marks as associated with these types of goods and that there may be much contention about use[658] in Metaverse platforms to come. Platforms may consider trying to address this in a clear manner up front by assessing 'use in commerce'[659] in relation to NFTs.

Not only whether a mark is being used, but when the mark was first used is important.[660] In the context of when a mark was first used in a mobile app, in *Gearsource Holdings, LLC v. Google LLC*,[661] the dispute centred around use[662] and specifically 'when [the] [p]laintiff began to display its G-SUITE mark on its downloadable mobile app'.[663] The court found that 'Google's [f]oreign [p]riority [f]iling [d]ate'[664]

Post) https://blog.ericgoldman.org/archives/2015/08/hashtags-are-not-trademarks-eksouzian-v-albanese-guest-blog-post-2.htm accessed January 2024.

648. Alexandra Roberts, 'Hashtags Are Not Trademarks: Eksouzian v. Albanese' (*Guest Blog Post*) https://blog.ericgoldman.org/archives/2015/08/hashtags-are-not-trademarks-eksouzian-v-albanese-guest-blog-post-2.htm accessed January 2024.
649. USPTO, 'TMEP 1301.04(h)(iv)(C) USPTO Trademark Manual of Examining Procedure May 2024' https://tmep.uspto.gov/RDMS/TMEP/current#/current/TMEP-1300d1e1.html accessed July 2024.
650. Alexandra Roberts, 'Tagmarks' (2015) 105 California Law Review 599.
651. *Yuga Labs, Inc. v. Ripps*, 2022 U.S. Dist. LEXIS 234124 (C.D. Cal., 16 December 2022).
652. *Yuga Labs, Inc. v. Ripps*, 2023 U.S. Dist. LEXIS 192487.
653. *Yuga Labs, Inc. v. Ripps*, 2023 U.S. Dist. LEXIS 71336.
654. *Ibid.*
655. *Ibid.*
656. CourtListerner, 'Yuga Labs Inc. v. Ripps, C.D. Cal., No. 2:22-cv-04355, summary judgment 4/21/23' https://storage.courtlistener.com/recap/gov.uscourts.cacd.855658/gov.uscourts.cacd.855658.225.0.pdf accessed January 2024.
657. *Yuga Labs, Inc. v. Ripps*, Case No. 24-879, 2025 WL 2056060 (9th Cir. 23 July 2025).
658. TRIPS, Art. 16; EUTMR, Art. 18; 15 U.S. Code § 1127.
659. 15 U.S. Code § 1127.
660. Under 15 U.S. Code § 1126(d), there is a '[r]ight of [p]riority' subject to, *inter alia*, a 'statement that the applicant has a bona fide intention to use the mark in commerce'.
661. *Gearsource Holdings, LLC v. Google LLC*, 2020 U.S. Dist. LEXIS 119892.
662. 15 U.S. Code § 1127.
663. *Gearsource Holdings, LLC v. Google LLC*, 2020 U.S. Dist. LEXIS 119892.
664. *Ibid.*

was prior to the plaintiffs 'constructive use date',[665] which are the relevant operative dates based on the 'metadata [which] undisputedly demonstrated that the screenshots'[666] were from 2018 rather than the contended 2016.[667] Mobile and other platforms may consider their discretion to look back at records which prove when a mark may have first been utilised within their platforms.

Under the UK Trade Marks Act 1994, a mark may be revoked if 'within the period of five years following the date of completion of the registration procedure it has not been put to genuine use in the United Kingdom, by the proprietor or with his consent, in relation to the goods or services for which it is registered'.[668] Likewise, in Canada, 'use, in relation to a trademark, means any use that by section 4 is deemed to be a use in association with goods or services'.[669]

In line with the above, policies/platforms should consider specifically how a mark may be utilised to determine whether there is actual use,[670] providing guidelines for the same. They may also consider source information on when a mark was first utilised, if relevant.

3.2.1.2 Place of Use Concept

Digital trademarks are used in various places on the Internet. For example, as was seen in Chapter 2, marks are used within domain names, e-commerce marketplace listings, search ads, social media[671] activity, social media ads, mobile app names, mobile app activity, Metaverse avatars, NFTs in the Metaverse, Metaverse concerts, etc. However, it is important to consider where, or which place within these digital environments, the mark is actually being used. However, 'place of use'[672] has traditionally been considered with respect to where, geographically, a mark has been used, or generally, where on the Internet it is used. EUIPO Guidelines use the terminology 'place of use'[673] to simply describe the context of whether the mark is being used in trade, 'in the territory where the trademark is protected',[674] for EUTMs in the EU,[675] or in the case of national marks, 'in the relevant Member State'.[676] It is a phrase often used in connection with where a mark is used and what needs to be proven in that respect.[677] This was

665. *Ibid.*
666. *Ibid.*
667. *Ibid.*
668. UK Trade Marks Act 1994, s. 46(1)(a).
669. Canadian Trademarks Act R.S.C., 1985, c. T-13, s. 2.
670. TRIPS, Art. 16; EUTMR, Art. 18; 15 U.S. Code § 1127; UK Trade Marks Act 1994, s. 46(1)(a); Canadian Trademarks Act R.S.C., 1985, c. T-13, s. 2.
671. Lisa P Ramsey, 'Brandjacking on Social Networks: Trademark Infringement by Impersonation of Markholders' (2010) 58 Buffalo Law Review 851.
672. EUIPO, '3 Place of Use' (*EUIPO Trade mark guidelines* 2024) https://guidelines.euipo.europa.eu/2214311/1982069/trade-mark-guidelines/3-place-of-use accessed January 2024.
673. *Ibid.*
674. *Ibid.*
675. *Ibid.*
676. *Ibid.*
677. Stefan Martin, 'Limits of Trade Marks: Parody' (*EUIPO Academy Learning Portal*, 31 January 2017) https://euipo.europa.eu/knowledge/course/view.php?id=2844 accessed January

reinforced in *Standard v. EUIPO*, where it became a key consideration[678] as the GC said that 'place of use'[679] of the mark (such as in online advertising and otherwise) should not have been confused with 'place of provision of the service' (the foreign hotel).[680] In the US, the 'place of use'[681] concept is recognised in the context of 'concurrent registration'[682] under 15 U.S. Code § 1052 where 'more than one person'[683] may be entitled to registration with restrictions as to the 'place of use'[684] where they may use the mark referring to a territory or geographic area (discussed further in section 3.2.6 *Digital Jurisdictional and Territorial Considerations* Jurisdiction below).[685]

However, it is important for platforms to note that the 'place of use'[686] in the context of this model focuses not only on, but platforms should consider, specifically where on the Internet (which platform) the mark is being utilised, but in what specific place within the various platforms. For example, the 'place of use'[687] may be within a domain name, on a listing webpage, with the headline or description of a search ad, within a social media username, within a social media ad, within social media activity, within a mobile app name, on the mobile app icon, within a mobile app ad, in a Metaverse game, or in a Metaverse store, Metaverse fashion show, or Metaverse concert. This is because each of these may raise different considerations and platforms should consider and address whether actual use[688] is being made of the mark in each such place.[689] Platforms may consider whether a particular 'place of use'[690] in the above lends itself to a particularly favoured result as opposed to others, for example, favouring infringement for use[691] of trademarks in domain names, in social media usernames, and in mobile app names, however disfavouring concluding trademark use[692] in search ads to market accessories of a trademarked product clearly by a third party.[693]

2024; Stefan Martin, 'Well Known Marks and Parody: Dilution and Denigration? Unfair Advantage?' (*EUIPO*, 2017), https://euipo.europa.eu/knowledge/pluginfile.php/77920/mod_resource/content/8/Limits%20of%20trade%20marks%2C%20Parody%2018-5-2017.pdf accessed January 2024.

678. Case T-768/20 *Standard International Management LLC v. EUIPO* ECLI:EU:T:2022:458.
679. *Ibid.*
680. *Ibid.*
681. 15 U.S. Code § 1052.
682. *Ibid.*
683. *Ibid.*
684. *Ibid.*
685. *Ibid.*
686. EUIPO, '3 Place of Use' (*EUIPO Trade mark guidelines*, 2024) https://guidelines.euipo.europa.eu/2214311/1982069/trade-mark-guidelines/3-place-of-use accessed January 2024.
687. *Ibid.*
688. TRIPS, Art. 16; EUTMR, Art. 18; 15 U.S. Code § 1127; UK Trade Marks Act 1994, s. 46(1)(a); Canadian Trademarks Act R.S.C., 1985, c. T-13, s. 2.
689. EUIPO, '3 Place of Use' (*EUIPO Trade mark guidelines* 2024) https://guidelines.euipo.europa.eu/2214311/1982069/trade-mark-guidelines/3-place-of-use accessed January 2024.
690. WIPO, 'WIPO Overview of WIPO Panel Views on Selected UDRP Questions, Third Edition, ('WIPO Jurisprudential Overview 3.0') (*WIPO*, 2017) https://www.wipo.int/amc/en/domains/search/overview3.0/ accessed June 2025.
691. TRIPS, Art. 16; EUTMR, Art. 18; 15 U.S. Code § 1127; UK Trade Marks Act 1994, s. 46(1)(a); Canadian Trademarks Act R.S.C., 1985, c. T-13, s. 2.
692. *Ibid.*
693. EUTMR, Art. 14.

3.2.1.3 *Property Theory and Use*

Another way of looking at trademark 'use'[694] is through the lens of using one's 'property'[695] and McCarthy considers that 'protection of the trademark holder's property right is another important goal of trademark law'.[696] Bently says that 'trademarks law, originally conceived as a legal mechanism for preventing fraud or protecting consumers, has been reconceptualised' and this time as 'property'[697] and further that a 'communication-based model'[698] was confronted by 'a property'[699] based one.[700] Landes and Posner say that '[t]he ownership of a valid trademark does not carry with it as broad a right to exclude others from using it as the ownership of a piece of land does'[701] unless, for example, 'dilution'[702] or the 'likelihood of confusion' exists.[703] It is important for platforms to recognise such views as they put things into context. As aptly noted by Kamperman Sanders, trademarks as intellectual property concern 'property in intangibles'.[704] Intellectual property rights 'are by definition considered property and as such ... are protected against interference by third parties'.[705] Drexl says that the 'property claim'[706] serves to justify 'demands for higher levels of IP protection on the international level'.[707] He says there is 'no inherent conflict between

694. TRIPS, Art. 16; EUTMR, Art. 18; 15 U.S. Code § 1127; UK Trade Marks Act 1994, s. 46(1)(a); Canadian Trademarks Act R.S.C., 1985, c. T-13, s. 2.
695. J Thomas McCarthy, *McCarthy on Trademarks and Unfair Competition* (4th edn, vol. 69, Thomson Reuters, 2014) in Lisa L Ouellette, 'The Google Shortcut to Trademark Law' (2014) 102 California Law Review 351, 358; Lionel Bently, 'From Communication to Thing: Historical Aspects of the Conceptualisation of Trade Marks as Property' in Graeme B Dinwoodie and Mark D Janis (eds), *Trademark Law and Theory: A Handbook of Contemporary Research* (Edward Elgar, 2008) 3-41.
696. J Thomas McCarthy, *McCarthy on Trademarks and Unfair Competition* (4th edn, vol. 69, Thomson Reuters, 2014) in Lisa L Ouellette, 'The Google Shortcut to Trademark Law' (2014) 102 California Law Review 351; Lisa L Ouellette, 'The Google Shortcut to Trademark Law' (2014) 102 California Law Review 351, 358.
697. J Thomas McCarthy, *McCarthy on Trademarks and Unfair Competition* (4th edn, vol. 69, Thomson Reuters, 2014) as seen in Lisa L Ouellette, 'The Google Shortcut to Trademark Law' (2014) 102 California Law Review 351, 358; Lionel Bently, 'From Communication to Thing: Historical Aspects of the Conceptualisation of Trade Marks as Property' in Graeme B Dinwoodie and Mark D Janis (eds), *Trademark Law and Theory: A Handbook of Contemporary Research* (Edward Elgar, 2008) 3-41.
698. Lionel Bently, 'From Communication to Thing: Historical Aspects of the Conceptualisation of Trade Marks as Property' in Graeme B Dinwoodie and Mark D Janis (eds), *Trademark Law and Theory: A Handbook of Contemporary Research* (Edward Elgar, 2008) 3-41.
699. *Ibid.*
700. *Ibid.*
701. William M Landes and Richard A Posner, 'Trademark Law: An Economic Perspective' (1987) 30 The Journal of Law and Economics 265, 300 https://doi.org/10.1086/467138.
702. *Ibid.*
703. *Ibid.*
704. Anselm Kamperman Sanders, *Unfair Competition Law: The Protection of Intellectual and Industrial Creativity* (Oxford University Press 1997) 109.
705. Anselm Kamperman Sanders and Christopher Heath (eds), *Intellectual Property and International Dispute Resolution* (Wolters Kluwer 2019) Chapter 7.
706. Josef Drexl, 'European and International Intellectual Property Law between Propertization and Regulation: How a Fundamental Rights Approach Can Mitigate the Tension' (2016) 47 The University of Pennsylvania Law Review 199, 200.
707. *Ibid.*

the two concepts of IP as a property right, and IP as a regulatory tool'.[708] Further, 'human achievement lies at the foundation'[709] and a trademark as a property asset of this kind is often sought to be protected. However, as Gangjee notes, 'the judicial recognition of brands as property objects is a controversial development'[710] because it minimises the aspect of consumer involvement in the creation of a brand,[711] which is discussed further in section 3.2.4.1. As Dinwoodie and Ohly recognise, labelling intellectual property as 'property … is often abused to extend the scope of protection, modern property theories have demystified the concept … and … [if] used analytically rather than rhetorically, the notion of property may well have its doctrinal virtues'.[712] Mossoff recognises that trademarks rights are 'use-right-based property rights that are appurtenant to larger estates, such as easements and riparian interests'.[713] Hence, while trademarks are property, they are intangible, and there are limitations. Overall, it is clear that while trademarks are a form of property, albeit intellectual, they must be used[714] in specific ways.

In the EU, even though a mark is a kind of property, 'genuine use'[715] is still required,[716] without which the property rights may be lost.[717] In the same way, under U.S. law, a trademark is considered intangible property; there are limitations because the mark is required to be put into 'use'[718] or at least there must be an 'intent to use'[719] the trademark in commerce.[720] There remains little doubt that a trademark is the intellectual property of an owner, and in the international context, registration of a mark may be undertaken in all relevant jurisdictions. However, it appears from an Internet perspective that 'use'[721] of such property cannot unconditionally be made and

708. *Ibid.*
709. *Ibid.*
710. Dev Gangjee, 'Property in Brands' (12 April 2013). LSE Legal Studies Working Paper No. 8/2013 http://dx.doi.org/10.2139/ssrn.2249765.
711. *Ibid.*
712. Niklas Bruun et al. (eds), *Transition and Coherence in Intellectual Property Law: Essays in Honour of Annette Kur* (Cambridge University Press 2021) 5.
713. Adam Mossoff, 'Trademark as a Property Right' (2017) George Mason Law & Economics Research Paper No. 17-15 https://ssrn.com/abstract=2941763 accessed 4 August 2025.
714. TRIPS, Art. 16; EUTMR, Art. 18; 15 U.S. Code § 1127; UK Trade Marks Act 1994, s. 46(1)(a); Canadian Trademarks Act R.S.C., 1985, c. T-13, s. 2.
715. EUTMR, Art. 18.
716. Stephen L Carter, 'Does It Matter Whether Intellectual Property Is Property?' https://digitalcommons.law.yale.edu/fss_papers/2259/ accessed 4 August 2025; EUTMR, Art. 15(1); Emily Bolton, 'Defining Genuine Use Requirements of Community Trade Marks in Light of an Expanding European Union' (*WIPO*) http://www.wipo.int/edocs/mdocs/mdocs/en/wipo_ipr_ge_11/wipo_ipr_ge_11_topic3.pdf accessed January 2024.
717. EUTMR, Art. 58(1)(a); 15 U.S. Code § 1127; 15 U.S. Code § 1064; UK Trade Marks Act 1994, s. 46(1)(a); Canadian Trade-marks Regulation, s. 45.
718. TRIPS, Art. 16; EUTMR, Art. 18; 15 U.S. Code § 1127; UK Trade Marks Act 1994, s. 46(1)(a); Canadian Trademarks Act R.S.C., 1985, c. T-13, s. 2.
719. USPTO, 'Trademark Applications: Intent-to-Use (ITU) Basis' (*USPTO*) https://www.uspto.gov/trademarks-application-process/filing-online/intent-use-itu-applications accessed January 2024.
720. 15 U.S. Code § 1127.
721. *Ibid.*

even within various jurisdictions, it must be made in certain ways[722] and even in the context of certain goods or services. Nevertheless, in general, a digital trademark may potentially be accessed by consumers worldwide, despite where it is registered or claim made.

The UDRP already assesses rights in a mark based on registration or, in the case of unregistered marks, whether it is distinctive.[723] Based on the implications of the property theory,[724] the platforms should consider whether the user of the trademark has property ownership of a mark and/or authorisation to use it, and how that may be assessed for purposes of their enforcement policies.

3.2.1.4 Summary of Platform Considerations for Digital Use and Place of Use

The UDRP and platforms may be well informed by the use theory[725] and select aspects of the legal frameworks in that they clarify use[726] requirements in a trademark context. While the UDRP considers trademarks used in domain names, and some platforms consider use within their services, the requirement of 'use as a mark'[727] must be specifically or adequately considered. Based on the above, while some differences do exist, there appears to substantial similarity for certain aspects of use in the EU and the US. For example, even though the terminology is slightly different, specifically, 'genuine use in the Union in connection with the goods or services in respect of which it is registered'[728] and 'use in commerce',[729] it appears that the common thread can be found in the TRIPS agreement terminology of use 'in the course of trade'[730] which sums it up well and platforms may consider this inclusive terminology. Platforms may

722. TRIPS, Art. 16; EUTMR, Art. 18; 15 U.S. Code § 1127; UK Trade Marks Act 1994, s. 46(1)(a); Canadian Trademarks Act R.S.C., 1985, c. T-13, s. 2.
723. WIPO, 'WIPO Overview of WIPO Panel Views on Selected UDRP Questions, Third Edition, ('WIPO Jurisprudential Overview 3.0') (*WIPO*, 2017) https://www.wipo.int/amc/en/domains/search/overview3.0/ accessed June 2025.
724. J Thomas McCarthy, *McCarthy on Trademarks and Unfair Competition* (4th edn, vol. 69, Thomson Reuters, 2014) in Lisa L Ouellette, 'The Google Shortcut to Trademark Law' (2014) 102 California Law Review 351, 358; Lionel Bently, 'From Communication to Thing: Historical Aspects of the Conceptualisation of Trade Marks as Property' in Graeme B Dinwoodie and Mark D Janis (eds), *Trademark Law and Theory: A Handbook of Contemporary Research* (Edward Elgar, 2008) 3-41.
725. Graeme B Dinwoodie and Mark D Janis, 'Confusion Over Use: Contextualism in Trademark Law' (2007) 92 Iowa Law Review 1597 *Articles by Maurer Faculty*. Paper 361; Stephen L Carter, 'Does It Matter Whether Intellectual Property Is Property?' https://digitalcommons.law.yale.edu/fss_papers/2259/ accessed 4 August 2025; William Fisher, 'Theories of Intellectual Property' (*Harvard Law*) https://cyber.harvard.edu/people/tfisher/iptheory.pdf accessed 4 August 2025; Shontavia J Johnson, 'Memetic Theory, Trademarks & the Viral Meme Mark' (2013) 13 The John Marshall Law School Review of Intellectual Property Law 96.
726. EUTMR, Art. 18; 15 U.S. Code § 1127.
727. Eric Goldman, 'In a SAD Scheme Case, Court Rejects Injunction over "Emoji" Trademark' (*Technology & Marketing Law Blog*, 5 October 2023) https://blog.ericgoldman.org/archives/2023/10/in-a-sad-scheme-case-court-rejects-injunction-over-emoji-trademark.htm accessed January 2024.
728. EUTMR, Art. 18.
729. 15 U.S. Code § 1127.
730. TRIPS, Art. 16.

interpret this based on common elements amongst the jurisdictions, including the connection which is required on the Internet to the goods and services. Based on this, the UDRP and platforms need to consider whether a mark is being used as a mark.[731] This should be incorporated directly into their policies and expounded upon in their guidance. Platforms should also consider whether the user of a mark has a property right or authorisation based on implications of the 'use theory'[732] and the property theory.[733]

3.2.2 Digital Bad Faith and Abuse

This section looks at the concept of bad faith,[734] registration in bad faith,[735] and bad faith in domain names,[736] including ccTLDs.[737] The concept of abuse[738] is also considered. How these inform the model and the resulting considerations for the UDRP and platforms are summarised.

3.2.2.1 Concept of Bad Faith and Registration

The concept of bad faith[739] operates in different aspects of trademarks. Mostert and Wu rightly recognise that 'the advent of digital technology has also contributed to the

731. Graeme B Dinwoodie and Mark D Janis, 'Confusion Over Use: Contextualism in Trademark Law' (2007) 92 Iowa Law Review 1597.
732. *Ibid., Articles by Maurer Faculty.* Paper 361.; Stephen L Carter, 'Does It Matter Whether Intellectual Property Is Property?' https://digitalcommons.law.yale.edu/fss_papers/2259/ accessed 4 August 2025; William Fisher, 'Theories of Intellectual Property' (*Harvard Law*) https://cyber.harvard.edu/people/tfisher/iptheory.pdf accessed 4 August 2025; Shontavia J Johnson, 'Memetic Theory, Trademarks & the Viral Meme Mark' (2013) 13 The John Marshall Law School Review of Intellectual Property Law, 96.
733. Lionel Bently, 'From Communication to Thing: Historical Aspects of the Conceptualisation of Trade Marks as Property' in Graeme B Dinwoodie and Mark D Janis (eds), *Trademark Law and Theory: A Handbook of Contemporary Research* (Edward Elgar, 2008) 3-41.
734. Paris Convention, Art. 6bis; EUTMR, Art. 59; TTAB, 'Fighting Bad Faith Trademark Filings in the United States' (*The Honorable Karen S. Kuhlke Administrative Trademark Judge*) https://www.jpo.go.jp/e/news/kokusai/tm5/document/bad_faith_seminar2/01.pdf accessed July 2024; UDRP, 4(a)(iii).
735. *Ibid.*
736. UDRP, 4(a)(iii).
737. WIPO, 'WIPO Domain Name Dispute Resolution Service for .EU (and.ею and.ευ)' (*WIPO*) https://www.wipo.int/amc/en/domains/cctld/eu/index.html accessed July 2024; Registry Services, 'UsTLD Dispute Resolution Policy' (*Registry Services, LLC*, 2021) https://www.about.us/documents/policies/usTLD_Dispute_Resolution_Policy_(usDRP).pdf accessed July 2024.
738. WIPO, 'WIPO Overview of WIPO Panel Views on Selected UDRP Questions, Third Edition, ('WIPO Jurisprudential Overview 3.0') (WIPO, 2017) https://www.wipo.int/amc/en/domains/search/overview3.0/ accessed June 2025.
739. Paris Convention, Art. 6bis; EUTMR, Art. 59; TTAB, 'Fighting Bad Faith Trademark Filings in the United States' (*The Honorable Karen S. Kuhlke Administrative Trademark Judge*) https://www.jpo.go.jp/e/news/kokusai/tm5/document/bad_faith_seminar2/01.pdf accessed July 2024; UDRP, 4(a)(iii).

importance of bad faith'[740] and point to the fact that those intended to act in 'bad faith ... can simply rely on a host of internet and website information to copy and pre-empt the owners of foreign marks'.[741] They state that the concept 'was originally derived from the Twelve Tables ("Lex Duodecim Tabularum") of Ancient Rome'[742] and in the context of 'bad faith possession'[743] potentially lead to 'punitive damages'[744] and that this 'fundamental legal principle was also highlighted in later years by Roman Law scholars in Europe'.[745] The Cornell Legal Information Institute definition recognises that 'bad faith'[746] can mean different things in different legal settings, including but not limited to a 'dishonest belief or purpose'.[747]

Article 6bis of The Paris Convention specifically recognises 'bad faith'[748] and says: '(3) No time limit shall be fixed for requesting the cancellation or the prohibition of the use of marks registered or used in bad faith'.[749] In the EU under Article 59(1)(b) EUTMR, 'bad faith'[750] is an 'absolute grounds for invalidity'[751] in situations 'where the applicant was acting in bad faith when he filed the application for the trademark'.[752] The EUIPO Guidelines recognise that 'it is not defined, delimited or even described in any way in the legislation'.[753] Davis and Żelechowski note that bad faith[754] is 'based entirely on undefined concepts and require a value judgement to be made by the adjudicating authorities'.[755] In Lindt Goldhase,[756] AG Sharpston noted this as the 'conduct which departs from accepted principles of ethical behaviour or honest commercial and business practices'.[757] In fact, according to Sitko, 'EU case-law has long considered trademark applications made in bad faith to be dishonest practice that

740. Frederick Mostert and Gloria Wu, 'The Importance of the Element of Bad Faith in International Trade Mark Law and Its Relevance under the New Chinese Trade Mark Law Provisions' (2017) 12 Journal of Intellectual Property Law & Practice 650, 650 https://doi.org/10.1093/jiplp/jpx063.
741. *Ibid.*
742. *Ibid.*
743. *Ibid.*
744. *Ibid.*
745. *Ibid.*
746. Cornell, 'Bad Faith' (*Cornell LII*) https://www.law.cornell.edu/wex/bad_faith accessed January 2024.
747. *Ibid.*
748. Paris Convention, Art. 6bis.
749. *Ibid.*
750. EUTMR, Art. 59.
751. *Ibid.*
752. *Ibid.*
753. EUIPO, '3.3.2 Concept of Bad Faith' (*EUIPO Trade mark guidelines* 2024) https://guidelines.euipo.europa.eu/2214311/2047218/trade-mark-guidelines/3-3-2-concept-of-bad-faith accessed January 2024.
754. Jennifer Davis and and Łukasz Zelechowski, 'Bad Faith, Public Policy and Morality: How Open Concepts Shape Trade Mark Protection' (2023) 54 International Review of Intellectual Property and Competition Law 54, 859-890 https://doi.org/10.1007/s40319-023-01350-7.
755. *Ibid.*
756. AG Opinion in C-529/07, *Lindt Goldhase*, EU:C:2009:148.
757. *Ibid.*

involves a sign used by a third party'[758] and, potentially 'when it has nothing to do with a third-party sign but instead involves a dishonest strategy for protecting the applicant's own trademarks'.[759] Sitko notes the mandatory factors to consider bad faith,[760] which include: '1) identity/similarity of the trademark applied for to the third-party sign; 2) awareness of use of the sign by the opposing third party; 3) dishonest intention on the part of the applicant'.[761] However, 'non mandatory factors'[762] include: '1) identity/similarity of goods/services; 2) other circumstances, e.g. the extent of reputation enjoyed by the sign, the commercial strategy involved, use of the sign prior to seeking registration, etc.'[763] In the context of bad faith registration,[764] in *Flatworld Solutions,*[765] the issue of bad faith[766] was considered and confirmed. Two companies (an applicant for cancellation and a proprietor) were in discussions about a potential business relationship surrounding outsourcing services.[767] Shortly after failed negotiations, the proprietor registered a substantially similar trademark to the applicant's unregistered trademark that was already being used[768] to market outsourcing services in Germany via the Internet.[769] Services by the proprietor were being provided using a logo and the domain name www.outsource2india.com.[770] It was initially considered 'that the proprietor had intentionally sought to appropriate the applicant's mark and thus acted in bad faith when filing for registration'.[771] In this case, 'bad faith'[772] was confirmed since 'the proprietor knew that the applicant was using that wording in its logo, in its non-registered mark and in its domain names'.[773] It was clear that the proprietor sought collaboration in Germany using that mark and it was important that

758. Joanna Sitko, 'The Significance of Bad-Faith Premises for the Strategy of Trade Mark Protection in the Light of the Latest EU Case-Law' (2023) 54 International Review of Intellectual Property and Competition Law, 1381, abstract https://doi.org/10.1007/s40319-023-01374-z.
759. *Ibid.*
760. Joanna Sitko, 'The Significance of Bad-Faith Premises for the Strategy of Trade Mark Protection in the Light of the Latest EU Case-Law' (2023) 54 International Review of Intellectual Property and Competition Law, 1381, 1384 https://doi.org/10.1007/s40319-023-01374-z.
761. *Ibid.*
762. *Ibid.*
763. *Ibid.*
764. Case T-340/16 *Outsource 2 India* (fig.); *Flatworld Solutions Pvt Ltd v. EUIPO* EU:T:2018:314.
765. *Ibid.*
766. *Ibid.*
767. *Ibid.*; EUIPO, 'Overview of GC/CJ Case Law 2018' (*International Cooperation and Legal Affairs Department*, 2018) 302 https://euipo.europa.eu/tunnel-web/secure/webdav/guest/document_library/contentPdfs/law_and_practice/yearly_overview/yearly_overview_2018.pdf accessed 4 August 2025.
768. EUTMR, Art. 18.
769. Case T-340/16 *Outsource 2 India (fig.)*; *Flatworld Solutions Pvt Ltd v. EUIPO* EU:T:2018:314; EUIPO, 'Overview of GC/CJ Case Law 2018' (*International Cooperation and Legal Affairs Department*, 2018) 302 https://euipo.europa.eu/tunnel-web/secure/webdav/guest/document_library/contentPdfs/law_and_practice/yearly_overview/yearly_overview_2018.pdf accessed 4 August 2025.
770. *Ibid.*
771. *Ibid.*
772. EUTMR, Art. 59(1)(b).
773. Case T-340/16 *Outsource 2 India (fig.)*; *Flatworld Solutions Pvt Ltd v. EUIPO* EU:T:2018:314.

'the proprietor filed to register the contested mark shortly after the termination of its pre-contractual relationship with the applicant'.[774]

Recently, in the cancellation matter of *Holzer y Cia v. EUIPO*,[775] 'bad faith'[776] was confirmed by the GC, which included some references to activity on Facebook. The holder of the contested mark, ANN TAYLOR (for watches and jewellery), was found to have registered it in 'bad faith'[777] under Article 59(1)(b) EUTMR as 'highly similar'[778] to a mark registered in numerous countries, ANN TAYLOR (for clothing etc.).[779] The GC, in upholding the earlier decision confirming 'bad faith',[780] relied, *inter alia*, on the fact that the applicant 'had sought to associate its goods with those of the intervener'[781] and took action 'to promote them by publishing on the Facebook page of the intervener relating to the ANN TAYLOR LOFT mark links to its own Facebook page'[782] which was specific to 'ANN TAYLOR watches'[783] and on such page held itself as 'the legitimate owner of the trademark registrations for ANN TAYLOR (watches and jewellery) in Mexico, Switzerland, the European Union'.[784] It was noted that the 'Mexican distributor of the applicant's goods, TiempoMania had used, with a view to the promotion of watches sold by the applicant under its Mexican ANN TAYLOR mark, digitally altered copies of advertisements of the intervener in which, inter alia, well-known actresses featured promoting the ANN TAYLOR mark for clothing goods.'[785] The 'evidence further highlighted the fact that the applicant had sought to pretend to be a licensee of the intervener'.[786] The GC cited that, as before the Board of Appeals, 'all of those facts show that the applicant had attempted to "lay his hands" on the ANN TAYLOR mark, in a manner contrary to the standards of acceptable commercial behaviour'[787] and that 'the Board of Appeal was entitled to consider that those circumstances constituted a first indication of bad faith on the part of the applicant'.[788] In fact the applicant was found to have posted a Facebook message 'on the intervener's Facebook page, originating from the Facebook account named 'Ann Taylor Watches' and containing'[789] an English based promotion indicating: 'There is definitely no time to waste, so take a look at our new fan page for AnnTaylor watches'[790] and which also included 'a reproduction of one of the watches promoted and an indication that the applicant is the rightful owner of the ANN TAYLOR trademark registrations for watches and jewellery

774. *Ibid.*
775. T-3/18 & T-4/18, *ANN TAYLOR/ANNTAYLOR et al.*, EU:T:2019:357.
776. *Ibid.*
777. *Ibid.*
778. *Ibid.*
779. *Ibid.*
780. *Ibid.*
781. *Ibid.*
782. *Ibid.*
783. *Ibid.*
784. *Ibid.*
785. *Ibid.*
786. *Ibid.*
787. *Ibid.*
788. *Ibid.*
789. *Ibid.*
790. *Ibid.*

in Mexico, in Switzerland and in the European Union'.[791] The 'link in question appears, prima facie, to be taken from the Facebook page'[792] designated as 'AnnTaylor Watches'[793] and 'which the applicant does not dispute as being under its control'.[794] The cancellation was confirmed by the GC, confirming the 'bad faith'[795] intention at the time of registration and also considering other facts leading to the same.[796]

Likewise, in the US, bad faith registration[797] of a mark may be where there is 'token use'[798] on the Internet 'to sustain registration'.[799] Also, where there is 'no intention of using'[800] the mark but only to sell the mark, it may be considered 'bad faith'.[801] Further, it may be found where there is 'intention of using the mark on same, related or unrelated goods to trade off of goodwill of another party'.[802] Various cases are discussed in the following section relating to domain names.

Platforms may consider whether a username, mobile app name, Metaverse avatar name or other like registration utilising a mark was registered in 'bad faith'[803] within their platforms. This consideration is not intended to override legitimate uses (*see* section 3.2.7 *Digital Justification* below).

3.2.2.2 Bad Faith and Domain Names (Including ccTLDs)

Importantly, bad faith[804] is already considered in the context of domain name trademark disputes, such as under the UDRP, general domain name cybersquatting legislation (ACPA) and in the context of .us and .eu (and various other)[805] ccTLDs. The EU does not have similar general domain name-oriented legislation to the ACPA, although

791. *Ibid.*
792. *Ibid.*
793. *Ibid.*
794. *Ibid.*
795. *Ibid.*
796. *Ibid.*
797. TTAB USPTO, 'Fighting Bad Faith Trademark Filings in the United States' https://www.jpo.go.jp/e/news/kokusai/tm5/document/bad_faith_seminar2/01.pdf accessed January 2024.
798. *Ibid.*
799. *Ibid.*
800. *Ibid.*
801. *Ibid.*
802. *Ibid.*
803. Paris Convention, Art. 6bis; EUTMR, Art. 59; TTAB, 'Fighting Bad Faith Trademark Filings in the United States' (*The Honorable Karen S. Kuhlke Administrative Trademark Judge*) https://www.jpo.go.jp/e/news/kokusai/tm5/document/bad_faith_seminar2/01.pdf accessed July 2024; UDRP, 4(a)(iii).
804. *Ibid.*
805. WIPO, 'WIPO Domain Name Dispute Resolution Service for .EU (and.ею and.ευ)' (*WIPO*) https://www.wipo.int/amc/en/domains/cctld/eu/index.html accessed July 2024; Registry Services, 'UsTLD Dispute Resolution Policy' (*Registry Services, LLC*, 2021) https://www.about.us/documents/policies/usTLD_Dispute_Resolution_Policy_(usDRP).pdf accessed July 2024.

some Member States do cover cybersquatting under unfair competition or other legislation.[806]

To provide some historical context for the US, the Federal Trademark Dilution Act (FTDA) 15 U.S. Code § 1125(c) was previously used to lodge claims of dilution of marks, and later began to be used to counter claims of cybersquatting, which resulted in expanding the scope of the Act.[807] One of the early cases to do so was *Panavision v. Toeppen*,[808] where Panavision, 'a well-known motion picture equipment company',[809] sued on the basis that the domain panavision.com was registered to try and get it to purchase the domain for USD 13,000.[810] The Court sided with Panavision because 'the defendant was in the business of registering trademarks as domain names and then selling them back to the rightful trademark holders, and this constituted commercial use of the domain name'.[811] Additionally, dilution[812] was found based on the fact that 'that a domain name is not simply an address marker, but also serves to identify the entity that owns the website'.[813] Later, the ACPA[814] was enacted 'in an attempt to prevent cybersquatters from registering Internet domain names containing trademarks for the purpose of selling those ... back to the trademark owner'.[815] More specifically, it is covered under 15 U.S. Code § 1125(d) in the context of 'cybersquatting'.[816] Similar to the UDRP, the ACPA covers the 'bad faith'[817] utilisation of marks in domain names; however, no such similar provisions exist in legislation applicable to search advertising, social media,[818] mobile apps or Metaverse platforms. Back in 2010, Curtin recommended that the ACPA be updated to incorporate social media,[819] as others have

806. CMS, 'Protection of Trade Marks: Online Use and Anticybersquatting a European Perspective' (*CMS*, March 2007) https://www.cms-lawnow.com/~/media/lawnow/pdfs/cms%20publications/sector%20specific%20publications/tmc/ip/cmsanticybersquattingguide.pdf accessed 4 August 2025.
807. Tamara Kurtzman, 'The Continued Hijacking and Ransoming of the Domain Name System by Modern-Day Corporate Privateers' (*Cyber Center*, 20 June 2016) https://www.americanbar.org/groups/business_law/publications/blt/2016/06/cyber_center_kurtzman/ accessed January 2024.
808. *Panavision Int'l, L.P. v. Toeppen*. 141 F.3d 1316 (9th Cir. 1998); Tamara Kurtzman, 'The Continued Hijacking and Ransoming of the Domain Name System by Modern-Day Corporate Privateers' (*Cyber Center*, 20 June 2016) https://www.americanbar.org/groups/business_law/publications/blt/2016/06/cyber_center_kurtzman/ accessed January 2024.
809. Tamara Kurtzman, 'The Continued Hijacking and Ransoming of the Domain Name System by Modern-Day Corporate Privateers' (*Cyber Center*, 20 June 2016) https://www.americanbar.org/groups/business_law/publications/blt/2016/06/cyber_center_kurtzman/ accessed January 2024.
810. *Ibid.*
811. *Ibid.*
812. *Ibid.*
813. *Ibid.*
814. 15 U.S. Code § 1125(d).
815. Tamara Kurtzman, 'The Continued Hijacking and Ransoming of the Domain Name System by Modern-Day Corporate Privateers' (*Cyber Center*, 20 June 2016) https://www.americanbar.org/groups/business_law/publications/blt/2016/06/cyber_center_kurtzman/ accessed January 2024.
816. *Ibid.*
817. *Ibid.*
818. Thomas J Curtin, 'The Name Game: Cybersquatting and Trademark Infringement on Social Media Websites' (2010-2011) 19 Journal of Law and Policy 353, 359.
819. *Ibid.*

over time.[820] However, the ACPA has some key relevant provisions that are informative to platforms.

Under 15 U.S. Code § 1125(d)(1)(A):

> (A) A person shall be liable in a civil action by the owner of a mark, including a personal name which is protected as a mark under this section, if, without regard to the goods or services of the parties, that person –
>
> (i) has a bad faith intent to profit from that mark, including a personal name which is protected as a mark under this section; and
> (ii) registers, traffics in, or uses a domain name that –
> (I) in the case of a mark that is distinctive at the time of registration of the domain name, is identical or confusingly similar to that mark;
> (II) in the case of a famous mark that is famous at the time of registration of the domain name, is identical or confusingly similar to or dilutive of that mark; or
> (III) is a trademark, word, or name protected by reason of section 706 of title 18 or section 220506 of title 36.[821]

Under the above provision, a 'bad faith intent to profit'[822] must be present with other factors for a civil action to be successful against a domain name registrant.[823]

Under 15 U.S. Code § 1125(d)(1)(B):

> (B) (i) In determining whether a person has a bad faith intent described under subparagraph (A), a court may consider factors such as, but not limited to –
> (I) the trademark or other intellectual property rights of the person, if any, in the domain name;
> (II) the extent to which the domain name consists of the legal name of the person or a name that is otherwise commonly used to identify that person;
> (III) the person's prior use, if any, of the domain name in connection with the bona fide offering of any goods or services;
> (IV) the person's bona fide noncommercial or fair use of the mark in a site accessible under the domain name;
> (V) the person's intent to divert consumers from the mark owner's online location to a site accessible under the domain name that could harm the goodwill represented by the mark, either for commercial gain or with the intent to tarnish or disparage the mark, by creating a likelihood of

820. Rajeev Sachdev, 'Towards an Improved Framework for Trade-Mark Law and Regulation in Social Media Usernames: A Study of the Canadian, U.S., and U.K. Positions' (2016) 28 Intellectual Property Journal I.P.J. 379; Daniel Doft, 'Facebook, Twitter, and the Wild West of IP Enforcement on Social Media: Weighing the Merits of a Uniform Dispute Resolution Policy' (2016) 49 The John Marshall Law Review 959; Thomas J Curtin, 'The Name Game: Cyber-squatting and Trademark Infringement on Social Media Websites' (2010-2011) 19 Journal of Law and Policy 353; Heels EJ, '* How to Twittersquat the Top 100 Brands' (* *GiantPeople*) http://www.giantpeople.com/1298.html accessed 4 August 2025; Paul D McGrady, *McGrady on Social Media: 2018* (LexisNexis 2018).
821. 15 U.S. Code § 1125(d)(1)(A).
822. *Ibid.*
823. *Ibid.*

confusion as to the source, sponsorship, affiliation, or endorsement of the site;

(VI) the person's offer to transfer, sell, or otherwise assign the domain name to the mark owner or any third party for financial gain without having used, or having an intent to use, the domain name in the bona fide offering of any goods or services, or the person's prior conduct indicating a pattern of such conduct;

(VII) the person's provision of material and misleading false contact information when applying for the registration of the domain name, the person's intentional failure to maintain accurate contact information, or the person's prior conduct indicating a pattern of such conduct;

(VIII) the person's registration or acquisition of multiple domain names which the person knows are identical or confusingly similar to marks of others that are distinctive at the time of registration of such domain names, or dilutive of famous marks of others that are famous at the time of registration of such domain names, without regard to the goods or services of the parties; and

(IX) the extent to which the mark incorporated in the person's domain name registration is or is not distinctive and famous within the meaning of subsection (c).

(ii) Bad faith intent described under subparagraph (A) shall not be found in any case in which the court determines that the person believed and had reasonable grounds to believe that the use of the domain name was a fair use or otherwise lawful.[824]

The above includes various specific factors which may be considered with respect to whether 'bad faith'[825] exists. It is rare that such detailed guidance is provided in the context of Internet trademark situations. The provisions do not restrict the courts to those factors listed, which allows for further discretion as reiterated in the U.S. case of *Alston v. www.calculator.com,*[826] also citing *S. Grouts & Mortars v. 3M.*[827] The court said that an 'analysis of whether a defendant had the bad faith intent to profit necessary to a cybersquatting claim is not based on a score card of the statutory factors'.[828] It summarised that 'the factors are permissive considerations'[829] and 'must be assessed on a case-by-case basis'.[830] Likewise, in the U.S. case of *ServPro v. Blanton,*[831] it was found that there was 'a genuine dispute about whether Blanton bought ServPro.click with bad faith intent to profit from the misuse of the domain name'.[832] The court considered the ACPA factors and stated that these were a 'guide'[833] in the analysis and not a replacement for proper assessment.[834] The defendant indicated that the domain

824. 15 U.S. Code § 1125(d)(1)(B).
825. *Ibid.*
826. *Alston v. www.calculator.com*, 2020 U.S. Dist. LEXIS 137360.
827. *S. Grouts & Mortars, Inc. v. 3M Co.*, 575 F.3d 1235, 1249 (11th Cir. 2009).
828. *Alston v. www.calculator.com*, 2020 U.S. Dist. LEXIS 137360; *S. Grouts & Mortars, Inc. v. 3M Co.*, 575 F.3d 1235, 1249 (11th Cir. 2009).
829. *Ibid.*
830. *Ibid.*
831. *ServPro Intellectual Property, Inc. v. Blanton*, 2020 WL 1666121 (W.D. Ky. 3 April 2020).
832. *Ibid.*
833. *Ibid.*
834. *Ibid.*

name was not purchased 'with the intent to divert customer away from Servpro for its own commercial gain'[835] and rather, was done 'to collect information and perform analytical research on the domain names with an eye towards testing consumer responses to various domain names in conjunction with specific key word searches when running Google AdWords advertisements'.[836] The defendant also contended 'that the website the domain name pointed to did not advertise that it was ServPro, and the contact information on the website pointed to his personal cellphone'.[837] Also, 'when answering calls made to that number, he identified himself as affiliated with Emergency Services and never identified himself as affiliated with ServPro'.[838] Thus, summary judgment on cybersquatting was denied[839] and the ACPA factors were considered in the overall assessment, resulting in this finding. In this case, consideration went beyond the domain to the associated website and was even related to receipt of phone inquiries.[840] Further, in another U.S. case, *NYP Holdings v. N.Y. Post,*[841] it was recognised that, in a bad faith analysis, the court could take into consideration 'the unique circumstances of the case'[842] and are not limited to the factors listed in the ACPA.[843] Nevertheless, the court did not seem to have difficulty concluding that '[m]any of the factors enumerated in 15 U.S. Code § 1125(d)(1)(B)(i) weigh in favour of NYP Holdings'.[844] This was especially because the defendants 'acquired and began operating the ... Website with the express purpose of diverting consumers from NYPost.com to newyorkpostpublishinginc.com and that Defendants deliberately attempted to mislead consumers as to the connection ...'.[845] The court adopted the 'whole course of conduct'[846] approach set out in Gioconda Law Grp. PLLC, 941 F.Supp.2d at 433. In the U.S. case of *Black v. Irving Materials,*[847] the court weighed the nine ACPA factors and found 'numerous genuine disputes of material fact as to whether Black acted with bad faith intent'.[848] In the case of *Dent v. Lotto Sport Italia,*[849] the court found that 'registration and use to date of the domain names <lottostore.com> and <lottoworks.com> are not unlawful under the ACPA or the Lanham

835. *Ibid.*
836. *Ibid.*
837. *Ibid.*
838. *Ibid.*
839. *Ibid.*
840. *Ibid.*
841. *NYP Holdings v. N.Y. Post Publ. Inc.*, 63 F. Supp. 3d 328.
842. *Ibid.*
843. *Ibid.*
844. *Ibid.*
845. *Ibid.*
846. *Ibid.*
847. *Black v. Irving Materials, Inc.*, 17-CV-06734-LHK (N.D. Cal 2019/2020).
848. *Ibid.*
849. *Dent v. Lotto Sport Italia SpA*, CV-17-00651-PHX-DMF (D. Arizona 10 March 2020).

Act'.[850] Levine says that the court 'arrived at this determination by focusing more carefully on two factors … 1) domain name creation date; and 2) website content'.[851]

The above provisions of the ACPA provide some clear factors and the cases described show how these have been interpreted. The ACPA factors and interpretations raise various important considerations for platforms, including how bad faith may be determined even if not in domain name scenarios. For example, an 'offer to transfer, sell, or otherwise assign'[852] the domain without using it or intending to use it[853] may be a factor. While the UDRP considers domain names under its purview, the ACPA raises considerations for platforms because of the part similarity between domain names and social media usernames,[854] mobile app names, avatar names in the Metaverse, etc. Platforms should consider when marks are being used in these settings in 'bad faith'[855] and some of the factors under the ACPA and their interpretation above are informative, as are UDRP considerations of 'bad faith'.[856]

The World Intellectual Property Organization (WIPO) has a WIPO Domain Name Dispute Resolution Service for.eu[857] and the United States Top-Level Domain (usTLD) Dispute Resolution Policy (applicable to .us domains)[858] has adopted identical or similar provisions to the UDRP bad faith requirement.[859] However, under the policies applicable to .eu and .us, in addition to other requirements, it is enough to prove that the registration was in bad faith[860] OR use is in bad faith[861] (not both as under the UDRP).[862] While there are some differences, such as but not limited to the policy for .eu domains outlining some very specific timelines and alternative basis,[863] much of the

850. *Dent v. Lotto Sport Italia SpA*, No. CV-17-00651-PHX-DMF (D. Ariz. 10 March 2020); Domainnamewire, 'Dent v. Lotto Sport Italia SpA' (*Lottosport*) https://domainnamewire.com/wp-content/lottosport.pdf accessed January 2024.
851. Gerald M Levine, 'Cybersquatting and Reverse Domain Name Hijacking: UDRP to ACPA' (*IP Legal Corner*, 30 March 2020) https://circleid.com/posts/20200330-cybersquatting-and-reverse-domain-name-hijacking-udrp-to-acpa accessed January 2024.
852. UDRP, 4(a)(iii).
853. 15 U.S. Code § 1125(d)(1)(B).
854. Rajeev Sachdev, 'Towards an Improved Framework for Trade-Mark Law and Regulation in Social Media Usernames: A Study of the Canadian, U.S., and U.K. Positions' (2016) 28 Intellectual Property Journal, 379, 379-418; Lisa P Ramsey, 'Brandjacking on Social Networks: Trademark Infringement by Impersonation of Markholders' (2010) 58 Buffalo Law Review 851; Danny Friedmann, *Trademarks and Social Media: Towards Algorithmic Justice* (Edward Elgar Publishing, 2015); Paul D McGrady, *McGrady on Social Media and the Metaverse* (Mathew Bender & Company, Inc. 2023) §12.
855. 15 U.S. Code § 1125(d).
856. UDRP, 4(a)(iii).
857. WIPO, 'WIPO Domain Name Dispute Resolution Service for .EU (and.ею and.ευ)' (*WIPO*) https://www.wipo.int/amc/en/domains/cctld/eu/index.html accessed July 2024.
858. Registry Services, 'UsTLD Dispute Resolution Policy' (*Registry Services, LLC*, 2021) https://www.about.us/documents/policies/usTLD_Dispute_Resolution_Policy_(usDRP).pdf accessed July 2024.
859. UDRP, 4(a)(iii).
860. *Ibid.*
861. WIPO, 'WIPO Domain Name Dispute Resolution Service for .EU (and.ею and.ευ)' (*WIPO*) https://www.wipo.int/amc/en/domains/cctld/eu/index.html accessed July 2024.
862. *Ibid.*; https://www.icann.org/resources/pages/policy-2012-02-25-en. Under the policy applicable to.ca, registration in bad faith is required.uk etc.
863. WIPO, 'WIPO Domain Name Dispute Resolution Service for .EU (and.ею and.ευ)' (*WIPO*) https://www.wipo.int/amc/en/domains/cctld/eu/index.html accessed July 2024.

text of the policies is very similar, many times adopting the same or similar language as seen below.

For .eu, '[u]nder the ADR Rules, the examples of registration or use of a disputed domain name in bad faith include':[864]

(1) circumstances indicating that the domain name was registered or acquired primarily for the purpose of selling, renting, or otherwise transferring the domain name to the holder of a name, in respect of which a right is recognized or established by national and/or European Union law, or to a public body; or
(2) the domain name has been registered in order to prevent the holder of such a name in respect of which a right is recognized or established by national and/or European Union law, or a public body, from reflecting this name in a corresponding domain name, provided that:
  (i) the Respondent has engaged in a pattern of such conduct; or
  (ii) the domain name has not been used in a relevant way for at least two years from the date of registration; or
  (iii) there are circumstances where, at the time the ADR Proceeding was initiated, the Respondent has declared its intention to use the domain name, in respect of which aright is recognized or established by national and/or European Union law or which corresponds to the name of a public body, in a relevant way but failed to do so within six months of the day on which the ADR Proceeding was initiated;
(3) the domain name was registered primarily for the purpose of disrupting the professional activities of a competitor; or
(4) the domain name was intentionally used to attract Internet users, for commercial gain to the Respondent's website or other online location, by creating a likelihood of confusion with a name on which a right is recognized or established, by national and/or European Union law, or it is a name of a public body, such likelihood arising as to the source, sponsorship, affiliation or endorsement of the website or location or of a product or service on the website or location of the Respondent; or
(5) the domain name is a personal name for which no demonstrable link exists between the Respondent and the domain name registered.[865]

Under 4b of the usTLD Dispute Resolution Policy (applicable to .us domains):[866]

b) Evidence of Registration or Use in Bad Faith – For the purposes of Paragraph 4(a)(1)(iii), the following circumstances, in particular but without limitation, if found by the Panel to be present, shall be evidence of the registration or use of a domain name in bad faith:
  (i) Circumstances indicating that you have registered or you have acquired the domain name primarily for the purpose of selling, renting, or otherwise transferring the domain name registration to the Complainant who is the owner of the trademark or service mark or to a competitor of that Complainant, for valuable consideration in excess of your documented out of-pocket costs directly related to the domain name;

864. *Ibid.*
865. *Ibid.*
866. Registry Services, 'UsTLD Dispute Resolution Policy' (*Registry Services, LLC,* 2021) https://www.about.us/documents/policies/usTLD_Dispute_Resolution_Policy_(usDRP).pdf accessed July 2024.

(ii) You have registered the domain name in order to prevent the owner of the trademark or service mark from reflecting the mark in a corresponding domain name;

(iii) You have registered the domain name primarily for the purpose of disrupting the business of a competitor; or

(iv) By using the domain name, you have intentionally attempted to attract, for commercial gain, Internet users to your web site or other on- line location, by creating a likelihood of confusion with the Complainant's mark as to the source, sponsorship, affiliation, or endorsement of your web site or location or of a product or service on your web site or location.[867]

The implementation of a similar policy to the above ccTLD policies relating to bad faith[868] which are also similar to the UDRP is very informative to platforms. In fact, similar policies have been implemented across various jurisdictions in the case of ccTLDs[869] and in the case of the UDRP globally. Even if these are not all the same, it appears that a more uniform approach is very possible when it comes to a bad faith requirement[870] and platforms could draw from the benefits of a similar uniform approach.

Other jurisdictions are informative. Canada does not have legislation similar to the ACPA; however, in the recent Canadian case of *Blossman v. Alliance*[871] with respect to a mark that was used, among other places, on a website, the court noted that the conclusions, *inter alia*, to invalidate a trademark on the bases of bad faith under section 18(1)(e) of the Canadian Trademarks Act 'are consistent with the approach to bad faith in the European Union and the United Kingdom, where it has been a ground of invalidity for decades'.[872] This is significant to platforms because, even if not the same provisions, it shows acceptance in the application of bad faith within jurisdictions.

The UDRP already addresses bad faith as an element.[873] Considerations for platforms involve the inclusion of bad faith[874] and how it will be assessed. The EU and US approaches to bad faith registration and, more specifically, the U.S. ACPA factors and interpretive case law can inform platforms by assisting in their interpretation. Domain name policies from .eu and .us and various other jurisdictions have adopted

867. *Ibid.*
868. WIPO, 'WIPO Domain Name Dispute Resolution Service for .EU (and.ею and.ευ)' (*WIPO*) https://www.wipo.int/amc/en/domains/cctld/eu/index.html accessed July 2024; Registry Services, 'UsTLD DisputeResolution Policy' (*Registry Services, LLC*, 2021) https://www.about.us/documents/policies/usTLD_Dispute_Resolution_Policy_(usDRP).pdf accessed July 2024.
869. Likewise, several other ccTLDs have adopted similar provisions such as the CIRA Domain Name Dispute Resolution Policy (applicable to.ca) where 'bad faith' registration is required, or the.au Dispute Resolution Policy (for Australia) where registration or use are alternatives; CIIDRC, CIRA Domain Name Dispute Resolution Policy (*CIIDRC*) https://ciidrc.org/domain-name-disputes/cdrp-policy/ accessed January 2024; auDA, '.au Dispute Resolution Policy (auDRP) (2016-01) (*auDA*)' https://www.auda.org.au/policy/au-dispute-resolution-policy-audrp-2016-01 accessed January 2024.
870. UDRP.
871. *Blossman Gas, Inc. v. Alliance Autopropane Inc.* 2022 FC 1794.
872. *Ibid.*
873. UDRP, 4(a)(iii).
874. *Ibid.*

similar policies to the UDRP and platforms should consider incorporating similar provisions into their policies.

3.2.2.3 *Concept of Abuse*

Domain name abuse[875] is recognised under the UDRP to include multiple[876] incidents of 'bad faith'[877] with respect to domain registrations that violate UDRP rules. For example, when proving the element of bad faith,[878] '[a] pattern of abuse has also been found where the respondent registers, simultaneously or otherwise, multiple trademark-abusive domain names corresponding to the distinct marks of individual brand owners'.[879]

Under the policy applicable to .eu,[880] bad faith may be found where:

> (2) the domain name has been registered in order to prevent the holder of such a name in respect of which a right is recognized or established by national and/or European Union law, or a public body, from reflecting this name in a corresponding domain name, provided that:
>
> (i) the Respondent has engaged in a pattern of such conduct; or … .[881]

Under the ACPA, patterns of conduct are recognised and may be considered abusive. Under 15 U.S. Code § 1125(d)(1)(B):

> (VI) the person's offer to transfer, sell, or otherwise assign the domain name to the mark owner or any third party for financial gain without having used, or having an intent to use, the domain name in the bona fide offering of any goods or services, or the person's prior conduct indicating a pattern of such conduct;
>
> (VII) the person's provision of material and misleading false contact information when applying for the registration of the domain name, the person's intentional failure to maintain accurate contact information, or the person's prior conduct indicating a pattern of such conduct.[882]

The UDRP, the policy applicable to .eu, and the ACPA, references to conduct patterns[883] are relevant to platforms when considering whether such actions are

875. WIPO, 'WIPO Overview of WIPO Panel Views on Selected UDRP Questions, Third Edition' ('WIPO Jurisprudential Overview 3.0') (*WIPO*, 2017) https://www.wipo.int/amc/en/domains/search/overview3.0/ accessed June 2025.
876. *Ibid.*
877. *Ibid.*
878. ICANN, 'Uniform Domain-Name Dispute-Resolution Policy' (*ICANN* 25 February 2012) https://www.icann.org/resources/pages/policy-2012-02-25-en accessed June 2025.
879. WIPO, 'WIPO Overview of WIPO Panel Views on Selected UDRP Questions, Third Edition' ('WIPO Jurisprudential Overview 3.0') (*WIPO*, 2017) https://www.wipo.int/amc/en/domains/search/overview3.0/ accessed June 2025.
880. WIPO, 'WIPO Domain Name Dispute Resolution Service for .EU (and.ею and.ευ)' (*WIPO*) https://www.wipo.int/amc/en/domains/cctld/eu/index.html accessed July 2024.
881. *Ibid.*
882. 15 U.S. Code § 1125(d)(1)(B).
883. WIPO, 'WIPO Overview of WIPO Panel Views on Selected UDRP Questions, Third Edition, ('WIPO Jurisprudential Overview 3.0') (*WIPO*, 2017) https://www.wipo.int/amc/en/domains

abusive[884] and warrant further consequences. In the broader context of the Internet, including in e-commerce marketplace, search ad, social media, mobile app, and Metaverse platforms, platforms may consider recognising abuse[885] if, for example, there is repeated 'bad faith'[886] by an individual or organisation, where the repercussion of such actions should be greater. Platforms should consider the consequences of abuse[887] within their platforms and ensure these are within their policies if not already accounted for.

3.2.2.4 Summary of Platform Considerations for Digital Bad Faith and Abuse

The above concepts inform the model by eliciting angles from which 'bad faith'[888] may be considered. As seen above, 'bad faith'[889] considerations are incorporated in the UDRP, ACPA, some ccTLD domains, and EU and U.S. 'bad faith'[890] registration. Platforms should consider including 'bad faith'[891] and guidelines on how it should be assessed, especially from the perspective of the UDRP, ACPA 'bad faith'[892] factors and relevant case law, as well as ccTLD domain name policies such as the .eu and .us and others. Platforms should also consider incorporating 'abuse'[893] as repeated 'bad faith'[894] and how it should be dealt with should be considered by platforms.

/search/overview3.0/ accessed June 2025; 15 U.S. Code § 1125(d)(1)(B); WIPO, 'WIPO Domain Name Dispute Resolution Service for .EU (and.ею and.ευ)' (*WIPO*) https://www.wipo.int/amc/en/domains/cctld/eu/index.html accessed July 2024.

884. WIPO, 'WIPO Overview of WIPO Panel Views on Selected UDRP Questions, Third Edition, ('WIPO Jurisprudential Overview 3.0') (*WIPO*, 2017) https://www.wipo.int/amc/en/domains/search/overview3.0/ accessed June 2025.
885. *Ibid.*
886. Paris Convention 1967, Art. 6bis; *See* ICANN, 'Uniform Domain-Name Dispute-Resolution Policy' (ICANN, 25 February 2012) https://www.icann.org/resources/pages/policy-2012-02-25-en; 15 U.S. Code § 1125(d).
887. WIPO, 'WIPO Overview of WIPO Panel Views on Selected UDRP Questions, Third Edition, ('WIPO Jurisprudential Overview 3.0') (*WIPO*, 2017). https://www.wipo.int/amc/en/domains/search/overview3.0/ accessed June 2025.
888. Paris Convention, Art. 6bis; EUTMR, Art. 59; TTAB, 'Fighting Bad Faith Trademark Filings in the United States' (*The Honorable Karen S. Kuhlke Administrative Trademark Judge*) https://www.jpo.go.jp/e/news/kokusai/tm5/document/bad_faith_seminar2/01.pdf accessed July 2024; UDRP, 4(a)(iii).
889. *Ibid.*
890. *Ibid.*
891. *Ibid.*
892. 15 U.S. Code § 1125(d).
893. WIPO, 'WIPO Overview of WIPO Panel Views on Selected UDRP Questions, Third Edition' ('WIPO Jurisprudential Overview 3.0') (*WIPO*, 2017) https://www.wipo.int/amc/en/domains/search/overview3.0/ accessed June 2025.
894. *Ibid.*

3.2.3 Digital Confusion

This section covers confusion theory,[895] prohibition against confusion,[896] and related concepts that inform the model. It summarises the resulting considerations for the UDRP and platforms.

3.2.3.1 *Confusion Theory*

There is no doubt that 'confusion'[897] is a major trademark theory and has been applied in the trademark context from an early time.[898] Kamperman Sanders rightly declared that 'the principles of the Paris Convention are covered in all countries described'[899] and that '[t]he paradigm of the common norm is the prevention of the creation of confusion or avoidable confusion in the marketplace.'[900] Fhima and Gangjee note, in their deep dive into this area, that '[t]he likelihood of confusion test is inextricably linked to the principal justification for trademark protection'.[901]

Confusion[902] was discussed by the work of Landes and Posner, and is as a whole informed by the so-called law and economics approach which sees trademark as an incentive to create information, for the benefit of markets'.[903] 'Consumer confusion'[904] may be classified as an 'economic theory'[905] based on one of its functions which allows

895. Ilanah Fhima and Dev S Gangjee, 'Assessing Likelihood of Confusion', *The Confusion Test in European Trade Mark Law* (New York, 2019; online edn, Oxford Academic), https://doi.org/10.1093/oso/9780199674336.003.0006, pp. 160-203; Giovanni B Ramello, 'What's in a Sign? Trademark Law And Economic Theory' (2006) 20 Journal of Economic Surveys 547, 551 https://doi.org/10.1111/j.1467-6419.2006.00255.x; Stacey L Dogan and Mark A Lemley, 'Trademarks and Consumer Search Costs on the Internet' (2004) 41 Houston Law Review 777 in Graeme B Dinwoodie and Mark D Janis, 'Confusion Over Use: Contextualism in Trademark Law' (2007) 92 Iowa Law Review 1597; Mark P McKenna, 'A Consumer Decision-Making Theory of Trademark Law' 98 Virginia Law Review 67.
896. Paris Convention, Art. 6bis; TRIPS, Art. 16.
897. *Ibid.*
898. *Ibid.*
899. Anselm Kamperman Sanders, 'Badges of Trade: The Protection of Trade Marks and Related Intangibles in Unfair Competition Law' (Intellectual Property Law Unit of the Centre for Commercial Law Studies, Queen Mary and Westfield College, University of London 1995) 55, 78.
900. *Ibid.*
901. Ilanah Fhima and Dev S Gangjee, 'Assessing Likelihood of Confusion', *The Confusion Test in European Trade Mark Law* (New York, 2019; online edn, Oxford Academic) 160, 160 https://doi.org/10.1093/oso/9780199674336.003.0006.
902. Giovanni B Ramello, 'What's in a Sign? Trademark Law And Economic Theory' (2006) 20 Journal of Economic Surveys 547, 551 https://doi.org/10.1111/j.1467-6419.2006.00255.x.
903. *Ibid.*
904. Mark P McKenna, 'A Consumer Decision-Making Theory of Trademark Law' 98 Virginia Law Review 67.
905. Stacey L Dogan and Mark A Lemley, 'Trademarks and Consumer Search Costs on the Internet' (2004) 41 Houston Law Review 777, 786; Graeme B Dinwoodie and Mark D Janis, 'Confusion Over Use: Contextualism in Trademark Law' (2007) 92 Iowa Law Review 1597; Mark P McKenna, 'A Consumer Decision-Making Theory of Trademark Law' 98 Virginia Law Review 67.

consumers to reduce 'search costs'.[906] As noted by Dogan and Lemley, '[t]he general principle is always to avoid creating any confusion, in the minds of consumers, as to the origin of the goods'[907] and conclude, after discussing a number of rules in a trademark analysis, that '[c]ourts must be mindful of long-standing legal rules, and even more so of the fundamental normative goal that underlies those rules - the reduction of consumer search costs'.[908] Ohly recognises confusion[909] as the traditional form of infringement[910] and says that 'the investment made by trademark owners is sufficiently safeguarded when the law makes sure that consumers can distinguish correctly between high-end products and imitations'.[911] Non mark holders are prohibited from confusing[912] others about the 'source of particular goods or services'.[913] The idea is that a consumer may make an erroneous decision if confused[914] and what is sought to be avoided is the costs[915] a consumer may need to expend in order to locate a good or service, including that of a particular mark holder.[916] Ramello says there could be a 'market failure caused by the information asymmetry to consumers'[917] because they do not know where the product comes from, or its source.[918] This ultimately results in the 'economics of information problem'[919] identified by Akerlof, and a market which 'is impoverished in terms of both transactions and quality'.[920]

906. *Ibid.*
907. *Ibid.*
908. Stacey L Dogan and Mark A Lemley, 'Trademarks and Consumer Search Costs on the Internet' (2004) 41 Houston Law Review 777, 838.
909. Angsar Ohly, '"Buy Me Because I'm Cool": The "Marketing Approach" and the Overlap Between Design, Trade Mark and Unfair Competition Law' in Annette Kur, Marianne Levin and Jens Schovsbo (eds), *The EU Design Approach: A Global Appraisal* (Edward Elgar 2018) 114-116.
910. *Ibid.*
911. Angsar Ohly, '"Buy Me Because I'm Cool": The "Marketing Approach" and the Overlap Between Design, Trade Mark and Unfair Competition Law' in Annette Kur, Marianne Levin and Jens Schovsbo (eds), *The EU Design Approach: A Global Appraisal* (Edward Elgar 2018) 114.
912. *Ibid.*
913. Mark P McKenna, 'A Consumer Decision-Making Theory of Trademark Law' 98 Virginia Law Review 67; William M Landes and Richard A Posner, 'Trademark Law: An Economic Perspective' (1987) 30 The Journal of Law and Economics 265 https://doi.org/10.1086/467138; Lisa L Ouellette, 'The Google Shortcut to Trademark Law' (2014) 102 California Law Review 351Lisa L Ouellette, 'The Google Shortcut to Trademark Law' (2014) 102 California Law Review 351, 358.
914. Paris Convention, Art. 6bis; TRIPS, Art. 16(1); EUTMR, Art. 8(1)(b) and Art. 9(2)(b); 15 U.S. Code § 1114;15 U.S. Code § 1125.
915. Stacey L Dogan and Mark A Lemley, 'Trademarks and Consumer Search Costs on the Internet' (2004) 41 Houston Law Review 777 in Graeme B Dinwoodie and Mark D Janis, 'Confusion Over Use: Contextualism in Trademark Law' (2007) 92 Iowa Law Review 1597; Mark P McKenna, 'A Consumer Decision-Making Theory of Trademark Law' 98 Virginia Law Review 67.
916. Lisa L Ouellette, 'The Google Shortcut to Trademark Law' (2014) 102 California Law Review 351. 358.
917. Giovanni B Ramello, 'What's in a Sign? Trademark Law And Economic Theory' (2006) 20 Journal of Economic Surveys 547, 561https://doi.org/10.1111/j.1467-6419.2006.00255.x.
918. *Ibid.*
919. George A Akerlof, 'The Market for Lemons: Quality Uncertainty and the Market Mechanism' (1970) 84 Quarterly Journal of Economics 488 https://doi.org/10.2307/1879431.
920. Giovanni B Ramello, 'What's in a Sign? Trademark Law And Economic Theory' (2006) 20 Journal of Economic Surveys 547, 563 https://doi.org/10.1111/j.1467-6419.2006.00255.x;

Trademarks provide 'information relating to the quality of products',[921] resulting in better 'consumer purchase decisions'[922] and 'leveraging the reputation of producers',[923] which results in better quality products and services.[924] This is the case when consumers have information about brands and associate a particular quality with them. For many years, 'consumer confusion'[925] has been a basis of liability for trademark infringement.[926] Consumers who confuse[927] a trademark may be led in a direction not intended by the consumer. Relatedly, the 'consumer decision making'[928] theory narrows in on a more specific area of 'confusion'[929] as analysed by McKenna and others. A specific confusion[930] is required, namely, 'confusion about the identity of a product's actual source'.[931] McKenna says that confusion[932] theories are often developed to protect trademark holders and not consumers;[933] however, this has not stopped the courts from making case decisions based on 'consumer protection terms'[934] because of the link to the 'search costs theory'.[935]

However, some theorists have criticised the 'consumer confusion'[936] theory, stating that confusion is insufficient alone, and that there are 'inconsistencies'[937] and

George A Akerlof, 'The Market for Lemons: Quality Uncertainty and the Market Mechanism' (1970) 84 Quarterly Journal of Economics 488 https://doi.org/10.2307/1879431.

921. Armen Alchian and William R Allen, *Exchange and Production* (Wadsworth 1977); William M Landes and Richard A Posner, 'Trademark Law: An Economic Perspective' (1987) 30 The Journal of Law and Economics 265 https://doi.org/10.1086/467138; John R Lott Jr, 'Brand Names, Ignorance, and Quality Guaranteeing Premiums' (1988) 20 Applied Economics 165 https://doi.org/10.1080/00036848800000002; Nicholas V Economides, 'The Economics of Trademarks' (1988) 78 Trademark Reporter 523; Peter S Menell, 'Intellectual Property General Theories' in Giovanni B Ramello, 'What's in a Sign? Trademark Law And Economic Theory' (2006) 20 Journal of Economic Surveys 547, 551 https://doi.org/10.1111/j.1467-6419.2006.00255.x.
922. *Ibid.*
923. *Ibid.*
924. *Ibid.*
925. Graeme B Dinwoodie and Mark D Janis, 'Confusion Over Use: Contextualism in Trademark Law' (2007) 92 Iowa Law Review 1597.
926. *Ibid.*
927. *Ibid.*
928. Mark P McKenna, 'A Consumer Decision-Making Theory of Trademark Law' 98 Virginia Law Review 67, 70.
929. Paris Convention, Art. 6bis; TRIPS, Art. 16(1); EUTMR, Art. 8(1)(b) and Art. 9(2)(b); 15 U.S. Code § 1114;15 U.S. Code § 1125.
930. Mark P McKenna, 'A Consumer Decision-Making Theory of Trademark Law' 98 Virginia Law Review 67, 70.
931. *Ibid.*
932. *Ibid.*
933. *Ibid.*
934. *Ibid.*
935. *Ibid.*
936. Graeme B Dinwoodie and Mark D Janis, 'Confusion Over Use: Contextualism in Trademark Law' (2007) 92 Iowa Law Review 1597.
937. Barton Beebe, 'An Empirical Study of the Multifactor Tests for Trademark Infringement' (2006) 94 California Law Review 1581 https://doi.org/10.2307/20439078 in Robert G Bone, 'Taking the Confusion out of "Likelihood of Confusion": Toward a More Sensible Approach to Trademark Infringement' (2012) 106 Northwestern University Law Review 1307, 1308.

'uncertainty'[938] surrounding it.[939] Bone strongly opposes the theory and argues that 'the test is a mess'[940] and that confusion[941] is not enough without legal wrongdoing or consequences.[942] In line with this, the UDRP certainly considers confusion,[943] but along with other required factors.[944] He says that it is based on 'inadequately justified and normatively incomplete premise',[945] which 'assumes that the ultimate goal of trademark law is to prevent consumer confusion'.[946] Likewise, Beebe opines that consumer confusion[947] is 'in a severe state of disrepair'[948] and, in the context of the US, complains in particular about its 'inconsistent formulation and application across circuits'.[949] McGeveran 'criticized the test's uncertainty and the high litigation costs it generates'.[950] He says that mark holders 'exploit this uncertainty and high cost to chill legitimate uses of marks'.[951] Confusion[952] is said only to be what the law wishes to put into check and other laws step in only when this reaches higher levels.[953] McGeveran and McKenna argue, as it relates to the root objective of the law relating to trademarks, that 'confusion isn't everything'[954] and this results in enhanced conflict 'with open markets and free speech'.[955] Despite the issues surrounding this theory, and the fact

938. William McGeveran, 'Rethinking Trademark Fair Use' (2008) 94 Iowa Law Review 49; Robert G Bone, 'Taking the Confusion out of "Likelihood of Confusion": Toward a More Sensible Approach to Trademark Infringement' (2012) 106 Northwestern University Law Review 1307, 1309.
939. Barton Beebe, 'An Empirical Study of the Multifactor Tests for Trademark Infringement' (2006) 94 California Law Review 1581 https://doi.org/10.2307/20439078 in Robert G Bone, 'Taking the Confusion out of "Likelihood of Confusion": Toward a More Sensible Approach to Trademark Infringement' (2012) 106 Northwestern University Law Review 1307, 1308.
940. Robert G Bone, 'Taking the Confusion out of "Likelihood of Confusion": Toward a More Sensible Approach to Trademark Infringement' (2012) 106 Northwestern University Law Review 1307, abstract.
941. Robert G Bone, 'Taking the Confusion out of "Likelihood of Confusion": Toward a More Sensible Approach to Trademark Infringement' (2012) 106 Northwestern University Law Review 1307, introduction.
942. *Ibid.*
943. UDRP, 4(a).
944. *Ibid.*
945. Robert G Bone, 'Taking the Confusion out of "Likelihood of Confusion": Toward a More Sensible Approach to Trademark Infringement' (2012) 106 Northwestern University Law Review 1307, introduction.
946. *Ibid.*
947. Barton Beebe, 'An Empirical Study of the Multifactor Tests for Trademark Infringement' (2006) 94 California Law Review 1581 https://doi.org/10.2307/20439078 in Robert G Bone, 'Taking the Confusion out of "Likelihood of Confusion": Toward a More Sensible Approach to Trademark Infringement' (2012) 106 Northwestern University Law Review 1307, 1308.
948. *Ibid.*
949. *Ibid.*
950. William McGeveran, 'Rethinking Trademark Fair Use' (2008) 94 Iowa Law Review 49; Robert G Bone, 'Taking the Confusion out of "Likelihood of Confusion": Toward a More Sensible Approach to Trademark Infringement' (2012) 106 Northwestern University Law Review 1307, 1309.
951. *Ibid.*
952. *Ibid.*
953. *Ibid.*
954. *Ibid.*
955. *Ibid.*

that there is 'confusion about confusion',[956] it is embedded in fundamental documents such as the Paris Convention and TRIPS[957] and courts apply a confusion[958] analysis to Internet trademark disputes despite any limitations identified. This will be discussed next.

3.2.3.2 Prohibition Against Confusion and Confusion-Related Concepts

Platforms will be well informed by the prohibition against confusion[959] in the Paris Convention, TRIPS, UDRP, and EU and U.S. approaches.[960] While there is difficulty surrounding the application of confusion[961] in any context, especially in the Internet context, it is important to review select aspects to see where overlap may exist. This section covers various aspects of confusion[962] which inform the model and in turn raise considerations for platforms, which will be summarised at the end of the section.

Confusion[963] is incorporated in both the Paris Convention and TRIPS.

Paris Convention 1967, Article 6bis states:

> (1) The countries of the Union undertake, ex officio if their legislation so permits, or at the request of an interested party, to refuse or to cancel the registration, and to prohibit the use, of a trademark which constitutes a reproduction, an imitation, or a translation, liable to create confusion, of a mark considered by the competent authority of the country of registration or use to be well known in that country as being already the mark of a person entitled to the benefits of this Convention and used for identical or similar goods. These provisions shall also apply when the essential part of the mark constitutes a reproduction of any such well-known mark or an imitation liable to create confusion therewith.[964]

TRIPS, Article 16(1) says:

> The owner of a registered trademark shall have the exclusive right to prevent all third parties not having the owner's consent from using in the course of trade identical or similar signs for goods or services which are identical or similar to those in respect of which the trademark is registered where such use would result in a likelihood of confusion. In case of the use of an identical sign for identical goods or services, a likelihood of confusion shall be presumed. The rights described above shall not prejudice any existing prior rights, nor shall they affect the possibility of Members making rights available on the basis of use.[965]

956. Graeme W Austin, 'Tolerating Confusion About Confusion: Trademark Policies and Fair Use' (2008) 50 Arizona Law Review 157, 160.
957. Paris Convention, Art. 6bis; TRIPS, Art. 16.
958. *Ibid.*
959. Paris Convention, Art. 6bis; TRIPS, Art. 16(1); EUTMR, Art. 8(1)(b) and Art. 9(2)(b); 15 U.S. Code § 1114; 15 U.S. Code § 1125.
960. *Ibid.*
961. *Ibid.*
962. *Ibid.*
963. Paris Convention, Art. 6bis; TRIPS, Art. 16.
964. *Ibid.*
965. TRIPS, Art. 16(1).

Platforms may be informed by the above core implementation of confusion,[966] especially the terminology 'likelihood of confusion',[967] similar to what some jurisdictions have adopted, as will be seen below.

Platforms may also be informed by the way in which the UDRP implements confusion,[968] especially as it is done uniformly in the context of domain names, since platforms may deal with similar issues, such as in social media usernames[969] and mobile app names. The UDRP incorporates confusion under 4(a)(i) as 'identical or confusingly similar to a trademark or service mark in which the complainant has rights'.[970]

Under EU provisions, confusion[971] is also a key aspect under the preamble to the EUTMR:

> (11) The protection afforded by an EU trade mark, the function of which is in particular to guarantee the trade mark as an indication of origin, should be absolute in the case of identity between the mark and the sign and the goods or services. The protection should apply also in cases of similarity between the mark and the sign and the goods or services. An interpretation should be given for the concept of similarity in relation to the likelihood of confusion. The likelihood of confusion, the appreciation of which depends on numerous elements and, in particular, on the recognition of the trade mark on the market, the association which can be made with the used or registered sign, the degree of similarity between the trade mark and the sign and between the goods or services identified, should constitute the specific condition for such protection.[972]

The 'likelihood of confusion'[973] is covered under Article 9(2) EUTMR, which states:

> 1. The registration of an EU trade mark shall confer on the proprietor exclusive rights therein.
> 2. Without prejudice to the rights of proprietors acquired before the filing date or the priority date of the EU trade mark, the proprietor of that EU trade mark shall be entitled to prevent all third parties not having his consent from using in the course of trade, in relation to goods or services, any sign where:
>   (a) the sign is identical with the EU trademark and is used in relation to goods or services which are identical with those for which the EU trademark is registered;

---

966. *Ibid.*
967. *Ibid.*
968. UDRP, 4(a)(i).
969. Rajeev Sachdev, 'Towards an Improved Framework for Trade-Mark Law and Regulation in Social Media Usernames: A Study of the Canadian, U.S., and U.K. Positions' (2016) 28 Intellectual Property Journal, 379, 379-418; Lisa P Ramsey, 'Brandjacking on Social Networks: Trademark Infringement by Impersonation of Markholders' (2010) 58 Buffalo Law Review 851; Danny Friedmann, *Trademarks and Social Media: Towards Algorithmic Justice* (Edward Elgar Publishing, 2015); Paul D McGrady, *McGrady on Social Media and the Metaverse* (Mathew Bender & Company, Inc. 2023) §12.
970. ICANN, 'Uniform Domain-Name Dispute-Resolution Policy' (*ICANN*, 25 February 2012) https://www.icann.org/resources/pages/policy-2012-02-25-en accessed June 2025.
971. EUTMR, Art. 8(1)(b) & Art. 9(2)(c).
972. EUTMR, Preamble 11.
973. EUTMR, Art. 7.

> (b) the sign is identical with, or similar to, the EU trademark and is used in relation to goods or services which are identical with, or similar to, the goods or services for which the EU trademark is registered, if there exists a likelihood of confusion on the part of the public; the likelihood of confusion includes the likelihood of association between the sign and the trademark.[974]

Article 9(2)(a) EUTMR is also known as 'double identity'[975] whereas, in the context of 'likelihood of confusion'[976] under Article 9(2)(b) EUTMR, this may either be 'direct confusion'[977] or 'indirect confusion'[978] ('also referred to as sponsorship confusion or the likelihood of commercial association').[979] In other words, confusion[980] could result from consumers mistakenly believing that the relevant products are from 'economically-linked undertakings'.[981]

It also forms a 'relative grounds for refusal'[982] under Article 8(1)(b) EUTMR and 'the trademark applied for shall not be registered':

> if, because of its identity with, or similarity to, the earlier trade mark and the identity or similarity of the goods or services covered by the trade marks there exists a likelihood of confusion on the part of the public in the territory in which the earlier trade mark is protected; the likelihood of confusion includes the likelihood of association with the earlier trade mark.[983]

As noted by Aytekin et al., in the EU, 'the most common opposition to trademark registration is the likelihood of confusion based on the identity or similarity of the trademark, sign, and the identity or similarity of the goods or services concerned'.[984]

Fhima and Gangjee remind us that in the landmark case of *SABEL v. Puma*,[985] the Court clarified that '[t]he likelihood of confusion must ... be appreciated globally, taking into account all factors relevant to the circumstances of the case ... [t]hat global appreciation of the visual, aural or conceptual similarity of the marks in question, must be based on the overall impression given by the marks, bearing in mind, in particular,

974. EUTMR, Art. 8(1)(b) & Art. 9(b).
975. Anna Tischner and Katarzyna Stasiuk, 'Spare Parts, Repairs, Trade Marks and Consumer Understanding' (2023) 54 International Review of Intellectual Property and Competition Law 26, 34 https://doi.org/10.1007/s40319-022-01274-8.
976. EUTMR, Art. 9(2)(b).
977. Martin Senftleben, 'Bringing EU Trademark Protection Back Into Shape: Lessons to Learn From Keyword Advertising' https://www.researchgate.net/publication/228174475_Adapting_EU_Trademark_Law_to_New_Technologies_-_Back_to_Basics accessed January 2024.
978. *Ibid.*
979. Ilanah Fhima and Dev S Gangjee, 'Assessing Likelihood of Confusion', *The Confusion Test in European Trade Mark Law* (New York, 2019; online edn, Oxford Academic) 160, 160 https://doi.org/10.1093/oso/9780199674336.003.0006.
980. *Ibid.*; Case C-39/97 *Canon Kabushiki Kaisha v. Metro-Goldwyn-Mayer Inc* (CJEU) EU:C:1998:442.
981. *Ibid.*
982. EUTMR, Art. 8(1)(b) and Art. 9(2)(c).
983. *Ibid.*
984. Ceren Aytekin et al., 'Trademarks in the United States and European Union' (2023) 27(4) Young Lawyer https://www.americanbar.org/groups/young_lawyers/resources/tyl/practice-areas/trademarks-the-united-states-and-european-union-neutralization-and-use/ accessed 4 August 2025.
985. Case C-251/95 *SABEL v. Puma AG, Rudolf Dassler Sport* (CJEU) EU:C:1997:528.

their distinctive and dominant components ... In that perspective, the more distinctive the earlier mark, the greater will be the likelihood of confusion'.[986] Likewise, according to 2024 EUIPO Guidelines, '[t]he likelihood of confusion is assessed in the following steps, taking into account multiple factors: comparison of goods and services; relevant public and degree of attention; comparison of signs; distinctiveness of the earlier mark; any other factors; global assessment of the likelihood of confusion'.[987] Further, citing *Canon v. Metro-Goldwyn-Maye*[988] and 'additional factors',[989] the Guidelines state that '[t]he Court has identified the following factors for determining whether goods/services are similar: their nature, their intended purpose, their method of use, whether they are complementary or not, whether they are in competition or interchangeable, their distribution channels/points of sale, their relevant public, their usual origin'.[990] With reference to the *Canon*[991] factors, the Guidelines state that '[a]s a result of weighing all these factors in accordance with their respective importance in relation to the goods/services at issue, similarity may be found to various degrees: low, average or high'.[992]

In fact, the guidelines also state that, alongside 'distribution channels',[993] the 'method of use'[994] and 'relevant public'[995] factors are 'less important'.[996] Specifically as to the 'distribution channels factor',[997] the Guidelines state: 'even dissimilar goods can be sold in the same section of stores depending on different display practices'.[998] It is notable that the guidelines do not make direct mention of the Internet in this regard; however, a recent case is illustrative. In the 2021 EU case of *Zoom,*[999] it was stated while '[t]he same distribution channels (App Store/Google Play Store) are a factor to be

986. *Ibid.*
987. EUIPO, '4.2 List of Factors for Assessing the Likelihood of Confusion' (*EUIPO Trade mark guidelines* 2024) https://guidelines.euipo.europa.eu/2214311/2227748/trade-mark-guidelines/4-2-list-of-factors-for-assessing-the-likelihood-of-confusion accessed July 2024.
988. C-39/97, *Canon*, EU:C:1998:442.
989. EUIPO, 'Similarity Factors' (*EUIPO Trade mark guidelines* 2024) https://guidelines.euipo.europa.eu/2058843/2135996/trade-mark-guidelines/3-1-1-similarity-factors accessed July 2024.
990. C-39/97, *Canon*, EU:C:1998:442; EUIPO, '3.4.1 Fact and Law: Similarity of Goods/Services and of Signs' (*EUIPO Trade mark guidelines* 2024) https://guidelines.euipo.europa.eu/2214311/2046921/trade-mark-guidelines/3-4-1-fact-and-law-%E2%80%94-similarity-of-goods-services-and-of-signs accessed July 2024.
991. C-39/97, *Canon*, EU:C:1998:442.
992. EUIPO, '3.3 Relation Between Different Factors' (*EUIPO Trade mark guidelines* 2024) https://guidelines.euipo.europa.eu/2214311/1937813/trade-mark-guidelines/3-3-relation-between-different-factors accessed July 2024.
993. EUIPO, '3.3.2 Importance of Each Factor' (*EUIPO Trade mark guidelines* 2024) https://guidelines.euipo.europa.eu/2214311/1924406/trade-mark-guidelines/3-3-2-importance-of-each-factor accessed July 2024.
994. *Ibid.*
995. *Ibid.*
996. *Ibid.*
997. *Ibid.*
998. *Ibid.*
999. T-204/20, *ZOOM/ZOOM* (fig.) et al., EU:T:2021:391; EUIPO, 'Overview of GC/CJ Case-Law Status: 01/01/2019 – 30/09/2023' (*Board of Appeals Operations Area*) https://euipo.europa.eu/tunnel-web/secure/webdav/guest/document_library/contentPdfs/about_euipo/boards_of_appeal/case-law/case-law_overview_2019-2023_Q3_en.pdf accessed January 2024.

taken into account ... a multitude of software with radically different functions can be found in physical/virtual stores'[1000] and '[c]onsumers will not automatically believe they have the same origin'.[1001] The court went on to describe their understanding of a consumer app search and said that '[u]sers generally identify the desired function and then launch a search for all the applications available that perform that function ... [and] ... [e]ven if a consumer searches for the desired application by name, the search will ultimately be guided by the desired function'.[1002] While the products both involve software, 'the intended purpose of the goods covered by the earlier figurative mark is to edit and alter sounds while recording, whereas the intended purpose of the goods covered by the contested mark is to enable users to secure and access mobile devices through multidimensional facial recognition identification'[1003] and as a result, '[t]here is only a low degree of similarity between the goods'.[1004]

In the context of e-commerce, in the now infamous *France.com v. EUIPO*[1005] case, it was found that the domain france.com could not be registered as an EU mark.[1006] The domain was being used in relation to an e-commerce travel website, and an application to register a figurative mark incorporating the domain france.com, along with a logo depicting the Eiffel Tower and using the colours of the flag of France, was made.[1007] The GC ruled that there was a 'likelihood of confusion'[1008] with a registered mark of the country of France, which included the word France along with the Eiffel Tower and the colours of the flag of France.[1009] Even though the court found the signs only 'slightly visually similar',[1010] it considered that 'many consumers'[1011] will make reference to france.com by the term 'France'[1012] with the.com aspect simply 'being perceived as referring to a website'.[1013] The two signs were considered 'conceptually similar'[1014] because they 'convey[ed] the same concept'.[1015] A related case in the U.S. Fourth Circuit was dismissed for 'lack of subject matter jurisdiction'.[1016] In another e-commerce platform case, similarity was also at issue. In *Wallapop,*[1017] figurative signs were in contest under 8(1)(b) EUTMR. In this case, the e-commerce services provided

1000. *Ibid.*
1001. *Ibid.*
1002. *Ibid.*
1003. *Ibid.*
1004. *Ibid.*
1005. Case T-71/17 *France.com, Inc. v. EUIPO* EU:T:2018:381.
1006. General Court of the European Union, 'Press Release No 91/18' (*Press and Information*, 26 June 2018) https://curia.europa.eu/jcms/upload/docs/application/pdf/2018-06/cp180091en.pdf accessed January 2024.
1007. *Ibid.*
1008. *Ibid.*
1009. *Ibid.*
1010. *Ibid.*
1011. *Ibid.*
1012. *Ibid.*
1013. *Ibid.*
1014. *Ibid.*
1015. *Ibid.*
1016. *France.com, Inc. v. French Republic*, No. 20-1016 (4th Cir. 25 March 2021); United States Court of Appeals for the Fourth District, 'No: 20-1016' (*USCourts*) https://www.ca4.uscourts.gov/opinions/201016.P.pdf accessed 4 August 2025.
1017. Case T-186/17 *WALLAPOP (fig.)/WALA W (fig.) et al.; Unipreus, SL v. EUIPO* EU:T:2018:640.

related to 'intermediation or online market management services for buyers and sellers of goods and services, including providing commercial information relevant to the conduct of sales'.[1018] Wallapop's attempt to register a figurative European Union Trade mark (EUTM) under class 35 with respect to 'online trade ...'[1019] etc. was challenged based on an earlier registered Spanish trademark, under class 35 with the description of 'Retailing of sporting articles'.[1020] It was noted in the appeal that even though the parties were 'weak competitors',[1021] consumers were able to 'analyse the offer for the same product both on the "www.walashop.com" website and on the "www.wallapop.com" website'.[1022] The GC decided that the services were 'at the very least, weakly similar, therefore, the BoA wrongly deemed that these services were different'.[1023] Further, that 'the notion of "retail" includes both sales in physical premises and online sales'.[1024] On appeal, in *Wallapop v. EUIPO,*[1025] relevant questions surrounded the interpretation of: 'online trading services relating to the operation of an online marketplace' compared to or included in the 'notion of' 'retailing services'.[1026] The Advocate General opined, in the context of whether the 'distribution channels' were similar, that '[t]he traditional distinction between outlets selling to customers in physical premises, on the one hand, and those entities engaging in direct online sales, on the other, has in recent years been undermined – almost to the point of collapse – by both technological developments and changing patterns of consumer behaviour'.[1027] Further that, 'from the point of view of a consumer seeking to purchase the goods in question, Wallapop's platform and Unipreus' site are similar channels of distribution ... [i]t is at that point that the risk of confusion between the two slightly similar marks might most acutely come into play'.[1028] In siding with the GC's overall decision, the Advocate General raised some points pertinent to the growing nature of online or virtual platforms.[1029] Wallapop ultimately withdrew its appeal.[1030]

Confusion[1031] with respect to trademarks and search ads have had specific attention in EU jurisprudence over time. Senftleben states that the CJ requires 'keyword advertisers to ensure clarity about the commercial origin of advertised goods or services'[1032] and 'thus bans the risk of initial interest confusion from the outset'.[1033] Fhima and Gangjee make clear that EU courts have generally found the concept of

1018. *Ibid.*
1019. *Ibid.*
1020. *Ibid.*
1021. *Ibid.*
1022. *Ibid.*
1023. *Ibid.*
1024. *Ibid.*
1025. *Ibid.*
1026. *Ibid.*
1027. Case C-763/18 *P Wallapop, SL v. EUIPO, Unipreus, SL* EU:C:2020:497.
1028. *Ibid.*
1029. *Ibid.*
1030. *Ibid.*
1031. Martin Senftleben, 'Rights Conferred' in Annette Kur and Martin Senftleben (eds), *European Trade Mark Law* (Oxford University Press 2017) 326.
1032. *Ibid.*
1033. *Ibid.*

'initial interest confusion'[1034] unhelpful as seen in several cases which are discussed below, although believe the 'door may not entirely be closed'.[1035] Seftleben further comments that '[a]n unauthorized advertising message leaving Internet users to wonder whether it stems from the trademark proprietor or a competitor will readily be actionable – regardless of a potential later correction of wrongful origin assumptions on the advertisers' webpage'.[1036] He also says that since 'the general confusion test is configured so broadly in keyword advertising cases ... it is unnecessary to recognize initial interest confusion as a distinct species of actionable confusion'.[1037] Further, the relevant attention given when searching online is also relevant. Fhima and Gangjee summarise that recent concept of the 'average Internet user'[1038] has emerged 'in the context of search engines and Internet advertising'[1039] and predict that '[t]he attributes and perceptions of the latter could evolve as Internet literacy changes over time'.[1040] Even though the 'degree of attention is likely to vary according to the category of goods or services in question',[1041] this may also differ in relation to different areas of the Internet. The Guidelines For Examination of European Union Trade Marks state that a 'higher degree of care'[1042] is usual in 'expensive purchases';[1043] times have changed and consumers regularly search for and purchase expensive items online.

In Google France,[1044] as was discussed in section 3.2.1 above, a key issue was that an ad 'does not enable normally informed and reasonably attentive internet users, or enable them only with difficulty, to ascertain whether the goods or services referred to by the ad originate from the proprietor of the trademark or an undertaking economically connected to it or, on the contrary, originate from a third party'.[1045] Fhima and Gangjee declare that '[s]ignificantly, *Google France* therefore established that an Internet keyword advertisement, which generated some ambiguity that might

1034. Ilanah Fhima and Dev S Gangjee, 'Assessing Likelihood of Confusion', *The Confusion Test in European Trade Mark Law* (New York, 2019; online edn, Oxford Academic) 160, 167 https://doi.org/10.1093/oso/9780199674336.003.0006.
1035. *Ibid.*
1036. *Ibid.*
1037. *Ibid.*
1038. *Ibid.*
1039. Ilanah Fhima and Dev S Gangjee, 'Assessing Likelihood of Confusion', *The Confusion Test in European Trade Mark Law* (New York, 2019; online edn, Oxford Academic) 160-203 https://doi.org/10.1093/oso/9780199674336.003.0006.
1040. *Ibid.*
1041. C-342/97 *Lloyd Schuhfabrik* EU:C:1999:323; EUIPO, 'Guidelines for Examination of European Union Trade Marks Part C Opposition' (*EUIPO* 2017) https://guidelines.euipo.europa.eu/2302857/1951405/trade-mark-guidelines/3-1-1-expensive-purchases accessed January 2024.
1042. EUIPO, 'Guidelines For Examination of European Union Trade Marks' (*EUIPO*, 2017) https://guidelines.euipo.europa.eu/2302857/1951405/trade-mark-guidelines/3-1-1-expensive-purchases accessed January 2024.
1043. *Ibid.*
1044. *Ibid.*
1045. Case C-236/08 *Google France SARL and Google Inc. v. Louis Vuitton Malletier SA*, C-237/08 *Google France SARL v. Viaticum SA and Luteciel SARL* and C-238/08 *Google France SARL v. Centre national de recherche en relations humaines (CNRRH) SARL and Others* EU:C:2010:159.

ultimately be dispelled "with difficulty," could nevertheless be infringing'.[1046] That, '[i]n effect, either straight up confusion or increased cognitive processing effort – which might even be read as transient confusion – was deemed sufficient to jeopardise the origin function *specifically in the context of double identity infringement* and *in relation to keywords*'.[1047] Fhima and Gangjee review that in BergSpechte,[1048] the result in Google France 'was applied by analogy to likelihood of confusion cases in the Internet context'.[1049] In this case, the parties offered tour services and party, trekking.at Reisen, bid on keywords for paid search ads related to BergSpechte's registered mark, specifically the terms 'Edi Koblmüller' and/or 'Bergspechte.'[1050] By reference for preliminary ruling, the CJ decided that 'it will be for the national court to hold whether there is a likelihood of confusion when internet users are shown, on the basis of a keyword similar to a mark, a third party's ad which does not enable normally informed and reasonably attentive internet users, or enable them only with difficulty, to ascertain whether the goods or services referred to by the ad originate from the proprietor of the trademark or an undertaking economically connected to it or, on the contrary, originate from a third party'.[1051] Following Google France and BergSpechte, in *Portakabin v. Primakabin,*[1052] Portakabin sued a company which bought keywords related to the term 'Portakabin'[1053] to sell 'used portakabin'[1054] products. The CJ ruled that trademark holders do have the right to stop advertisers from using their mark 'where that advertising does not enable average internet users, or enables them only with difficulty, to ascertain whether the goods or services referred to by the ad originate from the proprietor of the trademark or from an undertaking economically linked to it or, on the contrary, originate from a third party'.[1055] At the same time, generally, the trademark holder cannot stop an advertiser from using[1056] the trademarks to advertise the 'resale of genuine goods ... as long as it is at the same time in accordance with honest practices in industrial and commercial matters'[1057] and some EU cases[1058] have

1046. Ilanah Fhima and Dev S Gangjee, 'Assessing Likelihood of Confusion', *The Confusion Test in European Trade Mark Law* (New York, 2019; online edn, Oxford Academic) 204-230 https://doi.org/10.1093/oso/9780199674336.003.0006.
1047. *Ibid.*
1048. Case C-278/08 *Die BergSpechte Outdoor Reisen und Alpinschule Edi Koblmüller GmbH v. Günter Guni and trekking.at Reisen GmbH* EU:C:2010:163.
1049. Ilanah Fhima and Dev S Gangjee, 'Assessing Likelihood of Confusion', *The Confusion Test in European Trade Mark Law* (New York, 2019; online edn, Oxford Academic) 1-16 https://doi.org/10.1093/oso/9780199674336.003.0006.
1050. *Ibid.*
1051. Case C-278/08 *Die BergSpechte Outdoor Reisen und Alpinschule Edi Koblmüller GmbH v. Günter Guni and trekking.at Reisen GmbH* EU:C:2010:163.
1052. Case C-558/08 *Portakabin Ltd and Portakabin BV v. Primakabin BV* EU:C:2010:416.
1053. *Ibid.*
1054. IPKitten, 'Portakabin Ruling: A Bad Result for Trade Mark Owners?' (*ipkitten*) http://ipkitten.blogspot.com/2010/07/portakabin-ruling-bad-result-for-trade.html accessed 4 August 2025.
1055. *Ibid.*
1056. *Ibid.*; EUTMR, Art. 18.
1057. IPKitten, 'Portakabin Ruling: A Bad Result for Trade Mark Owners?' (*ipkitten*) http://ipkitten.blogspot.com/2010/07/portakabin-ruling-bad-result-for-trade.html accessed 4 August 2025; EUTMR, Recital 21.
1058. Annette Kur and Martin Senftleben, 'Limitations, Defences, and Genuine Use' in Annette Kur and Martin Senftleben (eds), *European Trade Mark Law* (Oxford University Press 2017) 407.

dealt with trademarks in search ads such as relating to 'accessories or spare parts'[1059] for trademarked goods.

One aspect of 'confusion'[1060] in social media was considered in *Hello Media Group v. EUIPO*[1061] with respect to utilising social media symbols.[1062] The GC found 'likelihood of confusion'[1063] between the figurative mark, which incorporated the phrase '#hello digitalmente diferentes'[1064] and the earlier mark 'HELLO!'.[1065] It found that the word 'hello'[1066] in the above phrase 'was the dominant element of the EUTM application'[1067] and that the #[1068] symbol 'would largely be understood as a reference to metadata used in social networks'.[1069] The Internet and certainly the Metaverse also raise the concept of 'interdimensional confusion'[1070] as discussed by Tenkhoff et al.[1071] For example, a trademark which has been registered for and is normally used on a physical good in the physical world may itself or something similar to it be utilised with a virtual good, such as an NFT.[1072] However, Tenkhoff et al. raise a key question, which is 'whether similarity within the meaning of Art. 9(2)(b) EUTMR can exist between virtual goods and their physical counterparts'.[1073] In recognising that the potential outcome would be very fact-dependant and that 'it seems fair to conclude that a finding of a likelihood of confusion is at the very least a possibility',[1074] recognising Kur has a more 'sceptical view'.[1075]

NFTs have also reached the courts in Italy. In the Italian case of *Juventus v. Blockeras,*[1076] where 'defendant offered NFTs representing collectable cards which

1059. EUTMR, Art. 14(1)(c).
1060. EUTMR, Art. 9.
1061. Case T-330/16 *hello digitalmente diferentes/HELLO! et al.; Hello Media Group SL v. EUIPO* EU:T: 2017:762.
1062. *Ibid.*
1063. EUTMR, Art. 9(2)(b).
1064. Case T-330/16 *hello digitalmente diferentes/HELLO! et al. Hello Media Group SL v. EUIPO*; Judgment of 26 October 2017; EU:T: 2017:762.
EUIPO, 'Overview of GC/CJ Case Law 2017' (*International Cooperation and Legal Affairs Department*, 2017) 176-178 https://euipo.europa.eu/tunnel-web/secure/webdav/guest/document_library/contentPdfs/law_and_practice/yearly_overview/yearly_overview_2017.pdf accessed January 2024.
1065. *Ibid.*
1066. *Ibid.*
1067. *Ibid.*
1068. *Ibid.*
1069. *Ibid.*
1070. Christian Tenkhoff, Phillip Grotkamp and Sylvia Burgess-Tate, 'Brands in the Metaverse: The Concept of "Interdimensional Confusion" Between the Physical and the Virtual Space under EU Trade Mark Law' 72 GRUR International 643 https://doi.org/10.1093/grurint/ikad045.
1071. *Ibid.*
1072. *Ibid.*
1073. Christian Tenkhoff, Phillip Grotkamp and Sylvia Burgess-Tate, 'Brands in the Metaverse: The Concept of "Interdimensional Confusion" Between the Physical and the Virtual Space under EU Trade Mark Law' 72 GRUR International 643, 647 https://doi.org/10.1093/grurint/ikad045.
1074. *Ibid.*
1075. Annette Kur, 's 9 para 17' in Annette Kur, Verena von Bomhard and Friedrich Albrecht (eds), *BeckOK Markenrecht* (CH Beck 2023).
1076. *Juventus F.C. v. Blockeras s.r.l.*, No. 32072/2022.

contained or were offered in connection with, among others, the mark JUVE'.[1077] The Court of Rome found that 'there was a high risk that the public might believe that the unauthorised NFTs were associated with the football club, especially in light of the club's recent expansion into the field of crypto and blockchain games and subsequent activity in the same commercial sector as the contested goods'.[1078] Confusion was likely as a result.[1079]

Platforms may consider various aspects of the above examples of treatment of confusion[1080] on the Internet. Specifically, there is no single factor that can lead to a determination. It is assessed with 'global appreciation'[1081] with various or multiple factors and platforms should consider which factors may be relevant to an analysis within their service. For example, as EU courts have recognised, consumer may not always be confused[1082] about various apps within platforms and the relevancy of being in the 'same distribution channels'[1083] may not be as important.[1084] However, when it comes to physical offline settings and digital settings, such as NFTs in the Metaverse, some consumers may confuse[1085] trademarks in these environments if a known brand has entered the Metaverse in some way, for example.[1086]

With respect to the U.S. framework, Bone says that the 'likelihood of confusion test'[1087] is the main 'infringement standard'[1088] and liability exists 'if an appreciable number of consumers are likely to be confused by the defendant's use of its mark'.[1089] Confusion[1090] is well-embedded in the law and is widely applicable today, and thus informs platforms. It is recognised by the U.S. Lanham Act, such as, for registered trademarks, under 15 U.S. Code § 1114, which prohibits *'reproduction, counterfeit, copy, or colorable imitation ... likely to cause confusion ...'*.[1091] Similar rules apply for

1077. Christian Tenkhoff, Phillip Grotkamp and Sylvia Burgess-Tate, 'Brands in the Metaverse: The Concept of "Interdimensional Confusion" Between the Physical and the Virtual Space under EU Trade Mark Law' 72 GRUR International 643, 647 https://doi.org/10.1093/grurint/ikad045.
1078. *Ibid.*
1079. *Ibid.*
1080. Paris Convention, Art. 6bis; TRIPS, Art. 16(1); EUTMR, Art. 8(1)(b) and Art. 9(2)(b); 15 U.S. Code § 1114;15 U.S. Code § 1125.
1081. Case C-251/95 *SABEL v. Puma AG, Rudolf Dassler Sport* (CJEU) EU:C:1997:528.
1082. Paris Convention, Art. 6bis; TRIPS, Art. 16(1); EUTMR, Art. 8(1)(b) and Art. 9(2)(b); 15 U.S. Code § 1114;15 U.S. Code § 1125.
1083. T-204/20, *ZOOM/ZOOM* (fig.) et al., EU:T:2021:391; EUIPO, 'Overview of GC/CJ Case-Law Status: 01/01/2019 – 30/09/2023' (*Board of Appeals Operations Area*) https://euipo.europa.eu/tunnel-web/secure/webdav/guest/document_library/contentPdfs/about_euipo/boards_of_appeal/case-law/case-law_overview_2019-2023_Q3_en.pdf accessed January 2024.
1084. *Ibid.*
1085. Paris Convention, Art. 6bis; TRIPS, Art. 16(1); EUTMR, Art. 8(1)(b) and Art. 9(2)(b); 15 U.S. Code § 1114;15 U.S. Code § 1125.
1086. *Juventus F.C. v. Blockeras s.r.l.*, No. 32072/2022.
1087. Robert G Bone, 'Taking the Confusion out of "Likelihood of Confusion": Toward a More Sensible Approach to Trademark Infringement' (2012) 106 Northwestern University Law Review 1307, abstract.
1088. *Ibid.*
1089. *Ibid.*
1090. Paris Convention 1967, Art. 6bis; TRIPS, Art. 16(1); EUTMR, Art. 8(1)(b) and Art. 9(2)(b); 15 U.S. Code § 1114;15 U.S. Code § 1125.
1091. 15 U.S. Code § 1114.

unregistered marks under 15 U.S. Code § 1125. In the US, various circuit courts use different factors to assess confusion.[1092] For example, the Ninth Circuit Sleekcraft factors,[1093] the Sixth Circuit Frisch factors,[1094] and the Second Circuit Polaroid Test[1095] are among the tests used. While some of the factors differ between circuits, which may result in inconsistencies, and although 'the specific number and description of these factors vary according to jurisdiction',[1096] as Batholomew et al note, these are some common factors that may be considered:

- Similarity of the plaintiff's and defendant's marks.
- Strength of the plaintiff's mark.[1097]

1092. *AMF Inc. v. Sleekcraft Boats*, 599 F.2d 341 (9th Cir. 1979); *Frisch's Rest., Inc. v. Shoney's Inc.*, 759 F.2d 1261 (6th Cir. 1985); *Kibler v. Hall*, Case No. 14-10017 (E.D. Mich. 9 November 2015); *CFE Racing Prods., Inc. v. BMF Wheels, Inc.*, 793 F.3d 571 (6th Cir. 2015); *Polaroid Corp. v. Polarad Elecs. Corp.*, 287 F.2d 492 (2d Cir.1961).

1093. *AMF, Inc. v. Sleekcraft Boats*, 599 F.2d 341 (9th Cir. 1979); Berkman Klein Center, 'AMF' (*AMF, Inc.*) https://cyber.harvard.edu/metaschool/fisher/domain/tmcases/amf.htm accessed 4 August 2025. These factors include as stated in the case '*1. strength of the mark; 2. proximity of the goods; 3. similarity of the marks; 4. evidence of actual confusion;5. marketing channels used; 6. type of goods and the degree of care likely to be exercised by the purchaser; 7. defendant's intent in selecting the mark; and 8. likelihood of expansion of the product lines*'.

1094. *Frisch's Rest., Inc. v. Shoney's Inc.*, 759 F.2d 1261, 1264 (6th Cir. 1985) These factors include: '*1) strength of the plaintiff's mark, 2) relatedness of the products, 3) similarity of the marks, 4) evidence of actual confusion, 5) parties' marketing channels, 6) likely degree of purchaser care, 7) defendant's intent in selecting the mark, and 8) probability that the product lines will expand*'. *See Kibler v. Hall*, Case No. 14-10017 (E.D. Mich. 9 November 2015) https://www.govinfo.gov/content/pkg/USCOURTS-ca6-15-02516/pdf/USCOURTS-ca6-15-02516-0.pdf accessed 4 August 2025; *Frisch's Rest., Inc. v. Shoney's Inc.*, 759 F.2d 1261, 1264 (6th Cir. 1985); *CFE Racing Prods., Inc. v. BMF Wheels, Inc.*, 793 F.3d 571, 592 (6th Cir. 2015).

1095. *Polaroid Corp. v. Polarad Elecs. Corp.*, 287 F.2d 492, 495 (2d Cir.1961). These factors include: '*(1) the strength of the plaintiff's mark; (2) the degree of similarity between the two marks; (3) the proximity of the products; (4) the likelihood that the owner will bridge the gap; (5) evidence of actual confusion; (6) defendant's good faith in adopting the mark; (7) the quality of defendant's product; and (8) the sophistication of the consumers will likely cause confusion with plaintiff's mark*'. *See* Cornell Law, 'Trademarks-Demonstrating Actual Consumer Confusion' (*Cornell University Law School Social Science and Law*) https://courses2.cit.cornell.edu/sociallaw/topics/Trademarks-confusion.htm#:~:text=For%20example%2C%20in%20the%20Second,confusion%3B%20(6)%20defendant's%20good accessed January 2024; *Polaroid Corp. v. Polarad Elecs. Corp.*, 287 F.2d 492, 495 (2d Cir.1961).

1096. Mark Bartholomew et al., 'A New Addition to the Trademark Litigator's Tool Kit: A Neuroscientific Index of Mark Similarity' (2023) 113 The Trademark Reporter 785, 792 https://www.inta.org/wp-content/uploads/public-files/resources/the-trademark-reporter/TMR-Vol-113-No-6-November-December-2023_12182023-Secured.pdf accessed July 2024.

1097. *Joseph Phelps Vineyards, LLC v. Fairmont Holdings LLC*, 857 F.3d 1323, 122 U.S.P.Q.2d 1733 (Fed. Cir. 2017); J Thomas McCarthy, 'Commentary: Trademark Strength and Fame: The Federal Circuit Corrects the Trademark Trial and Appeal Board' 108 (May-June 2018) The Trademark Reporter 904. In *Joseph Phelps*, the first factor related to 'strength', was clarified to include the fact that 'strength should be a sliding scale' rather than a 'yes/no decision'. In *Kibler v. Hall, Case No. 14-10017 (E.D. Mich. Nov. 9, 2015)*, it was discussed how 'strength', the first of the Frich factors are assessed from the perspective of social media marketing. The court identified specific types of evidence that would have contributed to the assessment of the 'strength' and made this statement: '[p]romotion on platforms such as Twitter and Facebook not only constitutes marketing, but is among the most popular and effective advertising strategies today'. The court indicated that certain types of social media specific evidence would be helpful. For example, it stated that certain questions were relevant including the number and 'kind of Twitter followers'. It said that a 'large number of followers,

- Intent of the defendant.
- Purchaser sophistication.
- Presence of actual confusion.
- Relatedness of the goods or services at issue.[1098]

Lim suggests the use of only three factors, including 'actual confusion',[1099] 'similarity',[1100] and 'proximity',[1101] based on what Lim believes to be some duplication and the lack of need for others.[1102]

Relatedly, some circuit courts in the US also adopt the concept of 'initial interest confusion'.[1103] This has often been relevant in search advertising cases, although it may have application to other areas of the Internet, such as searching in social media or for mobile apps. Under *Ayse Sen,*[1104] '[c]lear labeling can eliminate the likelihood of initial interest confusion in cases involving internet search terms'.[1105] However, it has been opined that 'development of initial interest confusion just happened to coincide with the explosion of e-commerce and digital marketing'.[1106]

The ACPA is also informative since domain names and social media usernames or mobile app names have some overlapping considerations, even if these are different. The ACPA 'generally prevents use of domain names and designations that (1) create a likelihood of confusion among consumers regarding the origin of a registered trademark owner's product or service or (2) are similar to a registered trademark'.[1107] The

or celebrities likely to re-tweet Kibler's messages to their large number of followers, for example, would suggest that many types of people know his work and mark'. The same comment was made for 'the number and kind of Kibler's Facebook fans, likes, posts, and re-posts'; however, this evidence was not provided.

1098. Mark Bartholomew et al., 'A New Addition to the Trademark Litigator's Tool Kit: A Neuroscientific Index of Mark Similarity' (2023) 113 The Trademark Reporter 785, 792 https://www.inta.org/wp-content/uploads/public-files/resources/the-trademark-reporter/TMR-Vol-113-No-6-November-December-2023_12182023-Secured.pdf accessed July 2024.
1099. Daryl Lim, 'Trademark Confusion Simplified: A New Framework for Multifactor Tests' (2022) 37 Berkeley Technology Law Journal 867, 913-916.
1100. *Ibid.*
1101. *Ibid.*
1102. Daryl Lim, 'Trademark Confusion Simplified: A New Framework for Multifactor Tests' (2022) 37 Berkeley Technology Law Journal 867, 916.
1103. *Playboy Enters. v. Netscape Commc'ns Corp.*, 354 F.3d 1020, 1022-23 (9th Cir. 2004); Zachary J Zweihorn, 'Searching for Confusion: The Initial Interest Confusion Doctrine and Its Misapplication to Search Engine Sponsored Links' (September 2006) 91 Cornell Law Reveiw 1343 https://scholarship.law.cornell.edu/cgi/viewcontent.cgi?article=3041&context=clr accessed 4 August 2025; Johnny Walsh, 'Confusion Mélange: A Call to Revise the Law on Trademark Infringement, Initial Interest Confusion, and Digital Marketing' (2023) 57 Indiana Law Review 281 https://doi.org/10.18060/27650. While other confusion concepts exist, the latter work mainly focuses on 'likelihood of confusion'.
1104. *Ayse Sen v. Amazon.com*, Inc., 2020 U.S. Dist. LEXIS 142850; *Multi Time Mach., Inc. v. Amazon.com*, Inc., 804 F.3d 930 (9th Cir. 2015).
1105. *Ibid.*
1106. Johnny Walsh, 'Confusion Mélange: A Call to Revise the Law on Trademark Infringement, Initial Interest Confusion, and Digital Marketing' (2023) 57 Indiana Law Review 281, 311 https://doi.org/10.18060/27650.
1107. CEB, *Internet Law Practice in California* (Continuing Education of the Bar, the Regents of the University of California, 2015).

ACPA, under 15 U.S. Code § 1125(d)(1)(A)(ii)(I), prevents use[1108] of a domain name which, 'in the case of a mark that is distinctive at the time of registration of the domain name, is identical or confusingly similar to that mark'.[1109] ACPA cases have also considered confusion factors.[1110]

Circuits have long utilised and applied factors to determine 'likelihood of confusion';[1111] however, many courts have recognised that the factors are not all required to tip in one side's favour, courts have discretion as to the relevance of the factors to the case, and they may be adapted.[1112] While not used in all circuits, the factor of 'similarity of advertising methods'[1113] or 'marketing channels'[1114] has sometimes taken centre stage, while in others, it becomes questionable as platforms become flooded with marketing.[1115] In the context of social media, in *Uber Promotions v. Uber Technologies,*[1116] a seven-factor Eleventh Circuit test[1117] was applied, and one of the factors was the 'similarity of advertising methods'[1118] being social media.[1119] Even though the parties' ads looked different, 'both companies´ extensive use of social media ... raises the likelihood that consumers will come into contact with both marks, which in turn raises the likelihood of confusion'.[1120] Similarly, in relation to mobile apps, in *Updateme v. Se,*[1121] the plaintiff contended a majority of (without pleading) the *Sleekcraft* factors[1122] including that '(i) they have a strong mark ... ; (ii) both products are news aggregation apps ... ; (iii) the upday mark is confusingly similar to the updatemi mark in appearance, sound, and meaning ... ; (iv) both apps are marketed through Google Play ... ; (v) consumers are unlikely to take care in distinguishing between the pre-downloaded apps or apps on the Google Play store ... ; and (vi) defendant intentionally copied the updatemi mark'.[1123] The court determined that 'these allegations sufficiently allege a likelihood of confusion'.[1124] This was an issue in *ServPro v. Blanton,*[1125] under the ACPA, and the court weighed the eight Sleekcraft

1108. 15 U.S. Code § 1125(d)(1)(A)(ii)(I).
1109. *Ibid.*
1110. *Passport Health, LLC v. Avance Health Sys.*, No. 5:17-CV-187-BO (E.D.N.C. 26 January 2021); *Passport Health, LLC v. Avance Health Sys.*, No. 19-1061 (4th Cir. 13 August 2020).
1111. *Multi Time Mach., Inc. v. Amazon.com, Inc.*, 804 F.3d 930 (9th Cir. 2015); *Brookfield Commc'ns v. West Coast Entm't Corp.*, 174 F.3d 1036, 1054 (9th Cir.1999); *Passport Health, LLC v. Avance Health Sys.*, No. 19-1061 (4th Cir. 13 August 2020).
1112. *Ibid.*
1113. *Uber Promotions, Inc. v. Uber Technologies, Inc.* 162 F.Supp.3d 1253 (N.D. Fla. 2016).
1114. *AMF Inc. v. Sleekcraft Boats*, 599 F.2d 341, 348-349 (9th Cir. 1979).
1115. *Multi Time Mach., Inc. v. Amazon.com, Inc.*, 804 F.3d 930 (9th Cir. 2015); *Brookfield Commc'ns v. West Coast Entm't Corp.*, 174 F.3d 1036, 1054 (9th Cir.1999); *Passport Health, LLC v. Avance Health Sys.*, No. 19-1061 (4th Cir. 13 August 2020).
1116. *Uber Promotions, Inc. v. Uber Technologies, Inc.* 162 F.Supp.3d 1253 (N.D. Fla. 2016).
1117. *Tana v. Dantanna's*, 611 F.3d 767 (11th Cir. 2010).
1118. *Uber Promotions, Inc. v. Uber Technologies, Inc.* 162 F.Supp.3d 1253 (N.D. Fla. 2016).
1119. *Ibid.*
1120. *Ibid.*
1121. *Updateme Inc. v. Se*, 2017 U.S. Dist. LEXIS 195468.
1122. *Ibid.*
1123. *Ibid.*
1124. *Ibid.*
1125. *ServPro Intellectual Property, Inc. v. Blanton*, 2020 WL 1666121 (W.D. Ky. 3 April 2020).

factors.[1126] It was reiterated that the 'ultimate question remains whether relevant consumers are likely to believe that the products or services offered by the parties are affiliated in some way'.[1127] The court found that the defendant directly used[1128] the ServePro mark; however weighed the 'actual confusion'[1129] factor 'neutrally'.[1130] However, the court went on to recognise that 'most businesses advertise online'[1131] and decided that it was not enough to generally allege 'that both parties market their goods through the Internet or social media'[1132] as shown under *Tailgate Beer v. Boulevard Brewing.*[1133] The court identified that, 'to consider whether an overlap in online marketing denotes a likelihood of confusion',[1134] there are three questions that must be asked, including: '[f]irst, do the parties use the internet as a substantial marketing channel? ... [s]econd, are the parties' marks used with web-based products? ... [t]hird, do the parties' marketing channels overlap in any other way?'[1135] Further, in *RIPL v. Google,*[1136] the Sleekcraft[1137] factor of 'marketing channels'[1138] was also considered. The plaintiff claimed 'that RIPL and Ripples share the same marketing channel because the products are marketed over the internet'.[1139] However, the court decided that '[m]ere use of the internet ... is insufficient to show that the parties operate within the same marketing channel'.[1140] This was further reinforced in *Network Automation,*[1141] in which it was stated that '[t]oday, it would be the rare commercial retailer that did not advertise online, and the shared use of a ubiquitous marketing channel does not shed much light on the likelihood of consumer confusion'.[1142]

However, the Sleekcraft[1143] factors were again put to the test in *Multi Time Mach. v. Amazon.com*[1144] which also cited *Dreamwerks v. SKG*[1145] and indicated that the 'test

1126. *AMF Inc. v. Sleekcraft Boats*, 599 F.2d 341, 348-349 (9th Cir. 1979).
1127. *ServPro Intellectual Property, Inc. v. Blanton, 2020 WL 1666121* (W.D. Ky. 3 April 2020); *Daddy's Junky Music Stores, Inc. v. Big Daddy's Family Music Ctr.*, 109 F.3d 275, 280 (6th Cir. 1997).
1128. *ServPro Intellectual Property, Inc. v. Blanton*, 2020 WL 1666121 (W.D. Ky. 3 April 2020).
1129. *AMF Inc. v. Sleekcraft Boats*, 599 F.2d 341, 348–49 (9th Cir. 1979); *ServPro Intellectual Property, Inc. v. Blanton*, 2020 WL 1666121 (W.D. Ky. 3 April 2020).
1130. *ServPro Intellectual Property, Inc. v. Blanton*, 2020 WL 1666121 (W.D. Ky. 3 April 2020).
1131. *Ibid.*
1132. *ServPro Intellectual Property, Inc. v. Blanton*, 2020 WL 1666121 (W.D. Ky. 3 April 2020); *Tailgate Beer, LLC v. Boulevard Brewing Co.*, No. 3:18-CV-00563, 2019 WL 5208186, at *9 (M.D. Tenn. 16 October 2019).
1133. *Tailgate Beer, LLC v. Boulevard Brewing Co.*, No. 3:18-CV-00563, 2019 WL 5208186, (M.D. Tenn. 16 October 2019).
1134. *ServPro Intellectual Property, Inc. v. Blanton*, 2020 WL 1666121 (W.D. Ky. 3 April 2020); *Kibler v. Hall*, 843 F.3d 1068, 1079 (6th Cir. 2016).
1135. *Ibid.*
1136. *RIPL Corp. v. Google Inc.*, 2014 U.S. Dist. LEXIS 47210.
1137. *AMF Inc. v. Sleekcraft Boats*, 599 F.2d 341, 348-349 (9th Cir. 1979).
1138. *Ibid.*
1139. *RIPL Corp. v. Google Inc.*, 2014 U.S. Dist. LEXIS 47210.
1140. *Ibid.*; *Network Automation, Inc. v. Advanced Sys. Concepts*, 638 F.3d 1137.
1141. *Network Automation, Inc. v. Advanced Sys. Concepts*, 638 F.3d 1137.
1142. *Ibid.*
1143. *AMF Inc. v. Sleekcraft Boats*, 599 F.2d 341 (9th Cir. 1979).
1144. *Multi Time Mach., Inc. v. Amazon.com, Inc.*, 804 F.3d 930 (9th Cir. 2015).
1145. *Dreamwerks Prod. Group v. SKG Studio*, 142 F.3d 1127, 1129 (9th Cir. 1998).

for likelihood of confusion is whether a "reasonably prudent consumer"[1146] who, "in the marketplace is likely to be confused as to the origin of the good or service bearing one of the marks"'.[1147] In this case, Amazon's search function was at issue where consumers who searched for a 'military-style wristwatch',[1148] namely the 'MTM Special Ops',[1149] using the search terms 'mtm special ops'[1150] would be shown results for 'other brands of military style watches'.[1151] Putting '*Sleekcraft* aside',[1152] the court said that 'the ultimate test for determining likelihood of confusion'[1153] boils down to the 'reasonably prudent consumer',[1154] one who is 'in the marketplace'[1155] and 'is likely to be confused as to the origin of the goods'.[1156] Therefore, the matter would be 'resolved simply by an evaluation of the web page at issue and the relevant consumer'.[1157] The court in *Multi* Time[1158] stated that the analysis 'will turn on the answers to the following two questions: (1) Who is the relevant reasonable consumer?; and (2) What would he reasonably believe based on what he saw on the screen?'[1159] The court found in favour of Amazon, a decision which was later affirmed.[1160] *Multi* Time[1161] also made clear that the Sleekcraft[1162] factors are 'adaptable'[1163] and the 'relative importance of each individual factor will be case-specific'.[1164] Citing *Multi Time*, in

1146. *Multi Time Mach., Inc. v. Amazon.com, Inc.*, 804 F.3d 930 (9th Cir. 2015).
1147. *Dreamwerks Prod. Group v. SKG Studio*, 142 F.3d 1127, 1129 (9th Cir. 1998); *Multi Time Mach., Inc. v. Amazon.com, Inc.*, 804 F.3d 930 (9th Cir. 2015).
1148. *Ibid.*
1149. *Ibid.*
1150. *Ibid.*
1151. *Multi Time Mach., Inc. v. Amazon.com, Inc.*, 804 F.3d 930 (9th Cir. 2015).
1152. *Ibid.*
1153. *Ibid.*
1154. *Ibid.*
1155. *Ibid.*
1156. *Multi Time Mach., Inc. v. Amazon.com, Inc.*, 804 F.3d 930 (9th Cir. 2015); *Dreamwerks Prod. Group v. SKG Studio*, 142 F.3d 1127, 1129 (9th Cir. 1998).
1157. *Multi Time Mach., Inc. v. Amazon.com, Inc.*, 804 F.3d 930 (9th Cir. 2015); *Brookfield Commc'ns v. West Coast Entm't Corp.*, 174 F.3d 1036, 1054 (9th Cir.1999).
1158. *Multi Time Mach., Inc. v. Amazon.com, Inc.*, 804 F.3d 930 (9th Cir. 2015).
1159. *Ibid.*
1160. https://www.law.berkeley.edu/wp-content/uploads/2016/05/Multi-Time-Machine-v-Amazon-804_F.3d_930.pdf accessed 4 August 2025. Likewise in *USA Nutraceuticals Group, Inc. and Ultra-Lab Nutrition, Inc. v. BPI Sports, LLC et al 2016 U.S. Dist. LEXIS 21132*, search results on amazon.com were at issue. By buying some of BPI's trademarked keywords or keywords using their product names and utilising them to sell their own products, BPI alleged trademark infringement. However, in this case, a banner ad would appear as a paid advertisement when certain phrases of BPI marks or products were searched. The court confirmed that the 'essential element … is proof by the plaintiff that the alleged infringement by the defendant creates a likelihood of confusion on the part of consumers as to the source of the goods'. After applying the Eleventh Circuit factors, the court decided that BPI did not succeed in establishing confusion would result from such activity, it failed 'to demonstrate a substantial likelihood of success on the merits'.
1161. *Multi Time Mach., Inc. v. Amazon.com, Inc.*, 804 F.3d 930 (9th Cir. 2015).
1162. *AMF Inc. v. Sleekcraft Boats*, 599 F.2d 341, 348-349 (9th Cir. 1979).
1163. *Multi Time Mach., Inc. v. Amazon.com, Inc.*, 804 F.3d 930 (9th Cir. 2015); *Brookfield Commc'ns v. West Coast Entm't Corp.*, 174 F.3d 1036, 1054 (9th Cir.1999).
1164. *Ibid.*

Health v. Avance,[1165] it was argued that '[b]ecause Avance's advertisement'[1166] took 'consumers to Avance's website and not Passport's, Avance contends that any confusion from the appearance of Passport's marks'[1167] was 'ultimately dispelled'[1168] as the 'the labelling and appearance of the advertisements and the surrounding context on the screen displaying the results page'[1169] as shown in *MultiTime* and *Network Automation* which were considered relevant.[1170]

The Polaroid factors were also considered in the 2021 decision in *AM General v. Activision,*[1171] where the court found that Humvee-branded and marked trucks were utilised in the extremely popular online game, Call of Duty.[1172] While the mark was no doubt considered strong, the 'degree of similarity between the two marks'[1173] was decided in favour of the defendant based, *inter alia,* on the fact that the mark was being used 'for different purposes',[1174] and 'proximity'[1175] was not found based on the parties'[1176] very different products (even though one was a digitally depicted version of the other). The owner of the Humvee mark was not expected to 'bridge the gap'[1177] by entering the 'video game industry'[1178] and while 'some'[1179] confusion was found, this did not tantamount to 'actual confusion'.[1180] The 'good faith'[1181] factor also favoured the defendant, who was not considered to have used the mark in 'bad faith'[1182] and as to 'quality of defendant's product',[1183] no evidence was provided to support or deny this. Finally, the 'sophistication of the buyers'[1184] was considered high for Humvees and video gamers were not considered 'any less astute'.[1185] On balance, the Polaroid factors favoured Activision and their Call of Duty game. Ultimately, 'artistic freedom'[1186] was the important consideration for the motion for summary judgment

1165. *Health v. Avance Health Sys.*, 2020 U.S. App. LEXIS 25737.
1166. *Ibid.*
1167. *Ibid.*
1168. *Ibid.*
1169. *Ibid.*
1170. Which was considered an appropriate but different approach than taken by the court in *Rosetta Stone Ltd. v. Google, Inc.*, 676 F.3d 144 which included a 'nominative fair use' argument.
1171. *AM General LLC v. Activision Blizzard, Inc. and others* 1:2017cv08644 (SDNY 2020).
1172. *Ibid.*
1173. *Ibid.*
1174. *Ibid.*
1175. *Ibid.*
1176. *Ibid.*
1177. *Ibid.*
1178. *Ibid.*
1179. *Ibid.*
1180. *Ibid.*
1181. *Ibid.*
1182. *Ibid.*
1183. *Ibid.*
1184. *Ibid.*
1185. *Ibid.*
1186. *AM General LLC v. Activision Blizzard, Inc. and others* 1:2017cv08644 (SDNY 2020).

granted in this case, as will be discussed in section 3.2.7 on *Digital Justification* later in this chapter.[1187]

NFTs-related trademarks have also made their way to the U.S. courts. In the 2023 decision in *Hermes v. Rothschild,*[1188] the district court granted an injunction to stop one Rothschild from marketing MetaBirkin NFTs on the website metabirkins.com, finding, *inter alia,* that they were confusing against popularly branded physical Birkin handbags.[1189] In fact, as result of the survey put forth by Hermes, note, '18% of respondents reflected actual consumer confusion'[1190] and major magazines in the fashion industry were confused that Hermes had entered the NFT space.[1191] Confirming confusion under the Polaroid factors among other reasoning, the injunction was issued against Rothschild in order to prevent the continuation of the infringing activity.[1192] However, Gery argues that this case 'highlighted the flaws of the Polaroid factors and their singular focus on determining consumer confusion'.[1193] Another case dealing with NFTs is *Yuga Labs v. Ripps,*[1194] where the Sleekcraft factors were applied. The court found, in summary judgment proceedings, that there was a likelihood of confusion because 'the majority of the Sleekcraft factors weigh in favor of Yuga and those factors that do not weigh in favor of Yuga are neutral'.[1195] The NFTs were considered 'both conceptually and commercially strong',[1196] even though 'the NFT market is relatively new'. Also, 'recognition'[1197] and 'significant goodwill'[1198] had been established and were considered 'one of the top-selling and highest-valued NFT collections and Yuga has used its BAYC Marks to brand this success in connection with Yuga's website, events, social media pages, marketing, partnerships, products, and services'.[1199] The court found that 'the conflicting marks are identical or virtually identical'[1200] and that they were similar in 'sight, sound, and meaning'.[1201] The defendants 'knowingly and intentionally used'[1202] the marks in question and both parties used the same 'marketing channels',[1203] namely the 'same NFT marketplaces ("OpenSea and x2y2") and social

1187. *Ibid.* The Polaroid factors were used to assess the second prong of the *Rogers v. Grimaldi*, 875 F.2d 994 (2d Cir. 1989) test relating to the U.S. First Amendment which is discussed later in this chapter in the section Digital Justification.
1188. *Hermes Int'l v. Rothschild*, 22-cv-384 (JSR) (S.D.N.Y. 23 June 2023).
1189. *Ibid.*
1190. *Ibid.*
1191. *Ibid.*
1192. *Ibid.*
1193. Michelle Gery, 'Understanding the MetaBirkin: Trademark Law and an Appropriate Legal Standard for NFTs' (20 September 2024) Columbia Journal of Law & the Arts https://doi.org/10.52214/jla.v47i4.13098.
1194. CourtListerner, 'Yuga Labs Inc. v. Ripps, C.D. Cal., No. 2:22-cv-04355, Summary Judgment 4/21/23' https://storage.courtlistener.com/recap/gov.uscourts.cacd.855658/gov.uscourts.cacd.855658.225.0.pdf accessed January 2024.
1195. *Ibid.*
1196. *Ibid.*
1197. *Ibid.*
1198. *Ibid.*
1199. *Ibid.*
1200. *Ibid.*
1201. *Ibid.*
1202. *Ibid.*
1203. *Ibid.*

media (Twitter) to promote them'.[1204] The 'specialized knowledge'[1205] required to authenticate NFTs was used to show that the purchasers would have confusion identifying them as different. Expansion of 'product lines'[1206] was not considered dispositive.[1207] However, in 2025, the 9th Circuit reversed the 'grant of summary judgment for Yuga on its trademark-infringement and cybersquatting claims because it has not proven as a matter of law that Defendants' actions are likely to cause consumer confusion'.[1208]

Other jurisdictions, in line with TRIPS, have a 'likelihood of confusion' provision.[1209] The UK, under the Trade Marks Act 1994 (as amended), likewise considers infringement where 'there exists a likelihood of confusion on the part of the public, which includes the likelihood of association with the trademark'.[1210] In the UK case of *Match Group v. Muzmatch,*[1211] where a reputable dating service alleged that the use of keyphrases related to match support 'likelihood of confusion'.[1212] While there was little evidence of 'actual confusion', this did not prevent a finding of 'likelihood of confusion'.[1213] In Canada, confusion[1214] is prohibited under section 6 of the Canadian Trademarks Act and being 'confusing with another trademark'[1215] is prohibited.[1216] In a recent opposition proceeding, in *Greater Edmonton v. Tappcar,*[1217] the opponent owned the marks 'TAPP, TAPP YOUR CAB and TAPP YOUR RIDE, in word and design form'[1218] and utilised these 'in association with goods and services including taxi services'.[1219] The applicant wished to register the mark, 'TAPPCAR'[1220] and the Board continued with a confusion[1221] analysis under section 6 of the Canadian Trademarks Act, remarking that the list was 'not exhaustive and different weight will be given to each one in a context specific assessment'.[1222] It also made reference to the test in

1204. *Ibid.*
1205. *Ibid.*
1206. *Ibid.*
1207. *Ibid.*
1208. *Yuga Labs, Inc. v. Ripps*, Case No. 24-879, 2025 WL 2056060 (9th Cir. 23 July 2025).
1209. Paris Convention, Art. 6bis; TRIPS, Art. 16(1); EUTMR, Art. 8(1)(b) and Art. 9(2)(b); 15 U.S. Code § 1114;15 U.S. Code § 1125.
1210. UK Trade Marks Act 1995, s. 10(2).
1211. *Match Group v. Muzmatch* [2022] EWHC 941 (IPEC).
1212. Yana Zhou, Adelin Weber Bain and Hannah Cramp 'Overview of United Kingdom Trade Mark, Design and Copyright Cases 2022' (2023) 54 International Review of Intellectual Property and Competition Law 412-430 https://doi.org/10.1007/s40319-023-01303-0.
1213. *Ibid.*
1214. Canadian Trademarks Act R.S.C., 1985, c. T-13, s. 6.
1215. *Ibid.*
1216. In Canada, the factors to assess confusion under 6(5) include: '*(a) the inherent distinctiveness of the trademarks or trade names and the extent to which they have become known; (b) the length of time the trademarks or trade names have been in use; (c) the nature of the goods, services or business; (d) the nature of the trade; and (e) the degree of resemblance between the trademarks or trade names, including in appearance or sound or in the ideas suggested by them*'.
1217. *Greater Edmonton Taxi Service Inc. v. Tappcar Inc.*, 2021 TMOB 158 (CanLII).
1218. *Ibid.*
1219. *Ibid.*
1220. *Ibid.*
1221. *Ibid.*
1222. *Ibid.*; *Mattel, Inc v. 3894207 Canada Inc*, 2006 SCC 22, [2006] 1 SCR 772 (SCC).

Veuve v. Boutiques[1223] which was 'a casual consumer somewhat in a hurry who sees the [mark] at a time when he or she has no more than an imperfect recollection of the [prior] trademarks and does not pause to give the matter any detailed consideration or scrutiny, nor to examine closely the similarities and differences between the marks'.[1224] The 'probability of confusion'[1225] was found based on 'all of the surrounding circumstances, and in particular the high degree of resemblance between the trademarks' as well as the fact that the services were 'related'.[1226] It was found that 'at best the probability of confusion'[1227] was 'evenly balanced between a finding of confusion and no confusion'[1228] though, due to the 'onus'[1229] being 'on the [a]pplicant to demonstrate on a balance of probabilities that there is no reasonable likelihood of confusion between the marks',[1230] the case was decided 'against the [a]pplicant'[1231] and the application to register the mark was refused.[1232]

From the above, it appears that there are some common principles that apply to a confusion[1233] analysis, even if the standards for confusion may be confusing in themselves.[1234] Like the EU, the US uses a factor approach to a confusion

1223. *Veuve Clicquot Ponsardin v. Boutiques Cliquot Ltée*, 2006 SCC 23 (CanLII), [2006] 1 SCR 824.
1224. *Ibid.*
1225. *Ibid.*
1226. *Greater Edmonton Taxi Service Inc. v. Tappcar Inc.*, 2021 TMOB 158 (CanLII). Based on the above factors and test, the marks were considered to 'possess a limited degree of inherent distinctiveness' because they were 'highly suggestive of goods and services related to the acquisition of transportation services (by car or cab) through a mobile application (ie, through the tap of an app)'. The 'extent known and length of time in use' factor weighed 'only slightly' in favour of the [o]pponent. Relating to the '[n]ature of the goods, services, or business, and trade' factors, it was found that 'the parties' goods, services, and business' were 'sufficiently related'. One of the key factors was that there was 'a significant degree of resemblance between the parties' marks as the most striking element' was considered 'identical'. However, what is surprising is the reference to the applicant's 'business model' being 'innovation-based' in that a mobile app in 2021 was still considered to be offering of 'newer technologies' which made it different. In relation to the 'degree of resemblance' factor, 'the most striking element of the [o]pponent's trademark' was considered 'to be the prefix TAPP' because the term 'CAB' was considered 'descriptive of the [o]pponent's taxi services'. The term 'YOUR' was considered 'simply a pronoun' which assisted 'to form the phrase'. In relation to the mark applied for, it was likewise found that 'the most striking element was 'the prefix TAPP' with the term 'CAR' being 'similarly descriptive of the [a]pplicant's taxi and transportation services, and suggestive of the character of the [a]pplicant's computer software insofar as it is relates to the coordination of transportation by car'. There was 'a significant degree of resemblance between the parties' marks' because 'the most striking element in both marks' was considered 'identical'. In relation to 'the ideas suggested', it was found that both marks were a 'play on words' since they 'suggest' that the consumer would 'tap' the 'app' in order 'to obtain car transportation services'. Although, the court stated that 'there can be no monopoly in this idea'. *Greater Edmonton Taxi Service Inc. v. Tappcar Inc.*, 2021 TMOB 158 (CanLII).
1227. *Greater Edmonton Taxi Service Inc. v. Tappcar Inc.*, 2021 TMOB 158 (CanLII).
1228. *Ibid.*
1229. *Ibid.*
1230. *Ibid.*
1231. *Ibid.*
1232. *Ibid.*
1233. Paris Convention, Art. 6bis; TRIPS, Art. 16(1); EUTMR, Art. 8(1)(b) and Art. 9(2)(b); 15 U.S. Code § 1114;15 U.S. Code § 1125.
1234. Graeme W Austin, 'Tolerating Confusion About Confusion: Trademark Policies and Fair Use', 50 Arizona Law Review 157, 160 (2008).

analysis.[1235] Some common or similar factors appear to include the similarity/relatedness of goods,[1236] strength/distinctiveness of the earlier/plaintiffs mark,[1237] and similarity of the marks/comparison of signs[1238] and platforms should consider adopting some of these in their own analysis.

3.2.3.3 Summary of Platform Considerations for Digital Confusion

As noted by García-Pérez, '[t]he concept of risk of confusion has a prominent role in any trademark system'.[1239] Platforms should consider applying a form of a confusion[1240] test, as does the UDRP.[1241] They may be informed by key aspects of the 'confusion theory'[1242] and some key factors as commonly used by the jurisdictions, despite the confusion surrounding confusion[1243] on the Internet. While some jurisdictions use different confusion concepts, platforms should consider the 'likelihood of

1235. C-39/97, *Canon*, EU:C:1998:442; EUIPO, '3.4.1 Fact and Law: Similarity of Goods/Services and of Signs' (*EUIPO Trade mark guidelines* 2024) https://guidelines.euipo.europa.eu/2214311/2046921/trade-mark-guidelines/3-4-1-fact-and-law-%E2%80%94-similarity-of-goods-services-and-of-signs accessed July 2024; EUIPO, '3.4.1 Fact and Law: Similarity of Goods/Services and of Signs' (*EUIPO Trade mark guidelines* 2024) https://guidelines.euipo.europa.eu/2214311/2135996/trade-mark-guidelines/3-1-1-similarity-factors accessed July 2024; *Joseph Phelps Vineyards, LLC v. Fairmont Holdings LLC*, 857 F.3d 1323, 122 U.S.P.Q.2d 1733 (Fed. Cir. 2017); J Thomas McCarthy, 'Commentary: Trademark Strength and Fame - The Federal Circuit Corrects the Trademark Trial and Appeal Board' (14 October 2018) http://dx.doi.org/10.2139/ssrn.3266138; Mark Bartholomew et al., 'A New Addition to the Trademark Litigator's Tool Kit: A Neuroscientific Index of Mark Similarity' (2023) 113 The Trademark Reporter 785, 792 https://www.inta.org/wp-content/uploads/public-files/resources/the-trademark-reporter/TMR-Vol-113-No-6-November-December-2023_12182023-Secured.pdf accessed July 2024.
1236. *Ibid.*
1237. *Ibid.*
1238. *Ibid.*
1239. Rafael García-Pérez, 'Some Certainties and Some Uncertainties in European Union Trade Mark Law' (2023) 72 GRUR International 1018, 1020 https://doi.org/10.1093/grurint/ikad087.
1240. Paris Convention, Art. 6bis; TRIPS, Art. 16(1); EUTMR, Art. 8(1)(b) and Art. 9(2)(b); 15 U.S. Code § 1114;15 U.S. Code § 1125.
1241. UDRP, 4(a)(i).
1242. Ilanah Fhima and Dev S Gangjee, 'Assessing Likelihood of Confusion', *The Confusion Test in European Trade Mark Law* (New York, 2019; online edn, Oxford Academic) 160-203 https://doi.org/10.1093/oso/9780199674336.003.0006; Graeme B Dinwoodie and Mark D Janis, 'Confusion Over Use: Contextualism in Trademark Law' (2007) 92 Iowa Law Review 1597; Mark P McKenna, 'A Consumer Decision-Making Theory of Trademark Law' 98 Virginia Law Review 67; William M Landes and Richard A Posner, 'Trademark Law: An Economic Perspective' (1987) 30 The Journal of Law and Economics 265 https://doi.org/10.1086/467138; Lisa L Ouellette, 'The Google Shortcut to Trademark Law' (2014) 102 California Law Review 351; Lisa L Ouellette, 'The Google Shortcut to Trademark Law' (2014) 102 California Law Review 351, 358.
1243. Graeme W Austin, 'Tolerating Confusion About Confusion: Trademark Policies and Fair Use' (2008) 50 Arizona Law Review 157.

confusion'[1244] as the common thread and as implemented by the UDRP, incorporating 'confusing similarity'.[1245] Platforms should consider rejecting confusion concepts[1246] which are not commonly used in jurisdictions in favour of common confusion principles,[1247] such as the similarity/relatedness of goods,[1248] strength/distinctiveness of the earlier/plaintiffs mark,[1249] and similarity of the marks/comparison of signs.[1250] Some common factors should be considered in the overall analysis and explained in guidance.

3.2.4 Digital Unfair Competition

Unfair competition,[1251] including unfair acts,[1252] trade practices,[1253] and unfair competition[1254] on the Internet, raises many considerations for policies/platforms and includes a number of related concepts. This section first introduces unfair competition theory[1255] and the prohibition against unfair competition[1256] and the related concept of passing off,[1257] while also linking this to relevant theories/concepts of marketing &

1244. Paris Convention, Art. 6bis; TRIPS, Art. 16(1); EUTMR, Art. 8(1)(b) and Art. 9(2)(b); 15 U.S. Code § 1114;15 U.S. Code § 1125.
1245. UDRP, 4(a)(i).
1246. Ilanah Fhima and Dev S Gangjee, 'Assessing Likelihood of Confusion', *The Confusion Test in European Trade Mark Law* (New York, 2019; online edn, Oxford Academic) 160 https://doi .org/10.1093/oso/9780199674336.003.0006.
1247. Paris Convention, Art. 6bis; TRIPS, Art. 16(1); EUTMR, Art. 8(1)(b) and Art. 9(2)(b); 15 U.S. Code § 1114;15 U.S. Code § 1125.
1248. *Ibid.*
1249. *Ibid.*
1250. *Ibid.*
1251. *Ibid.*
1252. Anselm Kamperman Sanders, *Unfair Competition Law: The Protection of Intellectual and Industrial Creativity* (Oxford University Press, 1997) 8; Frauke Henning-Bodewig, *Unfair Competition Law European Union and Member States* (Kluwer Law International 2006) xv-xvi; Martin Senftleben, Michael Handler and Irene Calboli, 'Protection Against Unfair Competition Around the Globe' (2024) 19 Journal of Intellectual Property Law & Practice 79, 79-80 https://doi.org/10.1093/jiplp/jpad121; Paris Convention, Art. 10bis; EUTMR, Art. 9(2)(c); 15 U.S.C. § 1125(c)(2)(B).
1253. *Ibid.*
1254. *Ibid.*
1255. Anselm Kamperman Sanders, *Unfair Competition Law: The Protection of Intellectual and Industrial Creativity* (Oxford University Press 1997) 6-10; Anselm Kamperman Sanders, 'A Consumer Trademark: protection Based on Origin and Quality' (1993) 15 European Intellectual Property Review 406; Anselm Kamperman Sanders, 'Unfair Competition and Ethics' in Spyros M Maniatis and Lionel Bently (eds), *Intellectual Property and Ethics* (Sweet & Maxwell 1998) 227-230.
1256. *Ibid.*
1257. Ethan Horwitz and Benjamin Levi, 'Fifty Years of the Lanham Act: A Retrospective of Section 43(a)E' (1996) 7 Fordham Intellectual Property, Media and Entertainment Law Journal Article 6; David Bainbridge, *Intellectual Property* (Pearson Education Limited 2018) Chapter 30; EUTMR, Art. 17(2); 15 U.S.C. §1125.

branding,[1258] comparative advertising,[1259] as well as symbols & signs.[1260] Following this, other related concepts are established, including famous,[1261] well-known,[1262] reputable,[1263] strong,[1264] and marks with goodwill.[1265] Then, dilution theory,[1266] unfair advantage,[1267] free riding,[1268] and misappropriation[1269] are covered. Finally, distinctiveness[1270] is reviewed. In all, there are linkages and inter-relations between the various aspects covered in this section, and are therefore collectively summarised as titled, *Digital Unfair Competition*. These raise various considerations for the UDRP and platforms, which will then be summarised.

3.2.4.1 *Unfair Competition Theory and Prohibition, Passing Off, Comparative Advertising, Marketing & Branding, and Symbols & Signs*

Trademark law can be seen as a narrow body of tort law and Kamperman Sanders analysed 'unfair competition'[1271] to a great extent, from an economics

1258. Angsar Ohly, '"Buy Me Because I'm Cool": The "Marketing Approach" and the Overlap Between Design, Trade Mark and Unfair Competition Law' in Annette Kur, Marianne Levin and Jens Schovsbo (eds), *The EU Design Approach: A Global Appraisal* (Edward Elgar 2018) 108-141.
1259. Michal Bohaczewski, *Special Protection of Trade Marks with a Reputation under European Union Law* (Kluwer Law International 2020) §2.02.
1260. Barton Beebe, 'The Semiotic Account of Trademark Doctrine and Trademark Culture' in Graeme B Dinwoodie and Mark D Janis (eds), *Trademark Law and Theory: A Handbook of Contemporary Research* (Edward Elgar, 2008) 42.
1261. Stefan Martin, 'Well Known Marks and Parody: Dilution and Denigration? Unfair Advantage?' (*EUIPO*, 2017), https://euipo.europa.eu/knowledge/pluginfile.php/77920/mod_resource/content/8/Limits%20of%20trade%20marks%2C%20Parody%2018-5-2017.pdf accessed January 2024.
1262. *Ibid.*
1263. EUTMR, Arts 8(5) and 9(1)(c).
1264. Timothy D Greene and Jeff Wilkerson, 'Understanding Trademark Strength' (2013) 16 Stanford Technology Law Review 535-582, abstract.
1265. TTAB USPTO, 'Fighting Bad Faith Trademark Filings in the United States' https://www.jpo.go.jp/e/news/kokusai/tm5/document/bad_faith_seminar2/01.pdf accessed January 2024.
1266. Anselm Kamperman Sanders, 'Odol: The Introduction of a Watery Concept with Steeled Resilience' in Christopher Heath and Anselm Kamperman Sanders (eds), *Landmark Intellectual Property Cases and Their Legacy* (Wolters Kluwer 2011) 51-56; Graeme B Dinwoodie, 'Dilution as Unfair Competition: European Echoes' in Rochelle C Dreyfuss and Jane C Ginsburg (eds) *Intellectual Property at the Edge: The Contested Contours of IP* (Cambridge University Press 2014) 100; Frank I Schechter, 'The Rational Basis of Trademark Protection' (1927) 40 Harvard Law Review 813 https://doi.org/10.2307/1330367;15 U.S. Code § 1125(c); Keola R Whitaker, 'Trademark Dilution in a Global Age' (2006) 27 University of Pennsylvania Journal of International Economic Law 907.
1267. EUTMR, Art. 9(2)(c); 15 U.S.C. § 1125(c)(2)(B).
1268. Josef Drexl and Anselm Kamperman Sanders (eds), *The Innovation Society and Intellectual Property*, European Intellectual Property Institutes Network series (Edward Elgar Publishing 2019) 146-159.
1269. David Barnes, 'Misappropriation of Trademark' (2008) 9 North Carolina Journal of Law & Technology 171.
1270. EUTMR, Recital 21.
1271. Anselm Kamperman Sanders, *Unfair Competition Law: The Protection of Intellectual and Industrial Creativity* (Oxford University Press 1997) 6-10; Anselm Kamperman Sanders, 'A

perspective.[1272] He looked at the nature of the remedies provided for 'free riding on the back of another's achievement'[1273] and 'appropriating and building on others' achievements'.[1274] This is a very important theory because it pervades the basic notions of the trademark itself and puts it into the context of competition, in which environment trademarks may be utilised in platforms.[1275] For example, trademarks can be utilised in a competitive setting and often assist one business to distinguish[1276] themselves from their competitors. When one's labour[1277] results in some sort of 'achievement',[1278] this may be taken advantage of by others.[1279] Specifically, in this regard, Kamperman Sanders notes that '[w]here exploitation of another's achievements becomes inequitable, unfair competition law acts provides a remedy'.[1280] For example, 'the taking of fruits of another's industry and investment is unjust enrichment and parasitic competition'.[1281]

Also, 'the law of unfair competition is primarily comprised of torts that cause economic injury to a business through a deceptive or wrongful business practice'[1282] and Port argues that trademarks should be seen through the eyes of tort law rather than 'property'.[1283] It is of course recognised that a common example of unfair competition[1284] is that which is done in relation to trademarks.[1285] Landes and Posner indicate

---

Consumer Trademark: protection Based on Origin and Quality' (1993) 15 European Intellectual Property Review 406; Anselm Kamperman Sanders, 'Unfair Competition and Ethics' in Spyros M Maniatis and Lionel Bently (eds), *Intellectual Property and Ethics* (Sweet & Maxwell 1998) 227-230.

1272. *Ibid.*
1273. WIPO 'Protection Against Unfair Competition: Analysis of the Present World Situation' (*Geneva WIPO Publication No. 725(E)* 1994) 54 https://tind.wipo.int/record/20405/files/wipo_pub_725_en_protection_against_unfair_competition.pdf?ln=en accessed July 2024; Anselm Kamperman Sanders, *Unfair Competition Law: The Protection of Intellectual and Industrial Creativity* (Oxford University Press 1997) 6-10.
1274. Anselm Kamperman Sanders, *Unfair Competition Law: The Protection of Intellectual and Industrial Creativity* (Oxford University Press 1997) 6-10.
1275. WIPO, 'WIPO Overview of WIPO Panel Views on Selected UDRP Questions, Third Edition' ('WIPO Jurisprudential Overview 3.0') (*WIPO*, 2017) https://www.wipo.int/amc/en/domains/search/overview3.0/ accessed June 2025; Facebook, 'Facebook Terms of Service' (*Facebook*) https://www.facebook.com/legal/terms; Instagram, 'Trademark' (*Instagram Help Center Trademark*) https://help.instagram.com/222826637847963.
1276. TRIPS, Art. 15; Paris Convention, Art. 6bis.
1277. The Bridge, 'Economic Analysis of Intellectual Property' (*Berkman Klein Center*) https://cyber.harvard.edu/bridge/LawEconomics/ip.htm accessed January 2024.
1278. Anselm Kamperman Sanders, *Unfair Competition Law: The Protection of Intellectual and Industrial Creativity* (Oxford University Press 1997) 6-10.
1279. *Ibid.*
1280. Anselm Kamperman Sanders, *Unfair Competition Law: The Protection of Intellectual and Industrial Creativity* (Oxford University Press 1997) 8.
1281. Anselm Kamperman Sanders, *Unfair Competition Law: The Protection of Intellectual and Industrial Creativity* (Oxford University Press 1997) 29.
1282. Cornell LII, 'Unfair Competition' (*Legal Information Institute*) https://www.law.cornell.edu/wex/unfair_competition accessed January 2024.
1283. Kenneth L Port, 'The "Unnatural" Expansion of Trademark Rights: Is a Federal Dilution Statute Necessary?' 18 Seton Hall Legislative Journal 433 in Peter S Menell, 'Intellectual Property General Theories' 157 https://reference.findlaw.com/lawandeconomics/1600-intellectual-property-general-theories.pdf accessed 4 August 2025.
1284. *Ibid.*
1285. *Ibid.*

that in 'some respects trademark law is closer to tort law'[1286] and especially under 'unfair competition'.[1287] Importantly, Kamperman Sanders notes that the legislation pertaining to 'unfair competition'[1288] considers 'the functioning of the free market as a whole'[1289] as opposed to traditional intellectual property entitlements. Even though in the early days, Schechter challenged the adequacy of passing off[1290] for purposes of trademark protection,[1291] unfair competition[1292] has since developed into a way 'to ensure that free and fair competition is maintained'.[1293] The notion at the time was that, only where there is direct competition, can there be trademark protection under 'unfair competition'.[1294]

Riffel concludes that there is a 'line of argument put forward when the doc-trine of unfair competition is employed to fill gaps in the intellectual property system due to the occurrence of new technology'.[1295] This is especially relevant in the context of the Internet because it consistently raises new considerations. The doctrine's 'flexibility makes it a suitable remedy for the solution of unsettled legal problems, such as when novel technologies emerge'.[1296] Riffel believes that '[u]nfair competition law thus appears to be a preliminary stage to intellectual property protection'.[1297] He argues that '[b]y filling lacunae in the intellectual property system, it offers a legal basis to fit new needs'.[1298] New needs[1299] may be raised consistently in the Internet environment and

1286. William M Landes and Richard A Posner, *The Economic Structure of Intellectual Property Law* (Harvard University Press, 2009) 166.
1287. *Ibid.*
1288. Anselm Kamperman Sanders, 'Unfair Competition: Complementary or Alternative to Intellectual Property in the EU?' in Christophe Geiger (ed.), *Constructing European Intellectual Property* (Edward Elgar Publishing, 2013) 329, abstract.
1289. *Ibid.*
1290. Frank I Schechter, 'The Rational Basis of Trademark Protection' (1927) 40 Harvard Law Review 813 https://doi.org/10.2307/1330367; Jeremy N Sheff, 'The (Boundedly) Rational Basis of Trademark Liability' (2007) 15 Texas Intellectual Property Law Journal 331, 334.
1291. *Ibid.*
1292. Anselm Kamperman Sanders, *Unfair Competition Law: The Protection of Intellectual and Industrial Creativity* (Oxford University Press 1997) 6-10.
1293. Anselm Kamperman Sanders, 'Unfair Competition: Complementary or Alternative to Intellectual Property in the EU?' in Christophe Geiger (ed.), *Constructing European Intellectual Property* (Edward Elgar Publishing, 2013) 329, abstract.
1294. Rudolf Callmann, 'Trade-Mark Infringement and Unfair Competition' (1949) 14 Law and Contemporary Problems 185 https://doi.org/10.2307/1189831 http://scholarship.law.duke.edu/cgi/viewcontent.cgi?article=2403&context=lcp accessed 4 August 2025.
1295. Christian Riffel, *Protection Against Unfair Competition in the WTO TRIPS Agreement: The Scope and Prospects of Article 10bis of the Paris Convention for the Protection of Industrial Property* (Brill 2016) 223-224.
1296. Christian Riffel, *Protection Against Unfair Competition in the WTO TRIPS Agreement: The Scope and Prospects of Article 10bis of the Paris Convention for the Protection of Industrial Property* (Brill 2016) 22.
1297. *Ibid.*; Anselm Kamperman Sanders, *Unfair Competition Law: The Protection of Intellectual and Industrial Creativity* (Oxford University Press 1997) 6-10.
1298. Christian Riffel, *Protection Against Unfair Competition in the WTO TRIPS Agreement: The Scope and Prospects of Article 10bis of the Paris Convention for the Protection of Industrial Property* (Brill 2016) 23.
1299. *Ibid.*

'unfair competition'[1300] is an important basis on which remedies may be sought. The doctrine of 'unfair competition'[1301] covers a wide variety of possibilities, including, as Riffel notes, 'misdirecting a rival's customers to one's own internet homepage'.[1302] At the same time, generally in the context of 'unfair competition',[1303] Ohly recognises that drawing 'a line between what is fair and what is unfair is notoriously difficult',[1304] which is especially true in relation to digital trademarks.

Ohly says that 'trademark law also creates an incentive for producers to offer high-quality or high-reputation products'.[1305] Further, as aptly noted by Tyagi in the context of innovation by digital platforms, '[i]nnovation laws, most notably intellectual property law, and competition law offer an important impetus to ... innovation, by offering the right and balanced set of incentives for firms to innovate'.[1306] These incentives and impetus result in new products and innovation demanded by consumers.[1307] Taking 'unfair advantage',[1308] misappropriating,[1309] acting 'detrimental to',[1310] or engaging in 'free riding'[1311] of reputable,[1312] and distinctive[1313] marks are important

1300. Anselm Kamperman Sanders, *Unfair Competition Law: The Protection of Intellectual and Industrial Creativity* (Oxford University Press 1997) 6-10.
1301. Anselm Kamperman Sanders, *Unfair Competition Law: The Protection of Intellectual and Industrial Creativity* (Oxford University Press 1997) 1.
1302. Christian Riffel, *Protection Against Unfair Competition in the WTO TRIPS Agreement: The Scope and Prospects of Article 10bis of the Paris Convention for the Protection of Industrial Property* (Brill 2016) 3.
1303. *Ibid.*
1304. Angsar Ohly, '"Buy Me Because I'm Cool": The "Marketing Approach" and the Overlap Between Design, Trade Mark and Unfair Competition Law' in Annette Kur, Marianne Levin and Jens Schovsbo (eds), *The EU Design Approach: A Global Appraisal* (Edward Elgar 2018) 131.
1305. Angsar Ohly, '"Buy Me Because I'm Cool": The "Marketing Approach" and the Overlap Between Design, Trade Mark and Unfair Competition Law' in Annette Kur, Marianne Levin and Jens Schovsbo (eds), *The EU Design Approach: A Global Appraisal* (Edward Elgar 2018) 113.
1306. Kalpana Tyagi, 'Content, Competition, and Data' in Kalpana Tyagi, Anselm Kamperman Sanders and Caroline Cauffman (eds) *Digital Platforms, Competition Law, and Regulation* (Hart Publishing 2024) 241.
1307. Angsar Ohly, '"Buy Me Because I'm Cool": The "Marketing Approach" and the Overlap Between Design, Trade Mark and Unfair Competition Law' in Annette Kur, Marianne Levin and Jens Schovsbo (eds), *The EU Design Approach: A Global Appraisal* (Edward Elgar 2018) 113; Kalpana Tyagi, 'Content, Competition, and Data' in Kalpana Tyagi, Anselm Kamperman Sanders and Caroline Cauffman (eds) *Digital Platforms, Competition Law, and Regulation* (Hart Publishing 2024) 241.
1308. EUTMR, Art. 9(2)(c).
1309. David Barnes, 'Misappropriation of Trademark' (2008) 9 North Carolina Journal of Law & Technology 171.
1310. EUTMR, Art. 9(2)(c).
1311. Angsar Ohly, 'Free-Riding on the Repute on Trademarks: Does Protection Generate Innovation?' in Josef Drexl and Anselm Kamperman Sanders (eds), *The Innovation Society and Intellectual Property, European Intellectual Property Institutes Network series* (Edward Elgar Publishing 2019) 146.
1312. EUTMR, Art. 9(1)(c).
1313. *Ibid.*

considerations. Kamperman Sanders persuasively concludes that 'our economic development'[1314] as well as 'our culture'[1315] is conditioned 'upon appropriating and building on others' achievements'.[1316] He says, '[w]here exploitation of another's achievements becomes inequitable, unfair competition law ... provides a remedy'.[1317] It is important for certain concepts related to unfair acts[1318] to be incorporated by platforms in this regard.

Ohly further says that unfair competition law responds to marketing aspects[1319] and expands on the crucial relationship between marketing and 'unfair competition'.[1320] Ohly recognises that in 'modern marketing, trademarks also convey messages of lifestyle, which have be-come more and more detached from the identity of the manufacturer or even the qualities of the product'.[1321] He says that the law 'has developed well beyond a mere protection device for indications of source'.[1322] Sachdev notes that platforms and increasing smart environments have great potential for digital marketing[1323] and trademarks may be widely used in these forums. One relevant way of looking at marketing theory is through the 'branding'[1324] perspective, in which

1314. Christian Riffel, *Protection Against Unfair Competition in the WTO TRIPS Agreement: The Scope and Prospects of Article 10bis of the Paris Convention for the Protection of Industrial Property* (Brill 2016) 213; Anselm Kamperman Sanders, *Unfair Competition Law: The Protection of Intellectual and Industrial Creativity* (Oxford University Press 1997) 6-10.
1315. *Ibid.*
1316. *Ibid.*
1317. Anselm Kamperman Sanders, *Unfair Competition Law: The Protection of Intellectual and Industrial Creativity* (Oxford University Press 1997) 6-10; Christian Riffel, *Protection Against Unfair Competition in the WTO TRIPS Agreement: The Scope and Prospects of Article 10bis of the Paris Convention for the Protection of Industrial Property* (Brill 2016) 224.
1318. Anselm Kamperman Sanders, *Unfair Competition Law: The Protection of Intellectual and Industrial Creativity* (Oxford University Press, 1997) 8; Frauke Henning-Bodewig, *Unfair Competition Law European Union and Member States* (Kluwer Law International 2006) xv-xvi; Martin Senftleben, Michael Handler and Irene Calboli, 'Protection Against Unfair Competition Around the Globe' (2024) 19 Journal of Intellectual Property Law & Practice 79, 79-80 https://doi.org/10.1093/jiplp/jpad121; Paris Convention, Art. 10bis; EUTMR, Art. 9(2)(c); 15 U.S.C. § 1125(c)(2)(B).
1319. Angsar Ohly, '"Buy Me Because I'm Cool": The "Marketing Approach" and the Overlap Between Design, Trade Mark and Unfair Competition Law' in Annette Kur, Marianne Levin and Jens Schovsbo (eds), *The EU Design Approach: A Global Appraisal* (Edward Elgar 2018) 108-141.
1320. *Ibid.*
1321. Angsar Ohly, '"Buy Me Because I'm Cool": The "Marketing Approach" and the Overlap Between Design, Trade Mark and Unfair Competition Law' in Annette Kur, Marianne Levin and Jens Schovsbo (eds), *The EU Design Approach: A Global Appraisal* (Edward Elgar 2018) 117.
1322. Angsar Ohly, '"Buy Me Because I'm Cool": The "Marketing Approach" and the Overlap Between Design, Trade Mark and Unfair Competition Law' in Annette Kur, Marianne Levin and Jens Schovsbo (eds), *The EU Design Approach: A Global Appraisal* (Edward Elgar 2018) 140-141.
1323. Raj Sachdev, *Digital Marketing* (McGraw Hill, 2024).
1324. Devan R Desai, 'From Trademarks to Brands' (2012) 64 Florida Law Review 981; Jonathan E Schroeder, 'Brand Culture: Trade Marks, Marketing and Consumption' in Lionel Bently, Jennifer Davis and Jane C Ginsburg (eds), *Trade Marks and Brands: An Interdisciplinary Critique* (Cambridge University Press 2008) 161; Apostolos Chronopoulos, 'Legal and Economic Arguments for the Protection of Advertising Value Through Trade Mark Law' (2014) 4 Queen Mary Journal of Intellectual Property 256 https://doi.org/10.4337/qmjip.2014.04.01.

trademarks may be recognised as brands,[1325] even if not all brands are protected trademarks. Also, to protect value in a brand through 'unfair competition',[1326] it is important to protect 'achievements'[1327] which may be a possible result of marketing activity, such as 'sustained investment in the advertising value and reputation'.[1328] Kamperman Sanders says, from an advertising perspective, that there is emphasis placed on the 'recognition of the enhanced advertising function of the trademark over the traditional origin function'.[1329] This is plausible because this serious function of marks should not be able to be taken advantage of without recourse. Desai formulated the brand theory,[1330] arguing that 'trademark law is blinkered and confused'[1331] and as a result does not address 'all the interests at stake in the modern business environment'.[1332] He argues that a trademark is a brand and the focus on that is lost.[1333] He opines that marks go beyond an 'information-based understanding'[1334] to one that highlights marks as 'information resources for all stakeholders in a brand'.[1335] This theory can help bring the law of trademark 'into the information age'.[1336] Griffiths shows that trademarks have extensive importance in the field of marketing as they can be utilised to 'stimulate or strengthen specific demand for its goods and services'.[1337] Menell, Lemley, Merges and Balganesh say that marks enhance possibilities of implementing 'efficient new business models, such as franchising, which generate economies of scale and scope in marketing'[1338] and may also enhance business growth spanning large regions.[1339] As one major function of the trademark is for marketing purposes, this may be protected, as one means, through 'unfair competition'.[1340] At the

1325. Devan R Desai, 'From Trademarks to Brands' (2012) 64 Florida Law Review 981; Jonathan E Schroeder, 'Brand Culture: Trade Marks, Marketing and Consumption' in Lionel Bently, Jennifer Davis and Jane C Ginsburg (eds), *Trade Marks and Brands: An Interdisciplinary Critique* (Cambridge University Press 2008) 161; Apostolos Chronopoulos, 'Legal and Economic Arguments for the Protection of Advertising Value Through Trade Mark Law' (2014) 4 Queen Mary Journal of Intellectual Property 256 https://doi.org/10.4337/qmjip.2014.04.01.
1326. Anselm Kamperman Sanders, *Unfair Competition Law: The Protection of Intellectual and Industrial Creativity* (Oxford University Press 1997) 6-10.
1327. Anselm Kamperman Sanders, *Unfair Competition Law: The Protection of Intellectual and Industrial Creativity* (Oxford University Press 1997) 107-110.
1328. *Ibid.*; Apostolos Chronopoulos, 'Legal and Economic Arguments for the Protection of Advertising Value Through Trade Mark Law' (2014) 4 Queen Mary Journal of Intellectual Property 256 https://doi.org/10.4337/qmjip.2014.04.01.
1329. Anselm Kamperman Sanders and Spyros M Maniatis, 'A Consumer Trade Mark: Protection Based on origin and Quality' (1993) 15 European Intellectual Property Review 406 in Anselm Kamperman Sanders, *Unfair Competition Law: The Protection of Intellectual and Industrial Creativity* (Oxford University Press 1997) 107.
1330. Devan R Desai, 'From Trademarks to Brands' (2012) 64 Florida Law Review 981.
1331. *Ibid.*
1332. *Ibid.*
1333. *Ibid.*
1334. *Ibid.*
1335. *Ibid.*
1336. *Ibid.*
1337. Andrew Griffiths, *An Economics Perspective on Trade Mark Law* (Edward Elgar, 2011) 1.
1338. Peter S Menell et al., *Intellectual Property in the New Technological Age: 2020* (Clause 8 Publishing 2020) 27.
1339. *Ibid.*
1340. Anselm Kamperman Sanders, *Unfair Competition Law: The Protection of Intellectual and Industrial Creativity* (Oxford University Press 1997).

same time, consumers are bombarded with 'signs and symbols'[1341] related to marketing every day. Sheltering of trademarks is essentially 'the law's recognition of the psychological function of symbols'.[1342] There is no doubt that '[i]f it is true that we live by symbols, it is no less true that we purchase goods by them'.[1343] Beebe argues that 'economic theories'[1344] need to be complemented by a 'semiotic account'[1345] which incorporates 'consumers' demand'[1346] for 'signs',[1347] 'distinctions'[1348] and 'differences'.[1349] Signs and symbols also have relation to the larger discussion on 'search costs',[1350] where decisions can be made by consumers based upon these.[1351] However, this can also result in 'irrational behaviour'[1352] on the part of the consumer, such as paying a higher price based on the 'reputation'[1353] of the trademark (including as a symbol or sign)[1354] without consideration to quality.[1355] Thus, trademarks may be protected, given the psychological function that they also play.[1356] This function promotes the fact that a sign may play a larger role than other factors in determining how consumers react to trademarks. For example, a sign may provide the necessary psychological element to making a decision on the part of a consumer.[1357] They may

1341. Mooij MKde, *Global Marketing and Advertising: Understanding Cultural Paradoxes* (SAGE 2010) 54.
1342. *Mishawaka Rubber & Woolen Mfg, Co, v. S.S, Kresge Co.*, 316 US 203, 205 (1942) in Jeremy N Sheff, 'The (Boundedly) Rational Basis of Trademark Liability' (2007) 15 Texas Intellectual Property Law Journal 331, 335.
1343. *Mishawaka Rubber & Woolen Mfg, Co, v. S.S, Kresge Co.*, 316 US 203, 205 (1942) in Jeremy N Sheff, 'The (Boundedly) Rational Basis of Trademark Liability' (2007) 15 Texas Intellectual Property Law Journal 331, 334.
1344. Barton Beebe, 'The Semiotic Account of Trademark Doctrine and Trademark Culture' in Graeme B Dinwoodie and Mark D Janis (eds), *Trademark Law and Theory: A Handbook of Contemporary Research* (Edward Elgar, 2008) 42, 64; Lisa L Ouellette, 'The Google Shortcut to Trademark Law' (2014) 102 California Law Review 351.
1345. *Ibid.*
1346. *Ibid.*
1347. *Ibid.*
1348. *Ibid.*
1349. *Ibid.*
1350. William M Landes and Richard A Posner, 'Trademark Law: An Economic Perspective' (1987) 30 The Journal of Law and Economics 265 https://doi.org/10.1086/467138; Stacey L Dogan and Mark A Lemley, 'Trademarks and Consumer Search Costs on the Internet' (2004) 41 Houston Law Review 777; Graeme B Dinwoodie and Mark D Janis, *Trademark Law and Theory: A Handbook of Contemporary Research* (Edward Elgar, 2008) 65.
1351. *Ibid.*
1352. A Samuel Oddi, 'Consumer Motivation in Trademark and Unfair Competition Law: On the Importance of Source' (1986) 31 Villanova Law Review 1, 5; Hanne Kirk, 'How to Prove Use and Reputation' (*IP Case Law Conference,* May 2016) https://euipo.europa.eu/tunnel-web/secure/webdav/guest/document_library/contentPdfs/law_and_practice/mediation/IP_CL_Conference_05-05-2016/Hanne_Kirk_en.pdf accessed 4 August 2025.
1353. *Ibid.*
1354. Anselm Kamperman Sanders, *Unfair Competition Law: The Protection of Intellectual and Industrial Creativity* (Oxford University Press 1997) 41.
1355. Anselm Kamperman Sanders and Spyros M Maniatis, 'A Consumer Trade Mark: Protection Based on Origin and Quality' (Sweet & Maxwell 1993) 11 European Intellectual Property Review 406.
1356. A Samuel Oddi, 'Consumer Motivation in Trademark and Unfair Competition Law: On the Importance of Source' (1986) 31 Villanova Law Review 1.
1357. Judith L Zaichkowsky, *The Psychology Behind Trademark Infringement and Counterfeiting* (Taylor & Francis 2006) Chapter 2.

choose to purchase something (or not) on the basis of a sign.[1358] Unfair acts[1359] may lead consumers to make a decision they did not intend. However, Gangjee aptly recognises the changing times in marketing where '[c]urrent research views consumers and other intermediaries as active partners or co-creators of brand significance'[1360] and that this 'suggests that brand formation is dialogic and iterative, as opposed to being the result of a one-way broadcast'.[1361] This raises the point that consumers may be partners in the making of a brand and brands may need to recognise this joint effort.[1362]

Unfair competition[1363] is specifically covered under Article 10bis of the Paris Convention, which states that: '[a]ny act of competition contrary to honest practices in industrial or commercial matters constitutes an act of unfair competition'.[1364] Thus, it should be a fundamental consideration for policies/platforms.

In the EU, an action may be made under the 'civil liability and unfair competition'[1365] law of the Member State.[1366] Also, 'comparative advertising that presents the advertiser's products as an imitation of a product bearing a trademark is inconsistent with fair competition and thus unlawful'.[1367] Further, 'false allegations ... as to discredit'[1368] and where utilisation of a mark would 'mislead the public'[1369] are also prohibited.

In the context of cybersquatting, and although there is no specific cybersquatting legislation at the EU level (other than for.eu domains),[1370] national laws of the Member States have addressed the issue from the perspective of trademark infringement, unfair competition',[1371] and/or 'passing off'.[1372] Bainbridge says that this has been 'very useful in controlling'[1373] it. Even though this work does not generally delve into specific

1358. *Ibid.*
1359. *Ibid.*
1360. Dev Gangjee and Jonathan Griffiths, 'Property in Brands: The Commodification of Conversation' in Helena R. Howe (ed.) *Concepts of Property in Intellectual Property Law* (Cambridge University Press 2013) 29, 58.
1361. *Ibid.*
1362. *Ibid.*
1363. Anselm Kamperman Sanders, *Unfair Competition Law: The Protection of Intellectual and Industrial Creativity* (Oxford University Press 1997) 6-10; EUTMR, Art. 8(5).
1364. Paris Convention for the Protection of Industrial Property, Art. 10bis.
1365. EUTMR, Art. 17.
1366. At the EU level, and while not a main focus of this research, it should be noted that the Digital Services Act (DSA) is intended, *inter alia,* to combat counterfeiting, and Digital Market Act (DMA) to allow inter-operation and contracting outside of a platform and puts into place various measures to reach that goal to such platforms to which it they apply. *See* European Commission, 'The Digital Services Act package' (*European Commission*) https://digital-strategy.ec.europa.eu/en/policies/digital-services-act-package accessed July 2024.
1367. C-324/09 *L'Oreal SA v. eBay International AG* [2012] Bus. L.R. 1369 (ECLI:EU:C:2011:474).
1368. *Ibid.*
1369. Paris Convention for the Protection of Industrial Property, Art. 10bis.
1370. Regulation (EU) 2019/517 of the European Parliament and of the Council of 19 March 2019 on the implementation and functioning of the .eu top-level domain name.
1371. CMS, 'Protection of Trade Marks: Online Use and Anticybersquatting a European Perspective' (*CMS,* March 2007) https://www.cms-lawnow.com/~/media/lawnow/pdfs/cms%20publications/sector%20specific%20publications/tmc/ip/cmsanticybersquattingguide.pdf accessed January 2024.
1372. David Bainbridge, *Intellectual Property* (Pearson Education Limited 2018) Chapter 30.
1373. *Ibid.*

Member State law, it is nevertheless useful to provide a brief overview of how some Member States have addressed the issue of cybersquatting. For example, the Belgian Code of Economic Law Article XII.22 prohibits registering domain names 'in which no right or legitimate interest can be invoked, with the intent to harm a third party or to obtain an unfair advantage, if that domain name is identical with or similar to such an extent that it may create confusion with, amongst others, a trademark ... belonging to someone else'.[1374] Further, under Article XII.23, the above Article 'shall be applied without prejudice to other legal provisions, such as any legal provision protecting trademarks ... as well as any legal provision concerning unfair competition, market practices and the information and protection of the consumer'.[1375] In Germany, a specific law does not exist,[1376] although cybersquatting claims may be filed under sections 14 and 15 of the 'German Trademark Act',[1377] section 12 of the 'German Civil Code',[1378] sections 3, 4, and 5 of the 'German Act Against Unfair Competition'[1379] or under tort law sections 823 and 826 of the 'German Civil Code'.[1380] Likewise, there is no specific cybersquatting legislation in the Netherlands, however, 'domaingrabbing'[1381] which is 'the registration of a domain name with the intention of selling it to the owner of a corresponding trademark or trade name or of misleadingly diverting Internet users to the website offered under the domain name (for instance through typosquatting)',[1382] may be claimed under trademark law, for example, under Article 2.20 of the Benelux Convention on Intellectual Property (BCIP)[1383] or a claim may be made under the general law of torts.[1384] Thus, several Member States do have mechanisms to address cybersquatting, although they may encompass specific provisions and peculiarities and even though general cybersquatting is not specifically covered under EU law.

In the US, 'unfair competition'[1385] is legislated federally under 15 U.S. Code § 1125 and is also a matter of state law.[1386] A common law claim may be made through

1374. Johan Vandendriessche, 'Belgian Code of Economic Law: Book XII. The Law of the Electronic Economy Unofficial English Translation: Consolidated Version' (*SAS University of London Open Journals*) https://journals.sas.ac.uk/deeslr/article/download/2315/2266/3540 accessed July 2024.
1375. *Ibid.*
1376. Torsten Bettinger, 'GERMANY (".de")' in Torsten Bettinger and Allegra Waddell (eds) *Domain Name Law And Practice: An International Handbook* (Oxford University Press 2015) 359-453 https://academic.oup.com/book/41089 accessed July 2024.
1377. *Ibid.*
1378. *Ibid.*
1379. *Ibid.*
1380. *Ibid.*
1381. Adonna Alkema, 'Netherlands (".nl")' in Torsten Bettinger and Allegra Waddell (eds) *Domain Name Law And Practice: An International Handbook* (Oxford University Press 2015) 359-453 https://academic.oup.com/book/41089 accessed July 2024.
1382. *Ibid.*
1383. *Ibid.*
1384. *Ibid.*
1385. Anselm Kamperman Sanders, *Unfair Competition Law: The Protection of Intellectual and Industrial Creativity* (Oxford University Press 1997) 6-10.
1386. Cornell LII, 'Unfair Competition' (*Legal Information Institute*) https://www.law.cornell.edu/wex/unfair_competition#:~:text=The%20law%20of%20unfair%20competition%20is%20mainly%20governed%20by%20state,1125%20of%20the%20Lanham%20Act. accessed

'an action of deceit'.[1387] Previously considered 'passing off'[1388] legislation, Horwitz and Levi note that 15 U.S. Code § 1125 'has increased in scope to include infringement of common law marks, trade dress infringement, and false advertising – including trade libel and product disparagement'.[1389] Various types of claims may be made under the Lanham Act and its scope has been expanded beyond 'passing off'.[1390] On a federal level, there is a relationship between 'unfair competition'[1391] law and trademark law more generally. For example, under 15 U.S. Code § 1125, the activities envisioned are similar to 'unfair competition'[1392] law more generally and even though 'unfair competition'[1393] is not specifically mentioned by name, the provisions are considered 'unfair competition'.[1394] In *Two Pesos v. Taco Cabana*,[1395] it was indicated that the Lanham Act's 'protection of trademarks and of trade dress'[1396] has 'the same statutory purpose of preventing deception and unfair competition'.[1397] Welch and Schwimmer note that the issue with 15 U.S. Code § 1125 is that it 'includes both the false association and the false advertising prongs that comprise federal unfair competition, in a single sentence'.[1398] Likewise, Bone argues 'for eliminating the distinction and applying a unitary approach'[1399] and that '[c]ourts should craft injunctions in all trademark cases based on the competing interests and policies at stake'.[1400] He says that '[t]he high litigation

January 2024. It should be noted that the FTC Act, the Sherman Antitrust Act of 1890 15 U.S. Code §§ 1-38 together with the Clayton Antitrust Act of 1914 15 U.S. Code § 12 form the major federal antitrust laws (*See* FTC, 'The Antitrust Laws' (*Federal Trade Commission*, 15 December 2017) https://www.ftc.gov/tips-advice/competition-guidance/guide-antitrust-laws/antitrust-laws accessed January 2024; William M Landes and Richard A Posner, 'Market Power in Antitrust Cases' (March 1981) 94 Harvard Law Review 937 https://doi.org/10.2307/1340687.

1387. Peter Groves, *Sourcebook on Intellectual Property* (Routeledge 1997) 516; Zechariah Chafee Jr, 'Does Equity Follow the Law of Torts?' (1926) 75 University of Pennsylvania Law Review and American Law Register 1 https://doi.org/10.2307/3307903.
1388. Ethan Horwitz and Benjamin Levi, 'Fifty Years of the Lanham Act: A Retrospective of Section 43(a)E' (1996) 7 Fordham Intellectual Property, Media and Entertainment Law Journal 6.
1389. *Ibid.*
1390. *Ibid.*
1391. *Ibid.*
1392. *Ibid.*
1393. *Ibid.*
1394. Cornell LII, 'Unfair Competition' (*Legal Information Institute*) https://www.law.cornell.edu/wex/unfair_competition#:~:text=The%20law%20of%20unfair%20competition%20is%20mainly%20governed%20by%20state,1125%20of%20the%20Lanham%20Act. accessed January 2024.
1395. *Two Pesos, Inc. v. Taco Cabana, Inc.*, 505 U.S. 763 (1992).
1396. *Ibid.*
1397. *Ibid.*
1398. John L Welch and Martin B Schwimmer, 'US Law Inches Towards Protecting Trademark Reputation Without Use' (*World Trademark Review Lexology*, 1 October 2019) https://www.lexology.com/library/detail.aspx?g=312238ac-bf71-4053-991f-e43cb756985b accessed January 2024. Note that the court in *Lexmark Int'l, Inc. v. Static Control Components, Inc.*, 572 U.S. 118 instituted a new test with respect to false advertising under 15 U.S. Code § 1125(a) and stated that to 'come within the zone of interests in a suit for false advertising' under the Act, 'a plaintiff must allege an injury to a commercial interest in reputation or sales'.
1399. Robert G Bone, 'Rights and Remedies in Trademark Law: The Curious Distinction between Trademark Infringement and Unfair Competition' (2020) 98 Texas Law Review 1187.
1400. *Ibid.*

costs and risks of trademark cases can chill socially desirable uses ... and innovative uses of marks on the internet'.[1401]

Specifically, under 15 U.S. Code § 1125(a), 'any false designation of origin, false or misleading description of fact, or false or misleading representation of fact, which ... is likely to cause confusion, or to cause mistake, or to deceive as to the affiliation, connection, or association of such person with another person, or as to the origin, sponsorship, or approval of his or her goods, services, or commercial activities by another person, or ... in commercial advertising or promotion, misrepresents the nature, characteristics, qualities, or geographic origin of his or her or another person's goods, services, or commercial activities'[1402] may result in civil liability.[1403]

Outfit 7 v. Nanjing[1404] related to mobile apps. It was commented that, 'there's no exact case law on whether the Lanham Act's counterfeiting sections explicitly apply to mobile apps - nonphysical products that have existed for only a few years'.[1405] However, the above case 'might have been one of the first to address that question'.[1406] Outfit, owner of the 'Talking Tom'[1407] and 'Friends'[1408] mobile app games, found apps by others, including 'Talking Tom 3'[1409] and 'Talking Tom 4',[1410] available in mobile app stores and successfully sued for trademark infringement.[1411] The judgment in that case 'shows that courts are willing to find companies like NanJing liable under the Lanham Act's counterfeit rules for pushing fake apps'.[1412] It 'broke new ground'[1413] outside of copyright law and was based on the 'counterfeiting provision of the Lanham Act'.[1414] It was noted that 'the language of the provision on its face'[1415] is 'not limited to physical products'.[1416] Therefore, it would appear that newer technologies are being

1401. *Ibid.*
1402. 15 U.S. Code § 1125(a)(1)(B).
1403. 15 U.S. Code § 1125(a)(1).
1404. *Out Fit 7 Limited et al v. NanJing Oooo3D Information Technology Co. LTD,* case No. 3:13-cv-00050 in the U.S. District Court for the Northern District of California.
1405. Law360, 'Out Fit 7 Limited et al v. NanJing Oooo3D Information Technology Co. LTD, case number 3:13-cv-00050' in Bill Donahue, 'Mobile Apps the New Frontier for Counterfeiting' (*Law360,* 5 March 2014) http://www.law360.com/articles/515464/mobile-apps-the-new-frontier-for-counterfeiting accessed January 2024.
1406. Law360, 'Out Fit 7 Limited et al v. NanJing Oooo3D Information Technology Co. LTD, case number 3:13-cv-00050' in Bill Donahue, 'Mobile Apps the New Frontier for Counterfeiting' (*Law360,* 5 March 2014) http://www.law360.com/articles/515464/mobile-apps-the-new-frontier-for-counterfeiting accessed January 2024; Outfit7, 'Outfit7 Celebrates Legal Win Against Counterfeit App Publisher in China' (*OUTFIT7*) https://outfit7.com/2014/02/outfit7-celebrates-legal-win-against-counterfeit-app-publisher-in-china/ accessed January 2024.
1407. Law360, 'Out Fit 7 Limited et al v. NanJing Oooo3D Information Technology Co. LTD, case number 3:13-cv-00050' in Bill Donahue, 'Mobile Apps the New Frontier for Counterfeiting' (*Law360,* 5 March 2014) http://www.law360.com/articles/515464/mobile-apps-the-new-frontier-for-counterfeiting accessed January 2024.
1408. *Ibid.*
1409. *Ibid.*
1410. *Ibid.*
1411. *Ibid.*
1412. *Ibid.*
1413. *Ibid.*
1414. *Ibid.*
1415. *Ibid.*
1416. *Ibid.*

treated similarly to traditional situations. It was also commented, however, that '[s]ometimes it's just easier to rely on the terms and conditions, or the user policy, of the particular site'[1417] or in this case, mobile apps. In *Tichy v. Hyatt,*[1418] the court noted in relation to an '[o]nline [t]ravel [a]gency'[1419] that 'it's economically irrational to restrict [such agency] from competitive keyword ads'.[1420] It indicated that this offers a 'second chance'[1421] opportunity 'to win the customer's business'.[1422] Goldman says '[h]owever, the court acknowledges that vertical ad restrictions aren't as inherently anti-competitive as horizontal restrictions'.[1423] This case further exemplifies that search advertising contains various angles and the difficulty in assessing trademarks from the perspective of unfair competition[1424] principles as applied to the trademark context.

Another relevant area of consideration is comparative advertising.[1425] As stated in the most recent trademark guidelines issued by the EUIPO and in *L'Oreal v. eBay,*[1426] 'comparative advertising that presents the advertiser's products as an imitation of a product bearing a trademark is inconsistent with fair competition and thus unlawful'.[1427] These state that 'any advantage gained by the advertiser through such advertising will have been achieved as a result of unfair competition and must be regarded as taking unfair advantage of the reputation of that mark'.[1428] In the 2004 WIPO Intellectual Property Handbook: Policy, Law and Use,[1429] the three examples of 'unfair competition'[1430] provided under Article 10bis of the Paris Convention are explained to include the possibility of creating confusion in relation to competitors,[1431] 'false allegations ... as to discredit'[1432] (recognising that it is up to the Member States to

1417. *Ibid.*
1418. *Tichy v. Hyatt Hotels Corp.*, 2019 WL 1318674 (N.D. Ill. 22 March 2019).
1419. Eric Goldman, 'Rounding Up Three Recent Keyword Advertising Cases–*Comphy v. Amazon & More*' (*Eric Goldman* 29 March 2019) https://blog.ericgoldman.org/archives/2019/03/rounding-up-three-recent-keyword-advertising-cases-comphy-v-amazon-more.htm accessed January 2024.
1420. *Tichy v. Hyatt Hotels Corp.*, 2019 WL 1318674 (N.D. Ill. 22 March 2019); Eric Goldman, 'Rounding Up Three Recent Keyword Advertising Cases–Comphy v. Amazon & More' (*Eric Goldman,* 29 March 2019) https://blog.ericgoldman.org/archives/2019/03/rounding-up-three-recent-keyword-advertising-cases-comphy-v-amazon-more.htm accessed January 2024.
1421. *Ibid.*
1422. *Ibid.*
1423. *Ibid.*
1424. *Ibid.*
1425. Michal Bohaczewski, *Special Protection of Trade Marks with a Reputation under European Union Law* (Kluwer Law International 2020) §2.02.
1426. Case C-324/09 *L'Oreal SA v. eBay International AG* 1369 EU:C:2011:474.
1427. *Ibid.*
1428. *Ibid.*
1429. WIPO, 'WIPO Intellectual Property Handbook: Policy, Law and Use' 2nd edn (*WIPO*, 2004) 259 https://tind.wipo.int/record/28661?ln = en&v = pdf accessed 4 August 2025.
1430. Paris Convention, Art. 10bis.
1431. *Ibid.*
1432. *Ibid.*

interpret and apply this)[1433] and where it would 'mislead the public'[1434] from a consumer protection perspective.[1435] This is a 'non-exhaustive list'[1436] and it is important to note that there is a 'continuing evolution of provisions governing the practice of comparative advertising'.[1437] On the Internet, comparative adverting[1438] may take place in many forums and such provisions should include Internet-specific considerations. An illustrative case, although not specifically Internet-related, is *L'Oréal and Others,*[1439] which clarified 'advantage taken unfairly'[1440] with respect to a reputable mark.[1441] It was explained that the 'advantage arising from the use by a third party of a sign similar to a mark with a reputation is an advantage taken unfairly by that third party of the distinctive character or the repute of that mark where that party seeks by that use to ride on the coat-tails of the mark with a reputation in order to benefit from the power of attraction, the reputation and the prestige of that mark and to exploit, without paying any financial compensation, the marketing effort expended by the proprietor of the mark in order to create and maintain the mark's image'.[1442] Importantly, Kamperman Sanders notes that this case links 'trademark law and the law on comparative advertising'[1443] and concludes that the 'case highlighted the dividing lines in European thinking on the role of unfair competition in trademark law'.[1444]

In fact, some of these principles are laid down in the Misleading and Comparative Advertising Directive,[1445] which recognises the 'exclusive rights'[1446] of mark holders in Recital 13, the importance of 'making reference to a trademark'[1447] in 'comparative advertising'[1448] in Recital 14, and provides protection for those using mark of others in comparative advertising under conditions laid out in the Directive.[1449] Specifically, Article 4 of the Directive prohibits comparative advertising that will 'discredit or

1433. WIPO, 'WIPO Intellectual Property Handbook: Policy, Law and Use' 2nd edn (*WIPO*, 2004) 259 https://tind.wipo.int/record/28661?ln = en&v = pdf accessed 4 August 2025.
1434. Paris Convention, Art. 10bis.
1435. WIPO, 'WIPO Intellectual Property Handbook: Policy, Law and Use' 2nd edn (*WIPO*, 2004) 259 https://tind.wipo.int/record/28661?ln = en&v = pdf accessed 4 August 2025.
1436. *Ibid.*
1437. *Ibid.*
1438. Michal Bohaczewski, *Special Protection of Trade Marks with a Reputation under European Union Law* (Kluwer Law International 2020) §2.02.
1439. Case C-487/07 *L'Oréal and Others* EU:C:2009:378.
1440. *Ibid.*
1441. *Ibid.*
1442. *Ibid.*
1443. Anselm Kamperman Sanders, 'The Legacy of Odol: Cross-Atlantic Parallel Import' in Christopher Heath and Anselm Kamperman Sanders (eds), *Landmark Intellectual Property Cases and Their Legacy* (Kluwer Law International 2011) 58.
1444. Anselm Kamperman Sanders, 'The Legacy of Odol: Cross-Atlantic Parallel Import' in Christopher Heath and Anselm Kamperman Sanders (eds), *Landmark Intellectual Property Cases and Their Legacy* (Kluwer Law International 2011) 58-59.
1445. Directive 2006/114/EC of the European Parliament and of the Council of 12 December 2006 concerning misleading and comparative advertising.
1446. *Ibid.*
1447. *Ibid.*
1448. *Ibid.*
1449. *Ibid.*

denigrate'[1450] the trademark (but also covers 'trade names' and more)[1451] or such comparative advertising that will 'take unfair advantage of the reputation of a trademark',[1452] that which presents 'imitations or replicas'[1453] of goods or services 'bearing a protected trademark'[1454] or creates 'confusion'.[1455] Similarly, the Unfair Commercial Practices Directive (aimed at consumers), under Article 6, prohibits 'any marketing of a product, including comparative advertising, which creates confusion with any products, trademarks ... of a competitor'[1456] and Article 3a covers similar provisions on comparative advertising to the Misleading and Comparative Advertising Directive.[1457] While a detailed analysis of the above Directives is beyond the scope of this work, the above clearly recognise relevant principles.

From the US perspective, based on the intersection between unfair competition[1458] and antitrust principles,[1459] in *1-800 CONTACTS v. FTC,*[1460] the respondent brief argues that the 'central question in this case is whether the competing sellers may agree to limit the comparative advertisements consumers see under the guise of protecting their trademarked names'.[1461] The initial matter at issue alleged that '1-800 Contacts and its competitors entered into agreements which prevented the other online contact lens retailers from bidding for search engine keywords in advertising auctions conducted by internet search engines, such as Google and Yahoo'.[1462] The Federal Trade Commission (FTC) found that the actions complained of 'violated Section 5 of the FTC Act and harmed competition in bidding for search engine keywords and by artificially reducing the prices that 1-800 Contacts pays as well as the quality of search engine results delivered to consumers'.[1463] It is interesting how the 'quality of search

1450. *Ibid.*
1451. *Ibid.*
1452. *Ibid.*
1453. *Ibid.*
1454. *Ibid.*
1455. *Ibid.*
1456. Directive 2005/29/EC of the European Parliament and of the Council of 11 May 2005 concerning unfair business-to-consumer commercial practices in the internal market and amending Council Directive 84/450/EEC, Directives 97/7/EC, 98/27/EC and 2002/65/EC of the European Parliament and of the Council and Regulation (EC) No. 2006/2004 of the European Parliament and of the Council ('Unfair Commercial Practices Directive').
1457. *Ibid.*; Directive 2006/114/EC of the European Parliament and of the Council of 12 December 2006 concerning misleading and comparative advertising.
1458. FTC, '1-800 Contacts, Inc, in the Matter of' (*FTC Cases and Proceedings* 6 August 2021) https://www.ftc.gov/legal-library/browse/cases-proceedings/141-0200-1-800-contacts-inc-matter accessed July 2024.
1459. *Ibid.*
1460. *1-800 Contacts, Inc. v. Federal Trade Commission*, 2021 WL 2385274, Case No. 18-3848 (2nd Cir. 11 June 2021).
1461. FTC, 'Brief of the Federal Trade Commission (Final Form) 1-800 CONTACTS, *INC. v. FTC* Case 18-3848, Document 153, 10/07/2019, 2674661' (*FTC*, 10 July 2019) https://www.ftc.gov/system/files/documents/cases/1-800_contacts_ca2_ftc_answering_brief_10-7-19.pdf accessed January 2024.
1462. Antitrust Advocate, '1-800 Contacts Settles Class Action Lawsuit with Roots in FTC Action' (*Lexology*) https://www.lexology.com/library/detail.aspx?g=e1d6a951-7a3f-4cbb-825d-3b5cc423c0d8 accessed January 2024.
1463. *Ibid.*

engine results'[1464] would be a factor under consideration, as it does not appear that the enforcement body specifically regulates quality other than where violation occurs under the Act. On appeal to the Second Circuit Court of Appeals[1465] 1-800 Contacts challenges, *inter alia*, that 'the Commission's decision to avoid a full analysis of competitive effects by both invoking the presumptively unlawful standard and, concluding, in the alternative, that a restriction on advertising that is the result of a bona fide assertion of trademark rights is sufficient to establish competitive harm'.[1466] In vacating the FTC decision, the Court said that 'while trademark settlements are not immune from antitrust scrutiny, the FTC improperly deemed'[1467] that these agreements were 'inherently suspect'[1468] and erroneously decided that they were against the 'rule of reason'[1469] under antitrust law. The Court reiterated 'the procompetitive benefits of trademark enforcement'[1470] and clarified that the FTC's decision was 'antithetical to the procompetitive goals of trademark policy'.[1471]

In the context of other jurisdictions, as Gangjee confirms, that while the 'UK lacks a unified legal basis', it 'offers up an unfair competition menu consisting of individual torts or equitable wrongs (primarily passing off, injurious falsehood, defamation and the breach of confidence), the prohibition of misleading practices under consumer protection law, trademark law and codes of advertising regulation'.[1472] Further, he opines that 'their cumulative coverage, these regimes overlap considerably with the protection available under civilian unfair competition regimes'.[1473] In Canada, 'unfair competition'[1474] is directly prohibited as specified in section 7 of the Canadian Trademarks Act, including making a 'false and misleading statement'[1475] and prohibition against passing off.[1476] If an imposter passes off[1477] as a mark holder while displaying a mark for financial gain, this may be prevented.

1464. *Ibid.*
1465. FTC, 'Brief of the Federal Trade Commission (Final Form) 1-800 CONTACTS, INC. v. FTC Case 18-3848, Document 153, 10/07/2019, 2674661' (*FTC*, 10 July 2019) https://www.ftc.gov/system/files/documents/cases/1-800_contacts_ca2_ftc_answering_brief_10-7-19.pdf accessed January 2024; Antitrust Advocate, '1-800 Contacts Settles Class Action Lawsuit With Roots in FTC Action' (*Lexology*) https://www.lexology.com/library/detail.aspx?g=e1d6a951-7a3f-4cbb-825d-3b5cc423c0d8 accessed January 2024.
1466. Gregory Battersby and Charles Grimes (eds), *2020 Licensing Update* (Wolters Kluwer 2020) 13.
1467. *1-800 Contacts, Inc. v. Federal Trade Commission*, 2021 WL 2385274, Case No. 18-3848 (2nd Cir. 11 June 2021).
1468. *Ibid.*
1469. *Ibid.*
1470. *Ibid.*
1471. *Ibid.*
1472. Dev Saif Gangjee, 'Law(s) Against Unfair Competition: The Legitimacy of the UK Approach' (2024) 19 Journal of Intellectual Property Law & Practice 90 https://doi.org/10.1093/jiplp/jpad105.
1473. *Ibid.*
1474. Canadian Trademarks Act R.S.C., 1985, c. T-13, s. 7.
1475. *Ibid.*
1476. *Ibid.*
1477. Anselm Kamperman Sanders, *Unfair Competition Law: The Protection of Intellectual and Industrial Creativity* (Oxford University Press 1997) 134-136; Hossein Bidgoli, *The Internet Encyclopedia* (John Wiley & Sons, vol. 3, 2004) 452.

Platforms should consider common principles pertinent to 'unfair acts',[1478] trade practices,[1479] or 'unfair competition'[1480] and incorporate this directly into their policies if not already considered. Even if a specific concept is not legislated in various jurisdictions, the umbrella term 'unfair competition'[1481] appears to be inclusive of the different types of related unfair actions[1482] that might exist across jurisdictions.[1483] Because the analysis can be considered beyond one of confusion,[1484] it is imperative to specifically consider spelling out a related provision. Specifically, actions such as 'passing off'[1485] should be prohibited. As much digital marketing is conducted within all platforms considered, it is crucial to ensure 'unfair competition'[1486] is incorporated in the analysis based on the connection between these.[1487] Comparative advertising should be permitted conditionally within bounds.

3.2.4.2 *Famous, Well-Known, Reputable, Strong, and Marks with Goodwill*

Ramsey surmises that on certain social media sites, 'users may be more likely to believe false statements of identity and authorship, and rely to their detriment on the imposter's expression'.[1488] A marks 'reputation may be harmed by the third party's disclosure of untruthful information, or posts that are offensive or inappropriate'.[1489] However, as noted by García-Pérez, the CJ 'has established that trademark law does not protect signs with a reputation against their mere evocation',[1490] even if this is done online. Ohly says that 'trademark law also creates an incentive for producers to offer

1478. EUTMR, Art. 9(2)(c) and Art. 17(2); 15 U.S.C. §1125.
1479. Anselm Kamperman Sanders, *Unfair Competition Law: The Protection of Intellectual and Industrial Creativity* (Oxford University Press 1997) 134-136; Hossein Bidgoli, *The Internet Encyclopedia* (John Wiley & Sons, vol. 3, 2004) 452.
1480. Anselm Kamperman Sanders, *Unfair Competition Law: The Protection of Intellectual and Industrial Creativity* (Oxford University Press, 1997) 8; EUTMR, Art. 9(2)(c) and Art. 17(2); 15 U.S.C. §1125.
1481. *Ibid.*
1482. *Ibid.*
1483. *Ibid.*
1484. Paris Convention, Art. 6bis; TRIPS, Art. 16(1); EUTMR, Art. 8(1)(b) and Art. 9(2)(b); 15 U.S. Code § 1114;15 U.S. Code § 1125.
1485. EUTMR, Art. 17(2); 15 U.S.C. §1125.
1486. Anselm Kamperman Sanders, *Unfair Competition Law: The Protection of Intellectual and Industrial Creativity* (Oxford University Press, 1997) 8; EUTMR, Art. 9(2)(c) and Art. 17(2); 15 U.S.C. §1125.
1487. Angsar Ohly, '"Buy Me Because I'm Cool": The "Marketing Approach" and the Overlap Between Design, Trade Mark and Unfair Competition Law' in Annette Kur, Marianne Levin and Jens Schovsbo (eds), *The EU Design Approach: A Global Appraisal* (Edward Elgar 2018) 108-141.
1488. Lisa P Ramsey, 'Brandjacking on Social Networks: Trademark Infringement by Impersonation of Markholders' (2010) 58 Buffalo Law Review 851, 856.
1489. *Ibid.*
1490. Rafael García-Pérez, 'Some Certainties and Some Uncertainties in European Union Trade Mark Law' (2023) 72 GRUR International 1018, 1022 https://doi.org/10.1093/grurint/ikad087.

high-quality or high-reputation products'[1491] and this reputation may be harmed online.

Under 6bis of the Paris Convention:

> (1) The countries of the Union undertake, ex officio if their legislation so permits, or at the request of an interested party, to refuse or to cancel the registration, and to prohibit the use, of a trademark which constitutes a reproduction, an imitation, or a translation, liable to create confusion, of a mark considered by the competent authority of the country of registration or use to be well known in that country as being already the mark of a person entitled to the benefits of this Convention and used for identical or similar goods. These provisions shall also apply when the essential part of the mark constitutes a reproduction of any such well-known mark or an imitation liable to create confusion therewith.
> (2) A period of at least five years from the date of registration shall be allowed for requesting the cancellation of such a mark. The countries of the Union may provide for a period within which the prohibition of use must be requested.
> (3) No time limit shall be fixed for requesting the cancellation or the prohibition of the use of marks registered or used in bad faith.[1492]

Article 16(2) TRIPS says:

> Article 6bis of the Paris Convention (1967) shall apply, mutatis mutandis, to services. In determining whether a trademark is well-known, Members shall take account of the knowledge of the trademark in the relevant sector of the public, including knowledge in the Member concerned which has been obtained as a result of the promotion of the trademark.[1493]

In the EU, 'well known'[1494] marks, 'highly renowned marks'[1495] and 'marks with market recognition'[1496] may be given additional protection. For example, 'well known'[1497] marks with greater distinctiveness[1498] will generally be afforded more protection.[1499] This is 'provided the earlier mark has developed a reputation'[1500] and this is in line with the provision that all Member States must 'provide protection

1491. Angsar Ohly, '"Buy Me Because I'm Cool": The "Marketing Approach" and the Overlap Between Design, Trade Mark and Unfair Competition Law' in Annette Kur, Marianne Levin and Jens Schovsbo (eds), *The EU Design Approach: A Global Appraisal* (Edward Elgar 2018) 113.
1492. Paris Convention, Art. 6bis.
1493. TRIPS, Art. 16(1).
1494. EUTMR, Art. 8; Paris Convention, Art. 6bis.
1495. Stefan Martin, 'Limits of Trade Marks: Parody' (*EUIPO – Boards of Appeal*, 31 January 2017) https://euipo.europa.eu/knowledge/course/view.php?id = 2844 accessed January 2024.
1496. *Ibid.*
1497. EUTMR, Art. 8(2)(c).
1498. EUTMR, Arts 8 and 9.
1499. Frouke Hekker, 'Nina Ricci and the Importance of Trademark Reputation' (*The Impact of Fake News: Economy – part 2 – Lexology*, 9 January 2017) https://www.lexology.com/library/detail.aspx?g = 38ba13ed-57d9-4e21-ab27-c5ec4b70e552 accessed January 2024.
1500. Anne-Laure Covin and Edward J Fennesey, *Trademarks Throughout the World* (Thomson West 2007) §54:18.

without use for well known marks'.[1501] Article 8(2)(c) EUTMR permits opposition by the owner of an 'earlier mark'[1502] which is 'well known in a Member State, in the sense in which the words 'well known' are used in Article 6*bis* of the Paris Convention'.[1503] However, in addition to the term 'well known'[1504] in Article 8(2)(c) EUTMR, the terminology used in Article 8(5) and Article 9(2)(c) EUTMR is 'repute'[1505] or 'reputation',[1506] and other sources have used terms such as 'famous marks',[1507] 'highly renowned marks'[1508] and 'marks with market recognition'.[1509] As marketing in the form of advertising can help a brand achieve high levels of brand image and the EUIPO Guidelines warn that it is common to confuse 'well known marks'[1510] under Article 8(2)(c) EUTMR with 'marks with reputation'[1511] under Article 8(5) EUTMR. For example, the latter 'aims at protecting this advertising function and the investment made in creating a certain brand image by granting protection to reputed trademarks, irrespective of the similarity of the goods or services or of a likelihood of confusion, provided it can be demonstrated that use of the contested application without due cause would take unfair advantage of, or be detrimental to, the distinctive character or repute of the earlier mark'.[1512] According to EUIPO Guidelines, practically speaking, 'the threshold for establishing whether a trademark is well-known or enjoys reputation will usually be the same'.[1513] Specific factors were used to assess reputation[1514] in *General Motors Corporation v. Yplon*[1515] to make an assessment. These factors included 'the market share held by the trademark, the intensity, geographical extent and duration of its use, and the size of the investment made by the undertaking in

1501. Bardehle Pagenberg, 'Trademark Protection in Europe' (*Bardehle Pagenberg*, 2015) https://media.bardehle.com/contentdocuments/broschures/Trademark-Protection_BARDEHLE_PAGENBERG_IP-brochure.pdf accessed 4 August 2025.
1502. EUTMR, Art. 8.
1503. *Ibid.*
1504. EUTMR, Art. 8(2)(c).
1505. EUTMR, Art. 8(5).
1506. *Ibid.*
1507. Stefan Martin, 'Well Known Marks and Parody: Dilution and Denigration? Unfair Advantage?' (*EUIPO*, 2017), https://euipo.europa.eu/knowledge/pluginfile.php/77920/mod_resource/content/8/Limits%20of%20trade%20marks%2C%20Parody%2018-5-2017.pdf accessed January 2024.
1508. *Ibid.*
1509. *Ibid.*
1510. EUIPO, '2.1.2 Relationship Between Marks with Reputation (Article 8(5) EUTMR) and Well-Known Marks (Article 8(2)(c) EUTMR)' (*EUIPO Trade mark guidelines*, 2024) https://guidelines.euipo.europa.eu/2214311/2227283/trade-mark-guidelines/2-1-2-relationship-between-marks-with-reputation--article-8-5--eutmr--and-well-known-marks--article-8-2--c--eutmr- accessed July 2024.
1511. *Ibid.*
1512. EUIPO, '1.1 Purpose of Article 8(5) EUTMR' (*EUIPO Trade mark guidelines* 2024) https://guidelines.euipo.europa.eu/2214311/2045468/trade-mark-guidelines/1-1-purpose-of-article-8-5--eutmr accessed July 2024.
1513. EUIPO, '2.1.2 Relationship Between Marks with Reputation (Article 8(5) EUTMR) and Well-Known Marks (Article 8(2)(c) EUTMR)' (*EUIPO Trade mark guidelines* 2024) https://guidelines.euipo.europa.eu/2214311/2227283/trade-mark-guidelines/2-1-2-relationship-between-marks-with-reputation--article-8-5--eutmr--and-well-known-marks--article-8-2--c--eutmr- accessed July 2024.
1514. Case C-375/97 *General Motors Corporation v. Yplon SA.* EU:C:1999:408.
1515. *Ibid.*

promoting it'.[1516] Platforms may consider the extent of investment;[1517] however, on the Internet, there may be a different type of investment[1518] that is used to garner 'reputation',[1519] which may not be entirely financial. Furthermore, such reputation[1520] may be able to be gained online in a much faster way considering the nature of the Internet. For example, some marks quickly become widely prevalent online based on something going viral.[1521]

Some guidance on factors that may be used to determine 'reputation'[1522] was provided in *HAWKERS*,[1523] where it was found that '[t]he evidence to establish the presence of the earlier trademark on the internet is an additional element making it possible to establish the reputation of that trademark'.[1524] In this case, it was decided that 'a significant presence of the earlier trademark on the internet, given the number of subscribers to accounts dedicated to this trademark on social networks, or the number of visitors to blogs mentioning this trademark, constitutes an element making it possible to establish the knowledge of the trademark by the public concerned and therefore its reputation'.[1525]

The concept of trademark strength[1526] also plays a role. Trademark strength[1527] is recognised in the EU in matters of 'dilution'[1528] and EU law protects marks which are strong.[1529] 'Strength'[1530] may also be relevant to taking 'unfair advantage'[1531] of the mark.[1532]

In the US, 'a mark is famous if it is widely recognized by the general consuming public of the United States as a designation of source of the goods or services of the mark's owner'.[1533] The factors that are used to assess this include:

(i) The duration, extent, and geographic reach of advertising and publicity of the mark, whether advertised or publicized by the owner or third parties.
(ii) The amount, volume, and geographic extent of sales of goods or services offered under the mark.

1516. *Ibid.*
1517. *Ibid.*
1518. *Ibid.*
1519. EUTMR, Art. 8.
1520. *Ibid.*
1521. Karine Nahon and Jeff Hemsley, *Going Viral* (Polity 2013) 16.
1522. Case T-651/18 *HAWKERS (fig.)/HAWKERS (fig.) et al.* EU:T:2019:444.
1523. *Ibid.*
1524. *Ibid.*
1525. *Ibid.*
1526. Timothy D Greene and Jeff Wilkerson, 'Understanding Trademark Strength' (2013) 16 Stanford Technology Law Review 535-582, abstract.
1527. *Ibid.*
1528. Frank I Schechter, 'The Rational Basis of Trademark Protection' (1927) 40 Harvard Law Review 813 https://doi.org/10.2307/1330367; EUTMR, Art. 8(5); 15 U.S. Code § 1125(c); Keola R Whitaker, 'Trademark Dilution in a Global Age' (2006) 27 University of Pennsylvania Journal of International Economic Law 907.
1529. EUTMR, Art. 8(5).
1530. Timothy D Greene and Jeff Wilkerson, 'Understanding Trademark Strength' (2013) 16 Stanford Technology Law Review 535.
1531. *Ibid.*
1532. *Ibid.*
1533. 15 U.S. Code § 1125(c)(2)(C).

(iii) The extent of actual recognition of the mark.
(iv) Whether the mark was registered under the Act of March 3, 1881, or the Act of February 20, 1905, or on the principal register.[1534]

In *Alston v. www.calculator.com,*[1535] it was considered that the mark calculator.com 'acquired name recognition and invaluable customer goodwill'[1536] and it had 'ultimately achieved a secondary meaning such that the public throughout the regions in which calculator.com does business associates this mark with Plaintiff's reliable online calculator services'.[1537] Some of the factors considered included that the site garnered 'approximately 166,000 daily active users on a monthly basis from all over the world who utilise the calculator services offered',[1538] and that it was 'essential to the markets, individuals, and clients from all around the world that rely on the calculator services offered'[1539] due to 'the sole location'[1540] these are provided.[1541] In the context of reputation,[1542] it is possible for e-commerce websites to gain fame[1543] within a short time frame such as when a site goes viral.[1544] However, such fame[1545] may also fade away in a short time. How this may affect the definition of fame[1546] must be addressed, such as in cases where a mark on an e-commerce website were to gain fame[1547] in a matter of days (or sometimes even hours), possibly in conjunction with other sources of digital marketing. In *De Beers v. DeBeers Diamond Syndicate,*[1548] it was commented that 'the famous marks doctrine is particularly desirable in a world where international travel is commonplace and where the Internet and other media facilitate the rapid creation of business goodwill that transcends borders'.[1549] In *Rovio Entm't v. Royal Plush Toys,*[1550] 'famous'[1551] or 'reputation'[1552] was assessed using, in part, the number of app downloads and a statement relating to its substantial success.[1553] In *Rovio v. Angry Clubs,*[1554] a case was filed by the maker of Angry Birds against Angry Clubs who

1534. *Ibid.*
1535. *Alston v. www.calculator.com,* 2020 U.S. Dist. LEXIS 137360.
1536. *Ibid.*
1537. *Ibid.*
1538. *Ibid.*
1539. *Ibid.*
1540. *Ibid.*
1541. *Ibid.*
1542. 15 U.S. Code § 1125(c)(2)(C).
1543. 15 U.S. Code § 1125(2)(A).
1544. Karine Nahon and Jeff Hemsley, *Going Viral* (Polity 2013) 16.
1545. 15 U.S. Code § 1125(2)(A).
1546. *Ibid.*
1547. *Ibid.*
1548. *De Beers LV Trademark Ltd. v. DeBeers Diamond Syndicate, Inc.*, 2005 U.S. Dist. LEXIS 9307.
1549. *Ibid.*; Barton Beebe, 'Trademark Law: An Open-Source Casebook Version 7.0' (2020) 319 https://www.tmcasebook.org/wp-content/uploads/2020/08/BeebeTMLaw-v7-digital_edition.pdf accessed July 2024.
1550. *Rovio Entm't, Ltd. v. Royal Plush Toys, Inc.*, 2012 U.S. Dist. LEXIS 169020.
1551. 15 U.S. Code § 1125(c)(2)(C).
1552. *Ibid.*
1553. *Rovio Entm't, Ltd. v. Royal Plush Toys, Inc.*, 2012 U.S. Dist. LEXIS 169020.
1554. *Rovio Entertainment, Ltd. v. Angry Clubs, LLC et al,* docket No. 1:13-cv-23619 (s.d. Fla. 8 October 2013).

was alleged to have violated trademark rights, including infringement under 15 U.S. Code § 1114, dilution[1555] under 15 U.S. Code § 1125(c), as well as unfair competition [1556] under 15 U.S. Code § 1125(a) along with local state claims.[1557] Rovio Entertainment had won several awards and worldwide fame based on its games carrying the trademark ANGRY BIRDS,[1558] and although this case was not a case of app infringement,[1559] it was based partially upon the success of the plaintiff's apps and trademark use[1560] therein.[1561] A 'final judgment and permanent injunction against Angry Clubs, LLC'[1562] was entered. In settlement, 'Angry Clubs did not admit liability, but agreed to stop using the name Angry Clubs or the "A" logo ... on its products.'[1563] This case shows that trademark names can, at least partially, become famous[1564] through mobile apps, which can enhance the distinctiveness[1565] of a trademark.[1566] In *Rovio v. Royal Plush Toys,*[1567] it was stated that the 'Angry Birds game has been downloaded over one billion times across all platforms, including both regular and special editions.'[1568] At the time, the court indicated that some have called this 'the largest mobile app success the world has seen so far'.[1569] Also, Angry Birds' growing 'popularity led to versions of Angry Birds being created for personal computers and gaming consoles, a market for merchandise featuring its characters, and even long-term plans for a feature film or television series'.[1570]

Green and Wilkerson argue, in the context of trademark strength[1571] and based on lack of theory, that decisions are often inconsistent because courts depend on 'their own peculiar heuristics for determining whether a trademark is strong or weak'.[1572] They argue that the courts and lawyers are unsuccessful in answering 'what should be a relatively easy question: how many other trademark uses can the mark-at-issue keep out of the stream of commerce'.[1573] They further say that the lack of success with this

1555. *Ibid.*
1556. *Ibid.*
1557. *Ibid.*
1558. *Ibid.*
1559. *Ibid.*
1560. *Ibid.*
1561. *Ibid.*
1562. *Ibid.*
1563. Gabriella Khorasanee, 'Angry Birds Trademark Suit Settled, and Policing Trademarks' (*In House*) http://blogs.findlaw.com/in_house/2013/12/angry-birds-trademark-suit-settled-and-policing-trademarks.html#sthash.oEU33Fel.dpuf accessed January 2024.
1564. 15 U.S. Code § 1125(c).
1565. *Ibid.*
1566. *Ibid.*
1567. *Rovio Entm't, Ltd. v. Royal Plush Toys, Inc.*, 2012 U.S. Dist. LEXIS 169020.
1568. *Ibid.*
1569. *Ibid.*
1570. *Ibid.*
1571. Timothy D Greene and Jeff Wilkerson, 'Understanding Trademark Strength' (2013) 16 Stanford Technology Law Review 535.
1572. *Ibid.*
1573. *Ibid.*

concept is due mainly to the 'backlash against the Abercrombie taxonomy'.[1574] Various '[s]cholars and judges have long lambasted the taxonomy'[1575] due to its 'oversimplification of trademark strength'.[1576] Those in opposition argue that while initial 'strength'[1577] is informative, what is most important 'is how consumers in the marketplace react to the mark'.[1578] A U.S. court has defined it (as stated by Judge Pierre Level) in terms of the 'legal muscle'[1579] a mark has.

Other jurisdictions likewise recognise such marks. The UK Trade Marks (Amendment) Regulations 2022 update the Trade Marks Act 1994 to reflect that the protection applies to well-known[1580] marks in the UK and extends protection even to unregistered well-known[1581] marks under a 'new remedy'.[1582] Also, under Canadian law, strength[1583] may be considered in relation to 'depreciation of goodwill'.[1584] For example, a mark which does not have such strength,[1585] may not have the requisite goodwill and thus may not be able to have goodwill depreciated,[1586] even if these terms may not be synonymous and that this would be decided on a case by case basis.

Platforms should consider adding protection to marks which are well-known[1587] as grounded in the Paris Convention and TRIPS and also incorporated in the jurisdictions as seen above. Platforms may also consider their own data or other platforms' data relating to the mark. For example, brand popularity in e-commerce listings, brand impressions and clicks on branded search ads, social media following, mobile app downloads, or Metaverse users, etc. However, none of these might be considered dispositive and must be carefully assessed if being used alongside other factors. For example, there may be reasons for high clicks or following, including bots,[1588] which are software that may be programmed to click on search ads, inflating the actual number that consumers are clicking on the ad.[1589]

1574. *Abercrombie & Fitch Co. v. Hunting World, Inc.*, 537 F.2d 4 (2d Cir. 1976) in Timothy D Greene and Jeff Wilkerson, 'Understanding Trademark Strength' (2013) 16 Stanford Technology Law Review 535-582, 536.
1575. Timothy D Greene and Jeff Wilkerson, 'Understanding Trademark Strength' (2013) 16 Stanford Technology Law Review 535-582, 536.
1576. *Ibid.*
1577. *Scandia Down Corp. v. Euroquilt, Inc.*, 772 F.2d 1423 (7th Cir. 1985) in Timothy D Greene and Jeff Wilkerson, 'Understanding Trademark Strength' (2013) 16 Stanford Technology Law Review 535, 537.
1578. *Ibid.*
1579. Pierre N Leval, 'Trademark: Champion of Free Speech' (2004) 27 Columbia Journal of Law & the Arts 187, 191 in Timothy D Greene and Jeff Wilkerson, 'Understanding Trademark Strength' (2013) 16 Stanford Technology Law Review 535.
1580. UKIPO, 'Guidance Changes for Well Known Marks (WKM)' (*UKIPO*, 19 December 2022) https://www.gov.uk/government/publications/changes-for-well-known-marks/changes-for-well-known-marks-wkm accessed January 2024.
1581. *Ibid.*
1582. *Ibid.*
1583. Canadian Trademarks Act R.S.C., 1985, c. T-13, s. 22.
1584. *Ibid.*
1585. *Ibid.*
1586. *Ibid.*
1587. Paris Convention, Art. 6bis; TRIPS, Art. 16(2); EUTMR, Art. 8(2)(c).
1588. Cloudfare, 'What Is Click Fraud? | How Click Bots Work' (*Cloudfare*) https://www.cloudflare.com/learning/bots/what-is-click-fraud/ accessed January 2024.
1589. *Ibid.*

3.2.4.3 *Distinctiveness*

The related concept of distinctiveness[1590] is also relevant. It is one aim of trademark law to be able to defend 'distinctive marks'[1591] which are designed to 'identify the source of goods or services and distinguish those products from others in the marketplace'.[1592] McKenna says that the 'distinctiveness plays a critical doctrinal role'[1593] as it 'differentiates designations that warrant trademark protection from those that do not'.[1594] A major factor is how much the information or mark identifies its source.[1595] However, not all believe that the concept of 'distinctiveness'[1596] follows original trademark purposes from a consumer angle because it permits holder of 'famous'[1597] marks to still prohibit utilisation of their mark even when there is no 'consumer confusion'.[1598] Brauneis and Moerland put forth the example of where consumers do not know what a famous word in a foreign language (or jurisdiction) may mean and a 'new entrant',[1599] say in a foreign jurisdiction, may face 'anti-competitive burdens',[1600] even if in the minds of the consumers, the term is 'a fanciful, newly-coined word'.[1601] This may be the case even though it may be an extremely popular mark in another country and even sold online through the proprietor's website.[1602] They argue that 'in most cases, foreign words should be analysed for distinctiveness in the context of their own languages, and should be excluded from protection if they are generic, or protected only upon a showing of secondary meaning if they are descriptive'.[1603] With this approach, they argue that the 'distinctiveness doctrine fully serves its purpose of preventing the owner of a mark from inhibiting competition in the sale of particular goods or services'.[1604]

1590. Mark P McKenna, 'Teaching Trademark Theory Through the Lens of Distinctiveness' (2008) 52 St Louis University Law Journal 843, 847; Timothy D Greene and Jeff Wilkerson, 'Understanding Trademark Strength' (2013) 16 Stanford Technology Law Review 535.
1591. *Ibid.*
1592. Lisa L Ouellette, 'The Google Shortcut to Trademark Law' (2014) 102 California Law Review 351Lisa L Ouellette, 'The Google Shortcut to Trademark Law' (2014) 102 California Law Review 351, 352.
1593. Mark P McKenna, 'Teaching Trademark Theory Through the Lens of Distinctiveness' (2007) 52 St Louis University Law Journal 847.
1594. *Ibid.*
1595. *Ibid.*
1596. Mark P McKenna, 'Teaching Trademark Theory Through the Lens of Distinctiveness' (2008) 52 St Louis University Law Journal 843, 847; Timothy D Greene and Jeff Wilkerson, 'Understanding Trademark Strength' (2013) 16 Stanford Technology Law Review 535.
1597. Paris Convention, Art. 6bis; TRIPS, Art. 16; 15 U.S. Code § 1125(c).
1598. Mark P McKenna, 'Teaching Trademark Theory Through the Lens of Distinctiveness' (2008) 52 St Louis University Law Journal 843; 15 U.S. Code § 1125(c)(1).
1599. Anke Moerland and Robert Brauneis, 'Monopolizing Matratzen in Malaga: The Mistreatment of Distinctiveness of Foreign Terms in EU and US Trademark Law' 2020-55 GW Legal Studies Research Paper No. 2020-61 https://cris.maastrichtuniversity.nl/ws/portalfiles/portal/135820363/Moerland_2020_Monopolizing_Matratzen_in_Malaga.pdf accessed January 2024.
1600. *Ibid.*
1601. *Ibid.*
1602. *Ibid.*
1603. *Ibid.*
1604. *Ibid.*

The UDRP recognises distinctiveness through an overview of the policy stating that 'where acquired distinctiveness/secondary meaning is demonstrated in a particular UDRP case, unregistered rights have been found to support standing to proceed with a UDRP case ...'.[1605]

In the EU, under Article 7(1)(b) EUTMR, it is an absolute ground for refusal if a mark is 'devoid of any distinctive character'.[1606] In the EU, there is a 'distinctiveness'[1607] requirement under Article 8(5) EUTMR and simply translating websites into different languages will not qualify.[1608] Ohly says that 'threshold of distinctiveness takes account of the competition concerns'[1609] and ensures 'that words, devices or shapes are protected only if they can function as signs'.[1610] He believes that '[p]rotection should be restricted to the sign function of trademarks'.[1611] Also, 'descriptive'[1612] signs do not generally qualify as having 'distinctive character acquired through use'[1613] although exceptions may apply.[1614]

In the context of Internet searches using a trademark, in an earlier case, the issue of descriptiveness was considered in *TrekStor Ltd v. OHIM*[1615] for the mark SMARTTV STATION.[1616] The court decided that it was not relevant that Internet consumers entered the phrase 'smarttv station'[1617] into a search engine because it is adequate that such 'expression'[1618] may 'be understood as a descriptive indication of the products'.[1619] The court held that if 'screenshots of the search results of Google, excerpts of the online encyclopedia Wikipedia, a list of products linked to the sign sold on the online shop and screenshots relating to products linked to the sign from the site

1605. WIPO, 'WIPO Overview of WIPO Panel Views on Selected UDRP Questions, Third Edition' ('WIPO Jurisprudential Overview 3.0') (*WIPO*, 2017) https://www.wipo.int/amc/en/domains/search/overview3.0/ accessed June 2025.
1606. Article 7(1)(b) EUTMR.
1607. EUTMR, Art. 8(5).
1608. *Case T-553/12 Compagnie des Bateaux-Mouches v. OHIM – fr* ECLI:EU:T:2014:264.
1609. Angsar Ohly, '"Buy Me Because I'm Cool": The "Marketing Approach" and the Overlap Between Design, Trade Mark and Unfair Competition Law' in Annette Kur, Marianne Levin and Jens Schovsbo (eds), *The EU Design Approach: A Global Appraisal* (Edward Elgar 2018) 120.
1610. *Ibid.*
1611. Angsar Ohly, '"Buy Me Because I'm Cool": The "Marketing Approach" and the Overlap Between Design, Trade Mark and Unfair Competition Law' in Annette Kur, Marianne Levin and Jens Schovsbo (eds), *The EU Design Approach: A Global Appraisal* (Edward Elgar 2018) 113.
1612. William A Finkelstein and James R Sims, *The Intellectual Property Handbook: A Practical Guide for Franchise, Business and IP Counsel* (American Bar Association 2005) 6.
1613. EUIPO, 'Trade Mark guidelines' (*EUIPO*, 2025) guidelines.euipo.europa.eu/2302857/2214737/trade-mark-guidelines/1-introduction.
1614. *Ibid.*
1615. Case T-649/13 *SmartTV Station TrekStor Ltd v. OHIM – DE* EU:T:2015:800; Alicante News, 'IP Caselaw Conference at OHIM' (*IPCLC IP Case Law Conference*, January 2016) 29-30 https://euipo.europa.eu/tunnel-web/secure/webdav/guest/document_library/contentPdfs/about_euipo/alicante_news/alicantenews_January_2016_print_en.pdf accessed January 2024; The EUIPO was formerly the Office for Harmonization of the Internal Market (OHIM).
1616. *Ibid.*
1617. *Ibid.*
1618. *Ibid.*
1619. *Ibid.*

Amazon'[1620] were submitted, 'such documents do not suffice to prove that the sign had acquired distinctive character through use'.[1621] However, more recently, distinctiveness[1622] was considered in *bet365 v. EUIPO*[1623] also in the context of search engines. In this case, in conjunction with visits to and ranking of its website, 'the number of times the contested mark or its derived marks had been the subject of a search using internet search engines is information which can help to show that the contested mark has acquired distinctive character through use'.[1624] It should be clarified here that search engine ads are different from 'organic search results'[1625] as explained in Chapter 2, and a search may result in one or both of these types of results being presented.

In *PDF Expert*,[1626] the mark 'pdf expert'[1627] was sought to be registered and it was considered how the '[u]se of a verbal element in combination with the icon of an app'[1628] impacts the analysis. Apps were argued to be 'rather unconventional goods'[1629] and it was further argued that the 'traditional evidence of distinctiveness acquired through use, such as statements by professional associations or market studies, does not readily apply'.[1630] However, the GC rejected this argument and noted that 'the case-law on evidence of distinctive character acquired through use ... does not distinguish between goods and services, and in particular does not make any distinction as to the types of evidence corresponding to each of those categories'.[1631] In this case, the mobile app 'icon was not a registered trademark'[1632] and it was decided that the 'word element'[1633] or phrase 'pdf expert'[1634] used 'in combination with that icon'[1635] was 'not sufficient to establish that the element ... has acquired distinctiveness through the use which has been made of it'.[1636] Based on the fact that the mobile app icon was considered 'predominant'[1637] as well as the fact that it was 'most often used completely separately from the word element',[1638] this didn't 'confer distinctiveness on that element in itself'.[1639] Advertising in relation to the app was considered only 'secondary'[1640] in terms of 'evidence of distinctive character acquired through

1620. *Ibid.*
1621. *Ibid.*
1622. EUTMR, Art. 8(5).
1623. T-304/16 *BET 365; bet365 Group Ltd v. EUIPO* EU:T:2017:912.
1624. Case T-304/16 *bet365 Group Ltd v. EUIPO* EU:T:2017:912.
1625. Google, 'Organic Search Result' (*Google*) https://support.google.com/google-ads/answer/6054492?hl=en accessed January 2024.
1626. Case T-404/18 *PDF Expert* EU:T:2019:666.
1627. *Ibid.*
1628. Case T-404/18 *PDF Expert* EU:T:2019:666; Case T-492/18 *Zhadanov v. EUIPO (Scanner Pro)* EU:T:2019:667.
1629. Case T-404/18 *PDF Expert* EU:T:2019:666.
1630. *Ibid.*
1631. *Ibid.*
1632. *Ibid.*
1633. *Ibid.*
1634. *Ibid.*
1635. *Ibid.*
1636. *Ibid.*
1637. *Ibid.*
1638. *Ibid.*
1639. *Ibid.*
1640. *Ibid.*

use';[1641] however, the GC did recognise that statistics of 'internet searches for the keyword ... could be capable of demonstrating that a mark has acquired distinctive character through use',[1642] but only in 'special circumstances'.[1643] In this case, 'the applicant had failed to establish that the searches in question had been performed in order to find his app'[1644] and as a result was not sufficient 'evidence that the mark applied for had acquired distinctive character through use'.[1645] A similar result was found in *Zhadanov v. EUIPO*.[1646]

In the 2022 decision in *Louis Vuitton v. EUIPO*,[1647] the GC made a preliminary observation relating to 'evidence concerning the use of the contested mark on the internet',[1648] that 'with the expansion of electronic commerce and, more generally, the growing importance of the internet in the course of trade, the relevant public's perception may, nowadays, be largely influenced by the presence and promotion of a brand in the virtual realm'.[1649] That '[s]uch evidence may thus be likely to play an increasingly important role in assessing distinctive character acquired through use of a trademark'.[1650] Although it was noted that '[f]or that type of evidence to be relevant for that purpose, however, the proprietor of the mark at issue must demonstrate that the websites in question and, in particular, the internet pages on which that mark was displayed, promoted or marketed, target or are consulted by a significant part of the relevant public in the Member States in which the mark is, *ab initio*, devoid of inherent distinctiveness'.[1651] Platforms no doubt recognise the growing importance of their platforms in digital marketing, in line with the above recognition, while understanding that the 'relevant public'[1652] needs to be considered.

As noted by Ramírez-Montes in relation to distinctiveness and NFTs, in *Puma v. Nike*,[1653] the Cancellation Division at the EUIPO, as was the case in earlier UK-related actions, found that FOOTWARE was not descriptive for the classes Nike sought to register them which did not include shoes or footwear but rather included hardware and software, etc.[1654] Further, on appeal, Puma raised new arguments pertaining to a growing '[digitalized] footwear industry'[1655] and that FOOTWARE is a descriptive element of 'purely digital footwear'[1656] such as that used to adorn a digital avatar or

1641. *Ibid.*
1642. *Ibid.*
1643. *Ibid.*
1644. *Ibid.*
1645. *Ibid.*
1646. Case T-492/18 *Zhadanov v. EUIPO (Scanner Pro)* EU:T:2019:667.
1647. Case T-275/21, *Louis Vuitton Malletier v. EUIPO* EU:T:2022:654.
1648. *Ibid.*
1649. *Ibid.*
1650. *Ibid.*
1651. *Ibid.*
1652. *Ibid.*
1653. Case R-2173/2021-5 *PUMA SE v. Nike Innovate*, European Union Intellectual Property Office Fifth Board of Appeal [EUIPO], 5 (9 January 2023); César Ramírez-Montes, 'EU Trademarks in the Metaverse' 63 IDEA 557, 604-612.
1654. *Ibid.*
1655. *Ibid.*
1656. *Ibid.*

used as NFT footwear.[1657] Nike countered with the fact that, in an ever-changing Metaverse environment, PUMA's arguments related to the Metaverse in 2020-2021, whereas the relevant date of assessment was 2019.[1658] As Ramírez-Montes notes, Nike argued that FOOTWARE 'was not descriptive for average consumers on the relevant date' and did not cover 'digital footwear'[1659] or 'digital shoes'.[1660] However, despite excluding some of PUMA's evidence, the Board still found that FOOTWARE was descriptive and sent the message that the software covered in the class included 'data processing devices intended to be used within a shoe'.[1661]

There is also the related issue of language in relation to distinctiveness.[1662] Simply having a website in multiple languages relevant to various Member States does not in itself guarantee distinctiveness[1663] as considered in *Compagnie des Bateaux-Mouches v. OHIM.*[1664] In this case, the 'GC confirmed that the document filed by the applicant does not demonstrate acquired distinctiveness for the Belgian and Luxembourgish territories'[1665] and it was not considered decisive that the applicant's website was 'available in 10 languages'.[1666] Also related to language, in *SilverTours GmbH v. EUIPO,*[1667] the mark 'billiger-mietwagen.de' was refused registration 'as it was found to be devoid of distinctive character and descriptive'.[1668] The BoA dismissed based on the finding 'that the contested mark will be understood as a reference to an internet portal for motor vehicle hire with favourable conditions and therefore is descriptive'.[1669] The GC found that 'the relevant public is the German-speaking public of the EU'[1670] based on the language in which the word mark is expressed.[1671] In finding that the mark 'consists of three elements, "billiger" [cheap], "mietwagen" [hire car] and ".de"[1672] which is the German ccTLD,[1673] it was decided that the immediate understanding of the relevant public would be that this relates to 'making a favourable offer for hiring a motor vehicle'[1674] and that this service is being made available 'online via an internet portal'.[1675] In *Oatly v. EUIPO,*[1676] it was stated that '[i]t must, however, be borne in mind that the English-speaking part of the European Union does not only consist of the

1657. *Ibid.*
1658. *Ibid.*
1659. *Ibid.*
1660. *Ibid.*
1661. *Ibid.*
1662. EUTMR, Recital 21.
1663. *Ibid.*
1664. Case T-553/12 *BATEAUX-MOUCHES; Compagnie des Bateaux-Mouches v. OHIM – fr* EU:T:2014:264.
1665. *Ibid.*
1666. *Ibid.*
1667. Case T-866/16 *billiger-mietwagen.de; SilverTours GmbH v. EUIPO* EU:T:2018:32.
1668. Case T-866/16 *SilverTours v. EUIPO (billiger-mietwagen.de)* EU:T:2018:32.
1669. *Ibid.*
1670. *Ibid.*
1671. *Ibid.*
1672. *Ibid.*
1673. *Ibid.*
1674. *Ibid.*
1675. *Ibid.*
1676. Case T-253/20 *Oatly AB v. EUIPO* EU:T:2021:21.

countries in which English is an official language, but also of those in which, at the very least, English is widely understood, which includes, in particular, Denmark, the Netherlands, Finland and Sweden ... [and] ... since the consumers in those countries are deemed to be part of the English-speaking public, the evidence which the applicant put forward for the purposes of explaining their perception of the mark applied for is relevant ...'.[1677] While '[v]ery basic English terms can be understood in the whole of the EU',[1678] it is also recognised that 'the public's understanding of English expressions is broader than basic terms'[1679] in countries where English is 'widely understood'.[1680]

In the US, under 15 U.S. Code § 1125(c)(1), even without 'confusion',[1681] a 'famous'[1682] mark which is distinctive[1683] may be protected. Specifically, '[s]ubject to the principles of equity, the owner of a famous mark that is distinctive, inherently or through acquired distinctiveness, shall be entitled to an injunction against another person who, at any time after the owner's mark has become famous, commences use of a mark or trade name in commerce that is likely to cause dilution by blurring or dilution by tarnishment of the famous mark, regardless of the presence or absence of actual or likely confusion, of competition, or of actual economic injury'.[1684] Menell, Lemley, Merges and Balganesh say that 'trademark protection for descriptive terms can impede competition'.[1685] 'Hashtag [m]arks'[1686] are specifically covered in the TMEP 1202.18, which indicates that these are 'often used in social-networking sites to identify or facilitate a search for a keyword or topic of interest'.[1687] It is also clear that 'addition of the term HASHTAG or the hash symbol (#) to an otherwise unregistrable mark typically will not render it registrable'[1688] and that such hashtag 'combined with

1677. *Ibid.*
1678. EUIPO, '4.3.1 Relevant Territory and Objections Based on EU National Languages' (*EUIPO Trade mark guidelines*, 2024) https://euipo01app.sdlproducts.com/2214311/2066125/trade-mark-guidelines/4-3-1-relevant-territory-and-objections-based-on-eu-national-languages accessed July 2024.
1679. *Ibid.*
1680. *Ibid.*
1681. Paris Convention, Art. 6bis; TRIPS, Art. 16.
1682. *Ibid.*; 15 U.S. Code § 1125(c).
1683. Mark P McKenna, 'Teaching Trademark Theory Through the Lens of Distinctiveness' (2008) 52 St Louis University Law Journal 843, 847; Timothy D Greene and Jeff Wilkerson, 'Understanding Trademark Strength' (2013) 16 Stanford Technology Law Review 535.
1684. 15 U.S. Code § 1125(c)(1).
1685. Peter S Menell et al., *Intellectual Property in the New Technological Age: 2020* (Clause 8 Publishing 2020) 28.
1686. USPTO, 'TMEP 1202.18 USPTO Trademark Manual of Examining Procedure May 2024' (*USPTO, 2024*) https://tmep.uspto.gov/RDMS/TMEP/current#/current/TMEP-1200d1e1.html accessed January 2024.
1687. *Ibid.*
1688. USPTO, 'TMEP 1202.18 USPTO Trademark Manual of Examining Procedure May 2024' (*USPTO, 2024*) https://tmep.uspto.gov/RDMS/TMEP/current#/current/TMEP-1200d1e1.html accessed January 2024; Barton Beebe, 'Trademark Law: An Open-Source Casebook Version 7.0' (2020), 51 https://www.tmcasebook.org/wp-content/uploads/2020/08/BeebeTMLaw-v7-digital_edition.pdf accessed July 2024; Alexandra J Roberts, 'Tagmarks' 105 California Law Review 599 (2017).

wording that is merely descriptive or generic for the goods or services'[1689] is not acceptable and therefore does not render it distinctive.[1690]

One way that the 'distinctiveness'[1691] theory has been applied is through the renowned Abercrombie categories,[1692] which include 'generic marks',[1693] 'descriptive marks',[1694] 'suggestive marks',[1695] and 'fanciful marks'.[1696] These provide levels by which trademarks may be categorised and Beebe favours the Abercrombie categorisation[1697] as a 'relatively accurate'[1698] way of forecasting whether a trademark holder can create a 'successful and distinctive mark'.[1699] Marks may be protected where they have managed to have 'acquired distinctiveness',[1700] also referred to as 'secondary meaning',[1701] to the extent that customers look at these as 'distinctive of a unique source'.[1702] It should be noted that '[i]nherent distinctiveness'[1703] is analysed through 'conceptual strength',[1704] whereas 'distinctiveness'[1705] will be based on 'commercial strength'.[1706] However, it is often difficult in practice to make such determination of distinctiveness;[1707] the tests are not very well defined and practical application of these has often led to a high level of discretion, leading to less certainty.[1708] Also, in the US, the

1689. USPTO, 'TMEP 1202.18 USPTO Trademark Manual of Examining Procedure May 2024' https://tmep.uspto.gov/RDMS/TMEP/current#/current/TMEP-1200d1e1.html accessed 4 August 2025.
1690. *Ibid.*
1691. Mark P McKenna, 'Teaching Trademark Theory Through the Lens of Distinctiveness' (2008) 52 St Louis University Law Journal 843.
1692. *Abercrombie & Fitch Co. v. Hunting World, Inc.*, 537 F.2d 4 (2nd Cir. 1976).
1693. *Ibid.*
1694. *Ibid.*
1695. *Ibid.*
1696. *Ibid.*
1697. *Ibid.*
1698. Timothy D Greene and Jeff Wilkerson, 'Understanding Trademark Strength' (2013) 16 Stanford Technology Law Review 535.
1699. *Ibid.*
1700. Lisa L Ouellette, 'The Google Shortcut to Trademark Law' (2014) 102 California Law Review 351, 353; Barton Beebe, 'The Semiotic Account of Trademark Doctrine and Trademark Culture' in Graeme B Dinwoodie and Mark D Janis (eds), *Trademark Law and Theory: A Handbook of Contemporary Research* (Edward Elgar, 2008) 42, 64.
1701. *Ibid.*
1702. *Ibid.*
1703. J Thomas McCarthy, *McCarthy on Trademarks and Unfair Competition* (4th edn, vol. 69, Thomson Reuters, 2014) as seen in Lisa L Ouellette, 'The Google Shortcut to Trademark Law' (2014) 102 California Law Review 351, 353.
1704. *Ibid.*
1705. *Ibid.*
1706. *Ibid.*
1707. Lisa L Ouellette, 'The Google Shortcut to Trademark Law' (2014) 102 California Law Review 351, 353.
1708. *Ibid.*

Trademark Trial and Appeal Board (TTAB) considers that this is largely a matter of application of intuition instead of a 'precisely logical analysis'.[1709]

In *Steelbuilding.com,*[1710] this domain was found to be 'highly descriptive'.[1711] Mattress.com was generic for mattresses and related items,[1712] as found in the case *1800mattress.com.*[1713] The same result was found for lawyers.com in *Reed Elsevier Properties*.[1714] This traditional approach was initially followed in the non-precedential case of *Booking.com,*[1715] where the Board found that booking.com could not be registered for lack of 'distinctiveness',[1716] under 15 U.S. Code § 1052(f).[1717] It found that the term *booking* was a 'very highly descriptive term'[1718] and if a term is 'descriptive'[1719] and has not attained 'distinctiveness',[1720] it cannot be registered under U.S. law. However, in what may be considered a landmark case, the U.S. Supreme Court in *Booking.com*[1721] recently affirmed the Court of Appeals decision and held that booking.com 'could receive federal trademark protection',[1722] regardless of whether the term 'Booking'[1723] by itself was unable to achieve such protection.[1724] This is especially where, as Litman reports, 'consumers do not perceive them as generic'.[1725] It is opined that this case will launch a reconsideration of how 'distinctiveness'[1726] may

1709. J Thomas McCarthy, *McCarthy on Trademarks and Unfair Competition* (4th edn, vol. 69, Thomson Reuters, 2014) in Lisa L Ouellette, 'The Google Shortcut to Trademark Law' (2014) 102 California Law Review 351, 353.
1710. *In re Steelbuilding.com*, 415 F.3d 1293, 1297 (Fed. Cir. 2005).
1711. J Thomas McCarthy, *McCarthy on trademarks and unfair competition* (4th edn, vol. 69, Thomson Reuters, 2014) in Lisa L Ouellette, 'The Google Shortcut to Trademark Law' (2014) 102 California Law Review 351, 353.
1712. *Ibid.*
1713. *In re 1800mattress.com IP, LLC*, 586 F.3d 1359 (Fed. Cir. 2009).
1714. J Thomas McCarthy, *McCarthy on trademarks and unfair competition* (4th edn, vol. 69, Thomson Reuters, 2014) in Lisa L Ouellette, 'The Google Shortcut to Trademark Law' (2014) 102 California Law Review 351, 353; *In re Reed Elsevier Properties, Inc.*, 482 F.3d 1376, 82 U.S.P.Q.2d 1378 (Fed. Cir. 2007).
1715. *In re Booking.com B.V.*, S.N. 79114998 (18 February 2016).
1716. 15 U.S. Code § 1125.
1717. *In re Booking.com B.V., S.N.* 79114998 (18 February 2016).
1718. *Allen's Trademark Digest* (Wolters Kluwer 29 April 2016); *In re Booking.com B.V., S.N.* 79114998 (18 February 2016).
1719. *Ibid.*
1720. Mark P McKenna, 'Teaching Trademark Theory Through the Lens of Distinctiveness' (2008) 52 St Louis University Law Journal 843, 847.
1721. *Patent and Trademark Office v. Booking.com B. V.*, No. 19-46 (U.S. 30 June 2020).
1722. Bloomberg Law, 'Supreme Court Affirms Validity of 'Booking.com' Trademark (1)' (*Bloomberg Law,* 30 June 2020) https://news.bloomberglaw.com/ip-law/supreme-court-affirms-validity-of-booking-com-trademark accessed January 2024.
1723. *Ibid.*
1724. *Ibid.*
1725. Jessica Litman, 'Opinion analysis: Court Holds That "generic.com" Marks May Be Registered Trademarks or Service Marks When Consumers Do Not Perceive Them as Generic' (*Scotus Blog,* 30 June 2020) https://www.scotusblog.com/2020/06/opinion-analysis-court-holds-that-generic-com-marks-may-be-registered-trademarks-or-service-marks-when-consumers-do-not-perceive-them-as-generic/ accessed January 2024.
1726. 15 U.S. Code § 1127.

be assessed and even potentially open the floodgates to litigation.[1727] This also impacts social media usernames, mobile app names and the like since these raise some of the same issues.

In the UK, marks 'devoid of distinctive character'[1728] may be refused registration under section 3(1)(b) of the UK Trade Marks Act 1994. Likewise, in Canada, 'distinctiveness'[1729] is recognised under section 5(a) of the Canadian Trademarks Act.

Platforms should consider, as the UDRP may and as the jurisdictions do, as seen above, providing protection to distinctive[1730] marks. While descriptive[1731] or generic[1732] marks may not receive protection, platforms should consider whether there is a relevant level of distinctiveness.[1733] Platforms should not consider the additional elements, such as hashtags, in a distinctiveness analysis absent other elements.[1734] Platforms should consider treading carefully relating to matters of language unless the platform is itself targeting a specific language-speaking public, a matter discussed further in section 3.2.6 *Digital Jurisdictional and Territorial Considerations* further below.

3.2.4.4 Dilution Theory, Unfair Advantage, Free Riding, and Misappropriation

Related to these concepts is the theory of dilution,[1735] which Dinwoodie sees from a 'misappropriation'[1736] angle both in the EU and the US.[1737] This is suggested from cases such as *L'Oréal*[1738] in the sense that 'unlimited protection of property'[1739] need not be

1727. Bloomberg Law, 'Supreme Court Affirms Validity of 'Booking.com' Trademark (1)' (*Bloomberg Law*, 30 June 2020) https://news.bloomberglaw.com/ip-law/supreme-court-affirms-validity-of-booking-com-trademark.
1728. UK Trade Marks Act 1994, s. 3(1)(b).
1729. Canadian Trademarks Act R.S.C., 1985, c. T-13, s. 6.
1730. Mark P McKenna, 'Teaching Trademark Theory Through the Lens of Distinctiveness' (2008) 52 St Louis University Law Journal 843, 847; Timothy D Greene and Jeff Wilkerson, 'Understanding Trademark Strength' (2013) 16 Stanford Technology Law Review 535.
1731. *Abercrombie & Fitch Co. v. Hunting World, Inc.*, 537 F.2d 4 (2nd Cir. 1976).
1732. *Ibid.*
1733. *Ibid.*
1734. Alexandra Roberts, 'Hashtags Are Not Trademarks: Eksouzian v. Albanese' (*Guest Blog Post*) https://blog.ericgoldman.org/archives/2015/08/hashtags-are-not-trademarks-eksouzian-v-albanese-guest-blog-post-2.htm accessed January 2024.
1735. Graeme B Dinwoodie, 'Dilution as Unfair Competition: European Echoes' in Rochelle C Dreyfuss and Jane C Ginsburg (eds) *Intellectual Property at the Edge: The Contested Contours of IP* (Cambridge University Press 2014) 100; EU misappropriation is the other part of EUTMR, s. 9(c).
1736. *Ibid.*
1737. *Ibid.*
1738. C-487/07 *L'Oréal and Others* EU:C:2009:378.
1739. Graeme B Dinwoodie, 'Dilution as Unfair Competition: European Echoes' in Rochelle C Dreyfuss and Jane C Ginsburg (eds) *Intellectual Property at the Edge: The Contested Contours of IP* (Cambridge University Press 2014) 100.

the ultimate goal.[1740] In the context of *Odol,*[1741] it has been said that 'dilution law'[1742] is a matter of 'unfair competition'.[1743] Friedman, in the context of social media trademarks, says that 'trademark dilution is premised on the need to prevent against harming the trademark'.[1744] Protection against 'dilution'[1745] is a concept that developed based on the need to guard 'achievements'[1746] such as the 'advertising value of a mark'[1747] and to defend against 'misappropriation of a reputation',[1748] which are all related to 'unfair competition'.[1749] The concept of 'dilution'[1750] was raised back in 1924 in the *Odol*[1751] decision, where the German court had to decide whether there was legal justification to cancel a trademark based on a 'non-competing'[1752] use by a 'steel producer'.[1753] The court decided that such activity was not acceptable because of the consumers' association of 'quality'[1754] with the name *Odol*, and this caused the mark to be 'diluted'[1755] and to 'lose in selling power'.[1756] The European theory of 'dilution'[1757]

1740. *Ibid.*
1741. Graeme B Dinwoodie, 'Dilution as Unfair Competition: European Echoes' in Rochelle C Dreyfuss and Jane C Ginsburg (eds) *Intellectual Property at the Edge: The Contested Contours of IP* (Cambridge University Press 2014) 100; Odol Case: Reichsgericht (NJW 1925, 264) 14 September 1924 13. O. 89/24, GEWERBLICHER RECHTSSCHUTZ UND URHEBERRECHT [GRUR] 204 (1924); Anselm Kamperman Sanders, 'Odol: The Introduction of a Watery Concept with Steeled Resilience' in Christopher Heath and Anselm Kamperman Sanders (eds), *Landmark Intellectual Property Cases and Their Legacy* (Wolters Kluwer 2011) 51-56.
1742. *Ibid.*
1743. *Ibid.*
1744. Danny Friedmann, *Trademarks and Social Media: Towards Algorithmic Justice* (Edward Elgar Publishing 2015) 3-15.
1745. Frank I Schechter, 'The Rational Basis of Trademark Protection' (1927) 40 Harvard Law Review 813 https://doi.org/10.2307/1330367;15 U.S. Code § 1125(c); Keola R Whitaker, 'Trademark Dilution in a Global Age' (2006) 27 University of Pennsylvania Journal of International Economic Law 907.
1746. Anselm Kamperman Sanders, *Unfair Competition Law: The Protection of Intellectual and Industrial Creativity* (Oxford University Press 1997) 6-10.
1747. Anselm Kamperman Sanders, *Unfair Competition Law: The Protection of Intellectual and Industrial Creativity* (Oxford University Press 1997) 10.
1748. *Ibid.*
1749. *Ibid.*
1750. Frank I Schechter, 'The Rational Basis of Trademark Protection' (1927) 40 Harvard Law Review 813 https://doi.org/10.2307/1330367;15 U.S. Code § 1125(c); Keola R Whitaker, 'Trademark Dilution in a Global Age' (2006) 27 University of Pennsylvania Journal of International Economic Law 907.
1751. Christopher Heath, Anselm Kamperman Sanders (eds), *Landmark Intellectual Property Cases and Their Legacy* (Kluwer Law International 2011) 51-62.
1752. Peter Groves, *Sourcebook on Intellectual Property* (Routeledge 1997) 520; Christopher Heath, Anselm Kamperman Sanders (eds), *Landmark Intellectual Property Cases and Their Legacy* (Kluwer Law International 2011) 51-62.
1753. *Ibid.*
1754. *Ibid.*
1755. *Ibid.*
1756. *Ibid.*
1757. Frank I Schechter, 'The Rational Basis of Trademark Protection' (1927) 40 Harvard Law Review 813 https://doi.org/10.2307/1330367; Keola R Whitaker, 'Trademark Dilution in a Global Age' (2006) 27 University of Pennsylvania Journal of International Economic Law 907, 913.

was brought to light in the US by Frank Schechter ('[t]he father of dilution theory')[1758] in his 'seminal article, The Rational Basis of Trademark Protection'.[1759] He defined it as the 'gradual whittling away or dispersion of the identity and hold upon the public mind of the mark or name by its use upon non-competing goods'.[1760] Schechter was apprehensive about what can be done when others utilised a 'unique'[1761] mark in relation to 'non-competing goods'.[1762] Kamperman Sanders says that *Odol*[1763] is a case which has focused on 'the persuasive advertising function'[1764] of 'well known'[1765] marks. This is in line with the fundamental protections afforded to marks. Kamperman Sanders indicates that the German *Odol*[1766] case 'has been a key factor in supporting the transition of a tort against unfair competition into a property right in the persuasive advertising function that well known trademarks may perform in the marketplace'.[1767] He recognises that this was 'the first case considering protection of a trademark beyond the notion of confusion and similarity of goods'.[1768] Kamperman Sanders also notes that this case 'found its first supporters across the Atlantic in the United States, only to be rediscovered in Europe later'.[1769] McCabe says that dilution[1770] would require the utilisation of an 'identical or substantially similar'[1771] mark to one that already exists and where a consumer would make a 'mental association'[1772] that the second mark was actually the first would cause an 'eroding'[1773] of the 'strength of the original mark'.[1774]

1758. Keola R Whitaker, 'Trademark Dilution in a Global Age' (2006) 27 University of Pennsylvania Journal of International Economic Law 907, 913.
1759. Frank I Schechter, 'The Rational Basis of Trademark Protection' (1927) 40 Harvard Law Review 813 https://doi.org/10.2307/1330367; Keola R Whitaker, 'Trademark Dilution in a Global Age' (2006) 27 University of Pennsylvania Journal of International Economic Law 907, 913.
1760. Kathleen B McCabe, 'Dilution-by-Blurring: A Theory Caught in the Shadow of Trademark Infringement' (2000) 68 Fordham Law Review 1827, 1846.
1761. *Ibid.*
1762. *Ibid.*
1763. Anselm Kamperman Sanders, 'The Legacy of Odol: Cross-Atlantic Parallel Import' in Christopher Heath and Anselm Kamperman Sanders (eds), *Landmark Intellectual Property Cases and Their Legacy* (Kluwer Law International 2011) 58.
1764. *Ibid.*
1765. *Ibid.*
1766. *Ibid.*
1767. *Ibid.*
1768. Anselm Kamperman Sanders, 'Dilution and Damage beyond Confusion in the European Union' in Irene Calboli and Jane C Ginsburg, *The Cambridge Handbook of International and Comparative Trademark Law* (Cambridge University Press 2020) summary.
1769. Anselm Kamperman Sanders, 'The Legacy of Odol: Cross-Atlantic Parallel Import' in Christopher Heath and Anselm Kamperman Sanders (eds), *Landmark Intellectual Property Cases and Their Legacy* (Kluwer Law International 2011) 51.
1770. Frank I Schechter, 'The Rational Basis of Trademark Protection' (1927) 40 Harvard Law Review 813 https://doi.org/10.2307/1330367; 15 U.S. Code § 1125(c); Keola R Whitaker, 'Trademark Dilution in a Global Age' (2006) 27 University of Pennsylvania Journal of International Economic Law 907, 913.
1771. Kathleen B McCabe, 'Dilution-by-Blurring: A Theory Caught in the Shadow of Trademark Infringement' (2000) 68 Fordham Law Review 1827, 1828.
1772. *Ibid.*
1773. *Ibid.*
1774. *Ibid.*

McCabe proposes that 'the doctrine of dilution is alive, but not well'.[1775] This is especially because of misapplication of dilution[1776] standards, including confusion between this and an 'infringement'[1777] analysis. At the same time, Lemley and McKenna argue that '[t]he claim that trademark owners are injured by not being able to control use in a remote market is ultimately a circular claim-mark owners are injured if, but only if, we define their trademark rights ex ante to include control over that remote market'.[1778] They, however, propose that injury, defined as including that which 'flows from confusion'[1779] and is 'material to consumer purchasing decisions',[1780] must take precedence in their trademark injury doctrine.[1781] It should also be considered that 'dilution'[1782] has the aim of preventing 'junior users from free riding on the labor and investments of the senior user'.[1783] It appears that there are competing arguments, especially as to how dilution[1784] should be applied.

Preventing 'dilutive use'[1785] of a mark is considered a function of 'protecting the fame embodied in a trademark'[1786] and this has had 'an uneasy and torturous history in trademark dilution law'.[1787] This can be contrasted with 'freeriding',[1788] which has been defined by the WIPO as 'any act that a competitor or another market participant undertakes with the intention of directly exploiting another person's industrial or commercial achievement for his own business purposes without substantially departing from the original achievement'.[1789]

Likewise, Riffel says, 'appropriating an intangible asset without authorization and capitalizing on it constitutes competitive behaviour'.[1790] In line with this, Ohly further says, in cases where 'the trademark has a reputation, EU law also grants

1775. *Ibid.*
1776. *Ibid.*
1777. *Ibid.*
1778. Mark A Lemley and Mark P McKenna, 'Owning Mark(Et)s' (2010) 109 Michigan Law Review 137, 141.
1779. *Ibid.*
1780. *Ibid.*
1781. *Ibid.*
1782. Frank I Schechter, 'The Rational Basis of Trademark Protection' (1927) 40 Harvard Law Review 813 https://doi.org/10.2307/1330367;15 U.S. Code § 1125(c); Keola R Whitaker, 'Trademark Dilution in a Global Age' (2006) 27 University of Pennsylvania Journal of International Economic Law 907, 913.
1783. Irena D Manta, 'Hedonic Trademarks' (2013) 74 Ohio State Law Journal 241, 261.
1784. *Ibid.*
1785. Laura R Bradford, 'Emotion, Dilution, and the Trademark Consumer' (2008) 23 Berkeley Technology Law Journal 1227, 1231 in Xuan-Thao Nguyen, 'Fame Law: Requiring Proof of National Fame in Trademark Law' (2011) 33 Cardozo Law Review 91, 92.
1786. *Ibid.*
1787. *Ibid.*
1788. WIPO, 'WIPO Intellectual Property Handbook: Policy, Law and Use' 2nd edn (*WIPO* 2004) 138 https://tind.wipo.int/record/28661?ln=en&v=pdf accessed January 2024.
1789. *Ibid.*
1790. *Ibid.*

protection against misappropriation'.[1791] This protection for 'misappropriation'[1792] is when utilisation of the mark is 'undue'.[1793] Further, engaging in the act of 'free riding'[1794] in relation to 'the achievements of competitors'[1795] is prohibited, especially in the context of reputable[1796] marks. On the Internet, there are many possibilities of where 'exploitation'[1797] or 'misappropriation'[1798] may take place, and in fact may enhance the possibility that it can due to the global reach and multiple ways in which marks can be utilised online. Relatedly, Chronopoulos says that '[t]he free-riding theory of protection'[1799] is most relevant to 'the legal evaluation of the branding activity because it can squarely address the diverse interests involved in the respective disputes'.[1800] Also, 'free-riding'[1801] should not be permitted and can be used to evaluate, from a legal perspective, an advertising and marketing pursuit.[1802] This may especially be considered to protect against 'overbroad trademark monopolies',[1803] and a simple 'waste of economic resources'[1804] spent on advertising.[1805]

Stibbe raises a good question regarding the fact that 'courts have not quite figured out what standard to apply to the online marketing context: how they can protect brand equity and the producers of brand equity while also endeavouring to prevent a clog

1791. Angsar Ohly, '"Buy Me Because I'm Cool": The "Marketing Approach" and the Overlap Between Design, Trade Mark and Unfair Competition Law' in Annette Kur, Marianne Levin and Jens Schovsbo (eds), *The EU Design Approach: A Global Appraisal* (Edward Elgar 2018) 129.
1792. WIPO, 'WIPO Intellectual Property Handbook: Policy, Law and Use' 2nd edn (*WIPO* 2004) 138 https://tind.wipo.int/record/28661?ln=en&v=pdf accessed January 2024.
1793. *Ibid.*
1794. *Ibid.*
1795. *Ibid.*
1796. EUTMR, Art. 9(1)(c).
1797. Christian Riffel, *Protection Against Unfair Competition in the WTO TRIPS Agreement: The Scope and Prospects of Article 10bis of the Paris Convention for the Protection of Industrial Property* (Brill 2016) 213; Anselm Kamperman Sanders, *Unfair Competition Law: The Protection of Intellectual and Industrial Creativity* (Oxford University Press 1997) 6-10.
1798. David Barnes, 'Misappropriation of Trademark' (2008) 9 North Carolina Journal of Law & Technology 171.
1799. Apostolos Chronopoulos, 'Legal and Economic Arguments for the Protection of Advertising Value Through Trade Mark Law' (2014) 4 Queen Mary Journal of Intellectual Property 256, 276 https://doi.org/10.4337/qmjip.2014.04.01.
1800. *Ibid.*
1801. Andrew Griffiths, *An Economics Perspective on Trade Mark Law* (Edward Elgar, 2011) 32; Apostolos Chronopoulos, 'Legal and Economic Arguments for the Protection of Advertising Value Through Trade Mark Law' (2014) 4 Queen Mary Journal of Intellectual Property 256 https://doi.org/10.4337/qmjip.2014.04.01.
1802. *Ibid.*
1803. Apostolos Chronopoulos, 'Legal and Economic Arguments for the Protection of Advertising Value Through Trade Mark Law' (2014) 4 Queen Mary Journal of Intellectual Property 256, abstract https://doi.org/10.4337/qmjip.2014.04.01.
1804. *Ibid.*
1805. *Ibid.*

in the online advertising market'.[1806] Stibbe says that the courts can only try their best, considering dilution[1807] requirements and balancing interests.[1808]

As Farley notes, the TRIPS Agreement is considered to cover dilution under Article 16(3), which reads:

> Article 6bis of the Paris Convention (1967) shall apply, mutatis mutandis, to goods or services which are not similar to those in respect of which a trademark is registered, provided that use of that trademark in relation to those goods or services would indicate a connection between those goods or services and the owner of the registered trademark and provided that the interests of the owner of the registered trademark are likely to be damaged by such use.[1809]

In the EU, under Article 9(2)(c) EUTMR, a mark holder can prevent others from using a mark if 'the sign is identical with, or similar to, the EU trademark irrespective of whether it is used in relation to goods or services which are identical with, similar to or not similar to those for which the EU trademark is registered, where the latter has a reputation in the Union and where use of that sign without due cause takes unfair advantage of, or is detrimental to, the distinctive character or the repute of the EU trademark'.[1810] This is essentially the concept of dilution.[1811] Likewise, a mark may be refused registration under Article 8(5) EUTMR where 'the use without due cause of the trademark applied for would take unfair advantage of, or be detrimental to, the distinctive character or the repute of the earlier trademark'.[1812] This will not pass muster unless all elements are met.[1813] The Guidelines for Examination in the Office, Part C, Opposition, indicate that this 'requires that the advantage be "unfair,"[1814] in that there is no justification for the applicant's profit'.[1815] As Ohly recognises, 'free riding on the repute of trademarks'[1816] can be a source of 'unfair advantage'[1817] and no 'likelihood of confusion'[1818] finding[1819] is necessary.[1820]

1806. Paul F Stibbe, 'Pushing the Boundaries of the Trademark Dilution by Tarnishment Claim: The Tarnishment Claim in an Ever-Expanding Keyword Search Market' (2012) 17 Virginial Journal of Law & Technology 244.
1807. *Ibid.*
1808. *Ibid.*
1809. TRIPS, Art. 16.3.
1810. EUTMR, Art. 9(2)(c).
1811. Anselm Kamperman Sanders, 'The Legacy of Odol: Cross-Atlantic Parallel Import' in Christopher Heath and Anselm Kamperman Sanders (eds), *Landmark Intellectual Property Cases and Their Legacy* (Kluwer Law International 2011) 58.
1812. WIPO, *Intellectual Property Handbook* (World Intellectual Property Organization 2008) 153 https://tind.wipo.int/record/28661/files/wipo_pub_489.pdf accessed 4 August 2025.
1813. *Ibid.*
1814. *Ibid.*
1815. *Ibid.*
1816. Angsar Ohly, 'Free-Riding on the Repute on Trade Marks: Does Protection Generate Innovation?' in Josef Drexl and Anselm Kamperman Sanders (eds), *The Innovation Society and Intellectual Property, European Intellectual Property Institutes Network series* (Edward Elgar Publishing 2019) 146.
1817. EUTMR, Art. 8(5).
1818. EUTMR, Art. 8(1)(b) and Art. 9(2)(c).
1819. Jane C Ginsburg, 'Response Euro-Yearnings? Moving Toward A "Substantive" Registration-Based Trademark Regime' (2017) 130 Harvard Law Review Forum 95.
1820. *Ibid.*

As noted by Ramírez-Montes, '[u]nfair advantage actions concern the protection of the proprietor's marketing efforts and investment in creating a positive image or positive characteristics around the EU trademark'.[1821] Relatedly, *L'Oréal SA v. Bellure*[1822] recognised the marketing perspective and covered 'comparative advertising'.[1823] The CJ noted that '[t]he advantage arising from the use by a third party of a sign similar to a mark with a reputation is an advantage taken unfairly by that third party of the distinctive character or the repute of that mark where that party seeks by that use to ride on the coat-tails of the mark in order to benefit from the power of attraction, the reputation and prestige of that mark and to exploit, without paying any financial compensation, the marketing effort expended by the proprietor of the mark in order to create and maintain the mark's image'.[1824] Specifically, in the context of marketing imitations, 'an advertiser who states explicitly or implicitly in comparative advertising that the product marketed by him is an imitation of a product bearing a well-known trademark presents ... goods or services as imitations or replicas'.[1825] Further, '[t]he advantage gained by the advertiser as a result of such unlawful comparative advertising must be considered to be an advantage taken unfairly of the reputation of that mark'.[1826]

Unfair advantage[1827] was also relevant in *Coca-Cola v. EUIPO*.[1828] In this case, 'the contested mark Master (in combination with the term "cola")'[1829] was used in Syria and the Middle East, and evidence from the website www.mastercola.com was mainly in the Arabic language.[1830] It was stated that this could be used to determine 'whether use of that mark in the EU would take unfair advantage of the reputation of the four earlier Coca-Cola EUTMs'.[1831] 'Free riding'[1832] was considered based on the 'fact that presentational features'[1833] such as 'the red label',[1834] the contested mark being 'written in white',[1835] 'the characteristic shape of the container'[1836] and 'the red cap and the Spenserian script'[1837] were being 'used on the applicant's website'.[1838] This was

1821. César Ramírez-Montes, 'EU Trademarks in the Metaverse' 63 IDEA 557, 673; Case C-487/07, *L'Oréal SA v. Bellure NV*, 2009 E.C.R. I5185, ¶ 47 (18 June 2009).
1822. Case C-487/07 *L'Oréal SA v. Bellure NV* EU:C:2009:378.
1823. *Ibid.*
1824. *Ibid.*
1825. *Ibid.*
1826. *Ibid.*
1827. EUTMR, Art. 8(5).
1828. Case T-61/16 *MASTER/COCA-COLA et al.; The Coca-Cola Company v. EUIPO* EU:T:2017:877.
1829. Case T-61/16 *Coca-Cola v. EUIPO – Mitico (Master)* EU:T:2017:877; EUIPO, 'Overview of GC/CJ Case Law 2017' (*International Cooperation and Legal Affairs Department*, 2017) 247 https://euipo.europa.eu/tunnel-web/secure/webdav/guest/document_library/contentPdfs/law_and_practice/yearly_overview/yearly_overview_2017.pdf accessed January 2024.
1830. *Ibid.*
1831. *Ibid.*
1832. *Ibid.*
1833. *Ibid.*
1834. *Ibid.*
1835. *Ibid.*
1836. *Ibid.*
1837. *Ibid.*
1838. Case T-61/16 *Coca-Cola v. EUIPO – Mitico (Master)* EU:T:2017:877, EUIPO, 'Overview of GC/CJ Case Law 2017' (*International Cooperation and Legal Affairs Department*, 2017) 247

considered to possibly 'reinforce the logical inference that there was a risk of free-riding and that an amended form of those features could be used in the future on that website in order to target consumers in the EU'.[1839] As can be seen, there are various e-commerce website considerations beyond the domain name itself. Also, in *Interflora,* [1840] discussed earlier in the section 3.2.3 *Digital Confusion*, the CJ equated 'unfair advantage'[1841] with 'inter alia, free-riding'[1842] and '[d]etriment to the distinctive character of a mark with a reputation',[1843] which was considered a reference to 'inter alia, dilution'.[1844] However, when reverted back to the UK court after reference, 'dilution'[1845] and 'unfair advantage'[1846] were not found by the UK High Court as it did not find an 'adverse effect on the origin function'.[1847] It should be noted that the defence of 'comparative advertising'[1848] was not raised in this case, even though briefly discussed.[1849]

Ramírez-Montes says that 'brand owners in the metaverse may have better chances of success by claiming unfair advantage',[1850] specifically referring to where, under Environmental Mfg. LLP,[1851] 'by reason of a transfer of the image of the mark or of the characteristics which it projects to the goods identified by the identical or similar sign, there is clear exploitation on the coat-tails of the mark with a reputation'.[1852]

On a related note, and although the UK is no longer an EU member,[1853] interestingly, the Nominet Dispute Resolution Policy applicable to.uk domains defines 'abusive registration'[1854] as:

> i. was registered or otherwise acquired in a manner which, at the time when the registration or acquisition took place, took unfair advantage of or was unfairly detrimental to the Complainant's Rights; or ii. is being or has been used in a

https://euipo.europa.eu/tunnel-web/secure/webdav/guest/document_library/contentPdfs/law_and_practice/yearly_overview/yearly_overview_2017.pdf accessed January 2024.

1839. *Ibid.*
1840. *Interflora Inc. v. Marks & Spencer plc* EU:C:2011:604.
1841. EUTMR, Art. 9(2)(c).
1842. *Interflora Inc and another v. Marks and Spencer plc and another* [2013] EWHC 1291 (Ch) (21 May 2013).
1843. *Interflora Inc. v. Marks & Spencer plc* EU:C:2011:604.
1844. *Ibid.*
1845. *Ibid.*
1846. *Ibid.*
1847. *Interflora Inc and another v. Marks and Spencer plc and another* [2013] EWHC 1291 (Ch).
1848. *Ibid.*
1849. Lexology, 'English High Court Holds Marks & Spencer's Use of Interflora Keywords Infringed Trade Marks' (*Lexology*) https://www.lexology.com/library/detail.aspx?g=41410e79-6b39-46e1-bb02-b4d135da299e; *Interflora Inc and another v. Marks and Spencer plc and another* [2013] EWHC 1291 (Ch) https://www.bailii.org/ew/cases/EWHC/Ch/2013/1291.html accessed 4 August 2025.
1850. César Ramírez-Montes, 'EU Trademarks in the Metaverse' 63 IDEA 557, 672.
1851. Case C-383/12 P, *Environmental Mfg. LLP v. OHIM*, ECLI:EU:C:2013:741.
1852. *Ibid.*
1853. European Parliament, 'The United Kingdom' (*European Parliament*, April 2024) https://www.europarl.europa.eu/factsheets/en/sheet/216/the-united-kingdom.
1854. Nominet, 'Dispute Resolution Service Policy' (*Nominet*, 2024) https://nominet.uk/wp-content/uploads/2025/03/Dispute-Resolution-Service-Policy-post-1st-Oct-2016.pdf accessed August 2025.

manner which has taken unfair advantage of or has been unfairly detrimental to the Complainant's Rights.[1855]

This language is familiar to provisions in the EUTMR and the UK Trade Marks Act 1994 and is very relevant to platforms. This provision shows that dispute resolution procedures can and do take into consideration concepts such as unfair acts[1856] on the Internet.

In the US, the FTDA protected against dilutive use of trademarks.[1857] Following that, the Trademark Dilution Revision Act (TDRA) of 2006 was developed to address that 'likelihood'[1858] was sufficient and 'actual dilution'[1859] was not needed as was required in *Moseley v. V Secret.*[1860] Whitaker says this needs to be interpreted 'in light of foreign and international law'.[1861] The U.S. opinion in *Moseley v. V Secret* resulted in a major change to dilution[1862] law, ending in legislation enacted following the decision.[1863] The TDRA was passed in view of further protection for 'famous trademarks'[1864] because the U.S. Supreme Court had 'set an extremely high bar for plaintiffs to prove trademark dilution',[1865] 'fame'[1866] being a requirement.[1867] However, 'courts continue to struggle with anti-dilution law protection for famous trademarks'[1868] and

1855. *Ibid.*
1856. Anselm Kamperman Sanders, *Unfair Competition Law: The Protection of Intellectual and Industrial Creativity* (Oxford University Press, 1997) 8; Frauke Henning-Bodewig, *Unfair Competition Law European Union and Member States* (Kluwer Law International 2006) xv-xvi; Martin Senftleben, Michael Handler and Irene Calboli, 'Protection Against Unfair Competition Around the Globe' (2024) 19 Journal of Intellectual Property Law & Practice 79, 79-80 https://doi.org/10.1093/jiplp/jpad121; Paris Convention, Art. 10bis; EUTMR, Art. 9(2)(c); 15 U.S.C. § 1125(c)(2)(B).
1857. 15 U.S. Code § 1125; Xuan-Thao Nguyen, 'Fame Law: Requiring Proof of National Fame in Trademark Law' (2011) 33 Cardozo Law Review 89, 93.
1858. Britt N Lovejo, 'Tarnishing the Dilution By Tarnishment Cause of Action: Starbucks Corp. v. Wolfe's Borough Coffee, Inc. and V Secret Catalogue, Inc. v. Moseley, Compared' 26 Berkeley Technology Law Journal 623.
1859. *Ibid.*
1860. Britt N Lovejo, 'Tarnishing the Dilution By Tarnishment Cause of Action: Starbucks Corp. v. Wolfe's Borough Coffee, Inc. and V Secret Catalogue, Inc. v. Moseley, Compared' 26 Berkeley Technology Law Journal 623; *Moseley v. V Secret Catalogue, Inc. (Moseley 1)*, 537 U.S. 418 (2003).
1861. Keola R Whitaker, 'Trademark Dilution in a Global Age' (2006) 27 University of Pennsylvania Journal of International Economic Law 907.
1862. Blake R Bertagna, 'Poaching Profits: An Examination of the Ability of a Trademark Owner to Recover an Infringer's Profits Under the Lanham Act' (2008) 16 Texas Intellectual Property Law Journal 257, 265; Matthew J Slowik, 'Ahead of the Curve? The Effect of the Trademark Dilution Revision Act of 2006 on the Federal Circuit' (2009) 18 Federal Circuit Bar Journal 349 in Xuan-Thao Nguyen, 'Fame Law: Requiring Proof of National Fame in Trademark Law' (2011) 33 Cardozo Law Review 91, 93.
1863. *Ibid.*
1864. Keola R Whitaker, 'Trademark Dilution in a Global Age' (2006) 27 University of Pennsylvania Journal of International Economic Law, 907.
1865. *Ibid.*
1866. *Ibid.*
1867. *Ibid.*
1868. Xuan-Thao Nguyen, 'Fame Law: Requiring Proof of National Fame in Trademark Law' (2011) 33 Cardozo Law Review 89, 94.

Nguyen argues that it is hard to assess the 'level of fame'.[1869] The problem is that 'courts have continued to ignore the distinction between infringement and dilution, and have failed to appreciate the different protection offered by each theory'[1870] and related concepts and models.[1871] While U.S. courts have had considerable difficulty applying national dilution[1872] law 'to obligations under international law',[1873] it should be noted that courts worldwide have difficulty differentiating 'trademark infringement'[1874] and 'trademark dilution'.[1875] However, Whitaker argues that 'likelihood of confusion'[1876] should be enlarged to include 'dilution'.[1877] Under the U.S. law, the 'likelihood of confusion'[1878] test is codified in the Lanham Act 15 U.S. Code §§ 1051-1129 and 'has long been used to apply liability for trademark infringement under the rubric of unfair competition'.[1879] However, Sheff argues that confusion[1880] standards help little in a dilution[1881] analysis, competition is not a factor, and it has been problematic to integrate dilution[1882] concepts into law.[1883] Likewise, Pote says, 'the Act applies even in the absence of competition and likelihood of confusion'.[1884]

As defined in 15 U.S. Code § 1125(c)(2)(B), 'dilution by blurring'[1885] is the 'association arising from the similarity between a mark or trade name and a famous mark that impairs the distinctiveness of the famous mark'.[1886] Fisher says that '[b]lurring occurs when the power of the mark is weakened through its identification with dissimilar goods'.[1887] Specifically, 15 U.S.C. § 1125(c)(2)(B) states that 'the court may consider all relevant factors, including the following:

(i) The degree of similarity between the mark or trade name and the famous mark.
(ii) The degree of inherent or acquired distinctiveness of the famous mark.
(iii) The extent to which the owner of the famous mark is engaging in substantially exclusive use of the mark.
(iv) The degree of recognition of the famous mark.

1869. *Ibid.*
1870. 15 U.S. Code § 1127; Kathleen B McCabe, 'Dilution-by-Blurring: A Theory Caught in the Shadow of Trademark Infringement' (2000) 68 Fordham Law Review 1827.
1871. *Ibid.*
1872. Keola R Whitaker, 'Trademark Dilution in a Global Age' (2006) 27 University of Pennsylvania Journal of International Economic Law 907, 908.
1873. *Ibid.*
1874. *Ibid.*
1875. *Ibid.*
1876. Paris Convention, Art. 6bis; TRIPS, Art. 16.
1877. *Ibid.*
1878. *Ibid.*
1879. Jeremy N Sheff, 'The (Boundedly) Rational Basis of Trademark Liability' (2007) 15 Texas Intellectual Property Law Journal 331, 332.
1880. *Ibid.*
1881. *Ibid.*
1882. *Ibid.*
1883. *Ibid.*
1884. Daniel R Pote, 'A Domain by Any Other Name: The Federal Trademark Dilution Act of 1995 Applied to Internet Domain Names' (Spring 1997) 37 Jurimetrics 301 https://www.jstor.org/stable/29762473.
1885. 15 U.S. Code § 1125(c)(2)(B).
1886. *Ibid.*
1887. William Fisher, 'Overview of Trademark Law' (*Harvard*) cyber.law.harvard.edu/metaschool/fisher/domain/tm.htm#8 accessed January 2024.

(v) Whether the user of the mark or trade name intended to create an association with the famous mark.
(vi) Any actual association between the mark or trade name and the famous mark.[1888]

Also, under 15 U.S. Code § 1125(c)(2)(C), 'dilution by tarnishment'[1889] is the 'association arising from the similarity between a mark or trade name and a famous mark that harms the reputation of the famous mark'.[1890] Fisher also summarises that tarnishment[1891] happens when a trademark is 'cast in an unflattering light'[1892] and this is often in the case of 'inferior or unseemly products or services'.[1893] However, Bedi and Reibstein remark that the 'basic definition is deceptively simple'.[1894] In a recent study, Linford, Sevier, and Willis propose that 'the case for tarnishment might be weak in circumstances where courts have been most willing to presume tarnishment occurs ... much of what courts have presumed about the tarnishing effect of sex-, drug, and sacrilege-related uses may be more mythic than material'.[1895] Similarly, the concept of 'free-riding'[1896] is prohibited under the above U.S. Lanham Act provision. For example, '[f]ree riding occurs when the owner of a lesser known mark creates an association with a more famous mark to improve the lesser known mark's reputation or reach by exploiting the famous mark's success'.[1897]

Further, in the context of domain names, 'Congress implemented the ACPA to bridge the gaps in the Anti-Dilution Act.'[1898] Specifically, under 15 U.S. Code § 1125(d): '(II) in the case of a famous mark that is famous at the time of registration of the domain name, is identical or confusingly similar to or dilutive of that mark; or ...'.[1899] In *Toys 'R' Us v. Akkaoui,*[1900] in which *adultsrus.com* was deemed to be tarnishing the Toys 'R' Us mark.[1901] Also, in *Moseley v. V Secret,*[1902] the utilisation of 'Victor's Little Secret'[1903] was at issue. The Supreme Court reversed and remanded the case to the Sixth

1888. 15 U.S.C. § 1125(c)(2)(B).
1889. 15 U.S. Code § 1125(c)(2)(C).
1890. *Ibid.*
1891. William Fisher, 'Overview of Trademark Law' (*Harvard*) cyber.law.harvard.edu/metaschool/fisher/domain/tm.htm#8 accessed January 2024.
1892. *Ibid.*
1893. *Ibid.*
1894. Suneal Bedi and David Reibstein, 'Measuring Trademark Dilution by Tarnishment' (2020) 95 Indiana Law Journal 683.
1895. Jake Linford, Justin Sevier and Allyson Willis, 'Trademark Tarnishmyths' (2023) 55 Arizona State Law Journal https://ssrn.com/abstract=4183500 accessed 4 August 2025.
1896. 15 U.S. Code § 1125(c).
1897. Ryder Hogan, .Examining the Unconstitutionality of Dilution by Tarnishment after Tam. (2019) 27 American University Journal of Gender, Social Policy & the Law 466, 471; World Intellectual Property Organization, Pub. No. 725(E), Protection Against Unfair Competition 55 (1994) https://tind.wipo.int/record/20405?v=pdf accessed January 2024.
1898. CEB, *Internet Law Practice in California* (Continuing Education of the Bar, the Regents of the University of California 2015) §3.22.
1899. 15 U.S. Code § 1125(d).
1900. *Toys 'R' Us v. Akkaoui,* 40 U.S.P.Q. 2d (BNA) 1836 (N.D. Cal. 29 October 1996).
1901. William Fisher, 'Overview of Trademark Law' (*Harvard*) cyber.law.harvard.edu/metaschool/fisher/domain/tm.htm#8 accessed January 2024.
1902. *Moseley v. V Secret Catalogue, Inc.* (01-1015) 537 U.S. 418 (2003) 259 F.3d 464.
1903. *Ibid.*

Circuit[1904], which decided that there was tarnishment.[1905] It appears that single or multiple domains or 'inferior products or services'[1906] which associate with an original mark may be considered dilutive[1907] of that original mark.[1908] Bedi and Reibstein note that, in *Mattel v. Internet Dimensions,*[1909] it was determined that the website *barbiesplaypen.com* which 'portrayed Barbie dolls in lewd sex acts tarnished the Barbie brand'.[1910] In *Williams-Sonoma v. Friendfinder,*[1911] various defendants in default were 'permanently enjoined from infringing or diluting in any manner WSI's POTTERY BARN family of marks'.[1912] The court found that Friendfinder utilised 'Pottery Barn',[1913] a protected mark, 'to direct internet users to sex oriented websites'.[1914] Some of these decisions were made based on the domain name, while others appeared to factor in the content on the associated websites to make the determination. In *Nike v. Nikepal,*[1915] a strictly online business (operating through nikepal.com) marketed laboratory and related products and held a registered trademark for NIKEPAL.[1916] The District Court found dilution based on the fame associated with the NIKE mark and under 15 U.S.C. § 1125(c)(2)(B) assessed the six factors in favour of Nike.[1917] Specifically in the context of websites, NIKEPAL registered several domains including 'nikepal.biz, nikepal.net, nikepal.us, nikepal.info and nikepal.tv'[1918] and the court found that related 'under construction'[1919] pages promoting NIKE products caused 'actual association',[1920] one of the six factors, with NIKE.

1904. *Ibid.*
1905. *V Secret Catalogue, Inc., et al. v. Moseley, et al.* No. 08-5793 https://www.opn.ca6.uscourts.gov/opinions.pdf/10a0144p-06.pdf accessed 4 August 2025; IP Watchdog, 'Trademark Tarnishment: Trademark Law's Dirty Little Secret' (*IPWatchdog.com | Patents & Patent Law* 9 April 2014) http://www.ipwatchdog.com/2010/10/21/trademark-tarnishment-trademark-law-dirty-little-secret/id=12905/ accessed January 2024.
1906. *Ibid.*
1907. *Ibid.*
1908. *Ibid.*
1909. *Mattel, Inc. v. Internet Dimensions Inc.*, No. 99 Civ. 10066(HB), 2000 U.S. Dist. LEXIS 9747 *(S.D.N.Y.* 13 July 2000).
1910. Suneal Bedi and David Reibstein, 'Measuring Trademark Dilution by Tarnishment' (2020) 95 Indiana Law Journal 683; *Mattel, Inc. v. Internet Dimensions Inc.*, No. 99 Civ. 10066(HB), 2000 US Dist. LEXIS 9747 *(S.D.N.Y.* 13 July 2000).
1911. *Williams-Sonoma, Inc. v. Friendfinder, Inc.*, 2007 U.S. Dist. LEXIS 98118.
1912. *Ibid.*
1913. *Ibid.*
1914. Suneal Bedi and David Reibstein, 'Measuring Trademark Dilution by Tarnishment' (2020) 95 Indiana Law Journal 683; *Williams-Sonoma, Inc. v. Friendfinder, Inc.*, 2007 U.S. Dist. LEXIS 98118.
1915. *Nike, Inc. v. Nikepal Intern., Inc.* 84 U.S.P.Q.2d 1820 (E.D. Cal. 2007); Barton Beebe, 'Trademark Law: An Open-Source Casebook Version 10' (2020), 444-461 https://www.tmcasebook.org/wp-content/uploads/2023/07/BeebeTMLaw-v10-digital-edition.pdf accessed July 2024.
1916. *Ibid.*
1917. *Ibid.*
1918. *Ibid.*
1919. *Ibid.*
1920. *Ibid.*

In *Rosetta Stone v. Google,*[1921] the dilution[1922] holding was vacated[1923] and the dilution[1924] claim under the TDRA failed because the 'brand awareness had only increased'.[1925] In *Tiffany v. eBay,*[1926] rejection of the dilution[1927] claim was affirmed 'because eBay ... never used the [Tiffany] Marks to refer to eBay's own product'.[1928] Franklyn and Hyman recognise that 'most of the litigation involving trademarks as search engine keywords features competitors who are selling similar goods to those bearing the trademark, which is quite different than the typical dilution by blurring or by tarnishment cause of action'.[1929]

In the NFT dilution context, in *Hermès v. Rothschild,*[1930] as discussed in section 3.2.3 *Digital Confusion*, the jury found dilution from the Metabirkin bags marketed by Rothschild, necessarily finding that the marks were famous.[1931] On motions filed, the District Court found that 'Rothschild's use of Hermes' trademarks do not qualify as First Amendment protected speech that is exempt from anti-dilution laws'[1932] which will be discussed in the section 3.2.7 *Digital Justification*.

Section 10(3) of the UK Trade Marks Act 1994 protects against 'unfair advantage'.[1933] Dilution[1934] in Canada was initially included in the Trade Marks Act 1953 as 'depreciation of goodwill',[1935] which may potentially be even stronger than U.S. dilution laws.[1936] This is also enacted in Canada under section 22 of the Canadian Trademarks Act, although, as Janis and Yu say was 'largely ignored in the Courts until 2006, when the Supreme Court of Canada ... invoked section 22 as the basis for relief against dilution'.[1937]

1921. *Rosetta Stone Ltd. v. Google Inc.*, 730 F.Supp.2d 531, 550-53 (E.D. Va. 2010).
1922. 15 U.S. Code § 1125(c)(2)(B).
1923. David J Franklyn and David A Hyman, 'Trademarks as Search Engine Keywords: Much Ado About Something?' 26 Harvard Journal of Law & Technology 481 (2013).
1924. 15 U.S. Code § 1125(c)(2)(B).
1925. *Ibid.*
1926. *Tiffany (NJ) Inc. and Tiffany and Company v. eBay, Inc.* 600 F.3d 93 (2d Cir. 2010).
1927. Berkman Klein Center, 'Tiffany (NJ) Inc. and Tiffany and Company v. eBay, Inc. 600 F.3d 93 (2d Cir. 2010)' (*Tiffany Abridged,* 2010) https://cyber.harvard.edu/people/tfisher/IP/2010%20Tiffany%20Abridged.pdf accessed 4 August 2025.
1928. *Ibid.*
1929. David J Franklyn and David A Hyman, 'Trademarks as Search Engine Keywords: Much Ado About Something?' (2013) 26 Harvard Journal of Law & Technology 481.
1930. *Hermès International v. Rothschild* (22-cv-384, US District Court SD New York, 2023).
1931. Moish Peltz, 'Hermès v. Rothschild: A Landmark Decision for Trademarks and NFTs' (*Falcon, Rappaport& Berkan LLP,* 10 February 2023) https://frblaw.com/hermes-v-rothschild-a-landmark-decision-for-trademarks-and-nfts/ accessed January 2024.
1932. *Hermès International v. Rothschild* (22-cv-384, US District Court SD New York, 2023).
1933. *Ibid.*
1934. Canadian Trade Marks Act 1953.
1935. Canadian Trademarks Act R.S.C., 1985, c. T-13, s. 22.
1936. Keola R Whitaker, 'Trademark Dilution in a Global Age' (2006) 27 University of Pennsylvania Journal of International Economic Law 907, 926.
1937. Mark D Janis and Peter K Yu, 'International and Comparative Aspects of Trademark Dilution, Symposium issue of Transnational Law and Contemporary Problems' (2008) 17 Transnational Law & Contemporary Problems 603.

Platforms and the UDRP should consider directly incorporating dilution,[1938] misappropriation,[1939] and 'unfair advantage'[1940] into their policies where absent. One way of implementing this is through the terminology 'unfair competition',[1941] which includes 'unfair acts',[1942] trade practices,[1943] or 'unfair competition'.[1944]

3.2.4.5 *Summary of Platform Considerations for Digital Unfair Competition*

Several theories and concepts inform the model from the perspective of unfair competition,[1945] including unfair acts,[1946] trade practices,[1947] or unfair competition.[1948] The UDRP and platforms should consider specifically incorporating aspects of these. Specifically, unfair competition[1949] should be considered explicitly as a major element related to trademark and unfair competition law and theory. Likewise, they should consider famous,[1950] well-known,[1951] reputable,[1952] and strong[1953] marks, and afford greater protection under general trademark principles. Relatedly, platforms should

1938. 15 U.S.C. § 1125(c)(2)(B); EUTMR, Art. 9(2)(c).
1939. Dima Basma, 'Dilution Versus Unfair Advantage: Myths and Realities' (2021) 52 International Review of Intellectual Property and Competition Law 1217-1257 https://doi.org/10.1007/s40319-021-01116-z; David Barnes, 'Misappropriation of Trademark' (2008) 9 North Carolina Journal of Law & Technology 171.
1940. EUTMR, Art. 9(2)(c).
1941. Anselm Kamperman Sanders, *Unfair Competition Law: The Protection of Intellectual and Industrial Creativity* (Oxford University Press, 1997) 8.
1942. EUTMR, Art. 9(2)(c) and Art. 17(2); 15 U.S.C. §1125.
1943. Anselm Kamperman Sanders, *Unfair Competition Law: The Protection of Intellectual and Industrial Creativity* (Oxford University Press 1997) 134-136; Hossein Bidgoli, *The Internet Encyclopedia* (John Wiley & Sons, vol. 3, 2004) 452.
1944. Anselm Kamperman Sanders, *Unfair Competition Law: The Protection of Intellectual and Industrial Creativity* (Oxford University Press, 1997) 8; EUTMR, Art. 9(2)(c) and Art. 17(2); 15 U.S.C. §1125.
1945. *Ibid.*
1946. Anselm Kamperman Sanders, *Unfair Competition Law: The Protection of Intellectual and Industrial Creativity* (Oxford University Press, 1997) 8; Frauke Henning-Bodewig, *Unfair Competition Law European Union and Member States* (Kluwer Law International 2006) xv-xvi; EUTMR, Art. 9(2)(c) and Art. 17(2); 15 U.S.C. §1125.
1947. Anselm Kamperman Sanders, *Unfair Competition Law: The Protection of Intellectual and Industrial Creativity* (Oxford University Press, 1997) 8; Frauke Henning-Bodewig, *Unfair Competition Law European Union and Member States* (Kluwer Law International 2006) xv-xvi.
1948. Anselm Kamperman Sanders, *Unfair Competition Law: The Protection of Intellectual and Industrial Creativity* (Oxford University Press, 1997) 8; EUTMR, Art. 9(2)(c) and Art. 17(2); 15 U.S.C. §1125.
1949. *Ibid.*
1950. Stefan Martin, 'Well Known Marks and Parody: Dilution and Denigration? Unfair Advantage?' (*EUIPO*, 2017), https://euipo.europa.eu/knowledge/pluginfile.php/77920/mod_resource/content/8/Limits%20of%20trade%20marks%2C%20Parody%2018-5-2017.pdf accessed January 2024.
1951. Paris Convention, Art. 6bis; TRIPS, Art. 16(2); EUTMR, Art. 8(2)(c).
1952. EUTMR, Arts 8(5) and 9(1)(c).
1953. Timothy D Greene and Jeff Wilkerson, 'Understanding Trademark Strength' (2013) 16 Stanford Technology Law Review 535-582, abstract.

consider dilution[1954] theory and law, unfair advantage,[1955] free riding,[1956] and misappropriation[1957] concepts, including distinctive marks.[1958] It is argued that 'unfair competition'[1959] covers all of the acts covered in this section and this terminology is recommended for the UDRP and platforms alike without the need to reference each related concept within their terms and policies.

3.2.5 Digital Terms, Policies, and Disclaimers

Generally, there is little trademark theory that addresses Terms, Policies, and Disclaimers specifically for trademarks, even though contract or related law may play a significant role.[1960] Various terms and conditions are used in the Internet context in different settings. In e-commerce marketplace, search ad, social media, mobile app, and Metaverse platforms, there are possibilities to include various terms, conditions, policies or disclaimers. For example, an e-commerce marketplace or mobile app platform may have 'Terms of Use'[1961] of that website or app with various possible titles such as Terms, User Agreement, Terms and Conditions etc. When running a search advertising campaign, terms and conditions are generally agreed to upon signup, as is the case with social media accounts and mobile app platforms. Some platforms have begun to offer specialised programmes such as the Amazon Brand Registry,[1962] as will be seen further in Chapter 5. Fromer and McKenna argue that this registry is a 'cheaper and more efficient way to resolve disputes'[1963] but that its rules have a great impact on the trademark system itself.[1964] Platforms such as Amazon and others need to consider the text of their terms, conditions and/or policies which drive such programmes and

1954. EUTMR, Art. 9(2)(c); 15 U.S.C. § 1125(c)(2)(B).
1955. *Ibid.*
1956. EUTMR, Art. 9(2)(c) and Art. 17(2); 15 U.S.C. §1125.
1957. *Ibid.*
1958. EUTMR, Recital 21.
1959. Anselm Kamperman Sanders, *Unfair Competition Law: The Protection of Intellectual and Industrial Creativity* (Oxford University Press, 1997) 8; EUTMR, Art. 9(2)(c) and Art. 17(2); 15 U.S.C. §1125.
1960. Europa, 'Consumer Contracts Law' (*Europa*, 1 August 2018) https://commission.europa.eu/law/law-topic/consumer-protection-law/consumer-contract-law_en accessed January 2024; Oliver Herzfeld, 'Are Website Terms of Use Enforceable?' (*Forbes*, 20 March 2015) https://www.forbes.com/sites/oliverherzfeld/2013/01/22/are-website-terms-of-use-enforceable/#3975e7a1f4a7 accessed January 2024; Christopher P Knight, 'Canada: What Makes Standard Terms and Conditions Enforceable?' http://www.mondaq.com/canada/x/90528/Contract Law/What Makes Standard Terms And Conditions Enforceable accessed January 2024.
1961. Google, 'Google Terms of Service' (*Google Privacy and Terms*) https://policies.google.com/terms?hl=en&gl=us accessed January 2024; Apple, 'Legal: Apple Media Services - Apple' (*Apple Canada*) https://www.apple.com/legal/internet-services/itunes/us/terms.html accessed January 2024.
1962. Amazon, 'Let's Protect the Brand You Built' (*Amazon Brand Registry*) https://brandservices.amazon.com/ accessed July 2024.
1963. *Ibid.*
1964. Jeanne Fromer and Mark McKenna, 'Amazon's Quiet Overhaul of the Trademark System' (2024 forthcoming 2025) 113 California Law Review 3, NYU Law and Economics Research Paper Forthcoming, Public Law Research Paper Forthcoming https://ssrn.com/abstract=4870984 accessed 4 August 2025.

ensure there is sufficient coverage for the types of issues that trademarks in their platforms raise (as seen through the model) and uniform[1965] approaches based on aspects of common principles legal frameworks could result in consistent application across platforms as will be seen in the following chapters.

In the EU, interestingly, and as it relates to platforms, the Regulation (EU) 2019/1150 of the European Parliament and of the Council of 20 June 2019 on promoting fairness and transparency for business users of online intermediation services makes specific mention of terms and conditions. Specifically, Preamble 17 states:

> The ownership and control of intellectual property rights online can have significant economic importance for both the providers of online intermediation services and their business users. To ensure clarity and transparency for business users and for their better understanding, providers of online intermediation services should within their terms and conditions include general, or more detailed, information if they so wish, regarding the overall effects, if any, of those terms and conditions on the ownership and control of intellectual property rights of the business user. Such information could, inter alia, include information such as the general usage of logos, trademarks or brand names.[1966]

Although it is voluntary to include such clarity in terms, it is incumbent on platforms to strongly consider this because of the role trademarks have on the Internet.

In the US, as a matter of law, certain terms and conditions or policies may be effective for specific purposes. Although there is no federal law requiring websites to contain terms, there are state laws such as the California Online Privacy Protection Act (Calif. Bus. & Prof. Code § 22575) which require specific statements on website. Under Calif. Bus. & Prof. Code § 22575(a), '[a]n operator of a commercial Web site or online service that collects personally identifiable information through the Internet about individual consumers residing in California who use or visit its commercial Web site or online service shall conspicuously post its privacy policy on its Web site …'.[1967] The Code 'requires the operator of a commercial web site or online service to disclose in its privacy policy how it responds to a web browser "Do Not Track" signal or similar

1965. Rajeev Sachdev, 'Towards an Improved Framework for Trade-Mark Law and Regulation in Social Media Usernames: A Study of the Canadian, U.S., and U.K. Positions' (2016) 28 Intellectual Property Journal 379, 379-418; Daniel Doft, 'Facebook, Twitter, and the Wild West of IP Enforcement on Social Media: Weighing the Merits of a Uniform Dispute Resolution Policy' (2016) 49 The John Marshall Law Review 959; Thomas J Curtin, 'The Name Game: Cybersquatting and Trademark Infringement on Social Media Websites' (2010-2011) 19 Journal of Law and Policy 353; Erick J Heels, 'How to Twittersquat the Top 100 Brands' (*GiantPeople*, 8 January 2009) http://www.giantpeople.com/1298.html accessed 4 August 2025; Paul D McGrady, *McGrady on Social Media and the Metaverse* (Mathew Bender & Company, Inc. 2023) §12; John McElwaine and Christopher D Casavale, 'Tackling Bad Faith Registration of Domain Names in a Fast-Changing Landscape' (*WIPO Magazine*, December 2019) https://www.wipo.int/wipo_magazine/en/2019/06/article_0006.html accessed June 2025.

1966. Regulation (EU) 2019/1150 of the European Parliament and of the Council of 20 June 2019 on promoting fairness and transparency for business users of online intermediation services, Preamble 17.

1967. Calif. Bus. & Prof. Code § 22575(a).

mechanisms'[1968] among other requirements. However, in the context of trademarks, there is no such requirement. Further, terms and conditions may be subject to scrutiny by the FTC and should not be misleading.[1969]

Uniform policies such as the UDRP and ccTLD dispute resolution policies are informative to the model as they provide context for dealing with trademarks in the context of domain names. The UDRP is discussed in more depth in the next chapter, and reference to ccTLDs has been made in this chapter. Sachdev,[1970] Curtin,[1971] Doft,[1972] Heels,[1973] Pesochinsk,[1974] Levy and Dorrain,[1975] and McGrady[1976] all discussed the potential for uniform policies for social media and Internet situations. Platforms should consider the UDRP and its long history of resolving trademarks in domain names in a uniform way, and consider adopting similar policies.[1977]

Disclaimers are also relevant to a trademark analysis. Under the UDRP, 'a clear and sufficiently prominent disclaimer would lend support to circumstances suggesting

1968. Calif. Bus. & Prof. Code § 22575; NCSL, 'State Laws Related to Internet Privacy' (*NCSL*, 22 June 2022) https://www.ncsl.org/technology-and-communication/state-laws-related-to-digital-privacy.
1969. FTC, 'Advertising and Marketing on the Internet: Rules of the Road' (*Federal Trade Commission*) https://www.ftc.gov/system/files/ftc_gov/pdf/bus28-rulesroad-2023_508.pdf accessed January 2024; FTC, 'Snapchat Settles FTC Charges That Promises of Disappearing Messages Were False' (*Federal Trade Commission*) https://www.ftc.gov/news-events/news/press-releases/2014/05/snapchat-settles-ftc-charges-promises-disappearing-messages-were-false accessed January 2024.
1970. Rajeev Sachdev, 'Towards an Improved Framework for Trade-Mark Law and Regulation in Social Media Usernames: A Study of the Canadian, U.S., and U.K. Positions' (2016) 28 Intellectual Property Journal 379.
1971. Thomas J Curtin, 'The Name Game: Cybersquatting and Trademark Infringement on Social Media Websites' (2010-2011) 19 Journal of Law and Policy 353, 359 notes.
1972. Daniel Doft, 'Facebook, Twitter, and the Wild West of IP Enforcement on Social Media: Weighing the Merits of a Uniform Dispute Resolution Policy' (2016) 49 The John Marshall Law Review 959.
1973. Erick J Heels, 'How to Twittersquat the Top 100 Brands' (*GiantPeople*, 8 January 2009) http://www.giantpeople.com/1298.html accessed 4 August 2025.
1974. Zorik Pesochinsky, 'Almost Famous: Preventing Username Squatting on Social Networking Websites' (2010) 28 Cardozo Arts & Entertainment Law Journal 223, 224-225; Daniel Doft, 'Facebook, Twitter, and the Wild West of IP Enforcement on Social Media: Weighing the Merits of a Uniform Dispute Resolution Policy' (2016) 49 The John Marshall Law Review 959, 1009-1011.
1975. Daniel Doft, 'Facebook, Twitter, and the Wild West of IP Enforcement on Social Media: Weighing the Merits of a Uniform Dispute Resolution Policy' (2016) 49 The John Marshall Law Review 959, 1009-1011.
1976. Daniel Doft, 'Facebook, Twitter, and the Wild West of IP Enforcement on Social Media: Weighing the Merits of a Uniform Dispute Resolution Policy' (2016) 49 The John Marshall Law Review 959, 1007-1009; Paul D McGrady, *McGrady on Social Media and the Metaverse* (Mathew Bender & Company, Inc. 2023) §12.
1977. Rajeev Sachdev, 'Towards an Improved Framework for Trade-Mark Law and Regulation in Social Media Usernames: A Study of the Canadian, U.S., and U.K. Positions' (2016) 28 Intellectual Property Journal 379; Daniel Doft, 'Facebook, Twitter, and the Wild West of IP Enforcement on Social Media: Weighing the Merits of a Uniform Dispute Resolution Policy' (2016) 49 The John Marshall Law Review 959; Thomas J Curtin, 'The Name Game: Cybersquatting and Trademark Infringement on Social Media Websites' (2010-2011) 19 Journal of Law and Policy 353; Heels EJ, 'How to Twittersquat the Top 100 Brands' (* *GiantPeople*) http://www.giantpeople.com/1298.html accessed 4 August 2025; Paul D McGrady, *McGrady on Social Media: 2018* (LexisNexis 2018).

its good faith'.[1978] In the context of social media, Peukert says that, if a platform does not incorporate a jurisdiction-specific option,[1979] 'the global web presence of the user on this platform has to be supplemented with a disclaimer'.[1980] In other words, if it is not obvious through the service itself to which jurisdiction the social media account and associated trademark are in reference to, a disclaimer may be one way of making that clear.[1981] In the EU/UK case of *Interflora,*[1982] although appealed on other grounds, following the response from the CJ on reference of specific questions, the UK judge held in Interflora[1983] that '[t]he defendants should have prevented the risk of confusion by appropriate design of the advertisements, such as by including a disclaimer'.[1984] It seems to suggest that the use of a disclaimer may have helped to prevent confusion.[1985] In the US, disclaimers have been recognised in the context of trademarks, on occasion, since early days. In *Singer v. June,*[1986] the court 'enjoined'[1987] the non mark holder's use of SINGER[1988] 'or any equivalent thereto, in advertisements in relation to sewing machines, without clearly and unmistakably stating in all said advertisements that the machines are made by'[1989] the non mark holder.[1990] However, disclaimers have only sometimes been recognised to avoid liability, while in other cases, they have had no effect and even the opposite effect.[1991] However, in *Gruma v. Mexican Rests,*[1992] it was stated that '[d]isclaimers are appropriate when they can effectively make the presentation of particular information no longer deceptive or misleading'.[1993] However, it was

1978. *Evolution Gaming Group AB v. Domains By Proxy, LLC/Engin Talih, Tum Ltd.* Case No. D2020-1666 https://www.wipo.int/amc/en/domains/search/text.jsp?case=D2020-1666.
1979. Alexander Peukert, 'The Coexistence of Trade Mark Laws and Rights on the Internet, and the Impact of Geolocation Technologies' (2016) 47 International Review of Intellectual Property and Competition Law 60, 81 https://doi.org/10.1007/s40319-015-0427-8.
1980. *Ibid.*
1981. *Ibid.*
1982. *Interflora Inc and another v. Marks and Spencer plc and another* [2013] EWHC 1291 (Ch).
1983. *Ibid.*
1984. *Ibid.*
1985. Robert Burrell and Michael Handler, 'Keyword Advertising and Actionable Consumer Confusion' (2020) 15 in Aplin Tanya (ed.) *Research Handbook on Intellectual Property and Digital Technologies* (Edward Elgar 2020); UNSW Law Research Paper No. 21-11 https://ssrn.com/abstract=3776895 accessed 4 August 2025.
1986. *Singer Mfg. Co. v. June Mfg. Co.*, 163 U.S. 169, 204 (1896).
1987. *Ibid.*; Timothy D Greene and Jeff Wilkerson, 'Understanding Trademark Strength' (2013) 16 Stanford Technology Law Review 535, 542.
1988. *Ibid.*
1989. *Ibid.*
1990. *Ibid.*
1991. Robert Burrell and Michael Handler, 'Keyword Advertising and Actionable Consumer Confusion' (2020) 15 in Aplin Tanya (ed.), *Research Handbook on Intellectual Property and Digital Technologies* (Edward Elgar 2020); UNSW Law Research Paper No. 21-11 https://ssrn.com/abstract=3776895 accessed 4 August 2025; Jake Linford 'Brief of Trademark and Internet Law Professors as *Amici Curiae* in Support of Respondent' (18 February 2020). FSU College of Law, Public Law Research Paper No. 923, FSU College of Law, Law, Business & Economics Paper No. 20-10, https://ssrn.com/abstract=3541921 accessed 4 August 2025 or http://dx.doi.org/10.2139/ssrn.3541921; Johnny Walsh, 'Confusion Mélange: A Call to Revise the Law On Trademark Infringement, Initial Interest Confusion, and Digital Marketing' (2020) 57 Indiana Law Review 281, 295 https://doi.org/10.18060/27650.
1992. *Gruma Corp. v. Mexican Rests., Inc.*, 2013 U.S. Dist. LEXIS 200183.
1993. *Ibid.*

also recognised that 'the mere presence of a disclaimer does not necessarily prevent consumer confusion ... [and] ... 'an obscure or inconspicuous disclaimer will not be sufficient ... to reduce confusion'.[1994] Conversely, 'a conspicuous disclaimer can reduce or eliminate any confusion of source or affiliation'.[1995] In *Hermes v. Rothschild,*[1996] discussed in section 3.2.3 *Digital Confusion*, Rothschild insisted that the disclaimer used that 'MetaBirkins are artworks by Mason Rothschild and are not affiliated with or endorsed or sponsored by Hermes' should be effective.[1997] The court disagreed, citing the recent case of *Jack Daniels*[1998] as well as referring back to the trial of the matter where this same disclaimer 'failed to convince jurors that he was not-liable under the Lanham Act'.[1999] It appears that a disclaimer with respect to counterfeit products would be ineffective.

In line with this, a Canadian case is informative. A disclaimer in the form of a 'warning'[2000] that goods were in fact 'high quality replicas',[2001] in other words, counterfeit,[2002] did not work for the defendant in the Canadian case of *Lululemon*.[2003] The court said that '[i]t is no defence to assert that the defendant added information intended to warn the consumer that the goods were not those of the plaintiff'.[2004] Also, the court reiterated that 'the addition of distinguishing features or designs is not a defence if the defendant uses the exact trademark or a confusing one'.[2005]

Platforms should consider enforcing clear and conspicuous disclaimers[2006] where a reasonable consumer would immediately believe there was no association and not be confused.[2007]

3.2.5.1 Summary of Platform Considerations for Digital Terms, Policies, and Disclaimers

Platforms should consider clear terms and conditions pertinent to trademarks within their services. More specifically, platforms should consider UDRP-like uniform policies in lieu of existing policies.[2008] Platforms should consider clear and conspicuous

---

1994. *Ibid.*
1995. *Ibid.*; *Pebble Beach Co. v. Tour* 18 I Ltd., 155 F.3d 526.
1996. *Hermes Int'l v. Rothschild*, 22-cv-384 (JSR) (S.D.N.Y. 23 June 2023).
1997. *Ibid.*
1998. *Jack Daniel's Props., Inc. v. VIP Products, L.L.C.*, No. CV14-023057-PHX-SMM, 2021 WL 5710730 (D. Ariz. 8 October 2021).
1999. *Hermes Int'l v. Rothschild*, 22-cv-384 (JSR) (S.D.N.Y. 23 June 2023).
2000. *Lululemon Athletica Canada Inc. v. Campbell* 2022 FC 194.
2001. *Ibid.*
2002. *Ibid.*
2003. *Ibid.*
2004. *Ibid.*
2005. *Ibid.*
2006. WIPO, 'WIPO Overview of WIPO Panel Views on Selected UDRP Questions, Third Edition' ('WIPO Jurisprudential Overview 3.0') (*WIPO*, 2017) https://www.wipo.int/amc/en/domains/search/overview3.0/ accessed June 2025.
2007. Paris Convention, Art. 6bis; TRIPS, Art. 16(1); EUTMR, Art. 8(1)(b) and Art. 9(2)(b); 15 U.S. Code § 1114;15 U.S. Code § 1125.
2008. Rajeev Sachdev, 'Towards an Improved Framework for Trade-Mark Law and Regulation in Social Media Usernames: A Study of the Canadian, U.S., and U.K. Positions' (2016) 28

disclaimers[2009] as effective within platforms. However, hidden, buried, inconspicuous, or unclear disclaimers should be rejected.[2010]

3.2.6 Digital Jurisdictional and Territorial Considerations

Ohly says, '[i]n the global world created by the internet, national boundaries lose their significance'[2011] and that IP law 'which is firmly rooted in the notion of territoriality, therefore faces new challenges'.[2012] Scholars such as Peukert have raised the issue of digital trademarks and opine that 'trademark conflicts on the internet continue to raise intricate questions'.[2013] Peukert says that the '[f]reedom of online communication is subject to national/supranational trademark laws, and these laws are subject to the principle of territoriality',[2014] such principle also being recognised by Calboli.[2015] And as aptly noted by Calboli, 'national trademark laws have been largely harmonized in the past century through several multilateral treaties';[2016] however, the utilisation of

Intellectual Property Journal 379, 379-418; Daniel Doft, 'Facebook, Twitter, and the Wild West of IP Enforcement on Social Media: Weighing the Merits of a Uniform Dispute Resolution Policy' (2016) 49 The John Marshall Law Review 959; Thomas J Curtin, 'The Name Game: Cybersquatting and Trademark Infringement on Social Media Websites' (2010-2011) 19 Journal of Law and Policy 353; Erick J Heels, 'How to Twittersquat the Top 100 Brands' (*GiantPeople*, 8 January 2009) http://www.giantpeople.com/1298.html accessed 4 August 2025; Paul D McGrady, *McGrady on Social Media and the Metaverse* (Mathew Bender & Company, Inc. 2023) §12; John McElwaine and Christopher D Casavale, 'Tackling Bad Faith Registration of Domain Names in a Fast-Changing Landscape' (*WIPO Magazine*, December 2019) https://www.wipo.int/wipo_magazine/en/2019/06/article_0006.html accessed June 2025.

2009. WIPO, 'WIPO Overview of WIPO Panel Views on Selected UDRP Questions, Third Edition' ('WIPO Jurisprudential Overview 3.0') (*WIPO*, 2017) https://www.wipo.int/amc/en/domains/search/overview3.0/ accessed June 2025; Alexander Peukert, 'The Coexistence of Trade Mark Laws and Rights on the Internet, and the Impact of Geolocation Technologies' (2016) 47 International Review of Intellectual Property and Competition Law 60, 81 https://doi.org/10.1007/s40319-015-0427-8; Leslie Fair, 'Full Disclosure' (*FTC Business Blog*, 23 September 2014) https://www.ftc.gov/business-guidance/blog/2014/09/full-disclosure accessed June 2025; *Gruma Corp. v. Mexican Rests., Inc.*, 2013 U.S. Dist. LEXIS 200183.
2010. *Ibid.*
2011. Ansgar Ohly, 'Choice of Law in the Digital Environment: Problems and Possible Solutions' in Josef Drexl and Annette Kur (eds), *Intellectual Property and Private International Law: Heading for the Future* (Bloomsbury Publishing 2005) 241.
2012. *Ibid.*
2013. Alexander Peukert, 'The Coexistence of Trade Mark Laws and Rights on the Internet, and the Impact of Geolocation Technologies' (2016) 47 International Review of Intellectual Property and Competition Law 60, 61 https://doi.org/10.1007/s40319-015-0427-8.
2014. Alexander Peukert, 'The Coexistence of Trade Mark Laws and Rights on the Internet, and the Impact of Geolocation Technologies' (2016) 47 International Review of Intellectual Property and Competition Law 60, 81 https://doi.org/10.1007/s40319-015-0427-8.
2015. Irene Calboli and Jane Ginsburg, 'Preface', in Irene Calboli and Jane Gindburg JC (eds), *The Cambridge Handbook of International and Comparative Trademark Law* (Cambridge University Press 2020) XXI.
2016. Irene Calboli, 'Trademarks' in Jan Smits, Jaako Husa, Catherine Valcke and Madalena Narciso, *Elgar Encyclopedia of Comparative Law* (Elgar Online 2023) 499, 499.

digital trademarks on platforms raises complicated jurisdictional and territorial considerations. Peukert further opines that 'the fragmented character of these disputes'[2017] contributes to the problem and that these are 'often adjudicated before different courts according to different laws'.[2018] As Daniel notes with respect to the digital context, assessing the 'place of infringement'[2019] for IP rights termed 'localization of infringement'[2020] and specifically when 'the act is done over the internet, is a complex matter that is addressed differently by different countries'.[2021]

3.2.6.1 *Jurisdictional and Territorial*

Clearly, trademark law is 'regional/territorial'.[2022] This is complicated by the fact that 'domain names' (but also social media usernames, mobile app names and the like) 'are utilized in every region of the globe and are not restricted in the kinds of goods or services to which they might refer'.[2023] However, Garnett proposed a 'single, transnational, IP right'[2024] in line with the EUTM, although he recognised that such would be unlikely to be implemented.[2025] Garnett argued the 'unilateralism'[2026] approach involving the 'unilateral application of domestic law to transnational disputes'[2027] in line with an approach used by the ACPA.[2028] Despite various studies[2029] having been conducted and even though the preamble to the Joint Recommendation Concerning Provisions on

2017. Alexander Peukert, 'The Coexistence of Trade Mark Laws and Rights on the Internet, and the Impact of Geolocation Technologies' (2016) 47 International Review of Intellectual Property and Competition Law 60, 61 https://doi.org/10.1007/s40319-015-0427-8.
2018. *Ibid.*
2019. Naama Daniel, 'Transnational Competition: From Enforcement of Foreign Unfair Competition Judgments to Global Trademarks' (2023) 64 IDEA 31, 103.
2020. *Ibid.*
2021. *Ibid.*
2022. Julien Chaisse, 'The Merging of Two Worlds: Cyber Law and Trade Law Normative Convergence on Internet Domain Names' (2019) 37 Boston University International Law Journal 281; Brendan J Witherell, 'Trademark Law: The Extraterritorial Application of the Lanham Act: The First Circuit Cuts the Fat from the Vanity Fair Test' (2006) 29 Western New England Law Review 193, 197.
2023. Julien Chaisse and Danny Friedmann, 'Law of the Digital Domain: Trademarks, Domain Names, and the AI Frontier' (2024) 64 IDEA 399, 427.
2024. Richard L Garnett, 'Trademarks and the Internet: Resolution of International IP Disputes by Unilateral Application of U.S. Laws' (2005) 30 Brooklyn Journal of International Law 925, 926.
2025. *Ibid.*
2026. Richard L Garnett, 'Trademarks and the Internet: Resolution of International IP Disputes by Unilateral Application of U.S. Laws' (2005) 30 Brooklyn Journal of International Law 925, 926-927.
2027. *Ibid.*
2028. *Ibid.*
2029. Josef Drexl and Annette Kur (eds), *Intellectual Property and Private International Law: Heading for the Future* (Bloomsbury Publishing 2005) 241; Alexander Peukert, 'The Coexistence of Trade Mark Laws and Rights on the Internet, and the Impact of Geolocation Technologies' (2016) 47 International Review of Intellectual Property and Competition Law 60, 66 https://doi.org/10.1007/s40319-015-0427-8; Torsten Bettinger and Dorthee Thum, 'Territorial Trademark Rights in the Global Village: International Jurisdiction, Choice of Law and Substantive Law for Trademark Disputes on the Internet' (2000) 31 International Review of Intellectual Property and Competition Law 285, 285-308; Yelena Simonyuk, 'The Extraterritorial Reach of Trademarks on the Internet' (*Duke Law Scholarship*, 2002)

the Protection of Marks, and Other Industrial Property Rights in Signs, on the Internet (2001)[2030] indicated 'that a sign used on the Internet is simultaneously and immediately accessible irrespective of territorial location',[2031] movement in the direction of uniform approaches[2032] has been limited. Certainly, one mainly successful application of a common approach has been the UDRP, which is largely based on general trademark principles.[2033] From a technological angle, Peukert argues that a 'territorial approach can ... be realized by implementing adequate geolocation technologies'[2034] especially if a consumer is 'shown a version of the web site that contains additional information about the origin of the products or the location of the enterprise'.[2035]

There are clear difficulties in determining the 'place of infringement'[2036] when it comes to digital trademarks.[2037] For example, where a case may be heard or whether a court has jurisdiction over the parties or the subject matter can be complicated. This is especially a problem when considering the significant and numerous jurisdictions utilising a trademark on the Internet can implicate.

---

https://scholarship.law.duke.edu/cgi/viewcontent.cgi?article=1050&context=dltr; Graeme Dinwoodie, 'Private International Aspects of the Protection of Trademarks' (*WIPO Doc. No. WIPO/PIL/01/4*, 2001) https://scholarship.kentlaw.iit.edu/fac_schol/899/ accessed 4 August 2025; WIPO, 'Joint Recommendation Concerning Provisions on the Protection of Marks, and Other Industrial Property Rights in Signs, on the Internet' https://www.wipo.int/edocs/pubdocs/en/wipo_pub_845.pdf accessed January 2024'.

2030. WIPO, 'Joint Recommendation Concerning Provisions on the Protection of Marks, and Other Industrial Property Rights in Signs, on the Internet' https://www.wipo.int/edocs/pubdocs/en/wipo_pub_845.pdf accessed January 2024.
2031. WIPO, 'Joint Recommendation Concerning Provisions on the Protection of Marks, and Other Industrial Property Rights in Signs, on the Internet' 5 https://www.wipo.int/edocs/pubdocs/en/wipo_pub_845.pdf accessed January 2024.
2032. Rajeev Sachdev, 'Towards an Improved Framework for Trade-Mark Law and Regulation in Social Media Usernames: A Study of the Canadian, U.S., and U.K. Positions' (2016) 28 Intellectual Property Journal 379, 379-418; Daniel Doft, 'Facebook, Twitter, and the Wild West of IP Enforcement on Social Media: Weighing the Merits of a Uniform Dispute Resolution Policy' (2016) 49 The John Marshall Law Review 959; Thomas J Curtin, 'The Name Game: Cybersquatting and Trademark Infringement on Social Media Websites' (2010-2011) 19 Journal of Law and Policy 353; Erick J Heels, 'How to Twittersquat the Top 100 Brands' (*GiantPeople*, 8 January 2009) http://www.giantpeople.com/1298.html accessed 4 August 2025; Paul D McGrady, *McGrady on Social Media and the Metaverse* (Mathew Bender & Company, Inc. 2023) §12; John McElwaine and Christopher D Casavale, 'Tackling Bad Faith Registration of Domain Names in a Fast-Changing Landscape' (*WIPO Magazine*, December 2019) https://www.wipo.int/wipo_magazine/en/2019/06/article_0006.html accessed June 2025.
2033. WIPO, 'WIPO Overview of WIPO Panel Views on Selected UDRP Questions, Third Edition' ('WIPO Jurisprudential Overview 3.0') (*WIPO*, 2017) https://www.wipo.int/amc/en/domains/search/overview3.0/ accessed June 2025.
2034. Alexander Peukert, 'The Coexistence of Trade Mark Laws and Rights on the Internet, and the Impact of Geolocation Technologies' (2016) 47 International Review of Intellectual Property and Competition Law 60, 81 https://doi.org/10.1007/s40319-015-0427-8.
2035. *Ibid.*
2036. Eleonora Rosati, 'International Jurisdiction in Online EU Trade Mark Infringement Cases: Where Is the Place of Infringement Located?' (2016) 38(8) European Intellectual Property Review 482-491https://ssrn.com/abstract=2714310 accessed 4 August 2025.
2037. *Ibid.*

In the EU, under Article 97(5) EUTMR, actions may be brought 'in the courts of the Member State in which the act of infringement has been committed or threatened',[2038] which is rather unhelpful. However, various factors may be considered in Internet infringement situations. For example, jurisdiction may be established where 'offers for sale are directed are located'[2039] under *AMS Neve v. Heritage*.[2040] The court decided that 'the proprietor of a European Union trademark ... may bring an infringement action against that third party before a European Union trademark court of the Member State within which the consumers or traders to whom that advertising and those offers for sale are directed are located, notwithstanding that that third party took decisions and steps in another Member State to bring about that electronic display'.[2041] The 'direction'[2042] may implicate where an action may be filed in the EU and while in the case of certain online advertising that is targeted at certain geographic locations, this might be clear, it is not always clear to whom and where such 'direction'[2043] might be taking place. The CJ addressed some additional elements of 'direction'[2044] in *Lännen v. Berky,*[2045] where two related Finnish companies bid on *Lännen* 's trademark WATERMASTER[2046] on Google's 'national top-level domain'[2047] website, www.google .fi, through its search ad programme.[2048] The Finnish Court referred, *inter alia*, the question of whether 'advertising is directed at consumers'[2049] under such advertising .[2050] Further whether the Finnish court had jurisdiction to hear the case where while such advertising was taking place, the websites indicate that services are offered 'globally'[2051] and 'the geographical area where the goods are to be supplied is not specified, at least not expressly';[2052] however, at the same time, 'no individual Member State is expressly excluded from that area'.[2053] And importantly, the Finnish Court asked what 'factors, if any, should be taken into account in determining whether the advertisement is directed'.[2054] The CJ concluded that using such 'national top-level

2038. *Ibid.*
2039. Eckhard Ratjen, 'International Jurisdiction for Infringement of an EU Trade Mark by Advertising on the Internet' (*Boehmert & Boehmert*, 1 May 2020) https://www.boehmert.de/en/international-jurisdiction-for-infringement-of-an-eu-trade-mark-by-advertising-on-the-internet/ accessed January 2024; Case C-172/18 AMS *Neve Ltd and Others v. Heritage Audio SL and Pedro Rodríguez Arribas* EU:C:2019:674.
2040. Case C-172/18 AMS *Neve Ltd and Others v. Heritage Audio SL and Pedro Rodríguez Arribas* EU:C:2019:674.
2041. *Ibid.*
2042. *Ibid.*
2043. *Ibid.*
2044. *Ibid.*
2045. Case C-104/22 *Lännen MCE Oy v. Berky GmbH, Senwatec GmbH & Co. KG.* EU:C:2023:343.
2046. *Ibid.*
2047. *Ibid.*
2048. *Ibid.*
2049. *Ibid.*
2050. *Ibid.*
2051. *Ibid.*
2052. *Ibid.*
2053. *Ibid.*
2054. *Ibid.*

domain'[2055] for 'paid referencing on a search engine'[2056] implicates trademark rights in the related Member State and that the court had jurisdiction despite no other specific targeting as the targeted advertising was a 'sufficient connecting factor'[2057] beyond simply being 'visible online in Finland'[2058] which would not suffice.[2059]

The court's jurisdiction and where 'declining jurisdiction'[2060] under Article 136(1)(a) EUTMR is necessary was considered in *Merck v. Merck & Co. Inc. and Others.*[2061] The mark *MERCK* was at issue,[2062] and although the 'applicant and the defendants in the main proceedings were initially part of the same group of companies',[2063] they had been separate for many years.[2064] The defendant operated many websites on which 'the dissemination of information'[2065] was 'not geographically targeted'[2066] and 'all of the content'[2067] was essentially 'accessible in the same form worldwide'.[2068] Cases were filed in the UK as well as the Regional Court in Hamburg and various questions were referred to the CJ relating to jurisdiction.[2069] Under Article 136(1)(a) EUTMR, '*actions for infringement involving the same cause of action and between the same parties are brought in the courts of different Member States, one seised on the basis of an EU trademark and the other seised on the basis of a national trademark … the court other than the court first seised shall of its own motion decline jurisdiction in favour of that court where the trademarks concerned are identical and valid for identical goods or services*'.[2070] In this case, it was decided that the 'same cause of action'[2071] will be 'satisfied where actions for infringement between the same parties, on the basis of a national trademark and an EU trademark respectively, are brought before the courts of different Member States, only in so far as those actions relate to an alleged infringement of a national trademark and an identical EU trademark in the territory of the same Member States'.[2072]

2055. *Ibid.*
2056. *Ibid.*
2057. *Ibid.*
2058. *Ibid.*
2059. *Ibid.*
2060. EUTMR, Art. 136.
2061. *Case C-231/16 Merck; Merck KCaA v. Merck & Co. Inc. and Others* EU:C:2017:771; EUIPO, 'Overview of GC/CJ Case Law 2017' (*International Cooperation and Legal Affairs Department,* 2017) 312-314 https://euipo.europa.eu/tunnel-web/secure/webdav/guest/document_library/contentPdfs/law_and_practice/yearly_overview/yearly_overview_2017.pdf accessed January 2024.
2062. *Ibid.*
2063. *Ibid.*
2064. *Ibid.*
2065. *Ibid.*
2066. *Ibid.*
2067. *Ibid.*
2068. *Ibid.*
2069. *Ibid.*
2070. EUTMR, Art. 136(1)(a).
2071. *Ibid.*
2072. Case C-231/16 *Merck; Merck KCaA v. Merck & Co. Inc. and Others* EU:C:2017:771; EUIPO, 'Overview of GC/CJ Case Law 2017' (*International Cooperation and Legal Affairs Department, 2017*) 312-314 https://euipo.europa.eu/tunnel-web/secure/webdav/guest/document_library/contentPdfs/law_and_practice/yearly_overview/yearly_overview_2017.pdf accessed January 2024.

In the US, the issue of 'specific personal jurisdiction'[2073] was considered in *Alston v. www.calculator.com.*[2074] Such jurisdiction was challenged and based on the 'ongoing pattern of acts in Florida – i.e., by targeting Florida residents through location-specific advertising on its website and generating significant, continuous revenue from these Florida-tailored advertisements – is sufficient to establish a general course of business activity'[2075] in such state.[2076] In the context of domain names specifically, and different from the geographical limitations of trademark registration, as noted by Beebe, domain name 'exclusivity is world-wide'.[2077] In *Snow Systems v. Sneller's Landscaping,*[2078] the issue of 'personal jurisdiction'[2079] was also raised and the term 'snow systems'[2080] was in dispute. It was considered that the 'defendant had no clients outside Michigan'[2081] and did not 'market outside the state'.[2082] Additionally, their site was 'geared toward clients and potential clients in Michigan, not Illinois'[2083] and there was an express statement that 'it provides services in Grand Rapids and Lansing, Michigan'.[2084] Further, it provided 'weather reports local to those areas alone'[2085] and 'company contact information'[2086] was 'local to the area'.[2087] Based on these facts, the 'defendant's motion to dismiss for lack of jurisdiction was granted'.[2088] However, in the 2023 case of *Herbal Brands v. Photoplaza,*[2089] the Ninth Circuit ruled that 'the sale of a product via an interactive website' is enough as it provides the 'minimum contacts' which 'support jurisdiction over a non-resident defendant in a state where the defendant causes the product to be delivered'.[2090]

2073. *Alston v. www.calculator.com*, 2020 U.S. Dist. LEXIS 137360.
2074. *Ibid.*
2075. *Ibid.*; *Spigot, Inc.*, 2020 U.S. Dist. LEXIS 71973.
2076. *Ibid.*
2077. Barton Beebe, 'Trademark Law: An Open-Source Casebook Version 7.0' (2020), 75 https://www.tmcasebook.org/wp-content/uploads/2020/08/BeebeTMLaw-v7-digital_edition.pdf accessed July 2024.
2078. *Snow Systems, Inc. v. Sneller's Landscaping, LLC,* 2019 WL 1317746 (N.D. Ill. 22 March 2019).
2079. *Ibid.*; Eric Goldman, 'Rounding Up Three Recent Keyword Advertising Cases: *Comphy v. Amazon & More*' (*Technology & Marketing Law Blog,* 29 March 2019) https://blog.ericgoldman.org/archives/2019/03/rounding-up-three-recent-keyword-advertising-cases-comphy-v-amazon-more.htm accessed January 2024.
2080. *Ibid.*
2081. *Ibid.*
2082. *Ibid.*
2083. *Ibid.*
2084. *Ibid.*
2085. *Ibid.*
2086. *Ibid.*
2087. *Snow Systems, Inc. v. Sneller's Landscaping, LLC,* 2019 WL 1317746 (N.D. Ill. 22 March 2019); Eric Goldman, 'Rounding Up Three Recent Keyword Advertising Cases: *Comphy v. Amazon & More*' (*Eric Goldman,* 29 March 2019) https://blog.ericgoldman.org/archives/2019/03/rounding-up-three-recent-keyword-advertising-cases-comphy-v-amazon-more.htm accessed January 2024.
2088. *Snow Systems Inc. v. Sneller's Landscaping, LLC,* No. 1:2018cv05842 – Document 22 (N.D. Ill. 2019).
2089. *Herbal Brands Inc v. Photoplaza Inc* (21-17001; 9th Cir; 5 July 2023); WTR, 'Ninth Circuit Defines Personal Jurisdiction in Interactive Website Dispute' https://www.worldtrademarkreview.com/article/ninth-circuit-defines-personal-jurisdiction-in-interactive-website-dispute? accessed January 2024.
2090. *Ibid.*

Some District courts have dealt with territorial limitations. In *Belmora v. Bayer Consumer Care,*[2091] the court 'addressed the territorial limits of trademark rights and the standing of a foreign trademark owner to assert claims based on conduct in the United States'.[2092] This case illustrates 'that foreign trademark holders can bring Lanham Act claims in the U.S. when based upon commercial use of the mark only in foreign nations, but not in the United States'.[2093] Also, 'trademark holders can use the procedures available ... to block competitors from use of their foreign marks'.[2094] Also, in *Updateme Inc. v. Se,*[2095] the '[e]xtraterritorial [a]pplication of the Lanham Act'[2096] was considered. It was stated that '[t]he Lanham Act applies extraterritorially if: (1) the alleged violations ... create some effect on American foreign commerce; (2) the effect [is] sufficiently great to present a cognizable injury to the plaintiffs under the Lanham Act; and (3) the interests of and links to American foreign commerce [are] sufficiently strong in relation to those of other nations to justify an assertion of extraterritorial authority'.[2097] The first two prongs were considered to be met partly based on the fact that the app was made 'available for download in the United States from the Google Play store online'[2098] and the 'domestic economic activity'[2099] was considered. Also, a 'defendant's foreign activities need not have a substantial or even significant effect on American commerce, rather, "some effect" may be sufficient'.[2100] However, the third prong was not met, and the plaintiff did not allege 'significance of effects'[2101] which can include factors 'such as number of downloads or popularity in the United States in relation to plaintiff's product'.[2102] Also, whether 'direct effect on interstate commerce' in the US,[2103] whether an 'ongoing pattern of acts',[2104] 'location-specific advertising',[2105] 'continuous revenue',[2106] specific mention of geographic targeting, targeted

2091. *Belmora LLC v. Bayer Consumer Care AG,* 819 F.3d 697 (4th Cir. 2016), cert. denied, 2017 WL 737826 (U.S. 27 February 2017).
2092. Paul C Llewellyn, 'Supreme Court Lets Stand Court of Appeals Ruling that Owner of a Foreign Trademark May Sue Under the Lanham Act for Conduct in the United States' (*Arnold & Porter,* 6 March 2017) https://www.arnoldporter.com/en/perspectives/publications/2017/03/supreme-court-lets-stand-court-of-appeals accessed January 2024.
2093. Jennifer Itzkoff, 'International Trademark Lessons from the Bayer-Belmora FLANAX Trademark Fight' (*IPWatchdog,* 14 November 2018) https://www.ipwatchdog.com/2018/11/14/international-trademark-bayer-belmora-flanax/id = 103101/ accessed January 2024.
2094. *Ibid.*
2095. *Updateme Inc. v. Se,* 2017 U.S. Dist. LEXIS 195468.
2096. *Ibid.*
2097. *Ibid.*; *Trader Joe's Co. v. Hallatt,* 835 F.3d 960.
2098. *Updateme Inc. v. Se,* 2017 U.S. Dist. LEXIS 195468.
2099. *Ibid.*; *Trader Joe's Co. v. Hallatt,* 835 F.3d 960.
2100. *Ibid.*
2101. *Ibid.*
2102. *Updateme Inc. v. Se,* 2017 U.S. Dist. LEXIS 195468.
2103. USPTO, 'Trademark Manual of Examining Procedure (TMEP)' (*TMEP*) https://tmep.uspto.gov/RDMS/TMEP/current#/current/TMEP-900d1e98.html accessed 4 August 2025.
2104. *Alston v. www.calculator.com,* 2020 U.S. Dist. LEXIS 137360; *Spigot, Inc.,* 2020 U.S. Dist. LEXIS 71973, 2020 WL 1955360.
2105. *Ibid.*
2106. *Ibid.*

information to particular geographical areas,[2107] and shipping locations would be considered. However, a 2023 Supreme Court decision made the territoriality issue clear. In the US, the '[u]se of a mark in a foreign country does not give rise to rights in the United States if the goods or services are not sold or rendered in the United States'.[2108] As was seen in section 3.2.1 under *Digital Use and Place of Use*, in the 2023 case of *Abitron v. Hetronic,*[2109] Lanham Act provisions 'are not extraterritorial and apply only to infringing uses of protected marks in U.S. commerce'.[2110]

A WIPO study on online infringement highlights that different jurisdictions employ an approach based on 'targeting'.[2111] In the UK, such 'targeting'[2112] is used and this may be the case even if advertising is directed to UK customers through a UK website, and the court in the 2024 decision (while post-Brexit was decided based on EU law applicable to the timing of the events) in *Lifestyle Equities v. Amazon* recognised that 'the marketing and sale of goods on the internet knows no … territorial boundaries'.[2113] Such 'targeting'[2114] was found based upon 'displaying the USA Branded Goods on its USA website and marking them available for shipment to the UK'.[2115] The WIPO study also indicates that a 'targeting approach'[2116] can be applied in Metaverse situations, regardless of where the defendant is 'established or domiciled'.[2117]

As with the UDRP, platforms should consider working to clarify jurisdictional matters and apply general principles of trademark law[2118] to seek to avoid the complicated issues of jurisdiction, as seen from the above. An approach based on

2107. Case C-231/16 *Merck; Merck KCaA v. Merck & Co. Inc. and Others* [2017] EU:C:2017:771 http://curia.europa.eu/juris/document/document.jsf?text=&docid=195738&pageIndex=0&doclang=EN&mode=lst&dir=&occ=first&part=1&cid=2315703.
2108. USPTO, 'Trademark Manual of Examining Procedure (TMEP)' (*TMEP*) https://tmep.uspto.gov/RDMS/TMEP/current#/current/TMEP-900d1e98.html accessed 4 August 2025.
2109. *Abitron Austria GmbH v. Hetronic International, Inc.*, 600 U.S. 412.
2110. Lydia Lundstedt, 'SCOTUS Holds that Lanham Act Does Not Apply to Trademark Infringement Abroad' (*EAPIL Blog*, 12 July 2023) https://eapil.org/2023/07/12/scotus-holds-that-lanham-act-does-not-apply-to-trademark-infringement-abroad/ accessed January 2024.
2111. WIPO, 'Building Respect for IP Study: The Localization of IP Infringements in the Online Environment: From Web 2.0 to Web 3.0 and the Metaverse' (*WIPO*, September 2023) https://www.wipo.int/export/sites/www/respect-for-ip/en/docs/case-strudy-the-localiaztion-of-ip-infringement.pdf accessed January 2024.
2112. *Lifestyle Equities CV v. Amazon UK Services Ltd* [2022] EWCA Civ 552.
2113. *Ibid.*
2114. *Ibid.*
2115. *Ibid.*
2116. WIPO, 'Building Respect for IP Study: The Localization of IP Infringements in the Online Environment: From Web 2.0 to Web 3.0 and the Metaverse' (*WIPO*, September 2023) https://www.wipo.int/export/sites/www/respect-for-ip/en/docs/case-strudy-the-localiaztion-of-ip-infringement.pdf accessed January 2024.
2117. *Ibid.*
2118. WIPO, 'WIPO Overview of WIPO Panel Views on Selected UDRP Questions, Third Edition' ('WIPO Jurisprudential Overview 3.0') (*WIPO*, 2017) https://www.wipo.int/amc/en/domains/search/overview3.0/ accessed June 2025.

targeting[2119] and 'sufficient'[2120] forms of 'direction'[2121] appears to be a useful consideration for platforms because of its broad applicability and one which is based on factors conducive to online environments.

3.2.6.2 *Coexistence*

Bettinger and Thum state that 'the use of a sign on the Internet can result in disputes even though the marks have hitherto coexisted without dispute, because their use in general business activity has been restricted to a domestic market'.[2122] Peukert addresses situations where the legal 'coexistence … of signs'[2123] online may take place and proposes an approach whereby a 'fairness proviso is intended to minimize a potential distortion of competition resulting from coexistence'[2124] of marks. This approach 'requires courts to consider all circumstances of the case and to balance the interests involved'.[2125] For example, '[c]onflicting and yet concurrent online use of a sign is even more warranted if the contested use does not concern direct competition on the product market but merely general commercial information about the company or the products of the user'.[2126] He concludes that 'the balance of interests can lead to

2119. WIPO, 'Building Respect for IP Study: The Localization of IP Infringements in the Online Environment: From Web 2.0 to Web 3.0 and the Metaverse' (*WIPO*, September 2023) https://www.wipo.int/export/sites/www/respect-for-ip/en/docs/case-strudy-the-localiaztion-of-ip-infringement.pdf accessed January 2024.
2120. Case C-172/18 *AMS Neve Ltd and Others v. Heritage Audio SL and Pedro Rodríguez Arribas* EU:C:2019:674; Case C-104/22 *Lännen MCE Oy v. Berky GmbH, Senwatec GmbH & Co. KG.* EU:C:2023:343; *Alston v. www.calculator.com*, 2020 U.S. Dist. LEXIS 137360; *Spigot, Inc.*, 2020 U.S. Dist. LEXIS 71973.
2121. Case C-172/18 *AMS Neve Ltd and Others v. Heritage Audio SL and Pedro Rodríguez Arribas* EU:C:2019:674; Case C-104/22 *Lännen MCE Oy v. Berky GmbH, Senwatec GmbH & Co. KG.* EU:C:2023:343; *Alston v. www.calculator.com*, 2020 U.S. Dist. LEXIS 137360; *Spigot, Inc.*, 2020 U.S. Dist. LEXIS 71973; *Lifestyle Equities CV v. Amazon UK Services Ltd* [2022] EWCA Civ 552; WIPO, 'Building Respect for IP Study: The Localization of IP Infringements in the Online Environment: From Web 2.0 to Web 3.0 and the Metaverse' (*WIPO*, September 2023) https://www.wipo.int/export/sites/www/respect-for-ip/en/docs/case-strudy-the-localiaztion-of-ip-infringement.pdf accessed January 2024.
2122. Torsten Bettinger and Dorthee Thum, 'Territorial Trademark Rights in the Global Village: International Jurisdiction, Choice of Law and Substantive Law for Trademark Disputes on the Internet' (2000) 31 International Review of Intellectual Property and Competition Law 285, 285-308.
2123. Alexander Peukert, 'The Coexistence of Trade Mark Laws and Rights on the Internet, and the Impact of Geolocation Technologies' (2016) 47 International Review of Intellectual Property and Competition Law 60, 65 https://doi.org/10.1007/s40319-015-0427-8.
2124. *Ibid.*
2125. *Ibid.*
2126. Alexander Peukert, 'The Coexistence of Trade Mark Laws and Rights on the Internet, and the Impact of Geolocation Technologies' (2016) 47 International Review of Intellectual Property and Competition Law 60, 79 https://doi.org/10.1007/s40319-015-0427-8.

the conclusion that conflicting uses with substantial effect in the country of protection'[2127] and this approach highlights consideration of the impact in particular jurisdictions.[2128] Beebe says, in relation to the 'commercial use of a mark on an internet website accessible anywhere in the country',[2129] that courts have said 'common law rights based only on internet use should extend geographically only so far as the mark owner can show actual market penetration'.[2130]

In the EU, coexistence,[2131] while difficult to prove, may be argued.[2132] The EUIPO Guidelines clarify the conditions which must be met, including, there being a 'comparable situation'[2133] with 'identical' marks and covering the same goods, in relation to relevant countries,[2134] being 'in the marketplace' (not just on the register),[2135] with consideration to the 'period of coexistence',[2136] and that it must have been 'peaceful' coexistence, etc.[2137] Further, in *Ornua v. Tindale & Stanton,*[2138] the CJ held that 'the fact that, in part of the European Union, an EU trademark and a national mark peacefully coexist, does not allow the conclusion that in another part of the European Union, where peaceful coexistence between that EU trademark and the sign identical to that national mark is absent, there is no likelihood of confusion between that EU trademark and that sign'.[2139] Likewise, it was decided that 'the fact that, in part of the European Union, an EU trademark with a reputation and a sign peacefully coexist, does not allow the conclusion that in another part of the European Union, where that peaceful coexistence is absent, there is due cause legitimising the use of that sign'.[2140]

In the US, under 15 U.S. Code § 1052(d), 'concurrent registrations may be issued to such persons when they have become entitled to use such marks as a result of their concurrent lawful use in commerce' under certain conditions.[2141] In *Hyperheal Hyperbarics v. Shapiro,*[2142] it was stated that '[i]nevitably, the lack of geographic limitations with a website domain registration leads to a clash with trademark law'.[2143] In this

2127. Alexander Peukert, 'The Coexistence of Trade Mark Laws and Rights on the Internet, and the Impact of Geolocation Technologies' (2016) 47 International Review of Intellectual Property and Competition Law 60, 80 https://doi.org/10.1007/s40319-015-0427-8.
2128. *Ibid.*
2129. Barton Beebe, 'Trademark Law: An Open-Source Casebook Version 7.0' (2020), 282 https://www.tmcasebook.org/wp-content/uploads/2020/08/BeebeTMLaw-v7-digital_edition.pdf accessed July 2024.
2130. *Ibid.*
2131. EUIPO, '3.1 Coexistence Between the Marks Involved in the Opposition' (*EUIPO Trade mark guidelines* 2024) https://guidelines.euipo.europa.eu/2214311/2043906/trade-mark-guidelines/3-1-coexistence-between-the-marks-involved-in-the-opposition accessed January 2024.
2132. *Ibid.*
2133. *Ibid.*
2134. *Ibid.*
2135. *Ibid.*
2136. *Ibid.*
2137. *Ibid.*
2138. Case C-93/16 *Ornua Co-operative Ltd v. Tindale & Stanton Ltd España SL* ECLI:EU:C:2017:571.
2139. *Ibid.*
2140. *Ibid.*
2141. 15 U.S. Code § 1052(d).
2142. *Hyperheal Hyperbarics, Inc. v. Shapiro*, 2019 U.S. Dist. LEXIS 129289.
2143. *Ibid.*; *Harrods Ltd. v. Sixty Internet Domain Names*, 2002 U.S. App. LEXIS 17530.

case, 'the geographic scope of protection'[2144] was an issue and it was stated that the common law mark holder 'can only prevent others ... from using its name and trademark in the geographic territories where it has senior rights'.[2145] This is because 'trademark laws allow concurrent use of the same mark by multiple adopters so long as each adopter's use of the mark does not unreasonably intrude on another user's geographic zone of exclusivity'.[2146]

In some cases, a co-existence agreement may be used.[2147] Co-existence[2148] is implemented nationally in Canada, if the Federal Court permits 'continued use'[2149] of a 'confusing trademark'[2150] in 'a defined territorial area concurrently with the use of the registered trademark'.[2151]

Platforms should consider recognising co-existence of trademarks, and under Peukert's approach, employing this only in very narrow and fair circumstances using a balanced approach.[2152]

3.2.6.3 *Summary of Platform Considerations for Digital Jurisdictional and Territorial Considerations*

The UDRP already permits the consideration of national law, such as when the parties are from the same jurisdiction.[2153] Platforms should consider not resorting to local laws unless there are special circumstances in line with the UDRP approach, and common trademark principles should largely be considered.[2154] Platforms should further consider whether there is any specific and relevant online targeting[2155] of specific jurisdictions. For example, this might be clearer in the case of search or social media ads targeting a specific area, but not in the case of a Metaverse concert open to all. Essentially, whether the activity involves any limits on the extent of geographic reach

2144. *Hyperheal Hyperbarics, Inc. v. Shapiro*, 2019 U.S. Dist. LEXIS 129289.
2145. *Ibid.*
2146. *Ibid.*; *Harrods Ltd. v. Sixty Internet Domain Names*, 2002 U.S. App. LEXIS 17530.
2147. Tamara Nanayakkara, 'IP and Business: Trademark Coexistence' (*WIPO*, November 2006) https://www.wipo.int/wipo_magazine/en/2006/06/article_0007.html accessed June 2025.
2148. *Ibid.*
2149. Canadian Trademarks Act R.S.C., 1985, c. T-13, s. 21(1).
2150. *Ibid.*
2151. *Ibid.*
2152. Alexander Peukert, 'The Coexistence of Trade Mark Laws and Rights on the Internet, and the Impact of Geolocation Technologies' (2016) 47 International Review of Intellectual Property and Competition Law 60, 81 https://doi.org/10.1007/s40319-015-0427-8.
2153. WIPO, 'WIPO Overview of WIPO Panel Views on Selected UDRP Questions, Third Edition' ('WIPO Jurisprudential Overview 3.0') (*WIPO*, 2017) https://www.wipo.int/amc/en/domains/search/overview3.0/ accessed June 2025.
2154. *Ibid.*
2155. *DealDash Oyj v. Contextlogic Inc.*, 2018 U.S. Dist. LEXIS 135531; *Lifestyle Equities CV and another v. Amazon UK Services Ltd and others* [2022] EWCA Civ 552.

should be considered.[2156] Platforms should consider how language[2157] plays a role, such as in their guidelines.

3.2.7 Digital Justification

Various Constitutional provisions, human rights laws, defences, and justifications play a role in the utilisation of trademarks online.[2158] These create defences and limitations to the trademark protections set out in legal frameworks and are very informative to the UDRP and platforms.

3.2.7.1 Fair Use, Freedom of Expression, Freedom of Artistic Expression or Use, Free Speech, and Parody

Under TRIPS, Article 17, 'Members may provide limited exceptions to the rights conferred by a trademark, such as fair use of descriptive terms, provided that such exceptions take account of the legitimate interests of the owner of the trademark and of third parties.'

The UDRP considers a fair use[2159] defence under circumstances where there is no 'affiliation with the trademark owner'.[2160] Additionally, marks in domain names may be used 'for referential use, commentary, criticism, praise, or parody'[2161] will be considered as long as it 'is not misleading as to source or sponsorship, and is not a pretext for tarnishment or commercial gain'.[2162]

In the EU, as noted in Recital 21 EUTMR, marks 'used fairly and thus in accordance with honest practices in industrial and commercial matters'[2163] are permissible. Specifically, 'the use of descriptive or non-distinctive signs or indications in general', the 'resale of genuine goods that were originally sold by or with the consent of the proprietor'[2164] or 'by third parties for the purpose of artistic expression'[2165] are

2156. WIPO, 'Building Respect for IP Study: The Localization of IP Infringements in the Online Environment: From Web 2.0 to Web 3.0 and the Metaverse' (*WIPO*, September 2023) https://www.wipo.int/export/sites/www/respect-for-ip/en/docs/case-strudy-the-localiazt ion-of-ip-infringement.pdf accessed January 2024.
2157. Anke Moerland and Robert Brauneis, 'Monopolizing Matratzen in Malaga: The Mistreatment of Distinctiveness of Foreign Terms in EU and US Trademark Law' 2020-55 GW Legal Studies Research Paper No. 2020-61 https://cris.maastrichtuniversity.nl/ws/portalfiles/portal/1358 20363/Moerland_2020_Monopolizing_Matratzen_in_Malaga.pdf accessed January 2024.
2158. The Constitution of the United States of America, the Charter of Fundamental Rights of the European Union; Constitution Act, 1982, Canadian Charter of Rights and Freedoms; Paris Convention, Art. 6bis; TRIPS, Art. 16; EUTMR, Art. 18; 15 U.S. Code § 1127; Canadian Trademarks Act R.S.C., 1985, c. T-13.
2159. WIPO, 'WIPO Overview of WIPO Panel Views on Selected UDRP Questions, Third Edition' ('WIPO Jurisprudential Overview 3.0') (*WIPO*, 2017) https://www.wipo.int/amc/en/domains/search/overview3.0/ accessed June 2025.
2160. *Ibid.*
2161. *Ibid.*
2162. *Ibid.*
2163. EUTMR, Recital 21.
2164. *Ibid.*
2165. *Ibid.*

permitted. However, these must be done 'in accordance with honest practices in industrial and commercial matters'.[2166] Under Article 14 EUTMR, mark holders may not prevent the use of a personal name of a natural person, non-distinctive signs, and 'accessories or spare parts'.[2167] Kur and Senftleben recognise that utilisation of a trademark is 'subject to an additional scrutiny concerning its compatibility with fairness in trade'.[2168] Therefore, these are acceptable, again, 'where the use made by the third party is in accordance with honest practices in industrial or commercial matters'.[2169] As Ramirez opines, 'while the inclusion of referential use and non-distinctive fair use defenses are a welcome development in EU law, the role that fundamental rights will play in the application of the whole of EU trademark law remains to be seen'.[2170] Further, under Article 15 EUTMR, a mark may be used where 'goods which have been put on the market … under that trademark by the proprietor or with his consent' unless 'there exist[s] legitimate reasons for the proprietor to oppose further commercialisation of the goods, especially where the condition of the goods is changed or impaired after they have been put on the market'.[2171] Additionally, comparative advertising portraying a mark is permitted unless, under Article 9(3)(f) EUTMR, done 'in a manner that is contrary to Directive 2006/114/EC'[2172] such as, but not limited to ways which are 'misleading',[2173] 'confusing',[2174] takes 'unfair advantage',[2175] or presents 'imitations or replicas'.[2176]

In the EU, 'right of freedom of expression and information'[2177] is recognised under Article 10 of the European Convention on Human Rights (ECHR) and Article 11 of the EU Charter of Fundamental Rights; however, in many cases, this right is limited.[2178] In the context of trademarks, Recital 21 of the EUTMR states, 'this Regulation should be applied in a way that ensures full respect for fundamental rights and freedoms, and in particular the freedom of expression'.[2179] Schovsbo believes that the incorporation of this provision in the EUTMR expands the application of fundamental rights in trademark cases, more so than what was intended in trademark

2166. *Ibid.*
2167. EUTMR, Art. 15.
2168. Annette Kur and Martin Senftleben, 'Limitations, Defences, and Genuine Use' in Annette Kur and Martin Senftleben (eds), *European Trade Mark Law* (Oxford University Press 2017) 407.
2169. EUTMR, Art. 14(2).
2170. César Ramírez-Montes, 'EU Trademarks in the Metaverse' 63 IDEA 557, 717.
2171. EUTMR, Art. 15.
2172. EUTMR, Art. 9(3)(f).
2173. *Ibid.*
2174. *Ibid.*
2175. *Ibid.*
2176. Stefan Martin, 'Well Known Marks and Parody: Dilution and Denigration? Unfair Advantage?' (*EUIPO*, 2017), https://euipo.europa.eu/knowledge/pluginfile.php/77920/mod_resource/content/8/Limits%20of%20trade%20marks%2C%20Parody%2018-5-2017.pdf accessed January 2024.
2177. European Convention for the Protection of Human Rights, Art. 10; EU Charter of Fundamental Rights, Art. 11.
2178. *Ibid.*; Gordon Humphreys, 'Freedom of Speech and Trademarks: Gauging Public Sensitivities or Curtailing Civil Liberties?' (March 2009).
2179. EUTMR, Recital 21.

history, even if free speech has always been a part of the analysis.[2180] However, Bohaczewski argues that 'conflicts between the freedom of expression and trademark rights are often illusory'[2181] and that 'the freedom of commercial expression'[2182] must be guarded by 'fundamental rights'.[2183] Geiger confirms that there are limits to freedom of expression under EU law and concludes that such freedom assists in fostering innovation through expression and creativity.[2184] As Senftleben recognises, 'artistic expression'[2185] in the EU may be 'deemed fair';[2186] however, as seen above, 'as long as it is at the same time in accordance with honest practices in industrial and commercial matters'.[2187] Although, he argues that this is a 'double-edged sword'[2188] and 'artists are expected to align their artistic activity with behavioural standards in the field of industry and commerce'[2189] instead of a proposed approach whereby 'a legal presumption of fair use'[2190] is introduced putting the onus on the trademark holder to show confusion,[2191] dilution,[2192] unfair advantage of a reputable mark, etc.[2193] Recently, in *Constantin v. EUIPO,*[2194] the 'freedom of expression'[2195] was at issue when a German phrase, 'Fack Ju Göhte'[2196] which means 'Fuck You Goethe'[2197] in English, and also 'the title of the blockbuster German film comedy produced by the appellant'[2198] was refused registration as 'vulgar and offensive'.[2199] However, the CJ decided that it 'was not perceived as morally unacceptable by the German-speaking public ... [and] ...

2180. Jens Schovsbo, '"Mark My Words": Trademarks and Fundamental Rights in the EU' (2018) 8 U.C. Irvine Law Review 555.
2181. Michal Bohaczewski, 'Conflicts Between Trade Mark Rights and Freedom of Expression Under EU Trade Mark Law: Reality or Illusion?' (2020) 51 International Review of Intellectual Property and Competition Law 856, 858 https://doi.org/10.1007/s40319-020-00964-5.
2182. *Ibid.*
2183. *Ibid.*
2184. Christophe Geiger, 'Trade Marks and Freedom of Expression: The Proportionality of Criticism' (2007) 38 International Review of Intellectual Property and Competition Law 317, 324.
2185. EUTMR, Recital 21.
2186. Martin Senftleben, 'Robustness Check: Evaluating and Strengthening Artistic Use Defences in EU Trademark Law' (2022) 53 International Review of Intellectual Property and Competition Law 567, 567 https://doi.org/10.1007/s40319-022-01182-x; EUTMR, Recital 21.
2187. *Ibid.*
2188. *Ibid.*
2189. *Ibid.*
2190. Martin Senftleben, 'Robustness Check: Evaluating and Strengthening Artistic Use Defences in EU Trademark Law' (2022) 53 International Review of Intellectual Property and Competition Law 567, 591 https://doi.org/10.1007/s40319-022-01182-x.
2191. Martin Senftleben, 'Robustness Check: Evaluating and Strengthening Artistic Use Defences in EU Trademark Law' (2022) 53 International Review of Intellectual Property and Competition Law 567, 588 https://doi.org/10.1007/s40319-022-01182-x.
2192. *Ibid.*
2193. *Ibid.*
2194. Case C-240/18 P *Constantin Film Produktion GmbH v. European Union Intellectual Property Office (EUIPO)* ECLI:EU:C:2020:118.
2195. Columbia University, 'Constantin Film Produktion v. EUIPO' (*Columbia University Global Freedom of Expression*) https://globalfreedomofexpression.columbia.edu/cases/constantin-film-produktion-v-euipo/ accessed January 2024.
2196. *Ibid.*
2197. *Ibid.*
2198. *Ibid.*
2199. *Ibid.*

there was no concrete evidence to explain the perception of the word sign "Fack Ju Göhte" as going against the fundamental moral values and standards of society when it is used as a trademark'.[2200] Reference was made back to Recital 21 EUTMR, which states the importance of ensuring 'full respect for fundamental rights and freedoms, in particular freedom of expression'.[2201] The mark was subsequently registered as seen from the register.[2202]

In the context of parody in the EU, this could be in the form of 'artistic expression'[2203] but also one which sends a 'social message' (such as against a brand),[2204] 'expresses humour or mockery',[2205] expresses opinion,[2206] or a type of 'consumer speech', etc.[2207] However, a parody under EU trademark law does not extend to confusing or unfair advantage, free riding situations.[2208] Kurr and Senftleben discuss how parodic[2209] utilisation of marks is unclear, such as when a mark is used in a video on social media which can go viral.[2210] For example, video-based social media fake advertising[2211] which incorporates the mark of others might be done to 'gain credit for the maker's creativeness, as a kind of digital business card meant to attract the attention of advertising agencies or film producers'.[2212] Pontes anticipates, based on a parody[2213] decision in copyright law, that 'the European system [is] along a new path by accepting a broader concept of parody, which is generally treated in the US as unprotected sattire'.[2214] In a recent Belgian referral to the CJ, in *IKEA v. Algemeen,*[2215]

2200. *Ibid.*
2201. Case C-240/18 P *Constantin Film Produktion GmbH v. European Union Intellectual Property Office (EUIPO)* ECLI:EU:C:2020:118.
2202. EUIPO, 'Fack Ju Göhte 013971163' https://euipo.europa.eu/eSearch/#details/trademarks/013971163 accessed January 2024.
2203. Stefan Martin, 'Well Known Marks and Parody: Dilution and Denigration? Unfair Advantage?' (*EUIPO*, 2017), https://euipo.europa.eu/knowledge/pluginfile.php/77920/mod_resource/content/8/Limits%20of%20trade%20marks%2C%20Parody%2018-5-2017.pdf accessed January 2024.
2204. *Ibid.*
2205. *Ibid.*
2206. *Ibid.*
2207. *Ibid.*
2208. Lucas Fischer, *Parody and Trademarks: A Comparative Analysis of EU and US Legislation and Case Law*, Stanford-Vienna TTLF Working Paper No. 79 http://ttlf.stanford.edu accessed January 2024; Stefan Martin, 'Well Known Marks and Parody: Dilution and Denigration? Unfair Advantage?' (*EUIPO*, 2017), https://euipo.europa.eu/knowledge/pluginfile.php/77920/mod_resource/content/8/Limits%20of%20trade%20marks%2C%20Parody%2018-5-2017.pdf accessed January 2024; Martin Senftleben, 'Robustness Check: Evaluating and Strengthening Artistic Use Defences in EU Trademark Law' (2022) 53 International Review of Intellectual Property and Competition Law 567, 588 https://doi.org/10.1007/s40319-022-01182-x.
2209. Annette Kur and Martin Senftleben, 'Limitations, Defences, and Genuine Use' in Annette Kur and Martin Senftleben (eds), *European Trade Mark Law* (Oxford University Press 2017) 430.
2210. *Ibid.*
2211. *Ibid.*
2212. *Ibid.*
2213. Leonardo M Pontes, 'Trademark and Freedom of Speech: A Comparison Between the U.S. and the EU System in the Awakening of Johan Deckmen v. Helena Vandersteen' www.wipo.int/edocs/mdocs/mdocs/en/wipo_ipl_ge_15/wipo_ipl_ge_15_t3.pdf accessed July 2024.
2214. *Ibid.*
2215. *Inter IKEA Systems BV v. Algemeen Vlaams Belang vzw* (C-298/23).

a political party put forth a mark as can be seen in different places on the Internet, using the mark IKEA, the furniture brand, but instead an acronym for 'Immigratie Kan Echt Anders'[2216] translating to 'Immigration Really Can Be Different'[2217] and which used the blue and yellow colours already associated with IKEA.[2218] Based on the reliance on parody, the Belgian court referred some key questions to the CJ including whether 'freedom of expression, including the freedom to express political opinions and political parody, as guaranteed by Article 10 of the European Convention for the Protection of Human Rights and Fundamental Freedoms and Article 11 of the Charter of Fundamental Rights of the European Union, constitute "due cause" for using a sign identical or similar to a well-known trademark'.[2219] If yes, what the criteria would be to balance 'those fundamental rights'[2220] and whether 'commercial character ... competitive motives ... public interest ... degree of reputation ... extent of infringing use ... expression, and the circumstances accompanying that expression ... are detrimental to the reputation, distinctive character ... original contribution ... attempt ... .to avoid confusion ... or commercial or other connection'[2221] would be applicable in the assessment.[2222] The case is yet to be decided at time of writing.

Various defences are also available under U.S. law. Menell, Lemley, Merges and Balganesh say that '[t]rademark protection can also interfere with both communicative and creative expression'.[2223] However, as they also say, 'various doctrines limit such adverse effects'.[2224] These are important for platforms to consider. In the context of comparative advertising, '[t]he Lanham Act does not restrict the fair use of a trademark in both nominative uses and comparative advertising'.[2225] Equitable defences[2226] are also available and include 'equitable principles, including laches, estoppel, and acquiescence'.[2227]

The defence of 'fair use'[2228] 'allows commentary or criticism that incidentally involves the use of a trademark so long as such use is for a purpose other than that

2216. Noemi Parrotta and Andreas Lubberger, 'INTA Attempts to File Amicus Brief with CJEU in Preliminary Ruling Case' (*INTA News*, 10 January 2024) https://www.inta.org/news-and-press/inta-news/inta-attempts-to-file-amicus-brief-with-cjeu-in-preliminary-ruling-case-involving-ikea/ accessed July 2024.
2217. *Ibid.*
2218. *Ibid.*
2219. Case C-298/23 *Inter IKEA Systems BV v. Algemeen Vlaams Belang VZW and Others* https://curia.europa.eu/juris/document/document.jsf;jsessionid = 1E7243B226A8FA96FD66EF948FAAF70D?text = &docid = 276324&pageIndex = 0&doclang = en&mode = req&dir = &occ = first&part = 1&cid = 1043972 accessed 4 August 2025.
2220. *Ibid.*
2221. *Ibid.*
2222. *Ibid.*
2223. Peter S Menell et al., *Intellectual Property in the New Technological Age: 2020* (Clause 8 Publishing 2020) 28.
2224. *Ibid.*
2225. Benjamin Aitken, 'Keyword-Linked Advertising, Trademark Infringement, and Google's Contributory Liability' (2005) 21 Duke Law & Technology Review 1, conclusion.
2226. Cornell LII, 'Trademark Infringement' (*Cornell Legal information Institute*) https://www.law.cornell.edu/wex/trademark_infringement accessed January 2024.
2227. 15 U.S. Code § 1115.
2228. *Ibid.*

normally made of a trademark'.[2229] For example, utilisation of a 'personal name'[2230] may be permissible 'if the name is used solely to indicate truthfully the named person's connection with the goods, services, or business'.[2231] Also, '[d]escriptive [f]air [u]se' is found in 15 U.S. Code § 1115(b)(4) which indicates that it is acceptable to utilise a mark 'which is descriptive of and used fairly and in good faith only to describe the goods and services of such party, or their geographic origin'.[2232] Further, 'nominative fair use'[2233] may be available where a 'junior user uses another's trademark deliberately to refer to that party'[2234] such as for 'commentary',[2235] or 'comparative advertising'.[2236] In the US, 'Fair use allows commentary or criticism that incidentally involves the use of a trademark so long as such use is for a purpose other than that normally made of a trademark.'[2237] Under 15 U.S. Code § 1115, a mark may be 'used fairly and in good faith only to describe the goods or services of such party, or their geographic origin'.[2238] Fair use[2239] has been recognised in the courts such as in the U.S. case of *Playboy v. Welles,*[2240] where the decision was that the '[u]se of metatags may be nominative fair use so long as three conditions are met'[2241] and Saunders argues that the purchase of competitive search keywords are generally 'fair use'[2242] specifically 'treated as a form of lawful comparative advertising'.[2243] In *Align Tech Inc v. Strauss Diamond,*[2244] the court relied upon the test set out in *Playboy v. Welles,*[2245] where three factors control a

2229. Cornell LII, 'Trademark Infringement' (*Cornell Legal information Institute*) https://www.law.cornell.edu/wex/trademark_infringement accessed January 2024.
2230. William J Murphy, 'Intellectual Property in E-Commerce' (*On-line Tutorial Project*, 2001) mod 3, 15 https://scholars.unh.edu/law_facpub/171/ accessed 4 August 2025.
2231. *Ibid.*
2232. 15 U.S. Code § 1115(b)(4).
2233. Louis S Ederer, 'Nominative Fair Use: Legitimate Advertising or Trademark Infringement?' (*Arnold & Porter LLP*) https://www.arnoldporter.com/~/media/files/perspectives/publications/2012/12/nominative-fair-use-legitimate-advertising-or-tr__/files/publication/fileattachment/nominative-fair-use.pdf accessed January 2024.
2234. Greg R Vetter, 'Classic vs. Nominative Fair Use' https://www.law.uh.edu/faculty/gvetter/classes/TrademarksSpring2016/TrademarksSpring2016_Module4_SlideSetA(OH212to224).pdf accessed 4 August 2025; Louis S Ederer, 'Nominative Fair Use: Legitimate Advertising or Trademark Infringement?' (*Arnold & Porter LLP*) https://www.arnoldporter.com/~/media/files/perspectives/publications/2012/12/nominative-fair-use-legitimate-advertising-or-tr__/files/publication/fileattachment/nominative-fair-use.pdf accessed January 2024.
2235. Louis S Ederer, 'Nominative Fair Use: Legitimate Advertising or Trademark Infringement?' (*Arnold & Porter LLP*) https://www.arnoldporter.com/~/media/files/perspectives/publications/2012/12/nominative-fair-use-legitimate-advertising-or-tr__/files/publication/fileattachment/nominative-fair-use.pdf accessed January 2024.
2236. *Ibid.*
2237. Cornell LII, 'Trademark Infringement' https://www.law.cornell.edu/wex/trademark_infringement accessed January 2024.
2238. 15 U.S. Code § 1115.
2239. EUTMR, Recital 21; 15 U.S. Code § 1115(b)(4); Canadian Trademarks Act R.S.C., 1985, c. T-13, s. 22.
2240. *Playboy v. Welles*, 279 F.3d.
2241. Aaron Schwabach, *Internet and the Law: Technology, Society, and Compromises* (ABC-CLIO 2006).
2242. Kurt M Saunders, 'Confusion Is the Key: A Trademark Law Analysis of Keyword Banner Advertising' (2002) 71 Fordham Law Review 543.
2243. *Ibid.*
2244. *Align Tech Inc v. Strauss Diamond Instrus Inc,* Case 18-cv-06663-TSH (ND Cal 12 April 2019).
2245. *Playboy Enters., Inc. v. Welles*, 279 F.3d 796, 801 (9th Cir. 2002).

'nominative fair use'[2246] situation: 'First, the product or service in question must be one not readily identifiable without use of the trademark; second, only so much of the mark or marks may be used as is reasonably necessary to identify the product or service; and third, the user must do nothing that would, in conjunction with the mark, suggest sponsorship or endorsement by the trademark holder.'[2247] The defendant used the plaintiff's marks in hashtags in social media advertising 'to refer to its *own* product'[2248] as well as 'used more of the marks than is reasonably necessary to identify the product'.[2249] Thus, they were not entitled to a defence under 'nominative fair use'.[2250] Fair use[2251] is also a defence to dilution[2252] under 15 U.S. Code § 1125 for comparing goods and services, 'identifying and parodying, criticizing, or commenting',[2253] 'news reporting and news commentary',[2254] and 'noncommercial' uses.[2255] Under the ACPA, specifically 15 U.S. Code § 1125(d)(1)(B)(IV), one factor to be assessed is 'the person's bona fide noncommercial or fair use of the mark in a site accessible under the domain name'.[2256] An noted by Bradley, the Tenth Circuit's test is 'that it must be immediately apparent to anyone visiting a parodic website that it was not the trademark owner's website'[2257] while the Fourth Circuit considers 'whether the domain name at issue conveys two simultaneous, yet contradictory, messages: that it is the original and that it is not the original and is instead a parody'.[2258]

The application of the First Amendment also factors into the trademark legal framework in that 'freedom of speech'[2259] is protected, which can include 'parody'.[2260] Specifically, the First Amendment to the U.S. Constitution, in part, states that 'Congress shall make no law … abridging the freedom of speech …'[2261] McGeveran argues that '[t]here is no shortage of law review articles and books warning that overly broad interpretation of trademark rights imperil free speech values'.[2262] It has been said that, if analysed properly, 'precedent, and the free expression ideal enshrined in the First

2246. *Ibid.*
2247. *Ibid.*; *Align Tech Inc v. Strauss Diamond Instrus Inc*, Case 18-cv-06663-TSH (ND Cal 12 April 2019).
2248. *Align Tech Inc v. Strauss Diamond Instrus Inc*, Case 18-cv-06663-TSH (ND Cal 12 April 2019).
2249. *Ibid.*
2250. *Ibid.*
2251. 15 U.S. Code § 1125.
2252. *Ibid.*
2253. *Ibid.*
2254. *Ibid.*
2255. *Ibid.*
2256. 15 U.S. Code § 1125(d)(1)(B).
2257. Monique Bradley, 'Why the Fair Use Defense of Free Speech or Parody under the Anticybersquatting Consumer Protection Act Needs Judicial Review by the United States Supreme Court' (2010) 11 Minnesota Journal of Law, Science & Technology 267, 268.
2258. *Ibid.*
2259. Constitution of United States of America 1789 (rev. 1992), amendment I.
2260. Mark VB Partridge, 'Trademark Parody and the First Amendment: Humor in the Eye of the Beholder' (1996) 29 John Marshall Law Review 877.
2261. Constitution of United States of America 1789 (rev. 1992), amendment I.
2262. William McGeveran, 'Four Free Speech Goals for Trademark Law' (2008) 18 Fordham Intellectual Property, Media and Entertainment Law Journal 1205.

Amendment',[2263] trademark holders would not prevail in most circumstances.[2264] Reference here is to actions against those utilising trademarks for 'lighthearted humor, critical cultural commentary, parody or even simply to shock'.[2265] Ramsey develops a novel 'impersonation theory'[2266] which is designed to remedy 'conflicts between trademark and free speech rights in disputes involving expressive uses of marks'.[2267] She believes that liability should be limited to cases where there is confusion[2268] as to source, it actually confuses[2269] and there is nothing there to clarify.[2270] At the same time, free speech[2271] should take precedence over such rights if they do not strictly exist.[2272]

Artistic expression[2273] may also be protected under certain circumstances. In the context of 'artistic expression'[2274] through 'artistic or expressive works',[2275] in *AM General v. Activision Blizzard,*[2276] discussed earlier in section 3.2.3 *Digital Confusion*, it was found, under the Rogers Test, that the Humvee vehicles used in the Call of Duty game did in fact have 'above zero'[2277] (all that is needed) level of 'artistic relevance'[2278] as they evoke 'a sense of realism and lifelikeness to the player ... across a variety of computer-generated battlefields'.[2279] However, in *Hermès v. Rothschild,*[2280] discussed earlier in section 3.2.4.4, the jury was instructed that 'even the modest ... elements of artistic expression contained in Rothschild's works entitled him to total First Amendment protection against Hermes' claims unless Hermes proved that Rothschild intentionally misled consumers into believing that Hermes was backing its products, the jury had no difficulty in concluding that Hermes had so proved'.[2281] The jury found 'that Rothschild did use Hermes' marks with an intent to deceive',[2282] and as a result, 'any claim he might have to First Amendment protection was waived'.[2283] Gery 'makes a case for an expanded understanding of a copyright fair use defence in trademark

2263. Pratheepan Gulaskaram, 'Santa Clara Law Digital Commons' (2005) http://digitalcommons.law.scu.edu/facpubs/529/ accessed July 2024.
2264. *Ibid.*
2265. *Ibid.*
2266. Lisa P Ramsey, 'Brandjacking on Social Networks: Trademark Infringement by Impersonation of Markholders' (2010) 58 Buffalo Law Review 851.
2267. Lisa P Ramsey, 'An Impersonation Theory of Trademark Law' www.law.uh.edu/wipip2012/Abstracts/RamseyAbstract_WIPIP2012.pdf accessed July 2024.
2268. *Ibid.*
2269. *Ibid.*
2270. *Ibid.*
2271. The Constitution of the United States of America, Amendment I.
2272. *Ibid.*
2273. Susan Weller, 'First Amendment May Protect Use of Trademarks as Artistic Expression' (*The National Law Review*, 27 May 2020) https://www.natlawreview.com/article/first-amendment-may-protect-use-trademarks-artistic-expression accessed July 2024.
2274. *AM General LLC v. Activision Blizzard, Inc. and others* 1:2017cv08644 (SDNY 2020).
2275. *Ibid.*
2276. *Ibid.*
2277. *Ibid.*
2278. *Ibid.*
2279. *Ibid.*
2280. *Hermès Int'l v. Mason Rothschild*, 603 F. Supp. 3d 98 (S.D.N.Y. 2022).
2281. *Ibid.*
2282. *Ibid.*
2283. *Ibid.*

law'[2284] and argues that 'factors in the copyright fair use defence seem to strike directly at the heart of the most salient concerns in Hermes v. Rothschild'[2285] while opining that confusion factors[2286] may not cover the necessary ground of consideration.[2287] In the NFT case of *Yuga Labs v. Ripps,*[2288] discussed earlier in section 3.2.1.1, the court did not consider the NFTs as an 'expressive work'.[2289] Specifically, 'the RR/BAYC NFTs do not express an idea or point of view, but, instead, merely point to the same online digital images associated with the BAYC collection'.[2290] The court further agreed that the 'sale of RR/BAYC NFTs is no more artistic than the sale of a counterfeit handbag, making the Rogers test inapplicable'[2291] ... and even if applied, it concluded that 'use of the BAYC marks is explicitly misleading'.[2292] In 2025, the 9th Circuit, in recognizing 'a narrow First Amendment except to trademark infringement for expressive speech'[2293] concluded that because the marks were used 'as source identification',[2294] the exception does not apply.[2295] While not an Internet trademark case, the recent Supreme Court decision in *Jack Daniels v. VIP*[2296] is informative to digital marks dealing with 'freedom of artistic expression'.[2297] In that case, a firm created a dog toy which utilised various elements of the Jack Daniel's whiskey mark and the Supreme Court outlined the various similarities, including that the toy and the bottle are 'about the same size' and outlining stark similarities or copying of the labelling.[2298] As Mann summarises, Justice Kagan's review of the Rogers test is that it is 'limited to products that use the mark in a ... non-source-identifying way'.[2299] When used 'as a designation of source for [its] own goods',[2300] First Amendment protections cannot be applied

2284. Michelle Gery, 'Understanding the MetaBirkin: Trademark Law and an Appropriate Legal Standard for NFTs' (11 March 2023) Columbia Journal of Law & the Arts https://doi.org/10.52214/jla.v47i4.13098, Forthcoming https://ssrn.com/abstract=4475873 accessed 4 August 2025.
2285. *Ibid.*
2286. *Ibid.*
2287. *Ibid.*
2288. *Yuga Labs, Inc. v. Ripps,* 2023 U.S. Dist. LEXIS 192487.
2289. *Ibid.*
2290. *Ibid.*
2291. *Ibid.*
2292. *Ibid.*
2293. *Yuga Labs, Inc. v. Ripps,* Case No. 24-879, 2025 WL 2056060 (9th Cir. 23 July 2025).
2294. *Ibid.*
2295. *Ibid.*
2296. *Jack Daniel's Props., Inc. v. VIP Products, L.L.C.,* No. CV14-023057-PHX-SMM, 2021 WL 5710730 (D. Ariz. 8 October 2021).
2297. Max Vern, 'Yuga Labs prevail on a summary judgment, protecting Bored Ape Yacht Club NFTs' (The Trademark Lawyer, 18 May 2023) https://trademarklawyermagazine.com/yuga-labs-prevail-on-a-summary-judgment-protecting-bored-ape-yacht-club-nfts/# accessed July 2024.
2298. *Jack Daniel's Props., Inc. v. VIP Products, L.L.C.,* No. CV14-023057-PHX-SMM, 2021 WL 5710730 (D. Ariz. 8 October 2021); https://www.scotusblog.com/2023/06/jack-daniels-wins-big-in-challenge-to-spoofing-bad-spaniels-dog-toy/ accessed 4 August 2025.
2299. Ronald Mann, 'Jack Daniel's Wins Big in Challenge to Spoofing "Bad Spaniels" Dog Toy' (*SCOTUS Blog*, 9 June 2023) https://www.scotusblog.com/2023/06/jack-daniels-wins-big-in-challenge-to-spoofing-bad-spaniels-dog-toy/ accessed July 2024.
2300. *Jack Daniel's Props., Inc. v. VIP Products, L.L.C.,* No. CV14-023057-PHX-SMM, 2021 WL 5710730 (D. Ariz. 8 October 2021); Ronald Mann, 'Jack Daniel's Wins Big in Challenge to

when 'the copied mark is used in that way'.[2301] However, as Tushnet opines, 'Bad Spaniels is a fairly obvious parody, and the fact that a court found it likely to be confusing highlights that the ordinary trademark infringement test can encourage false positives in cases involving humor, commentary, and the like, especially in cases where the challenged speech is itself the product being sold.'[2302] As Ramsey notes, 'nothing in the opinion suggests that the display of parodies, jokes, or other messages on the surface of toys, T-shirts, or other types of expressive merchandise would, by itself, constitute a trademark use of another's mark or trade dress'.[2303] However, it is the way in which it was used that was objectionable and the decision was vacated and the case was remanded.[2304]

3.2.7.2 Summary of Platform Considerations for Digital Justification

As seen above, there is some overlap pertaining to Digital Justification. Platforms should consider defences and justification such as fair use,[2305] freedom of expression,[2306] free speech,[2307] and parody,[2308] drawing from where there are common approaches in the jurisdictions.

3.3 CONCLUSION

In conclusion, this chapter sought to answer how the Digital Trademark and Trade Practices Model is informed by select theories and concepts, and select aspects of the US and EU (with reference to other) legal frameworks, and what the resulting considerations for the UDRP and platform policies are.

Spoofing "Bad Spaniels" Dog Toy' (*SCOTUS Blog*, 9 June 2023) https://www.scotusblog.com/2023/06/jack-daniels-wins-big-in-challenge-to-spoofing-bad-spaniels-dog-toy/ accessed July 2024.

2301. *Ibid.*
2302. Rebecca Tushnet, 'Bad Spaniels, Counterfeit Methodists, and Lying Birds: How Trademark Law Reinvented Strict Scrutiny' (13 May 2023) https://ssrn.com/abstract=4387772 accessed July 2024.
2303. Lisa Ramsey, 'Resolving Conflicts Between Trademark and Free Speech Rights after Jack Daniel's v. VIP Products (Guest Blog Post)' (*Technology & Marketing Law Blog*, 21 June 2023) https://blog.ericgoldman.org/archives/2023/06/resolving-conflicts-between-trademark-and-free-speech-rights-after-jack-daniels-v-vip-products-guest-blog-post.htm accessed July 2024.
2304. SCOTUS Blog, 'Jack Daniel's Properties, Inc. v. VIP Products LLC' (*SCOTUS Blog*) https://www.scotusblog.com/case-files/cases/jack-daniels-properties-inc-v-vip-products-llc-2/ accessed July 2024.
2305. EUTMR, Recital 21; 15 U.S. Code § 1115(b)(4); Canadian Trademarks Act R.S.C., 1985, c. T-13, s. 22.
2306. European Convention on Human Rights (ECHR), Art. 10; EU Charter of Fundamental Rights of the EU, Art. 11; The Constitution of the United States of America, Amendment I; Lisa P Ramsey, 'Free Speech and International Obligations to Protect Trademarks' 35 The Yale Journal of International Law 405, 406.
2307. *Ibid.*
2308. Stefan Martin, 'Well Known Marks and Parody: Dilution and Denigration? Unfair Advantage?' (*EUIPO*, 2017), https://euipo.europa.eu/knowledge/pluginfile.php/77920/mod_resource/content/8/Limits%20of%20trade%20marks%2C%20Parody%2018-5-2017.pdf accessed January 2024.

Based on the above analysis, the model is highly informed by the various theories, concepts, and legal frameworks touched on in this chapter, and hence is an adapted model. Based on these, a number of considerations were raised for the UDRP and platforms, which are summarised in Table 3.1 at the beginning of this chapter. These considerations will now be utilised in the next two chapters as the UDRP and platforms are more specifically analysed to provide recommendations for the same.

CHAPTER 4

Adapting the UDRP in Light of the Digital Trademark and Trade Practices Model

In this chapter, an overview of the longstanding, efficient, and cost-effective UDRP and its background is provided. The UDRP is assessed in line with the Digital Trademark and Trade Practices Model. Following this, specific recommendations are given for the UDRP. It is not recommended that the UDRP be completely overhauled, yet some key changes are recommended in line with the model and the draft text of an adapted UDRP, named the UDNDRP, is provided. The UDNDRP is an adapted policy which is based on gaps identified through the model and which addresses some key considerations raised.

4.1 INTRODUCTION

This chapter addresses the recommendations that can be made for the UDRP in light of the Digital Trademark and Trade Practices Model.

First implemented in 1999, the UDRP is a long-standing policy which serves as a framework for resolving certain trademark disputes for domain names. This chapter looks at whether the UDRP is a sufficient policy for domain names. It is concluded that, while the UDRP is a very effective and simplistic method to resolve domain name disputes, it has limited application (only to domain names) and, based on the Digital Trademark and Trade Practices Model, there are some gaps that should be filled while still largely maintaining its simple and workable approach.

The structure of this chapter is as follows. First, a bit of descriptive background on WIPO and the Internet Corporation for Assigned Names and Numbers (ICANN) is provided for purposes of context. Second, the UDRP is briefly introduced. Then, the UDRP advantages, challenges, and ongoing review are outlined. Further, gaps are identified in light of the Digital Trademark and Trade Practices Model, and in the process, the applicability of the UDRP to domain names is discussed. A draft of an adapted UDRP is provided against the backdrop of gaps based on the model.

4.2 WIPO, ICANN, AND THE UDRP

4.2.1 WIPO

A UN Agency, the WIPO 'is the global forum for intellectual property services, policy, information and cooperation'.[2309] The WIPO deals with many areas of intellectual property and is regarded as an international forum for these matters. Trademarks are a major area under the WIPO and many countries are signatory to various treaties that it administers relating to the same. The WIPO provides ADR[2310] services including 'mediation, arbitration, expedited arbitration, and expert determination'.[2311] It recognises the need for '[i]nternational IP rules for a changing world'.[2312] Various 'standing committees'[2313] are formed to address pressing needs of the global community in relation to trademarks and other intellectual property.[2314] Additionally, it compiles a list of thousands of laws and treaties relating to intellectual property for roughly 200 different countries.[2315] A '[g]lobal [b]rand [d]atabase'[2316] is maintained to allow searches of 'internationally protected trademarks'[2317] and therefore also acts as a resource platform. The WIPO has been a leader in the area of addressing Internet trademark issues, especially from the perspective of domain name disputes through the UDRP mechanism.

The WIPO Arbitration and Mediation Center is an 'independent and impartial body'[2318] which offers ADR 'for the resolution of international commercial disputes between private parties'.[2319] ADR can be defined as a 'method of resolving disputes without litigation'.[2320] To have a central body for the resolution of important disputes through ADR can benefit business and society from the perspective of being able to have a central forum. Also, the centre has an international focus and arbitrates and mediates disputes originating in different jurisdictions.[2321] Its panels have made

2309. WIPO, 'Inside WIPO' (*World Intellectual Property Organization*) https://www.wipo.int/about-wipo/en/ accessed January 2024.
2310. *Ibid.*
2311. *Ibid.*
2312. *Ibid.*
2313. *Ibid.*
2314. *Ibid.*
2315. *Ibid.*
2316. WIPO, 'Global Brand Database' (*Global Brand Database*) http://www.wipo.int/reference/en/branddb/ accessed January 2024.
2317. *Ibid.*
2318. WIPO, 'WIPO Arbitration and Mediation Center' (*WIPO Arbitration and Mediation Center*) http://www.wipo.int/amc/en/center/background.html accessed January 2024.
2319. *Ibid.*
2320. LII Staff, 'Alternative Dispute Resolution' (*LII/Legal Information Institute*, 5 June 2017) https://www.law.cornell.edu/wex/alternative_dispute_resolution accessed January 2024.
2321. *Ibid.*

decisions on many legal questions arising in the sphere of domain disagreements under the UDRP, although panels from other sources also exist.[2322]

4.2.2 ICANN

ICANN is structured as 'a nonprofit public-benefit corporation with a community of participants from all over the world'.[2323] ICANN 'promotes competition and develops policy on the Internet's unique identifiers'.[2324] However, it believes that 'Internet governance should mimic the structure of the Internet itself-borderless and open to all.'[2325] ICANN adopted the UDRP,[2326] which was kick-started by WIPO proposals ending in a policy being accepted in late 1999.[2327] It also has a 'WHOIS Lookup'[2328] allowing the public to look up publicly available registered domain owners.[2329] ICANN makes it clear that '[c]omplaints regarding trademark infringement due to website content and domain names are outside of ICANN's scope and authority',[2330] though it refers to the UDRP[2331] as a potential method of resolution for domain names. The UDRP is administered by WIPO who themselves are not specifically involved in the decision-making.[2332] Since 2016, certain aspects of the Internet have been transferred to private control (to ICANN) as opposed to under the Internet Assigned Numbers Authority (IANA) contract.[2333] This gives more responsibility to ICANN with a precedential move where the government relinquished 'control'.[2334]

The UDRP is an example of a uniform policy developed to deal with some of the Internet trademark issues arising in early days of 'commercialization of the Internet'.[2335] This policy was designed to prevent misuse in domain names and there is great

2322. Eun-Joo Min and Matheus Lilleengen, *Collection of WIPO Domain Name Panel Decisions* (Kluwer Law International 2004) 1-2.
2323. ICANN, 'ICANN for Beginners' (*ICANN*, 2025) https://www.icann.org/en/beginners accessed August 2025.
2324. *Ibid.*
2325. *Ibid.*
2326. ICANN, 'Uniform Domain-Name Dispute-Resolution Policy' (*ICANN*, 25 February 2012) https://www.icann.org/resources/pages/policy-2012-02-25-en accessed June 2025.
2327. Diane Cabell, 'Overview of Domain Policy Development' (*Harvard Law*, 20 April 2000) https://cyber.harvard.edu/udrp/overview.html accessed July 2024.
2328. ICANN, 'ICANN WHOIS' (*WHOIS Search | ICANN WHOIS*) https://whois.icann.org/en accessed January 2024.
2329. *Ibid.*
2330. ICANN, 'About Trademark Infringement' (*ICANN*) www.icann.org/resources/pages/trademark-2013-05-03-en accessed July 2024.
2331. *Ibid.*
2332. WIPO, 'WIPO – World Intellectual Property Organization' (*WIPO*) http://www.wipo.int/ accessed January 2024.
2333. Karen McCarthy, 'Internet Handover Is Go-Go-Go! ICANN to Take IANA from US Govt' (*The Register*, 20 September 2016) theregister.co.uk/2016/09/30/internet_handover_is_go_go_go/ accessed January 2024.
2334. *Ibid.*
2335. Diane Cabell, 'Overview of Domain Policy Development' (*Harvard Law*, 20 April 2000) https://cyber.harvard.edu/udrp/overview.html accessed July 2024.

reliance on the UDRP as seen from publicly available statistics.[2336] As an indicator of UDRP's major provider, 2023 was a record filing year for WIPO's 'UDRP and national variation'[2337] filings, reaching almost 6,200.[2338] EU members reporting individually totalled 2,611 complainant filings in 2023.[2339] Although many Member States reported only a few cases per year, 1,327 were filed for France,[2340] 273 for Germany,[2341] 192 for Italy,[2342] 139 for Denmark,[2343] 134 for the Netherlands,[2344] and 108 for Sweden.[2345] US complainant filings steadily rose from 894 in 2016 to 2,167 in 2023.[2346] Overall, there has been an approximate average of a 6% increase every year since 2014 in filed complaints.[2347] From these statistics, it appears that the UDRP is well in use and there appears to be much promise in its continued reliance.

4.3 UDRP OVERVIEW

In the context of global trademark disputes, de Werra argues in favour of and for 'the growing importance of ... ADR ... mechanisms, specifically arbitration, for solving trademark ... disputes'.[2348] Further, he says that '[i]t is hardly disputed that the UDRP has been extremely successful and that it probably is, as of today, the most accomplished example of an affordable and efficient global alternative dispute resolution

2336. WIPO, 'WIPO Domain Name Dispute Resolution Statistics' (*WIPO*) https://www.wipo.int/amc/en/domains/statistics/ accessed July 2024.
2337. WIPO, 'Record Number of Domain Name Cases filed with WIPO in 2023' (*WIPO*) https://www.wipo.int/amc/en/domains/caseload.html#: ~ :text = Trademark%20owners%20from%20around%20the,France%2C%20and%20the%20United%20Kingdom. accessed July 2024.
2338. *Ibid.*
2339. WIPO, 'WIPO Domain Name Dispute Resolution Statistics' (*WIPO*) https://www.wipo.int/amc/en/domains/statistics/ accessed July 2024.
2340. WIPO, 'Complainant Filing by Country: France' (*WIPO*) https://www.wipo.int/amc/en/domains/statistics/countries_yr.jsp?party = C&country_id = 60 accessed July 2024.
2341. WIPO, 'Complainant Filing by Country: Germany' (*WIPO*) https://www.wipo.int/amc/en/domains/statistics/countries_yr.jsp?party = C&country_id = 45 accessed July 2024.
2342. WIPO, 'Complainant Filing by Country: Italy' (*WIPO*) https://www.wipo.int/amc/en/domains/statistics/countries_yr.jsp?party = C&country_id = 84 accessed July 2024.
2343. WIPO, 'Complainant Filing by Country: Denmark' (*WIPO*) https://www.wipo.int/amc/en/domains/statistics/countries_yr.jsp?party = C&country_id = 47 accessed July 2024.
2344. WIPO, 'Complainant Filing by Country: Netherlands' (*WIPO*) https://www.wipo.int/amc/en/domains/statistics/countries_yr.jsp?party = C&country_id = 130 accessed July 2024.
2345. WIPO, 'Complainant Filing by Country: Sweden' (*WIPO*) https://www.wipo.int/amc/en/domains/statistics/countries_yr.jsp?party = C&country_id = 153 accessed July 2024.
2346. WIPO, 'Complainant Filing by Country: United States of America' (*WIPO*) https://www.wipo.int/amc/en/domains/statistics/countries_yr.jsp?party = C&country_id = 178 accessed July 2024.
2347. ICANN, 'Revised Uniform Domain Name Dispute Resolution Policy (UDRP) Status Report' (*ICANN*, July 2022) https://gnso.icann.org/sites/default/files/file/field-file-attach/udrp-status-report-redlined-13jul22-en.pdf accessed July 2024; WIPO, 'Record Number of Domain Name Cases Filed with WIPO in 2023' (*WIPO*) https://www.wipo.int/amc/en/domains/caseload.html#: ~ :text = Trademark%20owners%20from%20around%20the,France%2C%20and%20the%20United%20Kingdom. accessed July 2024.
2348. Jacques de Werra, Alternative 'Dispute Resolution for Trademark Disputes' in Irene Calboli and Jane Ginsburg (eds), *The Cambridge Handbook of International and Comparative Trademark Law* (Cambridge University Press 2020) 142-158.

system for intellectual property disputes',[2349] even if some have criticised the UDRP as trademark owner favourable.[2350]

The UDRP is an early example of limited recognition of Internet trademark concerns in today's world. UDRP 'proceedings provide an efficient remedy against the bad faith, abusive registration of domain names that violate trademark rights'.[2351] The policy 'has been adopted by ICANN-accredited registrars' with respect to all Generic Top-Level Domains (gTLDs).[2352] It 'applies to.com,.net and.org, as well as to ... gTLDs ... such as.aero,.asia,.biz,.cat,.coop,.info,.jobs,.mobi,.museum,.name,.pro,.travel and.tel', etc.[2353] It also applies to certain ccTLDs,[2354] including those of several EU member countries.[2355] It further 'applies to all [n]ew gTLDs'.[2356] The policy specifically outlines the various actions that can be taken if the registration of a domain name violates others' rights and is a part of the agreement consented to at the time of domain name registration.[2357]

Filing a complaint under the UDRP 'initiates a binding arbitration proceeding that is administered by an ICANN-authorized arbitrator'.[2358] New domain name registrants 'are required to consent to UDRP's authority when registering a domain name with an ICANN-authorized registrar'[2359] and 'a dispute may be brought under the UDRP if it concerns a domain name that is infringing another's mark'.[2360] Procedures under current dispute resolution mechanisms for domain names also include the Uniform Rapid Suspension (URS),[2361] which 'is intended to offer a lighter complement to the

2349. Jacques de Werra, 'Alternative Dispute Resolution Mechanisms For Solving Trademark Disputes (Mediation, UDRP, Arbitration)' in Irene Calboli and Jacques de Werra (eds), *The Law and Practice of Trademark Transactions, A Global and Local Outlook* (Edward Elgar 2016) 300.
2350. Michael Geist, 'Fundamentally Fair.com? An Update on Bias Allegations and the ICANN UDRP' (*Michael Geist*, 17 September 2015) https://www.michaelgeist.ca/tag/fair-com/ (archived).
2351. WIPO, 'UDRP Procedures for Generic Top Level Domains (GTLDs)' (*WIPO UDRP*) http://www.wipo.int/amc/en/domains/gtld/udrp/ accessed July 2024.
2352. ICANN, 'Domain Name Dispute Resolution Policies' (*Domain Name Dispute Resolution Policies – ICANN*) https://www.icann.org/resources/pages/dndr-2012-02-25-en#udrp accessed July 2024.
2353. WIPO, 'UDRP Procedures for Generic Top Level Domains (GTLDs)' (*WIPO UDRP*) http://www.wipo.int/amc/en/domains/gtld/udrp/ accessed July 2024.
2354. ICANN, 'Resources for Country Code Managers' (*ICANN*) https://www.icann.org/resources/pages/cctlds-21-2012-02-25-en accessed July 2024.
2355. WIPO, 'WIPO Domain Name Cases' (*WIPO Domain Name Cases*) http://www.wipo.int/amc/en/domains/cases.html accessed July 2024.
2356. WIPO, 'Domain Name Dispute Resolution Service for Generic Top-Level Domains' https://www.wipo.int/amc/en/domains/gtld/ accessed July 2024.
2357. ICANN, 'Uniform Domain-Name Dispute-Resolution Policy' (*ICANN*, 25 February 2012) https://www.icann.org/resources/pages/policy-2012-02-25-en accessed June 2025.
2358. CEB, *Internet Law Practice in California* (Continuing Education of the Bar, the Regents of the University of California, 2015) §3.5.
2359. *Ibid.*
2360. *Ibid.*
2361. WIPO, 'Rights Protection Mechanisms for New Top-Level Domains (TLDs)' (*WIPO*) https://www.wipo.int/amc/en/domains/rpm/ accessed July 2024.

existing UDRP'.[2362] The URS is designed to provide a quick resolution for clear-cut cases rather than more complicated ones.[2363]

The UDRP requires an administrative proceeding when three elements are in dispute, namely where the domain name is 'identical or confusingly similar',[2364] where the respondent does not have 'rights or legitimate interests in respect of the domain name',[2365] and the 'domain name has been registered and is being used in bad faith'.[2366] This requires a mandatory proceeding subject to being 'without prejudice to recourse to competent courts'.[2367] In other words, a court action is also available under these provisions. However, it is discretionary on the part of a panel to decide whether to continue to decision in a matter that may have been filed with a court of law.[2368]

4.3.1 UDRP Advantages, Challenges, and Ongoing Review

The UDRP has long been an effective approach to dealing with trademarks in domain names. Mostert indicates that the UDRP has been described as a modern iteration of 'the law merchant - the customary rules that services in medieval times as the international law of commerce - for cyberspace'.[2369]

Rule notes that it is '[o]ne of the most successful examples of a global ADR system'.[2370] As noted by many,[2371] the UDRP is aimed at or has primarily been an effective mechanism for resolving trademark domain name disputes in an efficient and cost-effective way.[2372] Decisions under the UDRP can often be made substantially quicker[2373] than through the courts and may also be achieved at a much lower cost.[2374]

2362. *Ibid.*
2363. *Ibid.*
2364. ICANN, 'Uniform Domain-Name Dispute-Resolution Policy' (*ICANN*, 25 February 2012) https://www.icann.org/resources/pages/policy-2012-02-25-en accessed June 2025.
2365. *Ibid.*
2366. *Ibid.*
2367. *Ibid.*
2368. *Ibid.*
2369. Frederick Mostert, 'The Internet: Regulators Struggle to Balance Freedom with Risk', (*Financial Times*, 2019) https://www.ft.com/content/e49c39e6-967d-11e9-8cfb-30c211dcd229 accessed December 2024.
2370. Colin Rule, 'Online Dispute Resolution and the Future of Justice' 16 Annual Review of Law and Social Science 277, 288 https://doi.org/10.1146/annurev-lawsocsci-101518-043049.
2371. Brian J Winterfeldt and Griffin M Barnett, 'Trademark Rights Protection Mechanisms in the Domain Name System: Current Landscape and Efforts to Diminish Protection' (2020) 29 Intellectual Property & Technology Law Journal 17, 18; Alpana Roy and Althaf Marsoof, '"Bad Faith" and "Rights or Legitimate Interests" Under Domain Name Law: Emerging Themes from the UDRP and auDRP' (2015) 20 Media and Arts Law Review 282; Patrick Kelley, 'Emerging Patterns in Arbitration Under the Uniform Domain-Name Dispute-Resolution Policy' (*Berkeley Law*) https://www.law.berkeley.edu/files/bclt_AnnualReview_Emerging_Final.pdf accessed July 2024; Diane Cabell, 'Overview of Domain Policy Development' (*Harvard Law*, 20 April 2000) https://cyber.harvard.edu/udrp/overview.html accessed July 2024.
2372. *Ibid.*
2373. WIPO, 'WIPO Guide to the Uniform Domain Name Dispute Resolution Policy (UDRP)' (*Domain Name Disputes*) http://www.wipo.int/amc/en/domains/guide/ accessed July 2024.
2374. *Ibid.*

It has been used by mark holders worldwide and provides a single and rather simple approach to trademark disputes in domain names.[2375]

The policy alleviates the need to determine which jurisdiction to file in, to determine which legal rules apply, or to hire local legal counsel in whichever possible jurisdiction(s) for purposes of court litigation.[2376] However, remedies through litigation may be wider, if needed, although the legal cost may generally be much greater at the outset, with the Court deciding whether any such fees will be recoverable (actual recovery depends on various factors and/or rules).[2377] Zalnieriute recognised that the UDRP provides 'a degree of predictability to a field which would otherwise be an entirely fragmented international system consisting of different regimes'.[2378] There may be more legal uncertainty than in a litigation setting unless the issue at hand is well settled in the relevant jurisdiction. Further, Lee compares the UDRP with traditional arbitration and says it 'is an option that should be considered'.[2379] Importantly, Rule notes that the UDRP is a 'good example of a justice system that works the way the Internet works ... not bound by any particular jurisdiction ... global and transparent, the participants are not required to show up in person at a specified location to get a resolution, and all outcomes delivered are immediately and effectively enforced'.[2380] As Chaisse and Friedman note, '[t]he near-global adoption of the ... UDRP ... not only offers a reasonably satisfactory resolution to conflicts between domain names and trademarks, but it also inspires legislators to further refine the trademark system'.[2381] A textual study by Cogburn, Ochieng, and Wong found 'substantial evidence for the ongoing stability of the UDRP'.[2382] Rule describes this as '[o]ne of the most successful examples of a global [online dispute resolution] ODR system'.[2383] Further, it is a 'good example of a justice system that works the way the Internet works ... not bound by any particular jurisdiction, it is global and transparent, the participants are not required to show up in person at a specified location to get a resolution, and all outcomes delivered

2375. ICANN, 'Revised Uniform Domain Name Dispute Resolution Policy (UDRP) Status Report' (*ICANN*, July 2022) https://gnso.icann.org/sites/default/files/file/field-file-attach/udrp-status-report-redlined-13jul22-en.pdf accessed July 2024.
2376. WIPO, 'WIPO Guide to the Uniform Domain Name Dispute Resolution Policy (UDRP)' (*Domain Name Disputes*) http://www.wipo.int/amc/en/domains/guide/ accessed July 2024.
2377. *Ibid.*
2378. Monika Zalnieriute, 'Beyond the Governance Gap in International Domain Name Law: Bringing the UDRP in Line with Internationally Recognized Human Rights' (2020) 56 Stanford Journal of International Law 79.
2379. Ilhyung Lee, 'The Uniform Domain Name Dispute Resolution Policy (UDRP): Not Quite Arbitration, but Satisfying?' (2020) 15 in Aplin Tanya (ed.) *Research Handbook on Intellectual Property and Digital Technologies* (Edward Elgar 2020).
2380. Colin Rule, 'Online Dispute Resolution and the Future of Justice' 16 Annual Review of Law and Social Science 277, 288 https://doi.org/10.1146/annurev-lawsocsci-101518-043049.
2381. Julien Chaisse and Danny Friedmann, 'Law of the Digital Domain: Trademarks, Domain Names, and the AI Frontier' (2024) 64 IDEA 399.
2382. Derrick Cogburn, Theodore Ochieng, and Haiman Wong, 'Towards an Understanding of Global "Private Ordering" in ICANN: Text Mining 23 Years of Uniform Domain-Name Dispute-Resolution Policy (UDRP) Decisions' (2023) 8(2) Journal of Cyber Policy, 186-217.
2383. Colin Rule, 'Online Dispute Resolution and the Future of Justice' 16 Annual Review of Law and Social Science 277, 288 https://doi.org/10.1146/annurev-lawsocsci-101518-043049.

are immediately and effectively enforced'.[2384] These are the features that make this system work well.

However, the UDRP has not been without challenges. While simplified procedures are much welcomed, these need to be comprehensive to the extent that all relevant factors be considered while still retaining a simple structure. There are clear limitations, including level of enforcement and extent of remedies available.[2385] From an enforcement perspective, under paragraph 3, the UDRP gives the power to the appropriate authority to cancel, transfer or change a registration.[2386] Where the elements of a UDRP action are present, this provides a quick and generally cost-effective resolution. However, this provision is limiting because it provides only for specific outcomes. For example, complainants under the UDRP cannot receive compensation, damages, or lost profits for use of their trademarks, and they would need to seek recourse through competent courts. This means that complainants may need to file a court action to avail themselves of all possible remedies available. Under *The Thread.com LLC v. Poploff* WIPO Case No. D2000-1470, the UDRP decision-making bodies are not akin to a 'general domain name court and the UDRP is not designed to adjudicate all disputes of any kind that relate in any way to domain names'.[2387] While domain name registrants 'represent'[2388] that, to their knowledge, 'the registration of the domain name will not infringe upon or otherwise violate the rights of any third party'[2389] as well as the domain is not being registered for 'an unlawful purpose'[2390] and that registrants 'will not knowingly use the domain name in violation of any applicable laws or regulations',[2391] all violations of trademarks in domain names are not enforceable under the UDRP. In fact, as a recent 2022 UDRP panel in *Service List Registry Limited v. Chris Young, Peckham Data Centre* Case No. D2022-2500 decided that, where 'complex legal issues'[2392] are present, the UDRP may not be an adequate venue of choice, in this case involving complex matters of 'previous agreements or trust arrangements'[2393] that needed to be carefully assessed.[2394] Further, in *Gido Ltd. v. Vincenzo Cucco, Girotti Srl* Case No. D2022-0892 pertaining to the EU mark, GIROTTI, it was decided that the matter was actually a 'business dispute involving the insolvency

2384. *Ibid.*
2385. WIPO, 'The Limits of the UDRP in Trademark and Commercial Disputes' (*WIPO*, 21 July 2022) https://www.worldtrademarkreview.com/article/the-limits-of-the-udrp-in-trademark-and-commercial-disputes accessed July 2024.
2386. ICANN, 'Uniform Domain-Name Dispute-Resolution Policy' (*ICANN*, 25 February 2012) https://www.icann.org/resources/pages/policy-2012-02-25-en accessed June 2025.
2387. Jane Seager and Eliza Parr, 'If the Shoe Doesn't Fit ... Panel Finds That UDRP Did Not Apply on the Facts' (*WTR*, 20 September 2022) https://www.worldtrademarkreview.com/article/if-the-shoe-doesnt-fit-panel-finds-udrp-did-not-apply-the-facts accessed July 2024.
2388. ICANN, 'Uniform Domain-Name Dispute-Resolution Policy' (*ICANN*, 25 February 2012) https://www.icann.org/resources/pages/policy-2012-02-25-en accessed June 2025.
2389. *Ibid.*
2390. *Ibid.*
2391. *Ibid.*
2392. Jane Seager and Gabrielle Creppy, 'UDRP Not "In Service" for Complex Legal Issues' (*WTR*, 7 November 2022) https://www.worldtrademarkreview.com/article/udrp-not-in-service-complex-legal-issues accessed July 2024.
2393. *Ibid.*
2394. *Ibid.*

of a corporate entity, rather than a case of cybersquatting of the kind that the UDRP was created to address'.[2395] While it is recognised that not all matters pertinent to domain names can fall under and be enforced by such a policy, there is scope to add limited elements to be resolved in the same simplified manner, especially when an overview to the UDRP,[2396] which will be introduced in section 4.3.2 below, shows various considerations in UDRP cases beyond the strict wording of the policy.[2397] Therefore, while focus is on the three elements required in the UDRP, in fact, panels take into consideration a number of different aspects considered relevant to those three elements and it would be incorrect to assume that the UDRP is restricted to the strict wording of those elements.[2398] This will become much clearer in section 4.3.2 below.

The UDRP, while much used, is on its face limited to circumstances of confusion,[2399] rights or legitimate interests,[2400] *and* bad faith.[2401] As noted by Silva, these elements are 'are markedly different from those required to establish trademark infringement'[2402] in some jurisdictions. For example, 'even if the UDRP-like rules have not been violated, there may still be unfair competition'.[2403] Additionally, Farley concludes that, under the UDRP, 'the focus is not on confusion, dilution, or any harm to the public or to the trademark owner'[2404] and that 'bad faith'[2405] is central to success under the UDRP.[2406] However, under the Digital Trademark and Trade Practices Model, as will be seen in the sections that follow, there is scope to add important elements without sacrificing the simplicity the UDRP was designed based on. The UDRP does not directly or adequately cover key elements such as 'unfair competition'[2407] (and related concepts such as reputation,[2408] dilution,[2409] etc.), disclaimers,[2410] or jurisdictional

2395. Jane Seager and Eliza Parr, 'If the Shoe Doesn't Fit ... Panel Finds That UDRP Did Not Apply on the Facts' (*WTR*, 20 September 2022) https://www.worldtrademarkreview.com/article/if-the-shoe-doesnt-fit-panel-finds-udrp-did-not-apply-the-facts accessed July 2024.
2396. WIPO, 'WIPO Overview of WIPO Panel Views on Selected UDRP Questions, Third Edition' ('WIPO Jurisprudential Overview 3.0') (*WIPO*, 2017) https://www.wipo.int/amc/en/domains/search/overview3.0/ accessed June 2025.
2397. *Ibid.*
2398. *Ibid.*
2399. ICANN, 'Uniform Domain-Name Dispute-Resolution Policy' (*ICANN*, 25 February 2012) https://www.icann.org/resources/pages/policy-2012-02-25-en accessed June 2025.
2400. *Ibid.*
2401. *Ibid.*
2402. Nuno Sousa e Silva, '*Sportagus*: Domain Names and Trade Marks, a Close Albeit Uneasy Relationship' (2022) 53 International Review of Intellectual Property and Competition Law 845 https://doi.org/10.1007/s40319-022-01200-y.
2403. *Ibid.*
2404. Christine Haight Farley 'Confusing the Similarity of Trademarks Law in Domain Name Disputes' 52 Akron Law Review 607, 613.
2405. *Ibid.*
2406. *Ibid.*
2407. Anselm Kamperman Sanders, *Unfair Competition Law: The Protection of Intellectual and Industrial Creativity* (Oxford University Press, 1997) 8; EUTMR, Art. 9(2)(c) and Art. 17(2); 15 U.S.C. §1125.
2408. *Ibid.*
2409. EUTMR, Art. 9(2)(c); 15 U.S.C. § 1125(c)(2)(B).
2410. WIPO, 'WIPO Overview of WIPO Panel Views on Selected UDRP Questions, Third Edition' ('WIPO Jurisprudential Overview 3.0') (*WIPO*, 2017) https://www.wipo.int/amc/en/domains/search/overview3.0/ accessed June 2025; Alexander Peukert, 'The Coexistence of

considerations[2411] within the policy itself. This can be limiting because it reduces the basis on which a complaint might succeed under the UDRP (unless these are factored in) and recourse in the courts may be required. Moreover, as Farley indicates, under the UDRP, the 'focus is not on the consumer',[2412] as in the case of trademark law, but rather on the domain name registrant.[2413] The consumer view may be enhanced when all elements where problems exist with digital trademarks, in this case, domain names, are incorporated. Additionally, Zalnieriute says that the UDRP can breed inconsistent decisions and recommends 'supplemental rules'[2414] to fill these gaps[2415] while also recommending regular reviews of the UDRP.[2416] Under the model, and in line with Woodward's recommendation, a set of clear guidelines,[2417] expanding on existing overviews[2418] and beyond the largely procedural and administrative guides,[2419] is recommended to further clarify how concepts in the policy may be applied. This can help to reduce inconsistent decisions by providing further certainty, guidance on specific provisions which cannot only support a decision maker but it can also provide information to those who have or are considering registering domains.

Starting in 2020, the UDRP has been up for review, commencing just before a record-breaking year of cases in 2021 (5,128 cases).[2420] A UDRP Status Report was issued in May 2022 and updated with public comment in July 2022. It reviewed the

Trade Mark Laws and Rights on the Internet, and the Impact of Geolocation Technologies' (2016) 47 International Review of Intellectual Property and Competition Law 60, 81 https://doi.org/10.1007/s40319-015-0427-8; Leslie Fair, 'Full Disclosure' (*FTC Business Blog*, 23 September 2014) https://www.ftc.gov/business-guidance/blog/2014/09/full-disclosure accessed June 2025.

2411. Julien Chaisse, 'The Merging of Two Worlds: Cyber Law and Trade Law Normative Convergence on Internet Domain Names' (2019) 37 Boston University International Law Journal 281; Brendan J Witherell, 'Trademark Law: The Extraterritorial Application of the Lanham Act – The First Circuit Cuts the Fat from the Vanity Fair Test' (2006) 29 Western New England Law Review 193, 197.
2412. Christine Haight Farley 'Confusing the Similarity of Trademarks Law in Domain Name Disputes' 52 Akron Law Review 607, 614.
2413. *Ibid.*
2414. Monika Zalnieriute, 'Reinvigorating Human Rights in Internet Governance: The UDRP Procedure Through the Lens of International Human Rights Principles' (2019-2020) 43 Columbia Journal of Law & the Arts 197.
2415. *Ibid.*
2416. *Ibid.*
2417. Elizabeth C Woodard, 'The UDRP, ADR, and Arbitration: Using Proven Solutions to Address Perceived Problems with the UDRP' (2009) 19 Fordham Intellectual Property, Media and Entertainment Law Journal 1169, 1207.
2418. WIPO, 'WIPO Overview of WIPO Panel Views on Selected UDRP Questions, Third Edition' ('WIPO Jurisprudential Overview 3.0') (*WIPO*, 2017) https://www.wipo.int/amc/en/domains/search/overview3.0/ accessed June 2025.
2419. WIPO, 'WIPO Guide to the Uniform Domain Name Dispute Resolution Policy (UDRP)' (*WIPO*) https://www.wipo.int/amc/en/domains/guide/ accessed July 2024.
2420. Trevor Little, 'ICANN Opens UDRP Review Public Comment, as Data Reveals Usage Trends' (*WTR*, 7 March 2022) https://www.worldtrademarkreview.com/article/icann-opens-udrp-review-public-comment-data-reveals-usage-trends accessed July 2024.

UDRP against its goals of 'efficiency',[2421] 'fairness',[2422] and 'addressing abuse'.[2423] Relating to efficiency, 'an average growth rate of 6% per year since 2014'[2424] was found. It is clear that the UDRP has been availed of in the jurisdictions covered in this study and such approach has been welcomed by many mark holders as an avenue for quicker resolution. The public commented on issues with 'compliance with timing requirements',[2425] decision delays, and lack of consolidation of cases.[2426] If an investigation finds these to be valid concerns, there may be operational or other efficiencies that need to be enforced. On the second goal of 'fairness',[2427] it was noted in the report that complainants were successful in approximately 78% of the decisions.[2428] However, public comments included 'unfair costs to brand owners'[2429] and that there is no additional procedure in the event that the UDRP was misapplied or not consistently or fairly applied.[2430] Under the 'fairness'[2431] goal, the question to be answered by the report was whether the UDRP allows for 'all relevant rights and interests of the parties to be considered and ensure procedural fairness for all concerned parties'.[2432]

Prior to the review, McElwaine and Casavale posited that the review may consider, *inter alia*, changing the bad faith registration 'and' use requirement,[2433] replacing the 'and' with an 'or'.[2434] They also envisioned a discussion of a 'loser pays'[2435] element in line with EU opposition and cancellation proceedings.[2436] Further, they considered a discussion on an appeal procedure.[2437] Additionally, they considered a review of a possible bar 'on future domain name registrations for repeat offenders'.[2438] Under the Digital Trademark and Trade Practices Model, as will be seen in this chapter, adapting the UDRP to add limited additional or alternative elements will allow for further 'relevant rights and interests'[2439] to be considered and this may assist in

2421. ICANN, 'Revised Uniform Domain Name Dispute Resolution Policy (UDRP) Status Report' (*ICANN*, July 2022) https://gnso.icann.org/sites/default/files/file/field-file-attach/udrp-status-report-redlined-13jul22-en.pdf accessed July 2024.
2422. *Ibid.*
2423. *Ibid.*
2424. *Ibid.*
2425. *Ibid.*
2426. *Ibid.*
2427. *Ibid.*
2428. *Ibid.*
2429. *Ibid.*
2430. *Ibid.*
2431. *Ibid.*
2432. Trevor Little, 'ICANN Opens UDRP Review Public Comment, as data Reveals Usage Trends' (*WTR*, 7 March 2022) https://www.worldtrademarkreview.com/article/icann-opens-udrp-review-public-comment-data-reveals-usage-trends accessed July 2024.
2433. *Ibid.*
2434. John McElwaine and Christopher D Casavale,'Tackling Bad Faith Registration of Domain Names in a Fast-Changing Landscape' (*WIPO Magazine*, December 2019) https://www.wipo.int/wipo_magazine/en/2019/06/article_0006.html accessed June 2025.
2435. *Ibid.*
2436. *Ibid.*
2437. *Ibid.*
2438. *Ibid.*
2439. ICANN, 'Revised Uniform Domain Name Dispute Resolution Policy (UDRP) Status Report' (*ICANN*, July 2022) https://gnso.icann.org/sites/default/files/file/field-file-attach/udrp-status-report-redlined-13jul22-en.pdf accessed July 2024.

retaining a simple avenue to resolve further rights while still incorporating further interests that may otherwise needed court action. For example, in line with the point raised by McElwaine and Casavale, an abuse[2440] provision is recommended under the model, as will be discussed in the next section. As to the goal of 'addressing abuse',[2441] an 'annual growth rate of 300 complaints per year'[2442] was noted. This purportedly provides insight into the level of 'alleged abuse'[2443] by registrants. Relating to 'addressing abuse',[2444] public comments sought more guidance for registrants to balance the playing field between such registrants and mark holders.[2445] Faster proceedings in the case of 'fraud and phishing'[2446] were also called for. The next steps include a review by the Generic Names Supporting Organization (GNSO) of the report to decide on the scope of and start Phase 2 of the UDRP review process.[2447] This procedure appears to be ongoing at time of writing.[2448]

In late 2024, WIPO announced, in conjunction with the Internet Commerce Association (ICA), the 'WIPO-ICA UDRP Review'.[2449] This is led by the project team comprising Brian Beckham from WIPO, and Zak Muscovitch of the ICA and consultations with 'industry leaders and experts'[2450] undertaken for the purpose is to 'identify best practices, consensus, and potential areas for improvement of the UDRP'.[2451] Bekham and Muscovitch intended to find areas where the UDRP may be improved under the specific focus of their review project, including maintaining the UDRP and a policy of 'predictability and effectiveness'.[2452] A draft of an initial report was released in April 2025 calling for public input[2453] and '[a] final report will be shared with ICANN

2440. John McElwaine and Christopher D Casavale,'Tackling Bad Faith Registration of Domain Names in a Fast-Changing Landscape' (*WIPO Magazine*, December 2019) https://www.wipo.int/wipo_magazine/en/2019/06/article_0006.html accessed June 2025.
2441. ICANN, 'Revised Uniform Domain Name Dispute Resolution Policy (UDRP) Status Report' (*ICANN*, July 2022) https://gnso.icann.org/sites/default/files/file/field-file-attach/udrp-status-report-redlined-13jul22-en.pdf accessed July 2024.
2442. *Ibid.*
2443. *Ibid.*
2444. *Ibid.*
2445. *Ibid.*
2446. *Ibid.*
2447. *Ibid.*
2448. ICANN, 'Revised Uniform Domain Name Dispute Resolution Policy (UDRP) Status Report' (*ICANN*, July 2022) https://gnso.icann.org/sites/default/files/file/field-file-attach/udrp-status-report-redlined-13jul22-en.pdf accessed July 2024; Julien Chaisse and Danny Friedmann, Law of the Digital Domain: Trademarks, Domain Names, and the AI Frontier' (2024) 64 IDEA 399, 427.
2449. WIPO, 'WIPO-ICA UDRP Review' (*WIPO*) https://www.wipo.int/amc/en/domains/resources/wipo-icaudrpreview.html accessed December 2024.
2450. *Ibid.*
2451. *Ibid.*
2452. Jason Seashore and Patrick H.J. Hughes, 'Q&A: WIPO's Brian Beckham, ICA's Zak Muscovitch Aim to "Shape the Scope" of Domain Dispute Resolution' (*Westlaw*, 2024) https://today.westlaw.com/Document/I92ccf6c6a5e311efb5eab7c3554138a0/View/FullText.html?transitionType=CategoryPageItem&contextData=(sc.Default)&firstPage=true accessed December 2024.
2453. WIPO, 'Initial Report of the WIPO-ICA UDRP Review Project Team' (*WIPO*, 2025), https://www.wipo.int/export/sites/www/amc/en/docs/wipoicareportapril2025.pdf accessed 4 August 2025.

for consideration in any UDRP review undertaken by its GNSO'.[2454] The initial report covered much content that is not part of the subject matter of this book, although two considerations were relevant. In the initial report, one consideration was 'registration, and use of the disputed domain name in bad faith'[2455] and 'free speech', topics also covered within this book and which have been debated for some time.[2456] The initial report recommended that both these issues be considered in a 'Secondary Track'.[2457] Recommendations in line with this book were presented to the WIPO-ICA UDRP Review Team and it is hoped that this book may be relevant to and considered within any ongoing review of the UDRP.

Despite its limitations, the UDRP appears to have served those looking for quick and cost-effective resolution.[2458] Cogburn et al., in 2022, found 'substantial evidence for the ongoing stability of the UDRP'.[2459] As an effective, simple approach to domain names, it is, at the same time, a minimalist approach to the problem of digital trademarks, broadly speaking. It does not apply beyond domain names, considers only certain factors (confusion, rights or legitimate interests, and bad faith),[2460] and has limited enforcement mechanisms (transfer, cancellation).[2461] The UDRP may not be relevant to all types of trademark disputes and litigation through the courts may be more appropriate in some circumstances.[2462] Under the model, as will be seen below, if additional important elements can be incorporated while maintaining the simplicity with which the UDRP was designed, this can serve parties very well. This is expanded on in the following section and throughout the rest of the chapter.

4.3.2 UDRP in Light of Digital Trademark and Trade Practices Model

The following is an overview of key factors used in UDRP decision-making and a sample of some relevant decisions in light of the elements of the model. It shows where (and the extent to which) the UDRP considers elements of the model, and where it does not. This analysis is intended to highlight gaps in the UDRP, which the model intends to cover

2454. Jason Seashore and Patrick H.J. Hughes, 'Q&A: WIPO's Brian Beckham, ICA's Zak Muscovitch Aim to "Shape the Scope" of Domain Dispute Resolution' (*Westlaw*, 2024) https://today.westlaw.com/Document/I92ccf6c6a5e311efb5eab7c3554138a0/View/FullText.html?transitionType=CategoryPageItem&contextData=(sc.Default)&firstPage=true accessed December 2024.
2455. WIPO, 'Initial Report of the WIPO-ICA UDRP Review Project Team' (*WIPO*, 2025), https://www.wipo.int/export/sites/www/amc/en/docs/wipoicareportapril2025.pdf accessed 4 August 2025.
2456. *Ibid.*
2457. *Ibid.*
2458. Patrick Kelley, 'Emerging Patterns in Arbitration Under the Uniform DomainName Dispute-Resolution Policy' (*Berkeley Law*) https://www.law.berkeley.edu/files/bclt_AnnualReview_Emerging_Final.pdf accessed July 2024.
2459. Derrick L Cogburn, Theodore Andrew Ochieng and Haiman M Wong, 'Towards an Understanding of Global "Private Ordering" in ICANN: Text Mining 23 Years of Uniform Domain-Name Dispute-Resolution Policy (UDRP) Decisions' (2023) 8 Journal of Cyber Policy 186.
2460. *Ibid.*
2461. *Ibid.*
2462. WIPO, 'The Limits of the UDRP in Trademark and Commercial Disputes' (*WIPO*, 21 July 2022) https://www.worldtrademarkreview.com/article/the-limits-of-the-udrp-in-trademark-and-commercial-disputes accessed July 2024.

while retaining many of the elements of the UDRP and its simple and quick approach. In some cases, the gaps are not glaring omissions, but inadequate or lack of explicit coverage of items that are considerations, as will be seen below.[2463] For example, 'unfair competition'[2464] related concepts are only somewhat covered by the UDRP but should be more directly and adequately included in the policy itself, as will be seen.

The WIPO Overview of WIPO Panel Views on Selected UDRP Questions, Third Edition (Overview)[2465] is very helpful to this analysis and is informative to put the UDRP into context. However, it should be noted that the document is an overview rather than guidance to the UDRP, even though it is contemplated that it may be used as such by decision makers, domain registrants, and parties as a form of guidance. In fact, it has been referred to and linked directly from some decisions.[2466] While WIPO also publishes a guide,[2467] it does not generally cover, sufficiently, the elements and their necessary interpretations; it is more of an administrative and procedural guide, which is helpful in its own right.[2468]

It is important to consider the UDRP against the adapted model. In the table below, for each element of the model, it is noted whether an element is *generally or not directly covered*, or whether there is *only some coverage*. For example, under *Digital Use and Place of Use*, while use in domain names may be covered, but use in the 'course of trade'[2469] or some alternative terminology for the concept is not required, this would be considered *only some coverage* since the considerations for the entire element are not covered.

Table 4.1 Digital Trademark and Trade Practices Model and UDRP

Digital Trademark and Trade Practices Model	*UDRP*
Digital Use and Place of Use	Only some coverage. Any use of registered or unregistered marks in domain names which violate the policy.[2470]

2463. WIPO, 'WIPO Overview of WIPO Panel Views on Selected UDRP Questions, Third Edition' ('WIPO Jurisprudential Overview 3.0') (*WIPO*, 2017) https://www.wipo.int/amc/en/domains/search/overview3.0/ accessed June 2025.
2464. Anselm Kamperman Sanders, *Unfair Competition Law: The Protection of Intellectual and Industrial Creativity* (Oxford University Press, 1997) 8; EUTMR, Art. 9(2)(c) and Art. 17(2); 15 U.S.C. §1125.
2465. WIPO, 'WIPO Overview of WIPO Panel Views on Selected UDRP Questions, Third Edition' ('WIPO Jurisprudential Overview 3.0') (*WIPO*, 2017) https://www.wipo.int/amc/en/domains/search/overview3.0/ accessed June 2025.
2466. *Zitro International, S.àr.l. v. Alex Ortiz, Zitro Services LLC* Case No. D2023-3508.
2467. WIPO, 'WIPO Guide to the Uniform Domain Name Dispute Resolution Policy (UDRP)' (*WIPO*) https://www.wipo.int/amc/en/domains/guide/ accessed July 2024.
2468. *Ibid.*
2469. TRIPS, Art. 16.
2470. WIPO, 'WIPO Overview of WIPO Panel Views on Selected UDRP Questions, Third Edition' ('WIPO Jurisprudential Overview 3.0') (*WIPO*, 2017) https://www.wipo.int/amc/en/domains/search/overview3.0/ accessed June 2025.

Digital Trademark and Trade Practices Model	*UDRP*
Digital Bad Faith and Abuse	'Registration and use of a domain name in bad faith'[2471] (abuse is covered in overview).[2472]
Digital Confusion	'Confusing similarity' in domain names.[2473] 'intentionally attempted to attract, for commercial gain, Internet users to your web site or other on-line location, by creating a likelihood of confusion with the complainant's mark as to the source, sponsorship, affiliation, or endorsement of your web site or location or of a product or service on your web site or location'.[2474]
Digital Unfair Competition	Only some coverage. 'without intent for commercial gain to misleadingly divert consumers or to tarnish the trademark or service mark at issue'.[2475] 'registered or you have acquired the domain name primarily for the purpose of selling, renting, or otherwise transferring the domain name registration to the complainant who is the owner of the trademark or service mark or to a competitor of that complainant, for valuable consideration in excess of your documented out-of-pocket costs directly related to the domain name'.[2476] 'you have registered the domain name primarily for the purpose of disrupting the business of a competitor'.[2477]

2471. UDRP, 4b.
2472. ICANN, 'Uniform Domain-Name Dispute-Resolution Policy' (*ICANN*, 25 February 2012) https://www.icann.org/resources/pages/policy-2012-02-25-en accessed June 2025; WIPO, 'WIPO Overview of WIPO Panel Views on Selected UDRP Questions, Third Edition' ('WIPO Jurisprudential Overview 3.0') (*WIPO*, 2017) https://www.wipo.int/amc/en/domains/search/overview3.0/ accessed June 2025.
2473. ICANN, 'Uniform Domain-Name Dispute-Resolution Policy' (*ICANN*, 25 February 2012) https://www.icann.org/resources/pages/policy-2012-02-25-en accessed June 2025.
2474. *Ibid.*
2475. *Ibid.*
2476. *Ibid.*
2477. *Ibid.*

Digital Trademark and Trade Practices Model	*UDRP*
	The Overview states that '[a]lso noting the availability of trademark-like protection under certain national legal doctrines (e.g., unfair competition or passing-off) and considerations of parity, where acquired distinctiveness/secondary meaning is demonstrated in a particular UDRP case, unregistered rights have been found to support standing to proceed with a UDRP case including where the complainant is based in a civil law jurisdiction'.[2478] Unfair advantage considerations may fall under bad faith and abuse (*see* Overview).[2479] 'Distinctiveness' and 'secondary meaning' is recognized in Overview along with a list of factors that may be considered.[2480] 'Secondary meaning'[2481] is covered in the Overview. Overview also states that 'the strength of the complainant's mark may be considered relevant in evaluating the second and third elements'[2482] of the UDRP.
Digital Terms, Policies, and Disclaimers	Only some coverage. Is itself a uniform policy addressing covered domain names. Disclaimers have been treated briefly in Overview. In cases 'where the respondent appears to otherwise have a right or legitimate interest in a disputed domain name, a clear and sufficiently prominent disclaimer would lend support to circumstances suggesting its good faith'.[2483]

2478. WIPO, 'WIPO Overview of WIPO Panel Views on Selected UDRP Questions, Third Edition' ('WIPO Jurisprudential Overview 3.0') (*WIPO*, 2017) https://www.wipo.int/amc/en/domains/search/overview3.0/ accessed June 2025.
2479. *Ibid.*
2480. *Ibid.*
2481. *Ibid.*
2482. *Ibid.*
2483. *Ibid.*

Digital Trademark and Trade Practices Model	*UDRP*
Digital Jurisdictional and Territorial Considerations	Only some coverage. Changes to a domain name may be made based on court or arbitral tribunal of competent jurisdiction.[2484] Overview states that 'rules and principles of law'[2485] may be considered (this is discretionary), however, 'in its own terms UDRP jurisprudence generally would not require resort to particular national laws'.[2486] For example, guidance indicates that where 'the parties share a common nationality and the import of a specific national law concept is particularly germane to an issue in dispute, panels have applied national law principles in assessing the UDRP elements'.[2487] Otherwise, the UDRP applies regardless of where domain is registered or used.
Digital Justification	Only some coverage. Using marks for 'legitimate noncommercial or fair use'[2488] is recognized as a method to demonstrate 'rights and legitimate interests'.[2489] Fair use and freedom of speech are also covered in the Overview.[2490]

4.3.2.1 *Digital Use and Place of Use*

The UDRP covers many but not all domain names. It does not always differentiate based on the types of use[2491] being made on the Internet, as long as the UDRP factors

2484. ICANN, 'Uniform Domain-Name Dispute-Resolution Policy' (*ICANN*, 25 February 2012) https://www.icann.org/resources/pages/policy-2012-02-25-en accessed June 2025.
2485. WIPO, 'WIPO Overview of WIPO Panel Views on Selected UDRP Questions, Third Edition' ('WIPO Jurisprudential Overview 3.0') (*WIPO*, 2017) https://www.wipo.int/amc/en/domains/search/overview3.0/ accessed June 2025.
2486. *Ibid.*
2487. *Ibid.*
2488. ICANN, 'Uniform Domain-Name Dispute-Resolution Policy' (*ICANN*, 25 February 2012) https://www.icann.org/resources/pages/policy-2012-02-25-en accessed June 2025.
2489. *Ibid.*
2490. *Ibid.*
2491. TRIPS, Art. 16; EUTMR, Art. 18; 15 U.S. Code § 1127; UK Trade Marks Act 1994, s. 46(1)(a); Canadian Trademarks Act R.S.C., 1985, c. T-13, s. 2.

applicable in the proceeding are present. Specifically, 'the goods and/or services for which the mark is registered or used in commerce, the filing/priority date, date of registration, and date of claimed first use, are not considered relevant'[2492] when considering 'confusion';[2493] however, these may be relevant to the other elements under the UDRP.[2494] For example, it may be relevant when a 'personal name'[2495] is being 'used in commerce as a distinctive identifier of the complainant's goods or services'[2496] which may assist in establishing 'standing to filing a UDRP complaint'.[2497]

The UDRP applies to registered as well as unregistered marks as long as these are being utilised within domain names covered under the policy and under certain conditions.[2498] The UDRP applies to all utilisation in covered domain names, including those situations where the mark is not being used commercially which is a gap under TRIPS which requires 'use in the course of trade'[2499] as well as under the 'use theory'.[2500] Another gap is that the UDRP does not always directly require consideration of the utilisation of trademarks on websites associated with domain names, although these are sometimes considered in the analysis.[2501] Further, the UDRP does not apply beyond use[2502] in domain names, for example, to use in various platforms.[2503] While this is a gap not for use[2504] in domain names per se, it is more of a gap beyond domain names,[2505] as will be discussed in the next chapter.

2492. WIPO, 'WIPO Overview of WIPO Panel Views on Selected UDRP Questions, Third Edition' ('WIPO Jurisprudential Overview 3.0') (*WIPO*, 2017) https://www.wipo.int/amc/en/domains/search/overview3.0/ accessed June 2025.
2493. *Ibid.*
2494. *Ibid.*
2495. *Ibid.*
2496. *Ibid.*
2497. *Ibid.*
2498. *Ibid.*
2499. TRIPS, Art. 16.
2500. Graeme B Dinwoodie and Mark D Janis, 'Confusion Over Use: Contextualism in Trademark Law' (2007) 92 Iowa Law Review 1597 *Articles by Maurer Faculty.* Paper 361.; Stephen L Carter, 'Does It Matter Whether Intellectual Property Is Property?' https://digitalcommons.law.yale.edu/fss_papers/2259/ accessed 4 August 2025; William Fisher, 'Theories of Intellectual Property' (*Harvard Law*) https://cyber.harvard.edu/people/tfisher/iptheory.pdf accessed 4 August 2025; Shontavia J Johnson, 'Memetic Theory, Trademarks & the Viral Meme Mark' (2013) The John Marshall Law School Review of Intellectual Property Law, 13 John Marshall Review of Intellectual Property Law 96; EUIPO, '3 Place of Use' (*EUIPO Trade mark guidelines* 2024) https://guidelines.euipo.europa.eu/2214311/1982069/trade-mark-guidelines/3-place-of-use accessed January 2024.
2501. WIPO, 'WIPO Overview of WIPO Panel Views on Selected UDRP Questions, Third Edition' ('WIPO Jurisprudential Overview 3.0') (*WIPO*, 2017) https://www.wipo.int/amc/en/domains/search/overview3.0/ accessed June 2025.
2502. TRIPS, Art. 16; EUTMR, Art. 18; 15 U.S. Code § 1127; UK Trade Marks Act 1994, s. 46(1)(a); Canadian Trademarks Act R.S.C., 1985, c. T-13, s. 2.
2503. Edward C Anderson and Timothy S Cole, 'The UDRP: A Model for Dispute Resolution in E-Commerce' (2002) 6 Journal of Small & Emerging Business Law 235; Rajeev Sachdev, 'Towards an Improved Framework for Trade-Mark Law and Regulation in Social Media Usernames: A Study of the Canadian, U.S., and U.K. Positions' (2016) 28 Intellectual Property Journal 379, 379-418; Daniel Doft, 'Facebook, Twitter, and the Wild West of IP Enforcement on Social Media: Weighing the Merits of a Uniform Dispute Resolution Policy' (2016) 49 The John Marshall Law Review 959; Thomas J Curtin, 'The Name Game: Cybersquatting and Trademark Infringement on Social Media Websites' (2010-2011) 19 Journal of Law and Policy 353; Erick J Heels, 'How to Twittersquat the Top 100 Brands' (*GiantPeople*, 8 January 2009)

Under the Digital Trademark and Trade Practices Model, it is recommended that the UDRP apply only to those instances where the mark is being used as a mark[2506] in the 'course of trade'.[2507] While this is not always clear, it may be prudent to look at the associated website recognising that the contents of such site may change.

4.3.2.2 Digital Bad Faith and Abuse

The UDRP clearly covers bad faith[2508] in domain names.[2509] The UDRP requires 'registration and use of a domain name in bad faith'[2510] (both), although a 2019 WIPO report surmised that these may, in the future, become alternative basis.[2511] In fact, as seen in Chapter 3, the WIPO Domain Name Dispute Resolution Service for .EU requires either the registration or the use of the domain to be in bad faith (not both).[2512] Likewise, the ACPA 15 U.S. Code § 1125(d)(1)(A)(i) requires 'bad faith intent to profit from that mark'[2513] alongside being 'identical or confusing similar'[2514] to a 'distinctive mark'[2515] or 'identical or confusingly similar to or dilutive of'[2516] a 'famous mark'.[2517] Bereskin says that, to prove bad faith,[2518] 'credible evidence of improper purpose for the registration and use of disputed domain name'[2519] is needed. The factors that may be considered for 'bad faith'[2520] include those that follow; however, the assessment

---

http://www.giantpeople.com/1298.html accessed 4 August 2025; Paul D McGrady, *McGrady on Social Media and the Metaverse* (Mathew Bender & Company, Inc. 2023) §12.

2504. TRIPS, Art. 16; EUTMR, Art. 18; 15 U.S. Code § 1127; UK Trade Marks Act 1994, s. 46(1)(a); Canadian Trademarks Act R.S.C., 1985, c. T-13, s. 2.

2505. Rajeev Sachdev, 'Towards an Improved Framework for Trade-Mark Law and Regulation in Social Media Usernames: A Study of the Canadian, U.S., and U.K. Positions' (2016) 28 Intellectual Property Journal 379, 379-418; Daniel Doft, 'Facebook, Twitter, and the Wild West of IP Enforcement on Social Media: Weighing the Merits of a Uniform Dispute Resolution Policy' (2016) 49 The John Marshall Law Review 959; Thomas J Curtin, 'The Name Game: Cybersquatting and Trademark Infringement on Social Media Websites' (2010-2011) 19 Journal of Law and Policy 353; Erick J Heels, 'How to Twittersquat the Top 100 Brands' (*GiantPeople*, 8 January 2009) http://www.giantpeople.com/1298.html accessed 4 August 2025; Paul D McGrady, *McGrady on Social Media and the Metaverse* (Mathew Bender & Company, Inc. 2023) §12.

2506. TRIPS, Art. 16.

2507. *Ibid.*

2508. UDRP, 4(a)(iii).

2509. *Ibid.*

2510. *Ibid.*

2511. John McElwaine and Christopher D Casavale, 'Tackling Bad Faith Registration of Domain Names in a Fast-Changing Landscape' (*WIPO Magazine*, December 2019) https://www.wipo.int/wipo_magazine/en/2019/06/article_0006.html accessed June 2025.

2512. WIPO, 'WIPO Domain Name Dispute Resolution Service for .EU (and.ею and.ευ)' (*WIPO*) https://www.wipo.int/amc/en/domains/cctld/eu/index.html accessed July 2024.

2513. 15 U.S. Code § 1125(d)(1)(A)(i).

2514. *Ibid.*

2515. *Ibid.*

2516. *Ibid.*

2517. *Ibid.*

2518. Daniel Bereskin, *Prosecuting and Defending Domain Name Disputes* (Elgar Online 2023) 148-175.

2519. *Ibid.*

2520. 15 U.S. Code § 1125(d)(1)(A)(i).

may not be limited to such factors under 4(b) of the UDRP and decision makers have discretion to find bad faith in other circumstances as these are 'non-exclusive and merely illustrative':[2521]

> (i) circumstances indicating that you have registered or you have acquired the domain name primarily for the purpose of selling, renting, or otherwise transferring the domain name registration to the complainant who is the owner of the trademark or service mark or to a competitor of that complainant, for valuable consideration in excess of your documented out-of-pocket costs directly related to the domain name; or
> (ii) you have registered the domain name in order to prevent the owner of the trademark or service mark from reflecting the mark in a corresponding domain name, provided that you have engaged in a pattern of such conduct; or
> (iii) you have registered the domain name primarily for the purpose of disrupting the business of a competitor; or
> (iv) by using the domain name, you have intentionally attempted to attract, for commercial gain, Internet users to your web site or other on-line location, by creating a likelihood of confusion with the complainant's mark as to the source, sponsorship, affiliation, or endorsement of your web site or location or of a product or service on your web site or location.[2522]

The above domain name-specific factors are explicitly outlined in the UDRP and can lead to a finding of bad faith.[2523] The listing of domain name-specific factors in this way is very helpful to decision makers of such disputes in order to reach legal conclusions on this as one of the key elements of a UDRP action.[2524] While Internet-specific factors are rare in legal frameworks, such domain name-specific provisions are particularly welcomed.

The UDRP appears to use some concepts drawn from unfair acts,[2525] practices,[2526] or competition[2527] in its 'bad faith'[2528] analysis, which not only should not be categorised under 'bad faith'[2529] but also should be a separate alternative ground to 'bad faith'[2530] as further discussed in the section on *Digital Unfair Competition*, below.

2521. *Ibid.*
2522. UDRP, 4(b)(iii).
2523. *Ibid.*
2524. WIPO, 'WIPO Overview of WIPO Panel Views on Selected UDRP Questions, Third Edition' ('WIPO Jurisprudential Overview 3.0') (*WIPO*, 2017) https://www.wipo.int/amc/en/domains/search/overview3.0/ accessed June 2025.
2525. Anselm Kamperman Sanders, *Unfair Competition Law: The Protection of Intellectual and Industrial Creativity* (Oxford University Press, 1997) 8; Frauke Henning-Bodewig, *Unfair Competition Law European Union and Member States* (Kluwer Law International 2006) xv-xvi; Martin Senftleben, Michael Handler and Irene Calboli, 'Protection Against Unfair Competition Around the Globe' (2024) 19 Journal of Intellectual Property Law & Practice 79, 79-80 https://doi.org/10.1093/jiplp/jpad121; Paris Convention, Art. 10bis; EUTMR, Art. 9(2)(c); 15 U.S.C. § 1125(c)(2)(B).
2526. *Ibid.*
2527. *Ibid.*
2528. UDRP, 4(b)(iii); WIPO, 'WIPO Overview of WIPO Panel Views on Selected UDRP Questions, Third Edition' ('WIPO Jurisprudential Overview 3.0') (*WIPO*, 2017) https://www.wipo.int/amc/en/domains/search/overview3.0/ accessed June 2025.
2529. UDRP, 4(b).
2530. *Ibid.*

For example, while registering or acquiring[2531] 'primarily for the purpose of selling, renting, or otherwise transferring the domain name registration … to a competitor of that complainant'[2532] as well as 'disrupting the business of a competitor' should be considered under the said section. Additionally, UDRP 4(b)(iv) incorporates a 'likelihood of confusion'[2533] analysis as a possible factor in a 'bad faith'[2534] analysis, which should not be the case because there is a distinct and separate requirement element of 'confusing similarity'[2535] already.

In the Overview, 'bad faith'[2536] under the UDRP is broadly understood to occur where a respondent takes 'unfair advantage of or otherwise abuses a complainant's mark'.[2537] In line with the discussion in the previous paragraph, the gap here is that 'unfair advantage'[2538] deserves distinct treatment alongside other relevant concepts. For example, 'misappropriation or free-riding considerations'[2539] or riding on 'the coattails of a famous mark'[2540] deserves a distinct analysis, as will be seen in the discussion on *Digital Unfair Competition* further below.

The Overview also addresses abuse[2541] of trademarks in domain names and states that 'establishing a pattern of bad faith conduct requires more than one, but as few as two instances of abusive domain name registration'.[2542] However, '[a] pattern of abuse has also been found where the respondent registers, simultaneously or otherwise, multiple trademark-abusive domain names corresponding to the distinct marks of individual brand owners'.[2543] The Overview first mentions 'a pattern of bad faith'[2544] and then switches to 'a pattern of abuse'.[2545] A clear distinction between 'bad faith'[2546] and 'abuse'[2547] is not present because it appears, in some cases, that 'abuse'[2548] is one

2531. *Ibid.*
2532. *Ibid.*
2533. *Ibid.*
2534. *Ibid.*
2535. UDRP, 4(a)(i).
2536. WIPO, 'WIPO Overview of WIPO Panel Views on Selected UDRP Questions, Third Edition' ('WIPO Jurisprudential Overview 3.0') (*WIPO*, 2017) https://www.wipo.int/amc/en/domains/search/overview3.0/ accessed June 2025.
2537. *Ibid.*
2538. Dima Basma, 'Dilution Versus Unfair Advantage: Myths and Realities' (2021) 52 International Review of Intellectual Property and Competition Law 1217-1257 https://doi.org/10.1007/s40319-021-01116-z.
2539. *Ibid.*
2540. Dima Basma, 'Dilution Versus Unfair Advantage: Myths and Realities' (2021) 52 International Review of Intellectual Property and Competition Law 1217-1257 https://doi.org/10.1007/s40319-021-01116-z; Anselm Kamperman Sanders, *Unfair Competition Law: The Protection of Intellectual and Industrial Creativity* (Oxford University Press, 1997).
2541. WIPO, 'WIPO Overview of WIPO Panel Views on Selected UDRP Questions, Third Edition' ('WIPO Jurisprudential Overview 3.0') (*WIPO*, 2017) https://www.wipo.int/amc/en/domains/search/overview3.0/ accessed June 2025.
2542. *Ibid.*
2543. *Ibid.*
2544. *Ibid.*
2545. *Ibid.*
2546. *Ibid.*
2547. *Ibid.*
2548. *Ibid.*

way to prove 'bad faith'.[2549] Instead, it should be a 'pattern'[2550] of repeated 'bad faith'[2551] or potentially one incident of a really 'abusive'[2552] type of 'bad faith'.[2553] Further, under UDRP 4(b)(ii), a factor is where someone tries to 'prevent the owner of the trademark or service mark from reflecting the mark in a corresponding domain name, provided that you have engaged in a pattern of such conduct'.[2554] However, the requirement of such 'pattern of conduct'[2555] should not be required, as this will prevent a mark holder from obtaining a remedy if the person engaging in what should be considered 'bad faith'[2556] (as they are effectively stopping the mark holder from so using their mark) has not engaged in such repeated conduct.[2557] If such 'pattern'[2558] is present, this should rather be considered 'abuse'[2559] but should not prevent a finding of 'bad faith'.[2560]

Additional factors under the Overview include:

> (i) the nature of the domain name (e.g., a typo of a widely-known mark, or a domain name incorporating the complainant's mark plus an additional term such as a descriptive or geographic term, or one that corresponds to the complainant's area of activity or natural zone of expansion), (ii) the chosen top-level domain (e.g., particularly where corresponding to the complainant's area of business activity or natural zone of expansion), (iii) the content of any website to which the domain name directs, including any changes in such content and the timing thereof, (iv) the timing and circumstances of the registration (particularly following a product launch, or the complainant's failure to renew its domain name registration), (v) any respondent pattern of targeting marks along a range of factors, such as a common area of commerce, intended consumers, or geographic location, (vi) a clear absence of rights or legitimate interests coupled with no credible explanation for the respondent's choice of the domain name, or (viii) other indicia generally suggesting that the respondent had somehow targeted the complainant.[2561]

Some cases will help to illustrate the 'bad faith'[2562] element under the UDRP, including 'abuse'.[2563] In *A Medium Corporation v. Protection of Private Person, REG.RU*

2549. *Ibid.*
2550. *Ibid.*
2551. *Ibid.*
2552. *Ibid.*
2553. *Ibid.*
2554. UDRP, 4(b)(ii).
2555. *Ibid.*
2556. UDRP, 4(b).
2557. UDRP, 4(b)(ii).
2558. *Ibid.*
2559. WIPO, 'WIPO Overview of WIPO Panel Views on Selected UDRP Questions, Third Edition' ('WIPO Jurisprudential Overview 3.0') (*WIPO*, 2017) https://www.wipo.int/amc/en/domains/search/overview3.0/ accessed June 2025.
2560. UDRP, 4(b)(ii).
2561. *Ibid.*
2562. *Ibid.*
2563. WIPO, 'WIPO Overview of WIPO Panel Views on Selected UDRP Questions, Third Edition' ('WIPO Jurisprudential Overview 3.0') (*WIPO*, 2017) https://www.wipo.int/amc/en/domains/search/overview3.0/ accessed June 2025.

Protection Service/Ivan Ivanov, Case No. D2018-2382, 'bad faith'[2564] was found based on the 'intentional misspelling'[2565] of the word *medium*.[2566] The domain used was *rnediurn.com*,[2567] which looks like, but is not the word *medium*, as the letter *r* and the letter *n* placed together mimic the letter *m* (used two times in the domain name in this case).[2568] In *Rockefeller & Co., Inc. v. James McCallum, Worlds-Wisdom-Inc.*, Case No. D2017-0009, based on a number of domain names, 'bad faith'[2569] was assessed using several 'observations'[2570] (following an earlier panel decision). These included that the mark had a 'strong reputation'[2571] and was 'widely known',[2572] that there was 'no evidence whatsoever of any actual or contemplated good faith',[2573] that the respondent registered a domain without using it,[2574] and even that communications were not replied to.[2575] In *TELUS Corporation v. Domain Administrator, See Privacy Guardian.org/Brandon Tursi*, Case No. D2018-2828, a Canadian company owning marks registered in Canada and the US, complained relating to the domain name teluspromos.com.[2576] In that case, 'bad faith'[2577] was found based on appearance of association[2578] with the markholder and 'promising'[2579] visitors 'the best promotions possible'.[2580] Also, 'further evidence of bad faith'[2581] was found where the respondent did not respond to communication to try and resolve the issue before filing, which was noted as being called 'cyberflight'.[2582] In 2022, Verizon was able to recover seventy-two domain names in *Verizon Trademark Services LLC v. Zhi Chao Yang*, Case No.

2564. *Ibid.*
2565. *A Medium Corporation v. Protection of Private Person, REG.RU Protection Service/Ivan Ivanov* Case No. D2018-2382 https://www.wipo.int/amc/en/domains/search/text.jsp?case=D2018-2382 accessed July 2024; Gerlad M Levine, 'Noteworthy Domain Name Decisions for 2018' https://iplegalcorner.com/noteworthy-domain-name-decisions-for-2018/ accessed July 2024.
2566. *Ibid.*
2567. *Ibid.*
2568. *Ibid.*
2569. *Ibid.*
2570. *Magazine Publishers Inc. and Les Publications Conde Nast S.A. v. ChinaVogue.com*, WIPO Case No. D2005-0615 https://www.wipo.int/amc/en/domains/decisions/html/2005/d2005-0615.html accessed July 2024.
2571. *Rockefeller & Co., Inc. v. James McCallum, Worlds-Wisdom-Inc.* Case No. D2017-0009 https://www.wipo.int/amc/en/domains/search/text.jsp?case=D2017-0009 accessed July 2024.
2572. *Ibid.*
2573. *Ibid.*
2574. *Ibid.*
2575. *Ibid.*
2576. *In TELUS Corporation v. Domain Administrator, See PrivacyGuardian.org/Brandon Tursi* Case No. D2018-2828 https://www.wipo.int/amc/en/domains/decisions/text/2018/d2018-2828.html accessed July 2024.
2577. ICANN, 'Uniform Domain-Name Dispute-Resolution Policy' (*ICANN*, 25 February 2012) https://www.icann.org/resources/pages/policy-2012-02-25-en accessed June 2025.
2578. *In TELUS Corporation v. Domain Administrator, See PrivacyGuardian.org/Brandon Tursi* Case No. D2018-2828 https://www.wipo.int/amc/en/domains/decisions/text/2018/d2018-2828.html accessed July 2024.
2579. *Ibid.*
2580. *Ibid.*
2581. *Ibid.*
2582. *Ibid.*

D2022-2224.[2583] Bad faith[2584] was determined based on the fact that 'the domains resolved to parked pages comprising pay-per-click links and the registrant did not respond to the complaint and had a history of abusive domain name disputes against third-party trademark owners'.[2585]

Reverse domain name hijacking (RDNH)[2586] may be found by a panel where a party uses 'the UDRP in bad faith to attempt to deprive a registered domain-name holder of a domain name'.[2587] In the recent case of *Scentsational Shoppe, Inc. v. Jeffrey Potts, The Common Scents, Inc.* Case No. D2023-3525, with respect to the disputed domain perfume-oils.com, RDNH[2588] was found based on the fact that counsel 'knew or should have known it could not succeed as to any of the required three elements of the Policy ... that its trademark rights were severely limited ... made no effort to support its allegations of bad faith ...'.[2589]

From the above, it appears that a variety of factors may be considered to meet the 'bad faith'[2590] element, including 'abuse'.[2591] Specific factors that may be considered to arrive at a conclusion of bad faith or abuse as outlined in the Overview are welcomed. Under the Digital Trademark and Trade Practices Model, while panels do consider 'abuse',[2592] and it is recognised in the Overview, it is important that it be covered more directly in the policy itself, beyond the reference to 'you have engaged in a pattern of such conduct'[2593] specific to one example in proving bad faith.[2594] The Overview mentions that 'to support a claim to rights or legitimate interests under the UDRP, the use of a disputed domain name must in any event not be abusive of third-party

2583. *Verizon Trademark Services LLC v. Zhi Chao Yang* Case No. D2022-2224 https://www.wipo.int/amc/en/domains/decisions/pdf/2022/d2022-2224.pdf accessed July 2024; Trevlor Little, 'Verizon's Biggest Ever UDRP Win Reminds Users of the Mechanism's Value' https://www.worldtrademarkreview.com/article/verizons-biggest-ever-udrp-win-reminds-users-of-the-mechanisms-value accessed July 2024.
2584. *Ibid.*
2585. *Ibid.*
2586. WIPO, 'WIPO Overview of WIPO Panel Views on Selected UDRP Questions, Third Edition' ('WIPO Jurisprudential Overview 3.0') (*WIPO*, 2017) https://www.wipo.int/amc/en/domains/search/overview3.0/ accessed June 2025.
2587. *Ibid.*
2588. *Ibid.*
2589. *Scentsational Shoppe, Inc. v. Jeffrey Potts, The Common Scents, Inc.* Case No. D2023-3525 https://www.wipo.int/amc/en/domains/decisions/pdf/2023/d2023-3525.pdf accessed July 2024.
2590. UDRP, 4(a)(iii).
2591. WIPO, 'WIPO Overview of WIPO Panel Views on Selected UDRP Questions, Third Edition' ('WIPO Jurisprudential Overview 3.0') (*WIPO*, 2017) https://www.wipo.int/amc/en/domains/search/overview3.0/ accessed June 2025.
2592. *Ibid.*
2593. UDRP, 4(b)(ii).
2594. UDRP, 4(a)(iii).

trademark rights'.[2595] However, it is more important to alert registrants within the policy itself and require a rule against 'abuse'[2596] with further explanation in guidance.

Overall, 'bad faith'[2597] and 'abuse'[2598] should be distinct from 'unfair competition'[2599] as these, even if some aspects are related, are effectively different sets of concepts. These should not be treated as the same thing under the policy, as this approach confuses, although it is not being recommended that both sets of concepts be required elements and these may be alternatives.

4.3.2.3 Digital Confusion

The UDRP addresses confusion in domain names through the terminology, 'confusing similarity'.[2600] The policy states that a 'mandatory administrative proceeding'[2601] is required if the complaint involves a domain name which 'is identical or confusingly similar to a trademark or service mark in which the complainant has rights'.[2602]

As explained in the Overview, the test for 'confusing similarity'[2603] will normally involve 'a side-by-side comparison of the domain name and the textual components'[2604] of the mark to determine if the trademark 'is recognizable'[2605] in the domain.[2606] It also includes 'recognizability by technological means such as search engine algorithms'[2607] and can involve 'a more holistic aural or phonetic comparison'[2608] between the mark and the domain to determine 'confusing similarity'.[2609] Also, if the domain includes the whole trademark, or if the 'dominant feature ... is

2595. WIPO, 'WIPO Overview of WIPO Panel Views on Selected UDRP Questions, Third Edition' ('WIPO Jurisprudential Overview 3.0') (*WIPO*, 2017) https://www.wipo.int/amc/en/domains/search/overview3.0/ accessed June 2025.
2596. *Scentsational Shoppe, Inc. v. Jeffrey Potts, The Common Scents, Inc.* Case No. D2023-3525 https://www.wipo.int/amc/en/domains/decisions/pdf/2023/d2023-3525.pdf accessed July 2024.
2597. UDRP, 4(a)(iii).
2598. WIPO, 'WIPO Overview of WIPO Panel Views on Selected UDRP Questions, Third Edition' ('WIPO Jurisprudential Overview 3.0') (*WIPO*, 2017) https://www.wipo.int/amc/en/domains/search/overview3.0/ accessed June 2025.
2599. Anselm Kamperman Sanders, *Unfair Competition Law: The Protection of Intellectual and Industrial Creativity* (Oxford University Press, 1997) 8; EUTMR, Art. 9(2)(c) and Art. 17(2); 15 U.S.C. §1125.
2600. UDRP, 4(a)(i).
2601. UDRP, 4(a).
2602. UDRP, 4(a)(i).
2603. WIPO, 'WIPO Overview of WIPO Panel Views on Selected UDRP Questions, Third Edition' ('WIPO Jurisprudential Overview 3.0') (*WIPO*, 2017) https://www.wipo.int/amc/en/domains/search/overview3.0/ accessed June 2025.
2604. *Ibid.*
2605. *Ibid.*
2606. *Ibid.*
2607. *Ibid.*
2608. *Ibid.*
2609. *Ibid.*

recognizable in the domain name',[2610] it will usually be deemed 'confusingly similar'.[2611] Of course, if the mark is 'identical',[2612] that will suffice.[2613] These specific methods to determine whether 'confusing similarity'[2614] exists under the UDRP provide some level of guidance as to how it will be assessed.

However, as noted by Farley and Sorkin, the 'confusing similarity test'[2615] can be different from a 'likelihood of confusion'[2616] or similar test under trademark law.[2617] An overview of some case decisions also helps to provide a glimpse into how 'confusing similarity'[2618] may be dealt with under the UDRP. In *Biogen MA Inc. v. Registration Private, Domains by Proxy, LLC/Jessica Raldi, Im Raldi Adventures,* Case No. D2018-0800, the exact mark was being utilised and was decided to be 'identical'.[2619] While this was a clear-cut case, many others are not and require guidance. In *Toyota Motor Sales, U.S.A. Inc. v. Domain Admin, Whois Privacy Corp.,* Case No. D2018-0801, a mark was found to be '[i]dentical or [c]onfusingly [s]imilar'[2620] based on the fact that it included the TOYOTA[2621] mark within the domain sunnysidetoyota.com.[2622] Incorporation[2623] of a mark is prohibited if done in a confusing[2624] manner and this case decided that the mark was confusing[2625] when utilised alongside the term 'sunnyside'.[2626] In *Orange Brand Services Limited v. Wangyang Zhang, Shen Zhen Shi Kai Xin Cheng Zi Ke Ji You Xian Gong Si,* Case No. D2018-0890, a mark was found to be 'confusingly similar'[2627] because the domain hi-orange.com took the trademark 'orange'[2628] and combined[2629] it with a 'descriptive and non-distinctive prefix',[2630] namely the word 'hi'.[2631] *Carrefour v. USDIET, Tony Mancini,* Case No. D20160571 involved a

2610. *Ibid.*
2611. *Ibid.*
2612. UDRP, 4(a)(i).
2613. *Ibid.*
2614. *Ibid.*
2615. David E Sorkin, 'Judicial Review of ICANN Domain Name Dispute Decisions' (2001) 18 Santa Clara Computer and High Technology Law Journal 35, 48; Christine Haight Farley 'Confusing the Similarity of Trademarks Law in Domain Name Disputes' 52 Akron Law Review 607.
2616. *Ibid.*
2617. *Ibid.*
2618. UDRP, 4(a)(i).
2619. *Biogen MA Inc. v. Registration Private, Domains by Proxy, LLC/Jessica Raldi, Im Raldi Adventures* Case No. D2018-0800 https://www.wipo.int/amc/en/domains/search/text.jsp?case=D2018-0800 accessed July 2024.
2620. *Toyota Motor Sales, U.S.A. Inc. v. Domain Admin, Whois Privacy Corp.* Case No. D2018-0801 https://www.wipo.int/amc/en/domains/search/text.jsp?case=D2018-0801.
2621. *Ibid.*
2622. *Ibid.*
2623. *Ibid.*
2624. *Ibid.*
2625. *Ibid.*
2626. *Ibid.*
2627. *Orange Brand Services Limited v. Wangyang Zhang, Shen Zhen Shi Kai Xin Cheng Zi Ke Ji You Xian Gong Si* Case No. D2018-0890 https://www.wipo.int/amc/en/domains/search/text.jsp?case=D2018-0890 accessed July 2024.
2628. *Ibid.*
2629. *Ibid.*
2630. *Ibid.*
2631. *Ibid.*

party from France and another from Los Angeles, California, and several domain names were disputed, including carrefournutrition.com, lapharmaciecarrefour.com, magasincarrefour.com and parapharmaciecarrefour.com.[2632] All of these included 'a dictionary term to the [c]omplainant's trademark',[2633] specifically, the words 'parapharmacie',[2634] 'pharmacie',[2635] 'nutrition'[2636] and 'magasin'[2637] respectfully, which means 'shop or stores in English'[2638] related to the business. All of these words were considered 'descriptive of some aspect of the [c]omplainant's business'[2639] and it was decided that the addition of 'a dictionary or descriptive term'[2640] would not serve to avoid 'confusing similarity'.[2641] It was noted that the complainant had been functioning on the Internet since 1995[2642] and retained registration of the mark CARREFOUR[2643] since 1968.[2644] Because the domain was different only with respect to the added 'dictionary terms',[2645] it was found that the non mark holder was cognizant 'of the potential for Internet user confusion'.[2646] This was sufficient to make a finding transferring the domain names to the complainant in this matter.[2647] A 'common, obvious, or intentional misspelling'[2648] will likely be deemed to be 'confusingly similar'.[2649] Further, a 'translation or transliteration'[2650] may also be determined as being 'identical or confusingly similar'.[2651] However, as seen in the recent case of *Meta Platforms, Inc. and Meta Platforms Technologies, LLC v. George Lamoureux*, Case No. D2023-4409, in the disputed domain of metaquesthelp.com, adding the term 'help'[2652] to a trademark 'does not prevent a finding of confusing similarity'.[2653]

2632. *Carrefour v. USDIET, Tony Mancini* Case No. D2016-0571 https://www.wipo.int/amc/en/domains/search/text.jsp?case=D2016-0571 accessed July 2024.
2633. *Ibid.*
2634. *Ibid.*
2635. *Ibid.*
2636. *Ibid.*
2637. *Ibid.*
2638. *Ibid.*
2639. *Ibid.*
2640. *Ibid.*
2641. *Ibid.*
2642. *Ibid.*
2643. *Ibid.*
2644. *Ibid.*
2645. *Ibid.*
2646. *Ibid.*
2647. *Ibid.*
2648. *Ibid.*
2649. *Ibid.*
2650. *Ibid.*
2651. *Ibid.*
2652. *Ibid.*
2653. *Meta Platforms, Inc. and Meta Platforms Technologies, LLC v. George Lamoureux* Case No. D2023-4409 https://www.wipo.int/amc/en/domains/decisions/pdf/2023/d2023-4409.pdf accessed July 2024.

As can be seen from the above cases, some decision makers under the UDRP have focused on 'determining the degree of resemblance',[2654] sometimes ignoring 'dictionary terms'.[2655] In other cases, decision makers may also consider 'distinctiveness of the mark, how well known the mark is, how long the mark has been used, and the nature of the goods and services'.[2656] For example, in *Canyon Bicycles GmbH v. Domains By Proxy, LLC/Rob van Eck* Case No. D2014-0206 (complainant from Germany, and respondents from the US and the Netherlands), the domain canyon.bike was at issue.[2657] It was decided that the gTLD (.bike) would be considered a part of the analysis, 'confusing similarity'[2658] was found, and the domain was ordered transferred to the complainant.[2659] Likewise, in *Marriott International, Inc. and Marriott Worldwide Corporation v. Miguel Sanchez Boat* Case No. D2018-0983 (complainant from the US and respondent from Spain), the domain marriott.social was found to be confusingly similar.[2660] However, as Farley indicates that the long-standing principle of ignoring the 'gTLD portion'[2661] is 'overstated'[2662] by the UDRP panels in these cases … and that it could certainly make a difference, as in the case of Farley's hypothetical example of amazon.books which would 'likely be found to be confusingly similar to the mark AMAZON'.[2663]

One issue with 'confusing similarity'[2664] under the UDRP is that, in only limited cases, the associated website or respondent's patterns of behaviour respecting the complainant's marks are considered.[2665] The Overview states that 'content of the website associated with the domain name is usually disregarded by panels when assessing confusing similarity'.[2666] Further, '[i]n some instances, panels have however taken note of the content of the website associated with a domain name to confirm

2654. *Carrefour v. USDIET, Tony Mancini* Case No. D2016-0571 https://www.wipo.int/amc/en/domains/search/text.jsp?case=D2016-0571 accessed July 2024.
2655. *Ibid.*
2656. *Columbia Insurance Company v. Pampered Gourmet* Case No. D2004-0649 https://www.wipo.int/amc/en/domains/decisions/html/2004/d2004-0649.html accessed July 2024; Christine Haight Farley 'Confusing the Similarity of Trademarks Law in Domain Name Disputes' 52 Akron Law Review 607, 615.
2657. *Canyon Bicycles GmbH v. Domains By Proxy, LLC/Rob van Eck* Case No. D2014-0206 https://www.wipo.int/amc/en/domains/decisions/text/2014/d2014-0206.html accessed July 2024; Christine Haight Farley 'Confusing the Similarity of Trademarks Law in Domain Name Disputes' 52 Akron Law Review 607, 620.
2658. *Ibid.*
2659. *Ibid.*
2660. *Marriott International, Inc. and Marriott Worldwide Corporation v. Miguel Sanchez Barco* Case No. D2018-0983 https://www-wipo-int.translate.goog/amc/en/domains/decisions/text/2018/d2018-0983.html?_x_tr_sl=es&_x_tr_tl=en&_x_tr_hl=en&_x_tr_pto=sc accessed July 2024; Christine Haight Farley 'Confusing the Similarity of Trademarks Law in Domain Name Disputes' 52 Akron Law Review 607.
2661. Christine Haight Farley 'Confusing the Similarity of Trademarks Law in Domain Name Disputes' 52 Akron Law Review 607, 632.
2662. *Ibid.*
2663. *Ibid.*
2664. UDRP, 4(a)(i).
2665. WIPO, 'WIPO Overview of WIPO Panel Views on Selected UDRP Questions, Third Edition' ('WIPO Jurisprudential Overview 3.0') (*WIPO*, 2017) https://www.wipo.int/amc/en/domains/search/overview3.0/ accessed June 2025.
2666. *Ibid.*

confusing similarity whereby it appears prima facie that the respondent seeks to target a trademark through the disputed domain name'.[2667] In some cases, the associated website has clearly been considered, while in others, it has been ignored.[2668] This causes uncertainty that needs to be resolved.

Another issue is that 'confusing similarity'[2669] is one required element of a UDRP proceeding (along with 'rights or legitimate interests'[2670] and 'bad faith')[2671] and cannot be used as a standalone argument to obtain an available remedy.[2672] In other words, both of these must also be proven. This leaves mark holders with the added burden to prove these two additional factors beyond 'confusion'.[2673] Under the WIPO Domain Name Dispute Resolution Service for.EU, the requirement is to 'demonstrate why the disputed domain name is identical or confusingly similar ... and, **either**: why the disputed domain name has been registered by its holder without rights or legitimate interests; **or** the disputed domain name should be considered as having been registered or being used in bad faith'.[2674] There is no cumulative requirement to demonstrate all three elements, as is the case under the UDRP.[2675]

Under the Digital Trademark and Trade Practices Model, while confusion[2676] is covered under the UDRP, it should be amply clear the circumstances under which the associated website to the disputed domain will be considered. For example, in some cases, such as clear-cut cases where the mark is the only or dominant aspect of a domain can be confusion[2677] and there may not be any need to consider the associated website. In other cases, confusion[2678] may not be as clear and consideration of the associated website may be warranted; however, this needs to be clear in guidance. Further, confusion,[2679] along with one additional factor, may be sufficient following the approach set out by the WIPO Domain Name Dispute Resolution Service for.EU described above.[2680] In the .eu policy,[2681] 'confusion'[2682] along with 'bad faith'[2683] (or

2667. *Ibid.*
2668. *Canyon Bicycles GmbH v. Domains By Proxy, LLC/Rob van Eck* Case No. D2014-0206 https://www.wipo.int/amc/en/domains/decisions/text/2014/d2014-0206.html accessed July 2024; Christine Haight Farley 'Confusing the Similarity of Trademarks Law in Domain Name Disputes' 52 Akron Law Review 607, 620; WIPO, 'WIPO Overview of WIPO Panel Views on Selected UDRP Questions, Third Edition' ('WIPO Jurisprudential Overview 3.0') (*WIPO*, 2017) https://www.wipo.int/amc/en/domains/search/overview3.0/ accessed June 2025.
2669. UDRP, 4(a).
2670. *Ibid.*
2671. *Ibid.*
2672. *Ibid.*
2673. *Ibid.*
2674. WIPO, 'WIPO Domain Name Dispute Resolution Service for .EU (and.ею and.ευ)' (*WIPO*) https://www.wipo.int/amc/en/domains/cctld/eu/index.html accessed July 2024.
2675. *Ibid.*
2676. UDRP, 4(a)(i).
2677. *Ibid.*
2678. *Ibid.*
2679. *Ibid.*
2680. WIPO, 'WIPO Domain Name Dispute Resolution Service for .EU (and.ею and.ευ)' (*WIPO*) https://www.wipo.int/amc/en/domains/cctld/eu/index.html accessed July 2024.
2681. *Ibid.*
2682. *Ibid.*

alternatively, 'no legitimate rights')[2684] is sufficient, and some form of alternative approach should be considered because 'confusion',[2685] along with one other element appears sufficient, especially if 'legitimate interests'[2686] is permitted as a justification for the respondent to prove (discussed under *Digital Justification*, below).

Digital Unfair Competition

There is no direct or specific mention in the UDRP of unfair competition,[2687] unfair acts,[2688] or unfair trade practices in domain names. However, some related provisions are present. For example, under 'Evidence of Registration and Use in Bad Faith',[2689] a complainant can show:

> (i) circumstances indicating that you have registered or you have acquired the domain name primarily for the purpose of selling, renting, or otherwise transferring the domain name registration to the complainant who is the owner of the trademark or service mark or to a competitor of that complainant, for valuable consideration in excess of your documented out-of-pocket costs directly related to the domain name; or
> (ii) you have registered the domain name in order to prevent the owner of the trademark or service mark from reflecting the mark in a corresponding domain name, provided that you have engaged in a pattern of such conduct; or
> (iii) you have registered the domain name primarily for the purpose of disrupting the business of a competitor; or ... .[2690]

Therefore, there are certain types of activities against competitors that could be used as evidence, but this is from the perspective of providing the bad faith[2691] element. However, these evidentiary elements of a UDRP action reflect some aspects of unfair competition,[2692] acts,[2693] or practices.[2694]

2683. *Ibid.*
2684. *Ibid.*
2685. *Ibid.*
2686. *Ibid.*
2687. Anselm Kamperman Sanders, *Unfair Competition Law: The Protection of Intellectual and Industrial Creativity* (Oxford University Press, 1997) 8; Frauke Henning-Bodewig, *Unfair Competition Law European Union and Member States* (Kluwer Law International 2006) xv-xvi; Martin Senftleben, Michael Handler and Irene Calboli, 'Protection Against Unfair Competition Around the Globe' (2024) 19 Journal of Intellectual Property Law & Practice 79, 79-80 https://doi.org/10.1093/jiplp/jpad121; Paris Convention, Art. 10bis; EUTMR, Art. 9(2)(c); 15 U.S.C. § 1125(c)(2)(B).
2688. *Ibid.*
2689. UDRP, 4(b).
2690. *Ibid.*
2691. *Ibid.*
2692. Anselm Kamperman Sanders, *Unfair Competition Law: The Protection of Intellectual and Industrial Creativity* (Oxford University Press, 1997) 8; Frauke Henning-Bodewig, *Unfair Competition Law European Union and Member States* (Kluwer Law International 2006) xv-xvi; Martin Senftleben, Michael Handler and Irene Calboli, 'Protection Against Unfair Competition Around the Globe' (2024) 19 Journal of Intellectual Property Law & Practice 79, 79-80 https://doi.org/10.1093/jiplp/jpad121; Paris Convention, Art. 10bis; EUTMR, Art. 9(2)(c); 15 U.S.C. § 1125(c)(2)(B).
2693. *Ibid.*
2694. *Ibid.*

In the context of 'How to Demonstrate Your Rights to and Legitimate Interests',[2695] unfair acts[2696] appear to creep into a justification context:

> (iii) you are making a legitimate noncommercial or fair use of the domain name, without intent for commercial gain to misleadingly divert consumers or to tarnish the trademark or service mark at issue'.[2697]

In other words, this is not an affirmative prohibition, but a method of proving 'rights and legitimate interests'[2698] from the perspective of 'noncommercial or fair use'[2699] of a domain name, so long as the specific (and potentially limited) unfair acts are not being engaged in.[2700] Only 'tarnishment'[2701] is named in the policy of the UDRP; however, taking 'unfair advantage'[2702] or 'dilution'[2703] generally or 'blurring'[2704] specifically are not mentioned.

Beyond the policy itself, the Overview states that '[a]lso noting the availability of trademark-like protection under certain national legal doctrines (e.g., unfair competition or passing-off) and considerations of parity, where acquired distinctiveness/ secondary meaning is demonstrated in a particular UDRP case, unregistered rights have been found to support standing to proceed with a UDRP case including where the complainant is based in a civil law jurisdiction'.[2705] Unfortunately, this appears to be more relevant to determining standing rather than as a standalone ground separate from the three elements of a UDRP action. This is especially true because an 'unfair competition,[2706] acts',[2707] or 'practices'[2708] analysis is different from a 'confusion'[2709]

2695. UDRP, 4(c).
2696. Anselm Kamperman Sanders, *Unfair Competition Law: The Protection of Intellectual and Industrial Creativity* (Oxford University Press, 1997) 8; Frauke Henning-Bodewig, *Unfair Competition Law European Union and Member States* (Kluwer Law International 2006) xv-xvi; Martin Senftleben, Michael Handler and Irene Calboli, 'Protection Against Unfair Competition Around the Globe' (2024) 19 Journal of Intellectual Property Law & Practice 79, 79-80 https://doi.org/10.1093/jiplp/jpad121; Paris Convention, Art. 10bis; EUTMR, Art. 9(2)(c); 15 U.S.C. § 1125(c)(2)(B).
2697. UDRP, 4(c)(iii).
2698. UDRP, 4(c).
2699. *Ibid.*
2700. *Ibid.*
2701. *Ibid.*
2702. Article 9(2)(c) EUTMR.
2703. EUTMR, Art. 9(2)(c); 15 U.S.C. § 1125(c)(2)(B).
2704. 15 U.S. Code § 1125(c)(2)(B).
2705. WIPO, 'WIPO Overview of WIPO Panel Views on Selected UDRP Questions, Third Edition' ('WIPO Jurisprudential Overview 3.0') (*WIPO*, 2017) https://www.wipo.int/amc/en/domains/search/overview3.0/ accessed June 2025.
2706. Anselm Kamperman Sanders, *Unfair Competition Law: The Protection of Intellectual and Industrial Creativity* (Oxford University Press, 1997) 8; Frauke Henning-Bodewig, *Unfair Competition Law European Union and Member States* (Kluwer Law International 2006) xv-xvi; Martin Senftleben, Michael Handler and Irene Calboli, 'Protection Against Unfair Competition Around the Globe' (2024) 19 Journal of Intellectual Property Law & Practice 79, 79-80 https://doi.org/10.1093/jiplp/jpad121; Paris Convention, Art. 10bis; EUTMR, Art. 9(2)(c); 15 U.S.C. § 1125(c)(2)(B).
2707. *Ibid.*
2708. *Ibid.*
2709. Paris Convention, Art. 6bis; TRIPS, Art. 16(1); EUTMR, Art. 8(1)(b) and Art. 9(2)(b); 15 U.S. Code § 1114;15 U.S. Code § 1125.

one. Further, the Overview states that 'the use of a domain name for illegal activity (e.g., the sale of counterfeit goods ... impersonation/passing off ...) can never confer rights or legitimate interests on a respondent'.[2710] While this is recognised in the Overview and has formed part of the decision-making in some UDRP cases, 'unfair acts',[2711] 'unfair competition',[2712] 'impersonation'[2713] or 'passing off'[2714] are not explicitly stated in the actual policy. Also, 'unfair advantage'[2715] appears to be covered only through the grounds of bad faith[2716] rather than instances of such that do not involve these aspects.[2717] For example, the Overview briefly mentions that 'behavior detrimental to the complainant's trademark'[2718] can satisfy the burden of establishing 'bad faith'.[2719] The Overview also covers 'unfair practices',[2720] 'unfairly passing itself off',[2721] 'unfairly capitalize',[2722] 'unfair advantage',[2723] 'behavior detrimental to'[2724] or 'abuse',[2725] but this again is in the context of proving the 'bad faith'[2726] element under the UDRP. The Overview also indicates that the 'lack of intent to unfairly profit from the complainant's reputation',[2727] or employing 'bait and switch ... or other related unfair trade practices'[2728] may be factors in 'legitimate rights and interests',[2729] the former supporting such rights of the respondent, and the latter working against any 'fair use'[2730] argument. Further, any 'counterfeit goods'[2731] or 'impersonation/passing off ... can never confer rights or legitimate interests on a respondent'.[2732] It appears that concepts covering unfair acts,[2733] practices,[2734] or competition[2735] are spread throughout the two prongs. However, while the coverage is commended, this approach may be problematic as these are not contained together in a single related element.

2710. WIPO 3rd edn.
2711. EUTMR, Art. 9(2)(c); EUTMR, Art. 17(2); 15 U.S.C. §1125.
2712. Anselm Kamperman Sanders, *Unfair Competition Law: The Protection of Intellectual and Industrial Creativity* (Oxford University Press, 1997) 8.
2713. Lisa P Ramsey, 'An Impersonation Theory of Trademark Law' www.law.uh.edu/wipip2012/Abstracts/RamseyAbstract_WIPIP2012.pdf accessed 4 August 2025.
2714. EUTMR, Art. 17(2); 15 U.S.C. §1125.
2715. EUTMR, Art. 9(2)(c).
2716. UDRP, 4(a)(iii).
2717. EUTMR, Art. 9(2)(c).
2718. WIPO, 'WIPO Overview of WIPO Panel Views on Selected UDRP Questions, Third Edition' ('WIPO Jurisprudential Overview 3.0') (*WIPO*, 2017) https://www.wipo.int/amc/en/domains/search/overview3.0/ accessed June 2025.
2719. *Ibid.*
2720. *Ibid.*
2721. *Ibid.*
2722. *Ibid.*
2723. *Ibid.*
2724. *Ibid.*
2725. *Ibid.*
2726. *Ibid.*
2727. *Ibid.*
2728. *Ibid.*
2729. *Ibid.*
2730. *Ibid.*
2731. *Ibid.*
2732. *Ibid.*
2733. Anselm Kamperman Sanders, *Unfair Competition Law: The Protection of Intellectual and Industrial Creativity* (Oxford University Press, 1997) 8; Frauke Henning-Bodewig, *Unfair Competition Law European Union and Member States* (Kluwer Law International 2006)

Not adequately covering unfair competition[2736] (which covers a number of related concepts) in the policy itself is limiting because the policy is not explicit about using a mark in these ways and does not emphasise their consideration. It is also considered only from the perspective of a 'rights and legitimate interests'[2737] or bad faith[2738] analysis, which is an issue when activity relating to the latter may not be directly involved.

While not directly stated in the UDRP, distinctiveness[2739] and reputation[2740] or recognition[2741] are evident in the Overview.[2742] For example, unregistered marks must be distinctive[2743] (have 'secondary meaning'),[2744] which is assessed using these factors:

> (i) the duration and nature of use of the mark, (ii) the amount of sales under the mark, (iii) the nature and extent of advertising using the mark, (iv) the degree of actual public (e.g., consumer, industry, media) recognition, and (v) consumer surveys.[2745]

The UDRP also considers where brands have achieved 'relatively rapid recognition due to a significant Internet presence',[2746] and some panels have paid attention to 'factors such as the type and scope of market activities and the nature of the complainant's goods and/or services'.[2747] The issue here is that focused attention on reputation is not evident under the UDRP, even though some panels have recognised the same.[2748] As seen in the discussion on bad faith[2749] above, guidance notes that '*(i) the nature of the domain name (e.g., a typo of a widely-known mark …*'[2750] may be considered.[2751] While reference to such a mark is welcome, there are two limiting aspects to this guidance. First, it recognises, only by way of example of a 'typo',[2752] a

xv-xvi; Martin Senftleben, Michael Handler and Irene Calboli, 'Protection Against Unfair Competition Around the Globe' (2024) 19 Journal of Intellectual Property Law & Practice 79, 79-80 https://doi.org/10.1093/jiplp/jpad121; Paris Convention, Art. 10bis; EUTMR, Art. 9(2)(c); 15 U.S.C. § 1125(c)(2)(B).

2734. *Ibid.*
2735. *Ibid.*
2736. *Ibid.*
2737. WIPO, 'WIPO Overview of WIPO Panel Views on Selected UDRP Questions, Third Edition' ('WIPO Jurisprudential Overview 3.0') (*WIPO*, 2017) https://www.wipo.int/amc/en/domains/search/overview3.0/ accessed June 2025.
2738. *Ibid.*
2739. *Ibid.*
2740. *Ibid.*
2741. *Ibid.*
2742. *Ibid.*
2743. *Ibid.*
2744. *Ibid.*
2745. *Ibid.*
2746. *Ibid.*
2747. *Ibid.*
2748. *Ibid.*
2749. *Ibid.*
2750. *Ibid.*
2751. *Ibid.*
2752. *Ibid.*

'widely-known'[2753] mark, rather than other possible uses of such a mark, even though not explicitly prohibited from consideration. This appears rather incidental as opposed to a deliberative incorporation of reputation[2754] of trademarks in domain names. Second, consideration of 'widely-known'[2755] marks is only in the context of a bad faith analysis rather than in their own right, which is an issue because these may raise different considerations.[2756] Being 'well known'[2757] was considered in *Meta Platforms, Inc. and Meta Platforms Technologies, LLC v. George Lamoureux* Case No. D2023-4409, with respect to the disputed domain metaquesthelp.com, the 'Complainant was using and announced use of the META QUEST Mark before Respondent registered the Domain Name'[2758] and bad faith[2759] was found based, in part, on the fact that 'MPT became well known worldwide for its virtual reality ... software and apparatus, which included the headset under the name "Oculus Quest",[2760] and a "rebranding from Oculus Quest to Meta Quest was widely publicized in late October 2021, about a year before Respondent's registration of the Domain Name"'.[2761] In another recent case, 'unfair advantage'[2762] and 'goodwill'[2763] were considered relevant.[2764] In *Zitro International, S.àr.l. v. Alex Ortiz, Zitro Services LLC* Case No. D2023-3508, the panellist found, in the context of the disputed domain zitrtechnologies.com and despite no reply to the complaint by the respondent, that 'the Complainant does not engage in any way with the fact that the Respondent appears to be running a business under the "Zitro" brand which does not seem to be in competition with the Complainant or to be taking unfair advantage of the Complainant's reputation or goodwill'.[2765] Further, the panellist indicated that '[n]o evidence has been provided supporting the Complainant's claims of being a worldwide leader in its field from which it might have been inferred that the Respondent may be seeking to capitalize on the Complainant's reputation and goodwill in its trademarks'.[2766] In determining that the respondent operates businesses using the 'Zitro prefix which are unrelated to the Complainant's line of business'[2767] and without targeting the complainant, the element of 'rights or legitimate interests'[2768] was not established.[2769]

2753. *Ibid.*
2754. *Ibid.*
2755. *Ibid.*
2756. *Ibid.*
2757. *Meta Platforms, Inc. and Meta Platforms Technologies, LLC v. George Lamoureux* Case No. D2023-4409 https://www.wipo.int/amc/en/domains/decisions/pdf/2023/d2023-4409.pdf accessed July 2024.
2758. *Ibid.*
2759. *Ibid.*
2760. *Ibid.*
2761. *Ibid.*
2762. *Zitro International, S.àr.l. v. Alex Ortiz, Zitro Services LLC* Case No. D2023-3508 https://www.wipo.int/amc/en/domains/decisions/pdf/2023/d2023-3508.pdf accessed July 2024.
2763. *Ibid.*
2764. *Ibid.*
2765. *Ibid.*
2766. *Ibid.*
2767. *Ibid.*
2768. *Ibid.*
2769. *Ibid.*

Third, it is not clear how 'wide'[2770] the mark must be 'known'[2771] discussed further in the section covering geographic considerations below. The Overview also states that '[i]ssues such as the strength of the complainant's mark or the respondent's intent to provide its own legitimate offering of goods or services without trading off the complainant's reputation, are decided under the second and third elements'.[2772] As stated in the Overview in reference to 'unregistered or common law'[2773] marks, the 'complainant must show that its mark has become a distinctive identifier which consumers associate with the complainant's goods and/or services'.[2774] The Overview also states that '[m]erely having a famous name (such as a businessperson or cultural leader who has not demonstrated use of their personal name in a trademark/source-identifying sense), or making broad unsupported assertions regarding the use of such name in trade or commerce, would not likely demonstrate unregistered or common law rights for purposes of standing to file a UDRP complaint'.[2775] It is helpful that there is guidance in the case of marks that are not registered and protection is afforded to the same.

In the recent case of *Scentsational Shoppe, Inc. v. Jeffrey Potts, The Common Scents, Inc.* Case No. D2023-3525, the disputed domain perfume-oils.com was found to contain generic terms which were not distinctive.[2776] The complainant owns the U.S. mark consisting, *inter alia*, the terms PO PERFUME OILS with a disclaimer as to the terms 'perfumes' and 'oils'.[2777] The panellist found, based on the generic terms, that 'secondary meaning'[2778] was required but not established.[2779]

2770. WIPO, 'WIPO Overview of WIPO Panel Views on Selected UDRP Questions, Third Edition' ('WIPO Jurisprudential Overview 3.0') (*WIPO*, 2017) https://www.wipo.int/amc/en/domains/search/overview3.0/ accessed June 2025.
2771. *Ibid.*
2772. *Ibid.*
2773. *Ibid.*
2774. *Ibid.*
2775. *Ibid.*
2776. *Scentsational Shoppe, Inc. v. Jeffrey Potts, The Common Scents, Inc.* Case No. D2023-3525 https://www.wipo.int/amc/en/domains/decisions/pdf/2023/d2023-3525.pdf accessed July 2024.
2777. *Ibid.*
2778. *Ibid.*
2779. *Ibid.*

Under the Digital Trademark and Trade Practices Model, it is recommended that unfair competition[2780] be a specific alternative ground. Also, 'unfair advantage'[2781] should extend beyond 'bad faith'[2782] and 'abuse'[2783] and be treated alongside the above set of concepts. Further, 'dilution'[2784] should be explicitly protected beyond its relevance to a 'bad faith'[2785] analysis in order to provide specific treatment to this and related concepts such as 'behavior detrimental to the complainant's trademark'.[2786] There should be added protection for reputable[2787] or 'well known'[2788] marks as originally contemplated under the TRIPS Agreement and the Paris Convention.[2789] However, this should be done in a clear and simplistic manner in line with the UDRP's current approach. To do this without losing the simplistic approach of the UDRP, and to make explicit some concepts in the policy itself, these grounds should be explicitly actionable, even if not absolutely required. Overall, it is recommended that unfair competition[2790] be added as an alternative ground as distinct from but alternative to 'bad faith'[2791] or 'abuse'.[2792]

4.3.2.4 Digital Terms, Policies, and Disclaimers

Evidence of a term, policy, or disclaimer[2793] might be proffered by a respondent in a UDRP complaint to avoid a complainant from successfully seeking recourse under the policy. However, it must usually be relevant to a necessary element of the claim (confusion,[2794] rights or legitimate interests,[2795] and bad faith)[2796] rather than serving to avoid recourse under the UDRP of its own accord.

2780. *Ibid.*
2781. EUTMR, Art. 9(2)(c).
2782. UDRP.
2783. WIPO, 'WIPO Overview of WIPO Panel Views on Selected UDRP Questions, Third Edition' ('WIPO Jurisprudential Overview 3.0') (*WIPO*, 2017) https://www.wipo.int/amc/en/domains/search/overview3.0/ accessed June 2025.
2784. 15 U.S.C. § 1125(c)(2)(B); EUTMR, Art. 9(2)(c).
2785. UDRP.
2786. WIPO, 'WIPO Overview of WIPO Panel Views on Selected UDRP Questions, Third Edition' ('WIPO Jurisprudential Overview 3.0') (*WIPO*, 2017) https://www.wipo.int/amc/en/domains/search/overview3.0/ accessed June 2025.
2787. EUTMR, Arts 8(5) and 9(1)(c).
2788. Paris Convention, Art. 6bis; TRIPS, Art. 16(2); EUTMR, Art. 8(2)(c).
2789. Paris Convention, Art. 6bis; TRIPS, Art. 16.
2790. *Ibid.*
2791. UDRP, 4(a)(iii).
2792. WIPO, 'WIPO Overview of WIPO Panel Views on Selected UDRP Questions, Third Edition' ('WIPO Jurisprudential Overview 3.0') (*WIPO*, 2017) https://www.wipo.int/amc/en/domains/search/overview3.0/ accessed June 2025.
2793. *Ibid.*; Alexander Peukert, 'The Coexistence of Trade Mark Laws and Rights on the Internet, and the Impact of Geolocation Technologies' (2016) 47 International Review of Intellectual Property and Competition Law 60, 81 https://doi.org/10.1007/s40319-015-0427-8; Leslie Fair, 'Full Disclosure' (*FTC Business Blog*, 23 September 2014) https://www.ftc.gov/business-guidance/blog/2014/09/full-disclosure accessed June 2025.
2794. UDRP, 4(a)(i).
2795. UDRP, 4(A)(ii).
2796. UDRP, 4(a)(iii).

As indicated in the Overview, 'a clear and sufficiently prominent disclaimer would lend support to circumstances suggesting its good faith'.[2797] However, this must be considered in light of only when website content associated with a domain name will be considered, something that is often unclear.[2798] The gap here, as was also seen in the earlier discussion on confusion,[2799] is that not all UDRP decision makers take into consideration the associated website to a domain name.[2800] Therefore, where the website is not considered, the disclaimer[2801] appears futile to a UDRP analysis.

The Overview also states that 'the presence of a clear and sufficiently prominent disclaimer can support a finding that the respondent has undertaken reasonable steps to avoid unfairly passing itself off as related to the complainant, or to otherwise confuse users'.[2802] However, it goes on to say that, '[o]n the other hand, where the overall circumstances of a case point to the respondent's bad faith, the mere existence of a disclaimer cannot cure such bad faith'.[2803] In fact, a disclaimer may actually work against a respondent and 'panels may consider the respondent's use of a disclaimer as an admission by the respondent that users may be confused'.[2804] While the circumstances that would lead to a 'bad faith'[2805] finding despite the disclaimer are not entirely clear, it is noted that '[p]articularly in the case of counterfeits …',[2806] it is likely that 'bad faith'[2807] will be found 'irrespective of any disclosure on the related website that such infringing goods are'[2808] what the actor will call 'replicas'[2809] or 'reproductions'[2810] and further relevant is 'indeed the use of such term [is] in the domain name itself'.[2811]

Under the Digital Trademark and Trade Practices Model, it is recommended that clear and conspicuous disclaimers[2812] serve to avoid liability if such disclaimer is sufficiently prominent and it is reasonably clear to a website visitor that the website utilising the mark is not associated with the mark holder. It should also be clear when the associated website will be considered. For example, where 'identical'[2813] use of a

2797. WIPO, 'WIPO Overview of WIPO Panel Views on Selected UDRP Questions, Third Edition' ('WIPO Jurisprudential Overview 3.0') (*WIPO*, 2017) https://www.wipo.int/amc/en/domains/search/overview3.0/ accessed June 2025.
2798. *Ibid.*
2799. *Ibid.*
2800. *Ibid.*
2801. *Ibid.*
2802. *Ibid.*
2803. *Ibid.*
2804. *Ibid.*
2805. *Ibid.*
2806. *Ibid.*
2807. *Ibid.*
2808. *Ibid.*
2809. *Ibid.*
2810. *Ibid.*
2811. *Ibid.*
2812. *Ibid.*; Alexander Peukert, 'The Coexistence of Trade Mark Laws and Rights on the Internet, and the Impact of Geolocation Technologies' (2016) 47 International Review of Intellectual Property and Competition Law 60, 81 https://doi.org/10.1007/s40319-015-0427-8; Leslie Fair, 'Full Disclosure' (*FTC Business Blog*, 23 September 2014) https://www.ftc.gov/business-guidance/blog/2014/09/full-disclosure accessed June 2025.
2813. UDRP.

mark is made in a domain name, a disclaimer may not be useful. Also, buried indication that a website is not owned or associated with a mark holder, such as within terms and conditions or policies, should not be eligible for protection because these may not be sufficiently conspicuous and may even be used to try and conceal that there is no relationship.

4.3.2.5 Digital Jurisdictional and Territorial Considerations

As recognised by Chaisse as well as Woodard, the UDRP 'is not specific to any locality or application of any territorial law'[2814] whereas trademark law is 'regional/territorial'.[2815] In fact, Caenegem notes, 'A UDRP decision also has worldwide effect, whereas the geographical jurisdiction of a national court may be limited.'[2816] The UDRP is highly beneficial as an international policy as it is one of the few legal frameworks that govern Internet-related trademark matters and avoids the need to establish jurisdiction (such as required in the Courts), and to potentially engage in lengthy geographical considerations. Notably, the UDRP has been designed as a 'geographically-detached approach'.[2817] Registrants agree to submit to arbitration under the policy as part of registration procedures.[2818]

In fact, the Overview confirms that due to 'the global nature of the Internet and Domain Name System, the jurisdiction(s) where the trademark is valid is not considered relevant to panel assessment'.[2819] However, at the same time, the UDRP Rules mention, under 15(a), that 'panels shall decide a complaint on the basis of the statements and documents submitted and in accordance with the Policy, these Rules and any rules and principles of law that it deems applicable'.[2820] Therefore, local law may play a factor in a UDRP decision, if a panel 'deems'[2821] that to be appropriate. The Overview also confirms that 'insofar as the UDRP system is designed to operate in a

2814. Julien Chaisse, 'The Merging of Two Worlds: Cyber Law and Trade Law Normative Convergence on Internet Domain Names' (2019) 37 Boston University International Law Journal 281, 291; Elizabeth C Woodard, 'The UDRP, ADR, and Arbitration: Using Proven Solutions to Address Perceived Problems with the UDRP (2009)' 19 Fordham Intellectual Property, Media and Entertainment Law Journal 1169, 1174-1175.
2815. Julien Chaisse, 'The Merging of Two Worlds: Cyber Law and Trade Law Normative Convergence on Internet Domain Names' (2019) 37 Boston University International Law Journal 281; Brendan J Witherell, 'Trademark Law: The Extraterritorial Application of the Lanham Act: The First Circuit Cuts the Fat from the Vanity Fair Test (2006) 29 Western New England Law Review 193, 197.
2816. W Van Caenegem, 'Domain Name, Website and Facebook Use of a Trade Mark: When Does It Infringe?' (2020) 22 Internet Law Bulletin 143, 143-146.
2817. Marketa Trimble, 'Territorialization of the Internet Domain Name System' (2018) 1020 Scholarly Works 623, 635 https://scholars.law.unlv.edu/cgi/viewcontent.cgi?article=2044&context=facpub.
2818. UDRP, 4(a).
2819. WIPO, 'WIPO Overview of WIPO Panel Views on Selected UDRP Questions, Third Edition' ('WIPO Jurisprudential Overview 3.0') (*WIPO*, 2017) https://www.wipo.int/amc/en/domains/search/overview3.0/ accessed June 2025.
2820. ICANN, 'Rules for Uniform Domain Name Dispute Resolution Policy (the "Rules")' (*ICANN*, 2013) https://www.icann.org/resources/pages/udrp-rules-2015-03-11-en accessed July 2024.
2821. *Ibid.*

global context, while rooted in general trademark law principles, in its own terms UDRP jurisprudence generally would not require resort to particular national laws'.[2822] Nevertheless, local law may be used by a panel if considered appropriate in the case such as when there is specific 'territorialization'[2823] and targeting towards territories.

Another provision pertinent to jurisdictional/territorial considerations, based on various factors, 'including the global nature of the Internet'[2824] is that if 'secondary meaning'[2825] is limited to 'a particular geographical area or market niche',[2826] this may not prevent one from 'establishing trademark rights'.[2827] This guidance is one method that may be used to give recognition to 'secondary meaning'.[2828] However, it should be noted that '[g]eographical terms used only in their ordinary geographical sense',[2829] unless they are registered marks,[2830] are not protected under the UDRP.[2831]

Another key difficulty is that while a domain name must be 'unique',[2832] trademarks may not be (such as a trademark owned by different mark holders in different industries and/or countries).[2833] However, because of the 'first-come-first served'[2834] policy, the first mark holder to register the domain name will prevail against another legitimate mark holder from another jurisdiction unless the other party proves the elements required under the UDRP, which success will be unlikely. Generally, co-existence[2835] is not possible with domain names for the exact same domain, although variants are possible.

2822. WIPO, 'WIPO Overview of WIPO Panel Views on Selected UDRP Questions, Third Edition' ('WIPO Jurisprudential Overview 3.0') (*WIPO*, 2017) https://www.wipo.int/amc/en/domains/search/overview3.0/ accessed June 2025.
2823. Marketa Trimble, 'Territorialization of the Internet Domain Name System' (2018) 1020 Scholarly Works 623, 635 https://scholars.law.unlv.edu/cgi/viewcontent.cgi?article=2044&context=facpub.
2824. WIPO, 'WIPO Overview of WIPO Panel Views on Selected UDRP Questions, Third Edition' ('WIPO Jurisprudential Overview 3.0') (*WIPO*, 2017) https://www.wipo.int/amc/en/domains/search/overview3.0/ accessed June 2025.
2825. *Ibid.*
2826. *Ibid.*
2827. *Ibid.*
2828. *Ibid.*
2829. *Ibid.*
2830. *Ibid.*
2831. *Ibid.*
2832. Diane Cabell, 'Overview of Domain Policy Development' (*Harvard Law*, 20 April 2000) https://cyber.harvard.edu/udrp/overview.html accessed July 2024.
2833. *Ibid.*
2834. Jane Seager and Laetitia Coguic, 'First Come, First Served' Is Key under the UDRP' (*WTR*, 12 November 2021) https://www.worldtrademarkreview.com/article/first-come-first-served-key-under-the-udrp.
2835. EUIPO, '3.1 Coexistence Between the Marks Involved in the Opposition' (*EUIPO Trade mark Guidelines*) https://guidelines.euipo.europa.eu/2058843/2043906/trade-mark-guidelines/3-1-coexistence-between-the-marks-involved-in-the-opposition accessed January 2024; 15 U.S. Code § 1052(d); Alexander Peukert, 'The Coexistence of Trade Mark Laws and Rights on the Internet, and the Impact of Geolocation Technologies' (2016) 47 International Review of Intellectual Property and Competition Law 60, 81 https://doi.org/10.1007/s40319-015-0427-8; Tamara Nanayakkara, 'IP and Business: Trademark Coexistence' (*WIPO*, November 2006) https://www.wipo.int/wipo_magazine/en/2006/06/article_0007.html accessed June 2025.

Further, as noted above in relation to reputation[2836] in the section on *Digital Unfair Competition*, it is not clear in the Overview how 'wide'[2837] a mark must be 'known'[2838] on the Internet in order to qualify as a 'widely-known'[2839] mark. This has jurisdictional/territorial implications as the assessment may need to take into consideration how 'wide'[2840] in a physical sense the mark is 'known'.[2841] Also, in an online sense, how to assess this, and whether that involves jurisdictional/territorial assessments, is unclear.

Under the Digital Trademark and Trade Practices Model, it is recommended that sufficient general trademark law be incorporated in the policy. Where the website is being used or targeted should be considered by the panel in order to concentrate the analysis on such areas in the event that is relevant to the analysis. For example, if a website clearly targets only a specific limited region, this should be considered.

4.3.2.6 Digital Justification

The UDRP provides protection, in the context of demonstrating rights and legitimate interests[2842] in the domain name, such as where there is 'legitimate noncommercial or fair use of the domain name, without intent for commercial gain to misleadingly divert consumers or to tarnish the trademark or service mark at issue'.[2843] However, one problematic area is that the policy requires the complainant to initially 'assert'[2844] that the other party does not have 'rights or legitimate interests'.[2845] There are several problems with the practical application of this element, as it is stated in the UDRP.[2846] First, the UDRP itself, rather than discussing how a complainant should prove this element (as it is their at least initial burden), puts forth a full paragraph on how the respondent can 'Demonstrate Your Rights to and Legitimate Interests in the Domain Name in Responding to a Complaint.'[2847] Even further, the Overview itself recognises this task as 'often impossible'[2848] because it is 'proving a negative'[2849] and reasons that the complainant only needs to put forth a 'prima facie case'[2850] after which the 'burden

2836. WIPO, 'WIPO Overview of WIPO Panel Views on Selected UDRP Questions, Third Edition' ('WIPO Jurisprudential Overview 3.0') (*WIPO*, 2017) https://www.wipo.int/amc/en/domains/search/overview3.0/ accessed June 2025.
2837. *Ibid.*
2838. *Ibid.*
2839. *Ibid.*
2840. *Ibid.*
2841. *Ibid.*
2842. *Ibid.*
2843. UDRP, 4(c)(iii).
2844. UDRP, 4(a).
2845. *Ibid.*
2846. *Ibid.*
2847. UDRP, 4(c).
2848. WIPO, 'WIPO Overview of WIPO Panel Views on Selected UDRP Questions, Third Edition' ('WIPO Jurisprudential Overview 3.0') (*WIPO*, 2017) https://www.wipo.int/amc/en/domains/search/overview3.0/ accessed June 2025.
2849. *Ibid.*
2850. *Ibid.*

of production on this element shifts to the respondent'.[2851] In fact, panels have also struggled with this element and have recognised the same issues as stated in *Belupo d.d. v. WACHEM d.o.o.* Case No. D2004-0110, which is that '[i]t involves the Complaint in the often impossible task of proving the negative'.[2852] While shifting of a burden is not a new concept, in a policy such as the UDRP, it might be a problematic shift to avoid intricacies of litigation and a more simplistic approach may be adopted because the list of methods for a respondent to show:

> (i) before any notice to you of the dispute, your use of, or demonstrable preparations to use, the domain name or a name corresponding to the domain name in connection with a bona fide offering of goods or services; or
> (ii) you (as an individual, business, or other organization) have been commonly known by the domain name, even if you have acquired no trademark or service mark rights; or
> (iii) you are making a legitimate noncommercial or fair use of the domain name, without intent for commercial gain to misleadingly divert consumers or to tarnish the trademark or service mark at issue.[2853]

However, all of these appear to be justifications and defences, properly the burden of the respondent. These are more suited to be recognised as a burden of the respondent in responding to a UDRP complaint.[2854]

Some UDRP decisions have shown that complainants prove their prima facie[2855] case by showing, to their knowledge, that the named respondent does not have the requisite 'rights or legitimate interests'[2856] and that 'permission'[2857] or 'authorization'[2858] has not been granted by the complainant[2859] or that 'there exists no connection

2851. *Ibid.*
2852. *Belupo d.d. v. WACHEM d.o.o.* Case No. D2004-0110 https://www.wipo.int/amc/en/domains/decisions/html/2004/d2004-0110.html accessed July 2024.
2853. UDRP, 4(c).
2854. WIPO, 'WIPO Overview of WIPO Panel Views on Selected UDRP Questions, Third Edition' ('WIPO Jurisprudential Overview 3.0') (*WIPO*, 2017) https://www.wipo.int/amc/en/domains/search/overview3.0/ accessed June 2025.
2855. *Ibid.*
2856. *Ibid.*
2857. *Belupo d.d. v. WACHEM d.o.o.* Case No. D2004-0110 https://www.wipo.int/amc/en/domains/decisions/html/2004/d2004-0110.html accessed July 2024.
2858. *Banco Itau S.A. v. Laercio Teixeira* Case No. D2007-0912 https://www.wipo.int/amc/en/domains/decisions/html/2007/d2007-0912.html accessed July 2024.
2859. *Belupo d.d. v. WACHEM d.o.o.* Case No. D2004-0110 https://www.wipo.int/amc/en/domains/decisions/html/2004/d2004-0110.html accessed July 2024; *Banco Itau S.A. v. Laercio Teixeira* Case No. D2007-0912 https://www.wipo.int/amc/en/domains/decisions/html/2007/d2007-0912.html accessed July 2024; https://www.wipo.int/amc/en/domains/decisions/html/2008/d2008-1393.html accessed 4 August 2025; *Malayan Banking Berhad v. Beauty, Success & Truth International* Case No. D2008-1393 https://www.wipo.int/amc/en/domains/decisions/html/2008/d2008-1393.html accessed July 2024; *Accor v. Eren Atesmen* Case No. D2009-0701 https://www.wipo.int/amc/en/domains/decisions/html/2009/d2009-0701.html accessed July 2024.

between the Parties'.[2860] If such little is required to prove a prima facie[2861] case, this might more properly be dealt with through a requirement of showing that the use was unauthorised.[2862]

In the Overview, it clarifies that 'fair use'[2863] will not be considered if there is a false suggested 'affiliation with the trademark owner'[2864] and 'the correlation between a domain name and the complainant's mark is often central to this inquiry'.[2865] Further, 'fair use'[2866] is not applicable where the utilisation of the mark can be 'seen as tending to suggest sponsorship or endorsement by the trademark owner'[2867] (such as *trademark-country.com*) but may be applicable where it 'tend[s] to communicate, prima facie at least, that there is no such affiliation'[2868] (such as trademarksuck-s.com).[2869] The Overview also states that '[a] domain name consisting of a trademark and a negative or pejorative term (such as <[trademark]sucks.com>.or … even <trademark.sucks>) is considered confusingly similar to the complainant's trademark'[2870] and that '[t]he merits of such cases, in particular as to any potential fair use, are typically decided under the second and third elements'.[2871] As the elements are cumulative, all must be proven, and even if 'confusingly similar',[2872] 'fair use'[2873] may apply under the other elements.

Also, 'beyond the domain name itself',[2874] 'whether the overall facts and circumstances of the case support a claimed fair use'[2875] may be informed by these 'illustrative'[2876] factors:

> (i) whether the domain name has been registered and is being used for legitimate purposes and not as a pretext for commercial gain or other such purposes inhering to the respondent's benefit, (ii) whether the respondent reasonably believes its use (whether referential, or for praise or criticism) to be truthful and well-founded, (iii) whether it is clear to Internet users visiting the respondent's website that it is not

---

2860. *Malayan Banking Berhad v. Beauty, Success & Truth International* Case No. D2008-1393 https://www.wipo.int/amc/en/domains/decisions/html/2008/d2008-1393.html accessed July 2024.
2861. WIPO, 'WIPO Overview of WIPO Panel Views on Selected UDRP Questions, Third Edition' ('WIPO Jurisprudential Overview 3.0') (*WIPO*, 2017) https://www.wipo.int/amc/en/domains/search/overview3.0/ accessed June 2025.
2862. *Banco Itau S.A. v. Laercio Teixeira* Case No. D2007-0912 https://www.wipo.int/amc/en/domains/decisions/html/2007/d2007-0912.html accessed July 2024.
2863. WIPO, 'WIPO Overview of WIPO Panel Views on Selected UDRP Questions, Third Edition' ('WIPO Jurisprudential Overview 3.0') (*WIPO*, 2017) https://www.wipo.int/amc/en/domains/search/overview3.0/ accessed June 2025.
2864. *Ibid.*
2865. *Ibid.*
2866. *Ibid.*
2867. *Ibid.*
2868. *Ibid.*
2869. *Ibid.*
2870. *Ibid.*
2871. *Ibid.*
2872. *Ibid.*
2873. *Ibid.*
2874. *Ibid.*
2875. *Ibid.*
2876. *Ibid.*

> operated by the complainant, (iv) whether the respondent has refrained from engaging in a pattern of registering domain names corresponding to marks held by the complainant or third parties, (v) where appropriate, whether a prominent link (including with explanatory text) is provided to the relevant trademark owner's website, (vi) whether senders of email intended for the complainant but (because of user confusion) directed to the respondent are alerted that their message has been misdirected, (vii) whether there is an actual connection between the complainant's trademark in the disputed domain name and the corresponding website content, and not to a competitor, or an entire industry, group, or individual, and (viii) whether the domain name registration and use by the respondent is consistent with a pattern of bona fide activity (whether online or offline).[2877]

Again, Internet-specific guidance in the form of factors can be very helpful to decision makers and this approach is particularly welcomed. However, the above mixes in 'confusion'[2878] and even types of unfair acts[2879] or 'unfair competition'[2880] might better be analysed under the latter. The Overview also makes clear that the associated website may be considered in a 'fair use'[2881] analysis, which provides for legal certainty. As an example, 'in cases where the combination of the mark and the TLD signals potential legitimate co-existence or fair use',[2882] the content on the associated website is considered.[2883]

Also, as the Overview indicates, whether the mark is actually being used 'for referential use, commentary, criticism, praise, or parody'[2884] will be considered as long as it 'is not misleading as to source or sponsorship, and is not a pretext for tarnishment or commercial gain'.[2885] However, '[t]o support fair use under UDRP paragraph 4(c)(iii), the respondent's criticism must be genuine and noncommercial; in a number of UDRP decisions where a respondent argues that its domain name is being used for free speech purposes the panel has found this to be primarily a pretext for cybersquatting, commercial activity, or tarnishment'.[2886] It is crucial to a finding for the respondent that they are 'making a legitimate noncommercial or fair use of the domain name, without intent for commercial gain to misleadingly divert consumers or to tarnish the trademark or service mark at issue'.[2887]

As Farley notes, porche.cars was decided to be 'confusingly similar to PORSHE'[2888] as the mark holder was in the business of cars with that mark.[2889] However,

2877. *Ibid.*
2878. *Ibid.*
2879. *Ibid.*
2880. Anselm Kamperman Sanders, *Unfair Competition Law: The Protection of Intellectual and Industrial Creativity* (Oxford University Press, 1997) 8; EUTMR, Art. 9(2)(c) and Art. 17(2); 15 U.S.C. §1125.
2881. *Ibid.*
2882. *Ibid.*
2883. *Ibid.*
2884. *Ibid.*
2885. *Ibid.*
2886. *Ibid.*
2887. *Ibid.*
2888. Christine Haight Farley 'Confusing the Similarity of Trademarks Law in Domain Name Disputes' 52 Akron Law Review 607.
2889. *Ibid.*

porshe.social, in the context of the gTLD .social, the associated website was considered and 'fair use'[2890] was found leading to a different result.[2891] Also, the associated website 'content will often also bear on assessment of the second and third elements, namely whether there may be legitimate co-existence or fair use, or an intent to create user confusion'.[2892]

As also noted in the Overview, '[i]n certain cases involving parties exclusively from the United States, some panels applying US First Amendment principles have found that even a domain name identical to a trademark used for a bona fide noncommercial criticism site may support a legitimate interest'.[2893] However, the Overview further recognises that 'even a general right to legitimate criticism does not necessarily extend to registering or using a domain name identical to a trademark (i.e., <trademark.tld> (including typos)); even where such a domain name is used in relation to genuine noncommercial free speech'[2894] as 'this creates an impermissible risk of user confusion through impersonation'.[2895] For example, 'a respondent's fan site must be active, genuinely noncommercial, and clearly distinct from any official complainant site' and this justification cannot be used 'primarily a pretext for cyber-squatting or commercial activity'.[2896] However, Zalnieriut notes that 'free speech advocates argued that the UDRP provided an uncontested forum for trademark owners to challenge any domain name that was remotely similar to one of their marks, thereby expanding trademark rights at the expense of free speech rights'.[2897] Komaitis notes that the UDRP fails to 'protect critical speech'.[2898] At a minimum, 'free speech'[2899] needs to be further made clear in detailed guidance with respect to the UDRP.

Under the Digital Trademark and Trade Practices Model, it is recommended that specific defences and justifications be directly incorporated within the policy itself under a requirement of 'rights or legitimate interests'.[2900] In other words, there should be no requirement for a complainant to prove the justification or defences of a

2890. *Ibid.*
2891. *Ibid.*
2892. *Ibid.*
2893. WIPO, 'WIPO Overview of WIPO Panel Views on Selected UDRP Questions, Third Edition' ('WIPO Jurisprudential Overview 3.0') (*WIPO*, 2017) https://www.wipo.int/amc/en/domains/search/overview3.0/ accessed June 2025.
2894. *Ibid.*
2895. *Ibid.*
2896. *Ibid.*
2897. Monika Zalnieriute, 'Beyond the Governance Gap in International Domain Name Law: Bringing the UDRP in Line with Internationally Recognized Human Rights' (2020) 56 Stanford Journal of International Law 79, 93; Oma Rabinovich-Einy, 'The Legitimacy Crisis and the Future of Courts' (2015) 17 Cardozo Journal of Conflict Resolution 23, 54; Nicholas Smith and Eric Wilbers, 'The UDRP: Design Elements of an Effective ADR Mechanism' (2004) 15 American Review of International Arbitration 215.
2898. Konstantinos Komaitis, 'Trade Mark Law's Increment Through the Uniform Domain Name Dispute Resolution Policy' (2011) 6 Journal of Intellectual Property Law & Practice 8, 553-567.
2899. WIPO, 'WIPO Overview of WIPO Panel Views on Selected UDRP Questions, Third Edition' ('WIPO Jurisprudential Overview 3.0') (*WIPO*, 2017) https://www.wipo.int/amc/en/domains/search/overview3.0/ accessed June 2025.
2900. UDRP, 4(a)(ii).

respondent, only that the use was 'unauthorized',[2901] and then a clear list of justifications or defences should be listed.

From the above review of the UDRP in light of the Digital Trademark and Trade Practices Model, it can be seen that the UDRP is a good, viable solution to deal with domain names. At the same time, there are some gaps that can be filled by incorporating some elements of the model. The Overview states that '[w]hile the UDRP does not operate on a strict doctrine of binding precedent, it is considered important for the overall credibility of the UDRP system that parties can reasonably anticipate the result of their case'.[2902] This is a valid consideration to enhance legal certainty. However, not incorporating key elements and considering them in an Overview does not promote legal certainty in the way that may be intended. By directly and adequately incorporating all relevant factors within the policy itself, parties may anticipate the outcomes of their matters, or better yet, act accordingly. By doing this, while retaining a simple structure, it will be crucial to success of such an adapted approach informed by the model.

While the Overview is extremely helpful to explain the UDRP policy, it appears that the interpretation goes beyond the directly stated elements, which can cause confusion and sometimes stretch deeply into elements which are not included. Notably, the Overview sometimes seems to incorporate some concepts in an attempt to classify them under one of the existing elements.[2903] For example, 'behavior detrimental to the complainant's trademark'[2904] is clumped under a 'bad faith'[2905] analysis. Also, 'fair use'[2906] may be considered under rights or legitimate interests[2907] or bad faith[2908] elements when it should be a separate and clear justification or defence. Further, 'strength of the complainant's mark ... are decided under the second and third elements'.[2909]

While an Overview is generally welcomed, incorporating interpretations of key concepts not shown in the policy itself, but only through the Overview and through various decisions, creates uncertainty as to what actually may be considered by a panel. By incorporating all relevant and key legal concepts within the policy itself, legal certainty can be enhanced, and guidelines may be used to interpret these concepts.

2901. WIPO, 'WIPO Overview of WIPO Panel Views on Selected UDRP Questions, Third Edition' ('WIPO Jurisprudential Overview 3.0') (*WIPO*, 2017) https://www.wipo.int/amc/en/domains/search/overview3.0/ accessed June 2025; *Banco Itau S.A. v. Laercio Teixeira* Case No. D2007-0912 https://www.wipo.int/amc/en/domains/decisions/html/2007/d2007-0912.html accessed July 2024.
2902. WIPO, 'WIPO Overview of WIPO Panel Views on Selected UDRP Questions, Third Edition' ('WIPO Jurisprudential Overview 3.0') (*WIPO*, 2017) https://www.wipo.int/amc/en/domains/search/overview3.0/ accessed June 2025.
2903. *Ibid.*
2904. *Ibid.*
2905. *Ibid.*
2906. *Ibid.*
2907. UDRP, 4(a)(ii).
2908. UDRP, 4(a)(iii).
2909. WIPO, 'WIPO Overview of WIPO Panel Views on Selected UDRP Questions, Third Edition' ('WIPO Jurisprudential Overview 3.0') (WIPO, 2017) https://www.wipo.int/amc/en/domains/search/overview3.0/ accessed June 2025.

While the Overview provides a central location for how decisions may have been made, it is not directly termed as guidelines. There should also be a clear document entitled Guidance to the UDRP, which interprets all elements, including some of the information already contained in the Overview.

With this in mind, under the Digital Trademark and Trade Practices Model, the following section is recommended as an adapted approach to resolve some of the key issues in the UDRP.

4.3.3 Recommended Adaptation of the UDRP

Uniform Domain Name Dispute Resolution Policy (UDNDRP)	Adapted or directly from the UDRP.[2910] The name change recommended is to include the phrase 'Domain Name' for clarity (the name is actually stated as the title of the policy, but still termed as UDRP).[2911] Otherwise, the current generic name could apply to any field. This policy would replace the current UDRP and be applicable to the same domain names to which it currently applies.
(1) *Purpose*. This Uniform Domain Name Dispute Resolution Policy ('Policy') has been adopted by the Internet Corporation for Assigned Names and Numbers ('ICANN'), is incorporated by reference into your Registration Agreement, and sets forth the terms and conditions in connection with a dispute between you and any party other than us (the registrar) over the registration and use of an Internet	Adapted or directly from the UDRP.[2912] No major changes to most of this Paragraph. However, to this was added a reference to Guidelines which should be created for the UDRP to cover the substantive content of the UDRP including an interpretation of all concepts. Much of the information contained in the Overview is recommended to be put in the form of guidance and included in the Guidelines to the UDRP.

2910. ICANN, 'Uniform Domain-Name Dispute-Resolution Policy' (*ICANN*, 25 February 2012) https://www.icann.org/resources/pages/policy-2012-02-25-en accessed June 2025.
2911. *Ibid.*
2912. *Ibid.*

domain name registered by you. Proceedings under Paragraph 4 of this Policy will be conducted according to the Rules for Uniform Domain Name Dispute Resolution Policy (the 'Rules of Procedure'), which are available at [URL for Rules], and the selected administrative-dispute-resolution service provider's supplemental rules. Guidelines to this policy are set forth in the document entitled: Guidelines to the UDRP.	Guidelines should be updated regularly (such as annually) to include any technology or other changes in the environment in which domain names exist without always having the need to update the policy where it is deemed that such is not needed. Guidelines may also be updated based on recommendations made by the public during commentary periods or otherwise, where relevant. The Rules of Procedure[2913] should be amended only to the extent of the changes recommended here, although no major recommendations are being made for the Rules, specifically.
(2) *Your Representations*. By applying to register a domain name, or by asking us to maintain or renew a domain name registration, you hereby represent and warrant to us that: (a) the statements that you made in your Registration Agreement are complete and accurate; (b) to your knowledge, the registration of the domain name will not infringe upon or otherwise violate the rights of any third party; (c) you are not registering the domain name for an unlawful purpose; and (d) you will not knowingly use the domain name in violation of any applicable laws or regulations. It is your responsibility to determine whether your domain name registration infringes or violates someone else's rights.	Adapted or directly from the UDRP.[2914] No changes recommended here.
(3) *Cancellations, Transfers, Changes, and Maintaining Status Quo.*	Adapted or directly from the UDRP.[2915] No major changes recommended here other than some consolidation of provisions.

2913. ICANN, 'Rules for Uniform Domain Name Dispute Resolution Policy (the "Rules")' (ICANN, 2013) https://www.icann.org/resources/pages/udrp-rules-2015-03-11-en accessed July 2024.
2914. *Ibid.*
2915. *Ibid.*

(a) Cancellations, Transfer, or Changes. We will cancel, transfer or otherwise make changes to domain name registrations under the following circumstances: (i) subject to the provisions of Paragraph 3b, our receipt of written or appropriate electronic instructions from you or your authorized agent to take such action; (ii) our receipt of an order from a court or arbitral tribunal, in each case of competent jurisdiction, requiring such action; and/or (iii) our receipt of a decision of an Administrative Panel requiring such action in any administrative proceeding to which you were a party and which was conducted under this Policy or a later version of this Policy adopted by ICANN; (iv) we may also cancel, transfer or otherwise make changes to a domain name registration in accordance with the terms of your Registration Agreement or other legal requirements. (b) Transfers During a Dispute: (i) Transfers of a Domain Name to a New Holder. You may not transfer your domain name registration to another holder: (a) during a pending administrative proceeding brought pursuant to Paragraph 4 or for a period of fifteen (15) business days (as observed in the location of our principal place of business) after such proceeding is concluded; or (b) during a pending court proceeding or arbitration commenced regarding your domain name unless the party to whom the domain name registration is being transferred agrees, in writing, to be	Some current provisions in the UDRP involving cancellations, transfers, changes, and maintaining status quo are related. They have been consolidated into this one Paragraph and renumbered where appropriate.

bound by the decision of the court or arbitrator. We reserve the right to cancel any transfer of a domain name registration to another holder that is made in violation of this subparagraph.

(ii) Changing Registrars. You may not transfer your domain name registration to another registrar during a pending administrative proceeding brought pursuant to Paragraph 4 or for a period of fifteen (15) business days (as observed in the location of our principal place of business) after such proceeding is concluded. You may transfer administration of your domain name registration to another registrar during a pending court action or arbitration, provided that the domain name you have registered with us shall continue to be subject to the proceedings commenced against you in accordance with the terms of this Policy. In the event that you transfer a domain name registration to us during the pendency of a court action or arbitration, such dispute shall remain subject to the domain name dispute policy of the registrar from which the domain name registration was transferred.

(c) Maintaining the Status Quo. We will not cancel, transfer, activate, deactivate, or otherwise change the status of any domain name registration under this Policy except as provided in this Paragraph.

(4) *Mandatory Administrative Proceeding and Remedies*. This Paragraph sets forth the type of disputes for which you are required to submit	Adapted or directly from the UDRP,[2916] Paris Convention,

2916. ICANN, 'Uniform Domain-Name Dispute-Resolution Policy' (*ICANN*, 25 February 2012) https://www.icann.org/resources/pages/policy-2012-02-25-en accessed June 2025.

to a mandatory administrative proceeding. These proceedings will be conducted before one of the administrative-dispute-resolution service providers listed at www.icann.org/en/dndr/udrp/approved-providers.htm accessed 4 August 2025 (each, a 'Provider'):

(a) Applicable Disputes. You are required to submit to a mandatory administrative proceeding in the event that a third party (a 'complainant') asserts to the applicable Provider, in compliance with the Rules of Procedure, that your domain name:
  (A) is identical or confusingly similar to a trademark in which a complainant has rights and which you are using on an unauthorised basis in the course of trade
  AND
  (B) (i) is being used to engage in unfair competition in the course of trade with respect to a trademark in the domain name OR (ii) has been registered or is being used in bad faith or is being abused.
  For clarity, in the administrative proceeding, the complainant must prove element A AND only one element from B (either i or ii) are present. Where abuse is found, a registrant may be barred from future domain name registrations for a period of one year in the first instance and a longer period or permanent ban in a single egregious circumstance or in further instances.

TRIPS, Dispute Resolution Service for .eu,[2917] Lanham Act 1946 15 U.S. Code §§ 1051 et seq. (as amended), the TDRA 2006 15 U.S. Code § 1125(c), EUTMR and the Digital Trademark and Trade Practices Model (*see* discussion below).

Key UDRP aspects have been retained. Some related provisions have been consolidated into this Paragraph. Some adaptations have been made. This Paragraph incorporates some changes recommended under the model while retaining the same simplistic approach of the UDRP. It incorporates principles set out in the Overview but which are not directly stated in the current policy. This includes those aspects recommended to be directly stated under the model.

All three elements in the UDRP are not required in this adapted version, and alternative grounds are preferred.[2918] However, 'legitimate interests'[2919] has been replaced with a section on permitted use which incorporates this and other justifications, the phrase 'on an unauthorized basis'[2920] in line with decisions in this regard[2921] was added to element A.

2917. WIPO, 'WIPO Domain Name Dispute Resolution Service for .EU (and.ею and.ευ)' (*WIPO*) https://www.wipo.int/amc/en/domains/cctld/eu/index.html accessed July 2024.
2918. *Ibid.*; 15 U.S. Code § 1125(d)(1)(A).
2919. UDRP, 4(c).
2920. *Banco Itau S.A. v. Laercio Teixeira* Case No. D2007-0912 https://www.wipo.int/amc/en/domains/decisions/html/2007/d2007-0912.html accessed July 2024.
2921. *Ibid.*

<table>
<tr>
<td>(b) Permitted use. Trademarks in domain names will be permitted if you demonstrate that you have rights or legitimate interests in respect of the domain name by showing one or more of these justifications: (i) you (as an individual, business, or other organization) have been commonly known by the domain name and are using it legitimately, (ii) you are making genuine noncommercial legitimate fair use of the trademark in the domain name, (iii) you are fairly utilising the trademark in the domain name in marketing of authorized, replacement, compatible or used goods or services, (iv) you are utilising the trademark in the domain name in an ordinary dictionary sense, (v) you are genuinely and noncommercially utilising the trademark in the domain name under freedom of speech and expression or legitimate criticism, parody, or review of the company, good or service associated with the trademark, OR (vi) you are making fair and legitimate use of the trademark in the domain name in comparative advertising.
(c) Remedies. The remedies available to a complainant pursuant to any proceeding before an Administrative Panel shall be limited to requiring the cancellation of your domain name or the transfer of your domain name registration to the complainant.</td>
<td>The ACPA requires 'bad faith'[2922] alongside one other element, 'confusingly similar'[2923] (in the case of 'distinctive' marks)[2924] or 'confusingly similar'[2925] or 'dilutive'[2926] (for 'famous' marks).[2927] A third possibility relating to special signs, etc., exists but is not relevant here.[2928] Further, the policy applicable to .eu[2929] requires 'confusing similarity'[2930] and either 'without rights or legitimate interests'[2931] OR 'bad faith'.[2932]</td>
</tr>
</table>

2922. 15 U.S. Code § 1125(d)(1)(A).
2923. *Ibid.*
2924. *Ibid.*
2925. *Ibid.*
2926. *Ibid.*
2927. *Ibid.*
2928. *Ibid.*
2929. WIPO, 'WIPO Domain Name Dispute Resolution Service for .EU (and.ею and.ευ)' (*WIPO*) https://www.wipo.int/amc/en/domains/cctld/eu/index.html accessed July 2024.
2930. *Ibid.*
2931. *Ibid.*
2932. *Ibid.*

(d) All Other Disputes. All other disputes between you and any party other than us regarding your domain name registration that are not brought pursuant to the mandatory administrative proceeding provisions of this Paragraph shall not be resolved through said proceeding.	Adapting from these while being reinforced by the fact that 'unfair competition'[2933] (including unfair acts,[2934] practices,[2935] or competition)[2936] is important, this adapted policy always requires 'confusing similarity'[2937] and, as another element, either 'unfair competition'[2938] OR 'bad faith or abuse'.[2939] Also, 'legitimate rights and interests'[2940] are factored in as permitted uses (justifications). Interpretation of this Paragraph should be set out in the Guidelines to the UDRP which will help to reduce inconsistencies and provide good guidance to decision makers.[2941] This should include all

2933. Anselm Kamperman Sanders, *Unfair Competition Law: The Protection of Intellectual and Industrial Creativity* (Oxford University Press, 1997) 8; EUTMR, Art. 9(2)(c) and Art. 17(2); 15 U.S.C. §1125.
2934. Anselm Kamperman Sanders, *Unfair Competition Law: The Protection of Intellectual and Industrial Creativity* (Oxford University Press, 1997) 8; Frauke Henning-Bodewig, *Unfair Competition Law European Union and Member States* (Kluwer Law International 2006) xv-xvi; Martin Senftleben, Michael Handler and Irene Calboli, 'Protection Against Unfair Competition Around the Globe' (2024) 19 Journal of Intellectual Property Law & Practice 79, 79-80 https://doi.org/10.1093/jiplp/jpad121; Paris Convention, Art. 10bis; EUTMR, Art. 9(2)(c); 15 U.S.C. § 1125(c)(2)(B).
2935. *Ibid.*
2936. *Ibid.*
2937. UDRP, 4(a)(i).
2938. Anselm Kamperman Sanders, *Unfair Competition Law: The Protection of Intellectual and Industrial Creativity* (Oxford University Press, 1997) 8; Frauke Henning-Bodewig, *Unfair Competition Law European Union and Member States* (Kluwer Law International 2006) xv-xvi; Martin Senftleben, Michael Handler and Irene Calboli, 'Protection Against Unfair Competition Around the Globe' (2024) 19 Journal of Intellectual Property Law & Practice 79, 79-80 https://doi.org/10.1093/jiplp/jpad121; Paris Convention, Art. 10bis; EUTMR, Art. 9(2)(c); 15 U.S.C. § 1125(c)(2)(B).
2939. ICANN, 'Uniform Domain-Name Dispute-Resolution Policy' (*ICANN*, 25 February 2012) https://www.icann.org/resources/pages/policy-2012-02-25-en accessed June 2025; WIPO, 'WIPO Overview of WIPO Panel Views on Selected UDRP Questions, Third Edition' ('WIPO Jurisprudential Overview 3.0') (*WIPO*, 2017) https://www.wipo.int/amc/en/domains/search/overview3.0/ accessed June 2025.
2940. UDRP, 4(a)(iii).
2941. Elizabeth C Woodard, 'The UDRP, ADR, and Arbitration: Using Proven Solutions to Address Perceived Problems with the UDRP' (2009) 19 Fordham Intellectual Property, Media and Entertainment Law Journal 1169, 1207.

	key concepts referred to in this section which should be interpreted in line with general trademark law and related, relevant, theoretical/conceptual principles. For example, in the course of trade,[2942] confusing similarity,[2943] unfair competition,[2944] bad faith,[2945] abuse,[2946] and permitted uses, etc., should be included in guidance in accordance with the following discussion. Based on the model, the following changes or amendments are recommended as implemented in this adapted UDRP. Further, concepts included in this section should be interpreted through guidance, as also discussed: Under *Digital Use and Place of Use*, the policy will apply to domain names that are covered under the existing policy but are being used in the 'course of trade'[2947] as indicated in TRIPS, Article 16 and EUTMR, Article 9(2). This may include 'course of trade, in relation to goods or services'[2948] or 'genuine use'[2949] or 'use in commerce'[2950] or what is incorporated in the UDRP 4(c)(i) as 'your use of, or demonstrable preparations to use, the domain

2942. TRIPS, Art. 16.
2943. UDRP, 4(a)(i).
2944. *Ibid.*
2945. UDRP, 4(a)(iii).
2946. WIPO, 'WIPO Overview of WIPO Panel Views on Selected UDRP Questions, Third Edition' ('WIPO Jurisprudential Overview 3.0') (*WIPO*, 2017) https://www.wipo.int/amc/en/domains/search/overview3.0/ accessed June 2025.
2947. TRIPS, Art. 16.
2948. EUTMR, Art. 9(2).
2949. EUTMR, Art. 18.
2950. 15 U.S. Code § 1127.

name or a name corresponding to the domain name in connection with a bona fide offering of goods or services'.[2951] Essentially, even if these concepts may not be the same, this interpretation should draw from the common threads of 'course of trade'.[2952]

Further, as opposed to one way of proving 'legitimate interests'[2953] for the complainant, being 'used in the course of trade'[2954] is directly included here. In line with use[2955] and property[2956] theories, complainants should be asked to provide proof of ownership/rights (such as registration), and/or use of the mark. Under *Digital Bad Faith and Abuse*, bad faith[2957] or abuse[2958] are an alternative ground under B, the other being unfair competition[2959] which are generally in the course of trade,[2960] whereas bad faith[2961] or

2951. UDRP 4(c)(i).
2952. TRIPS, Art. 16.
2953. UDRP, 4(c).
2954. TRIPS, Art. 16.
2955. Graeme B Dinwoodie and Mark D Janis, 'Confusion Over Use: Contextualism in Trademark Law' (2007) 92 Iowa Law Review 1597.
2956. J Thomas McCarthy, *McCarthy on Trademarks and Unfair Competition* (4th edn, vol. 69, Thomson Reuters, 2014) in Lisa L Ouellette, 'The Google Shortcut to Trademark Law' (2014) 102 California Law Review 351, 358; Lionel Bently, 'From communication to thing: Historical Aspects of the Conceptualisation of Trade Marks as Property' in Graeme B Dinwoodie and Mark D Janis (eds), *Trademark Law and Theory: A Handbook of Contemporary Research* (Edward Elgar, 2008) 3-41; Anselm Kamperman Sanders, *Unfair Competition Law: The Protection of Intellectual and Industrial Creativity* (Oxford University Press 1997) 109.
2957. UDRP, 4(a)(iii).
2958. WIPO, 'WIPO Overview of WIPO Panel Views on Selected UDRP Questions, Third Edition' ('WIPO Jurisprudential Overview 3.0') (*WIPO*, 2017) https://www.wipo.int/amc/en/domains/search/overview3.0/ accessed June 2025.
2959. *Ibid.*
2960. *Ibid.*
2961. UDRP, 4(a)(ii).

	abuse[2962] may or may not be. Guidelines should clearly differentiate between these two alternative grounds under the same element. The concept of abuse[2963] has been added which was not previously adequately stated even if recognized. This should be interpreted as any pattern[2964] or repetition of bad faith.[2965] A bar 'on future domain name registrations'[2966] for those that 'abuse'[2967] (a 'pattern of'[2968] or repeated bad faith)[2969] should be implemented. UDRP Paragraph 4b on *Evidence of Registration and Use in Bad Faith* and Paragraph 4c *How to Demonstrate Your Rights to and Legitimate Interests in the Domain Name in Responding to a Complaint* should all be moved to the Guidelines to the UDRP to be in one central place with any modifications. Although such guidelines would not be binding, they should show how decisions may be made in given circumstances. Guidelines should also state when the associated website[2970] will be considered

2962. WIPO, 'WIPO Overview of WIPO Panel Views on Selected UDRP Questions, Third Edition' ('WIPO Jurisprudential Overview 3.0') (*WIPO*, 2017) https://www.wipo.int/amc/en/domains/search/overview3.0/ accessed June 2025.
2963. *Ibid.*
2964. *Ibid.*
2965. *Ibid.*
2966. John McElwaine and Christopher D Casavale,'Tackling Bad Faith Registration of Domain Names in a Fast-Changing Landscape' (*WIPO Magazine*, December 2019) https://www.wipo.int/wipo_magazine/en/2019/06/article_0006.html accessed June 2025.
2967. WIPO, 'WIPO Overview of WIPO Panel Views on Selected UDRP Questions, Third Edition' ('WIPO Jurisprudential Overview 3.0') (*WIPO*, 2017) https://www.wipo.int/amc/en/domains/search/overview3.0/ accessed June 2025.
2968. *Ibid.*
2969. *Ibid.*
2970. *Ibid.*

	with respect to any of the elements in the adapted policy. Registration[2971] OR use[2972] in bad faith is acceptable and both are not required in accordance with how this is dealt with under the ACPA 15 U.S. Code § 1125(d)(1)(A) (even if in the context of confusion[2973] and dilution,[2974] etc.) as well as under the WIPO Domain Name Dispute Resolution Service for .EU[2975] which is preferred because both are not needed (also in line with 2019 WIPO report that suggested this could be a possibility in the future).[2976] Under *Digital Confusion*, confusing similarity[2977] is retained as a required element under A if done on an 'unauthorised'[2978] basis, alleviating the need to have a separate element for complainant to prove, even if on a prima facie[2979] basis, and must also be 'in the course of trade'.[2980] Common factors to assess 'confusing similarity'[2981] should be clarified in the Guidelines which should include common

2971. ICANN, 'Uniform Domain-Name Dispute-Resolution Policy' (*ICANN*, 25 February 2012) https://www.icann.org/resources/pages/policy-2012-02-25-en accessed June 2025.
2972. *Ibid.*
2973. 15 U.S. Code § 1125(d)(1)(A).
2974. *Ibid.*
2975. WIPO, 'WIPO Domain Name Dispute Resolution Service for .EU (and.ею and.ευ)' (*WIPO*) https://www.wipo.int/amc/en/domains/cctld/eu/index.html accessed July 2024.
2976. John McElwaine and Christopher D Casavale, 'Tackling Bad Faith Registration of Domain Names in a Fast-Changing Landscape' (*WIPO Magazine*, December 2019) https://www.wipo.int/wipo_magazine/en/2019/06/article_0006.html accessed June 2025.
2977. UDRP, 4(a)(i).
2978. *Banco Itau S.A. v. Laercio Teixeira* Case No. D2007-0912 https://www.wipo.int/amc/en/domains/decisions/html/2007/d2007-0912.html accessed July 2024.
2979. WIPO, 'WIPO Overview of WIPO Panel Views on Selected UDRP Questions, Third Edition' ('WIPO Jurisprudential Overview 3.0') (*WIPO*, 2017) https://www.wipo.int/amc/en/domains/search/overview3.0/ accessed June 2025.
2980. TRIPS, Art. 16.
2981. UDRP, 4(a)(i).

	trademark principles of a 'likelihood of confusion'[2982] test. Under *Digital Unfair Competition,* this has been directly stated as alternative grounds[2983] in line with Article 10bis of the Paris Convention. Guidelines should state that 'unfair acts',[2984] 'unfair trade practices'[2985] are part of this analysis and provide clarity on the common principles upon which these are built. Concepts such as 'unfair advantage',[2986] 'dilution',[2987] 'passing off'[2988] free riding,[2989] misappropriation[2990] and various related concepts are a part of this element and how these should be interpreted must be clarified. Key and important unfair competition principles should be incorporated with examples of prohibited behaviour. For example, the Overview recognizes, at least from one angle, 'national legal doctrines (e.g., unfair competition or

2982. Paris Convention, Art. 6bis; TRIPS, Art. 16(1); EUTMR, Art. 8(1)(b) and Art. 9(2)(b); 15 U.S. Code § 1114;15 U.S. Code § 1125.
2983. EUTMR, Art. 9(2)(c) and Art. 8(1)(b); 15 U.S. Code § 1125(c)(2)(B).
2984. Anselm Kamperman Sanders, *Unfair Competition Law: The Protection of Intellectual and Industrial Creativity* (Oxford University Press 1997) 6-10; Frauke Henning-Bodewig, *Unfair Competition Law European Union and Member States* (Kluwer Law International 2006) xv-xvi.
2985. *Ibid.*
2986. EUTMR, Art. 9(2)(c).
2987. 15 U.S. Code § 1125(c); 15 U.S. Code § 1125(d).
2988. Ethan Horwitz and Benjamin Levi, 'Fifty Years of the Lanham Act: A Retrospective of Section 43(a)E' (1996) 7 Fordham Intellectual Property, Media and Entertainment Law Journal Article 6; David Bainbridge, *Intellectual Property* (Pearson Education Limited 2018) Chapter 30.
2989. Anselm Kamperman Sanders, 'Odol: The Introduction of a Watery Concept with Steeled Resilience' in Christopher Heath and Anselm Kamperman Sanders (eds), *Landmark Intellectual Property Cases and Their Legacy* (Wolters Kluwer 2011) 51-56; Graeme B Dinwoodie, 'Dilution as Unfair Competition: European Echoes' in Rochelle C Dreyfuss and Jane C Ginsburg (eds) *Intellectual Property at the Edge: The Contested Contours of IP* (Cambridge University Press 2014) 100; Frank I Schechter, 'The Rational Basis of Trademark Protection' (1927) 40 Harvard Law Review 813 https://doi.org/10.2307/1330367;15 U.S. Code § 1125(c); Keola R Whitaker, 'Trademark Dilution in a Global Age' (2006) 27 University of Pennsylvania Journal of International Economic Law 907.
2990. *Ibid.*

passing-off)'.[2991] Further, the UDRP takes into consideration related concepts, including '*for the purpose of disrupting the business of a competitor; or …*'.[2992] The Guidelines must establish an interpretation of base principles of unfair competition[2993] in a clear way (as would be the case for confusion).

Further, 'well known'[2994] marks should be given added protection even if not registered.[2995] For example, famous,[2996] reputable[2997] marks with goodwill[2998] should be considered.[2999]

However, this ground should not be mixed up with 'bad faith'[3000] or 'abuse'[3001] as the latter concepts do not necessarily have to be in the 'course of trade'.[3002] Guidelines should set out clear distinctions between these concepts and how each may be proven. Pleading alternative

2991. WIPO, 'WIPO Overview of WIPO Panel Views on Selected UDRP Questions, Third Edition' ('WIPO Jurisprudential Overview 3.0') (*WIPO*, 2017) https://www.wipo.int/amc/en/domains/search/overview3.0/ accessed June 2025.
2992. UDRP, 4(b).
2993. Anselm Kamperman Sanders, *Unfair Competition Law: The Protection of Intellectual and Industrial Creativity* (Oxford University Press 1997) 6-10; Frauke Henning-Bodewig, *Unfair Competition Law European Union and Member States* (Kluwer Law International 2006) xv-xvi.
2994. TRIPS, Art. 16(2).
2995. *Ibid.*
2996. Paris Convention, Art. 6bis; TRIPS, Art. 16(2); EUTMR, Art. 8(5); EUTMR, Art. 9(2)(c); 15 U.S. Code § 1125; Timothy D Greene and Jeff Wilkerson, 'Understanding Trademark Strength' (2013) 16 Stanford Technology Law Review 535.
2997. *Ibid.*
2998. *Ibid.*
2999. *Ibid.*
3000. UDRP, 4(a)(iii).
3001. WIPO, 'WIPO Overview of WIPO Panel Views on Selected UDRP Questions, Third Edition' ('WIPO Jurisprudential Overview 3.0') (*WIPO*, 2017) https://www.wipo.int/amc/en/domains/search/overview3.0/ accessed June 2025.
3002. TRIPS, Art. 16.

	grounds is welcome as long as one is met. If a panellist deems one is met, deciding on the other is not needed, but may still be done. Under *Digital Terms, Policies, and Disclaimers*, adequate terms should be in place and Guidelines should provide relevant interpretations. The Guidelines should state when disclaimers are effective and that they need to be conspicuous.[3003] Whether these are present within the domain name (directly or indirectly) or whether a disclaimer on an associated website is acceptable should be clarified. For example, a clearly infringing domain name should not be able to rely on a disclaimer.[3004] Further, UDRP Paragraph 4c has a term that mandates that all other disputes be resolved through court or other proceedings. It is recommended that the UDRP, as a policy for domain names, not dictate how matters outside of the UDRP 'shall'[3005] be resolved. The provision 'shall be resolved between you and such other party through any court, arbitration or other proceeding that may be available'[3006] is especially problematic because it is submitted that there is no jurisdiction for such a policy to tell parties how their other

3003. WIPO, 'WIPO Overview of WIPO Panel Views on Selected UDRP Questions, Third Edition' ('WIPO Jurisprudential Overview 3.0') (*WIPO*, 2017) https://www.wipo.int/amc/en/domains/search/overview3.0/ accessed June 2025; Alexander Peukert, 'The Coexistence of Trade Mark Laws and Rights on the Internet, and the Impact of Geolocation Technologies' (2016) 47 International Review of Intellectual Property and Competition Law 60, 81 https://doi.org/10.1007/s40319-015-0427-8; Leslie Fair, 'Full Disclosure' (*FTC Business Blog*, 23 September 2014) https://www.ftc.gov/business-guidance/blog/2014/09/full-disclosure accessed June 2025.
3004. *Ibid.*
3005. UDRP, 5.
3006. UDRP, 4(c).

	disputes 'shall'[3007] be resolved. It does not even contemplate negotiation, mediation or other possibilities. Simply indicating that such matters will not be resolved by the administrative proceeding is the recommended alternative.
	Under *Digital Jurisdictional and Territorial Considerations*, when and how such considerations may be taken into account should be stated in the guidelines. For example, local law may be considered when the domain name is being used in a geographic area in which all parties operate or serve.
	While a domain name cannot, variations of domain names may be able to 'co-exist'[3008] if done in accordance with very narrow and fair circumstances.[3009]
	Under *Digital Justification*, justification and defences are directly included as a new section called Permitted use, and these justifications are expanded to include those covered in the Overview, and some in line with general trademark law and principles.

3007. *Ibid.*
3008. EUIPO, '3.1 Coexistence Between the Marks Involved in the Opposition' (*EUIPO Trade mark Guidelines*) https://guidelines.euipo.europa.eu/2058843/2043906/trade-mark-guidelines/3-1-coexistence-between-the-marks-involved-in-the-opposition accessed January 2024;15 U.S. Code § 1052(d); Alexander Peukert, 'The Coexistence of Trade Mark Laws and Rights on the Internet, and the Impact of Geolocation Technologies' (2016) 47 International Review of Intellectual Property and Competition Law 60, 81 https://doi.org/10.1007/s40319-015-0427-8; Tamara Nanayakkara, 'IP and Business: Trademark Coexistence' (*WIPO*, November 2006) https://www.wipo.int/wipo_magazine/en/2006/06/article_0007.html accessed June 2025.
3009. *Ibid.*

	Instead of the complainant having to prove the domain holder has 'no rights or legitimate interests',[3010] the term 'unauthorised'[3011] was incorporated into the required 'confusing similarity'[3012] element. Justifications and defences based on 'rights and legitimate interests'[3013] have been clearly listed to avoid a roundabout reasoning, and are made a clear burden on the respondent,[3014] and which directly state when a trademark may be utilised in a domain name. Common justifications and defences should be interpreted in line with general trademark law and principles stated in clear guidance. For example, 'fair use'[3015] cannot be legitimate if it is done to 'confuse'[3016] or to engage in an unfair act,[3017] practice,[3018] or competition.[3019]

3010. UDRP, 4(a)(ii).
3011. *Banco Itau S.A. v. Laercio Teixeira* Case No. D2007-0912 https://www.wipo.int/amc/en/domains/decisions/html/2007/d2007-0912.html accessed July 2024.
3012. UDRP, 4(a)(i).
3013. UDRP, 4(a)(ii).
3014. WIPO, 'WIPO Overview of WIPO Panel Views on Selected UDRP Questions, Third Edition' ('WIPO Jurisprudential Overview 3.0') (*WIPO*, 2017) https://www.wipo.int/amc/en/domains/search/overview3.0/ accessed June 2025.
3015. WIPO, 'WIPO Overview of WIPO Panel Views on Selected UDRP Questions, Third Edition' ('WIPO Jurisprudential Overview 3.0') (*WIPO*, 2017) https://www.wipo.int/amc/en/domains/search/overview3.0/ accessed June 2025.
3016. Anselm Kamperman Sanders, *Unfair Competition Law: The Protection of Intellectual and Industrial Creativity* (Oxford University Press, 1997) 8; Frauke Henning-Bodewig, *Unfair Competition Law European Union and Member States* (Kluwer Law International 2006) xv-xvi; Martin Senftleben, Michael Handler and Irene Calboli, 'Protection Against Unfair Competition Around the Globe' (2024) 19 Journal of Intellectual Property Law & Practice 79, 79-80 https://doi.org/10.1093/jiplp/jpad121; Paris Convention, Art. 10bis; EUTMR, Art. 9(2)(c); 15 U.S.C. § 1125(c)(2)(B).
3017. *Ibid.*
3018. *Ibid.*
3019. WIPO, 'WIPO Overview of WIPO Panel Views on Selected UDRP Questions, Third Edition' ('WIPO Jurisprudential Overview 3.0') (*WIPO*, 2017) https://www.wipo.int/amc/en/domains/search/overview3.0/ accessed June 2025.

(5) *Procedures and Our Involvement*: (a) Initiation of Proceeding and Process and Appointment of Administrative Panel. The Rules of Procedure state the process for initiating and conducting a proceeding and for appointing the panel that will decide the dispute (the 'Administrative Panel'). (b) Selection of Provider. The complainant shall select the Provider from among those approved by ICANN by submitting the complaint to that Provider. The selected Provider will administer the proceeding, except in cases of consolidation as described in Paragraph 5(c). (c) Consolidation. In the event of multiple disputes between you and a complainant, either you or the complainant may petition to consolidate the disputes before a single Administrative Panel. This petition shall be made to the first Administrative Panel appointed to hear a pending dispute between the parties. This Administrative Panel may consolidate before it any or all such disputes in its sole discretion, provided that the disputes being consolidated are governed by this Policy or a later version of this Policy adopted by ICANN. (d) Fees. All fees charged by a Provider in connection with any dispute before an Administrative Panel pursuant to this Policy shall be paid by the complainant, except in cases where you elect to expand the Administrative Panel from one to three panellists as provided in Paragraph 5(b)(iv) of the Rules of Procedure, in which case all fees will be split evenly by you and the complainant.	Adapted or directly from the UDRP.[3020] No major changes recommended for these provisions. Reorganized sections and consolidated related provisions into this paragraph.

3020. ICANN, 'Uniform Domain-Name Dispute-Resolution Policy' (*ICANN*, 25 February 2012) https://www.icann.org/resources/pages/policy-2012-02-25-en accessed June 2025.

(e) Our Involvement in Administrative Proceedings. We do not, and will not, participate in the administration or conduct of any proceeding before an Administrative Panel. In addition, we will not be liable as a result of any decisions rendered by the Administrative Panel.
(f) Our Involvement in Disputes. We will not participate in any way in any dispute between you and any party other than us regarding the registration and use of your domain name. You shall not name us as a party or otherwise include us in any such proceeding. In the event that we are named as a party in any such proceeding, we reserve the right to raise any and all defences deemed appropriate, and to take any other action necessary to defend ourselves.
(g) Notification and Publication. The Provider shall notify us of any decision made by an Administrative Panel with respect to a domain name you have registered with us. All decisions under this Policy will be published in full over the Internet, except when an Administrative Panel determines in an exceptional case to redact portions of its decision.
(h) Availability of Court Proceedings. The mandatory administrative proceeding requirements set forth in Paragraph 4 shall not prevent either you or the complainant from submitting the dispute to a court of competent jurisdiction for independent resolution before such mandatory administrative proceeding is commenced or after such proceeding is concluded. If an Administrative Panel decides that your domain name registration should be cancelled or transferred, we will wait ten (10) business days (as observed in the location of our principal office) after we are informed by the applicable Provider of the

Administrative Panel's decision before implementing that decision. We will then implement the decision unless we have received from you during that ten (10) business day period official documentation (such as a copy of a complaint, file-stamped by the clerk of the court) that you have commenced a lawsuit against the complainant in a jurisdiction to which the complainant has submitted under Paragraph 3(b)(xiii) of the Rules of Procedure. (In general, that jurisdiction is either the location of our principal office or of your address as shown in our Whois database. *See* Paragraphs 1 and 3(b)(xiii) of the Rules of Procedure for details.) If we receive such documentation within the ten (10) business day period, we will not implement the Administrative Panel's decision, and we will take no further action, until we receive (i) evidence satisfactory to us of a resolution between the parties; (ii) evidence satisfactory to us that your lawsuit has been dismissed or withdrawn; or (iii) a copy of an order from such court dismissing your lawsuit or ordering that you do not have the right to continue to use your domain name.	
(6) *Policy Modifications*. We reserve the right to modify this Policy at any time with the permission of ICANN. We will post our revised Policy at <URL> at least thirty (30) calendar days before it becomes effective. Unless this Policy has already been invoked by the submission of a complaint to a Provider, in which event the version of the Policy in effect at the time it was invoked will apply to you until the dispute is over, all such changes will be binding upon you with respect to any domain name registration dispute, whether the dispute arose before, on or after the effective date of our change. In the event that you object to a change in this	Adapted or directly from UDRP.[3021] No changes recommended for this provision.

3021. *Ibid.*

> Policy, your sole remedy is to cancel your domain name registration with us, provided that you will not be entitled to a refund of any fees you paid to us. The revised Policy will apply to you until you cancel your domain name registration.

The above adapted version of the UDRP, called the UDNDRP, is especially recommended because the Overview incorporates many concepts which are not directly covered in the policy itself. For example, 'in the course of trade'[3022] is the preferred terminology to be used in line with TRIPS. In addition to 'bad faith',[3023] the concept of 'abuse'[3024] should be directly incorporated in the policy to recognise any 'patterns'[3025] of 'bad faith'.[3026] With the revised version above, the UDRP should adequately and directly incorporate unfair competition,[3027] which includes various key principles and differentiates these from 'bad faith',[3028] which may not necessarily be done 'in the course of trade'.[3029] While the UDRP and the Overview recognise some of these concepts, they are either not adequately or directly covered in the policy itself which creates legal uncertainty (since the UDRP 'does not operate on a strict doctrine of binding precedent [and] it is considered important for the overall credibility of the UDRP system that parties can reasonably anticipate the result of their case').[3030] At the same time, not all elements should be required for a complaint to be successful and elements are not meant to be cumulative. For example, either 'unfair competition'[3031] is sufficient OR 'bad faith or abuse'[3032] may be present, but both are not required. The UDRP should be accompanied by clear guidelines that describe how these may be applied. Further, as stated in the revised version, specific guidelines should clarify

3022. TRIPS, Art. 16.
3023. UDRP, 4(a)(iii).
3024. WIPO, 'WIPO Overview of WIPO Panel Views on Selected UDRP Questions, Third Edition' ('WIPO Jurisprudential Overview 3.0') (*WIPO*, 2017) https://www.wipo.int/amc/en/domains/search/overview3.0/ accessed June 2025.
3025. *Ibid.*
3026. UDRP, 4(a)(iii).
3027. *Ibid.*
3028. UDRP, 4(a)(iii).
3029. TRIPS, Art. 16.
3030. WIPO, 'WIPO Overview of WIPO Panel Views on Selected UDRP Questions, Third Edition' ('WIPO Jurisprudential Overview 3.0') (*WIPO*, 2017) https://www.wipo.int/amc/en/domains/search/overview3.0/ accessed June 2025.
3031. Anselm Kamperman Sanders, *Unfair Competition Law: The Protection of Intellectual and Industrial Creativity* (Oxford University Press, 1997) 8; Frauke Henning-Bodewig, *Unfair Competition Law European Union and Member States* (Kluwer Law International 2006) xv-xvi; Martin Senftleben, Michael Handler and Irene Calboli, 'Protection Against Unfair Competition Around the Globe' (2024) 19 Journal of Intellectual Property Law & Practice 79, 79-80 https://doi.org/10.1093/jiplp/jpad121; Paris Convention, Art. 10bis; EUTMR, Art. 9(2)(c); 15 U.S.C. § 1125(c)(2)(B).
3032. UDRP, 4(a)(iii); WIPO, 'WIPO Overview of WIPO Panel Views on Selected UDRP Questions, Third Edition' ('WIPO Jurisprudential Overview 3.0') (*WIPO*, 2017) https://www.wipo.int/amc/en/domains/search/overview3.0/ accessed June 2025.

when the associate website[3033] is considered and specifically when disclaimers,[3034] etc., may be relevant to the analysis. Whether and when jurisdictional considerations may be considered (as is the case for application of local law)[3035] should also be made clear. Further, justifications and defences are more clearly incorporated and the Guidelines may be used to provide interpretations. This revised version is an example of how such policy may be adapted in order to incorporate these recommendations under the Digital Trademark and Trade Practices Model to cover the gaps identified.

At the same time, there are numerous trademark situations that are beyond the scope of uniform model, such as the adapted UDRP recommended above. Recourse in the courts will unlikely be avoided fully because there are many complex situations beyond the scope of simple adapted UDRP policy, especially those where damages are appropriate.

Further, the UDNDRP has benefits from the digital consumer perspective, especially amidst the numerous platforms and places where digital trademarks may be encountered. Digital consumers who engage with domain names and visit the associated websites may be faced not only with confusing[3036] domain names, but 'online unfair competition'[3037] can violate consumer rights,[3038] 'mislead consumers'[3039] and 'harm their interests'.[3040] Under this proposal, these consumers will benefit from

---

3033. WIPO, 'WIPO Overview of WIPO Panel Views on Selected UDRP Questions, Third Edition' ('WIPO Jurisprudential Overview 3.0') (*WIPO*, 2017) https://www.wipo.int/amc/en/domains/search/overview3.0/ accessed June 2025.

3034. WIPO, 'WIPO Overview of WIPO Panel Views on Selected UDRP Questions, Third Edition' ('WIPO Jurisprudential Overview 3.0') (WIPO, 2017) https://www.wipo.int/amc/en/domains/search/overview3.0/ accessed June 2025; Alexander Peukert, 'The Coexistence of Trade Mark Laws and Rights on the Internet, and the Impact of Geolocation Technologies' (2016) 47 International Review of Intellectual Property and Competition Law 60, 81 https://doi.org/10.1007/s40319-015-0427-8; Leslie Fair, 'Full Disclosure' (*FTC Business Blog*, 23 September 2014) https://www.ftc.gov/business-guidance/blog/2014/09/full-disclosure accessed June 2025.

3035. WIPO, 'WIPO Overview of WIPO Panel Views on Selected UDRP Questions, Third Edition' ('WIPO Jurisprudential Overview 3.0') (*WIPO*, 2017) https://www.wipo.int/amc/en/domains/search/overview3.0/ accessed June 2025.

3036. INTA, 'Contemporary Unfair Competition Practices in the Digital World' (*INTA*, 2020) https://www.inta.org/wp-content/uploads/public-files/advocacy/committee-reports/Modern-or-Contemporary-Unfair-Competition-Practices-Final-Report.pdf accessed June 2025.

3037. Yuhao Kang, *Research on Unfair Competition in the Digital Economy: Innovation, Regulation, and Balancing Strategies, 2024 International Conference on Sustainable Economy and Social Sciences* (SESS 2024), SHS Web Conf., 200 (2024) 01007 https://www.shs-conferences.org/articles/shsconf/abs/2024/20/shsconf_sess2024_01007/shsconf_sess2024_01007.html accessed June 2025.

3038. *Ibid.*

3039. INTA, 'Contemporary Unfair Competition Practices in the Digital World' (*INTA*, 2020) https://www.inta.org/wp-content/uploads/public-files/advocacy/committee-reports/Modern-or-Contemporary-Unfair-Competition-Practices-Final-Report.pdf accessed June 2025; Yuhao Kang, *Research on Unfair Competition in the Digital Economy: Innovation, Regulation, and Balancing Strategies, 2024 International Conference on Sustainable Economy and Social Sciences* (SESS 2024), SHS Web Conf., 200 (2024) 01007 https://www.shs-conferences.org/articles/shsconf/abs/2024/20/shsconf_sess2024_01007/shsconf_sess2024_01007.html accessed June 2025.

3040. Yuhao Kang, *Research on Unfair Competition in the Digital Economy: Innovation, Regulation, and Balancing Strategies, 2024 International Conference on Sustainable Economy and Social*

consumer protection afforded both by confusion principles[3041] as well as 'unfair competition'[3042] or bad faith,[3043] including cybersquatting or abuse,[3044] which can result in increased consumer trust and an erosion of 'consumer goodwill'.[3045] The UDNDRP provides an avenue for a clearly defined approach whereby consumers benefit when trademark holders are given more precisely defined alternative options to pursue without the need for litigating matters which can and should fall within the realm of the UDRP. By providing guidance on key areas of consideration using common threads from underlying principles, trademark owners can enforce rights to provide for a cleaner presence in domain names, resulting in less confusion and unfairness. Digital consumers will also benefit from conspicuous disclaimers as envisioned.

Additionally, smaller businesses can benefit from the UDNDRP. For small business trademark holders who may be compelled to bring litigation in cases which the UDRP does not clearly cover, this can be both costly and timely. The UDNDRP affords them an avenue where they may not need to give up their rights if they are not able to retain a lawyer and pursue litigation, and they may be able to more clearly pursue UDNDRP actions beyond the strict limits currently afforded in the text of the UDRP. Timing is also crucial for small businesses where the potential to lose much, or even everything, in the event they are not able to resolve trademark-related disputed in an expedient manner. Sometimes, loss of consumer trust for a small business could mean the loss of substantial business or even closure.

Overall, the UDNDRP retains a simplified approach, yet is clear as to what it actually incorporates, and encompasses key elements retaining the UDRP's template-like approach. Guidelines that are based on general trademark principles will help to clarify how the policy should be interpreted, sticking to broad applications rather than complicated legal analysis in order to retain an effective and simplified decision-making approach. It is submitted that these changes help clarify, streamline, and make certain, rather than seek to uplift or completely change the policy. In fact, such an approach is recommended to be extended to other platforms, as will be seen in the next chapter.

Sciences (SESS 2024), SHS Web Conf., 200 (2024) 01007 https://www.shs-conferences.org/articles/shsconf/abs/2024/20/shsconf_sess2024_01007/shsconf_sess2024_01007.html accessed June 2025.

3041. Paris Convention, Art. 6bis; TRIPS, Art. 16.

3042. Anselm Kamperman Sanders, *Unfair Competition Law: The Protection of Intellectual and Industrial Creativity* (Oxford University Press, 1997) 8; EUTMR, Art. 9(2)(c) and Art. 17(2); 15 U.S.C. §1125.

3043. UDRP, 4(a)(iii).

3044. WIPO, 'WIPO Overview of WIPO Panel Views on Selected UDRP Questions, Third Edition' ('WIPO Jurisprudential Overview 3.0') (WIPO, 2017) https://www.wipo.int/amc/en/domains/search/overview3.0/ accessed June 2025.

3045. INTA, 'Contemporary Unfair Competition Practices in the Digital World' (*INTA*, 2020) https://www.inta.org/wp-content/uploads/public-files/advocacy/committee-reports/Modern-or-Contemporary-Unfair-Competition-Practices-Final-Report.pdf accessed June 2025.

4.4 CONCLUSION

This chapter addressed recommendations for the UDRP in light of the Digital Trademark and Trade Practices model.

Considering the successful approach and benefits of the UDRP, and despite its limitations, it has been a long-standing policy which is currently in place. The adapted UDRP, namely the UDNDRP, is positioned as a simple policy which incorporates content from the Overview as well as being informed by the Digital Trademark and Trade Practices Model using general trademark principles. It is hoped that the recommended updates to the UDRP may be considered in future revisions.

Further, such adapted uniform approach can serve e-commerce marketplace,[3046] search ad, social media,[3047] mobile app, and Metaverse platforms well and the following chapter is dedicated to each of these platforms. The UDNDRP approach is applied to each platform after considering the gaps as a uniform[3048] solution to trademarks in each of those platforms.

3046. Edward C Anderson and Timothy S Cole, 'The UDRP: A Model for Dispute Resolution in E-Commerce' (2002) 6 Journal of Small & Emerging Business Law 235.

3047. Rajeev Sachdev, 'Towards an Improved Framework for Trade-Mark Law and Regulation in Social Media Usernames: A Study of the Canadian, U.S., and U.K. Positions' (2016) 28 Intellectual Property Journal 379, 379-418; Daniel Doft, 'Facebook, Twitter, and the Wild West of IP Enforcement on Social Media: Weighing the Merits of a Uniform Dispute Resolution Policy' (2016) 49 The John Marshall Law Review 959; Thomas J Curtin, 'The Name Game: Cybersquatting and Trademark Infringement on Social Media Websites' (2010-2011) 19 Journal of Law and Policy 353; Erick J Heels, 'How to Twittersquat The Top 100 Brands' (*GiantPeople*, 8 January 2009) http://www.giantpeople.com/1298.html accessed 4 August 2025; Paul D McGrady, *McGrady on Social Media and the Metaverse* (Mathew Bender & Company, Inc. 2023) §12; John McElwaine and Christopher D Casavale, 'Tackling Bad Faith Registration of Domain Names in a fast-Changing Landscape' (*WIPO Magazine*, December 2019) https://www.wipo.int/wipo_magazine/en/2019/06/article_0006.html accessed June 2025.

3048. *Ibid.*

CHAPTER 5

Towards Uniform Platform Policies for Trademarks in E-Commerce Marketplace, Search Ad, Social Media, Mobile App, and Metaverse Platforms Based on the Digital Trademark and Trade Practices Model

Platform trademark policies are overviewed for e-commerce marketplace, search advertising, social media, mobile, app, and Metaverse platforms. These are then considered in light of the Digital Trademark and Trade Practices Model. Specific recommendations are made for trademark policies for each type of platform. Then, based on a UDNDRP-type policy, the text of draft uniform platform trademark policies for each type of platform is provided. These draft policies, if implemented by platforms, will provide for legal certainty, uniformity, and cost-effective approaches to solve the problems and gaps with digital trademarks in platforms.

5.1 INTRODUCTION

This chapter intends to determine recommendations for platform trademark policies in light of the UDRP, recommendations for the UDRP, and the Digital Trademark and Trade Practices Model.

Trademarks are in much use across e-commerce marketplace, search ad, social media, mobile app, and Metaverse platforms. As was seen in Chapter 4, a uniform policy, the UDRP, is in place for trademark disputes for covered domain names.

However, there is no equivalent uniform policy for trademarks in platforms,[3049] which are generally dealt with by the platforms themselves or through available judicial processes.

This chapter will overview the trademark terms and policies for each platform separately.[3050] Based on the Digital Trademark and Trade Practices Model and related considerations raised for platforms in Chapter 3, gaps and problems for each of the platforms will be identified. To facilitate this, a table is provided for each type of platform in the sections below to summarise the terms and policies and compare them to each element of the model. In each of these tables, and for each element, it is noted whether an element is *generally or not directly covered*, or whether there is *only some coverage* of the element. For example, under *Digital Use and Place of Use*, while utilisation in a platform may be covered, but use in the 'course of trade'[3051] or some alternative terminology for the concept is not required, this would be considered *only some coverage* since considerations for the entire element were not covered. As another example, under *Digital Bad Faith and Abuse*, 'bad faith'[3052] may not be covered, but abuse[3053] may not be, in which the same notation will be made. Where an element in its entirety is not covered, the notation will be *generally or not directly covered*, even if some general reference may be present for that element. This is meant as a broad indication only.

Following that, a solution is offered based on the Digital Trademark and Trade Practices Model in line with the adapted UDRP (the UDNDRP as recommended and provided in Chapter 4) because of the huge benefits of simplicity, cost-effectiveness and 'predictability'[3054] this provides. It is argued that such uniform policy[3055] forms a

3049. Edward C Anderson and Timothy S Cole, 'The UDRP: A Model for Dispute Resolution in E-Commerce' (2002) 6 Journal of Small & Emerging Business Law 235; Rajeev Sachdev, 'Towards an Improved Framework for Trade-Mark Law and Regulation in Social Media Usernames: A Study of the Canadian, U.S., and U.K. Positions' (2016) 28 Intellectual Property Journal 379, 379-418; Daniel Doft, 'Facebook, Twitter, and the Wild West of IP Enforcement on Social Media: Weighing the Merits of a Uniform Dispute Resolution Policy' (2016) 49 The John Marshall Law Review 959; Thomas J Curtin, 'The Name Game: Cybersquatting and Trademark Infringement on Social Media Websites' (2010-2011) 19 Journal of Law and Policy 353; Erick J Heels, 'How to Twittersquat The Top 100 Brands' (*GiantPeople*, 8 January 2009) http://www.giantpeople.com/1298.html accessed 4 August 2025; Paul D McGrady, *McGrady on Social Media and the Metaverse* (Mathew Bender & Company, Inc. 2023) §12; John McElwaine and Christopher D Casavale, 'Tackling Bad Faith Registration of Domain Names in a Fast-Changing Landscape' (*WIPO Magazine*, December 2019) https://www.wipo.int/wipo_magazine/en/2019/06/article_0006.html accessed June 2025.

3050. Where the language of the terms or policies is not English (such as Dutch), a translation to English was conducted using browser translation tools such as but not limited to 'Translate' or 'Translate Page' or features to permit the setting of a language on a particular website etc.

3051. TRIPS, Art. 16.

3052. UDRP, 4(a)(iii).

3053. WIPO, 'WIPO Overview of WIPO Panel Views on Selected UDRP Questions, Third Edition' ('WIPO Jurisprudential Overview 3.0') (*WIPO*, 2017) https://www.wipo.int/amc/en/domains/search/overview3.0/ accessed June 2025.

3054. John McElwaine and Christopher D Casavale, 'Tackling Bad Faith Registration of Domain Names in a Fast-Changing Landscape' (*WIPO Magazine*, December 2019) https://www.wipo.int/wipo_magazine/en/2019/06/article_0006.html accessed June 2025.

3055. Rajeev Sachdev, 'Towards an Improved Framework for Trade-Mark Law and Regulation in Social Media Usernames: A Study of the Canadian, U.S., and U.K. Positions' (2016) 28

solid basis for each platform (adjustments for each platform are made as deemed necessary). Actual policies for each type of platform are drafted and presented, and it is proposed that platforms consider these for actual adoption. Platforms should consider adopting such uniform policies not only to resolve trademark disputes within their services in expedient and legally certain ways but also to build or enhance trust in their platforms, as consumers faced with confusion,[3056] counterfeit[3057] or other negative experiences may impact the platform and its viability. Therefore, problems and gaps may result in the potential for serious consequences.

5.2 MAJOR E-COMMERCE MARKETPLACE PLATFORM TRADEMARK TERMS AND POLICIES

Terms and policies of the two e-commerce marketplace platforms, Amazon and eBay will be overviewed here. Following that, gaps and problems will be identified and a unform[3058] solution recommended.

Intellectual Property Journal 379; Daniel Doft, "Facebook, Twitter, and the Wild West of IP Enforcement on Social Media: Weighing the Merits of a Uniform Dispute Resolution Policy" (2016) 49 The John Marshall Law Review 959; Thomas J Curtin, 'The Name Game: Cybersquatting and Trademark Infringement on Social Media Websites' (2010-2011) 19 Journal of Law and Policy 353; Heels EJ, '* How to Twittersquat The Top 100 Brands' (* *GiantPeople*) http://www.giantpeople.com/1298.html accessed 4 August 2025; Paul D McGrady, *McGrady on Social Media: 2018* (LexisNexis 2018); Edward C Anderson and Timothy S Cole, 'The UDRP – A Model for Dispute Resolution in E-Commerce' (2002) 6 Journal of Small & Emerging Business Law 235; John McElwaine and Christopher D Casavale, 'Tackling Bad Faith Registration of Domain Names in a Fast-Changing Landscape' (*WIPO Magazine*, December 2019) https://www.wipo.int/wipo_magazine/en/2019/06/article_0006.html accessed June 2025.

3056. Paris Convention, Art. 6bis; TRIPS, Art. 16(1); EUTMR, Art. 8(1)(b) and Art. 9(2)(b); 15 U.S. Code § 1114;15 U.S. Code § 1125.

3057. Amazon, 'Intellectual Property Policy for Sellers: FAQ about Trademarks' (*Amazon*) https://sellercentral.amazon.com/help/hub/reference/external/GZUQ6GBBXQVHQKF2 accessed June 2025; eBay, 'Forgeries, Replicas and Unauthorized Copies Policy' (*eBay NL*) https://www.ebay.nl/help/policies/prohibited-restricted-items/fake-items-policy?id=4276 accessed June 2025; Google, 'Counterfeit Goods' (*Google Advertising Policies Help*) https://support.google.com/adspolicy/answer/176017? accessed June 2025.

3058. Edward C Anderson and Timothy S Cole, 'The UDRP: A Model for Dispute Resolution in E-Commerce' (2002) 6 Journal of Small & Emerging Business Law 235; Rajeev Sachdev, 'Towards an Improved Framework for Trade-Mark Law and Regulation in Social Media Usernames: A Study of the Canadian, U.S., and U.K. Positions' (2016) 28 Intellectual Property Journal 379, 379-418; Daniel Doft, 'Facebook, Twitter, and the Wild West of IP Enforcement on Social Media: Weighing the Merits of a Uniform Dispute Resolution Policy' (2016) 49 The John Marshall Law Review 959; Thomas J Curtin, 'The Name Game: Cybersquatting and Trademark Infringement on Social Media Websites' (2010-2011) 19 Journal of Law and Policy 353; Erick J Heels, 'How to Twittersquat the Top 100 Brands' (*GiantPeople*, 8 January 2009) http://www.giantpeople.com/1298.html accessed 4 August 2025; Paul D McGrady, *McGrady on Social Media and the Metaverse* (Mathew Bender & Company, Inc. 2023) §12; John McElwaine and Christopher D Casavale, 'Tackling Bad Faith Registration of Domain Names in a Fast-Changing Landscape' (*WIPO Magazine*, December 2019) https://www.wipo.int/wipo_magazine/en/2019/06/article_0006.html accessed June 2025.

5.2.1 Amazon

Amazon operates a variety of sites geared to specific countries or regions and conditions of use and services may vary. This section will overview Amazon.com and Amazon.nl terms and policies as illustrative examples.

Under Amazon.com Conditions of Use and Amazon.nl Conditions of Use and Sale (and various others), it is stated that: 'Amazon respects the intellectual property of others. If you believe that your intellectual property rights are being infringed, please follow our Notice and Procedure for Making Claims of Copyright Infringement'[3059] or 'Rights Infringements.'[3060] Amazon.com Conditions of Use (and Sale) further note that: visitors may 'post … so [as] long as the content is not illegal … infringing of intellectual property rights …'.[3061]

Under Amazon.com Intellectual Property Policy for Sellers, compliance 'with all federal, state, and local laws and Amazon policies applicable to your products and product listings'[3062] must be maintained, as well as sellers 'may not violate the IP rights of brands or other rights owners'[3063] and a violation of this 'may result in loss of selling privileges or other legal consequences'.[3064]

Amazon.com's Intellectual property Policy generally discusses trademark law and indicates its protection against 'customer confusion about who provides, endorses, or is affiliated with particular goods or services'[3065] while specifically indicating that a mark holder may have the right to prevent others 'from using a particular mark, or a confusingly similar mark'[3066] where such use 'is likely to cause a customer to be confused about whether the product being sold is the trademark owner's product'.[3067]

While the above portion focuses on confusion,[3068] Amazon.nl's equivalent policy not only considers confusion but also discusses reputation, unfair advantage, etc. Specifically, it addresses, in a general discussion of trademark law, that it protects against 'misappropriation … by unauthorized third parties' and more specifically in the

3059. Amazon, 'Conditions of Use' (*Amazon*) https://www.amazon.com/gp/help/customer/display.html?nodeId=508088&ref_=footer_cou accessed June 2025; Amazon.nl, 'Amazon.nl Conditions of Use and Sale' (*Amazon.nl Legal Policies*) https://www.amazon.nl/-/en/gp/help/customer/display.html?nodeId=201909000&ref_=footer_cou accessed June 2025.
3060. Amazon.nl, 'Amazon.nl Conditions of Use and Sale' (*Amazon.nl Legal Policies*) https://www.amazon.nl/-/en/gp/help/customer/display.html?nodeId=201909000&ref_=footer_cou accessed June 2025.
3061. Amazon, 'Conditions of Use' (*Amazon*) https://www.amazon.com/gp/help/customer/display.html?nodeId=508088&ref_=footer_cou accessed June 2025; Amazon.nl, 'Amazon.nl Conditions of Use and Sale' (*Amazon.nl Legal Policies*) https://www.amazon.nl/-/en/gp/help/customer/display.html?nodeId=201909000&ref_=footer_cou accessed June 2025.
3062. Amazon, 'Amazon Intellectual Property Policy for Sellers' (*Amazon Seller Central*) https://sellercentral.amazon.com/help/hub/reference/external/G201361070 accessed June 2025.
3063. *Ibid.*
3064. *Ibid.*
3065. Amazon, 'Intellectual Property Policy for Sellers: FAQ about Trademarks' (*Amazon*) https://sellercentral.amazon.com/help/hub/reference/external/GZUQ6GBBXQVHQKF2 accessed June 2025.
3066. *Ibid.*
3067. *Ibid.*
3068. *Ibid.*

case of 'potential customer confusion about who provides, endorses, or is affiliated with such particular goods or services'.[3069] Further that a mark holder may prevent others from using a specific mark for 'identical'[3070] or 'similar'[3071] goods or services and in cases where 'it is likely that customers could be confused (even if the mark used is not identical but only similar)'.[3072] Further, prevention may be available if the mark 'has reputation in the relevant territory and where use of that same or a similar mark without due cause takes unfair advantage of, or is detrimental to, the distinctive character or the repute of the owner's mark'.[3073]

Under the Amazon.com Intellectual Property Policy for Sellers – FAQ about Trademarks, they indicate that a mark may be used if 'selling authentic goods'[3074] when 'using the trademark to identify an authentic product'[3075] or where used 'in its ordinary dictionary meaning'[3076] or for purposes of 'making truthful statements that a product is compatible with a trademarked product'[3077] (although logo use in this manner is not permitted).[3078] Further, a specific formatting may be required while factoring in the Amazon Brand Name Policy, or the listing may be removed.[3079]

Amazon.nl's Amazon Intellectual Property Policy generally indicates the same as above, except that (mostly) the reference in point b above to 'ordinary dictionary'[3080] is followed by 'descriptive meaning'.[3081] Also, in point c above, it states that '[a]ny statement you make about compatibility must be true'[3082] which is followed by 'and relevant for the customer's purchase decision (for example, if your product is actually compatible with all competitor products, it is not permissible to use the brands of these products, as the customer is not at risk of buying the "wrong" product without the compatibility statement)'.[3083] Further, making claims such as 'similar to'[3084] claims is addressed. For example, if a seller states that the goods they are selling are 'similar to Kindle'[3085] or 'equivalent to Find',[3086] they indicate that these 'may infringe trademark law, depending on the store and circumstances'[3087] and they encourage sellers to

3069. Amazon, 'Amazon Intellectual Property Policy' (*Amazon Seller Central*) https://sellercentral.amazon.nl/help/hub/reference/external/G201361070?locale=en-US accessed June 2025.
3070. *Ibid.*
3071. *Ibid.*
3072. *Ibid.*
3073. *Ibid.*
3074. Amazon, 'Intellectual Property Policy for Sellers: FAQ about Trademarks' (*Amazon*) https://sellercentral.amazon.com/help/hub/reference/external/GZUQ6GBBXQVHQKF2 accessed June 2025.
3075. *Ibid.*
3076. *Ibid.*
3077. *Ibid.*
3078. *Ibid.*
3079. *Ibid.*
3080. *Ibid.*
3081. Amazon, 'Amazon Intellectual Property Policy' (*Amazon Seller Central*) https://sellercentral.amazon.nl/help/hub/reference/external/G201361070?locale=en-US accessed June 2025.
3082. *Ibid.*
3083. *Ibid.*
3084. *Ibid.*
3085. *Ibid.*
3086. *Ibid.*
3087. *Ibid.*

'[s]eek legal counsel before making such comparisons'.[3088] Other aspects are largely the same except for a few words, which do not alter the point.

Under Amazon.com (and almost identically for Amazon.nl)[3089] Community Guidelines, it indicates, under 'Plagiarism, infringement, or impersonation',[3090] that one should only post their 'own content'[3091] or that for which they 'have permission to use on Amazon',[3092] including 'text, images, and videos'.[3093] They do not permit infringing content, including that which infringes trademarks 'or other proprietary rights'[3094] nor should any interactions 'with community members'[3095] result in infringement of such rights. Impersonation of individuals or organisations is banned.[3096]

Amazon.com's Intellectual Property Policy for Sellers – FAQ about Trademarks also says that infringing orders must not be fulfilled and customisation services involving infringing content must not be produced.[3097]

Both Amazon.com and Amazon.nl have a form for complaint procedures.[3098] In this regard, Amazon.com Conditions of Use say that '[w]e respond quickly to the concerns of rights owners about any alleged infringement, and we terminate repeat infringers in appropriate circumstances'.[3099] Amazon.nl likewise says that they, when receiving a complaint, may remove items, terminate 'repeat infringers in appropriate circumstances'[3100] and disclaim liability, reserve defences, and require indemnity.[3101]

Further, in connection with the Report Infringement Form, Amazon.com (and nearly identically for Amazon.nl)[3102] say that sellers on Amazon 'are expected to follow the law and Amazon's policies'[3103] and that they take 'claims of intellectual property

3088. *Ibid.*
3089. Amazon.nl, 'Community Guidelines' (*Amazon.nl Amazon Community*) https://www.amazon.nl/-/en/gp/help/customer/display.html?nodeId=GLHXEX85MENUE4XF accessed June 2025.
3090. Amazon, 'Community Guidelines' (*Amazon Help & Customer Service*) https://www.amazon.com/gp/help/customer/display.html?nodeId=GLHXEX85MENUE4XF accessed June 2025.
3091. *Ibid.*
3092. *Ibid.*
3093. *Ibid.*
3094. *Ibid.*
3095. *Ibid.*
3096. Amazon, 'Community Guidelines' (*Amazon Help & Customer Service*) https://www.amazon.com/gp/help/customer/display.html?nodeId=GLHXEX85MENUE4XF accessed June 2025.
3097. Amazon, 'Intellectual Property Policy for Sellers: FAQ about Trademarks' (*Amazon*) https://sellercentral.amazon.com/help/hub/reference/external/GZUQ6GBBXQVHQKF2 accessed June 2025.
3098. Amazon, 'Conditions of Use' (*Amazon*) https://www.amazon.com/gp/help/customer/display.html?nodeId=508088&ref_=footer_cou accessed June 2025; Amazon.nl, 'Amazon.nl Conditions of Use and Sale' (*Amazon.nl*) https://www.amazon.nl/gp/help/customer/display.html?ie=UTF8&nodeId=201909000&ref_=footer_cou&language=en_GB accessed June 2025.
3099. Amazon, 'Conditions of Use' (*Amazon*) https://www.amazon.com/gp/help/customer/display.html?nodeId=508088&ref_=footer_cou accessed June 2025.
3100. Amazon.nl, 'Amazon.nl Conditions of Use and Sale' (*Amazon.nl*) https://www.amazon.nl/gp/help/customer/display.html?ie=UTF8&nodeId=201909000&ref_=footer_cou&language=en_GB accessed June 2025.
3101. *Ibid.*
3102. Amazon, 'Amazon Intellectual Property Policy' (*Amazon Seller Central*) https://sellercentral.amazon.nl/help/hub/reference/external/G201361070?locale=en-US accessed June 2025.
3103. *Ibid.*

infringement seriously'.[3104] They may warn or suspend a seller even where the infringing actions was 'without knowledge'[3105] and state that sellers 'must consult a lawyer for help to ensure that your business has the right procedures in place to prevent IP infringement'.[3106]

Under the Using the Report Infringement Form, the same language appears for both, a 'valid trademark registration number that is enforceable in the jurisdiction of the Amazon store you're signed in to (for example, United States Patent and Trademark Office (USPTO) for amazon.com)',[3107] and a 'test buy'[3108] (unless 'reporting a complete ASIN').[3109] Likewise, a report of 'Counterfeit infringement requires a federally registered trademark. Common law and Pending trademark applications cannot be used as the basis for counterfeit infringement.'[3110]

The rules pertaining to trademarks are not all in one place and other policies are also operative. Under Amazon Business Acceptable Use Policy, there must be '[no illegal, harmful, or offensive use or content]'.[3111] Sellers may not 'use, or encourage, promote, facilitate or instruct others to use, Amazon Business for any illegal ... fraudulent, infringing or offensive use, or to transmit, store, display, distribute or otherwise make available content that is illegal, harmful, fraudulent, infringing or offensive'.[3112] While Amazon can, it does not have 'the obligation to monitor and edit or remove any activity or content' and a suspension or termination may result where there is a violation.[3113]

Under Amazon's Business Accounts terms and Conditions, there is a binding arbitration clause and Amazon 'may bring suit in court to enjoin infringement or other misuse of intellectual property rights'.[3114]

In the context of influencers, under Amazon Influencer Terms & Conditions For Sponsored Content, 'Prohibited Activities'[3115] content must 'not include ... (6) materials that infringe third-party ... trademark, tradename ... intellectual property rights,

3104. *Ibid.*
3105. *Ibid.*
3106. *Ibid.*
3107. Amazon, 'Using the Report Infringement Form' (*Amazon Seller Central*) https://sellercentral.amazon.com/help/hub/reference/external/GJFZJ63CR5BRSNAY accessed June 2025; Amazom.nl, 'Using the Report Infringement Form' (*Amazon.nl Seller Central*) https://sellercentral.amazon.nl/help/hub/reference/external/GJFZJ63CR5BRSNAY?locale=en-US accessed June 2025.
3108. *Ibid.*
3109. *Ibid.*
3110. *Ibid.*
3111. Amazon, 'Amazon Business Acceptable Use Policy' (*Amazon Terms and Conditions*) https://www.amazon.com/gp/help/customer/display.html?ref_=hp_left_v4_sib&nodeId=GFUSWPZP368LFFA9 accessed June 2025.
3112. *Ibid.*
3113. *Ibid.*
3114. Amazon, 'Amazon Business Accounts Terms and Conditions' (*Amazon Terms and Conditions*) https://www.amazon.com/gp/help/customer/display.html?ref_=hp_left_v4_sib&nodeId=G202119380 accessed June 2025.
3115. Amazon, 'Amazon Influencer Terms & Conditions For Sponsored Content' (*Amazon Legal Policies*) https://www.amazon.com/gp/help/customer/display.html?ref_=hp_left_v4_sib&nodeId=GA75EXWGGZPEFSQS accessed June 2025. However, it also defines Trademark as: 'Amazon's and its Affiliates' trademarks and logos'.

or other proprietary rights; or (7) illegal ... as determined by Amazon in its sole discretion'.[3116]

In the context of counterfeiting, under Amazon.com Intellectual Property Policy for Sellers – FAQ about Trademarks,

Amazon defines 'Counterfeiting ... [as] ... a specific type of trademark infringement ... an unlawful total or partial reproduction of a registered trademark or a mark that is very similar to a registered trademark in connection with the sale of a product that does not come from the trademark holder.'[3117] However, they, in general, state that this requires use 'on the product or packaging'.[3118] Reference is made to a 'brand name',[3119] 'logo',[3120] or 'the shape or look of the product itself'.[3121] But it is not considered counterfeit if it is 'sold on a separate product detail page and does not improperly use a registered trademark'[3122] except where 'a registered trademark protects the shape or appearance of a product itself, identical products may be counterfeit even if they do not feature a brand name or logo ...'.[3123] Further, that non-counterfeit products may still infringe intellectual property and the responsibility to ensure they do not is on the seller who must consult a lawyer for questions.[3124] Under Amazon.nl, some aspects are worded a bit differently and indicate that 'lookalike products may infringe upon trademark or other intellectual property rights, ... (in some countries) unfair competition/passing off'.[3125]

Under Amazon.com's Anti-Counterfeiting Policy, seller may only offer 'authentic'[3126] products and offering 'non-authentic products is strictly prohibited'.[3127] Sellers who do not follow this policy may lose the privilege of selling, monies being withheld, and even 'disposal of inventory in our possession'.[3128] Products that are 'not legal for sale, such as products that have been illegally replicated, reproduced, or manufactured' are not permitted and documentation may be required to be provided to Amazon on request. These include 'Bootlegs, fakes, or pirated copies of products or content'[3129] or other infringing products.[3130]

3116. *Ibid.*
3117. Amazon, 'Intellectual Property Policy for Sellers: FAQ about Trademarks' (*Amazon*) https://sellercentral.amazon.com/help/hub/reference/external/GZUQ6GBBXQVHQKF2 accessed June 2025.
3118. *Ibid.*
3119. *Ibid.*
3120. *Ibid.*
3121. *Ibid.*
3122. *Ibid.*
3123. *Ibid.*
3124. *Ibid.*
3125. Amazon, 'Amazon Intellectual Property Policy' (*Amazon Seller Central*) https://sellercentral.amazon.nl/help/hub/reference/external/G201361070?locale=en-US accessed June 2025.
3126. *Ibid.*
3127. *Ibid.*
3128. *Ibid.*
3129. *Ibid.*
3130. *Ibid.*

Amazon.com also has a 'counterfeit crimes unit'.[3131] It also offers Project Zero,[3132] which is identified as using 'advanced anti-counterfeiting technology'[3133] to help '[r]emove counterfeits-immediately'.[3134] Further, its 'Transparency Program' is designed to help brands 'stop inaccurate and counterfeit products'[3135] and is 'currently available in the US, Canada, Germany, France, Italy, Spain, the UK, Australia, India, and Japan'.[3136] There is a fee for 'Amazon-issued codes and for existing serial codes'[3137] shared with Amazon.[3138]

Importantly, Amazon also has a service called the Brand Registry,[3139] which is positioned to help 'detect and report suspected IP infringement'.[3140] It has a 'Report a Violation tool',[3141] which can be used to report a violation under the Brand Registry. While this is a welcome programme which helps brand owners find and complain about trademark violations[3142] along with other helpful services, this service is still based on Amazon's IP policy, from which Amazon will make a decision. The policy is generally applicable whether or not a brand is registered[3143] and the contents of such policy on which a programme is based are key to consider (and should be done in line with the model). Further, not all brands will be registered and brands that in fact are registered obviously do not represent the universe of trademarks. Thus, a system and adequate underlying trademark policy is still needed, such as the one recommended in this book.

Very interestingly, Amazon.com already uses a 'neutral patent evaluation'[3144] third-party service, which determines 'whether an asserted utility patent is infringed'.[3145] There does not appear to be an equivalent service for trademark violations.

5.2.2 ebay

The eBay.com User Agreement says that, when using their services, users 'agree to comply with this User Agreement, our policies, our terms, and all applicable laws, rules, and regulations, and you will not: ... infringe any Intellectual Property Rights

3131. Amazon, 'Amazon Counterfeit Crimes Unit (CCU)' (*Amazon Trustworthy Shopping*) https://brandservices.amazon.com/counterfeitcrimesunit accessed June 2025.
3132. Amazon, 'Amazon project Zero'(*Amazon Brand Services*) https://sell.amazon.com/brand-registry/project-zero accessed June 2025.
3133. *Ibid.*
3134. *Ibid.*
3135. Amazon, 'Transparency' (*Amazon*) https://sell.amazon.com/brand-registry/transparency accessed June 2025.
3136. *Ibid.*
3137. *Ibid.*
3138. *Ibid.*
3139. Amazon, 'Let's Protect the Brand You Built' (*Amazon Brand Registry*) https://sell.amazon.com/brand-registry accessed June 2025; Amazon.nl, 'Amazon Brand Registry' (*Amazon.nl*) https://sell.amazon.nl/brand-registry accessed June 2025.
3140. *Ibid.*
3141. *Ibid.*
3142. *Ibid.*
3143. *Ibid.*
3144. *Ibid.*
3145. *Ibid.*

that belong to third parties affected by your use of our Services or post content that does not belong to you'.[3146] Further, that users represent and warrant that they 'control all necessary rights'[3147] for content and 'that such content is accurate, appropriate, and legal'[3148] and 'that use of any such content (including derivative works) by us, our users, or others in contract with us ... does not and will not infringe any Intellectual Property Rights of any third party'.[3149] They take 'no responsibility'[3150] and assume 'no liability for any content provided'.[3151] Similarly, the eBay.nl User Agreement indicates representation that content 'complies with applicable law', that users 'own the intellectual property rights in the Content, that it does not infringe any third party rights, and that the Content is not the subject of any claim of infringement or on other grounds'.[3152] An indemnity is required for claims of intellectual property ... unfair and/or parasitic competition ...'.[3153] eBay.nl Counterfeits, Replicas and Unauthorised Copies Policy also indicates that 'Replicas may also infringe competition law.'[3154]

Both eBay.com and eBay.nl offer a 'Verified Rights Owner (VeRO) Program'[3155] to facilitate the reporting of 'listings that infringe'[3156] trademark rights.[3157] A Rights Violation form[3158] is available and includes intellectual property infringing items and '[c]ounterfeit or replica items'.[3159] A reason code is to be reported on the form to include, *inter alia*, 'item infringement',[3160] 'counterfeit product which infringes a trademark (provide trademark registration information)',[3161] 'content infringement'[3162] in a listing or 'unlawful use of trademark (provide trademark registration information)'[3163] in a listing.[3164]

3146. eBay, 'User Agreement' (*eBay Customer Service*) https://www.ebay.com/help/policies/member-behaviour-policies/user-agreement?id=4259 accessed June 2025.
3147. *Ibid.*
3148. *Ibid.*
3149. *Ibid.*
3150. *Ibid.*
3151. *Ibid.*
3152. eBay, 'User Agreement' (*eBay Customer Service*) https://www.ebay.nl/help/policies/member-behaviour-policies/user-agreement?id=4259 accessed June 2025.
3153. *Ibid.*
3154. eBay, 'Counterfeits, Replicas and Unauthorized Copies Policy' (*eBay NL*) https://www.ebay.nl/help/policies/prohibited-restricted-items/fake-items-policy?id=4276 accessed June 2025.
3155. eBay, 'Verified Rights Owner (VeRO) Policy' (*eBay Customer Service*) https://www.ebay.com/help/policies/listing-policies/selling-policies/intellectual-property-vero-program?id=4349 accessed June 2025.
3156. *Ibid.*
3157. eBay, 'Verified Rights Owner Program' (*eBay*) https://www.ebay.com/sellercenter/ebay-for-business/verified-rights-owner-program#m17-1-tb2 accessed June 2025; eBay.nl, 'Help Protect Intellectual Property' (*eBay.nl Vero Program*) https://pages.ebay.nl/vero/ accessed June 2025.
3158. eBay, 'Verified Rights Owner Program' (*eBay*) https://www.ebay.com/sellercenter/ebay-for-business/verified-rights-owner-program#m17-1-tb2 accessed June 2025.
3159. *Ibid.*
3160. *Ibid.*
3161. *Ibid.*
3162. *Ibid.*
3163. *Ibid.*
3164. eBay, 'Notice of Claimed Infringement', (*eBay*) https://ir.ebaystatic.com/pictures/aw/pics/pdf/us/help/community/EN-NOCI.pdf accessed June 2025.

Under eBay.com's Verified Rights Owner (VeRO) policy, '[o]ffers or products that infringe on the intellectual property rights of others are not permitted on eBay ... We do not allow products or offers that infringe the intellectual property rights of others. These include counterfeit products, replicas, unauthorized copies, and objects imported in parallel without permission.'[3165] Additionally, '[i]t is in eBay's interest to ensure that infringing items are removed from the site, as they are illegal, and erode the trust of our buyers and sellers'.[3166]

Further, users must 'follow this policy, the eBay User Agreement and all applicable laws, as well as respect the rights of third parties';[3167] otherwise, 'eBay may take action consistent with applicable laws and the eBay User Agreement, and may even be legally required to do so'[3168] including, for example, '[r]emoving the listing or other content, issuing a warning, restricting activity or account suspension'.[3169]

Similarly, but instead under eBay.nl's Intellectual Property Policy, '[o]ffers or products that infringe the intellectual property rights of others are not permitted on eBay'.[3170] Specifically, '[w]here branded goods have been marketed in the European Economic Area by the rightholder or with the consent of the rightholder, they may be resold within the European Economic Area without further consent'.[3171] However, a mark holder may object 'for example, if the condition of the goods has changed or if the goods have been damaged after the right holder has placed them on the market'.[3172] An 'illegal copy of (' counterfeits', 'product piracy')' a product is not permitted, including those with 'slightly changed brand names'[3173] where 'it wrongly gives the impression that the offer or object may come from the rights holder of the trademark'.[3174] Infringement may occur 'if the goods are expressly identified as copies in the offer'.[3175]

Moreover, eBay.nl selling policies state that '[i]tems or listings that infringe on third party trademarks are not allowed on eBay',[3176] including '[c]opied, counterfeit or

3165. eBay, 'Intellectual Property Policy' (*eBay*) https://www.ebay.nl/help/policies/listing-policies/selling-policies/vero-policy?id=4349 accessed June 2025.
3166. eBay, 'eBay Verified Rights Owner Program and Intellectual Property Policy' (*eBay*) https://export.ebay.com/en/regulations/ebay-policies/ebay-verified-rights-owner-program-and-intellectual-property-policy/ accessed June 2025.
3167. eBay, 'eBay's Intellectual Property Policy' (*eBay*) https://www.ebay.com/help/policies/member-behaviour-policies/ebays-intellectual-property-policy?id=4261 accessed June 2025.
3168. *Ibid.*
3169. *Ibid.*
3170. eBay, 'Intellectual Property Policy' (*eBay*) https://www.ebay.nl/help/policies/listing-policies/selling-policies/vero-policy?id=4349 accessed June 2025.
3171. *Ibid.*
3172. *Ibid.*
3173. *Ibid.*
3174. *Ibid.*
3175. *Ibid.*
3176. *Ibid.*

counterfeit goods under a protected trademark',[3177] those with 'a sign that confusingly resembles a protected trademark (including on packaging, if applicable) ... [o]riginal products not marketed in the European Economic Area with the consent of the trademark holder (parallel import) ... [m]isleading or excessive use of a protected trademark in the case of accessories or spare parts'.[3178] Additionally, those that 'falsely create the impression that there is an economic or organizational connection with the trademark holder ... for false comparative advertising ... [a]buse, defamation or unfair exploitation of the reputation of a well-known trademark ... [m]isleading use of a trademark as a keyword'.[3179]

Under the eBay.nl User Agreement, the following is prohibited: 'sell counterfeit items or otherwise infringe the copyright, trademark or other rights of third parties'.[3180] Under eBay.nl's Counterfeit Item Policy, 'Counterfeit objects, replicas and unauthorized copies of protected original objects are not permitted on eBay.'[3181] Further under the policy:

> [c]ounterfeit products are illegal and not allowed on eBay. These items may infringe on the copyright or trademark of others. Examples of counterfeit objects are: ... handbags, watched or sneakers.[3182]

Generally, eBay.nl requires that violation may result in a deletion of the listing/content, a warning, limitation of activities, or suspension.[3183]

5.2.3 Gaps and Problems with Current E-Commerce Marketplace Platform Trademark Terms and Policies

From the above, it can be seen that each of these e-commerce marketplace platforms has its own rules, trademark terms and policies, and FAQs or otherwise elaborate on trademarks. While some of these rules are the same or similar, others differ and coverage is not the same. Table 5.1 summarises the various elements of the Digital Trademark and Trade Practices Model that are incorporated by each of the e-commerce marketplace platforms in their terms or policies and which are not directly or adequately covered. The UDRP is also listed for ease of reference and comparison. This is followed by a discussion of each element relating to the policy.

3177. *Ibid.*
3178. *Ibid.*
3179. *Ibid.*
3180. eBay, 'User Agreement' (*eBay Customer Service*) https://www.ebay.com/help/policies/member-behaviour-policies/user-agreement?id=4259 accessed June 2025.
3181. eBay, 'Forgeries, Replicas and Unauthorized Copies Policy' (*eBay NL*) https://www.ebay.nl/help/policies/prohibited-restricted-items/fake-items-policy?id=4276 accessed June 2025.
3182. *Ibid.*
3183. *Ibid.*

Table 5.1 Digital Trademark and Trade Practices Model, UDRP, and E-Commerce Marketplace Platform Terms and Policies

Digital Trademark and Trade Practices Model	*UDRP*	*Amazon.com Amazon.nl*	*eBay.com eBay.nl*
Digital Use and Place of Use	Only some coverage. Any use of registered or unregistered marks in domain names which violate the policy.[3184]	Only some coverage. Use in Amazon When complaining about others using a mark, a trademark registration number is required.[3185]	Only some coverage. Use in eBay When complaining about others using a mark, a trademark registration number is required.[3186]
Digital Bad Faith and Abuse	'Registration and use of a domain name in bad faith'[3187] (abuse is covered in overview).[3188]	Only some coverage. Amazon.com Conditions of Use and Amazon.nl Conditions of Use and Sale: repeat infringer are terminated 'in appropriate circumstances'.[3189]	Only some coverage. eBay.com VeRO Policy: 'Removing the listing or other content, issuing a warning, restricting activity or account suspension.'[3190]
Digital Confusion	'Confusing similarity' in domain names.[3191]	Amazon.com IP Policy: 'listings that violate the intellectual property rights of brands or other rights owners'.[3192] Under Amazon.com FAQs general statement: 'Generally, trademark law protects sellers of goods and services from customer	Only some coverage. Under eBay.com and eBay.nl: items or listings that infringe intellectual property.[3193]

Digital Trademark and Trade Practices Model	*UDRP*	*Amazon.com Amazon.nl*	*eBay.com eBay.nl*
		confusion … or a confusingly similar mark, if using the mark is likely to cause a customer to be confused …'[3194] Amazon IP Policy: 'for goods or services that are similar to that of the registered mark if it is likely that customers could be confused (even if the mark used is not identical but only similar)'.[3195]	'unlawful use of trademark'.[3196] eBay IP Policy: 'Objects with a sign that confusingly resembles a protected trademark.'[3197]
Digital Unfair Competition	Only some coverage. The Overview states that '[a]lso noting the availability of trademark-like protection under certain national legal doctrines (e.g., unfair competition or passing-off) and considerations of parity, where acquired distinctiveness/secondary meaning is demonstrated in a particular UDRP case, unregistered rights have been found to support standing to	Only some coverage. Amazon.nl IP Policy: 'has reputation in the relevant territory and where use of that same or a similar mark without due cause takes unfair advantage of, or is detrimental to, the distinctive character or the repute of the owner's mark'.[3198] Amazon.com and Amazon.nl Community Guidelines: 'Impersonate someone or an organization'[3199]	Only some coverage. eBay.nl user Agreement: 'You indemnify eBay against any and all financial consequences of actions, claims or oppositions by persons claiming intellectual property rights in the Content, from claims of unfair and/or parasitic competition …'.[3200]

Digital Trademark and Trade Practices Model	*UDRP*	*Amazon.com Amazon.nl*	*eBay.com eBay.nl*
	proceed with a UDRP case including where the complainant is based in a civil law jurisdiction'.[3201] Unfair advantage considerations may fall under bad faith and abuse (*see* Overview).[3202] 'Distinctiveness' and 'secondary meaning' isrecognized in Overview along with a list of factors that may be considered.[3203] 'Secondary meaning'[3204] is covered in the Overview. Overview also states that 'the strength of the complainant's mark may be considered relevant in evaluating the second and third elements'[3205] of the UDRP.	Amazon.com and Amazon.nl Reporting Form: counterfeit report 'requires a federally registered trademark ... [c]ommon law and [p]ending trademark applications' are not sufficient.[3206] Amazon.com FAQs: 'Counterfeiting is a specific type of trademark infringement ... an unlawful total or partial reproduction ... very similar to a registered trademark in connection with the sale of a product that does not come from the trademark holder' ... 'An item that looks like or is identical to a trademarked item is not counterfeit if the item is sold on a separate product detail page and does not improperly use a registered trademark ...'.[3207]	eBay.com and eBay.nl 'Verified Rights Owner (VeRO) Program': 'Counterfeit or replica items.'[3208] Reporting form reason code: '1.1 Item(s) is a counterfeit product which infringes a trademark'[3209] eBay.nl IP Policy: 'illegal copy of ("counterfeits," "product piracy") ... 'use of slightly changed brand names ... if it wrongly gives the impression that the offer or object may come from the rights holder of the trademark ... may also be infringed if the goods are expressly marked as copies in the offer'.[3210]

Digital Trademark and Trade Practices Model	*UDRP*	*Amazon.com Amazon.nl*	*eBay.com eBay.nl*
		Amazon.nl: 'lookalike products may infringe upon trademark or other intellectual property rights, such as copyright or design rights, or constitute (in some countries) unfair competition/passing off'.[3211] Amazon.com's Anti-Counterfeiting Policy: 'Products offered for sale on Amazon must be authentic … sale of non-authentic products is strictly prohibited … products that are not legal for sale, such as products that have been illegally replicated, reproduced, or manufactured … Bootlegs, fakes, or pirated copies of products or content … illegally replicated, reproduced, or manufactured'[3212]	eBay.nl selling policies: 'infringe on third party trademarks … Copied, counterfeit or counterfeit goods under a protected trademark … Objects with a sign that confusingly resembles a protected trademark (including on packaging, if applicable) … Original products not marketed in the European Economic Area with the consent of the trademark holder (parallel import) … Misleading or excessive use of a protected trademark in the case of accessories or spare parts … Use of a protected trademark to falsely create the impression that there is an economic or organizational

Digital Trademark and Trade Practices Model	*UDRP*	*Amazon.com Amazon.nl*	*eBay.com eBay.nl*
			connection with the trademark holder (for example, via information about the seller account) … Use of a protected trademark for false comparative advertising … Abuse, defamation or unfair exploitation of the reputation of a well-known trademark … Misleading use of a trademark as a keyword'[3213] eBay.nl User Agreement: 'sell counterfeit items'.[3214] eBay.nl Counterfeit Item Policy: 'Counterfeit objects, replicas and unauthorized copies of protected original objects'.[3215] 'Counterfeit products are illegal … may infringe on the … trademark of others … [e]xamples … replica of a

Digital Trademark and Trade Practices Model	*UDRP*	*Amazon.com Amazon.nl*	*eBay.com eBay.nl*
			handbag, a watch or sneakers that are an imitation of a protected look, even if the original brand is not indicated'.[3216] 'Replicas may also infringe competition law.'[3217]
Digital Terms, Policies, and Disclaimers	Only some coverage. Is itself a uniform policy addressing covered domain names. Disclaimers have been treated briefly in Overview. In cases 'where the respondent appears to otherwise have a right or legitimate interest in a disputed domain name, a clear and sufficiently prominent disclaimer would lend support to circumstances suggesting its good faith'.[3218]	Generally or not directly covered. Trademark-related policies are contained in various documents.	Generally or not directly covered. Trademark-related policies are contained in various documents. 'Trademark infringement may also occur if the goods are expressly identified as copies in the offer'[3219] and this type of disclaimer may not work (and may even work against the seller)
Digital Jurisdictional and Territorial Considerations	Only some coverage. Changes to a domain name may be made based on court or arbitral tribunal of competent jurisdiction.[3220]	Generally or not directly covered.	Only some coverage. Slightly different terms may apply in between eBay.com and eBay.nl.

Digital Trademark and Trade Practices Model	*UDRP*	*Amazon.com Amazon.nl*	*eBay.com eBay.nl*
	Overview states that 'rules and principles of law'[3221] may be considered (this is discretionary); however, 'in its own terms UDRP jurisprudence generally would not require resort to particular national laws'.[3222] For example, guidance indicates that where 'the parties share a common nationality and the import of a specific national law concept is particularly germane to an issue in dispute, panels have applied national law principles in assessing the UDRP elements'.[3223] Otherwise, the UDRP applies regardless of where domain is registered or used.	Slightly different terms may apply in between Amazon.com and Amazon.nl.	eBay.nl IP Policy: 'branded goods have been placed on the market in the European Economic Area by the right holder or with the permission of the right holder, they may be resold within the European Economic Area without further permission. However, a rights holder may have legitimate reasons to object ... for example if the condition of the goods has changed or if the goods have been damaged after the rights holder has placed them on the market'.[3224] eBay.nl: 'eBay may take action in accordance with applicable law and the User Agreement from eBay. In some cases, eBay is even required to do so by law'.[3225]

Digital Trademark and Trade Practices Model	*UDRP*	*Amazon.com Amazon.nl*	*eBay.com eBay.nl*
Digital Justification	Only some coverage. Using marks for 'legitimate noncommercial or fair use'[3226] is recognized as a method to demonstrate 'rights and legitimate interests'.[3227] Fair use and freedom of speech are also covered in the Overview.[3228]	Only some coverage. Amazon.com Intellectual Property Policy for Sellers – FAQ about Trademarks: may be used if 'selling authentic goods'[3229] when 'using the trademark to identify an authentic product'[3230] or where used 'in its ordinary dictionary meaning'[3231] or for purposes of 'making truthful statements that a product is compatible with a trademarked product'[3232] (although logo use in this manner is not permitted).[3233] Further, a specific formatting may be required while factoring in the Amazon Brand Name Policy, or the listing may be removed.[3234] Similar policy for Amazon.nl, but Amazon.nl's Amazon Intellectual	Only some coverage. eBay.nl IP Policy: 'rightholder may have legitimate grounds for objecting to the sale, for example, if the condition of the goods has changed or if the goods have been damaged after the right holder has placed them on the market'.[3235]

Digital Trademark and Trade Practices Model	*UDRP*	*Amazon.com Amazon.nl*	*eBay.com eBay.nl*
		Property Policy: 'ordinary dictionary' is followed by 'descriptive meaning'.[3236] Also, in point c above, the statement 'Any statement you make about compatibility must be true' is followed by ', and relevant for the customer's purchase decision (for example, if your product is actually compatible with all competitor products, it is not permissible to use the brands of these products, as the customer is not at risk of buying the "wrong" product without the compatibility statement). "Similar to" claims (such as stating that goods are "similar to Kindle" or "equivalent to Find") may infringe trademark law, depending on the store and circumstances. Seek legal counsel before making such comparisons'.[3237]	

Digital Trademark and Trade Practices Model	*UDRP*	*Amazon.com Amazon.nl*	*eBay.com eBay.nl*
		Amazon.com Intellectual Property Policy for Sellers – FAQ about Trademarks: 'looks like or is identical to a trademarked item is not counterfeit if the item is sold on a separate product detail page and does not improperly use a registered trademark …'.[3238]	

3184. ICANN, 'Uniform Domain-Name Dispute-Resolution Policy' (*ICANN*, 25 February 2012) https://www.icann.org/resources/pages/policy-2012-02-25-en accessed June 2025; WIPO, 'WIPO Overview of WIPO Panel Views on Selected UDRP Questions, Third Edition' ('WIPO Jurisprudential Overview 3.0') (*WIPO*, 2017) https://www.wipo.int/amc/en/domains/search/overview3.0/ accessed June 2025.
3185. Amazon, 'Using the Report Infringement Form' (*Amazon Seller Central*) https://sellercentral.amazon.com/help/hub/reference/external/GJFZJ63CR5BRSNAY accessed June 2025; Amazon.nl, 'Using the Report Infringement Form' (*Amazon.nl Seller Central*) https://sellercentral.amazon.nl/help/hub/reference/external/GJFZJ63CR5BRSNAY?locale = en-US accessed June 2025.
3186. eBay, 'Notice of Claimed Infringement', (*eBay*) https://ir.ebaystatic.com/pictures/aw/pics/pdf/us/help/community/EN-NOCI.pdf accessed June 2025.
3187. UDRP, 4(b).
3188. WIPO, 'WIPO Overview of WIPO Panel Views on Selected UDRP Questions, Third Edition' ('WIPO Jurisprudential Overview 3.0') (*WIPO*, 2017) https://www.wipo.int/amc/en/domains/search/overview3.0/ accessed June 2025.
3189. Amazon, 'Conditions of Use' (*Amazon*) https://www.amazon.com/gp/help/customer/display.html?nodeId = 508088&ref_ = footer_cou accessed June 2025.
3190. eBay, 'Verified Rights Owner (VeRO) Policy' (*eBay*) https://www.ebay.com/help/policies/listing-policies/selling-policies/intellectual-property-vero-program?id = 4349 accessed June 2025.
3191. UDRP, 4(a)(i).
3192. Amazon, 'Amazon Intellectual Property Policy' (*Amazon Seller Central*) https://sellercentral.amazon.nl/help/hub/reference/external/G201361070? accessed June 2025.
3193. eBay, 'Verified Rights Owner Program' (*eBay*) https://www.ebay.com/sellercenter/ebay-for-business/verified-rights-owner-program#m17-1-tb2 accessed June 2025.
3194. Amazon, 'Intellectual Property Policy for Sellers: FAQ about Trademarks' (*Amazon*) https://sellercentral.amazon.com/help/hub/reference/external/GZUQ6GBBXQVHQKF2 accessed June 2025.
3195. Amazon, 'Amazon Intellectual Property Policy' (*Amazon Seller Central*) https://sellercentral.amazon.nl/help/hub/reference/external/G201361070?locale = en-US accessed June 2025.

3196. eBay, 'Notice of Claimed Infringement', (*eBay*) https://ir.ebaystatic.com/pictures/aw/pics/pdf/us/help/community/EN-NOCI.pdf accessed June 2025.
3197. eBay, 'Intellectual Property Policy' (*eBay*) https://www.ebay.nl/help/policies/listing-policies/selling-policies/vero-policy?id=4349 accessed June 2025.
3198. Amazon, 'Amazon Intellectual Property Policy' (*Amazon Seller Central*) https://sellercentral.amazon.nl/help/hub/reference/external/G201361070?locale=en-US accessed June 2025.
3199. Amazon.nl, 'Community Guidelines' (*Amazon.nl Amazon Community*) https://www.amazon.nl/-/en/gp/help/customer/display.html?nodeId=GLHXEX85MENUE4XF accessed June 2025.
3200. eBay, 'User Agreement' (*eBay Customer Service*) https://www.ebay.nl/help/policies/member-behaviour-policies/user-agreement?id=4259 accessed June 2025.
3201. WIPO, 'WIPO Overview of WIPO Panel Views on Selected UDRP Questions, Third Edition' ('WIPO Jurisprudential Overview 3.0') (*WIPO*, 2017) https://www.wipo.int/amc/en/domains/search/overview3.0/ accessed June 2025.
3202. *Ibid.*
3203. *Ibid.*
3204. *Ibid.*
3205. *Ibid.*
3206. Amazon, 'Using the Report Infringement Form' (*Amazon Seller Central*) https://sellercentral.amazon.com/help/hub/reference/external/GJFZJ63CR5BRSNAY accessed June 2025; Amazom.nl, 'Using the Report Infringement Form' (*Amazon.nl Seller Central*) https://sellercentral.amazon.nl/help/hub/reference/external/GJFZJ63CR5BRSNAY?locale=en-US accessed June 2025.
3207. Amazon, 'Intellectual Property Policy for Sellers: FAQ about Trademarks' (*Amazon*) https://sellercentral.amazon.com/help/hub/reference/external/GZUQ6GBBXQVHQKF2 accessed June 2025.
3208. eBay, 'Verified Rights Owner Program' (*eBay*) https://www.ebay.com/sellercenter/ebay-for-business/verified-rights-owner-program#m17-1-tb2 accessed June 2025.
3209. eBay, 'Notice of Claimed Infringement', (*eBay*) https://ir.ebaystatic.com/pictures/aw/pics/pdf/us/help/community/EN-NOCI.pdf accessed June 2025.
3210. eBay, 'Intellectual Property Policy' (*eBay*) https://www.ebay.nl/help/policies/listing-policies/selling-policies/vero-policy?id=4349 accessed June 2025.
3211. Amazon, 'Amazon Intellectual Property Policy' (*Amazon Seller Central*) https://sellercentral.amazon.nl/help/hub/reference/external/G201361070?locale=en-US accessed June 2025.
3212. Amazon, 'Amazon Anti-Counterfeiting Policy' (*Amazon Seller Central*) https://sellercentral.amazon.com/help/hub/reference/external/G201165970 accessed June 2025.
3213. *Ibid.*
3214. eBay.nl, 'User Agreement' (*ebay.nl*) https://www.ebay.nl/help/policies/member-behaviour-policies/user-agreement?id=4259 accessed June 2025.
3215. eBay, 'Counterfeits, Replicas and Unauthorized Copies Policy' (*eBay NL*) https://www.ebay.nl/help/policies/prohibited-restricted-items/fake-items-policy?id=4276 accessed June 2025.
3216. *Ibid.*
3217. *Ibid.*
3218. WIPO, 'WIPO Overview of WIPO Panel Views on Selected UDRP Questions, Third Edition' ('WIPO Jurisprudential Overview 3.0') (*WIPO*, 2017) https://www.wipo.int/amc/en/domains/search/overview3.0/ accessed June 2025.
3219. eBay, 'Intellectual property policy' (*eBay*) https://www.ebay.nl/help/policies/listing-policies/selling-policies/vero-policy?id=4349 accessed June 2025.
3220. ICANN, 'Uniform Domain-Name Dispute-Resolution Policy' (*ICANN*, 25 February 2012) https://www.icann.org/resources/pages/policy-2012-02-25-en accessed June 2025.

3221. WIPO, 'WIPO Overview of WIPO Panel Views on Selected UDRP Questions, Third Edition' ('WIPO Jurisprudential Overview 3.0') (*WIPO*, 2017) https://www.wipo.int/amc/en/domains/search/overview3.0/ accessed June 2025.
3222. *Ibid.*
3223. *Ibid.*
3224. eBay, 'Intellectual Property Policy' (*eBay*) https://www.ebay.nl/help/policies/listing-policies/selling-policies/vero-policy?id=4349 accessed June 2025.
3225. eBay, 'Counterfeits, Replicas and Unauthorized Copies Policy' (*eBay NL*) https://www.ebay.nl/help/policies/prohibited-restricted-items/fake-items-policy?id=4276 accessed June 2025.
3226. WIPO, 'WIPO Overview of WIPO Panel Views on Selected UDRP Questions, Third Edition' ('WIPO Jurisprudential Overview 3.0') (*WIPO*, 2017) https://www.wipo.int/amc/en/domains/search/overview3.0/ accessed June 2025.
3227. *Ibid.*
3228. *Ibid.*
3229. Amazon, 'Intellectual Property Policy for Sellers: FAQ about Trademarks' (*Amazon*) https://sellercentral.amazon.com/help/hub/reference/external/GZUQ6GBBXQVHQKF2 accessed June 2025.
3230. *Ibid.*
3231. *Ibid.*
3232. *Ibid.*
3233. *Ibid.*
3234. *Ibid.*
3235. eBay, 'Intellectual Property Policy' (*eBay*) https://www.ebay.nl/help/policies/listing-policies/selling-policies/vero-policy?id=4349 accessed June 2025.
3236. Amazon, 'Amazon Intellectual Property Policy' (*Amazon Seller Central*) https://sellercentral.amazon.nl/help/hub/reference/external/G201361070?locale=en-US accessed June 2025.
3237. *Ibid.*
3238. Amazon, 'Intellectual Property Policy for Sellers: FAQ about Trademarks' (*Amazon*) https://sellercentral.amazon.com/help/hub/reference/external/GZUQ6GBBXQVHQKF2 accessed June 2025.

As seen from the table above, several areas are not directly or adequately addressed by e-commerce marketplace platforms when applying the elements of the model and the considerations raised for platforms in Chapter 3.

5.2.3.1 Digital Use and Place of Use

E-Commerce marketplace platforms cover trademarks utilised within their services. There is no direct mention of use 'in the course of trade'[3239] or likewise, although most such activity is likely to be, considering the nature of an e-commerce marketplace platform. The place of use[3240] may be within listings, on product pages, or advertising; however, this is not clearly identified. When complaining about others using a mark,

3239. TRIPS, Art. 16.
3240. WIPO, 'WIPO Overview of WIPO Panel Views on Selected UDRP Questions, Third Edition' ('WIPO Jurisprudential Overview 3.0') (*WIPO*, 2017) https://www.wipo.int/amc/en/domains/search/overview3.0/ accessed June 2025.

a trademark registration number is required,[3241] which does not necessarily factor in use-based rights.[3242]

5.2.3.2 *Digital Bad Faith and Abuse*

The platforms do not directly or adequately address bad faith[3243] in the context presented by the model. Amazon does cover abuse[3244] in the form of addressing 'repeat infringers'.[3245] eBay.nl covers 'abuse'[3246] in the unfair context, as will be seen below.[3247] However, these should be directly and specifically included by the platforms in the context of the model, such as repeated bad faith[3248] constituting abuse.[3249]

5.2.3.3 *Digital Confusion*

A general infringement prohibition is stated by both platforms.[3250] While Amazon.com describes 'customer confusion ... or a confusingly similar mark ... likely to cause a customer to be confused'[3251] in FAQs,[3252] Amazon.nl incorporates it briefly in their IP policy as 'potential customer confusion'.[3253] eBay incorporates 'confusingly similar'[3254] and restricts this to registered trademarks.[3255] The language and where it sits across

3241. Amazon, 'Using the Report Infringement Form' (*Amazon Seller Central*) https://sellercentral .amazon.com/help/hub/reference/external/GJFZJ63CR5BRSNAY accessed June 2025; Amazom.nl, 'Using the Report Infringement Form' (*Amazon.nl Seller Central*) https:// sellercentral.amazon.nl/help/hub/reference/external/GJFZJ63CR5BRSNAY?locale = en-US accessed June 2025; eBay, 'Notice of Claimed Infringement', (eBay) https://ir.ebaystatic.com /pictures/aw/pics/pdf/us/help/community/EN-NOCI.pdf accessed June 2025.
3242. TRIPS, Art. 16; EUTMR, Art. 18; 15 U.S. Code § 1127; UK Trade Marks Act 1994, s. 46(1)(a); Canadian Trademarks Act R.S.C., 1985, c. T-13, s. 2.
3243. UDRP, 4(a)(iii).
3244. Amazon, 'Conditions of Use' (*Amazon*) https://www.amazon.com/gp/help/customer/ display.html?nodeId = 508088&ref_ = footer_cou accessed June 2025.
3245. *Ibid.*
3246. eBay, 'Intellectual Property Policy' (*eBay*) https://www.ebay.nl/help/policies/listing-policies /selling-policies/vero-policy?id = 4349 accessed June 2025.
3247. *Ibid.*
3248. *Ibid.*
3249. WIPO, 'WIPO Overview of WIPO Panel Views on Selected UDRP Questions, Third Edition' ('WIPO Jurisprudential Overview 3.0') (*WIPO*, 2017) https://www.wipo.int/amc/en/ domains/search/overview3.0/ accessed June 2025.
3250. Amazon, 'Amazon Intellectual Property Policy' (*Amazon Seller Central*) https://sellercentral. amazon.nl/help/hub/reference/external/G201361070? accessed June 2025; eBay, 'Verified Rights Owner Program' (*eBay*) https://www.ebay.com/sellercenter/ebay-for-business/ verified-rights-owner-program#m17-1-tb2 accessed June 2025.
3251. Amazon, 'Intellectual Property Policy for Sellers: FAQ about Trademarks' (*Amazon*) https:/ /sellercentral.amazon.com/help/hub/reference/external/GZUQ6GBBXQVHQKF2 accessed June 2025.
3252. *Ibid.*
3253. eBay, 'Intellectual Property Policy' (*eBay*) https://www.ebay.nl/help/policies/listing-policies /selling-policies/vero-policy?id = 4349 accessed June 2025.
3254. *Ibid.*
3255. *Ibid.*

platforms in this context is not entirely the same, although confusion[3256] is covered in some way by these platforms. Further guidance should be available on how to assess this.

5.2.3.4 Digital Unfair Competition

This element appears to have wider coverage from the perspective of counterfeit[3257] items, an obvious problem for e-commerce marketplace platforms. Amazon.com describes it in their policy FAQs as 'infringement',[3258] 'an unlawful total or partial reproduction'.[3259] Amazon.nl, however, covers 'lookalike products'[3260] and such actions as may 'constitute (in some countries) unfair competition/passing off'.[3261] The policies use some similar but some entirely different language. Amazon's Anti-Counterfeiting Policy which requires goods to be 'authentic'[3262] and those which are 'illegally replicated, reproduced, or manufactured ... Bootlegs, fakes, or pirated copies of products or content ... reproduced, or manufactured'[3263] are not permitted. eBay, but under VeRO, covers 'counterfeit or replica items';[3264] 'counterfeit' is also part of the reporting form[3265] and is also in the eBay.com IP Policy,[3266] eBay.nl Selling policies,[3267] eBay.nl User Agreement,[3268] and eBay.nl Counterfeit Item Policy[3269] with various descriptions for each. It further requires indemnity from claims of 'unfair and/or parasitic competition ...'.[3270]

The Amazon.nl IP Policy covers 'reputation in the relevant territory and where use of that same or a similar mark without due cause takes unfair advantage of, or is

3256. Paris Convention, Art. 6bis; TRIPS, Art. 16(1); EUTMR, Art. 8(1)(b) and Art. 9(2)(b); 15 U.S. Code § 1114;15 U.S. Code § 1125.
3257. Amazon, 'Intellectual Property Policy for Sellers: FAQ about Trademarks' (*Amazon*) https://sellercentral.amazon.com/help/hub/reference/external/GZUQ6GBBXQVHQKF2 accessed June 2025.
3258. *Ibid.*
3259. *Ibid.*
3260. Amazon, 'Amazon Intellectual Property Policy' (*Amazon Seller Central*) https://sellercentral.amazon.nl/help/hub/reference/external/G201361070?locale=en-US accessed June 2025.
3261. *Ibid.*
3262. *Ibid.*
3263. *Ibid.*
3264. eBay, 'Verified Rights Owner Program' (*eBay*) https://www.ebay.com/sellercenter/ebay-for-business/verified-rights-owner-program#m17-1-tb2 accessed June 2025.
3265. eBay, 'Notice of Claimed Infringement', (*eBay*) https://ir.ebaystatic.com/pictures/aw/pics/pdf/us/help/community/EN-NOCI.pdf accessed June 2025.
3266. eBay, 'Intellectual Property Policy' (*eBay*) https://www.ebay.nl/help/policies/listing-policies/selling-policies/vero-policy?id=4349 accessed June 2025.
3267. *Ibid.*
3268. eBay.nl, 'User Agreement' (*ebay.nl*) https://www.ebay.nl/help/policies/member-behaviour-policies/user-agreement?id=4259 accessed June 2025.
3269. eBay, 'Forgeries, Replicas and Unauthorized Copies Policy' (*eBay NL*) https://www.ebay.nl/help/policies/prohibited-restricted-items/fake-items-policy?id=4276 accessed June 2025.
3270. eBay, 'User Agreement' (*eBay Customer Service*) https://www.ebay.nl/help/policies/member-behaviour-policies/user-agreement?id=4259 accessed June 2025.

detrimental to, the distinctive character or the repute of the owner's mark'.[3271] eBay.nl covers the concepts of reputation and well-known by prohibiting: '[a]buse, defamation or unfair exploitation of the reputation of a well-known trademark …'.[3272]

While coverage for specific aspects of unfair acts, etc.,[3273] are included, these are not consistent or located in a single policy.

5.2.3.5 *Digital Terms, Policies, and Disclaimers*

While the terms and policies of e-commerce marketplace platforms form at least one major source of how trademarks might be utilised and regulated within the platform, trademark provisions are in various different places or policies and terms and FAQs.

Disclaimers[3274] are not adequately covered by these e-commerce marketplace platforms. For example, the effect of disclaimers[3275] is not mentioned. eBay.nl's selling policy mentions there 'may also be infringement on trademarks if the goods are expressly marked as a copy in the offer'.[3276] This alludes to a possible disclaimer (of sorts), the term 'copy'[3277] within a listing, which is clearly ineffective because of the potential illegal nature of the product being listed.

5.2.3.6 *Digital Jurisdictional and Territorial Considerations*

E-Commerce marketplace platforms are one of the few types of platforms that have various platforms dedicated to specific countries; however, not all countries are included, as some sites are applicable to different regions. For example, the eBay.nl IP Policy covers the permissible resale of goods within the European Economic Area,

3271. Amazon, 'Amazon Intellectual Property Policy' (*Amazon Seller Central*) https://sellercentral.amazon.nl/help/hub/reference/external/G201361070?locale=en-US accessed June 2025.
3272. eBay, 'Intellectual Property Policy' (*eBay*) https://www.ebay.nl/help/policies/listing-policies/selling-policies/vero-policy?id=4349 accessed June 2025.
3273. Anselm Kamperman Sanders, *Unfair Competition Law: The Protection of Intellectual and Industrial Creativity* (Oxford University Press, 1997) 8; Frauke Henning-Bodewig, *Unfair Competition Law European Union and Member States* (Kluwer Law International 2006) xv-xvi; Martin Senftleben, Michael Handler and Irene Calboli, 'Protection Against Unfair Competition Around the Globe' (2024) 19 Journal of Intellectual Property Law & Practice 79, 79-80 https://doi.org/10.1093/jiplp/jpad121; Paris Convention, Art. 10bis; EUTMR, Art. 9(2)(c); 15 U.S.C. § 1125(c)(2)(B).
3274. WIPO, 'WIPO Overview of WIPO Panel Views on Selected UDRP Questions, Third Edition' ('WIPO Jurisprudential Overview 3.0') (*WIPO*, 2017) https://www.wipo.int/amc/en/domains/search/overview3.0/ accessed June 2025; Alexander Peukert, 'The Coexistence of Trade Mark Laws and Rights on the Internet, and the Impact of Geolocation Technologies' (2016) 47 International Review of Intellectual Property and Competition Law 60, 81 https://doi.org/10.1007/s40319-015-0427-8; Leslie Fair, 'Full Disclosure' (*FTC Business Blog*, 23 September 2014) https://www.ftc.gov/business-guidance/blog/2014/09/full-disclosure accessed June 2025.
3275. *Ibid.*
3276. eBay, 'Intellectual Property Policy' (*eBay*) https://www.ebay.nl/help/policies/listing-policies/selling-policies/vero-policy?id=4349 accessed June 2025.
3277. *Ibid.*

subject to legitimate objection,[3278] although several EU country-specific sites are available.[3279] Non trademark-related matters may be dealt with through jurisdiction or territorial-specific terms; however, trademark aspects could be uniformly implemented. Co-existence[3280] is not identified.

5.2.3.7 Digital Justification

Justifications are covered to a larger extent by Amazon than eBay, as seen in the previous section. For example, it covers selling, under certain circumstances or requirements, 'authentic goods',[3281] 'compatible products',[3282] or using the 'ordinary dictionary meaning',[3283] or 'descriptive meaning'[3284] and a listing on a separate product page of an item that 'looks like'[3285] but does not 'improperly use a registered trademark'.[3286] eBay provides limited information on justifications. Various further or potential justifications and defences are not covered by these e-commerce marketplace platforms.

Overall, while some elements such as counterfeit[3287] products are covered extensively, there are areas, as was seen above, where there is no direct or adequate coverage for key elements. It is further contemplated that if an issue were to arise on both e-commerce marketplace platforms, there is potential for a different result or decision by each. This could result even from similar terms if no guidance is provided, or from those terms which are different. This may result in inconsistent decisions and lack of legal certainty. Further, decisions are not generally public, barring those

3278. *Ibid.*
3279. Amazon, 'Website (Country/Region)' (*Amazon*) https://www.amazon.com/customer-preferences/country? accessed June 2025.
3280. EUIPO, '3.1 Coexistence Between the Marks Involved in the Opposition' (*EUIPO Trade mark Guidelines*) https://guidelines.euipo.europa.eu/2058843/2043906/trade-mark-guidelines/3-1-coexistence-between-the-marks-involved-in-the-opposition accessed January 2024;15 U.S. Code § 1052(d); Alexander Peukert, 'The Coexistence of Trade Mark Laws and Rights on the Internet, and the Impact of Geolocation Technologies' (2016) 47 International Review of Intellectual Property and Competition Law 60, 81 https://doi.org/10.1007/s40319-015-0427-8; Tamara Nanayakkara, 'IP and Business: Trademark Coexistence' (*WIPO*, November 2006) https://www.wipo.int/wipo_magazine/en/2006/06/article_0007.html accessed December 2024.
3281. Amazon, 'Intellectual Property Policy for Sellers: FAQ about Trademarks' (*Amazon*) https://sellercentral.amazon.com/help/hub/reference/external/GZUQ6GBBXQVHQKF2 accessed June 2025.
3282. *Ibid.*
3283. *Ibid.*
3284. Amazon, 'Amazon Intellectual Property Policy' (*Amazon Seller Central*) https://sellercentral.amazon.nl/help/hub/reference/external/G201361070?locale=en-US accessed June 2025.
3285. Amazon, 'Intellectual Property Policy for Sellers: FAQ about Trademarks' (*Amazon*) https://sellercentral.amazon.com/help/hub/reference/external/GZUQ6GBBXQVHQKF2 accessed June 2025.
3286. *Ibid.*
3287. *Ibid.*; eBay, 'Forgeries, Replicas and Unauthorized Copies Policy' (*eBay NL*) https://www.ebay.nl/help/policies/prohibited-restricted-items/fake-items-policy?id=4276 accessed June 2025.

utilising trademarks within these platforms, to know how decisions are made causing legal uncertainty.

5.2.4 Solution: A Uniform Policy for Trademarks in E-Commerce Marketplace Platforms

E-Commerce is no stranger to Online Dispute Resolution (ODR).[3288] In fact, as noted by Rule, eBay was an early adopter of resolution through online means.[3289] Under the Digital Trademark and Trade Practices Model, it is recommended that e-commerce marketplace platforms adopt a uniform policy in line with the adapted UDRP (UDNDRP). In fact, back in 2002, just a short time after the UDRP was born, Anderson and Cole studied whether such approach was appropriate for e-commerce.[3290] They concluded that if cost considerations, enforceability with little 'outside intervention',[3291] and a 'mechanism'[3292] to bring this under ADR processes could be implemented, this could be a possible solution to look into further.[3293] While years have gone by since, the UDRP still stands as a successful procedure to quickly resolve domain disputes, and despite changes in e-commerce since then, it is argued that there is huge potential for a UDRP-like approach for e-commerce marketplace platforms.

Generally, e-commerce marketplace platforms have similar considerations with respect to trademarks in their platforms. Uniform rules will provide the basis for legal certainty and streamline the process for deciding complaints. For example, sellers marketing across these platforms may be permitted to, or face the same consequences of trademark utilisation between platforms, enhancing consistency. Further, this will provide an opportunity to clearly incorporate provisions which are not included and avoid legal uncertainty. As seen in the previous section, there are differences in coverage, terminology, application, and place where rules are addressed by the platforms. A uniform policy will alleviate the concerns that flow from these problems. Even where business models differ, such as Amazon selling its own goods or goods of others, this does not change the commonality of issues between platforms. If absolutely required, although it is argued that this is not necessary, country-specific rules may be supplemented, but not encouraged, in favour of uniform rules. Any peculiarities may also be dealt with through guidance while maintaining a uniform[3294] policy.

A recommended uniform policy is presented below in line with the adapted UDRP (UDNDRP) as seen in Chapter 4. However, before delving into the specific policy, it is important to consider how it could be implemented. Generally, there are two recommended ways a uniform policy can be adopted by e-commerce platforms,

3288. Colin Rule, 'Online Dispute Resolution and the Future of Justice' 16 Annual Review of Law and Social Science 277, 288 https://doi.org/10.1146/annurev-lawsocsci-101518-043049.
3289. *Ibid.*
3290. Edward C Anderson and Timothy S Cole, 'The UDRP: A Model for Dispute Resolution in E-Commerce' (2002) 6 Journal of Small & Emerging Business Law 235.
3291. *Ibid.*
3292. *Ibid.*
3293. *Ibid.*
3294. *Ibid.*

but as will be seen throughout the rest of this chapter, this can also be applied to all platforms:

(1) Platforms can individually adopt a uniform policy, implement it, and make their own decisions on complaints as they come in. Essentially, a set uniform policy will alleviate the need for platforms to come up with their own policies, will promote consistency, be comprehensive because it covers key elements of trademark disputes, and will set the stage for what may become a recognised uniform policy among various platforms in the future. Any individual e-commerce platform may adopt the uniform policy and is encouraged to do so by replacing their own with the text of what is shown below, to be displayed on their websites and services and agreed to by those using their services. The drawback here is that there is no central body or neutral third party such as the administrators and decision makers of the UDRP to decide on disputes, and platforms will need to handle these themselves (as they do now).
(2) Another approach is that this policy be adopted by any or various e-commerce platforms in the form administered, such as the UDRP, where panellists make the decisions, administered by WIPO or other bodies through neutral third-party panels. The benefits here are that the platform may only need to adopt the policy and implement the decisions made with a neutral third-party making the decision. The drawbacks here, for the platform, include that the platform will not be the decision maker.

In any of the cases described above, the processes are not intended to bar judicial proceedings, as is the case with the UDRP.

The following is sample text of such uniform trademark policy[3295] for major e-commerce marketplace platforms in line with the first option above, where they adopt the policy on their own and make their own decisions within their service.

Table 5.2 Uniform E-Commerce Marketplace Trademark Dispute Resolution Policy (UEMTDRP)

Uniform E-Commerce Marketplace Trademark Dispute Resolution Policy (UEMTDRP)	Adapted or directly from the UDRP[3296] and UDNDRP. The name reflects specifically the platform type and subject matter.

3295. ICANN, 'Uniform Domain-Name Dispute-Resolution Policy' (*ICANN*, 25 February 2012) https://www.icann.org/resources/pages/policy-2012-02-25-en accessed June 2025.
3296. *Ibid.*

(1) *Purpose.* This Uniform E-Commerce Marketplace Trademark Dispute Resolution Policy ('Policy') has been adopted by [E-Commerce Marketplace Platform] ('Platform' or 'We'), is incorporated by reference into the Terms of Use of Platform and your Seller Registration Agreement, and sets forth the terms and conditions in connection with a dispute between you and any party other than Platform over the utilisation of a trademark in Platform. Decisions under Paragraph 4 of this Policy will be made in accordance with the Policy. Guidelines to this policy are set forth in the document entitled: Guidelines to the UEMTDRP.	Adapted or directly from the UDRP[3297] and UDNDRP (Chapter 4). The policy refers to any disputed utilisation of a mark within the platforms.
(2) *Your Representations.* By creating an account, registering to sell, listing and/or advertising on Platform, you hereby represent and warrant to Platform that (a) the statements that you made in your Seller registration Agreement are complete and accurate; (b) to your knowledge, the listing and/or advertising will not infringe upon or otherwise violate the rights of any third party; (c) you are not registering to sell, listing and/or advertising for an unlawful purpose; and (d) you will not knowingly use Platform in violation of any applicable laws or regulations. It is your responsibility to determine whether your listing and/or advertising infringes or violates someone else's rights.	Adapted or directly from the UDRP[3298] and UDNRDP (Chapter 4).
(3) *Changes, Suspensions, and Cancellations.* We will make changes to, suspend, or cancel your account, listings and/or advertising on Platform under the following circumstances: (i) our receipt of written or appropriate electronic instructions from you or your authorized agent to take such action except that you may not transfer your account to another holder (a) during a pending administrative proceeding brought pursuant to Paragraph 4 or for a period of fifteen (15)	Adapted or directly from the UDRP[3299] and UDNDRP (Chapter 4). Updated based on services.

3297. *Ibid.*
3298. *Ibid.*
3299. *Ibid.*

business days after such proceeding is concluded; or (b) during a pending court proceeding or arbitration commenced regarding your account, listing and/or advertising or their content unless the court or party to whom the account is being transferred agrees, in writing, to be bound by the decision of the court or arbitrator. We reserve the right not to permit the transfer of your account to another party in accordance with this subparagraph; (ii) our receipt of an order from a court or arbitral tribunal, in each case of competent jurisdiction, requiring such action; (iii) our decision requiring such action based on a complaint received under this or a later version of this Policy; and/or (iv) in accordance with the terms of your Seller Registration Agreement (such as but not limited to where you have engaged in abuse with respect to one or more trademarks) or other legal requirements.	Added that 'abuse'[3300] can result in a change, suspension or cancellation and guidelines can be used to clarify when certain actions may take place.
(4) *Mandatory Decision Process and Remedies.* This Paragraph sets forth the type of disputes for which you are required to submit to a Mandatory Decision Process. A decision on a complaint lodged under this Policy will be made by Platform. a. Applicable Disputes. You are required to submit to a decision by Platform in the event that a third party (a 'complainant') asserts to Platform, through a Trademark Complaint Form < URL for Form > that your account, listing and/or advertising or their content: (A) is identical or confusingly similar to trademarks in which a complainant has rights and which you are using on an unauthorised basis in the course of trade AND	Adapted or directly from the UDRP,[3301] UDNDRP (Chapter 4), Paris Convention, TRIPS, Dispute Resolution Service for.eu,[3302]

3300. WIPO, 'WIPO Overview of WIPO Panel Views on Selected UDRP Questions, Third Edition' ('WIPO Jurisprudential Overview 3.0') (*WIPO*, 2017) https://www.wipo.int/amc/en/domains/search/overview3.0/ accessed June 2025.
3301. ICANN, 'Uniform Domain-Name Dispute-Resolution Policy' (*ICANN*, 25 February 2012) https://www.icann.org/resources/pages/policy-2012-02-25-en accessed June 2025.
3302. WIPO, 'WIPO Domain Name Dispute Resolution Service for .EU (and.ею and.ευ)' (*WIPO*) https://www.wipo.int/amc/en/domains/cctld/eu/index.html accessed July 2024.

(B) (i) is being used to engage in unfair competition in the course of trade with respect to a trademark OR (ii) is being used in bad faith or is being abused with respect to a trademark. For clarity, in the administrative proceeding, the complainant must prove element A AND one element from B (either i or ii) are present. (b) Permitted use. Trademarks will be permitted if you demonstrate that you have rights or legitimate interests in respect of your account, listing and/or advertising or their content by showing one or more of these justifications: (i) you (as an individual, business, or other organization) have been commonly known by the term and are using it legitimately (ii) you are making genuine noncommercial legitimate fair use of the trademark, (iii) you are fairly utilising the trademark in marketing of authorized, replacement, compatible or used goods or services, (iv) you are utilising the trademark in an ordinary dictionary sense, (v) you are genuinely and noncommercially utilising the trademark under freedom of speech and expression or legitimate criticism, parody, or review of the company, good or service associated with the trademark, OR (vi) you are making fair and legitimate use of the trademark in comparative advertising. (c) Remedies. The remedies available to a complainant pursuant to any decision by Platform shall be limited to requiring the cancellation of, suspending, or making changes to your account, listing and/or advertising.	EUTMR, Lanham Act 1946 15 U.S. Code §§ 1051 et seq. (as amended), the TDRA 2006 15 U.S. Code §1125(c), Amazon.com, Amazon.nl, eBay.com, eBay.nl trademark policies, terms, and guidelines.[3303] Key UDRP aspects have been retained including relevant concepts from the Overview.[3304] This uniform policy largely follows the UDNDRP (Chapter 4) but is adapted for e-commerce marketplace platforms. Please see Chapter 4 (section 4.3.3) for further details and explanations of the adaptations under the model.

3303. Amazon, 'Intellectual Property Policy for Sellers: FAQ about Trademarks' (*Amazon*) https://sellercentral.amazon.com/help/hub/reference/external/GZUQ6GBBXQVHQKF2 accessed June 2025; eBay, 'Verified Rights Owner (VeRO) Policy' (*eBay*) https://www.ebay.com/help/policies/listing-policies/selling-policies/intellectual-property-vero-program?id=4349 accessed June 2025.

3304. ICANN, 'Uniform Domain-Name Dispute-Resolution Policy' (*ICANN*, 25 February 2012) https://www.icann.org/resources/pages/policy-2012-02-25-en accessed June 2025; WIPO, 'WIPO Overview of WIPO Panel Views on Selected UDRP Questions, Third Edition' ('WIPO Jurisprudential Overview 3.0') (*WIPO*, 2017) https://www.wipo.int/amc/en/domains/search/overview3.0/ accessed June 2025.

(d) All Other Disputes. Any other disputes between you and any party other than Platform regarding your listing and/or advertising in Platform that are not brought pursuant to this Policy will not be resolved through a decision under this Policy. Platform reserves the right to make a decision on any matter outside of this policy as set forth in our Terms of Use available at < terms > including any remedies or actions it, in its sole discretion, deems appropriate.	For e-commerce platforms dedicated to specific jurisdictions, guidance should include that while decisions will be made based on general trademark principles, local law may be considered since the site is targeted to a jurisdiction (similar to the UDRP where local law may be considered, such as when parties are from the same jurisdiction).[3305] This should be the case in special circumstances, but decisions are expected to follow the general principles in most cases.
(5) *Procedures.* (a) Initiation of Proceeding. Submitting a Trade mark Complaint Form initiates the process for a decision by Platform. (b) Consolidation. In the event of multiple disputes between you and a complainant, either you or the complainant may request to consolidate the disputes for a single decision. Platform may consolidate before it any or all such disputes in its sole discretion, provided that the disputes being consolidated are governed by this Policy or a later version of this Policy. (c) Fees. No fees are charged to file a complaint under this Policy or to receive a decision by Platform. (d) Availability of Court Proceedings. The Mandatory Decision Process requirements set forth in Paragraph 4 shall not prevent either you or the complainant from submitting the dispute to a court of competent jurisdiction for independent resolution before such Mandatory Decision Process is commenced or after it is concluded. If we decide that your seller registration, listing and/or advertising should be cancelled, suspended, or changed, we will	Adapted or directly from the UDRP[3306] and UDNDRP (Chapter 4). Platforms may wish to include an indemnification provision here.

3305. WIPO, 'WIPO Overview of WIPO Panel Views on Selected UDRP Questions, Third Edition' ('WIPO Jurisprudential Overview 3.0') (*WIPO*, 2017) https://www.wipo.int/amc/en/domains/search/overview3.0/ accessed June 2025.

3306. ICANN, 'Uniform Domain-Name Dispute-Resolution Policy' (*ICANN*, 25 February 2012) https://www.icann.org/resources/pages/policy-2012-02-25-en accessed June 2025.

then implement the decision immediately unless we have received from you official documentation (such as a copy of a complaint, file-stamped by the clerk of the court) that you have commenced a lawsuit against the complainant in an appropriate jurisdiction. If we receive such documentation immediately following a decision, we will not implement the decision, and we will take no further action, until we receive (i) evidence satisfactory to us of a resolution between the parties; (ii) evidence satisfactory to us that your lawsuit has been dismissed or withdrawn; or (iii) a copy of an order from such court dismissing your lawsuit or ordering that you do not have the right to continue the listing and/or advertising.	
(6) *Policy Modifications*. Platform reserves the right to modify this Policy at any time. Platform will post any revised Policy at <URL> at least thirty (30) calendar days before it becomes effective. Unless this Policy has already been invoked by the submission of a Trade mark Complaint Form, in which event the version of the Policy in effect at the time it was invoked will apply to you until the dispute is over, all such changes will be binding upon you with respect to any listing and/or advertising trademark dispute, whether the dispute arose before, on or after the effective date of our change. In the event that you object to a change in this Policy, your sole remedy is to cancel your Account with us, provided that you will not be entitled to a refund of any fees you paid to us. The revised Policy will apply to you until you cancel your Account.	Adapted or directly from UDRP[3307] and UDNDRP (Chapter 4).

Overall, the above UEMTDRP will serve e-commerce marketplace platforms well because it is based on the UDRP and general trademark principles. How key concepts within the policy may be interpreted should be placed within Guidelines to the policy specific to trademarks in e-commerce marketplace platforms. It is envisioned that these Guidelines will provide a detailed analysis of relevant concepts and how they may be interpreted in line with common principles from the theories, concepts, and select aspects of the legal frameworks under this study. The UEMTDRP is further envisioned to be applicable to many e-commerce marketplace platforms beyond those under this study.

3307. *Ibid.*

The following is sample text of such uniform trademark policy[3308] for major e-commerce marketplace platforms in line with the second option above, where the platform adopts the policy through a UDRP-like approach with an administrative proceeding by panellists. The difference is mainly in the panellist decision-making process with the crux of the policy being identical to the above.

Table 5.3 Uniform E-Commerce Marketplace Trademark Dispute Resolution Policy (UEMTDRP)

Uniform E-Commerce Marketplace Trademark Dispute Resolution Policy (UEMTDRP)	Adapted or directly from the UDRP[3309] and UDNDRP. The name reflects specifically the platform type and subject matter.
(1) *Purpose.* This Uniform E-Commerce Marketplace Trademark Dispute Resolution Policy ('Policy') has been adopted by [E-Commerce Marketplace Platform] ('Platform' or 'We'), is incorporated by reference into the Terms of Use of Platform and your Seller Registration Agreement, and sets forth the terms and conditions in connection with a dispute between you and any party other than Platform over the utilisation of a trademark in Platform. Decisions under Paragraph 4 of this Policy will be made in accordance with the Policy. Guidelines to this policy are set forth in the document entitled: Guidelines to the UEMTDRP.	Adapted or directly from the UDRP[3310] and UDNDRP (Chapter 4). The policy refers to any disputed utilisation of a mark within the platforms.
(2) *Your Representations.* By registering to sell, listing and/or advertising on E-Commerce Marketplace Platform, you hereby represent and warrant to Platform that (a) the statements that you made in your Seller registration Agreement are complete and accurate; (b) to your knowledge, the listing and/or advertising will not infringe upon or otherwise violate the rights of any third party; (c) you are not registering to sell, listing and/or advertising for an unlawful purpose; and (d) you will not knowingly use Platform in violation of any applicable laws or regulations. It is your responsibility to determine whether your listing and/or advertising infringes or violates someone else's rights.	Adapted or directly from the UDRP[3311] and UDNRDP (Chapter 4).

3308. *Ibid.*
3309. *Ibid.*
3310. *Ibid.*
3311. *Ibid.*

(3) *Changes, Suspension, and Cancellations.* We will make changes to, suspend, or cancel your account, listings and/or advertising on Platform under the following circumstances: (i) our receipt of written or appropriate electronic instructions from you or your authorized agent to take such action except that you may not transfer your account to another holder (a) during a pending administrative proceeding brought pursuant to Paragraph 4 or for a period of fifteen (15) business days after such proceeding is concluded; or (b) during a pending court proceeding or arbitration commenced regarding your account, listing and/or advertising or their content unless the court or party to whom the account is being transferred agrees, in writing, to be bound by the decision of the court or arbitrator. We reserve the right not to permit the transfer of your account to another party in accordance with this subparagraph; (ii) our receipt of an order from a court or arbitral tribunal, in each case of competent jurisdiction, requiring such action; (iii) a panel decision requiring such action based on a complaint received under this or a later version of this Policy and/or (iv) in accordance with the terms of your Seller Registration Agreement (such as but not limited to where you have engaged in abuse with respect to one or more trademarks) or other legal requirements.	Adapted or directly from the UDRP[3312] and UDNDRP (Chapter 4). Updated based on services. Added that 'abuse'[3313] can result in a change, suspension or cancellation and guidelines can be used to clarify when certain actions may take place.
(4) *Mandatory Administrative Proceeding and Remedies.* This Paragraph sets forth the type of disputes for which you are required to submit to a mandatory Panel Decision. A decision on a complaint lodged under this Policy will be made by an appointed Panel.	Adapted or directly from the UDRP,[3314] UDNDRP (Chapter 4), Paris Convention, TRIPS, Dispute Resolution Service for.eu,[3315]

3312. *Ibid.*
3313. WIPO, 'WIPO Overview of WIPO Panel Views on Selected UDRP Questions, Third Edition' ('WIPO Jurisprudential Overview 3.0') (*WIPO*, 2017) https://www.wipo.int/amc/en/domains/search/overview3.0/ accessed June 2025.
3314. ICANN, 'Uniform Domain-Name Dispute-Resolution Policy' (*ICANN*, 25 February 2012) https://www.icann.org/resources/pages/policy-2012-02-25-en accessed June 2025.
3315. WIPO, 'WIPO Domain Name Dispute Resolution Service for .EU (and.ею and.ευ)' (*WIPO*) https://www.wipo.int/amc/en/domains/cctld/eu/index.html accessed July 2024.

a. Applicable Disputes. You are required to submit to a Panel Decision in the event that a third party (a 'complainant') asserts to Platform, through a Trademark Complaint Form < URL for Form > that your account, listing and/or advertising or their content:
   - (A) is identical or confusingly similar to trademarks in which a complainant has rights and which you are using on an unauthorised basis in the course of trade AND
   - (B) (i) is being used to engage in unfair competition in the course of trade with respect to a trademark OR (ii) is being used in bad faith or is being abused with respect to a trademark. For clarity, in the administrative proceeding, the complainant must prove element A AND one element from B (either i or ii) are present.

(b) Permitted use. Trademarks will be permitted if you demonstrate that you have rights or legitimate interests in respect of the listing and/or advertising or their content by showing one or more of these justifications: (i) you (as an individual, business, or other organization) have been commonly known by the term and are using it legitimately (ii) you are making genuine noncommercial legitimate fair use of the trademark, (iii) you are

EUTMR, Lanham Act 1946 15 U.S. Code §§ 1051 et seq. (as amended), the TDRA 2006 15 U.S. Code § 1125(c), Amazon.com, Amazon.nl, eBay.com, eBay.nl trademark policies, terms, and guidelines.[3316]

Key UDRP aspects have been retained including relevant concepts from the Overview.[3317]

This uniform policy largely follows the UDNDRP (Chapter 4) but is adapted for e-commerce marketplace platforms. Please see Chapter 4 (section 4.3.3) for further details and explanations of the adaptations under the model.

For e-commerce platforms dedicated to specific jurisdictions, guidance should include that while decisions will be made based on general trademark principles, local law may be considered since the site is targeted to a jurisdiction (similar to the UDRP where local law may be considered, such as when parties are from the same jurisdiction).[3318] This should be the case in special circumstances, but decisions are expected to follow the general principles in most cases.

3316. Amazon, 'Intellectual Property Policy for Sellers: FAQ about Trademarks' (*Amazon*) https://sellercentral.amazon.com/help/hub/reference/external/GZUQ6GBBXQVHQKF2 accessed June 2025; 'Verified Rights Owner (VeRO) Policy' (*eBay*) https://www.ebay.com/help/policies/listing-policies/selling-policies/intellectual-property-vero-program?id=4349 accessed June 2025.

3317. ICANN, 'Uniform Domain-Name Dispute-Resolution Policy' (*ICANN*, 25 February 2012) https://www.icann.org/resources/pages/policy-2012-02-25-en accessed June 2025; WIPO, 'WIPO Overview of WIPO Panel Views on Selected UDRP Questions, Third Edition' ('WIPO Jurisprudential Overview 3.0') (*WIPO*, 2017) https://www.wipo.int/amc/en/domains/search/overview3.0/ accessed June 2025.

3318. WIPO, 'WIPO Overview of WIPO Panel Views on Selected UDRP Questions, Third Edition' ('WIPO Jurisprudential Overview 3.0') (*WIPO*, 2017) https://www.wipo.int/amc/en/domains/search/overview3.0/ accessed June 2025.

fairly utilising the trademark in marketing of authorized, replacement, compatible or used goods or services, (iv) you are utilising the trademark in an ordinary dictionary sense, (v) you are genuinely and noncommercially utilising the trademark under freedom of speech and expression or legitimate criticism, parody, or review of the company, good or service associated with the trademark, OR (vi) you are making fair and legitimate use of the trademark in comparative advertising.

(c) Remedies. The remedies available to a complainant pursuant to any Panel Decision shall be limited to requiring the cancellation of, suspending, or making changes to your account, listing and/or advertising.

(d) All Other Disputes. Any other disputes between you and any party other than E-Commerce Marketplace Platform regarding your listing and/or advertising in that are not brought pursuant to this Policy will not be resolved through a Panel Decision. Platform reserves the right to make a decision on any matter outside of this policy as set forth in our Terms of Use available at <terms> including any remedies or actions it, in its sole discretion, deems appropriate.

(5) *Procedures.*

(a) Initiation of Proceeding. Submitting a Trade mark Complaint Form initiates the process for a Panel Decision.

(b) Consolidation. In the event of multiple disputes between you and a complainant, either you or the complainant may petition to consolidate the disputes before a single Panel. This petition shall be made to the Panel appointed to hear a pending dispute between the parties. This Panel may consolidate before it any or all such disputes in its sole discretion, provided that the disputes being consolidated are governed by this Policy or a later version of this Policy.

Adapted or directly from the UDRP[3319] and UDNDRP (Chapter 4).

3319. ICANN, 'Uniform Domain-Name Dispute-Resolution Policy' (*ICANN*, 25 February 2012) https://www.icann.org/resources/pages/policy-2012-02-25-en accessed June 2025.

(c) Fees. No fees are charged to file a complaint under this Policy or to receive a Panel Decision. (d) Availability of Court Proceedings. The Panel Decision proceeding requirements set forth in Paragraph 4 shall not prevent either you or the complainant from submitting the dispute to a court of competent jurisdiction for independent resolution before such Panel Decision is commenced or after such proceeding is concluded. If a Panel decides that your seller registration, listing and/or advertising should be cancelled, suspended, or changed, we will then implement the decision immediately unless we have received from you official documentation (such as a copy of a complaint, file-stamped by the clerk of the court) that you have commenced a lawsuit against the complainant in an appropriate jurisdiction. If we receive such documentation immediately following a decision, we will not implement the Panel's decision, and we will take no further action, until we receive (i) evidence satisfactory to us of a resolution between the parties; (ii) evidence satisfactory to us that your lawsuit has been dismissed or withdrawn; or (iii) a copy of an order from such court dismissing your lawsuit or ordering that you do not have the right to continue the listing and/or advertising.	Because platforms currently expend their own resources to make decisions on complaints they receive, these resources may be redirected to an online panel decision under the assumption that this will not raise costs by unreasonable sums. Platforms may wish to include an indemnification provision here.
(6) *Policy Modifications.* Platform reserves the right to modify this Policy at any time. Platform will post any revised Policy at <URL> at least thirty (30) calendar days before it becomes effective. Unless this Policy has already been invoked by the submission of a Trade mark Complaint Form, in which event the version of the Policy in effect at the time it was invoked will apply to you until the dispute is over, all such changes will be binding upon you with respect to any listing and/or advertising	Adapted or directly from UDRP[3320] and UDNDRP (Chapter 4).

3320. *Ibid.*

trademark dispute, whether the dispute arose before, on or after the effective date of our change. In the event that you object to a change in this Policy, your sole remedy is to cancel your Account with us, provided that you will not be entitled to a refund of any fees you paid to us. The revised Policy will apply to you until you cancel your Account.

5.3 MAJOR SEARCH AD PLATFORM TRADEMARK TERMS AND POLICIES

This section will review the three major search platform terms and policies, including Google, Yahoo, and Bing. Gaps and problems with the same will be uncovered, and a recommended policy will be provided.

5.3.1 Google

Google updated its Trademark policy pertinent to Google Ads effective 24 July 2023.[3321] Under the Ads Policy, they 'don't allow ads that infringe trademark rights'.[3322] If a mark holder lodges a complaint with Google relating to the use of their mark in Google Ads, Google 'will review it and may restrict use of the trademark'.[3323] They will consider 'where in the ad the trademark is used'.[3324] A mark is not permitted '[i]f the trademark is used in an ad from a direct competitor'[3325] or '[i]f the ad is using the trademark in a confusing, deceptive or misleading way'.[3326]

However, Google does not restrict 'use of trademarks as keywords'[3327] or 'in the second-level domain of the ad's display URL'.[3328] Further, certain activities are not restricted including where the 'landing page'[3329] for the search ad is mainly to sell or facilitation of selling 'products or services, components, replacement parts or compatible products or services corresponding to the trademark'[3330] so long as the page allows a method to buy and shows 'commercial information about them, such as rates or prices',[3331] and is 'clear as to whether the advertiser is a reseller or informational

3321. Google, 'Update to the Trademarks Policy (June 2023)' (*Google Advertising Policies Help*) https://support.google.com/adspolicy/answer/13594188? accessed June 2025.
3322. Google, 'Trademarks' (*Google Trademarks – Advertising Policies Help*) https://support.google.com/adspolicy/answer/6118?visit_id=638419270508802311-4094647794&rd=1 accessed June 2025.
3323. *Ibid.*
3324. *Ibid.*
3325. *Ibid.*
3326. *Ibid.*
3327. *Ibid.*
3328. *Ibid.*
3329. *Ibid.*
3330. *Ibid.*
3331. *Ibid.*

site'.[3332] Further, if the main goal 'is to provide informative details about products or services corresponding to the trademark, or an index of search results related to the trademark'[3333] or if 'the ad is using the trademark descriptively in its ordinary meaning'.[3334]

Under its Counterfeit Goods advertising policy, 'the sale or promotion for sale of counterfeit goods'[3335] is not permitted and are defined as those goods that 'contain a trademark or logo that is identical to or substantially indistinguishable from the trademark of another ... mimic the brand features of the product in an attempt to pass themselves off as a genuine product of the brand owner ... [t]his policy applies to the content of your ad and your website or app'.[3336] Specifically, 'knock off, replica, imitation, clone, faux, fake, mirror image, or similar terms when referring to a brand name in an attempt to pass themselves off as genuine products of the brand owner'[3337] or '[n]on-genuine products that mimic brand features in an attempt to pass themselves off as the genuine product'[3338] are not permitted. A violation of the Counterfeit Goods policy is an 'egregious violation',[3339] one that is 'so serious that it is unlawful or poses significant harm'[3340] to Google's users[3341] and Google will suspend the Account subject to an appeal process.[3342]

'For repeat violation's'[3343] strikes are issued, 'and penalties progressively increase with each subsequent strike leading up to account suspension'[3344] up to a 'maximum of 3 strikes per policy'.[3345] A Trademark Complaint Form is available to lodge a complaint, which references 'country of registration/use rights'.[3346]

Google requires that '[a]dvertisers must comply with the local laws and regulations of any area their ads target, in addition to the standard Google Ads policies'.[3347]

3332. *Ibid.*
3333. *Ibid.*
3334. *Ibid.*
3335. Google, 'Counterfeit Goods' (*Google Advertising Policies help*) https://support.google.com/adspolicy/answer/176017? accessed June 2025.
3336. *Ibid.*
3337. *Ibid.*
3338. *Ibid.*
3339. *Ibid.*
3340. *Ibid.*
3341. *Ibid.*
3342. *Ibid.*
3343. *Ibid.*
3344. Google, 'What Happens If You Violate Our Policies' (*Google*) https://support.google.com/adspolicy/answer/7187501?sjid=2768541143044478250-NA accessed June 2025.
3345. *Ibid.*
3346. Google, 'Report Content on Google' (*Google*) https://reportcontent.google.com/forms/legal_trademarks/trademark_ads accessed June 2025.
3347. Google, 'Legal Requirements' (*Google Advertising Policies help*) https://support.google.com/adspolicy/answer/6023676? accessed June 2025.

5.3.2 Yahoo!

Several years ago, in 2017, 'Yahoo and AOL joined to become a unified digital and mobile media company.'[3348] Interestingly, they are, as of 2018 and continuing into 2024, 'operating under these unified Yahoo Terms of Service'.[3349]

Yahoo Terms of Service indicate that they expect users to 'respect the intellectual property of others'[3350] and that they may, 'in appropriate circumstances and at our discretion, disable, terminate, and/or take other appropriate steps relating to the accounts of users who may be infringers'.[3351] This is reiterated in Yahoo's Community Guidelines, which say '[d]o not post content that violates a copyright, trademark, or other intellectual property right held by someone else'[3352] and '[w]e will remove such content if we discover it, or upon the request of the rights holder'.[3353]

Under its 'Repeat Infringer'[3354] policy, they have the right to 'terminate any user for actual or apparent infringement of intellectual property rights'.[3355] However, the policy goes on to say 'Yahoo will terminate, under appropriate circumstances, the accounts of users who are repeat copyright infringers'[3356] which appears to apply to copyright rather than trademark.[3357]

A specific Copyright and Intellectual Property Policy[3358] is available with respect to 'infringement on its Services'[3359] for 'content accessible on or through Yahoo's Services'.[3360] The policy also builds in an enforcement mechanism. Under this policy, Yahoo may '[i]n appropriate instances … remove allegedly infringing materials'.[3361] However, they also make clear that, '[u]pon review, we may decline to remove allegedly infringing materials – for example, if we determine they are not infringing, if we lack adequate information to determine that they are infringing, if we are unable to find the accused materials, or if the materials are protected by the fair use doctrine, among other reasons'.[3362]

Under its Counterfeit Policy, it 'forbids the sale or promotion of counterfeit products found on its Services'.[3363] They define these as 'unauthorized versions of

3348. Yahoo!, 'Yahoo Terms of Service' (*Yahoo!*) https://legal.yahoo.com/us/en/yahoo/terms/otos/index.html accessed June 2025.
3349. *Ibid.*
3350. *Ibid.*
3351. *Ibid.*
3352. Yahoo, 'Yahoo Community Guidelines' (*Yahoo!*) https://legal.yahoo.com/us/en/yahoo/guidelines/index.html accessed June 2025.
3353. *Ibid.*
3354. Yahoo! 'Copyright and Intellectual Property Policy' (*Yahoo!*) https://legal.yahoo.com/us/en/yahoo/ip/index.html accessed June 2025.
3355. *Ibid.*
3356. *Ibid.*
3357. *Ibid.*
3358. *Ibid.*
3359. *Ibid.*
3360. *Ibid.*
3361. *Ibid.*
3362. *Ibid.*
3363. Yahoo! 'Counterfeit Policy' (*Yahoo!*) https://legal.yahoo.com/us/en/yahoo/ip/counterfeits/index.html accessed June 2025.

goods that include the trademark or logo of the authentic brand owner ... sometimes referred to as counterfeits, replicas, knock-offs, in-the-same-style-as or fake'.[3364] A specific Counterfeit/Trademark reporting form is available.[3365]

Yahoo's Global Yahoo Advertising Policies[3366] apply to search ads internationally.[3367] It states that '[r]epeated or serious violations of our policies may result in account termination or suspension'.[3368] It 'prohibits infringement of trademarks and other intellectual property by advertisers'.[3369] Notably, 'fair use of trademarks in ad text; is permitted, for example, 'to identify a product, service or company' however, 'without suggesting' affiliation, endorsement, or sponsorship or using as 'ordinary dictionary definition of a term, rather than ... as a brand name ... to compare ... so long as the comparison is fair, accurate, and supported by independent research ... a reseller or distributor of authentic (not counterfeit) goods or services ... do not falsely say or imply that you are affiliated with the trademark owner or authorized to resell or distribute those goods or services'.[3370]

When a complaint is filed with Yahoo, it restricts where it will look for potential trademark violations[3371] to 'the text of a search ad only ... to ensure the quality and accuracy of our ad results and to help our users avoid confusion.'.[3372] However, with respect to some countries, it will investigate keywords in addition to ads such as in 'Brazil, France, Hong Kong, Indonesia, Ireland, Italy, Singapore, and United Kingdom ... [f]or these markets, advertisers may not bid on keywords, or use in the text of ads, any term whose use would infringe the trademark of any third party or otherwise be unlawful or in violation of the rights of any third party'.[3373]

Also, '[t]he display URL cannot mislead the consumer into believing they are going to a site not controlled or owned by our advertiser. The display URL cannot be used as another line of text or as an email address field'.[3374]

5.3.3 Microsoft Advertising (Bing)

Microsoft Advertising's Intellectual Property Rights Policy applicable to Bing indicates that '[a]s an advertiser, you are responsible for ensuring that your keywords and ad content, including trademarks and logos, do not infringe or violate the intellectual

3364. *Ibid.*
3365. Yahoo! 'Counterfeit/Trademark' (*Yahoo!*) https://www.yahooinc.com/ipr/en-US/forms/trademark accessed June 2025.
3366. Yahoo! 'Ad Specs Guide' (*Yahoo! Ad tech*) https://adspecs.yahooinc.com/pages/policies-guidelines/yahoo-ad-policy accessed June 2025.
3367. *Ibid.*
3368. *Ibid.*
3369. *Ibid.*
3370. *Ibid.*
3371. *Ibid.*
3372. *Ibid.*
3373. *Ibid.*
3374. *Ibid.*

property rights of others'.[3375] The policy directly states that Microsoft takes 'allegations of trademark infringement seriously'.[3376] Specifically, 'trademarks or other terms prone to nefarious tactics related to user safety may be proactively blocked to protect the network and our users'.[3377] An appeal process is available.[3378]

The policy also defines trademark placement as that which is 'used in text of the ad or keywords, as well as imagery contained in the creative'.[3379] While encouraging parties to discuss an alleged trademark violation amongst themselves first, Microsoft may conduct an investigation.[3380] In strikingly similar wording to the Yahoo policy seen earlier, leading to some level of uniformity: 'Microsoft will investigate a complaint about trademark infringement in the text of a Search ad ... to ensure the quality and accuracy of our ad results and to help our users avoid confusion.'[3381]

However, while advertisers must 'ensure ... keywords and ad content'[3382] do not violate, the above policy does not indicate that keywords will be investigated except for Taiwan.[3383]

Microsoft also factors in 'abuse'[3384] by saying: '[r]epeated use of trademark terms in a misleading way, including misleading ads created as a result of dynamic keyword insertion, may result in those trademark terms being blocked from use in your account'.[3385] Microsoft clarifies that, in terms of a complaint, '[t]he focus of the investigation is to "ensure the quality and accuracy of ... ad results and to help ... users avoid confusion"'.[3386]

Under their Counterfeit policy, advertising of goods 'that copies without permission the trademark and/or distinctive features of a product in order to misrepresent itself as the genuine product or promote a nearly identical replica or imitation of the original product'.[3387] Specifically, '[t]rademark or designer product brand names cannot be modified with "counterfeit," "fake," "replica," "copy of," "inspired by," "bootleg" or any synonym thereof'.[3388]

3375. Microsoft, 'Intellectual Property Policies' (*Microsoft*) https://help.ads.microsoft.com/#apex/ads/en/ext60211 accessed June 2025.
3376. *Ibid.*
3377. *Ibid.*
3378. *Ibid.*
3379. *Ibid.*
3380. *Ibid.*
3381. *Ibid.*
3382. *Ibid.*
3383. Microsoft, 'Intellectual Property Policies' (*Microsoft*) https://help.ads.microsoft.com/#apex/ads/en/60211/0-500 accessed June 2025.
3384. Microsoft, 'Intellectual property policies' (*Microsoft*) https://help.ads.microsoft.com/#apex/ads/en/ext60211 accessed June 2025.
3385. *Ibid.*
3386. *Ibid.*
3387. *Ibid.*
3388. *Ibid.*

An 'Intellectual Property Concern Form'[3389] is available and requires a trademark registration number.[3390] It also requires the 'exact phrase used in the search box that resulted in the ads in question'.[3391] Additionally, Microsoft Advertising Network Policies[3392] refer advertisers back to its intellectual property policies.[3393]

Microsoft does permit specific utilisation of marks under its Intellectual Property Policies and permits 'fair use of trademarks in ad text'[3394] including 'by a reseller of authentic goods or services … [i]nformational websites about goods or services represented by the trademark, such as product reviews … [or]dinary dictionary uses of a term … [c]omparative advertising (with restrictions)'.[3395] Thus, Microsoft appears to consider the associated website in the analysis and also consider whether competition is taking place.[3396]

5.3.4 Gaps and Problems with Current Search Advertising Platform Trademark Terms and Policies

As can be seen from the above, each search ad platform has its own rules relating to how it may deal with trademark matters within its search ads. Some of these rules are similar, while others differ. Table 5.4 below summarises the various elements of the Digital Trademark and Trade Practices Model that are incorporated by each of the search ad platforms in their search advertising terms or policies and which are not directly or adequately covered, even if they cover some aspects of the element. The UDRP elements are also shown for reference.

3389. Microsoft 'Intellectual Property Concern Form' (*Microsoft Advertising*) https://about.ads.microsoft.com/en-us/resources/policies/intellectual-property-complaint-form accessed June 2025.
3390. *Ibid.*
3391. *Ibid.*
3392. Microsoft, 'Microsoft Advertising Network Policies' (*Microsoft*) https://help.ads.microsoft.com/#apex/ads/en/60205/0 accessed June 2025.
3393. *Ibid.*
3394. Microsoft, 'Intellectual Property Policies' (*Microsoft*) https://help.ads.microsoft.com/#apex/ads/en/ext60211 accessed June 2025.
3395. *Ibid.*
3396. *Ibid.*

Table 5.4 Digital Trademark and Trade Practices Model, UDRP, and Search Advertising Platform Terms and Policies

Digital Trademark and Trade Practices Model	*UDRP*	*Google Ads*	*Yahoo!*	*Microsoft Advertising (Bing)*
Digital Use and Place of Use	Only some coverage. Any use of registered or unregistered marks in domain names which violate the policy.[3397]	Only some coverage. Use in Google Ads (and potentially related to websites that ads link to). Also, 'where in the ad the trademark is used'.[3398] However, does not restrict 'use of trademarks as keywords'[3399] or 'in the second-level domain of the ad's display URL'.[3400] When complaining about others using a mark, reference to registration/use rights is required.[3401]	Only some coverage. Use in Yahoo services including advertising. When complaining about others using a mark, a trademark registration number or application number is required.[3402] 'Yahoo will investigate ... in the text of a search ad only ...'.[3403] (However, see Digital Jurisdictional and Territorial Considerations below for countries where keywords will be investigated.[3404]	Only some coverage. Marks 'used in text of the ad or keywords, as well as imagery contained in the creative'.[3405] Use in 'keywords and ad content, including trademarks and logos ...'.[3406] 'Microsoft will investigate a complaint about trademark infringement in the text of a Search ad ...'.[3407] When complaining about others using a mark, a trademark registration number is required.[3408]

Digital Trademark and Trade Practices Model	*UDRP*	*Google Ads*	*Yahoo!*	*Microsoft Advertising (Bing)*
Digital Bad Faith and Abuse	'Registration and use of a domain name in bad faith'[3409] (abuse is covered in overview).[3410]	Only some coverage. 'For repeat violation's' strikes are issued 'and penalties progressively increase with each subsequent strike leading up to account suspension'[3411] up to a 'maximum of 3 strikes per policy'.[3412] A violation of the Counterfeit Goods policy is an 'egregious violation',[3413] one that is 'so serious that it is unlawful or poses significant harm' to Google's users[3414] and Google will suspend the Account subject to an appeal process.[3415]	Only some coverage. 'Repeat Infringer'[3416] policy says they have the right to 'terminate any user for actual or apparent infringement of intellectual property rights'.[3417] But goes on to say 'terminate, under appropriate circumstances, the accounts of users who are repeat copyright infringers'[3418] which appears to apply to copyright rather than trademark.[3419]	Only some coverage. Specifically, 'trademarks or other terms prone to nefarious tactics related to user safety may be proactively blocked to protect the network and our users'.[3420] An appeal process is available. 'Repeated use of trademark terms in a misleading way, including misleading ads created as a result of dynamic keyword insertion, may result in those trademark terms being blocked from use in your account.'[3421]

Digital Trademark and Trade Practices Model	*UDRP*	*Google Ads*	*Yahoo!*	*Microsoft Advertising (Bing)*
Digital Confusion	'Confusing similarity' in domain names.[3422]	A mark is not permitted … '[i]f the ad is using the trademark in a confusing … way'.[3423]	Generally or not directly covered. Required to 'respect the intellectual property of others'[3424] 'Do not post content that violates a copyright, trademark, or other intellectual property right held by someone else'[3425] 'The investigation is designed to ensure the quality and accuracy of our ad results and to help our users avoid confusion.'[3426] '[t]he display URL cannot mislead the consumer into believing they are going to a site not controlled or owned by our advertiser'.[3427]	Only some coverage. To 'ensure the quality and accuracy of … ad results and to help … users avoid confusion'.[3428]

Digital Trademark and Trade Practices Model	*UDRP*	*Google Ads*	*Yahoo!*	*Microsoft Advertising (Bing)*
Digital Unfair Competition	Only some coverage. The Overview states that '[a]lso noting the availability of trademark-like protection under certain national legal doctrines (e.g., unfair competition or passing-off) and considerations of parity, where acquired distinctiveness/ secondary meaning is demonstrated in a particular UDRP case, unregistered rights have been found to support standing to proceed with a UDRP case including where the complainant is based in a civil law jurisdiction'.[3429] Unfair advantage considerations may fall under bad faith and abuse (*see* Overview).[3430] 'Distinctiveness' and 'secondary meaning' isrecognized in Overview along with a list of factors that may be considered.[3431] 'Secondary meaning'[3432] is covered in the Overview.	Only some coverage. A mark is not permitted '[i]f the trademark is used in an ad from a direct competitor' or '[i]f the ad is using the trademark in a ... deceptive or misleading way'.[3433] Counterfeit Goods advertising policy: 'the sale or promotion for sale of counterfeit goods' is not permitted and are defined as those goods that 'contain a trademark or logo that is identical to or substantially indistinguishable from the trademark of another ... mimic the brand features of the product in an attempt to	Only some coverage. Counterfeit Policy it 'forbids the sale or promotion of counterfeit products found on its Services'.[3434] They define these as 'unauthorized versions of goods that include the trademark or logo of the authentic brand owner ... sometimes referred to as counterfeits, replicas, knock-offs, in-the-same-style-as or fake'.[3435]	Only some coverage. 'Comparative advertising (with restrictions)'.[3436] Under their Counterfeit policy, advertising of goods 'that copies without permission the trademark and/or distinctive features of a product in order to misrepresent itself as the genuine product or promote a nearly identical replica or imitation of the original product'.[3437]

Digital Trademark and Trade Practices Model	*UDRP*	*Google Ads*	*Yahoo!*	*Microsoft Advertising (Bing)*
	Overview also states that 'the strength of the complainant's mark may be considered relevant in evaluating the second and third elements'[3438] of the UDRP.	pass themselves off as a genuine product of the brand owner ... This policy applies to the content of your ad and your website or app'.[3439] Specifically, 'knock off, replica, imitation, clone, faux, fake, mirror image, or similar terms when referring to a brand name in an attempt to pass themselves off as genuine products of the brand owner'[3440] or 'Non-genuine products that mimic brand features in an attempt to pass themselves off as the genuine product'[3441] are not permitted.		Specifically, 'Trademark or designer product brand names cannot be modified with "counterfeit," "fake," "replica," "copy of," "inspired by," "bootleg" or any synonym thereof'.[3442]

Digital Trademark and Trade Practices Model	*UDRP*	*Google Ads*	*Yahoo!*	*Microsoft Advertising (Bing)*
Digital Terms, Policies, and Disclaimers	Only some coverage. Is itself a uniform policy addressing covered domain names. Disclaimers have been treated briefly in Overview. In cases 'where the respondent appears to otherwise have a right or legitimate interest in a disputed domain name, a clear and sufficiently prominent disclaimer would lend support to circumstances suggesting its good faith'.[3443]	Generally or not directly covered. Trademark-related policies are contained in various documents. Different terms and policies may potentially apply in different regions.	Generally or not directly covered. Trademark-related policies are contained in various documents. Different terms and policies may potentially apply in different regions. But 'now operating under these unified Yahoo Terms of Service'.[3444]	Generally or not directly covered. Trademark-related policies are contained in various documents. Different terms and policies may potentially apply in different regions.
Digital Jurisdictional and Territorial Considerations	Only some coverage. Changes to a domain name may be made based on court or arbitral tribunal of competent jurisdiction.[3445] Overview states that 'rules and principles of law'[3446] may be considered (this is discretionary);	Generally or not directly covered. Different terms may potentially apply to different regions where ads are targeted. '[a]dvertisers must comply with the local laws and regulations of any area their ads target, in addition to the standard Google Ads policies'.[3447]	Generally or not directly covered. Different terms may apply in different regions where ads are targeted.	Generally or not directly covered. Different terms may potentially apply to different regions where ads are targeted. 'If ads are shown outside of a targeted

Digital Trademark and Trade Practices Model	*UDRP*	*Google Ads*	*Yahoo!*	*Microsoft Advertising (Bing)*
	however, 'in its own terms UDRP jurisprudence generally would not require resort to particular national laws'.[3448] For example, guidance indicates that where 'the parties share a common nationality and the import of a specific national law concept is particularly germane to an issue in dispute, panels have applied national law principles in assessing the UDRP elements'.[3449] Otherwise, the UDRP applies regardless of where domain is registered or used.		'Ad and Keyword Investigations: Brazil, France, Hong Kong, Indonesia, Ireland, Italy, Singapore, and United Kingdom ... advertisers may not bid on keywords, or use in the text of ads, any term whose use would infringe the trademark of any third party or otherwise be unlawful or in violation of the rights of any third party.'[3450]	market due to an advertiser's account settings, we apply policies related to the geographical areas where the ads show'.[3451] 'investigate a complaint about trademark infringement in keyword use'[3452] for Taiwan.[3453]
Digital Justification	Only some coverage. Using marks for 'legitimate noncommercial or fair use'[3454] is recognized as a method to demonstrate 'rights and legitimate interests'.[3455] Fair use and freedom of speech are also covered in the Overview.[3456]	Only some coverage. Not restricted: 'products or services, components, replacement parts or compatible products or services corresponding to the	Only some coverage. '[u]pon review, we may decline to remove allegedly infringing materials – for example, ... if the materials are protected by the fair use doctrine, among other reasons'.[3457] Yahoo permits 'fair use of trademarks in ad text; is	Only some coverage. Microsoft permits 'fair use of trademarks in ad text'[3458]

Digital Trademark and Trade Practices Model	*UDRP*	*Google Ads*	*Yahoo!*	*Microsoft Advertising (Bing)*
		trademark' (under certain conditions; ad and landing page is considered)[3459] 'to provide informative details about products or services corresponding to the trademark, or an index of search results related to the trademark'[3460] 'descriptively in its ordinary meaning'[3461]	permitted, for example, 'to identify a product, service or company' however, 'without suggesting' affiliation, endorsement, or sponsorship or using as 'ordinary dictionary definition of a term, rather than … as a brand name … to compare … so long as the comparison is fair, accurate, and supported by independent research … a reseller or distributor of authentic (not counterfeit) goods or services … do not falsely say or imply that you are affiliated with the trademark owner or authorized to resell or distribute those goods or services'.[3462]	including 'by a reseller of authentic goods or services … [i]nformational websites about goods or services represented by the trademark, such as product reviews … [or]dinary dictionary uses of a term … [c]omparative advertising (with restrictions)'.[3463] Thus, Microsoft appears to consider the associated website in the analysis and also consider whether competition is taking place.[3464]

3397. ICANN, 'Uniform Domain-Name Dispute-Resolution Policy' (*ICANN*, 25 February 2012) https://www.icann.org/resources/pages/policy-2012-02-25-en accessed June 2025; WIPO, 'WIPO Overview of WIPO Panel Views on Selected UDRP Questions, Third Edition' ('WIPO Jurisprudential Overview 3.0') (*WIPO*, 2017) https://www.wipo.int/amc/en/domains/search/overview3.0/ accessed June 2025.
3398. Google, 'Trademarks' (*Google*) https://support.google.com/adspolicy/answer/6118?visit_id=638419270508802311-4094647794&rd=1 accessed June 2025.
3399. *Ibid.*
3400. *Ibid.*
3401. Google, 'Report Content on Google' (*Google*) https://reportcontent.google.com/forms/legal_trademarks/trademark_ads accessed June 2025.
3402. Yahoo! 'Counterfeit/Trademark' (*Yahoo!*) https://www.yahooinc.com/ipr/en-US/forms/trademark accessed June 2025.
3403. Yahoo! 'Ad Specs Guide' (*Yahoo! Ad tech*) https://adspecs.yahooinc.com/pages/policies-guidelines/yahoo-ad-policy accessed June 2025.
3404. *Ibid.*
3405. Microsoft, 'Intellectual Property Policies' (*Microsoft*) https://help.ads.microsoft.com/#apex/ads/en/ext60211 accessed June 2025.
3406. *Ibid.*
3407. *Ibid.*
3408. Microsoft 'Intellectual Property Concern Form' (*Microsoft Advertising*) https://about.ads.microsoft.com/en-us/resources/policies/intellectual-property-complaint-form accessed June 2025.
3409. UDRP, 4(b).
3410. ICANN, 'Uniform Domain-Name Dispute-Resolution Policy' (*ICANN*, 25 February 2012) https://www.icann.org/resources/pages/policy-2012-02-25-en accessed June 2025; WIPO, 'WIPO Overview of WIPO Panel Views on Selected UDRP Questions, Third Edition' ('WIPO Jurisprudential Overview 3.0') (*WIPO*, 2017) https://www.wipo.int/amc/en/domains/search/overview3.0/ accessed June 2025.
3411. Google, 'What Happens If You Violate Our Policies' (*Google*) https://support.google.com/adspolicy/answer/7187501?sjid=2768541143044478250-NA accessed June 2025.
3412. *Ibid.*
3413. Google, 'Counterfeit Goods' (*Google Advertising Policies help*) https://support.google.com/adspolicy/answer/176017? accessed June 2025.
3414. *Ibid.*
3415. *Ibid.*
3416. Yahoo! 'Copyright and Intellectual Property Policy' (*Yahoo!*) https://legal.yahoo.com/us/en/yahoo/ip/index.html accessed June 2025.
3417. *Ibid.*
3418. *Ibid.*
3419. *Ibid.*
3420. Microsoft, 'Intellectual Property Policies' (*Microsoft*) https://help.ads.microsoft.com/#apex/ads/en/ext60211 accessed June 2025.
3421. *Ibid.*
3422. UDRP, 4(a)(i).
3423. Google, 'Trademarks' (*Google*) https://support.google.com/adspolicy/answer/6118?visit_id=638419270508802311-4094647794&rd=1 accessed June 2025.
3424. Yahoo!, 'Yahoo Terms of Service' (*Yahoo!*) https://legal.yahoo.com/us/en/yahoo/terms/otos/index.html accessed June 2025.

3425. Yahoo, 'Yahoo Community Guidelines' (*Yahoo!*) https://legal.yahoo.com/us/en/yahoo/guidelines/index.html accessed June 2025.
3426. Yahoo! 'Ad Specs Guide' (*Yahoo! Ad tech*) https://adspecs.yahooinc.com/pages/policies-guidelines/yahoo-ad-policy accessed June 2025.
3427. *Ibid.*
3428. Microsoft, 'Intellectual Property Policies' (*Microsoft*) https://help.ads.microsoft.com/#apex/ads/en/ext60211 accessed June 2025.
3429. WIPO, 'WIPO Overview of WIPO Panel Views on Selected UDRP Questions, Third Edition' ('WIPO Jurisprudential Overview 3.0') (*WIPO*, 2017) https://www.wipo.int/amc/en/domains/search/overview3.0/ accessed June 2025.
3430. *Ibid.*
3431. *Ibid.*
3432. *Ibid.*
3433. Google, 'Trademarks' (*Google*) https://support.google.com/adspolicy/answer/6118?visit_id=638419270508802311-4094647794&rd=1 accessed June 2025.
3434. Yahoo! 'Counterfeit Policy' (*Yahoo!*) https://legal.yahoo.com/us/en/yahoo/ip/counterfeits/index.html accessed June 2025.
3435. *Ibid.*
3436. Microsoft, 'Intellectual Property Policies' (*Microsoft*) https://help.ads.microsoft.com/#apex/ads/en/ext60211 accessed June 2025.
3437. *Ibid.*
3438. *Ibid.*
3439. Google, 'Counterfeit Goods' (*Google Advertising Policies help*) https://support.google.com/adspolicy/answer/176017? accessed June 2025.
3440. *Ibid.*
3441. *Ibid.*
3442. *Ibid.*
3443. WIPO, 'WIPO Overview of WIPO Panel Views on Selected UDRP Questions, Third Edition' ('WIPO Jurisprudential Overview 3.0') (*WIPO*, 2017) https://www.wipo.int/amc/en/domains/search/overview3.0/ accessed June 2025.
3444. Yahoo!, 'Yahoo Terms of Service' (*Yahoo!*) https://legal.yahoo.com/xw/en/yahoo/terms/otos/index.html accessed June 2025.
3445. ICANN, 'Uniform Domain-Name Dispute-Resolution Policy' (*ICANN*, 25 February 2012) https://www.icann.org/resources/pages/policy-2012-02-25-en accessed June 2025.
3446. WIPO, 'WIPO Overview of WIPO Panel Views on Selected UDRP Questions, Third Edition' ('WIPO Jurisprudential Overview 3.0') (*WIPO*, 2017) https://www.wipo.int/amc/en/domains/search/overview3.0/ accessed June 2025.
3447. Google, 'Legal Requirements' (*Google Advertising Policies help*) https://support.google.com/adspolicy/answer/6023676? accessed June 2025.
3448. *Ibid.*
3449. *Ibid.*
3450. Yahoo! 'Ad Specs Guide' (*Yahoo! Ad tech*) https://adspecs.yahooinc.com/pages/policies-guidelines/yahoo-ad-policy accessed June 2025.
3451. Microsoft, 'Microsoft Advertising Network Policies' (*Microsoft*) https://help.ads.microsoft.com/#apex/ads/en/60205/0 accessed June 2025.
3452. Microsoft, 'Intellectual Property Policies' (*Microsoft*) https://help.ads.microsoft.com/#apex/ads/en/60211/0-500 accessed June 2025.
3453. *Ibid.*

3454. WIPO, 'WIPO Overview of WIPO Panel Views on Selected UDRP Questions, Third Edition' ('WIPO Jurisprudential Overview 3.0') (*WIPO*, 2017) https://www.wipo.int/amc/en/domains/search/overview3.0/ accessed June 2025.
3455. *Ibid.*
3456. *Ibid.*
3457. Yahoo! 'Copyright and Intellectual Property Policy' (*Yahoo!*) https://legal.yahoo.com/us/en/yahoo/ip/index.html accessed June 2025.
3458. Microsoft, 'Intellectual Property Policies' (*Microsoft*) https://help.ads.microsoft.com/#apex/ads/en/ext60211 accessed June 2025.
3459. Google, 'Trademarks' (*Google*) https://support.google.com/adspolicy/answer/6118?visit_id=638419270508802311-4094647794&rd=1 accessed June 2025.
3460. *Ibid.*
3461. *Ibid.*
3462. *Ibid.*
3463. *Ibid.*
3464. *Ibid.*

As seen in the table above, there are several gaps which are not directly or adequately addressed by the search ad platforms based on the elements of the model. It should be noted that while an element may be missing or not directly or adequately covered, it does not mean that the search ad platform does not consider it; however, whether it does is unclear and this results in a highly discretionary environment, which is a key problem with the search ad trademark policies.

5.3.4.1 Digital Use and Place of Use

The platforms' policies cover utilisation of trademarks within advertising (and other areas) of their services, some having ad-specific policies while some prefer overall policies applicable to their services. Google specifically addresses place of use[3465] by saying that they will look at 'where in the ad the trademark is used'[3466] and specifically does not restrict 'use of trademarks as keywords'[3467] or 'in the second-level domain of the ad's display URL'.[3468] Directly addressing the place of use[3469] is a good approach based on the fact that marks in different aspects of a search ad may raise different implications, as seen in Chapter 2. Yahoo indicates it will investigate 'trademark infringement in the text of a search ad only';[3470] however, it will investigate keywords for certain countries.[3471] Microsoft's policies appear to cover 'the text of the ad or

3465. Google, 'Trademarks' (*Google*) https://support.google.com/adspolicy/answer/6118?visit_id=638419270508802311-4094647794&rd=1 accessed June 2025.
3466. *Ibid.*
3467. *Ibid.*
3468. *Ibid.*
3469. *Ibid.*
3470. Yahoo! 'Ad Specs Guide' (*Yahoo! Ad tech*) https://adspecs.yahooinc.com/pages/policies-guidelines/yahoo-ad-policy accessed June 2025.
3471. *Ibid.*

keywords';[3472] however, it appears that 'trademark infringement in keyword use' may be applicable to Taiwan.[3473]

In the context of 'use'[3474] and 'property theory',[3475] on Yahoo's trademark form, the mark and associated 'Registration or Application #(s)'[3476] are required.[3477] If the mark is not registered, it is not clear whether remedy through Yahoo may be available or not. The form also asks for '[a]ssociated [g]oods and/or [s]ervices'[3478] which may not always be clear, and if there are none that are so associated, the complaint may potentially fail. For example, 'using in the course of trade'[3479] or 'in connection with goods or services'[3480] is not stated directly in the policy but appears in this way on the form.[3481] Microsoft also requires a trademark registration number.[3482]

5.3.4.2 *Digital Bad Faith and Abuse*

None of the search ad platforms directly or adequately addresses bad faith.[3483] There is a great opportunity for bad actors to engage in 'bad faith'[3484] with trademarks in search advertising. Google address 'abuse'[3485] through 'repeat violation's'[3486] (3 strikes)[3487]

3472. Microsoft, 'Intellectual Property Policies' (*Microsoft*) https://help.ads.microsoft.com/#apex/ads/en/60211/0-500 accessed June 2025.
3473. *Ibid.*
3474. TRIPS, Art. 16; EUTMR, Art. 18; 15 U.S. Code § 1127; UK Trade Marks Act 1994, s. 46(1)(a); Canadian Trademarks Act R.S.C., 1985, c. T-13, s. 2.
3475. J Thomas McCarthy, *McCarthy on Trademarks and Unfair Competition* (4th edn, vol. 69, Thomson Reuters, 2014) in Lisa L Ouellette, 'The Google Shortcut to Trademark Law' (2014) 102 California Law Review 351, 358; Lionel Bently, 'From Communication to Thing: Historical Aspects of the Conceptualisation of Trade Marks as Property' in Graeme B Dinwoodie and Mark D Janis (eds), *Trademark Law and Theory: A Handbook of Contemporary Research* (Edward Elgar, 2008) 3-41; Anselm Kamperman Sanders, *Unfair Competition Law: The Protection of Intellectual and Industrial Creativity* (Oxford University Press 1997) 109.
3476. Yahoo! 'Counterfeit/Trademark' (*Yahoo!*) https://www.yahooinc.com/ipr/en-US/forms/trademark accessed June 2025.
3477. *Ibid.*
3478. *Ibid.*
3479. TRIPS.
3480. EUTMR, Art. 18.
3481. Yahoo! 'Counterfeit/Trademark' (*Yahoo!*) https://www.yahooinc.com/ipr/en-US/forms/trademark accessed June 2025.
3482. Microsoft 'Intellectual Property Concern Form' (*Microsoft Advertising*) https://about.ads.microsoft.com/en-us/resources/policies/intellectual-property-complaint-form accessed June 2025.
3483. UDRP, 4(a)(iii).
3484. *Ibid.*
3485. Google, 'What Happens If You Violate Our Policies' (*Google*) https://support.google.com/adspolicy/answer/7187501?sjid=2768541143044478250-NA accessed June 2025.
3486. *Ibid.*
3487. *Ibid.*

and Yahoo through 'repeat infringer'[3488] policies. Google also considers counterfeit goods as an 'egregious violation'[3489] and Microsoft says 'trademarks or other terms prone to nefarious tactics related to user safety may be proactively blocked to protect the network and our users'.[3490] It is very unclear what the latter may mean and how specifically the trademark would need to be connected with 'user safety'.[3491]

5.3.4.3 *Digital Confusion*

While Google somewhat directly prohibits confusion[3492] through its policy stating that it will 'restrict'[3493] ads '[i]f the ad is using the trademark in a confusing ... way'.[3494] Yahoo prohibits general infringement[3495] and mentions that their investigation is 'to help our users avoid confusion'.[3496] Microsoft uses the same wording in this regard, which is 'to help our users avoid confusion'.[3497] While confusion[3498] has direct coverage with Google mentions this in a prohibitive way,[3499] while the other rely on general infringement or notation of what the investigation will, *inter alia*, focus on.[3500] Nevertheless, it is anticipated that the general infringement prohibition will serve to incorporate a confusion[3501] analysis.

3488. Yahoo! 'Copyright and Intellectual Property Policy' (*Yahoo!*) https://legal.yahoo.com/us/en/yahoo/ip/index.html accessed June 2025.
3489. Google, 'Counterfeit Goods' (Google Advertising Policies help) https://support.google.com/adspolicy/answer/176017? accessed June 2025.
3490. Microsoft, 'Intellectual Property Policies' (Microsoft) https://help.ads.microsoft.com/#apex/ads/en/ext60211 accessed June 2025.
3491. *Ibid.*
3492. Google, 'Trademarks' (*Google*) https://support.google.com/adspolicy/answer/6118?visit_id=638419270508802311-4094647794&rd=1 accessed June 2025.
3493. *Ibid.*
3494. *Ibid.*
3495. Yahoo!, 'Yahoo Terms of Service' (*Yahoo!*) https://legal.yahoo.com/us/en/yahoo/terms/otos/index.html accessed June 2025.
3496. Yahoo! 'Ad Specs Guide' (*Yahoo! Ad tech*) https://adspecs.yahooinc.com/pages/policies-guidelines/yahoo-ad-policy accessed June 2025.
3497. Microsoft, 'Intellectual Property Policies' (*Microsoft*) https://help.ads.microsoft.com/#apex/ads/en/ext60211 accessed June 2025.
3498. Google, 'Trademarks' (*Google*) https://support.google.com/adspolicy/answer/6118?visit_id=638419270508802311-4094647794&rd=1 accessed June 2025.
3499. *Ibid.*
3500. Yahoo! 'Ad Specs Guide' (*Yahoo! Ad tech*) https://adspecs.yahooinc.com/pages/policies-guidelines/yahoo-ad-policy accessed July 2024; Microsoft, 'Intellectual Property Policies' (*Microsoft*) https://help.ads.microsoft.com/#apex/ads/en/ext60211 accessed June 2025.
3501. Paris Convention, Art. 6bis; TRIPS, Art. 16(1); EUTMR, Art. 8(1)(b) and Art. 9(2)(b); 15 U.S. Code § 1114;15 U.S. Code § 1125.

5.3.4.4 *Digital Unfair Competition*

Unfair competition,[3502] unfair advantage,[3503] dilution,[3504] reputation,[3505] well-known,[3506] etc., are not directly mentioned by search ad trademark policies. However, some aspects of these are covered. Google does not permit '[i]f the trademark is used in an ad from a direct competitor'[3507] or '[i]f the ad is using the trademark in a ... deceptive or misleading way'.[3508] All three platforms have policies for counterfeit[3509] goods and cover them in some detail. Interestingly, Google extends the policy, in one sense, to websites and apps.[3510] Google specifically has a prohibition against 'an attempt to pass themselves off as a genuine product of the brand owner ...'.[3511] However, somehow they state that '[t]his policy applies to the content of your ad and your website or app'[3512] and while they would be able to enforce content within their ad or mobile app within their service, their reach to apps outside of their service or websites will unlikely be enforceable beyond the enforcement that can be done against the search ad or account. All three platforms have a counterfeit policy which also prohibit the use of certain terminology signifying counterfeit products.[3513] Microsoft makes some mention of '[c]omparative advertising (with restrictions)'[3514] although it is not immediately clear what those restrictions are.

3502. Anselm Kamperman Sanders, *Unfair Competition Law: The Protection of Intellectual and Industrial Creativity* (Oxford University Press, 1997) 8; Frauke Henning-Bodewig, *Unfair Competition Law European Union and Member States* (Kluwer Law International 2006) xv-xvi; Martin Senftleben, Michael Handler and Irene Calboli, 'Protection Against Unfair Competition Around the Globe' (2024) 19 Journal of Intellectual Property Law & Practice 79, 79-80 https://doi.org/10.1093/jiplp/jpad121; Paris Convention, Art. 10bis; EUTMR, Art. 9(2)(c); 15 U.S.C. § 1125(c)(2)(B).
3503. EUTMR, Art. 9(2)(c).
3504. EUTMR, Art. 9(2)(c); 15 U.S.C. § 1125(c)(2)(B).
3505. EUTMR, Arts 8(5) and 9(1)(c).
3506. Paris Convention, Art. 6bis; TRIPS, Art. 16(2); EUTMR, Art. 8(2)(c).
3507. Google, 'Trademarks' (*Google*) https://support.google.com/adspolicy/answer/6118?visit_id=638419270508802311-4094647794&rd=1 accessed June 2025.
3508. *Ibid.*
3509. Amazon, 'Intellectual Property Policy for Sellers: FAQ about Trademarks' (*Amazon*) https://sellercentral.amazon.com/help/hub/reference/external/GZUQ6GBBXQVHQKF2 accessed June 2025; eBay, 'Forgeries, Replicas and Unauthorized Copies Policy' (*eBay NL*) https://www.ebay.nl/help/policies/prohibited-restricted-items/fake-items-policy?id=4276 accessed June 2025; Google, 'Counterfeit Goods' (*Google Advertising Policies Help*) https://support.google.com/adspolicy/answer/176017?hl=en&ref_topic=1626336&sjid=17722085019300892729-NA accessed June 2025.
3510. Google, 'Counterfeit Goods' (*Google Advertising Policies help*) https://support.google.com/adspolicy/answer/176017? accessed June 2025.
3511. *Ibid.*
3512. *Ibid.*
3513. *Ibid.*; Yahoo! 'Counterfeit Policy' (Yahoo!) https://legal.yahoo.com/us/en/yahoo/ip/counterfeits/index.html accessed June 2025; Microsoft, 'Intellectual Property Policies' (*Microsoft*) https://help.ads.microsoft.com/#apex/ads/en/ext60211 accessed June 2025.
3514. https://help.ads.microsoft.com/#apex/ads/en/ext60211 accessed 4 August 2025.

5.3.4.5 *Digital Terms, Policies, and Disclaimers*

Significantly, Yahoo and Microsoft Bing use some similar language in their policies, adopting some uniformity.[3515] A significant approach is used by Microsoft Bing through its Intellectual Property form.[3516] Since Bing ads may also appear on Yahoo,[3517] and because 'Yahoo Search and Yahoo Images results are powered by Bing (including, but not limited to, [s]ponsored [l]istings and [a]ds results)',[3518] Bing incorporates Yahoo into their Intellectual property concern form where complainants may select from Bing, Yahoo, and/or Other search engine.[3519] This supports uniform approaches[3520] and it is argued that uniform policies[3521] will be able to work across all major search ad platforms.

The search ad platforms do not cover the utilisation or impact of disclaimers.[3522] While not directly a disclaimer, Google will permit certain trademarks such as ads

3515. Yahoo! 'Ad Specs Guide' (*Yahoo! Ad tech*) https://adspecs.yahooinc.com/pages/policies-guidelines/yahoo-ad-policy accessed July 2024; Microsoft, 'Intellectual Property Policies' (*Microsoft*) https://help.ads.microsoft.com/#apex/ads/en/ext60211 accessed June 2025.
3516. Microsoft 'Intellectual Property Concern Form' (*Microsoft Advertising*) https://about.ads.microsoft.com/en-us/resources/policies/intellectual-property-complaint-form accessed July 2024.
3517. Microsoft, 'Market Availability for Microsoft Advertising and Its Features' (*Microsoft Advertising*) https://help.ads.microsoft.com/apex/index/3/en-us/50873/ accessed June 2025.
3518. Yahoo! 'Copyright and Intellectual Property Policy' (*Yahoo!*) https://legal.yahoo.com/us/en/yahoo/ip/index.html accessed June 2025.
3519. Microsoft 'Intellectual Property Concern Form' (*Microsoft Advertising*) https://about.ads.microsoft.com/en-us/resources/policies/intellectual-property-complaint-form accessed June 2025.
3520. Rajeev Sachdev, 'Towards an Improved Framework for Trade-Mark Law and Regulation in Social Media Usernames: A Study of the Canadian, U.S., and U.K. Positions' (2016) 28 Intellectual Property Journal 379, 379-418; Daniel Doft, 'Facebook, Twitter, and the Wild West of IP Enforcement on Social Media: Weighing the Merits of a Uniform Dispute Resolution Policy' (2016) 49 The John Marshall Law Review 959; Thomas J Curtin, 'The Name Game: Cybersquatting and Trademark Infringement on Social Media Websites' (2010-2011) 19 Journal of Law and Policy 353; Erick J Heels, 'How to Twittersquat the Top 100 Brands' (*GiantPeople*, 8 January 2009) http://www.giantpeople.com/1298.html accessed 4 August 2025; Paul D McGrady, *McGrady on Social Media and the Metaverse* (Mathew Bender & Company, Inc. 2023) §12; John McElwaine and Christopher D Casavale, 'Tackling Bad Faith Registration of Domain Names in a Fast-Changing Landscape' (*WIPO Magazine*, December 2019) https://www.wipo.int/wipo_magazine/en/2019/06/article_0006.html accessed June 2025; Edward C Anderson and Timothy S Cole, 'The UDRP: A Model for Dispute Resolution in E-Commerce' (2002) 6 Journal of Small & Emerging Business Law 235.
3521. *Ibid.*
3522. WIPO, 'WIPO Overview of WIPO Panel Views on Selected UDRP Questions, Third Edition' ('WIPO Jurisprudential Overview 3.0') (*WIPO*, 2017) https://www.wipo.int/amc/en/domains/search/overview3.0/ accessed June 2025; Alexander Peukert, 'The Coexistence of Trade Mark Laws and Rights on the Internet, and the Impact of Geolocation Technologies' (2016) 47 International Review of Intellectual Property and Competition Law 60, 81 https://doi.org/10.1007/s40319-015-0427-8; Leslie Fair, 'Full Disclosure' (*FTC Business Blog*, 23 September 2014) https://www.ftc.gov/business-guidance/blog/2014/09/full-disclosure accessed June 2025.

selling 'products or services, components, replacement parts, or compatible products';[3523] however, '[t]he ad and landing page must be clear as to whether the advertiser is a reseller or informational site'.[3524]

5.3.4.6 *Digital Jurisdictional and Territorial Considerations*

While all search ad platforms have general policies applicable to all advertising, specific rules, such as whether or not the search platforms will investigate 'keywords',[3525] may apply to specific jurisdictions.[3526] It is anticipated that search ad platforms would want to deal with this uniformly, such that they all investigate 'keywords'[3527] for those jurisdictions which require it, or whether they investigate these for all countries. Co-existence[3528] is not discussed.

5.3.4.7 *Digital Justification*

Justification is covered only on a limited basis by search ad terms and policies. Google permits trademarks in ads for 'products or services, components, replacement parts or compatible products or services corresponding to the trademark'[3529] but only when the '[t]he ad and landing page must be clear as to whether the advertiser is a reseller or informational site'.[3530] Also, 'to provide informative details ... or an index of search results related to the trademark'[3531] or 'descriptively in its ordinary meaning',[3532] Google does not state justifications beyond these mentioned. Yahoo may remove an ad 'if the materials are protected by the fair use doctrine, among other reasons'.[3533] However, it is not clear what these other reasons may be. Microsoft permits 'fair

3523. Google, 'Trademarks' (*Google*) https://support.google.com/adspolicy/answer/6118?visit_id=638419270508802311-4094647794&rd=1 accessed June 2025.
3524. *Ibid.*
3525. Yahoo! 'Ad Specs Guide' (*Yahoo! Ad tech*) https://adspecs.yahooinc.com/pages/policies-guidelines/yahoo-ad-policy accessed July 2024; Microsoft, 'Microsoft Advertising Policies' (*Microsoft*) https://help.ads.microsoft.com/#apex/ads/en/60211/0-500 accessed June 2025.
3526. *Ibid.*
3527. *Ibid.*
3528. EUIPO, '3.1 Coexistence Between the Marks Involved in the Opposition' (*EUIPO Trade mark Guidelines*) https://guidelines.euipo.europa.eu/2058843/2043906/trade-mark-guidelines/3-1-coexistence-between-the-marks-involved-in-the-opposition accessed January 2024;15 U.S. Code § 1052(d); Alexander Peukert, 'The Coexistence of Trade Mark Laws and Rights on the Internet, and the Impact of Geolocation Technologies' (2016) 47 International Review of Intellectual Property and Competition Law 60, 81 https://doi.org/10.1007/s40319-015-0427-8; Tamara Nanayakkara, 'IP and Business: Trademark Coexistence' (*WIPO*, November 2006) https://www.wipo.int/wipo_magazine/en/2006/06/article_0007.html accessed June 2025.
3529. Google, 'Trademarks' (*Google*) https://support.google.com/adspolicy/answer/6118?visit_id=638419270508802311-4094647794&rd=1 accessed June 2025.
3530. *Ibid.*
3531. *Ibid.*
3532. *Ibid.*
3533. Yahoo! 'Copyright and Intellectual Property Policy' (*Yahoo!*) https://legal.yahoo.com/us/en/yahoo/ip/index.html accessed June 2025.

use'[3534] such as for reselling,[3535] 'informational websites' and product reviewing,[3536] 'ordinary dictionary use'[3537] and 'comparative advertising (with restrictions)'.[3538] While some justification and fair use are permitted, there is scope for other justifications and defences which are not directly addressed. For example, parody[3539] is not mentioned by the platforms even if may be a fair use.[3540]

Overall, by not directly or adequately incorporating certain basic elements within the policies, it makes enforcement through the search ad platform limited. It also makes it uncertain what rules apply beyond those directly indicated. Another major gap with having different policies (even if some elements overlap) is that there is ample opportunity for different decisions to be concluded by different search ad platforms in similar matters. With different bodies making decisions based on differently worded policies and internal procedures, this greatly enhances the chance to reach different conclusions breeding inconsistency. Further, unlike the UDRP, decisions are not made public and users may not be able to see what decisions were made unless privy to these decisions. This does not allow for those who are involved with using trademarks in these services or those involved in a dispute to be informed about decisions made.

5.3.5 Solution: A Uniform Policy for Trademarks in Search Advertising Platforms

Under the Digital Trademark and Trade Practices Model, it is recommended that a uniform policy apply to trademark disputes in search advertising platforms. Such uniform policy is proposed because of the commonalities between trademarks used in search advertising across platforms. While search engine algorithms and approaches may differ, key search advertising approaches are similar and a uniform policy can address the issues that they raise. The uniform policy should follow a UDNDRP approach as adapted from the UDRP and other sources, as seen in Chapter 4 and below.

There already is some overlap[3541] between two of these search ad platforms, as seen in the previous section; however, a consistent uniform policy[3542] implemented by

3534. *Ibid.*
3535. *Ibid.*
3536. *Ibid.*
3537. *Ibid.*
3538. *Ibid.*
3539. 15 U.S. Code § 1125.
3540. EUTMR, Recital 21; 15 U.S. Code § 1115(b)(4).
3541. Microsoft, 'Market Availability for Microsoft Advertising and Its features' (*Microsoft Advertising*) https://help.ads.microsoft.com/apex/index/3/en-us/50873/ accessed July 2024; Microsoft, 'Microsoft Advertising. Great Relationships Start Here.' (*Microsoft Advertising*) https://ads.microsoft.com/?n1pq=6d8f486e-e8c9-4233-8f4d-36a69d3c4bf0&fdmkt=en-us&fdiso=us&fdtz=-5 accessed July 2024.
3542. ICANN, 'Uniform Domain-Name Dispute-Resolution Policy' (*ICANN*, 25 February 2012) https://www.icann.org/resources/pages/policy-2012-02-25-en accessed June 2025; Rajeev Sachdev, 'Towards an Improved Framework for Trade-Mark Law and Regulation in Social Media Usernames: A Study of the Canadian, U.S., and U.K. Positions' (2016) 28 Intellectual Property Journal 379, 379-418; Daniel Doft, 'Facebook, Twitter, and the Wild West of IP Enforcement on Social Media: Weighing the Merits of a Uniform Dispute Resolution Policy'

search platforms may provide many benefits. Such uniform policy can help to make enforcement consistent across search ad platforms, as advertisers may choose to advertise across these channels. Further, this will provide an opportunity to clearly incorporate provisions which are not included and avoid legal uncertainty. For example, 'bad faith'[3543] is not adequately covered by search ad platforms, and concepts such as unfair acts,[3544] practices,[3545] and competition[3546] that are very relevant to advertising are not clearly incorporated, although some related concepts are. This will help to avoid the need for search ad platforms to state that other considerations may be taken into consideration and make clear what these are. The impact of disclaimers (such as in ads or the associated website to the ad) can be clarified. In this way, many gaps will be filled. As was seen in the recommendation for e-commerce marketplace platforms, it is recommended that this be achieved in one of two ways: either individually by search ad platforms making their own decisions on complaints, or by way of a panel decision approach, as with the UDRP.

The following is sample text of such uniform trademark policy[3547] for search advertising platforms to adopt on their own and make decisions through complaints to their platform.

Table 5.5 Uniform Search Ad Trademark Dispute Resolution Policy (USATDRP)

Uniform Search Ad Trademark Dispute Resolution Policy (USATDRP)	Adapted or directly from the UDRP[3548] and UDNDRP (Chapter 4). The name reflects specifically the platform type and subject matter.

(2016) 49 The John Marshall Law Review 959; Thomas J Curtin, 'The Name Game: Cybersquatting and Trademark Infringement on Social Media Websites' (2010-2011) 19 Journal of Law and Policy 353; Erick J Heels, 'How to Twittersquat the Top 100 Brands' (*GiantPeople*, 8 January 2009) http://www.giantpeople.com/1298.html accessed 4 August 2025; Paul D McGrady, *McGrady on Social Media and the Metaverse* (Mathew Bender & Company, Inc. 2023) §12; John McElwaine and Christopher D Casavale, 'Tackling Bad Faith Registration of Domain Names in a Fast-Changing Landscape' (*WIPO Magazine*, December 2019) https://www.wipo.int/wipo_magazine/en/2019/06/article_0006.html accessed June 2025.

3543. UDRP, 4(a)(iii).

3544. Anselm Kamperman Sanders, *Unfair Competition Law: The Protection of Intellectual and Industrial Creativity* (Oxford University Press, 1997) 8; Frauke Henning-Bodewig, *Unfair Competition Law European Union and Member States* (Kluwer Law International 2006) xv-xvi; Martin Senftleben, Michael Handler and Irene Calboli, 'Protection Against Unfair Competition Around the Globe' (2024) 19 Journal of Intellectual Property Law & Practice 79, 79-80 https://doi.org/10.1093/jiplp/jpad121; Paris Convention, Art. 10bis; EUTMR, Art. 9(2)(c); 15 U.S.C. § 1125(c)(2)(B).

3545. *Ibid.*

3546. *Ibid.*

3547. ICANN, 'Uniform Domain-Name Dispute-Resolution Policy' (*ICANN*, 25 February 2012) https://www.icann.org/resources/pages/policy-2012-02-25-en accessed June 2025.

3548. *Ibid.*

(1) *Purpose*. This Uniform Search Ad Trademark Dispute Resolution Policy ('Policy') has been adopted by [Search Ad Platform] ('Platform' or 'We'), is incorporated by reference into the Terms of Use of Platform and your Search Advertising Agreement, and sets forth the terms and conditions in connection with a dispute between you and any party other than Platform over the utilisation of a trademark in Platform. Decisions under Paragraph 4 of this Policy will be made in accordance with the Policy. Guidelines to this policy are set forth in the document entitled: Guidelines to the USATDRP.	Adapted or directly from the UDRP[3549] and UDNDRP (Chapter 4). The policy refers to any disputed utilisation of a mark within the platforms.
(2) *Your Representations*. By advertising on Platform, you hereby represent and warrant to us that (a) the statements that you made in your Search Advertising Agreement are complete and accurate; (b) to your knowledge, the advertising will not infringe upon or otherwise violate the rights of any third party; (c) you are not advertising for an unlawful purpose; and (d) you will not knowingly use Platform in violation of any applicable laws or regulations. It is your responsibility to determine whether your account and/or search advertising infringes or violates someone else's rights.	Adapted or directly from the UDRP[3550] and UDNRDP (Chapter 4).
(3) *Changes, Suspensions, and Cancellations*. We will make changes to, suspend, or cancel your account or search advertising on Platform under the following circumstances: (i) our receipt of written or appropriate electronic instructions from you or your authorized agent to take such action except that you may not transfer your account to another holder (a) during a pending administrative proceeding brought pursuant to Paragraph 4 or for a period of fifteen (15) business days after such proceeding is concluded; or (b) during a pending court proceeding or arbitration commenced regarding your account, search advertising	Adapted or directly from the UDRP[3551] and UDNDRP (Chapter 4). Updated based on services. Added that 'abuse'[3552] can result

3549. *Ibid.*
3550. *Ibid.*
3551. *Ibid.*
3552. WIPO, 'WIPO Overview of WIPO Panel Views on Selected UDRP Questions, Third Edition' ('WIPO Jurisprudential Overview 3.0') (*WIPO*, 2017) https://www.wipo.int/amc/en/domains/search/overview3.0/ accessed June 2025.

or their content unless the court or party to whom the account is being transferred agrees, in writing, to be bound by the decision of the court or arbitrator. We reserve the right not to permit the transfer of your account to another party in accordance with this subparagraph; (ii) our receipt of an order from a court or arbitral tribunal, in each case of competent jurisdiction, requiring such action; (iii) our decision requiring such action based on a complaint received under this or a later version of this Policy; and/or (iv) in accordance with the terms of your Search Advertising Agreement (such as but not limited to where you have engaged in abuse with respect to one or more trademarks) or other legal requirements.	in a change, suspension or cancellation and guidelines can be used to clarify when certain actions may take place.
(4) *Mandatory Decision Process and Remedies.* This Paragraph sets forth the type of disputes for which you are required to submit to a Mandatory Decision Process. A decision on a complaint lodged under this Policy will be made by Platform. (a) Applicable Disputes. You are required to submit to a decision by Platform in the event that a third party (a 'complainant') asserts to Platform, through a Trademark Complaint Form < URL for Form > that your search advertising or their content: (A) is identical or confusingly similar to trademarks in which a complainant has rights and which you are using on an unauthorized basis in the course of trade AND (B) (i) is being used to engage in unfair competition in the course of trade with respect to a trademark OR (ii) is being used in bad faith or is being abused with respect to a trademark. For clarity, in the administrative proceeding, the complainant must prove element A AND one element from B (either i or ii) are present.	Adapted or directly from the UDRP,[3553] UDNDRP, Paris Convention, TRIPS, Dispute Resolution Service for.eu,[3554]

3553. ICANN, 'Uniform Domain-Name Dispute-Resolution Policy' (*ICANN*, 25 February 2012) https://www.icann.org/resources/pages/policy-2012-02-25-en accessed June 2025.
3554. WIPO, 'WIPO Domain Name Dispute Resolution Service for .EU (and.ею and.ευ)' (*WIPO*) https://www.wipo.int/amc/en/domains/cctld/eu/index.html accessed July 2024.

(b) Permitted use. Trademarks will be permitted if you demonstrate that you have rights or legitimate interests in respect of the search advertising or their content by showing one or more of these justifications: (i) you (as an individual, business, or other organization) have been commonly known by the term and are using it legitimately (ii) you are making genuine noncommercial legitimate fair use of the trademark, (iii) you are fairly utilising the trademark in marketing of authorized, replacement, compatible or used goods or services, (iv) you are utilising the trademark in an ordinary dictionary sense, (v) you are genuinely and noncommercially utilising the trademark under freedom of speech and expression or legitimate criticism, parody, or review of the company, good or service associated with the trademark, OR (vi) you are making fair and legitimate use of the trademark in comparative advertising. (c) Remedies. The remedies available to a complainant pursuant to any decision by Platform shall be limited to requiring the cancellation of, suspending, or making changes to your account and/or search advertising.	EUTMR, Lanham Act 1946 15 U.S. Code §§ 1051 et seq. (as amended), the TDRA 2006 15 U.S. Code § 1125(c), Google, Yahoo, Microsoft terms and policies.[3555] Key UDRP aspects have been retained including relevant concepts from the Overview.[3556] This uniform policy largely follows the UDNDRP (Chapter 4) but is adapted for search advertising platforms. Please see Chapter 4 (section 4.3.3) for further details and explanations of the adaptations under the model. Interpretation of this Paragraph should be set out in the Guidelines. For search advertising dedicated to specific jurisdictions, guidance should include that while decisions will be made based on general trademark principles, local law may be considered since the site is targeted to a jurisdiction (similar to the UDRP where local law may be considered, such as when parties are from the same jurisdiction).[3557] This should be

3555. Google, 'Trademarks' (*Google*) https://support.google.com/adspolicy/answer/6118?visit_id=638419270508802311-4094647794&rd=1 accessed June 2025; Yahoo! 'Counterfeit/Trademark' (*Yahoo!*) https://www.yahooinc.com/ipr/en-US/forms/trademark accessed June 2025; Microsoft, 'Intellectual Property Policies' (*Microsoft*) https://help.ads.microsoft.com/#apex/ads/en/ext60211 accessed June 2025.
3556. ICANN, 'Uniform Domain-Name Dispute-Resolution Policy' (*ICANN*, 25 February 2012) https://www.icann.org/resources/pages/policy-2012-02-25-en accessed June 2025; WIPO, 'WIPO Overview of WIPO Panel Views on Selected UDRP Questions, Third Edition' ('WIPO Jurisprudential Overview 3.0') (*WIPO*, 2017) https://www.wipo.int/amc/en/domains/search/overview3.0/ accessed June 2025.
3557. WIPO, 'WIPO Overview of WIPO Panel Views on Selected UDRP Questions, Third Edition' ('WIPO Jurisprudential Overview 3.0') (*WIPO*, 2017) https://www.wipo.int/amc/en/domains/search/overview3.0/ accessed June 2025.

(d) All Other Disputes. All other disputes between you and any party other than Platform regarding your search advertising in Platform that are not brought pursuant to this Policy will not be resolved through a decision under this Policy. Platform reserves the right to make a decision on any matter outside of this policy as set forth in our Terms of Use available at < terms > including any remedies or actions it, in its sole discretion, deems appropriate.	the case in special circumstances, but decisions are expected to follow the general principles in most cases.
(5) *Procedures.* (a) Initiation of Proceeding. Submitting a Trade mark Complaint Form initiates the process for a decision by Platform. (b) Consolidation. In the event of multiple disputes between you and a complainant, either you or the complainant may request to consolidate the disputes for a single decision. Platform may consolidate before it any or all such disputes in its sole discretion, provided that the disputes being consolidated are governed by this Policy or a later version of this Policy. (c) Fees. No fees are charged to file a complaint under this Policy or to receive a decision by Platform. (d) Availability of Court Proceedings. The Mandatory Decision Process requirements set forth in Paragraph 4 shall not prevent either you or the complainant from submitting the dispute to a court of competent jurisdiction for independent resolution before such Mandatory Decision Process is commenced or after it is concluded. If we decide that your search advertising should be cancelled, suspended, or changed, we will then implement the decision immediately unless we have received from you official documentation	Adapted or directly from the UDRP[3558] and UDNDRP (Chapter 4). Platforms may wish to include an indemnification provision here.

3558. ICANN, 'Uniform Domain-Name Dispute-Resolution Policy' (*ICANN*, 25 February 2012) https://www.icann.org/resources/pages/policy-2012-02-25-en accessed June 2025.

(such as a copy of a complaint, file-stamped by the clerk of the court) that you have commenced a lawsuit against the complainant in an appropriate jurisdiction. If we receive such documentation immediately following a decision, we will not implement the decision, and we will take no further action, until we receive (i) evidence satisfactory to us of a resolution between the parties; (ii) evidence satisfactory to us that your lawsuit has been dismissed or withdrawn; or (iii) a copy of an order from such court dismissing your lawsuit or ordering that you do not have the right to continue the search advertising.	
(6) *Policy Modifications*. Platform reserves the right to modify this Policy at any time. Platform will post any revised Policy at <URL> at least thirty (30) calendar days before it becomes effective. Unless this Policy has already been invoked by the submission of a Trade mark Complaint Form, in which event the version of the Policy in effect at the time it was invoked will apply to you until the dispute is over, all such changes will be binding upon you with respect to any search advertising trademark dispute, whether the dispute arose before, on or after the effective date of our change. In the event that you object to a change in this Policy, your sole remedy is to cancel your Account with us, provided that you will not be entitled to a refund of any fees you paid to us. The revised Policy will apply to you until you cancel your Account.	Adapted or directly from UDRP[3559] and UDNDRP (Chapter 4).

The following is sample text of such uniform trademark policy[3560] for a panel-like approach in line with the UDRP for search ad platforms.

Table 5.6 Uniform Search Ad Trademark Dispute Resolution Policy (USATDRP)

Uniform Search Ad Trademark Dispute Resolution Policy (USATDRP)	Adapted or directly from the UDRP[3561] and UDNDRP (Chapter 4). The name reflects specifically the platform type and subject matter.

3559. *Ibid.*
3560. *Ibid.*
3561. *Ibid.*

(1) *Purpose.* This Uniform Search Ad Trademark Dispute Resolution Policy ('Policy') has been adopted by [Search Ad Platform] ('Platform' or 'We'), is incorporated by reference into the Terms of Use of Platform and your Search Advertising Agreement, and sets forth the terms and conditions in connection with a dispute between you and any party other than Platform over the utilisation of a trademark in Platform. Decisions under Paragraph 4 of this Policy will be made in accordance with the Policy. Guidelines to this policy are set forth in the document entitled: Guidelines to the USATDRP.	Adapted or directly from the UDRP[3562] and UDNDRP (Chapter 4). The policy refers to any disputed utilisation of a mark within the platforms.
(2) *Your Representations.* By advertising on Platform, you hereby represent and warrant to us that (a) the statements that you made in your Search Advertising Agreement are complete and accurate; (b) to your knowledge, the advertising will not infringe upon or otherwise violate the rights of any third party; (c) you are not advertising for an unlawful purpose; and (d) you will not knowingly use Platform in violation of any applicable laws or regulations. It is your responsibility to determine whether your account and/or search advertising infringes or violates someone else's rights.	Adapted or directly from the UDRP[3563] and UDNRDP (Chapter 4).
(3) *Changes, Suspensions, and Cancellations.* We will make changes to, suspend, or cancel your account or search advertising on Platform under the following circumstances: (i) our receipt of written or appropriate electronic instructions from you or your authorized agent to take such action except that you may not transfer your account to another holder (a) during a pending administrative proceeding brought pursuant to Paragraph 4 or for a period of fifteen (15) business days after such proceeding is concluded; or (b) during a pending court proceeding or arbitration commenced regarding your account, search advertising	Adapted or directly from the UDRP[3564] and UDNDRP (Chapter 4). Updated based on services. Added that 'abuse'[3565] can result

3562. *Ibid.*
3563. *Ibid.*
3564. *Ibid.*
3565. WIPO, 'WIPO Overview of WIPO Panel Views on Selected UDRP Questions, Third Edition' ('WIPO Jurisprudential Overview 3.0') (*WIPO*, 2017) https://www.wipo.int/amc/en/domains/search/overview3.0/ accessed June 2025.

or their content unless the court or party to whom the account is being transferred agrees, in writing, to be bound by the decision of the court or arbitrator. We reserve the right not to permit the transfer of your account to another party in accordance with this subparagraph; (ii) our receipt of an order from a court or arbitral tribunal, in each case of competent jurisdiction, requiring such action; (iii) a panel decision requiring such action based on a complaint received under this or a later version of this Policy; and/or (iv) in accordance with the terms of your Search Advertising Agreement (such as but not limited to where you have engaged in abuse with respect to one or more trademarks) or other legal requirements.	in a change, suspension or cancellation and guidelines can be used to clarify when certain actions may take place.
(4) *Mandatory Administrative Proceeding and Remedies*. This Paragraph sets forth the type of disputes for which you are required to submit to a mandatory Panel Decision. A decision on a complaint lodged under this Policy will be made by an appointed Panel. (a) Applicable Disputes. You are required to submit to a Panel Decision in the event that a third party (a 'complainant') asserts to Platform, through a Trademark Complaint Form < URL for Form > that that your search advertising or their content: (A) is identical or confusingly similar to trademarks in which a complainant has rights and which you are using on an unauthorized basis in the course of trade AND (B) (i) is being used to engage in unfair competition in the course of trade with respect to a trademark OR (ii) is being used in bad faith or is being abused with respect to a trademark. For clarity, in the administrative proceeding, the complainant must prove element A AND one element from B (either i or ii) are present.	Adapted or directly from the UDRP,[3566] UDNDRP, Paris Convention, TRIPS, Dispute Resolution Service for.eu,[3567]

3566. ICANN, 'Uniform Domain-Name Dispute-Resolution Policy' (*ICANN*, 25 February 2012) https://www.icann.org/resources/pages/policy-2012-02-25-en accessed June 2025.
3567. WIPO, 'WIPO Domain Name Dispute Resolution Service for .EU (and.ею and.ευ)' (*WIPO*) https://www.wipo.int/amc/en/domains/cctld/eu/index.html accessed July 2024.

(b) Permitted use. Trademarks will be permitted if you demonstrate that you have rights or legitimate interests in respect of the search advertising or their content by showing one or more of these justifications: (i) you (as an individual, business, or other organization) have been commonly known by the term and are using it legitimately (ii) you are making genuine noncommercial legitimate fair use of the trademark, (iii) you are fairly utilising the trademark in marketing of authorized, replacement, compatible or used goods or services, (iv) you are utilising the trademark in an ordinary dictionary sense, (v) you are genuinely and noncommercially utilising the trademark under freedom of speech and expression or legitimate criticism, parody, or review of the company, good or service associated with the trademark, OR (vi) you are making fair and legitimate use of the trademark in comparative advertising. (c) Remedies. The remedies available to a complainant pursuant to any Panel Decision shall be limited to requiring the cancellation of, suspending, or making changes to your account and/or search advertising.	EUTMR, Lanham Act 1946 15 U.S. Code §§ 1051 et seq. (as amended), the TDRA 2006 15 U.S. Code § 1125(c), Google, Yahoo, Microsoft terms and policies.[3568] Key UDRP aspects have been retained including relevant concepts from the Overview.[3569] This uniform policy largely follows the UDNDRP (Chapter 4) but is adapted for search advertising platforms. Please see Chapter 4 (section 4.3.3) for further details and explanations of the adaptations under the model. Interpretation of this Paragraph should be set out in the Guidelines. For search advertising dedicated to specific jurisdictions, guidance should include that while decisions will be made based on general trademark principles, local law may be considered since the site is targeted to a jurisdiction (similar to the UDRP where local law may be considered, such as when parties are from the same jurisdiction).[3570] This should be

3568. Google, 'Trademarks' (*Google*) https://support.google.com/adspolicy/answer/6118?visit_id=638419270508802311-4094647794&rd=1 accessed June 2025; Yahoo! 'Counterfeit/Trademark' (*Yahoo!*) https://www.yahooinc.com/ipr/en-US/forms/trademark accessed June 2025; Microsoft, 'Intellectual Property Policies' (*Microsoft*) https://help.ads.microsoft.com/#apex/ads/en/ext60211 accessed June 2025.
3569. ICANN, 'Uniform Domain-Name Dispute-Resolution Policy' (*ICANN*, 25 February 2012) https://www.icann.org/resources/pages/policy-2012-02-25-en accessed June 2025; WIPO, 'WIPO Overview of WIPO Panel Views on Selected UDRP Questions, Third Edition' ('WIPO Jurisprudential Overview 3.0') (*WIPO*, 2017) https://www.wipo.int/amc/en/domains/search/overview3.0/ accessed June 2025.
3570. WIPO, 'WIPO Overview of WIPO Panel Views on Selected UDRP Questions, Third Edition' ('WIPO Jurisprudential Overview 3.0') (*WIPO*, 2017) https://www.wipo.int/amc/en/domains/search/overview3.0/ accessed June 2025.

(d) All Other Disputes. All other disputes between you and any party other Platform regarding your search advertising in Platform that are not brought pursuant to this Policy will not be resolved through a Panel Decision. Platform reserves the right to make a decision on any matter outside of this policy as set forth in our Terms of Use available at < terms > including any remedies or actions it, in its sole discretion, deems appropriate.	the case in special circumstances, but decisions are expected to follow the general principles in most cases.
(5) *Procedures.* (a) Initiation of Proceeding. Submitting a Trade mark Complaint Form initiates the process for a Panel Decision. (b) Consolidation. In the event of multiple disputes between you and a complainant, either you or the complainant may petition to consolidate the disputes before a single Panel. This petition shall be made to the Panel appointed to hear a pending dispute between the parties. This Panel may consolidate before it any or all such disputes in its sole discretion, provided that the disputes being consolidated are governed by this Policy or a later version of this Policy. (c) Fees. No fees are charged to file a complaint under this Policy or to receive a Panel Decision. (d) Availability of Court Proceedings. The Panel Decision proceeding requirements set forth in Paragraph 4 shall not prevent either you or the complainant from submitting the dispute to a court of competent jurisdiction for independent resolution before such Panel Decision is commenced or after such proceeding is concluded. If a Panel decides that your search advertising should be cancelled, suspended, or changed, we will then implement the decision immediately unless we have received from you official documentation	Adapted or directly from the UDRP[3571] and UDNDRP (Chapter 4). Because platforms currently expend their own resources to make decisions on complaints they receive, these resources may be redirected to an online panel decision under the assumption that this will not raise costs by unreasonable sums.

3571. ICANN, 'Uniform Domain-Name Dispute-Resolution Policy' (*ICANN*, 25 February 2012) https://www.icann.org/resources/pages/policy-2012-02-25-en accessed June 2025.

(such as a copy of a complaint, file-stamped by the clerk of the court) that you have commenced a lawsuit against the complainant in an appropriate jurisdiction. If we receive such documentation immediately following a decision, we will not implement the Panel's decision, and we will take no further action, until we receive (i) evidence satisfactory to us of a resolution between the parties; (ii) evidence satisfactory to us that your lawsuit has been dismissed or withdrawn; or (iii) a copy of an order from such court dismissing your lawsuit or ordering that you do not have the right to continue the search advertising.	Platforms may wish to include an indemnification provision here.
(6) *Policy Modifications*. Platform reserves the right to modify this Policy at any time. Platform will post any revised Policy at <URL> at least thirty (30) calendar days before it becomes effective. Unless this Policy has already been invoked by the submission of a Trade mark Complaint Form, in which event the version of the Policy in effect at the time it was invoked will apply to you until the dispute is over, all such changes will be binding upon you with respect to any search advertising trademark dispute, whether the dispute arose before, on or after the effective date of our change. In the event that you object to a change in this Policy, your sole remedy is to cancel your Account with us, provided that you will not be entitled to a refund of any fees you paid to us. The revised Policy will apply to you until you cancel your Account.	Adapted or directly from UDRP[3572] and UDNDRP (Chapter 4).

5.4 MAJOR SOCIAL MEDIA PLATFORM TRADEMARK TERMS AND POLICIES

Social media services such as those by Facebook, X (formerly, Twitter), Pinterest, LinkedIn, and Snapchat require that users agree to certain terms and policies before an account can be opened (or username registered) to avail of such services as offered by these platforms.[3573] These terms and policies generally prohibit certain ways of

3572. ICANN, 'Uniform Domain-Name Dispute-Resolution Policy' (*ICANN*, 25 February 2012) https://www.icann.org/resources/pages/policy-2012-02-25-en.
3573. Meta, 'Terms of Service' (*Meta*) https://www.facebook.com/legal/terms accessed June 2025; X, 'X Terms of Service' (*X*) https://x.com/en/tos accessed June 2025; LinkedIn, 'User Agreement' (*LinkedIn*) https://www.linkedin.com/legal/user-agreement accessed June

utilising trademarks of others within these platforms, such as within usernames;[3574] however, disputes associated with these are generally handled by the platforms themselves unless resolved by the parties or litigation is commenced.[3575]

This section involves an overview of social media terms and policies pertinent to trademarks in their individual services. Some have previously reviewed or compared such terms and policies, including those pertaining to trademarks; however, these may change at any time and are often in a state of flux.[3576] Below is a summary of updated trademark provisions for each, followed by an identification of problems or gaps before turning to a proposed solution based on a uniform approach.[3577] Please note that with changes to some social media platform names or services, some terms and references still refer to previous names which have been retained.

5.4.1 Facebook

Facebook help pages say that '[w]hile there may be cases where this type of use can be reported for trademark infringement based on the context of its use, please note that not every use of your trademark in a username is necessarily a trademark infringement

2025; Pinterest, 'Terms of Service' (*Pinterest Policy*) https://policy.pinterest.com/en/terms-of-service accessed June 2025; Google, 'Google Terms of Service: Privacy & Terms' (*Google*) https://policies.google.com/terms?hl=en accessed June 2025.

3574. Rajeev Sachdev, 'Towards an Improved Framework for Trade-Mark Law and Regulation in Social Media Usernames: A Study of the Canadian, U.S., and U.K. Positions' (2016) 28 Intellectual Property Journal 379, 379-418; Daniel Doft, 'Facebook, Twitter, and the Wild West of IP Enforcement on Social Media: Weighing the Merits of a Uniform Dispute Resolution Policy' (2016) 49 The John Marshall Law Review 959; Thomas J Curtin, 'The Name Game: Cybersquatting and Trademark Infringement on Social Media Websites' (2010-2011) 19 Journal of Law and Policy 353; Erick J Heels, 'How to Twittersquat the Top 100 Brands' (*GiantPeople*, 8 January 2009) http://www.giantpeople.com/1298.html accessed 4 August 2025; Paul D McGrady, *McGrady on Social Media: 2018* (Lexis Nexis 2018) § 9.

3575. *Ibid.*

3576. Lisa P Ramsey, 'Brandjacking on Social Networks: Trademark Infringement by Impersonation of Markholders' (2010) 58 Buffalo Law Review 851; Danny Friedmann, *Trademarks and Social Media: Towards Algorithmic Justice* (Edward Elgar Publishing 2015); Rajeev Sachdev, 'Towards an Improved Framework for Trade-Mark Law and Regulation in Social Media Usernames: A Study of the Canadian, U.S., and U.K. Positions' (2016) 28 Intellectual Property Journal 379, 379-418; Paul D McGrady, *McGrady on Social Media and the Metaverse* (Mathew Bender & Company, Inc. 2023) §12.

3577. Rajeev Sachdev, 'Towards an Improved Framework for Trade-Mark Law and Regulation in Social Media Usernames: A Study of the Canadian, U.S., and U.K. Positions' (2016) 28 Intellectual Property Journal 379, 379-418; Daniel Doft, 'Facebook, Twitter, and the Wild West of IP Enforcement on Social Media: Weighing the Merits of a Uniform Dispute Resolution Policy' (2016) 49 The John Marshall Law Review 959; Thomas J Curtin, 'The Name Game: Cybersquatting and Trademark Infringement on Social Media Websites' (2010-2011) 19 Journal of Law and Policy 353; Erick J Heels, 'How to Twittersquat The Top 100 Brands' (*GiantPeople*, 8 January 2009) http://www.giantpeople.com/1298.html accessed 4 August 2025; Paul D McGrady, *McGrady on Social Media and the Metaverse* (Mathew Bender & Company, Inc. 2023) §12; John McElwaine and Christopher D Casavale, 'Tackling Bad Faith Registration of Domain Names in a Fast-Changing Landscape' (*WIPO Magazine*, December 2019) https://www.wipo.int/wipo_magazine/en/2019/06/article_0006.html accessed June 2025.

... [a] word or phrase that is used in a different context may not violate your trademark'.[3578] However, the specifics of such acceptable uses are not identified.

There are places where repeat infringement is covered and Facebook Terms mention that if they decide in their 'discretion' that there has been a serious or repeated breach of their 'Terms or Policies, including in particular the Community Standards', they 'may suspend or permanently disable ... access to Meta Company Products, and ... may permanently disable or delete [the] account'. For repeated infringement or under law, they may 'disable or delete' an account.[3579] Also, if upon removal, they will notify the party and indicate any 'review' possibilities with the exception of where a serious or repeated violation has occurred.[3580]

Facebook policies include rules that specifically prohibit content that 'infringes or violates someone else's rights, including their intellectual property rights (such as by infringing another's copyright or trademark, or distributing or selling counterfeit or pirated goods), unless an exception or limitation applies under applicable law'.[3581] Their help pages state: '[g]enerally, trademark infringement occurs when all three of the following requirements are met: A company or person uses a trademark owner's trademark (or similar trademark) without permission ... [t]hat use is in commerce, meaning that it's done in connection with the sale or promotion of goods or services ... [t]hat use is likely to confuse consumers about the source, endorsement or affiliation of the goods or services'.[3582] While not in its terms or community guidelines, Facebook's help centre provides general information about trademarks and some specific information pertinent to Facebook itself. It defines trademark and overviews that '[g]enerally, trademark law seeks to prevent consumers from being confused about who provides, endorses or is affiliated with a particular product or service'.[3583] If 'content violates Facebook's policies or is reported to Meta as infringing the intellectual property rights of another party, Facebook may remove that content'.[3584] Facebook Community Standards specific to intellectual property[3585] state that they 'enforce a policy against posting content that violates someone else's intellectual property rights, including copyright, trademark, or other legal rights'.[3586] They further state that '[u]pon receipt of a report from a rights holder or an authorized representative, we will remove or

3578. Facebook, 'Trademark' (*Facebook Help Center*) https://www.facebook.com/help/507663689427413?helpref=about_content accessed June 2025.
3579. Meta, 'Terms of Service' (*Meta*) https://www.facebook.com/legal/terms accessed June 2025.
3580. *Ibid.*
3581. *Ibid.*
3582. Meta, 'Trademark' (*Facebook Help Center*) https://www.facebook.com/help/507663689427413?helpref=about_content accessed June 2025.
3583. *Ibid.*
3584. Meta, 'How Can I Make Sure the Content I Post to Facebook Doesn't Violate Trademark Law?' (*Facebook Help Center*) https://www.facebook.com/help/189778307789711/ accessed June 2025.
3585. Meta, 'Third-Party Intellectual Property Infringement' (*Meta Transparency Center*) https://transparency.meta.com/policies/community-standards/intellectual-property/ accessed June 2025.
3586. *Ibid.*

restrict content that engages in ... [t]rademark infringement ... the sale or promotion of counterfeit goods ... false affiliation with brand(s) ... any other infringement ...'.[3587]

In general, Facebook help pages define 'counterfeit good'[3588] as 'a knockoff or replica version of another company's product ... usually copies the trademark (name or logo) and/or distinctive features of that other company's product to imitate a genuine product'.[3589] They say that '[t]he manufacture, promotion or sale of a counterfeit goods is a type of trademark infringement that is illegal in most countries, and is recognized as being harmful to consumers, trademark owners and honest sellers ... ... may be unlawful even if the seller explicitly says that the goods are counterfeit, or otherwise disclaims authenticity of the goods'.[3590] Their help pages further say, in general, that marks are 'protectable when it's used in a distinctive way to identify a product or service'[3591] and that '[p]rotection depends on a variety of factors, including how unique, generic or descriptive the trademark is and how it's used'.[3592] Generally, help pages state that '[t]rademark dilution may also be unlawful in certain countries ... [d]ilution, which applies to famous trademarks, may occur in certain circumstances when a trademark is used without permission in commerce'.[3593]

The help pages generally recognise that '[t]rademark rights are generally limited to the geographic territory where the trademark owner uses the trademark to identify their goods or services'.[3594] For example, 'if a trademark owner uses a trademark to refer to their restaurant in Country A, they likely won't be able to prevent another person from using the same term to refer to their own restaurant in Country B'.[3595] However, whether the mark is being used in one country within this platform is far from clear.

Generally, the Facebook help pages say 'while these matters are very fact-specific, trademark rights also often don't prevent: [t]he resale of legitimate goods or selling legitimate goods through channels that are not authorized by the trademark owner ... [t]he use of a trademarked word in its ordinary dictionary meaning ... [t]he use of a trademark in a way that is not related to the sale or promotion of products or services'.[3596] The Facebook help centre recommends that users ask themselves: '[d]oes my use of a trademark only refer to someone else's goods or services, or make some other type of non-infringing use of the trademark (example: using a trademarked word in its ordinary dictionary meaning, or using the trademark in a way that is not related to the sale or promotion of products or services)?'.[3597] Further, '[t]here are also many limits to trademark rights that can preclude a trademark infringement claim ... the

3587. *Ibid.*
3588. Meta, 'Trademark' (*Facebook Help Center*) https://www.facebook.com/help/507663689427413?helpref=about_content accessed June 2025.
3589. *Ibid.*
3590. *Ibid.*
3591. *Ibid.*
3592. *Ibid.*
3593. *Ibid.*
3594. *Ibid.*
3595. *Ibid.*
3596. *Ibid.*
3597. *Ibid.*

ability for someone to use your trademark to lawfully comment on or criticize your goods or services'.[3598]

There is a trademark report form which requires complaint submitters to confirm that 'have a good faith belief that the reported use described … in the manner … complained of, is not authorized by the intellectual property rights owner, its agent, or the law'.[3599] The form asks where the trademark is registered with a dropdown of countries (and a WIPO option to select instead of a country) to select from.[3600] When Facebook receives a trademark complaint from a mark holder claiming infringement, Facebook 'may need to promptly remove that content from Facebook'[3601] before contacting the user posting such material.[3602] Other remedies include claiming a username (transfer) or removing a username from a page.[3603]

Facebook also confirms that they cannot 'adjudicate disputes between third parties'[3604] and do not decide on 'trademark reports that require an in-depth trademark analysis or a real-world dispute outside of Facebook'[3605] where they say that the mark holders might contact the other party involved or seek redress through courts or other legal means.[3606]

Recently, Meta also introduced Brand Rights Protection, which is a service onto which brands may register using a registered trademark.[3607] It permits brands to 'identify and report content for counterfeit, trademark and copyright infringement and business impersonation'.[3608] This includes Facebook ads, '[s]hops, Facebook Marketplace, buy and sell groups … Pages, profiles or Groups … posts'.[3609] Upon submission of a request, Meta will 'verify that the report is complete and valid, and then we promptly remove the reported content … [and] … also attempt to remove bad actors, and disable the accounts of repeat infringers where appropriate'.[3610] Tools such as these are a welcomed approach; however, they appear to be based on the same underlying intellectual property/trademark policies as earlier discussed, for which recommendations are made in section 5.4.7 below.

3598. *Ibid.*
3599. Facebook, 'Trademark Report Form' (*Facebook Help Center*) https://www.facebook.com/help/contact/1057530390957243 accessed July 2024.
3600. *Ibid.*
3601. Meta, 'Trademark' (*Facebook Help Center*) https://www.facebook.com/help/507663689427413?helpref=about_content accessed June 2025.
3602. *Ibid.*
3603. *Ibid.*
3604. *Ibid.*
3605. *Ibid.*
3606. *Ibid.*
3607. Meta, 'Best Practices for Brand Rights Protection' (*Meta Business Help Center*) https://www.facebook.com/business/help/1124539191659664?id=4533021280101097 accessed June 2025.
3608. Meta, 'About Brand Rights Protection' (*Meta Business Help Center*) https://www.facebook.com/business/help/828925381043253?id=4533021280101097 accessed June 2025.
3609. *Ibid.*
3610. *Ibid.*

5.4.2 X (Formerly, Twitter)

X Terms of Service[3611] which also apply to the US and other countries (including its international terms which apply to the EU and other countries)[3612] and which are largely the same in the context of trademarks indicate that they 'reserve the right to remove Content that violates the User Agreement, including for example ... trademark violations or other intellectual property misappropriation, impersonation ...'.[3613] Under its specific trademark policy, X indicates that a user 'may not violate others' intellectual property rights, including ... trademark'.[3614] It overviews that '[t]rademark law may prevent others from using a trademark in an unauthorized or confusing manner'.[3615] It defines that '[u]sing another's trademark in a way that may mislead or confuse people about your affiliation may be a violation of our trademark policy'.[3616] If X determines that the trademark policy was violated, it may suspend the user's account.[3617] X may provide 'an opportunity to comply with our policies'[3618] based on the violation, or it may 'permanently suspend'[3619] an account on initial review[3620] or 'an account may be permanently suspended upon first review'.[3621]

Under X's 'Misleading and deceptive identities policy',[3622] 'impersonation'[3623] is not permitted and policy states that 'You may not impersonate other identities of individuals, groups, or organizations to deceive others ... [a]lthough you are not required to display your real identity on your profile, your account should not use false profile information to impersonate others.'[3624] Further, 'fake personas' are prohibited where one uses 'manufactured identities to engage in disruptive or deceptive behaviour ... [t]his may include using stock, stolen or AI-generated profile photos, copied or stolen profile bios, and/or misleading profile information for the purpose of deceiving others'.[3625] Further, '[w]e allow compliant Parody, Commentary, and Fan (PCF) accounts on X only if the purpose is to discuss, satirize or share information'.[3626] An

3611. X, 'Terms of Service' (*X*) https://twitter.com/en/tos accessed June 2025.
3612. X, 'Terms of Service' (*X International Terms*) https://twitter.com/en/tos#intlTerms accessed June 2025.
3613. X, 'X Terms of Service' (*X*) https://twitter.com/en/tos#update accessed June 2025.
3614. X, 'Trademark Policy' (*Trademark Policy*) https://help.x.com/en/rules-and-policies/x-trademark-policy accessed June 2025.
3615. *Ibid.*
3616. *Ibid.*
3617. *Ibid.*
3618. *Ibid.*
3619. *Ibid.*
3620. *Ibid.*
3621. *Ibid.*
3622. X, 'Misleading and Deceptive Identities Policy' (*X Help Center*) https://help.x.com/en/rules-and-policies/x-impersonation-and-deceptive-identities-policyaccessed June 2025.
3623. *Ibid.*
3624. *Ibid.*
3625. *Ibid.*
3626. *Ibid.*

impersonation-specific form is available.[3627] As a consequence of violating the 'Misleading and deceptive identities policy',[3628] X may employ enforcement such as 'restricting reach',[3629] 'temporary loss of access',[3630] requiring 'profile modifications'[3631] or even 'suspension'[3632] for 'severe violations'[3633] or 'requiring deletion of one or more posts to temporarily locking accounts'[3634] subject to appeal.[3635]

In the context of ads, '[c]ontent that may infringe on others' intellectual property rights, or that promotes the sale of counterfeit goods, is not eligible for monetization'[3636] and '[t]his includes (but not limited to): ... [m]isleading content on brand affiliation ... [p]romotion or sale of counterfeit goods or unauthorized access to digital goods'.[3637] Further, '[s]elling or promoting counterfeit goods on the platform is a violation of X's counterfeit policy'[3638] and these goods may 'attempt to deceive consumers into believing the counterfeit is a genuine product of the brand owner, or to represent themselves as faux, replicas or imitations of the genuine product'[3639] or 'pass themselves off as genuine products'.[3640]

However, 'using a trademark in a way that is outside the scope of the trademark registration e.g., in a different territory, or a different class of goods or services than that identified in the registration' is not a violation of the policy.[3641] Further, 'parody, commentary, or fan accounts'[3642] are permissible if they 'clearly indicate that they are unaffiliated'.[3643] However, they must (all are required) '[i]nclude a PCF label ... not use an identical avatar as the entity ... include terms such as "parody," "fake," "fan," or "commentary at the beginning of [the] account name; and include terms such as "parody," "fake," "fan," or "commentary in your bio or profile description'.[3644]

3627. X, 'Authenticity on X' (*X Help Center*) https://help.x.com/en/forms/authenticity/impersonation accessed June 2025.
3628. X, 'Misleading and Deceptive Identities Policy' (*X Help Center*) https://help.x.com/en/rules-and-policies/x-impersonation-and-deceptive-identities-policyaccessed June 2025.
3629. *Ibid.*
3630. *Ibid.*
3631. *Ibid.*
3632. *Ibid.*
3633. *Ibid.*
3634. *Ibid.*
3635. *Ibid.*
3636. X, 'Ads Policy: Brand Safety Policy' (*X Business*) https://business.x.com/en/help/ads-policies/product-policies/brand-safety-policy.html accessed June 2025.
3637. *Ibid.*
3638. X, 'Counterfeit Policy' (*X Business*) https://help.x.com/en/rules-and-policies/counterfeit-goods-policy accessed June 2025.
3639. *Ibid.*
3640. *Ibid.*
3641. X, 'Trademark Policy' (*Trademark Policy*) https://help.x.com/en/rules-and-policies/x-trademark-policy accessed June 2025.
3642. X, 'Misleading and Deceptive Identities Policy' (*X Help Center*) https://help.x.com/en/rules-and-policies/x-impersonation-and-deceptive-identities-policyaccessed June 2025.
3643. *Ibid.*
3644. *Ibid.*

There is a specific trademark report form which incorporates trademark infringement and counterfeit goods.[3645] A 'federal or international registration number is required'.[3646]

5.4.3 Pinterest

Pinterest Terms of Service prohibit posting of 'User Content that infringes the intellectual property rights of others (e.g ... trademark infringement or counterfeit), or that is otherwise unlawful, unless an exception or limitation applies under applicable law.'[3647] Similar general statements are under their Community Guidelines, including prohibiting intellectual property infringement or action or 'content that violates laws or regulations'.[3648] Under its Advertising Guidelines, '[y]our ads can't infringe upon or violate the rights of any third party, including ... trademark ... rights'.[3649]

Pinterest may take action by 'removing, restricting, or limiting access to, or distribution of, the content'.[3650] Pinterest can 'also suspend or terminate accounts of users who repeatedly or seriously infringe third-party intellectual property rights, violate the law, these Terms, or our policies, or where permitted or required to do so by law'.[3651] Under its specific Trademark Policy, it 'may disable access to content that misleads others or violates another's trademark rights ... suspend or terminate users who post or share such content ... transfer usernames as appropriate'.[3652] Pinterest also addresses repeat situations whereby 'in appropriate circumstances and at our discretion – to suspend or terminate the accounts of people who repeatedly infringe trademark rights or are repeatedly charged with infringing trademarks or other intellectual property rights'[3653] Also, '[a]ctions against such users may also include temporary suspension of their ability to post content, among other things'.[3654]

A specific 'Trademark Infringement Notification Form'[3655] is available, which includes a 'Counterfeit Report',[3656] 'Username transfer request',[3657] 'specific content',

3645. X, 'Help with Intellectual Property Issues' (*X Help Center*) https://help.x.com/en/forms/ipi/trademark/trademark-owner accessed June 2025.
3646. *Ibid.*
3647. Pinterest, 'Terms of Service' (*Pinterest Policy*) https://policy.pinterest.com/en/terms-of-service accessed June 2025.
3648. Pinterest. 'Community Guidelines' (*Pinterest Policy*) https://policy.pinterest.com/en/community-guidelines accessed June 2025.
3649. Pinterest, 'Advertising Guidelines' (*Pinterest Policy*) https://policy.pinterest.com/en/advertising-guidelines accessed June 2025.
3650. Pinterest, 'Terms of Service' (*Pinterest Policy*) https://policy.pinterest.com/en/terms-of-service accessed June 2025.
3651. *Ibid.*
3652. Pinterest, 'Trademark' (*Pinterest Policy*) https://policy.pinterest.com/en/trademark accessed June 2025.
3653. *Ibid.*
3654. *Ibid.*
3655. Pinterest, 'Trademark Infringement Notification' (*Pinterest*) https://www.pinterest.com/about/trademark/ accessed June 2025.
3656. *Ibid.*
3657. *Ibid.*

etc.[3658] A 'good faith belief that use of the trademark(s) described above infringes a trademark I own or whose owner I represent'[3659] is required, among other confirmations.[3660]

5.4.4 LinkedIn

LinkedIn terms require agreement with the rule against violating 'the intellectual property rights of others, including … trademarks …'.[3661] It requires that users 'agree to only provide content or information that does not violate the law nor anyone's rights (including intellectual property rights)'[3662] and '[c]omply with all applicable laws, including, without limitation … intellectual property laws … laws governing the content shared, and other applicable laws and regulatory requirements'.[3663]

LinkedIn's trademark policy links to a form to be filed if there is 'good faith believe that content posted by a member on our website infringes your trademark rights'[3664] and a counter notice form is available.[3665] The form requires proof of registration or may be 'summarily denied'.[3666] The form specifically mentions 'Groups, Company Pages, Profile, Rich Media, Other' as possible places where the trademark used might be complained of.[3667] They require users to use their 'real name'[3668] on their profile. Profiles and content may be reported through this form.[3669]

In the context of Ads, these 'must not use trademarks belonging to third parties unless express permission has been granted by the trademark owner or as otherwise permitted by applicable law … [y]ou should not use trademarks, logos, service marks or company names in a way that would be confusing to the user, or imply an affiliation or endorsement when there is none'.[3670]

Under its Professional Community policies, it states as follows: '[d]o not create a fake profile or falsify information … [w]e don't allow fake profiles or entities … [d]o not post misleading or deceptive information about … your business … affiliations …

3658. *Ibid.*
3659. *Ibid.*
3660. *Ibid.*
3661. LinkedIn, 'User Agreement' (*LinkedIn User Agreement*) https://www.linkedin.com/legal/user-agreement?trk=homepage-basic_footer-user-agreement accessed June 2025.
3662. *Ibid.*
3663. *Ibid.*
3664. LinkedIn, 'LinkedIn's Trademark Policy' (*LinkedIn Help*) https://www.linkedin.com/help/linkedin/answer/a1337296?trk=d_microsites-frontend_legal_copyright-policy&lang=en accessed June 2025.
3665. *Ibid.*
3666. LinkedIn, 'Reporting a Trademark Infringement Form' (*LinkedIn Help*) https://www.linkedin.com/help/linkedin/ask/TS-NTMI accessed June 2025.
3667. *Ibid.*
3668. LinkedIn, 'User Agreement' (*LinkedIn User Agreement*) https://www.linkedin.com/legal/user-agreement?trk=homepage-basic_footer-user-agreement accessed June 2025.
3669. LinkedIn, 'LinkedIn's Trademark Policy' (*LinkedIn Help*) https://www.linkedin.com/help/linkedin/answer/a1337296?trk=d_microsites-frontend_legal_copyright-policy&lang=en accessed June 2025.
3670. LinkedIn, 'LinkedIn Advertising Policies' (*LinkedIn*) https://www.linkedin.com/legal/ads-policy accessed June 2025.

[d]o not associate yourself on LinkedIn with a business or organization that you are not actually professionally associated with'.[3671] Under '[i]llegal, dangerous, and inappropriate commercial content',[3672] LinkedIn prohibits 'counterfeit items'.[3673] LinkedIn may 'limit the visibility of certain content, label it, or remove it entirely'[3674] which it deems violating its User Agreement or Professional Community Policies.[3675] Specific 'notices are sent in line with relevant laws in the regions where we operate'.[3676]

Further, '[r]epeated violations in the restriction of ... access to certain LinkedIn features'.[3677] Further, '[f]or certain egregious violations of our Professional Community Policies ... we may permanently restrict your account after a single violation'.[3678] Notably, an exception is provided '[c]ontent that would normally violate the letter of our policies may be allowed in cases where the content is being shared for awareness or to condemn'.[3679] Further, they state that '[i]n these cases, we may label and obscure the content for members who may find this content sensitive or disturbing, or otherwise do not want to view it. However, we won't remove the content or penalize the author for posting it'.[3680]

5.4.5 Snapchat

Under Snapchat's specific 'username infringement'[3681] support page, it says that 'Snapchat usernames are available on a first-come, first-serve basis and are generally not transferable.'[3682] However, it also states that '[m]ere use of a trademark in a username does not automatically violate Snap's trademark policy'.[3683] They further state that '[r]ather, the trademark owner must show ... that the Snapchat username is being used commercially, in a manner that leads others to believe that the Snapchat account is somehow affiliated with the trademark owner's brand'.[3684] The '[t]ypes of evidence'[3685] that may be considered 'include: (i) images or videos posted as a Story that would lead a viewer to think the content came from your company, or (ii) chat messages or Snaps delivered through an allegedly infringing username that are

3671. LinkedIn, 'Professional community policies' (*LinkedIn*) https://www.linkedin.com/legal/professional-community-policies accessed June 2025.
3672. LinkedIn, 'Illegal, Dangerous, and Inappropriate Commercial Activity' (*LinkedIn Help*) https://www.linkedin.com/help/linkedin/answer/a1349151 accessed June 2025.
3673. *Ibid.*
3674. LinkedIn, 'How We Enforce our Professional Community Policies' (*LinkedIn Help*) https://www.linkedin.com/help/linkedin/answer/a1342754 accessed June 2025.
3675. *Ibid.*
3676. *Ibid.*
3677. *Ibid.*
3678. *Ibid.*
3679. *Ibid.*
3680. *Ibid.*
3681. Snap, 'Username Infringement' (*Snapchat Support*) https://help.snapchat.com/hc/en-us/articles/7047503878804 accessed June 2025.
3682. *Ibid.*
3683. *Ibid.*
3684. *Ibid.*
3685. *Ibid.*

commercial in nature'.[3686] Therefore, commercial use[3687] is required. However, brand and trademark are not differentiated.[3688]

Trademark infringement forms include the ability to report trademark infringement in 'content, including in an Ad, Filter, Story, or Lens',[3689] in a 'Snapchat username'[3690] or '[t]o sell or promote counterfeit goods'.[3691] When reporting, a registration number and jurisdiction are required.[3692]

Snap Inc. Terms of Service (US)[3693] and Snap Group Limited Terms of Service (outside the US)[3694] do not permit utilisation which 'violate or infringe ... third party's ... trademarks, or other intellectual property rights, including by using the Services to submit, display, post, create or generate any infringing content'.[3695] Similarly, using Snapchat:

> in a manner that violates or infringes someone else's rights of ... trademark, or other intellectual property right'[3696] is not permitted. When a user provides content they 'agree and represent that ... [they] own that content, or ... have received all necessary permissions, clearances, and authorizations ... and grant the rights and licenses contained in these Terms for your content.[3697]

Snap Community Guidelines state that '[w]e prohibit pretending to be someone (or something) that you're not, or attempting to deceive people about who you are'[3698] and '[t]his includes impersonating ... celebrities ... brands, or other people or organizations for harmful, non-satirical purposes'.[3699] It also prohibits 'manipulating content for false or misleading purposes'[3700] and 'fraud and other deceptive practices ... including the promotion of fraudulent goods or services'.[3701]

Its support pages indicate that '[i]f someone is using your trademark to confuse people into thinking that they are you, or somehow affiliated with your business, it may be trademark infringement'.[3702] It also states that '[u]sing another's trademark to

3686. *Ibid.*
3687. *Ibid.*
3688. *Ibid.*
3689. Snap, 'Submit a Request' (*Snapchat Support*) https://help.snapchat.com/hc/en-us/requests/new?ticket_form accessed June 2025.
3690. *Ibid.*
3691. *Ibid.*
3692. *Ibid.*
3693. Snap, 'Snap Inc. Terms of Service' (*Snap Inc.*) https://www.snap.com/en-US/terms/ accessed June 2025.
3694. Snap, 'Snap Group Limited Terms of Service' (*Snap Group Limited*) https://www.snap.com/en-US/terms#sgl-terms accessed June 2025.
3695. Snap, 'Snap Inc. Terms of Service' (*Snap Inc.*) https://www.snap.com/en-US/terms/ accessed June 2025; Snap, 'Snap Group Limited Terms of Service' (*Snap Group Limited*) https://www.snap.com/en-US/terms#sgl-terms accessed June 2025.
3696. *Ibid.*
3697. *Ibid.*
3698. Snap, 'Community Guidelines' (*Snap Privacy, Safety, and Policy Hub*) https://values.snap.com/privacy/transparency/community-guidelines accessed June 2025.
3699. *Ibid.*
3700. *Ibid.*
3701. *Ibid.*
3702. Snapchat, 'About Trademark Infringement on Snapchat' (*Snapchat Support*) https://help.snapchat.com/hc/en-us/articles/7012343429652 accessed June 2025.

accurately reference the trademark owner's products or services, or compare them to other products or services, is not considered trademark infringement'.[3703]

3703. *Ibid.*

5.4.6 Gaps and Problems with Current Social Media Platform Trademark Terms and Policies

Table 5.7 Digital Trademark and Trade Practices Model, UDRP, and Social Media Platform Terms and Policies

Digital Trademark and Trade Practices Model	*UDRP*	*Facebook*	*X*	*Pinterest*	*LinkedIn*	*Snapchat*
Digital Use and Place of Use	Only some coverage. Any use of registered or unregistered marks in domain names which violate the policy.[3704]	Use in Facebook.[3705] 'That use is in commerce, meaning that it's done in connection with the sale or promotion of goods or services'.[3706] When complaining about others using a mark, a trademark registration number is required.[3707]	Only some coverage. Use in X. When complaining about others using a mark, a trademark registration number is required.[3708]	Only some coverage. Use in Pinterest services including usernames and content. When complaining about others using a mark, a trademark registration number may be provided 'if applicable'.[3709]	Only some coverage. Use in LinkedIn. LinkedIn 'Groups, Company Pages, Profile, Rich Media, Other'[3710] When complaining about others using a mark, a trademark registration number is required.[3711]	Only some coverage. Use in Snapchat. 'content, including in an [a]d, [f]ilter, or [s]tory',[3712] in a 'Snapchat username'[3713] 'Snapchat username is being used commercially, in a manner that leads others to believe that the Snapchat account is somehow affiliated with the trademark owner's brand.'[3714] When complaining about others using a mark, a trademark registration number is required.[3715]

Digital Bad Faith and Abuse	'Registration and use of a domain name in bad faith'[3716] (abuse is covered in overview).[3717]	Only some coverage. 'If we determine, in our discretion, that you have clearly, seriously or repeatedly breached our Terms or Policies, including in particular the Community Standards, we may suspend or permanently disable your access to Meta Company Products, and we may permanently disable or delete your account'.[3718] 'disable or delete your account if you repeatedly infringe other people's intellectual property rights or where we are required to do so	Only some coverage. 'remove Content that violates the User Agreement, including for example … trademark violations or other intellectual property misappropriation, impersonation …'.[3719] If X determines that the trademark policy was violated, it may suspend the user's account.[3720] X may provide 'an opportunity to comply with our policies'[3721] based on the violation or it may 'permanently suspend'[3722] an account on initial	Only some coverage. 'removing, restricting, or limiting access to, or distribution of, the content'.[3723] 'suspend or terminate accounts of users who repeatedly or seriously infringe third-party intellectual property rights, violate the law, these Terms, or our policies, or where permitted or required to do so by law'.[3724] Trademark Policy: 'may disable access to content	Only some coverage. '[r]epeated violations in the restriction of … access to certain LinkedIn features'.[3725] '[f]or certain egregious violations of our Professional Community Policies … we may permanently restrict your account after a single violation.'.[3726]	Not directly/adequately covered.

Digital Trademark and Trade Practices Model	*UDRP*	*Facebook*	*X*	*Pinterest*	*LinkedIn*	*Snapchat*
		for legal reasons'.[3727] Also, 'If we remove content that you have shared in violation of the Community Standards, we'll let you know and explain any options you have to request another review, unless you seriously or repeatedly violate these Terms …'.[3728] 'also attempt to remove bad actors, and disable the accounts of repeat infringers where appropriate'.[3729]	review[3730] or 'an account may be permanently suspended upon first review'.[3731] X may employ enforcement such as 'restricting reach',[3732] 'temporary loss of access',[3733] requiring 'profile modifications'[3734] or even 'suspension'[3735] for 'severe violations'[3736] or 'requiring deletion of one or more posts to temporarily locking accounts'[3737] subject to appeal.[3738]	that misleads others or violates another's trademark rights … suspend or terminate users who post or share such content … transfer usernames as appropriate'.[3739]		

Digital Confusion	'Confusing similarity' in domain names.[3740]	Only some coverage. Help Centre states: 'Generally, trademark law seeks to prevent confusion among consumers about who provides or is affiliated with a product or service'.[3741] Help Centre states: 'That use is likely to confuse consumers about the source, endorsement or affiliation of the goods or services'.[3742] 'enforce a policy against posting content that violates someone else's intellectual property rights, including copyright, trademark, or other legal rights'.[3743]	'Using another's trademark in a way that may mislead or confuse people about your affiliation may be a violation of our trademark policy.'[3744] 'Trademark law may prevent others from using a trademark in an unauthorized or confusing manner.'[3745]	Generally or not directly covered. Generally: 'User Content that infringes the intellectual property rights of others (e.g … trademark infringement'[3746]	Only some coverage. LinkedIn Ads Policy: 'trademarks belonging to third parties unless express permission has been granted by the trademark owner … You should not use trademarks, logos, service marks or company names in a way that would be confusing to the user, or imply an affiliation or endorsement when there is none'.[3747]	Generally or not directly covered. 'violate or infringe … third party's … trademarks, or other intellectual property rights, including by using the Services to submit, display, post, create or generate any infringing content'.[3748] 'may not use the Services … in a manner that violates or infringes someone else's rights of … trademark, or other intellectual property right. When you submit content to the Services, you agree and represent that you own that content, or that you have received all necessary permissions, clearances, and authorisations in

Digital Trademark and Trade Practices Model	*UDRP*	*Facebook*	*X*	*Pinterest*	*LinkedIn*	*Snapchat*
						order to submit it to the Services … and grant the rights and licenses contained in these Terms for your content'.[3749]
Digital Unfair Competition	Only some coverage. The Overview states that '[a]lso noting the availability of trademark-like protection under certain national legal doctrines (e.g., unfair competition or passing-off) and considerations of parity, where acquired distinctiveness/ secondary meaning is demonstrated in a	Only some coverage. Help Centre states 'A counterfeit good is a knockoff or replica version of another company's product. It usually copies the trademark (name or logo) and/or distinctive features of that other company's product to imitate a genuine product.'[3750]	Only some coverage. 'remove Content that violates the User Agreement, including for example … trademark violations or other intellectual property misappropriation, impersonation …'.[3751] 'You may not impersonate other identities of individuals, groups, or	Only some coverage. 'User Content that infringes the intellectual property rights of others (e.g … trademark infringement or counterfeit), or that is otherwise unlawful, unless an exception or	Only some coverage. Profiles and content may be reported through a form.[3752] 'Do not create a fake profile or falsify information … [w]e don't allow fake profiles or entities … Do not post misleading or deceptive information about … your business … affiliations … Do not associate yourself on LinkedIn with a business or	Only some coverage. Community Guidelines: 'prohibit pretending to be someone (or something) that you're not, or attempting to deceive people about who you are'[3753] and 'This includes impersonating … celebrities, brands, or other organizations'.[3754] Prohibits 'manipulating content for false or misleading purposes'[3755] and

	particular UDRP case, unregistered rights have been found to support standing to proceed with a UDRP case including where the complainant is based in a civil law jurisdiction'.[3756] Unfair advantage considerations may fall under bad faith and abuse (*see* Overview).[3757] 'Distinctiveness' and 'secondary meaning' is recognized in Overview along with a list of factors that may be considered.[3758] 'Secondary meaning'[3759] is covered in the Overview. Overview also states that 'the	Help Centre states that 'Trademark dilution may also be unlawful in certain countries. Dilution, which applies to famous trademarks, may occur in certain circumstances when a trademark is used without permission in commerce'.[3760]	organizations to deceive others … [a]lthough you are not required to display your real identity on your profile, your account should not use false profile information to impersonate others'.[3761] 'fake personas' are prohibited where one uses 'manufactured identities to engage in disruptive or deceptive behaviour … [t]his may include using stock, stolen or AI-generated profile photos, copied or stolen profile bios, and/or	limitation applies under applicable law.'[3762] 'Counterfeit Report.'[3763]	organization that you are not actually professionally associated with.'[3764] Under 'Illegal, dangerous, and inappropriate commercial content',[3765] LinkedIn prohibits 'counterfeit items'.[3766] LinkedIn may 'limit the visibility of certain content, label it, or remove it entirely'[3767] which it deems violating its User Agreement or Professional Community Policies.[3768]	'fraud and other deceptive practices, including the promotion of fraudulent goods or services'.[3769] '[t]o sell or promote counterfeit goods'.[3770] 'We prohibit pretending to be someone (or something) that you're not, or attempting to deceive people about who you are'[3771] 'This includes impersonating … celebrities, brands, or other organizations'.[3772] It also prohibits 'manipulating content for false or misleading purposes'[3773] and 'spam and deceptive practices'.[3774]

Digital Trademark and Trade Practices Model	*UDRP*	*Facebook*	*X*	*Pinterest*	*LinkedIn*	*Snapchat*
	strength of the complainant's mark may be considered relevant in evaluating the second and third elements'[3775] of the UDRP.		misleading profile information for the purpose of deceiving others'.[3776] 'Selling or promoting counterfeit goods on the platform is a violation of X's counterfeit policy'[3777] and these good may 'attempt to deceive consumers into believing the counterfeit is a genuine product of the brand owner, or to represent themselves as faux, replicas or imitations of the			'that the Snapchat username is being used commercially, in a manner that leads others to believe that the Snapchat account is somehow affiliated with the trademark owner's brand'.[3778] '[t]o sell or promote counterfeit goods'.[3779]

			genuine product'[3780] or 'pass themselves off as genuine products'.[3781]			
Digital Terms, Policies, and Disclaimers	Only some coverage. Is itself a uniform policy addressing covered domain names. Disclaimers have been treated briefly in Overview. In cases 'where the respondent appears to otherwise have a right or legitimate interest in a disputed domain name, a clear and sufficiently prominent disclaimer would lend support to circumstances suggesting its good faith'.[3782]	Generally or not directly covered. 'may be unlawful even if the seller explicitly … disclaims authenticity of the goods'.[3783]	Generally or not directly covered. Trademark-related policies are contained in various documents. A sort of disclaimer: 'clearly indicate that they are unaffiliated'.[3784]	Generally or not directly covered (disclaimers). Trademark-related policies are contained in various documents.	Generally or not directly covered (disclaimers). Trademark-related policies are contained in various documents.	Generally or not directly covered (disclaimers). Trademark-related policies are contained in various documents.

Digital Trademark and Trade Practices Model	*UDRP*	*Facebook*	*X*	*Pinterest*	*LinkedIn*	*Snapchat*
Digital Jurisdictional and Territorial Considerations	Only some coverage. Changes to a domain name may be made based on court or arbitral tribunal of competent jurisdiction.[3785] Overview states that 'rules and principles of law'[3786] may be considered (this is discretionary), however, 'in its own terms UDRP jurisprudence generally would not require resort to particular national laws'.[3787] For example, guidance indicates that where 'the parties share a	Only some coverage. 'Trademark rights are generally limited to the geographic territory where the trademark owner uses the trademark to identify their goods or services'.[3788] 'Please note that laws in different countries may vary'.[3789] 'There are also many limits to trademark rights that can preclude a trademark infringement claim. These include, among	Only some coverage. X Terms of Service[3790] which also apply to the U.S. and other countries (including its international terms which apply to the EU and other countries)[3791] and which are largely the same in the context of trademarks 'using a trademark in a way that is outside the scope of the trademark registration e.g., in a different territory … than	Generally or not directly covered.	Generally or not directly covered. '[c]omply with all applicable laws, including, without limitation … intellectual property laws … laws governing the content shared, and other applicable laws and regulatory requirements'.[3792] Specific 'notices are sent in line with relevant laws in the regions where we operate'.[3793]	Generally or not directly covered. Snap Inc. Terms of Service (U.S.)[3794] and Snap Group Limited Terms of Service (outside the U.S.)[3795] largely similar in the context of trademarks.

	common nationality and the import of a specific national law concept is particularly germane to an issue in dispute, panels have applied national law principles in assessing the UDRP elements'.[3796] Otherwise, the UDRP applies regardless of where domain is registered or used.	other things, geographic limitations ...'[3797]	that identified in the registration' is not a violation of the policy.[3798]			
Digital Justification	Only some coverage. Using marks for 'legitimate noncommercial or fair use'[3799] is recognised as a method to demonstrate 'rights and legitimate interests'.[3800]	Only some coverage. 'And while these matters are very fact-specific, trademark rights also often don't prevent: The resale of legitimate goods	Only some coverage. 'using a trademark in a way that is outside the scope of the trademark registration e.g., in a different territory, or a	Generally or not directly covered. 'is otherwise unlawful, unless an exception or limitation applies under applicable law'.[3801]	Only some coverage. 'unless express permission has been granted by the trademark owner or as otherwise permitted by applicable law'.[3802] 'Content that would normally violate the	Only some coverage. 'Using another's trademark to accurately reference the trademark owner's products or services, or compare them to other products or services, is not considered

Digital Trademark and Trade Practices Model	*UDRP*	*Facebook*	*X*	*Pinterest*	*LinkedIn*	*Snapchat*
	Fair use and freedom of speech are also covered in the Overview.[3803]	or selling legitimate goods through channels that are not authorised by the trademark owner The use of a trademarked word in its ordinary dictionary meaning The use of a trademark in a way that is not related to the sale or promotion of products or services.'[3804] 'non-infringing use of the trademark (example: using a trademarked word in its ordinary dictionary meaning, or using	different class of goods or services than that identified in the registration' is not a violation of the policy.[3805] '[w]e allow compliant Parody, Commentary, and Fan (PCF) accounts on X only if the purpose is to discuss, satirize or share information'.[3806]		letter of our policies may be allowed in cases where the content is being shared for awareness or to condemn'.[3807]	trademark infringement.'[3808] 'for harmful, non-satirical purposes'.[3809]

the trademark in a way that is not related to the sale or promotion of products or services)?'.[3810] Specifically in reference to usernames, infringement may be 'based on the context of its use'[3811] although Facebook notes 'that not every use … in a username is necessarily a trademark infringement'.[3812] For example, a 'word or phrase that is used in a different context'[3813] may not be violative.[3814] 'There are also many limits to trademark rights that can preclude

Digital Trademark and Trade Practices Model	*UDRP*	*Facebook*	*X*	*Pinterest*	*LinkedIn*	*Snapchat*
		a trademark infringement claim. These include, among other things, … the ability for someone to use your trademark to lawfully comment on or criticize your goods or services.'[3815]				

3704. ICANN, 'Uniform Domain-Name Dispute-Resolution Policy' (*ICANN*, 25 February 2012) https://www.icann.org/resources/pages/policy-2012-02-25-en accessed June 2025; WIPO, 'WIPO Overview of WIPO Panel Views on Selected UDRP Questions, Third Edition' ('WIPO Jurisprudential Overview 3.0') (*WIPO*, 2017) https://www.wipo.int/amc/en/domains/search/overview3.0/ accessed June 2025.
3705. Meta, 'Terms of Service' (*Meta, July 2022*) https://www.facebook.com/legal/terms accessed June 2025.
3706. Meta, 'Trademark' (*Facebook Help Center*) https://www.facebook.com/help/507663689427413?helpref = about_content accessed June 2025.
3707. Facebook, 'Trademark Report Form' (*Facebook Help Center*) https://www.facebook.com/help/contact/1057530390957243 accessed June 2025.
3708. X, 'Help with Intellectual Property Issues' (*X Help Center*) https://help.x.com/en/forms/ipi/trademark/trademark-owner accessed June 2025.
3709. Pinterest, 'Trademark Infringement Notification' (*Pinterest*) https://www.pinterest.com/about/trademark/ accessed June 2025.
3710. *Ibid.*
3711. LinkedIn, 'LinkedIn's Trademark Policy' (*LinkedIn Help*) https://www.linkedin.com/help/linkedin/answer/a1337296?trk = d_microsites-frontend_legal_copyright-policy&lang = en accessed June 2025.
3712. Snap, 'Submit a Request' (*Snapchat Support*) https://help.snapchat.com/hc/en-us/requests/new?ticket_form accessed June 2025.
3713. *Ibid.*
3714. Snap, 'Username Infringement' (*Snapchat Support*) https://help.snapchat.com/hc/en-us/articles/7047503878804 accessed June 2025.

3715. Snap, 'Submit a request' (*Snapchat Support*) https://help.snapchat.com/hc/en-us/requests/new?ticket_form accessed June 2025.
3716. UDRP, 4(b).
3717. ICANN, 'Uniform Domain-Name Dispute-Resolution Policy' (*ICANN*, 25 February 2012) https://www.icann.org/resources/pages/policy-2012-02-25-en accessed June 2025; WIPO, 'WIPO Overview of WIPO Panel Views on Selected UDRP Questions, Third Edition' ('WIPO Jurisprudential Overview 3.0') (*WIPO*, 2017) https://www.wipo.int/amc/en/domains/search/overview3.0/ accessed June 2025.
3718. Meta, 'Terms of Service' (*Meta, July 2022*) https://www.facebook.com/legal/terms accessed June 2025.
3719. X, 'X Terms of Service' (*X*) https://twitter.com/en/tos#update accessed June 2025.
3720. X, 'Trademark Policy' (*Trademark Policy*) https://help.x.com/en/rules-and-policies/x-trademark-policy accessed June 2025.
3721. *Ibid.*
3722. *Ibid.*
3723. Pinterest, 'Terms of Service' (*Pinterest Policy*) https://policy.pinterest.com/en/terms-of-service accessed June 2025.
3724. *Ibid.*
3725. LinkedIn, 'How We Enforce Our Professional Community Policies' (*LinkedIn*) https://www.linkedin.com/help/linkedin/answer/a1342754 accessed June 2025.
3726. *Ibid.*
3727. *Ibid.*
3728. *Ibid.*
3729. Meta, 'About Brand Rights Protection' (*Meta Business Help Center*) https://www.facebook.com/business/help/828925381043253?id=4533021280101097 accessed June 2025.
3730. *Ibid.*
3731. LinkedIn, 'How We Enforce Our Professional Community Policies' (*LinkedIn*) https://www.linkedin.com/help/linkedin/answer/a1342754 accessed June 2025.
3732. X, 'Misleading and Deceptive Identities Policy' (*X Help Center*) https://help.x.com/en/rules-and-policies/x-impersonation-and-deceptive-identities-policyaccessed June 2025.
3733. *Ibid.*
3734. *Ibid.*
3735. *Ibid.*
3736. *Ibid.*
3737. *Ibid.*
3738. *Ibid.*
3739. Pinterest, 'Trademark' (*Pinterest Policy*) https://policy.pinterest.com/en/trademark accessed June 2025.

3740. ICANN, 'Uniform Domain-Name Dispute-Resolution Policy' (*ICANN*, 25 February 2012) https://www.icann.org/resources/pages/policy-2012-02-25-en accessed June 2025.
3741. Facebook, 'Intellectual Property' (Facebook Help Center) https://www.facebook.com/help/399224883474207?ref=ccs accessed June 2025.
3742. Facebook, 'What Is Trademark Infringement' (*Facebook Help Center*) https://www.facebook.com/help/349534658401968/?helpref=related_articles accessed June 2025.
3743. Meta, 'Third-Party Intellectual Property Infringement' (*Meta Transparency Center*) https://transparency.meta.com/policies/community-standards/intellectual-property/ accessed June 2025.
3744. X, 'Trademark Policy' (*Trademark Policy*) https://help.x.com/en/rules-and-policies/x-trademark-policy accessed June 2025.
3745. *Ibid.*
3746. Pinterest, 'Terms of Service' (*Pinterest Policy*) https://policy.pinterest.com/en/terms-of-service accessed June 2025.
3747. LinkedIn, 'LinkedIn Advertising Policies' (*LinkedIn*) https://www.linkedin.com/legal/ads-policy accessed June 2025.
3748. Snap, 'Snap Inc. Terms of Service' (*Snap Inc.*) https://www.snap.com/en-US/terms/ accessed July 2024; Snap, 'Snap Group Limited Terms of Service' (*Snap Group Limited*) https://www.snap.com/en-US/terms#sgl-terms accessed June 2025.
3749. Snap, 'Snap Inc. Terms of Service' (*Snap Inc.*) https://www.snap.com/en-US/terms/ accessed July 2024; Snap, 'Snap Group Limited Terms of Service' (*Snap Group Limited*) https://www.snap.com/en-US/terms#sgl-terms accessed June 2025.
3750. Meta, 'Trademark' (*Facebook Help Center*) https://www.facebook.com/help/507663689427413?helpref=about_content accessed June 2025.
3751. X, 'X Terms of Service' (*X*) https://twitter.com/en/tos#update accessed June 2025.
3752. *Ibid.*
3753. Snap, 'Community Guidelines' (*Snap Privacy, Safety, and Policy Hub*) https://values.snap.com/privacy/transparency/community-guidelines accessed June 2025.
3754. *Ibid.*
3755. *Ibid.*
3756. WIPO, 'WIPO Overview of WIPO Panel Views on Selected UDRP Questions, Third Edition' ('WIPO Jurisprudential Overview 3.0') (*WIPO*, 2017) https://www.wipo.int/amc/en/domains/search/overview3.0/ accessed June 2025.
3757. *Ibid.*
3758. *Ibid.*
3759. *Ibid.*
3760. *Ibid.*
3761. X, 'Misleading and Deceptive Identities Policy' (*X Help Center*) https://help.x.com/en/rules-and-policies/x-impersonation-and-deceptive-identities-policyaccessed June 2025.
3762. Pinterest, 'Terms of Service' (*Pinterest Policy*) https://policy.pinterest.com/en/terms-of-service accessed June 2025.
3763. Pinterest, 'Trademark Infringement Notification' (*Pinterest*) https://www.pinterest.com/about/trademark/ accessed June 2025.

3764. LinkedIn, 'Professional community policies' (*LinkedIn*) https://www.linkedin.com/legal/professional-community-policies accessed June 2025.
3765. LinkedIn, 'Illegal, Dangerous, and Inappropriate Commercial Activity' (*LinkedIn Help*) https://www.linkedin.com/help/linkedin/answer/a1349151 accessed June 2025.
3766. *Ibid.*
3767. LinkedIn, 'How We Enforce Our Professional Community Policies' (*LinkedIn Help*) https://www.linkedin.com/help/linkedin/answer/a1342754 accessed June 2025.
3768. *Ibid.*
3769. *Ibid.*
3770. *Ibid.*
3771. *Ibid.*
3772. *Ibid.*
3773. *Ibid.*
3774. *Ibid.*
3775. *Ibid.*
3776. *Ibid.*
3777. X, 'Counterfeit Policy' (*X Business*) https://help.x.com/en/rules-and-policies/counterfeit-goods-policy accessed June 2025.
3778. *Ibid.*
3779. Snap, 'Submit a Request' (*Snapchat Support*) https://help.snapchat.com/hc/en-us/requests/new?ticket_form accessed June 2025.
3780. *Ibid.*
3781. *Ibid.*
3782. WIPO, 'WIPO Overview of WIPO Panel Views on Selected UDRP Questions, Third Edition' ('WIPO Jurisprudential Overview 3.0') (*WIPO*, 2017) https://www.wipo.int/amc/en/domains/search/overview3.0/ accessed June 2025.
3783. Meta, 'Trademark' (*Facebook Help Center*) https://www.facebook.com/help/507663689427413?helpref=about_content accessed June 2025.
3784. X, 'Misleading and Deceptive Identities Policy' (*X Help Center*) https://help.x.com/en/rules-and-policies/x-impersonation-and-deceptive-identities-policyaccessed June 2025.
3785. ICANN, 'Uniform Domain-Name Dispute-Resolution Policy' (*ICANN*, 25 February 2012) https://www.icann.org/resources/pages/policy-2012-02-25-en accessed June 2025.
3786. WIPO, 'WIPO Overview of WIPO Panel Views on Selected UDRP Questions, Third Edition' ('WIPO Jurisprudential Overview 3.0') (*WIPO*, 2017) https://www.wipo.int/amc/en/domains/search/overview3.0/ accessed June 2025.
3787. *Ibid.*

3788. Meta, 'Trademark' (*Facebook Help Center*) https://www.facebook.com/help/507663689427413?helpref=about_content accessed June 2025.
3789. *Ibid.*
3790. X, 'X Terms of Service' (*X*) https://twitter.com/en/tos#update accessed June 2025.
3791. X, 'X Terms of Service' (*X International Terms*) https://twitter.com/en/tos#intlTerms accessed June 2025.
3792. LinkedIn, 'User Agreement' (*LinkedIn User Agreement*) https://www.linkedin.com/legal/user-agreement?trk=homepage-basic_footer-user-agreement accessed June 2025.
3793. LinkedIn, 'How We Enforce Our Professional Community Policies' (*LinkedIn Help*) https://www.linkedin.com/help/linkedin/answer/a1342754 accessed June 2025.
3794. Snap, 'Snap Inc. Terms of Service' (*Snap Inc.*) https://www.snap.com/en-US/terms/ accessed June 2025.
3795. Snap, 'Snap Group Limited Terms of Service' (*Snap Group Limited*) https://www.snap.com/en-US/terms#sgl-terms accessed June 2025.
3796. *Ibid.*
3797. *Ibid.*
3798. X, 'Trademark Policy' (*Trademark Policy*) https://help.x.com/en/rules-and-policies/x-trademark-policy accessed June 2025.
3799. ICANN, 'Uniform Domain-Name Dispute-Resolution Policy' (*ICANN*, 25 February 2012) https://www.icann.org/resources/pages/policy-2012-02-25-en accessed June 2025.
3800. *Ibid.*
3801. Pinterest, 'Terms of Service' (*Pinterest Policy*) https://policy.pinterest.com/en/terms-of-service accessed June 2025.
3802. LinkedIn, 'LinkedIn Advertising Policies' (*LinkedIn*) https://www.linkedin.com/legal/ads-policy accessed June 2025.
3803. WIPO, 'WIPO Overview of WIPO Panel Views on Selected UDRP Questions, Third Edition' ('WIPO Jurisprudential Overview 3.0') (*WIPO*, 2017) https://www.wipo.int/amc/en/domains/search/overview3.0/ accessed June 2025.
3804. Meta, 'Trademark' (*Facebook Help Center*) https://www.facebook.com/help/507663689427413?helpref=about_content accessed June 2025.
3805. X, 'Trademark Policy' (*Trademark Policy*) https://help.x.com/en/rules-and-policies/x-trademark-policy accessed June 2025.
3806. *Ibid.*
3807. LinkedIn, 'How We Enforce Our Professional Community Policies' (*LinkedIn*) https://www.linkedin.com/help/linkedin/answer/a1342754 accessed June 2025.
3808. Snapchat, 'About Trademark Infringement on Snapchat' (*Snapchat Support*) https://help.snapchat.com/hc/en-us/articles/7012343429652 accessed June 2025.
3809. Snap, 'Community Guidelines' (*Snap Privacy, Safety, and Policy Hub*) https://values.snap.com/privacy/transparency/community-guidelines accessed June 2025.
3810. *Ibid.*
3811. *Ibid.*
3812. *Ibid.*

3813. *Ibid.*
3814. *Ibid.*
3815. Meta, 'Trademark' (*Facebook Help Center*) https://www.facebook.com/help/507663689427413?helpref=about_content accessed June 2025.

Although specific policies exist across social media, some are detailed while others are not. Even where help pages are available specifically discussing trademarks, there are some, but generally limited guidelines available on how the individual social media platform policies would apply. As social media policies differ in some or many respects, it is not always clear how some of the specific provisions will be interpreted, although some do provide a level of clarity in some cases. As was seen for other platforms, social media platforms have a high degree of discretion on how to apply their terms. This could even result in different decisions being made by different social media platforms in similar matters breeding the potential for inconsistency.

5.4.6.1 Digital Use and Place of Use

All social media trademark policies apply to utilisation of trademarks within their services, but only some, such as Facebook and Snapchat, specify some sort of use that relates to the goods or services or brand or in a commercial sense.[3816] It is unclear for other platforms whether such type of use is required. Sometimes, policies are specific to the place of use[3817] (such as usernames or content),[3818] more specifically, in a Facebook username,[3819] Pinterest username and content, LinkedIn 'Groups, Company Pages, Profile, Rich Media, Other',[3820] and Snapchat [a]d, [f]ilter, or [s]tory',[3821] in a 'Snapchat username'.[3822] Under Meta's Brand Rights Protection, the place may include Facebook ads, '[s]hops, Facebook Marketplace, buy and sell groups … Pages, profiles or Groups … posts'.[3823] Some complaint forms further identify place of use,[3824] while others do not. Likewise, only for some platforms, when complaining about others using a mark, a trademark registration number is required.[3825]

3816. Meta, 'Trademark' (*Facebook Help Center*) https://www.facebook.com/help/507663689427413?helpref=about_content accessed June 2025; Snap, 'Username Infringement' (*Snapchat Support*) https://help.snapchat.com/hc/en-us/articles/7047503878804 accessed June 2025.
3817. Meta, 'Trademark' (*Facebook Help Center*) https://www.facebook.com/help/507663689427413?helpref=about_content accessed June 2025; Snap, 'Submit a Request' (*Snapchat Support*) https://help.snapchat.com/hc/en-us/requests/new?ticket_form accessed June 2025.
3818. *Ibid.*
3819. Meta, 'Trademark' (*Facebook Help Center*) https://www.facebook.com/help/507663689427413?helpref=about_content accessed June 2025.
3820. *Ibid.*
3821. Snap, 'Submit a Request' (*Snapchat Support*) https://help.snapchat.com/hc/en-us/requests/new?ticket_form accessed June 2025.
3822. *Ibid.*
3823. Meta, 'About Brand Rights Protection' (*Meta Business Help Center*) https://www.facebook.com/business/help/828925381043253?id=4533021280101097 accessed June 2025.
3824. Meta, 'Trademark' (*Facebook Help Center*) https://www.facebook.com/help/507663689427413?helpref=about_content accessed June 2025; Snap, 'Submit a request' (*Snapchat Support*) https://help.snapchat.com/hc/en-us/requests/new?ticket_form accessed June 2025.
3825. Facebook, 'Trademark Report Form' (*Facebook Help Center*) https://www.facebook.com/help/contact/1057530390957243 accessed June 2025; Pinterest, 'Trademark Infringement Notification' (*Pinterest*) https://www.pinterest.com/about/trademark/ accessed June 2025; LinkedIn, 'LinkedIn's Trademark Policy' (*LinkedIn Help*) https://www.linkedin.com/help/linkedin/answer/a1337296?trk=d_microsites-frontend_legal_copyright-policy&lang=en accessed June 2025; Snap, 'Submit a Request' (*Snapchat Support*) https://help.snapchat.com/hc/en-us/requests/new?ticket_form accessed June 2025.

5.4.6.2 *Digital Bad Faith and Abuse*

None of the social media platforms incorporates bad faith[3826] directly (*see* discussion on counterfeit[3827] policies and related unfair acts[3828] below), and only some address abuse[3829] in some way. For example, Facebook, Pinterest and LinkedIn have repeat infringer-related policies[3830] and X recognises penalties based on 'initial review'[3831] if serious enough, while others such as LinkedIn address 'egregious violations'.[3832] There is no detailed approach to bad faith[3833] and abuse[3834] within the trademark policies, which means that it is not a concentrated part of the trademark analysis, although in some cases, it may play more of a role in the penalties or consequences applied. Bad faith[3835] should be an alternative ground since much bad faith[3836] can occur in social media.

3826. UDRP, 4(a)(iii).
3827. X, 'Counterfeit Policy' (*X Business*) https://help.x.com/en/rules-and-policies/counterfeit-goods-policy accessed June 2025.
3828. Meta, 'Trademark' (*Facebook Help Center*) https://www.facebook.com/help/507663689427413?helpref=about_content accessed June 2025; X, 'X Terms of Service' (*X*) https://twitter.com/en/tos#update accessed June 2025; Snap, 'Community Guidelines' (*Snap Privacy, Safety, and Policy Hub*) https://values.snap.com/privacy/transparency/community-guidelines accessed June 2025; X, 'Misleading and Deceptive Identities Policy' (*X Help Center*) https://help.x.com/en/rules-and-policies/x-impersonation-and-deceptive-identities-policy accessed June 2025.
3829. Facebook, 'Terms of Service' https://www.facebook.com/terms.php/ accessed June 2025; Pinterest, 'Terms of Service' (*Pinterest Policy*) https://policy.pinterest.com/en/terms-of-service accessed June 2025; LinkedIn, 'How We Enforce Our Professional Community Policies' (*LinkedIn*) https://www.linkedin.com/help/linkedin/answer/a1342754 accessed June 2025.
3830. *Ibid.*
3831. X, 'Trademark Policy' (*Trademark Policy*) https://help.x.com/en/rules-and-policies/x-trademark-policy accessed June 2025.
3832. LinkedIn, 'How We Enforce Our Professional Community Policies' (*LinkedIn*) https://www.linkedin.com/help/linkedin/answer/a1342754 accessed June 2025.
3833. Paris Convention, Art. 6bis; EUTMR, Art. 59; TTAB, 'Fighting Bad Faith Trademark Filings in the United States' (*The Honorable Karen S. Kuhlke Administrative Trademark Judge*) https://www.jpo.go.jp/e/news/kokusai/tm5/document/bad_faith_seminar2/01.pdf accessed July 2024; UDRP, 4(a)(iii).
3834. WIPO, 'WIPO Overview of WIPO Panel Views on Selected UDRP Questions, Third Edition' ('WIPO Jurisprudential Overview 3.0') (*WIPO*, 2017) https://www.wipo.int/amc/en/domains/search/overview3.0/ accessed June 2025.
3835. Paris Convention, Art. 6bis; EUTMR, Art. 59; TTAB, 'Fighting Bad Faith Trademark Filings in the United States' (*The Honorable Karen S. Kuhlke Administrative Trademark Judge*) https://www.jpo.go.jp/e/news/kokusai/tm5/document/bad_faith_seminar2/01.pdf accessed July 2024; UDRP, 4(a)(iii).
3836. *Ibid.*

5.4.6.3 *Digital Confusion*

Confusion[3837] is directly stated in X's Trademark Policy[3838] and in LinkedIn's Ads Policy,[3839] although referenced in Facebook help pages,[3840] through Pinterest's Terms[3841] and Snap Terms[3842] through general infringement with no direct or only an indirect reference to confusion.[3843] Confusion[3844] should be explicitly covered by all platforms in order to clarify it as a key ground that will be used to assess infringement.

5.4.6.4 *Digital Unfair Competition*

Unfair competition[3845] is not covered directly by name by any of the social media platforms. All social media platforms cover, in some way, counterfeit goods,[3846] although not always as part of their terms or policy.[3847] Relatedly, Facebook mentions 'knockoff'[3848] and 'replica'[3849] in help pages, X prohibits 'misappropriation',[3850] X's Terms and Snap Community Guidelines prohibit 'impersonation ...'.[3851] X prohibits 'fake personas',[3852] posing,[3853] and 'copied or stolen profile bios',[3854] 'imitation',[3855] LinkedIn prohibits a 'fake profile',[3856] LinkedIn Professional Community Policies

3837. X, 'Trademark Policy' (*Trademark Policy*) https://help.x.com/en/rules-and-policies/x-trademark-policy accessed June 2025.
3838. *Ibid.*
3839. LinkedIn, 'LinkedIn Advertising Policies' (*LinkedIn*) https://www.linkedin.com/legal/ads-policy accessed June 2025.
3840. Meta, 'Trademark' (*Facebook Help Center*) https://www.facebook.com/help/507663689427413?helpref=about_content accessed June 2025.
3841. Pinterest, 'Terms of Service' (*Pinterest Policy*) https://policy.pinterest.com/en/terms-of-service accessed June 2025.
3842. Snap, 'Snap Inc. Terms of Service' (*Snap Inc.*) https://www.snap.com/en-US/terms/ accessed June 2025; Snap, 'Snap Group Limited Terms of Service' (*Snap Group Limited*) https://www.snap.com/en-US/terms#sgl-terms accessed June 2025.
3843. Paris Convention, Art. 6bis; TRIPS, Art. 16(1); EUTMR, Art. 8(1)(b) and Art. 9(2)(b); 15 U.S. Code § 1114;15 U.S. Code § 1125.
3844. *Ibid.*
3845. *Ibid.*
3846. X, 'Counterfeit Policy' (*X Business*) https://help.x.com/en/rules-and-policies/counterfeit-goods-policy accessed June 2025.
3847. Meta, 'Trademark' (*Facebook Help Center*) https://www.facebook.com/help/507663689427413?helpref=about_content accessed June 2025.
3848. *Ibid.*
3849. *Ibid.*
3850. X, 'X Terms of Service' (*X*) https://twitter.com/en/tos#update accessed June 2025.
3851. X, 'X Terms of Service' (*X*) https://twitter.com/en/tos#update accessed June 2025; Snap, 'Community Guidelines' (*Snap Privacy, Safety, and Policy Hub*) https://values.snap.com/privacy/transparency/community-guidelines accessed June 2025.
3852. X, 'Misleading and Deceptive Identities Policy' (*X Help Center*) https://help.x.com/en/rules-and-policies/x-impersonation-and-deceptive-identities-policyaccessed June 2025.
3853. *Ibid.*
3854. *Ibid.*
3855. X, 'Counterfeit Policy' (*X Business*) https://help.x.com/en/rules-and-policies/counterfeit-goods-policy accessed June 2025.
3856. LinkedIn, 'Report Fake Profiles' (*LinkedIn Help*) https://www.linkedin.com/help/linkedin/answer/a1338436/ accessed June 2025.

prohibit 'misleading or deceptive information',[3857] and Snap Community Guidelines prohibit 'deceptive practices, including the promotion of fraudulent goods or services'.[3858] Dilution[3859] of a famous mark[3860] in commerce[3861] is only covered generally through Facebook help pages.[3862] However, there does not appear to be consistent policies or wording across the platforms with respect to these concepts, which can breed inconsistency and create legal uncertainty.

5.4.6.5 Digital Terms, Policies, and Disclaimers

All social media platforms have terms and policies governing trademarks in their platforms; however, these are often in various documents and are not consistent. In many cases, the rules or guidelines are spread through terms, policies, help centres, FAQs, or other options.

Facebook help pages very briefly note a type of disclaimer. They say counterfeit goods 'may be unlawful even if the seller explicitly says that the goods are counterfeit, or otherwise disclaims authenticity of the goods'.[3863] While not a disclaimer per se, X, under their Impersonation and Deceptive Identities Policy, requires users to 'clearly indicate that they are unaffiliated',[3864] such as by using 'parody',[3865] 'fun',[3866] 'fake',[3867] or 'commentary'[3868] in the account name and other requirements.[3869] This might act as a disclaimer of sorts. Most social media platforms do not directly address whether or how terms, conditions, and disclaimers may make a difference.

5.4.6.6 Digital Jurisdictional and Territorial Considerations

Facebook help pages make reference to the limitation of rights to a 'geographic territory',[3870] offering a generic example of a restaurant in one country and a restaurant in another. However, this does not offer much clarity to a Facebook user. LinkedIn

3857. LinkedIn, 'Professional Community Policies' (*LinkedIn*) https://www.linkedin.com/legal/professional-community-policies accessed June 2025.
3858. Snap, 'Community Guidelines' (*Snap Privacy, Safety, and Policy Hub*) https://values.snap.com/privacy/transparency/community-guidelines accessed June 2025.
3859. Meta, 'Trademark' (*Facebook Help Center*) https://www.facebook.com/help/507663689427413?helpref=about_content accessed June 2025.
3860. *Ibid.*
3861. *Ibid.*
3862. *Ibid.*
3863. *Ibid.*
3864. X, 'Misleading and Deceptive Identities Policy' (*X Help Center*) https://help.x.com/en/rules-and-policies/x-impersonation-and-deceptive-identities-policyaccessed June 2025.
3865. *Ibid.*
3866. *Ibid.*
3867. *Ibid.*
3868. *Ibid.*
3869. *Ibid.*
3870. Meta, 'Trademark' (*Facebook Help Center*) https://www.facebook.com/help/507663689427413?helpref=about_content accessed June 2025.

mentions that 'notices are sent in line with relevant laws in the regions where [they] operate'.[3871] Co-existence[3872] is not identified.

While some social media platforms have terms or policies pertinent to specific territories or geographic regions, it is rare to see substantially different trademark policies between them. It is unclear how or how much local law may impact decision-making by these platforms; however, anticipated that such may be taken into consideration. However, parties may be from different jurisdictions or territories and it is unclear how this will be taken into consideration with respect to a decision, or even if it may be considered at all.

5.4.6.7 Digital Justification

Justification is covered differently by most social media trademark policies. Facebook's help pages recognise 'resale of legitimate goods',[3873] Snapchat permits accurate references to goods and services and also for comparison[3874] and X recognises use for different goods or services is not violative.[3875] Facebook recognises 'ordinary dictionary meaning'.[3876] Facebook also recognises 'the context of its use'[3877] and 'not every use ... in a username is necessarily a trademark infringement'.[3878] X recognises 'compliant Parody, Commentary, and Fan (PCF) accounts on X only if the purpose is to discuss, satirize or share information'[3879] with specific requirements.[3880] LinkedIn permits content for 'awareness or to condemn'[3881] while Facebook recognises the ability to 'comment on or criticize ... goods or services'.[3882] Pinterest does not directly

3871. *Ibid.*
3872. EUIPO, '3.1 Coexistence Between the Marks Involved in the Opposition' (*EUIPO Trade mark Guidelines*) https://guidelines.euipo.europa.eu/2058843/2043906/trade-mark-guidelines/3-1-coexistence-between-the-marks-involved-in-the-opposition accessed January 2024;15 U.S. Code § 1052(d); Alexander Peukert, 'The Coexistence of Trade Mark Laws and Rights on the Internet, and the Impact of Geolocation Technologies' (2016) 47 International Review of Intellectual Property and Competition Law 60, 81 https://doi.org/10.1007/s40319-015-0427-8; Tamara Nanayakkara, 'IP and Business: Trademark Coexistence' (*WIPO*, November 2006) https://www.wipo.int/wipo_magazine/en/2006/06/article_0007.html accessed June 2025.
3873. Meta, 'Trademark' (*Facebook Help Center*) https://www.facebook.com/help/507663689427413?helpref=about_content accessed June 2025.
3874. Snapchat, 'About Trademark Infringement on Snapchat' (*Snapchat Support*) https://help.snapchat.com/hc/en-us/articles/7012343429652 accessed June 2025.
3875. X, 'Trademark Policy' (*Trademark Policy*) https://help.x.com/en/rules-and-policies/x-trademark-policy accessed June 2025.
3876. Meta, 'Trademark' (*Facebook Help Center*) https://www.facebook.com/help/507663689427413?helpref=about_content accessed June 2025.
3877. *Ibid.*
3878. *Ibid.*
3879. X, 'Misleading and Deceptive Identities Policy' (*X Help Center*) https://help.x.com/en/rules-and-policies/x-impersonation-and-deceptive-identities-policy accessed June 2025.
3880. *Ibid.*
3881. LinkedIn, 'How We Enforce Our Professional Community Policies' (*LinkedIn*) https://www.linkedin.com/help/linkedin/answer/a1342754 accessed June 2025.
3882. Meta, 'Trademark' (*Facebook Help Center*) https://www.facebook.com/help/507663689427413?helpref=about_content accessed June 2025.

address justification; however, it generalises that 'unless an exception or limitation applies under applicable law'.[3883] It does not state what those limitations may be.

Social media platforms do not offer a consistent approach which would allow for a more uniform understanding and greater legal certainty. Further, unlike the UDRP, and similar to other platforms, social media trademark-specific decisions are not generally made public (even if some publish statistics),[3884] which leads to further legal uncertainty. Interestingly, Meta mentions in its terms that '[i]n some cases, the Oversight Board may review our decisions, subject to its terms and bylaws'.[3885] This may be, for example, in decisions relating to 'free expression'[3886] and in line with the possible alternative of an external UDRP-like panel to make decisions pertaining to trademark complaints within these platforms.

5.4.7 Solution: A Uniform Policy for Trademarks in Social Media Platforms

As seen above, each individual social media company will be the decision-maker of any dispute relating to a trademarks in their service (unless filed with a court) because there is no UDRP for social media,[3887] as recommended by some.[3888] Rather than individual terms and conditions which are not uniform and highly discretionary on the part of the social media company, it is recommended that one uniform policy apply, which will result in consistent application of uniform rules on an expedited basis.[3889] Such uniform policy[3890] can help to resolve some of the key issues relating to trademarks utilised in social media, and, under the model, this recommendation is embraced. It is proposed that such policy be named the Uniform Social Media Trade

3883. Pinterest, 'Terms of Service' (*Pinterest Policy*) https://policy.pinterest.com/en/terms-of-service accessed July 2024.
3884. Meta, 'Notice and Takedown' (*Meta Transparency Center*) https://transparency.meta.com/reports/intellectual-property/notice-and-takedown/facebook/ accessed June 2025.
3885. Facebook, 'Terms of Service' https://www.facebook.com/terms.php/ accessed June 2025.
3886. Oversight Board, 'Improving How Meta Treats People and Communities Around the World' (*Oversight Board*) https://www.oversightboard.com/ accessed June 2025.
3887. Rajeev Sachdev, 'Towards an Improved Framework for Trade-Mark Law and Regulation in Social Media Usernames: A Study of the Canadian, U.S., and U.K. Positions' (2016) 28 Intellectual Property Journal 379, 379-418; Daniel Doft, 'Facebook, Twitter, and the Wild West of IP Enforcement on Social Media: Weighing the Merits of a Uniform Dispute Resolution Policy' (2016) 49 The John Marshall Law Review 959; Thomas J Curtin, 'The Name Game: Cybersquatting and Trademark Infringement on Social Media Websites' (2010-2011) 19 Journal of Law and Policy 353; Erick J Heels, 'How to Twittersquat the Top 100 Brands' (*GiantPeople*, 8 January 2009) http://www.giantpeople.com/1298.html accessed 4 August 2025; Paul D McGrady, *McGrady on Social Media and the Metaverse* (Mathew Bender & Company, Inc. 2023) §12; John McElwaine and Christopher D Casavale, 'Tackling Bad Faith Registration of Domain Names in a Fast-Changing Landscape' (*WIPO Magazine*, December 2019) https://www.wipo.int/wipo_magazine/en/2019/06/article_0006.html accessed June 2025.
3888. *Ibid.*
3889. *Ibid.*
3890. *Ibid.*

mark Dispute Resolution Policy (USMTDRP)[3891] and apply to all major social media companies.[3892] The policy should be based on the UDRP, UDNDRP, and individual social media terms, as similar considerations apply.[3893]

Although this will not be the first work to make arguments relating to a uniform approach,[3894] it outlines one comprehensive approach and provides the actual

3891. Rajeev Sachdev, 'Towards an Improved Framework for Trade-Mark Law and Regulation in Social Media Usernames: A Study of the Canadian, U.S., and U.K. Positions' (2016) 28 Intellectual Property Journal 379, 379-418; ICANN, 'Uniform Domain-Name Dispute-Resolution Policy' (*ICANN*, 25 February 2012) https://www.icann.org/resources/pages/policy-2012-02-25-en accessed June 2025; WIPO, 'WIPO Overview of WIPO Panel Views on Selected UDRP Questions, Third Edition' ('WIPO Jurisprudential Overview 3.0') (*WIPO*, 2017) https://www.wipo.int/amc/en/domains/search/overview3.0/ accessed June 2025.

3892. Rajeev Sachdev, 'Towards an Improved Framework for Trade-Mark Law and Regulation in Social Media Usernames: A Study of the Canadian, U.S., and U.K. Positions' (2016) 28 Intellectual Property Journal 379, 379-418; Daniel Doft, 'Facebook, Twitter, and the Wild West of IP Enforcement on Social Media: Weighing the Merits of a Uniform Dispute Resolution Policy' (2016) 49 The John Marshall Law Review 959; Thomas J Curtin, 'The Name Game: Cybersquatting and Trademark Infringement on Social Media Websites' (2010-2011) 19 Journal of Law and Policy 353; Erick J Heels, 'How to Twittersquat the Top 100 Brands' (*GiantPeople*, 8 January 2009) http://www.giantpeople.com/1298.html accessed 4 August 2025; Paul D McGrady, *McGrady on Social Media and the Metaverse* (Mathew Bender & Company, Inc. 2023) §12; John McElwaine and Christopher D Casavale, 'Tackling Bad Faith Registration of Domain Names in a Fast-Changing Landscape' (*WIPO Magazine*, December 2019) https://www.wipo.int/wipo_magazine/en/2019/06/article_0006.html accessed June 2025.

3893. Rajeev Sachdev, 'Towards an Improved Framework for Trade-Mark Law and Regulation in Social Media Usernames: A Study of the Canadian, U.S., and U.K. Positions' (2016) 28 Intellectual Property Journal 379, 379-418; Daniel Doft, 'Facebook, Twitter, and the Wild West of IP Enforcement on Social Media: Weighing the Merits of a Uniform Dispute Resolution Policy' (2016) 49 The John Marshall Law Review 959; Thomas J Curtin, 'The Name Game: Cybersquatting and Trademark Infringement on Social Media Websites' (2010-2011) 19 Journal of Law and Policy 353; Erick J Heels, 'How to Twittersquat the Top 100 Brands' (*GiantPeople*, 8 January 2009) http://www.giantpeople.com/1298.html accessed 4 August 2025; Paul D McGrady, *McGrady on Social Media and the Metaverse* (Mathew Bender & Company, Inc. 2023) §12; John McElwaine and Christopher D Casavale, 'Tackling Bad Faith Registration of Domain Names in a Fast-Changing Landscape' (*WIPO Magazine*, December 2019) https://www.wipo.int/wipo_magazine/en/2019/06/article_0006.html accessed June 2025; Facebook, 'Terms of Service' https://www.facebook.com/terms.php/ accessed June 2025; Pinterest, 'Terms of Service' (*Pinterest Policy*) https://policy.pinterest.com/en/terms-of-service accessed June 2025; LinkedIn, 'How We Enforce Our Professional Community Policies' (*LinkedIn*) https://www.linkedin.com/help/linkedin/answer/a1342754 accessed June 2025; Meta, 'Trademark' (*Facebook Help Center*) https://www.facebook.com/help/507663689427413?helpref=about_content accessed June 2025; X, 'X Terms of Service' (*X*) https://twitter.com/en/tos#update accessed June 2025; X, 'Misleading and Deceptive Identities Policy' (*X Help Center*) https://help.x.com/en/rules-and-policies/x-impersonation-and-deceptive-identities-policy accessed June 2025; X, 'Counterfeit Policy' (*X Business*) https://help.x.com/en/rules-and-policies/counterfeit-goods-policy accessed July 2024; Snap, 'Community Guidelines' (*Snap Privacy, Safety, and Policy Hub*) https://values.snap.com/privacy/transparency/community-guidelines accessed June 2025; Snap, 'Username Infringement' (*Snapchat Support*) https://help.snapchat.com/hc/en-us/articles/7047503878804 accessed June 2025.

3894. Rajeev Sachdev, 'Towards an Improved Framework for Trade-Mark Law and Regulation in Social Media Usernames: A Study of the Canadian, U.S., and U.K. Positions' (2016) 28 Intellectual Property Journal 379, 379-418; Daniel Doft, 'Facebook, Twitter, and the Wild West of IP Enforcement on Social Media: Weighing the Merits of a Uniform Dispute Resolution Policy' (2016) 49 The John Marshall Law Review 959; Thomas J Curtin, 'The Name Game:

proposed text of a specific uniform policy[3895] and applies a model approach informed by theories/concepts and select legal frameworks. Law student, at the time Thomas Curtin did not see a uniform approach[3896] such as the UDRP to be 'as potent of a remedy as the ACPA'[3897] type legislation for social media usernames,[3898] although he clearly recognised that working with social media administrators to resolve complaints could be highly beneficial.[3899] Law student, at the time, Daniel Doft reviewed that other's discussed uniform policies[3900] for social media, including a blog article by Erik Heels (attorney), a 'student-written note'[3901] by Zorik Pesochinsk,[3902] the idea raised by Steve Levy and Kristine Dorrain (attorneys),[3903] a work by Paul McGrady (author)[3904] and a work by Sachdev.[3905] Doft argued the benefits of a uniform procedure termed the Uniform Social Media Intellectual Property Dispute Resolution Policy (USRP),[3906] before dismissing it as the best solution.[3907] He argued that such an approach could not

Cybersquatting and Trademark Infringement on Social Media Websites' (2010-2011) 19 Journal of Law and Policy 353; Erick J Heels, 'How to Twittersquat the Top 100 Brands' (*GiantPeople*, 8 January 2009) http://www.giantpeople.com/1298.html accessed 4 August 2025; Paul D McGrady, *McGrady on Social Media and the Metaverse* (Mathew Bender & Company, Inc. 2023) §12; John McElwaine and Christopher D Casavale, 'Tackling Bad Faith Registration of Domain Names in a Fast-Changing Landscape' (*WIPO Magazine*, December 2019) https://www.wipo.int/wipo_magazine/en/2019/06/article_0006.html accessed June 2025.

3895. *Ibid.*

3896. Thomas J Curtin, 'The Name Game: Cybersquatting and Trademark Infringement on Social Media Websites' (2010-2011) 19 Journal of Law and Policy 353, 359 notes.

3897. *Ibid.*

3898. *Ibid.*

3899. *Ibid.*

3900. *Ibid.*

3901. Daniel Doft, 'Facebook, Twitter, and the Wild West of IP Enforcement on Social Media: Weighing the Merits of a Uniform Dispute Resolution Policy' (2016) 49 The John Marshall Law Review 959, 1009-1011.

3902. Zorik Pesochinsky, 'Almost Famous: Preventing Username Squatting on Social Networking Websites' (2010) 28 Cardozo Arts & Entertainment Law Journal 223, 224-225; Daniel Doft, 'Facebook, Twitter, and the Wild West of IP Enforcement on Social Media: Weighing the Merits of a Uniform Dispute Resolution Policy' (2016) 49 The John Marshall Law Review 959, 1009-1011.

3903. Daniel Doft, 'Facebook, Twitter, and the Wild West of IP Enforcement on Social Media: Weighing the Merits of a Uniform Dispute Resolution Policy' (2016) 49 The John Marshall Law Review 959, 1009-1011.

3904. Daniel Doft, 'Facebook, Twitter, and the Wild West of IP Enforcement on Social Media: Weighing the Merits of a Uniform Dispute Resolution Policy' (2016) 49 The John Marshall Law Review 959, 1007-1009; Paul D McGrady, *McGrady on Social Media and the Metaverse* § 12.06 (Mathew Bender & Company, Inc., 2023) §12.

3905. Rajeev Sachdev, 'Towards an Improved Framework for Trade-Mark Law and Regulation in Social Media Usernames: A Study of the Canadian, U.S., and U.K. Positions' (2016) 28 Intellectual Property Journal 379, 379-418.

3906. Daniel Doft, 'Facebook, Twitter, and the Wild West of IP Enforcement on Social Media: Weighing the Merits of a Uniform Dispute Resolution Policy' (2016) 49 The John Marshall Law Review 959, 962.

3907. Daniel Doft, 'Facebook, Twitter, and the Wild West of IP Enforcement on Social Media: Weighing the Merits of a Uniform Dispute Resolution Policy' (2016) 49 The John Marshall Law Review 959, 1007-1020.

work based on the consideration that each social media platform is different;[3908] however, this argument is not strong based on commonalities within social media.[3909] The differences in relation to trademarks in the context of social media can be resolved with a single uniform policy,[3910] as the issues raised are very similar, even if the platforms are different. He ultimately concludes that there is a 'need for transparency and predictability in the administration and creation of intellectual property policies on social media websites'[3911] in lieu of a uniform policy.[3912] However, while this may create a solution that may be 'accurate and consistent'[3913] within a particular social media platform, it does not address consistency across platforms when the same mark is utilised across these. A uniform policy[3914] can breed consistency[3915] across platforms as well as transparency[3916] all around. Sachdev proposed that a Uniform Social Media Username Dispute Resolution Procedure (USMUDRP)[3917] based on key benefits such as

3908. Daniel Doft, 'Facebook, Twitter, and the Wild West of IP Enforcement on Social Media: Weighing the Merits of a Uniform Dispute Resolution Policy' (2016) 49 The John Marshall Law Review 959.
3909. Rajeev Sachdev, 'Towards an Improved Framework for Trade-Mark Law and Regulation in Social Media Usernames: A Study of the Canadian, U.S., and U.K. Positions' (2016) 28 Intellectual Property Journal 379, 379-418; Thomas J Curtin, 'The Name Game: Cybersquatting and Trademark Infringement on Social Media Websites' (2010-2011) 19 Journal of Law and Policy 353; Erick J Heels, 'How to Twittersquat the Top 100 Brands' (*GiantPeople*, 8 January 2009) http://www.giantpeople.com/1298.html accessed 4 August 2025; Paul D McGrady, *McGrady on Social Media and the Metaverse* § 12.06 (Mathew Bender & Company, Inc., 2023) §12.
3910. Rajeev Sachdev, 'Towards an Improved Framework for Trade-Mark Law and Regulation in Social Media Usernames: A Study of the Canadian, U.S., and U.K. Positions' (2016) 28 Intellectual Property Journal 379, 379-418; Paul D McGrady, *McGrady on Social Media and the Metaverse* § 12.06 (Mathew Bender & Company, Inc., 2023) §12.
3911. Daniel Doft, 'Facebook, Twitter, and the Wild West of IP Enforcement on Social Media: Weighing the Merits of a Uniform Dispute Resolution Policy' (2016) 49 The John Marshall Law Review 959, 1017.
3912. *Ibid.*
3913. Daniel Doft, 'Facebook, Twitter, and the Wild West of IP Enforcement on Social Media: Weighing the Merits of a Uniform Dispute Resolution Policy' (2016) 49 The John Marshall Law Review 959, 1018.
3914. Rajeev Sachdev, 'Towards an Improved Framework for Trade-Mark Law and Regulation in Social Media Usernames: A Study of the Canadian, U.S., and U.K. Positions' (2016) 28 Intellectual Property Journal 379, 379-418; Daniel Doft, 'Facebook, Twitter, and the Wild West of IP Enforcement on Social Media: Weighing the Merits of a Uniform Dispute Resolution Policy' (2016) 49 The John Marshall Law Review 959; Thomas J Curtin, 'The Name Game: Cybersquatting and Trademark Infringement on Social Media Websites' (2010-2011) 19 Journal of Law and Policy 353; Erick J Heels, 'How to Twittersquat the Top 100 Brands' (*GiantPeople*, 8 January 2009) http://www.giantpeople.com/1298.html accessed 4 August 2025; Paul D McGrady, *McGrady on Social Media and the Metaverse* (Mathew Bender & Company, Inc. 2023) §12.
3915. Daniel Doft, 'Facebook, Twitter, and the Wild West of IP Enforcement on Social Media: Weighing the Merits of a Uniform Dispute Resolution Policy' (2016) 49 The John Marshall Law Review 959, 1018.
3916. Daniel Doft, 'Facebook, Twitter, and the Wild West of IP Enforcement on Social Media: Weighing the Merits of a Uniform Dispute Resolution Policy' (2016) 49 The John Marshall Law Review 959, 1017.
3917. Rajeev Sachdev, 'Towards an Improved Framework for Trade-Mark Law and Regulation in Social Media Usernames: A Study of the Canadian, U.S., and U.K. Positions' (2016) 28 Intellectual Property Journal 379, 379-418.

being a 'uniform method'[3918] with 'uniform rules and defences',[3919] not necessarily needing the 'identity'[3920] of an infringer, enhancing 'consistency',[3921] being applicable to 'each major social media platform',[3922] and a 'system of prompt address'[3923] while leaving litigation as an option.[3924] Sachdev also agreed, like others, that a UDRP-like approach with some provisions being similar would be beneficial.[3925] However, that work did not extend into the details included in this book, the theory, concepts or detailed law, the adapted model on which it is based, nor the text of the policy included below. Likewise, McGrady rightly argues that a uniform policy can help to counter specific problems such as 'inconsistencies in elements'[3926] considered, 'inconsistency of outcomes',[3927] and costs and risks for various parties.[3928] He took it further by putting together an example of the text of some key clauses of a possible uniform policy for social media usernames.[3929] His proposal, the 'Social Media Username Dispute Mechanism',[3930] follows the UDRP very closely and is a welcome approach as it moves towards a unified system.[3931] While having some similarities to the proposal outlined

3918. *Ibid.*; Daniel Doft, 'Facebook, Twitter, and the Wild West of IP Enforcement on Social Media: Weighing the Merits of a Uniform Dispute Resolution Policy' (2016) 49 The John Marshall Law Review 959; Thomas J Curtin, 'The Name Game: Cybersquatting and Trademark Infringement on Social Media Websites' (2010-2011) 19 Journal of Law and Policy 353; Erick J Heels, 'How to Twittersquat the Top 100 Brands' (*GiantPeople*, 8 January 2009) http://www.giantpeople.com/1298.html accessed 4 August 2025; Paul D McGrady, *McGrady on Social Media and the Metaverse* (Mathew Bender & Company, Inc. 2023) §12; John McElwaine and Christopher D Casavale, 'Tackling Bad Faith Registration of Domain Names in a Fast-Changing Landscape' (*WIPO Magazine*, December 2019) https://www.wipo.int/wipo_magazine/en/2019/06/article_0006.html accessed June 2025; ICANN, 'Uniform Domain-Name Dispute-Resolution Policy' (*ICANN*, 25 February 2012) https://www.icann.org/resources/pages/policy-2012-02-25-en accessed June 2025.

3919. *Ibid.*

3920. *Ibid.*

3921. *Ibid.*

3922. *Ibid.*

3923. *Ibid.*

3924. Rajeev Sachdev, 'Towards an Improved Framework for Trade-Mark Law and Regulation in Social Media Usernames: A Study of the Canadian, U.S., and U.K. Positions' (2016) 28 Intellectual Property Journal 379, 379-418; ICANN, 'Uniform Domain-Name Dispute-Resolution Policy' (*ICANN*, 25 February 2012) https://www.icann.org/resources/pages/policy-2012-02-25-en accessed June 2025.

3925. Rajeev Sachdev, 'Towards an Improved Framework for Trade-Mark Law and Regulation in Social Media Usernames: A Study of the Canadian, U.S., and U.K. Positions' (2016) 28 Intellectual Property Journal 379, 379-418; Paul D McGrady, *McGrady on Social Media and the Metaverse* (Mathew Bender & Company, Inc. 2023) §12; John McElwaine and Christopher D Casavale, 'Tackling Bad Faith Registration of Domain Names in a Fast-Changing Landscape' (*WIPO Magazine*, December 2019) https://www.wipo.int/wipo_magazine/en/2019/06/article_0006.html accessed June 2025; ICANN, 'Uniform Domain-Name Dispute-Resolution Policy' (*ICANN*, 25 February 2012) https://www.icann.org/resources/pages/policy-2012-02-25-en accessed June 2025.

3926. Paul D McGrady, *McGrady on Social Media and the Metaverse* § 12.06 (Mathew Bender & Company, Inc., 2023) §12.

3927. *Ibid.*

3928. *Ibid.*

3929. *Ibid.*

3930. *Ibid.*

3931. Rajeev Sachdev, 'Towards an Improved Framework for Trade-Mark Law and Regulation in Social Media Usernames: A Study of the Canadian, U.S., and U.K. Positions' (2016) 28

below, there are major differences and these represent alternative approaches.[3932] The USMTDRP below is expanded[3933] to cover not only social media usernames as with McGrady's approach[3934] but also content and advertising in social media. Further, his approach requires all three required elements of the UDRP in a username setting,[3935] whereas the USMTDRP incorporates an alternative grounds approach.[3936] For example, 'bad faith'[3937] is an alternative ground under the proposed USMTDRP. Further 'rights or legitimate interests'[3938] are framed as justifications instead of a requirement to be initially proven by the complainant as in the UDRP which has been problematic.[3939] Further, unfair competition is an alternative ground. Further, under the USMTDRP below, alongside 'bad faith',[3940] abusive[3941] situations are also taken into account, including repeat infringers.[3942] Additionally, McGrady's version has an associated cost to one or more parties,[3943] whereas the USMTDRP does not, as the cost would be borne by the social media platforms in line with not currently having a cost to decide on complaints within their platforms and having to expend resources to make decisions as they do currently. Further differences include creating guidelines for the USMTDRP to clarify the various specific situations that may arise in social media and how they may

Intellectual Property Journal 379, 379-418; Daniel Doft, 'Facebook, Twitter, and the Wild West of IP Enforcement on Social Media: Weighing the Merits of a Uniform Dispute Resolution Policy' (2016) 49 The John Marshall Law Review 959; Thomas J Curtin, 'The Name Game: Cybersquatting and Trademark Infringement on Social Media Websites' (2010-2011) 19 Journal of Law and Policy 353; Erick J Heels, 'How to Twittersquat the Top 100 Brands' (*GiantPeople,* 8 January 2009) http://www.giantpeople.com/1298.html accessed 4 August 2025; Paul D McGrady, *McGrady on Social Media and the Metaverse* (Mathew Bender & Company, Inc. 2023) §12.

3932. Rajeev Sachdev, 'Towards an Improved Framework for Trade-Mark Law and Regulation in Social Media Usernames: A Study of the Canadian, U.S., and U.K. Positions' (2016) 28 Intellectual Property Journal 379, 379-418; Paul D McGrady, *McGrady on Social Media and the Metaverse* (Mathew Bender & Company, Inc., 2023) § 12.06.
3933. Daniel Doft, 'Facebook, Twitter, and the Wild West of IP Enforcement on Social Media: Weighing the Merits of a Uniform Dispute Resolution Policy' (2016) 49 The John Marshall Law Review 959, 962.
3934. Paul D McGrady, *McGrady on Social Media and the Metaverse* (Mathew Bender & Company, Inc., 2023) Chapter 12; Daniel Doft, 'Facebook, Twitter, and the Wild West of IP Enforcement on Social Media: Weighing the Merits of a Uniform Dispute Resolution Policy' (2016) 49 The John Marshall Law Review 959, 1008.
3935. Paul D McGrady, *McGrady on Social Media and the Metaverse* (Mathew Bender & Company, Inc., 2023) §12.
3936. WIPO, 'WIPO Domain Name Dispute Resolution Service for .EU (and.ею and.ευ)' (*WIPO*) https://www.wipo.int/amc/en/domains/cctld/eu/index.html accessed July 2024.
3937. ICANN, 'Uniform Domain-Name Dispute-Resolution Policy' (ICANN, 25 February 2012) https://www.icann.org/resources/pages/policy-2012-02-25-en accessed June 2025.
3938. *Ibid.*
3939. WIPO, 'WIPO Overview of WIPO Panel Views on Selected UDRP Questions, Third Edition' ('WIPO Jurisprudential Overview 3.0') (*WIPO,* 2017) https://www.wipo.int/amc/en/domains/search/overview3.0/ accessed June 2025.
3940. UDRP, 4(a)(iii).
3941. Instagram, 'Instagram Help Center' (*Trademark | Instagram Help Center*) https://help.instagram.com/222826637847963 accessed July 2024.
3942. *Ibid.*
3943. Paul D McGrady, *McGrady on Social Media and the Metaverse* (Mathew Bender & Company, Inc., 2023) § 12.

be dealt with under the proposed policy. These may assist greatly in clarifying many aspects of trademarks in social media, even if not binding per se.

The text of the USMTDRP, as recommended under the Digital Trademark and Trade Practices Model, is as follows in the case of Platforms adopting it themselves and making their own decisions:

Table 5.8 Uniform Social Media Trademark Dispute Resolution Policy (USMTDRP)[3944]

Uniform Social Media Trademark Dispute Resolution Policy (USMTDRP)	Adapted or directly from the UDRP[3945] and UDNDRP (Chapter 4). The name reflects specifically the platform type and subject matter.
(1) *Purpose*. This Uniform Social Media Trademark Dispute Resolution Policy ('Policy') has been adopted by [Social Media Platform] ('Platform' or 'We'), is incorporated by reference into the Terms of Use of Platform and your Social Media Account Registration and/or Advertising Agreement, and sets forth the terms and conditions in connection with a dispute between you and any party other than Platform over the utilisation of a trademark in Platform. Decisions under Paragraph 4 of this Policy will be made in accordance with the Policy. Guidelines to this policy are set forth in the document entitled: Guidelines to the USMTDRP.	Adapted or directly from the UDRP[3946] and UDNDRP (Chapter 4) and Facebook, X, Pinterest,

3944. Rajeev Sachdev, 'Towards an Improved Framework for Trade-Mark Law and Regulation in Social Media Usernames: A Study of the Canadian, U.S., and U.K. Positions' (2016) 28 Intellectual Property Journal 379, 379-418; Daniel Doft, 'Facebook, Twitter, and the Wild West of IP Enforcement on Social Media: Weighing the Merits of a Uniform Dispute Resolution Policy' (2016) 49 The John Marshall Law Review 959; Thomas J Curtin, 'The Name Game: Cybersquatting and Trademark Infringement on Social Media Websites' (2010-2011) 19 Journal of Law and Policy 353; Erick J Heels, 'How to Twittersquat the Top 100 Brands' (*GiantPeople*, 8 January 2009) http://www.giantpeople.com/1298.html accessed 4 August 2025; Paul D McGrady, *McGrady on Social Media and the Metaverse* (Mathew Bender & Company, Inc. 2023) §12; John McElwaine and Christopher D Casavale, 'Tackling Bad Faith Registration of Domain Names in a Fast-Changing Landscape' (*WIPO Magazine*, December 2019) https://www.wipo.int/wipo_magazine/en/2019/06/article_0006.html accessed June 2025.

3945. ICANN, 'Uniform Domain-Name Dispute-Resolution Policy' (*ICANN*, 25 February 2012) https://www.icann.org/resources/pages/policy-2012-02-25-en.

3946. *Ibid.*

	LinkedIn, and Snapchat terms and policies.[3947] The policy refers to any disputed utilisation of a mark within the platforms. Guidelines should make clear that utilisation of a trademark includes in social media accounts, usernames, account names, profiles, identities, handles, pages, ID's or like accounts (collectively referred to as 'Username')[3948] registered by a user, as well as providing content within social media platform (including any activity, profiles, posts, pins, messages, infographics, live streams, images, pictures, polls, memes, filters, stories, reels, testimonials, snippets, contests, promotions, or any other content whatsoever in Social Media Platform whatever it may be called) and Advertising in Social Media Platform.[3949]

3947. Facebook, 'Terms of Service' https://www.facebook.com/terms.php/ accessed June 2025; Pinterest, 'Terms of Service' (*Pinterest Policy*) https://policy.pinterest.com/en/terms-of-service accessed June 2025; LinkedIn, 'How We Enforce Our Professional Community Policies' (*LinkedIn*) https://www.linkedin.com/help/linkedin/answer/a1342754 accessed June 2025; Meta, 'Trademark' (*Facebook Help Center*) https://www.facebook.com/help/507663689427413?helpref=about_content accessed June 2025; X, 'X Terms of Service' (*X*) https://twitter.com/en/tos#update accessed June 2025; X, 'Misleading and deceptive identities policy' (*X Help Center*) https://help.x.com/en/rules-and-policies/x-impersonation-and-deceptive-identities-policy accessed June 2025; X, 'Counterfeit Policy' (*X Business*) https://help.x.com/en/rules-and-policies/counterfeit-goods-policy accessed June 2025; Snap, 'Community Guidelines' (*Snap Privacy, Safety, and Policy Hub*) https://values.snap.com/privacy/transparency/community-guidelines accessed June 2025; Snap, 'Username Infringement' (*Snapchat Support*) https://help.snapchat.com/hc/en-us/articles/7047503878804 accessed June 2025.
3948. Lisa P Ramsey, 'Brandjacking on Social Networks: Trademark Infringement by Impersonation of Markholders' (2010) 58 Buffalo Law Review 851, 852; Rajeev Sachdev, 'Towards an Improved Framework for Trade-Mark Law and Regulation in Social Media Usernames: A Study of the Canadian, U.S., and U.K. Positions' (2016) 28 Intellectual Property Journal 379, 379-418.
3949. Rob Pugh, 'The 22 Different Types of Social Media Content' (*Jetpack*, 5 January 2024) https://jetpack.com/blog/types-of-social-media-content/ accessed July 2024.

(2) *Your Representations.* By registering an account, username, providing content, and/or advertising on Platform, you hereby represent and warrant to us that: (a) the statements that you made in your Social Media Account Registration and/or Advertising Agreement are complete and accurate; (b) to your knowledge, the username, content, and/or advertising will not infringe upon or otherwise violate the rights of any third party; (c) you are not registering an account, username, providing content, and/or advertising for an unlawful purpose; and (d) you will not knowingly use Platform in violation of any applicable laws or regulations. It is your responsibility to determine whether your account, username, content, and/or advertising infringes or violates someone else's rights.	Adapted or directly from the UDRP[3950] and UDNRDP (Chapter 4).
(3) *Changes, Suspensions, and Cancellations.* We will make changes to, suspend, or cancel your account, username, content, and/or advertising on Social Media Platform under the following circumstances: (i) our receipt of written or appropriate electronic instructions from you or your authorized agent to take such action except that you may not transfer your account or username to another holder: (a) during a pending administrative proceeding brought pursuant to Paragraph 4 or for a period of fifteen (15) business days after such proceeding is concluded; or (b) during a pending court proceeding or arbitration commenced regarding your account, username, content, and/or advertising or their content unless the court or party to whom the account is being transferred agrees, in writing, to be bound by the decision of the court or arbitrator. We reserve the right not to permit the transfer of your account or username to another party in accordance with this subparagraph;	Adapted or directly from the UDRP[3951] and UDNDRP. Updated based on services. Added that 'abuse'[3952] can result

3950. ICANN, 'Uniform Domain-Name Dispute-Resolution Policy' (*ICANN*, 25 February 2012) https://www.icann.org/resources/pages/policy-2012-02-25-en accessed June 2025.
3951. *Ibid.*
3952. WIPO, 'WIPO Overview of WIPO Panel Views on Selected UDRP Questions, Third Edition' ('WIPO Jurisprudential Overview 3.0') (*WIPO*, 2017) https://www.wipo.int/amc/en/domains/search/overview3.0/ accessed June 2025.

(ii) our receipt of an order from a court or arbitral tribunal, in each case of competent jurisdiction, requiring such action; (iii) our decision requiring such action based on a complaint received under this or a later version of this Policy; and/or (iv) in accordance with the terms of your Social Media Account Registration and/or Advertising Agreement (such as but not limited to where you have engaged in abuse with respect to one or more trademarks) or other legal requirements.	in a change, suspension or cancellation and guidelines can be used to clarify when certain actions may take place.
(4) *Mandatory Decision Process and Remedies.* This Paragraph sets forth the type of disputes for which you are required to submit to a Mandatory Decision Process. A decision on a complaint lodged under this Policy will be made by Platform. a. Applicable Disputes. You are required to submit to a decision by Platform in the event that a third party (a 'complainant') asserts to Platform, through a Trademark Complaint Form < URL for Form >, that your account, username, content, and/or advertising or their content: (A) is identical or confusingly similar to trademarks in which a complainant has rights and which you are using on an unauthorised basis in the course of trade AND (B) (i) is being used to engage in unfair competition in the course of trade with respect to a trademark OR (ii) is being used in bad faith or is being abused with respect to a trademark. For clarity, in the administrative proceeding, the complainant must prove element A AND one element from B (either i or ii) are present.	Adapted or directly from the UDRP,[3953] UDNDRP (Chapter 4), Paris Convention, TRIPS, Dispute Resolution Service for .eu,[3954] EUTMR, Lanham Act 1946 15 U.S. Code §§ 1051 et seq. (as amended), the TDRA 2006 15 U.S. Code §1125 (c), Facebook, X, Pinterest, LinkedIn, and Snapchat terms and policies.[3955]

3953. Paris Convention 1967, Art. 6bis; ICANN, 'Uniform Domain-Name Dispute-Resolution Policy' (*ICANN*, 25 February 2012) https://www.icann.org/resources/pages/policy-2012-02-25-en; 15 U.S. Code § 1125(d).

3954. WIPO, 'WIPO Domain Name Dispute Resolution Service for .EU (and.ею and.ευ)' (*WIPO*) https://www.wipo.int/amc/en/domains/cctld/eu/index.html accessed July 2024.

3955. Facebook, 'Terms of Service' https://www.facebook.com/terms.php/ accessed June 2025; Pinterest, 'Terms of Service' (*Pinterest Policy*) https://policy.pinterest.com/en/terms-of-service accessed June 2025; LinkedIn, 'How We Enforce Our Professional Community Policies' (*LinkedIn*) https://www.linkedin.com/help/linkedin/answer/a1342754 accessed June 2025; Meta, 'Trademark' (*Facebook Help Center*) https://www.facebook.com/help/507

(b) Permitted use. Trademarks will be permitted if you demonstrate that you have rights or legitimate interests in respect of the account, username, content, and/or advertising or their content by showing one or more of these justifications: (i) you (as an individual, business, or other organization) have been commonly known by the term and are using it legitimately (ii) you are making genuine noncommercial legitimate fair use of the trademark, (iii) you are fairly utilising the trademark in marketing of authorized, replacement, compatible or used goods or services, (iv) you are utilising the trademark in an ordinary dictionary sense, (v) you are genuinely and noncommercially utilising the trademark under freedom of speech and expression or legitimate criticism, parody, or review of the company, good or service associated with the trademark, OR (vi) you are making fair and legitimate use of the trademark in comparative advertising. (c) Remedies. The remedies available to a complainant pursuant to any decision by Platform shall be limited to requiring the cancellation of, suspending, or making changes to your account, username, content, and/or advertising.	Key UDRP aspects have been retained, including relevant concepts from the Overview.[3956] This uniform policy largely follows the UDNDRP (Chapter 4) but is adapted for social media platforms. Please see Chapter 4 (section 4.3.3) for further details and explanations of the adaptations under the model. Interpretation of this Paragraph should be set out in the Guidelines. For social media advertising dedicated to specific jurisdictions, guidance should include that while decisions will be made based on general trademark principles, local law may be considered since the site is targeted to a jurisdiction (similar to the UDRP where local law may be considered, such as when parties are from the same jurisdiction).[3957] This should be the case in special circumstances, but decisions are expected to follow the general principles in most cases.

663689427413?helpref=about_content accessed June 2025; X, 'X Terms of Service' (*X*) https://twitter.com/en/tos#update accessed June 2025; X, 'Misleading and Deceptive Identities Policy' (*X Help Center*) https://help.x.com/en/rules-and-policies/x-impersonation-and-deceptive-identities-policy accessed June 2025; X, 'Counterfeit Policy' (*X Business*) https://help.x.com/en/rules-and-policies/counterfeit-goods-policy accessed June 2025; Snap, 'Community Guidelines' (*Snap Privacy, Safety, and Policy Hub*) https://values.snap.com/privacy/transparency/community-guidelines accessed June 2025; Snap, 'Username Infringement' (*Snapchat Support*) https://help.snapchat.com/hc/en-us/articles/7047503878804 accessed June 2025.

3956. ICANN, 'Uniform Domain-Name Dispute-Resolution Policy' (*ICANN*, 25 February 2012) https://www.icann.org/resources/pages/policy-2012-02-25-en accessed June 2025; WIPO, 'WIPO Overview of WIPO Panel Views on Selected UDRP Questions, Third Edition' ('WIPO Jurisprudential Overview 3.0') (*WIPO*, 2017) https://www.wipo.int/amc/en/domains/search/overview3.0/ accessed June 2025.

3957. WIPO, 'WIPO Overview of WIPO Panel Views on Selected UDRP Questions, Third Edition' ('WIPO Jurisprudential Overview 3.0') (*WIPO*, 2017) https://www.wipo.int/amc/en/domains/search/overview3.0/ accessed June 2025.

(d) All Other Disputes. All other disputes between you and any party other than Platform regarding your account, username, content, and/or advertising or their content in Platform that are not brought pursuant to this Policy will not be resolved through a decision under this Policy. Platform reserves the right to make a decision on any matter outside of this policy as set forth in our Terms of Use available at < terms > including any remedies or actions it, in its sole discretion, deems appropriate.

(5) *Procedures.*

(a) Initiation of Proceeding. Submitting a Trade mark Complaint Form initiates the process for a decision by Platform.

(b) Consolidation. In the event of multiple disputes between you and a complainant, either you or the complainant may request to consolidate the disputes for a single decision. Platform may consolidate before it any or all such disputes in its sole discretion, provided that the disputes being consolidated are governed by this Policy or a later version of this Policy.

(c) Fees. No fees are charged to file a complaint under this Policy or to receive a decision by Platform.

(d) Availability of Court Proceedings. The Mandatory Decision Process requirements set forth in Paragraph 4 shall not prevent either you or the complainant from submitting the dispute to a court of competent jurisdiction for independent resolution before such Mandatory Decision Process is commenced or after it is concluded. If we decide that your accounts, username, content and/or advertising should be cancelled, suspended, or changed, we will then implement the decision immediately unless we have received from you official documentation

Adapted or directly from the UDRP[3958] and UDNDRP (Chapter 4).

Platforms may wish to include an indemnification provision here.

3958. ICANN, 'Uniform Domain-Name Dispute-Resolution Policy' (*ICANN*, 25 February 2012) https://www.icann.org/resources/pages/policy-2012-02-25-en accessed June 2025.

(such as a copy of a complaint, file-stamped by the clerk of the court) that you have commenced a lawsuit against the complainant in an appropriate jurisdiction. If we receive such documentation immediately following a decision, we will not implement the decision, and we will take no further action, until we receive (i) evidence satisfactory to us of a resolution between the parties; (ii) evidence satisfactory to us that your lawsuit has been dismissed or withdrawn; or (iii) a copy of an order from such court dismissing your lawsuit or ordering that you do not have the right to continue the account, username, content, and/or advertising.	
(6) *Policy Modifications*. Platform reserves the right to modify this Policy at any time. Platform will post any revised Policy at <URL> at least thirty (30) calendar days before it becomes effective. Unless this Policy has already been invoked by the submission of a Trade mark Complaint Form, in which event the version of the Policy in effect at the time it was invoked will apply to you until the dispute is over, all such changes will be binding upon you with respect to any account, username, content and/or advertising trademark dispute, whether the dispute arose before, on or after the effective date of our change. In the event that you object to a change in this Policy, your sole remedy is to cancel your Account with us, provided that you will not be entitled to a refund of any fees you paid to us. The revised Policy will apply to you until you cancel your Account.	Adapted or directly from UDRP[3959] and UDNDRP (Chapter 4).

The above specifically defined policy covers many aspects related to the problems identified. It also covers disputes between a mark holder and the user or registrant of a username and includes any content in social media and social media advertising. It helps to resolve many of the problems and gaps raised by current social media terms and policies. For example, it fills the gap of inconsistency[3960] and increases the likelihood that social media platforms or relevant decision makers will come to consistent decisions for like trademark complaints.[3961] Further, this proposed uniform

3959. *Ibid.*.
3960. Rajeev Sachdev, 'Towards an Improved Framework for Trade-Mark Law and Regulation in Social Media Usernames: A Study of the Canadian, U.S., and U.K. Positions' (2016) 28 Intellectual Property Journal 379, 379-418; Paul D McGrady, *McGrady on Social Media and the Metaverse* (Mathew Bender & Company, Inc. 2023) §12.
3961. *Ibid.*

policy[3962] applies key concepts uniformly such that clarity can be achieved, and confusion on applying it may be avoided. To do this, it is recommended that guidelines[3963] based on the policy be established. The USMTDRP Guidelines[3964] should supplement the above policy to provide further details, especially in the form of examples of how policy provisions would be interpreted. This is necessary to create consistency in application across the social media platforms and provide enhanced certainty[3965] for users and mark holders.

The text of the USMTDRP as recommended under the Digital Trademark and Trade Practices Model is as follows, where a UDRP-like approach is used.

3962. Rajeev Sachdev, 'Towards an Improved Framework for Trade-Mark Law and Regulation in Social Media Usernames: A Study of the Canadian, U.S., and U.K. Positions' (2016) 28 Intellectual Property Journal 379, 379-418; Daniel Doft, 'Facebook, Twitter, and the Wild West of IP Enforcement on Social Media: Weighing the Merits of a Uniform Dispute Resolution Policy' (2016) 49 The John Marshall Law Review 959; Thomas J Curtin, 'The Name Game: Cybersquatting and Trademark Infringement on Social Media Websites' (2010-2011) 19 Journal of Law and Policy 353; Erick J Heels, 'How to Twittersquat the Top 100 Brands' (*GiantPeople*, 8 January 2009) http://www.giantpeople.com/1298.html accessed 4 August 2025; Paul D McGrady, *McGrady on Social Media and the Metaverse* (Mathew Bender & Company, Inc. 2023) §12; John McElwaine and Christopher D Casavale, 'Tackling Bad Faith Registration of Domain Names in a Fast-Changing Landscape' (*WIPO Magazine*, December 2019) https://www.wipo.int/wipo_magazine/en/2019/06/article_0006.html accessed June 2025.

3963. WIPO, 'WIPO Overview of WIPO Panel Views on Selected UDRP Questions, Third Edition' ('WIPO Jurisprudential Overview 3.0') (*WIPO*, 2017) https://www.wipo.int/amc/en/domains/search/overview3.0/ accessed June 2025.

3964. *Ibid.*

3965. Rajeev Sachdev, 'Towards an Improved Framework for Trade-Mark Law and Regulation in Social Media Usernames: A Study of the Canadian, U.S., and U.K. Positions' (2016) 28 Intellectual Property Journal 379, 379-418; Paul D McGrady, *McGrady on Social Media and the Metaverse* (Mathew Bender & Company, Inc. 2023) §12.

Table 5.9 Uniform Social Media Trademark Dispute Resolution Policy (USMTDRP)[3966]

Uniform Social Media Trademark Dispute Resolution Policy (USMTDRP)	Adapted or directly from the UDRP[3967] and UDNDRP (Chapter 4). The name reflects specifically the platform type and subject matter.
(1) *Purpose.* This Uniform Social Media Trademark Dispute Resolution Policy ('Policy') has been adopted by [Social Media Platform] ('Platform' or 'We'), is incorporated by reference into the Terms of Use of Platform and your Social Media Account Registration and/or Advertising Agreement, and sets forth the terms and conditions in connection with a dispute between you and any party other than Platform over the utilisation of a trademark in Platform. Decisions under Paragraph 4 of this Policy will be made in accordance with the Policy. Guidelines to this policy are set forth in the document entitled: Guidelines to the USMTDRP.	Adapted or directly from the UDRP[3968] and UDNDRP (Chapter 4) and Facebook, X, Pinterest, LinkedIn, and Snapchat terms and policies.[3969]

3966. Rajeev Sachdev, 'Towards an Improved Framework for Trade-Mark Law and Regulation in Social Media Usernames: A Study of the Canadian, U.S., and U.K. Positions' (2016) 28 Intellectual Property Journal 379, 379-418; Daniel Doft, 'Facebook, Twitter, and the Wild West of IP Enforcement on Social Media: Weighing the Merits of a Uniform Dispute Resolution Policy' (2016) 49 The John Marshall Law Review 959; Thomas J Curtin, 'The Name Game: Cybersquatting and Trademark Infringement on Social Media Websites' (2010-2011) 19 Journal of Law and Policy 353; Erick J Heels, 'How to Twittersquat the Top 100 Brands' (*GiantPeople*, 8 January 2009) http://www.giantpeople.com/1298.html accessed 4 August 2025; Paul D McGrady, *McGrady on Social Media and the Metaverse* (Mathew Bender & Company, Inc. 2023) §12; John McElwaine and Christopher D Casavale, 'Tackling Bad Faith Registration of Domain Names in a Fast-Changing Landscape' (*WIPO Magazine*, December 2019) https://www.wipo.int/wipo_magazine/en/2019/06/article_0006.html accessed June 2025.

3967. ICANN, 'Uniform Domain-Name Dispute-Resolution Policy' (*ICANN*, 25 February 2012) https://www.icann.org/resources/pages/policy-2012-02-25-en accessed June 2025.

3968. *Ibid.*

3969. Facebook, 'Terms of Service' https://www.facebook.com/terms.php/ accessed June 2025; Pinterest, 'Terms of Service' (*Pinterest Policy*) https://policy.pinterest.com/en/terms-of-service accessed June 2025; LinkedIn, 'How We Enforce Our Professional Community Policies' (*LinkedIn*) https://www.linkedin.com/help/linkedin/answer/a1342754 accessed June 2025; Meta, 'Trademark' (*Facebook Help Center*) https://www.facebook.com/help/507663689427413?helpref=about_content accessed June 2025; X, 'X Terms of Service' (*X*) https://twitter.com/en/tos#update accessed June 2025; X, 'Misleading and Deceptive Identities Policy' (*X Help Center*) https://help.x.com/en/rules-and-policies/x-impersonation-and-deceptive-identities-policy accessed June 2025; X, 'Counterfeit Policy' (*X Business*) https://help.x.com/en/rules-and-policies/counterfeit-goods-policy accessed June 2025; Snap, 'Community Guidelines' (*Snap Privacy, Safety, and Policy Hub*) https://values.snap.com/

	The policy refers to any disputed utilisation of a mark within the platforms. Guidelines should make clear that utilisation of a trademark includes in social media accounts, usernames, account names, profiles, identities, handles, pages, ID's or like accounts (collectively referred to as 'Username')[3970] registered by a user, as well as providing content within social media platform (including any activity, profiles, posts, pins, messages, infographics, live streams, images, pictures, polls, memes, filters, stories, reels, testimonials, snippets, contests, promotions, or any other content whatsoever in Social Media Platform whatever it may be called) and Advertising in Social Media Platform.[3971]
(2) *Your Representations*. By registering an account, username, providing content, and/or advertising on Platform, you hereby represent and warrant to us that: (a) the statements that you made in your Social Media Account Registration and/or Advertising Agreement are complete and accurate; (b) to your knowledge, the username, content, and/or advertising will not infringe upon or otherwise violate the rights of any third party; (c) you are not registering an account, username, providing content, and/or advertising for an unlawful purpose; and (d) you will not knowingly use Platform in	Adapted or directly from the UDRP[3972] and UDNRDP (Chapter 4).

privacy/transparency/community-guidelines accessed June 2025; Snap, 'Username Infringement' (*Snapchat Support*) https://help.snapchat.com/hc/en-us/articles/7047503878804 accessed June 2025.

3970. Lisa P Ramsey, 'Brandjacking on Social Networks: Trademark Infringement by Impersonation of Markholders' (2010) 58 Buffalo Law Review 851, 852; Rajeev Sachdev, 'Towards an Improved Framework for Trade-Mark Law and Regulation in Social Media Usernames: A Study of the Canadian, U.S., and U.K. Positions' (2016) 28 Intellectual Property Journal 379, 379-418.

3971. Rob Pugh, 'The 22 Different Types of Social Media Content' (*Jetpack*, 5 January 2024) https://jetpack.com/blog/types-of-social-media-content/ accessed July 2024.

3972. ICANN, 'Uniform Domain-Name Dispute-Resolution Policy' (*ICANN*, 25 February 2012) https://www.icann.org/resources/pages/policy-2012-02-25-en.

violation of any applicable laws or regulations. It is your responsibility to determine whether your account, username, content, and/or advertising infringes or violates someone else's rights.	
(3) *Changes, Suspensions, and Cancellations.* We will make changes to, suspend, or cancel your account, username, content, and/or advertising on Social Media Platform under the following circumstances: (i) our receipt of written or appropriate electronic instructions from you or your authorized agent to take such action except that you may not transfer your account or username to another holder (a) during a pending administrative proceeding brought pursuant to Paragraph 4 or for a period of fifteen (15) business days after such proceeding is concluded; or (b) during a pending court proceeding or arbitration commenced regarding your account, username, content, and/or advertising or their content unless the court or party to whom the account is being transferred agrees, in writing, to be bound by the decision of the court or arbitrator. We reserve the right not to permit the transfer of your account or username to another party in accordance with this subparagraph; (ii) our receipt of an order from a court or arbitral tribunal, in each case of competent jurisdiction, requiring such action; (iii) a panel decision requiring such action based on a complaint received under this or a later version of this Policy; and/or (iv) in accordance with the terms of your Social Media Account Registration and/or Advertising Agreement (such as but not limited to where you have engaged in abuse with respect to one or more trademarks) or other legal requirements.	Adapted or directly from the UDRP[3973] and UDNDRP. Updated based on services. Added that 'abuse'[3974] can result in a change, suspension or cancellation and guidelines can be used to clarify when certain actions may take place.

3973. *Ibid.*
3974. WIPO, 'WIPO Overview of WIPO Panel Views on Selected UDRP Questions, Third Edition' ('WIPO Jurisprudential Overview 3.0') (*WIPO*, 2017) https://www.wipo.int/amc/en/domains/search/overview3.0/ accessed June 2025.

(4) *Mandatory Administrative Proceeding and Remedies.* This Paragraph sets forth the type of disputes for which you are required to submit to a mandatory Panel Decision. A decision on a complaint lodged under this Policy will be made by an appointed Panel.

(a) Applicable Disputes. You are required to submit to a Panel Decision in the event that a third party (a 'complainant') asserts to Platform, through a Trademark Complaint Form < URL for Form > that that your account, username, content, and/or advertising or their content:

(A) is identical or confusingly similar to trademarks in which a complainant has rights and which you are using on an unauthorised basis in the course of trade,
AND

(B) (i) is being used to engage in unfair competition in the course of trade with respect to a trademark, OR (ii) is being used in bad faith or is being abused with respect to a trademark. For clarity, in the administrative proceeding, the complainant must prove that element A AND one element from B (either i or ii) are present.

Adapted or directly from the UDRP,[3975] UDNDRP (Chapter 4), Paris Convention, TRIPS, Dispute Resolution Service for.eu,[3976] EUTMR, Lanham Act 1946 15 U.S. Code §§ 1051 et seq. (as amended), the TDRA 2006 15 U.S. Code § 1125(c), Facebook, X, Pinterest, LinkedIn, and Snapchat terms and policies.[3977] Key UDRP aspects have been retained, including relevant concepts from the Overview.[3978]

3975. Paris Convention 1967, Art. 6bis; ICANN, 'Uniform Domain-Name Dispute-Resolution Policy' (*ICANN*, 25 February 2012) https://www.icann.org/resources/pages/policy-2012-02-25-en; 15 U.S. Code § 1125(d).

3976. WIPO, 'WIPO Domain Name Dispute Resolution Service for .EU (and.ею and.ευ)' (*WIPO*) https://www.wipo.int/amc/en/domains/cctld/eu/index.html accessed July 2024.

3977. Facebook, 'Terms of Service' https://www.facebook.com/terms.php/ accessed June 2025; Pinterest, 'Terms of Service' (*Pinterest Policy*) https://policy.pinterest.com/en/terms-of-service accessed June 2025; LinkedIn, 'How We Enforce Our Professional Community Policies' (*LinkedIn*) https://www.linkedin.com/help/linkedin/answer/a1342754 accessed June 2025; Meta, 'Trademark' (*Facebook Help Center*) https://www.facebook.com/help/507663689427413?helpref=about_content accessed June 2025; X, 'X Terms of Service' (*X*) https://twitter.com/en/tos#update accessed June 2025; X, 'Misleading and Deceptive Identities Policy' (*X Help Center*) https://help.x.com/en/rules-and-policies/x-impersonation-and-deceptive-identities-policy accessed June 2025; X, 'Counterfeit Policy' (*X Business*) https://help.x.com/en/rules-and-policies/counterfeit-goods-policy accessed June 2025; Snap, 'Community Guidelines' (*Snap Privacy, Safety, and Policy Hub*) https://values.snap.com/privacy/transparency/community-guidelines accessed June 2025; Snap, 'Username Infringement' (*Snapchat Support*) https://help.snapchat.com/hc/en-us/articles/7047503878804 accessed June 2025.

3978. ICANN, 'Uniform Domain-Name Dispute-Resolution Policy' (*ICANN*, 25 February 2012) https://www.icann.org/resources/pages/policy-2012-02-25-en accessed June 2025; WIPO, 'WIPO Overview of WIPO Panel Views on Selected UDRP Questions, Third Edition' ('WIPO

(b) Permitted use. Trademarks will be permitted if you demonstrate that you have rights or legitimate interests in respect of the account, username, content, and/or advertising or their content by showing one or more of these justifications: (i) you (as an individual, business, or other organization) have been commonly known by the term and are using it legitimately (ii) you are making genuine noncommercial legitimate fair use of the trademark, (iii) you are fairly utilising the trademark in marketing of authorized, replacement, compatible or used goods or services, (iv) you are utilising the trademark in an ordinary dictionary sense, (v) you are genuinely and noncommercially utilising the trademark under freedom of speech and expression or legitimate criticism, parody, or review of the company, good or service associated with the trademark, OR (vi) you are making fair and legitimate use of the trademark in comparative advertising. (c) Remedies. The remedies available to a complainant pursuant to any Panel Decision shall be limited to requiring the cancellation of, suspending, or making changes to your account, username, content, and/or advertising. (d) All Other Disputes. All other disputes between you and any party other than Platform regarding your account, username, content, and/or advertising or their content in Platform that are not brought pursuant to this Policy will not be resolved through a Panel Decision. Platform reserves the right to make a decision on any matter outside of this policy as set forth in our Terms of Use available at <terms> including any remedies or actions it, in its sole discretion, deems appropriate.	This uniform policy largely follows the UDNDRP (Chapter 4) but is adapted for social media platforms. Please see Chapter 4 (section 4.3.3) for further details and explanations of the adaptations under the model. Interpretation of this Paragraph should be set out in the Guidelines. For social media advertising dedicated to specific jurisdictions, guidance should include that while decisions will be made based on general trademark principles, local law may be considered since the site is targeted to a jurisdiction (similar to the UDRP, where local law may be considered, such as when parties are from the same jurisdiction).[3979] This should be the case in special circumstances, but decisions are expected to follow the general principles in most cases.

Jurisprudential Overview 3.0') (*WIPO*, 2017) https://www.wipo.int/amc/en/domains/search/overview3.0/ accessed June 2025.

3979. WIPO, 'WIPO Overview of WIPO Panel Views on Selected UDRP Questions, Third Edition' ('WIPO Jurisprudential Overview 3.0') (*WIPO*, 2017) https://www.wipo.int/amc/en/domains/search/overview3.0/ accessed June 2025.

(5) *Procedures.* (a) Initiation of Proceeding. Submitting a Trade mark Complaint Form initiates the process for a Panel Decision. (b) Consolidation. In the event of multiple disputes between you and a complainant, either you or the complainant may petition to consolidate the disputes before a single Panel. This petition shall be made to the Panel appointed to hear a pending dispute between the parties. This Panel may consolidate before it any or all such disputes in its sole discretion, provided that the disputes being consolidated are governed by this Policy or a later version of this Policy. (c) Fees. No fees are charged to file a complaint under this Policy or to receive a Panel Decision. (d) Availability of Court Proceedings. The Panel Decision proceeding requirements set forth in Paragraph 4 shall not prevent either you or the complainant from submitting the dispute to a court of competent jurisdiction for independent resolution before such Panel Decision is commenced or after such proceeding is concluded. If a Panel decides that your accounts, username, content and/or advertising should be cancelled, suspended, or changed, we will then implement the decision immediately unless we have received from you official documentation (such as a copy of a complaint, file-stamped by the clerk of the court) that you have commenced a lawsuit against the complainant in an appropriate jurisdiction. If we receive such documentation immediately following a decision, we will not implement the Panel's decision, and we will take no further action, until we receive (i) evidence satisfactory to us of a resolution between the parties; (ii) evidence satisfactory to us that your lawsuit has been dismissed or withdrawn; or (iii) a copy	Adapted or directly from the UDRP[3980] and UDNDRP (Chapter 4). Because platforms currently expend their own resources to make decisions on complaints they receive, these resources may be redirected to an online panel decision under the assumption that this will not raise costs by unreasonable sums. Platforms may wish to include an indemnification provision here.

3980. ICANN, 'Uniform Domain-Name Dispute-Resolution Policy' (*ICANN*, 25 February 2012) https://www.icann.org/resources/pages/policy-2012-02-25-en accessed June 2025.

of an order from such court dismissing your lawsuit or ordering that you do not have the right to continue the account, username, content, and/or advertising.	
(6) *Policy Modifications*. Platform reserves the right to modify this Policy at any time. Platform will post any revised Policy at <URL> at least thirty (30) calendar days before it becomes effective. Unless this Policy has already been invoked by the submission of a Trade mark Complaint Form, in which event the version of the Policy in effect at the time it was invoked will apply to you until the dispute is over, all such changes will be binding upon you with respect to any account, username, content and/or advertising trademark dispute, whether the dispute arose before, on or after the effective date of our change. In the event that you object to a change in this Policy, your sole remedy is to cancel your Account with us, provided that you will not be entitled to a refund of any fees you paid to us. The revised Policy will apply to you until you cancel your Account.	Adapted or directly from UDRP[3981] and UDNDRP (Chapter 4).

5.5 MAJOR MOBILE APP PLATFORM TRADEMARK TERMS AND POLICIES

Apps may be downloaded from various platforms, sometimes known as mobile 'app stores',[3982] a phrase which itself has been the subject matter of a trademark dispute.[3983] These platforms have their own terms and conditions, which must be agreed to before app operators are able to offer mobile apps through their services.

This section will overview mobile app terms and policies pertinent to trademarks in their individual services. Below is a summary of updated provisions relating to trademarks for each platform, after which problems and gaps will be discussed prior to providing a proposed solution.

3981. *Ibid.*
3982. Artem Dogtiev, 'App Stores List' (*Business of Apps*, 30 January 2024) https://www.businessofapps.com/guide/app-stores-list/ accessed July 2024.
3983. Johnathan Stempel, 'Apple, Amazon End "App Store" Lawsuit' (*Reuters*, 9 July 2013) http://www.reuters.com/article/us-apple-amazon-appstore-lawsuit-idUSBRE9680TT20130709 accessed July 2024.

5.5.1 Apple App Store

Under 2.3.7 of Apple's App Store Review Guidelines, app operators are told that they should '[c]hoose a unique app name'[3984] and 'assign keywords that accurately describe your app, and don't try to pack any of your metadata with trademarked terms, popular app names, pricing information, or other irrelevant phrases just to game the system'.[3985] Under 2.5.2, '[e]gregious violations and repeat behavior will result in removal from the Apple Developer Program'.[3986] In 5.2 Intellectual Property, Apple warns that '[l]aws differ in different countries'[3987] and urges app operators to 'avoid ... common errors'[3988] followed by a list of such 'errors'.[3989] 5.2.1 states not to 'use protected third-party material such as trademarks ... without permission'[3990] and warns not to 'include misleading, false, or copycat representations, names, or metadata'[3991] within the 'app bundle or developer name'.[3992] Under 2.2.7, 'Apple may modify inappropriate keywords at any time or take other appropriate steps to prevent abuse.'[3993] There is also a complaint form that may be filed in cases of intellectual property infringement and a dispute may be lodged using this method.[3994] Specifically, the complaint form addresses both App Store Content as well as App Name disputes in different forms.[3995] Apple confirms that they do 'not investigate claims regarding branded terms used as Search Ads keywords'.[3996] However, Apple will first contact the party posting such content or registering such App name to encourage them to resolve the issue directly with the complainant.[3997]

Specific to '[a]pps with user-generated content'[3998] which may raise, *inter alia*, 'intellectual property infringement'[3999] concerns must include measures to 'filter',[4000] 'report',[4001] 'block'[4002] certain types of content, including blocking that by 'abusive users'.[4003]

3984. Apple Inc, 'App Store Review Guidelines' (*Apple*) https://developer.apple.com/app-store/review/guidelines/ accessed June 2025.
3985. *Ibid.*
3986. *Ibid.*
3987. *Ibid.*
3988. *Ibid.*
3989. *Ibid.*
3990. *Ibid.*
3991. *Ibid.*
3992. *Ibid.*
3993. *Ibid.*
3994. Apple, 'App Store Content Dispute' (*Apple*) https://www.apple.com/legal/intellectual-property/dispute-forms/app-store/ accessed June 2025.
3995. *Ibid.*
3996. *Ibid.*
3997. *Ibid.*
3998. Apple Inc, 'App Store Review Guidelines' (*Apple*) https://developer.apple.com/app-store/review/guidelines/ accessed June 2025.
3999. *Ibid.*
4000. *Ibid.*
4001. *Ibid.*
4002. *Ibid.*
4003. *Ibid.*

5.5.2 Google Play Store

Under Google Play Console Help Intellectual Property page, Google does not 'allow apps that infringe on others' trademarks'.[4004] Further, '[t]rademark infringement is improper or unauthorized use of an identical or similar trademark in a way that is likely to cause confusion as to the source of that product ... [i]f your app uses another party's trademarks in a way that is likely to cause confusion, your app may be suspended'.[4005] Additionally, Google does not 'allow apps that sell or promote for sale counterfeit goods ... [which] contain a trademark or logo that is identical to or substantially indistinguishable from the trademark of another ... mimic the brand features of the product in an attempt to pass themselves off as a genuine product of the brand owner'.[4006] Under its Google Play Console Help Impersonation page, they 'don't allow apps that mislead users by impersonating someone else (for example, another developer, company, entity) or another app'.[4007] They do not permit one to 'imply that your app is related to or authorized by someone that it isn't ... to use app icons, descriptions, titles, or in-app elements that could mislead users about your app's relationship to someone else or another app'.[4008]

Some terms in its Google Play Developer Distribution Agreement[4009] are relevant. Under 11.1, an app operator 'represent[s] and warrant[s]'[4010] that they 'have all Intellectual Property Rights in and to ... Product(s)'.[4011] Also, under 11.2, if using 'third-party materials',[4012] the app operator 'represent and warrant'[4013] that they 'have the right to distribute the third-party material in the Product'.[4014] Also, the operator agrees to 'not submit material to Google Play that is subject to third party Intellectual Property Rights'[4015] with the exception of if they 'are the owner of such rights or have permission from their rightful owner to submit the material'.[4016] Additionally, under 11.3, the mobile app operator is 'solely responsible for compliance worldwide with all applicable laws and other obligations'.[4017] Thus, the onus is put on the mobile app owner to ensure that appropriate rights are present for trademarks within the app. Under 8.1, even if an app is removed by the operator, they still 'agree to comply'[4018]

4004. Google, 'Intellectual Property' (*Google Play Console Help*) https://support.google.com/googleplay/android-developer/answer/9888072?hl=en&ref_topic=9876963 accessed June 2025.
4005. *Ibid.*
4006. *Ibid.*
4007. Google, 'Impersonation' (*Google Play Console Help*) https://support.google.com/googleplay/android-developer/answer/9888374 accessed June 2025.
4008. *Ibid.*
4009. Google, 'Google Play Developer Distribution Agreement' (*Google Play*) https://play.google.com/about/developer-distribution-agreement.html accessed June 2025.
4010. *Ibid.*
4011. *Ibid.*
4012. *Ibid.*
4013. *Ibid.*
4014. *Ibid.*
4015. *Ibid.*
4016. *Ibid.*
4017. *Ibid.*
4018. *Ibid.*

with the 'Agreement ... prior to removal.'[4019] However, under 8.2, 'in no event will Google maintain on any portion of Google Play ... any Product that ... [was] removed from Google Play and provided written notice to Google that such removal was due to (a) an allegation of infringement, or actual infringement, of any third party Intellectual Property Right; (b) an allegation of, or actual violation of, third party rights; or (c) an allegation or determination that such Product does not comply with applicable law ...'.[4020] Also, '[i]f a Product is removed from Google Play due to a Legal Takedown and an end user purchased such Product within a year (or a longer period as local consumer law mandates) before the date of takedown',[4021] then 'at Google's request',[4022] the app operator agrees 'to refund to the end user all amounts paid by such end user for such Product'.[4023] A specific form covering trademark infringement is available for Google Play and other services[4024] and clarifies the relevant action in the event a mobile app is removed based on a trademark violation and requires notice in such instances.[4025] However, they clarify that '[l]egal standards vary greatly by country/region ... [c]ontent that violates a specific law in one country/region may be legal in others'.[4026] Thus, they 'remove or restrict access to the content only in the country/region where it is deemed to be illegal' except when violating 'Google's content or product policies or Terms of Service' where they 'typically remove or restrict access globally'.[4027]

Also, under 14.1, '[t]o the maximum extent permitted by law',[4028] the app operator agrees 'to defend, indemnify, and hold harmless Google ... from and against any and all third party claims, actions, suits, or proceedings, as well as any and all losses, liabilities, damages, costs, and expenses (including reasonable attorneys' fees) arising out of or accruing from'[4029] the app operators 'use of the Play Console and Google Play in violation of this Agreement',[4030] 'infringement or violation ... of any Intellectual Property Right or any other right of any person'[4031] or 'violation of any law'[4032] pertaining to the app.

4019. *Ibid.*
4020. *Ibid.*
4021. *Ibid.*
4022. *Ibid.*
4023. *Ibid.*
4024. Google, 'Removing Content from Google: Legal Help' (*Google*) https://support.google.com/legal/troubleshooter/1114905#ts=13778295%2C1115643 accessed June 2025.
4025. *Ibid.*
4026. *Ibid.*
4027. *Ibid.*
4028. Google, 'Google Play Developer Distribution Agreement' (*Google Play*) https://play.google.com/about/developer-distribution-agreement.html accessed June 2025.
4029. *Ibid.*
4030. *Ibid.*
4031. *Ibid.*
4032. *Ibid.*

5.5.3 Gaps and Problems with Current Mobile App Platform Trademark Terms and Policies

Table 5.10 Digital Trademark and Trade Practices Model, UDRP, and Mobile App Platform Terms and Policies

Digital Trademark and Trade Practices Model	*UDRP*	*Apple App Store*	*Google Play*
Digital Use and Place of Use	Only some coverage. Any use of registered or unregistered marks in domain names which violate the policy.[4033]	Only some coverage. Use in Apple App Store app name, app bundle, keywords, etc.[4034]	Only some coverage. Use in Google Play apps. When complaining about others using a mark, reference to registration/use rights is required.[4035]
Digital Bad Faith and Abuse	'Registration and use of a domain name in bad faith'[4036] (abuse is covered in overview).[4037]	Only some coverage. Specific to '[a]pps with user-generated content'[4038] which may raise, *inter alia*, 'intellectual property infringement'[4039] concerns must include measures to 'filter',[4040] 'report',[4041] 'block'[4042] certain types of content, including blocking that by 'abusive users'.[4043] 'metadata'[4044] should not be packed[4045] 'with trademarked terms, popular app names, or other irrelevant phrases just to game the system'.[4046]	Only some coverage. Under 8.1, even if an app is removed by the operator, they still 'agree to comply'[4047] with the 'Agreement ... prior to removal.'[4048]

Digital Trademark and Trade Practices Model	*UDRP*	*Apple App Store*	*Google Play*
		'Apple may modify inappropriate keywords at any time or take other appropriate steps to prevent abuse.'[4049] 'Egregious violations and repeat behavior will result in removal from the Apple Developer Program.'[4050]	
Digital Confusion	'Confusing similarity' in domain names.[4051]	Only some coverage. 2.3.8 'Remember to ensure your metadata, including app name and icons (small, large, Apple Watch app, alternate icons, etc.), are similar to avoid creating confusion.'[4052] 5.2.1 states not to 'use protected third-party material such as trademarks ... without permissions'[4053] and warns not to 'include misleading, false, or copycat representations, names, or metadata'[4054] within the 'app bundle or developer name'.[4055]	Only some coverage. 'If your app uses another party's trademarks in a way that is likely to cause confusion, your app may be suspended.'[4056] Generally, 'Trademark infringement is improper or unauthorized use of an identical or similar trademark in a way that is likely to cause confusion as to the source of that product. If your app uses another party's trademarks in a way that is likely to cause confusion, your app may be suspended.'[4057]

Digital Trademark and Trade Practices Model	*UDRP*	*Apple App Store*	*Google Play*
Digital Unfair Competition	Only some coverage. The Overview states that '[a]lso noting the availability of trademark-like protection under certain national legal doctrines (e.g., unfair competition or passing-off) and considerations of parity, where acquired distinctiveness/secondary meaning is demonstrated in a particular UDRP case, unregistered rights have been found to support standing to proceed with a UDRP case including where the complainant is based in a civil law jurisdiction'.[4058] Unfair advantage considerations may fall under bad faith and abuse (*see* Overview).[4059] 'Distinctiveness' and 'secondary meaning' are recognised in Overview, along with a list of factors that may be considered.[4060] 'Secondary meaning'[4061] is covered in the Overview. Overview also states that 'the strength of the complainant's mark may be considered relevant in evaluating the second and third elements'[4062] of the UDRP.	Only some coverage. '[c]hoose a unique app name'[4063] and 'assign keywords that accurately describe'[4064] the app.[4065] 5.2.1 states not to 'use protected third-party material such as trademarks ... without permissions'[4066] and warns not to 'include misleading, false, or copycat representations, names, or metadata'[4067] within the 'app bundle or developer name'.[4068]	Only some coverage. 'We don't allow apps that sell or promote for sale counterfeit goods. Counterfeit goods contain a trademark or logo that is identical to or substantially indistinguishable from the trademark of another. They mimic the brand features of the product in an attempt to pass themselves off as a genuine product of the brand owner.'[4069] 'We don't allow apps that mislead users by impersonating someone else (for example, another developer, company, entity) or another app. Don't imply that your app is related to or authorized by someone that it isn't. Be careful not to use app icons, descriptions, titles, or in-app elements that could mislead users about your app's relationship to someone else or another app.'[4070]

Digital Trademark and Trade Practices Model	*UDRP*	*Apple App Store*	*Google Play*
Digital Terms, Policies, and Disclaimers	Only some coverage. Is itself a uniform policy addressing covered domain names. Disclaimers have been treated briefly in Overview. In cases 'where the respondent appears to otherwise have a right or legitimate interest in a disputed domain name, a clear and sufficiently prominent disclaimer would lend support to circumstances suggesting its good faith'.[4071]	Generally or not directly covered (disclaimers). Trademark-related policies are contained largely in a single policy.	Generally or not directly covered (disclaimers). Trademark-related policies are contained in various documents.
Digital Jurisdictional and Territorial Considerations	Only some coverage. Changes to a domain name may be made based on court or arbitral tribunal of competent jurisdiction.[4072] Overview states that 'rules and principles of law'[4073] may be considered (this is discretionary), however, 'in its own terms UDRP jurisprudence generally would not require resort to particular national laws'.[4074] For example, guidance indicates that where 'the parties share a common nationality and the import of a specific national law concept is particularly	Only some coverage. In 5.2 titled 'Intellectual Property', Apple warns that '[l]aws differ in different countries'[4075] and urges app operators to 'avoid ... common errors'[4076] followed by a list of such 'errors'.[4077]	Only some coverage. Mobile app operator is 'solely responsible for compliance worldwide with all applicable laws and other obligations'.[4078] 'Legal standards vary greatly by country/region. Content that violates a specific law in one country/region may be legal in others. Typically, we remove or restrict access to the content only in the country/region where it is deemed to be illegal. When content is found to

Digital Trademark and Trade Practices Model	*UDRP*	*Apple App Store*	*Google Play*
	germane to an issue in dispute, panels have applied national law principles in assessing the UDRP elements'.[4079] Otherwise, the UDRP applies regardless of where domain is registered or used.		violate Google's content or product policies or Terms of Service, however, we typically remove or restrict access globally.'[4080]
Digital Justification	Only some coverage. Using marks for 'legitimate noncommercial or fair use'[4081] is recognised as a method to demonstrate 'rights and legitimate interests'.[4082] Fair use and freedom of speech are also covered in the Overview.[4083]	Generally or not directly covered.	Only some coverage. The operator agrees to 'not submit material to Google Play that is subject to third party Intellectual Property Rights'[4084] with the exception of if they 'are the owner of such rights or have permission from their rightful owner to submit the material'.[4085]

4033. https://www.icann.org/resources/pages/policy-2012-02-25-en accessed 4 August 2025; WIPO, 'WIPO Overview of WIPO Panel Views on Selected UDRP Questions, Third Edition' ('WIPO Jurisprudential Overview 3.0') (*WIPO*, 2017) https://www.wipo.int/amc/en/domains/search/overview3.0/ accessed June 2025.

4034. Apple Inc, 'App Store Review Guidelines' (*Apple*) https://developer.apple.com/app-store/review/guidelines/ accessed June 2025.

4035. Google, 'Removing Content from Google: Legal Help' (*Google*) https://support.google.com/legal/troubleshooter/1114905#ts = 13778295%2C1115643 accessed June 2025.

4036. UDRP, 4(b).

4037. ICANN, 'Uniform Domain-Name Dispute-Resolution Policy' (*ICANN*, 25 February 2012) https://www.icann.org/resources/pages/policy-2012-02-25-en accessed June 2025; WIPO, 'WIPO Overview of WIPO Panel Views on Selected UDRP Questions, Third Edition' ('WIPO Jurisprudential Overview 3.0') (*WIPO*, 2017) https://www.wipo.int/amc/en/domains/search/overview3.0/ accessed June 2025.

4038. Apple Inc, 'App Store Review Guidelines' (*Apple*) https://developer.apple.com/app-store/review/guidelines/ accessed June 2025.

4039. *Ibid.*

4040. *Ibid.*

4041. *Ibid.*

4042. *Ibid.*

4043. *Ibid.*

4044. *Ibid.*
4045. *Ibid.*
4046. *Ibid.*
4047. Google, 'Google Play Developer Distribution Agreement' (*Google Play*) https://play.google.com/about/developer-distribution-agreement.html accessed June 2025.
4048. *Ibid.*
4049. Apple Inc, 'App Store Review Guidelines' (*Apple*) https://developer.apple.com/app-store/review/guidelines/ accessed June 2025.
4050. *Ibid.*
4051. UDRP, 4(a)(i).
4052. Apple Inc, 'App Store Review Guidelines' (*Apple*) https://developer.apple.com/app-store/review/guidelines/ accessed June 2025.
4053. *Ibid.*
4054. *Ibid.*
4055. *Ibid.*
4056. Google, 'Intellectual Property' (*Google Play Console Help*) https://support.google.com/googleplay/android-developer/answer/9888072?hl=en&ref_topic=9876963 accessed June 2025.
4057. *Ibid.*
4058. WIPO, 'WIPO Overview of WIPO Panel Views on Selected UDRP Questions, Third Edition' ('WIPO Jurisprudential Overview 3.0') (*WIPO*, 2017) https://www.wipo.int/amc/en/domains/search/overview3.0/ accessed June 2025.
4059. *Ibid.*
4060. *Ibid.*
4061. *Ibid.*
4062. *Ibid.*
4063. Apple Inc, 'App Store Review Guidelines' (*Apple*) https://developer.apple.com/app-store/review/guidelines/ accessed June 2025.
4064. *Ibid.*
4065. *Ibid.*
4066. *Ibid.*
4067. *Ibid.*
4068. *Ibid.*
4069. Google, 'Intellectual Property' (*Google Play Console Help*) https://support.google.com/googleplay/android-developer/answer/9888072?hl=en&ref_topic=9876963 accessed June 2025.
4070. Google, 'Impersonation' (*Google Play Console Help*) https://support.google.com/googleplay/android-developer/answer/9888374 accessed June 2025.
4071. WIPO, 'WIPO Overview of WIPO Panel Views on Selected UDRP Questions, Third Edition' ('WIPO Jurisprudential Overview 3.0') (*WIPO*, 2017) https://www.wipo.int/amc/en/domains/search/overview3.0/ accessed June 2025.
4072. ICANN, 'Uniform Domain-Name Dispute-Resolution Policy' (*ICANN*, 25 February 2012) https://www.icann.org/resources/pages/policy-2012-02-25-en accessed June 2025.
4073. WIPO, 'WIPO Overview of WIPO Panel Views on Selected UDRP Questions, Third Edition' ('WIPO Jurisprudential Overview 3.0') (*WIPO*, 2017) https://www.wipo.int/amc/en/domains/search/overview3.0/ accessed June 2025.
4074. *Ibid.*
4075. Apple Inc, 'App Store Review Guidelines' (*Apple*) https://developer.apple.com/app-store/review/guidelines/ accessed June 2025.
4076. *Ibid.*

4077. *Ibid.*
4078. Google, 'Google Play Developer Distribution Agreement' (*Google Play*) https://play.google.com/about/developer-distribution-agreement.html accessed June 2025.
4079. *Ibid.*
4080. Google, 'Removing Content from Google: Legal Help' (*Google*) https://support.google.com/legal/troubleshooter/1114905#ts=13778295%2C1115643 accessed June 2025.
4081. ICANN, 'Uniform Domain-Name Dispute-Resolution Policy' (*ICANN*, 25 February 2012) https://www.icann.org/resources/pages/policy-2012-02-25-en accessed June 2025; WIPO, 'WIPO Overview of WIPO Panel Views on Selected UDRP Questions, Third Edition' ('WIPO Jurisprudential Overview 3.0') (*WIPO*, 2017) https://www.wipo.int/amc/en/domains/search/overview3.0/ accessed June 2025.
4082. *Ibid.*
4083. WIPO, 'WIPO Overview of WIPO Panel Views on Selected UDRP Questions, Third Edition' ('WIPO Jurisprudential Overview 3.0') (*WIPO*, 2017) https://www.wipo.int/amc/en/domains/search/overview3.0/ accessed June 2025.
4084. Google, 'Google Play Developer Distribution Agreement' (*Google Play*) https://play.google.com/about/developer-distribution-agreement.html accessed June 2025.
4085. *Ibid.*

5.5.3.1 Digital Use and Place of Use

Both mobile app platform policies apply to utilisation of trademarks within their services. However, none make mention of commercial use[4086] or that which is associated with goods or services.[4087] This creates uncertainty about whether a mobile app name or content may be used which is not so connected or utilised. Place of use[4088] is recognised to a limited extent by recognising the places where marks may be utilised, such as the app name, app bundle, keywords, etc.[4089] For Google Play, when complaining about others using a mark, reference to registration/use rights is required.[4090]

5.5.3.2 Digital Bad Faith and Abuse

'Bad faith'[4091] is not directly mentioned in the policies. By not directly mentioning 'bad faith'[4092] registration of mobile app names and 'bad faith'[4093] use of content within or associated with apps, it is not clear how or whether such will be directly assessed.

4086. TRIPS, Art. 16; EUTMR, Art. 18; 15 U.S. Code § 1127; UK Trade Marks Act 1994, s. 46(1)(a); Canadian Trademarks Act R.S.C., 1985, c. T-13, s. 2.
4087. *Ibid.*
4088. EUIPO, '3 Place of Use' (*EUIPO Trade mark guidelines* 2024) https://guidelines.euipo.europa.eu/2214311/1982069/trade-mark-guidelines/3-place-of-use accessed January 2024.
4089. Apple Inc, 'App Store Review Guidelines' (*Apple*) https://developer.apple.com/app-store/review/guidelines/ accessed July 2024.
4090. Google, 'Removing Content from Google: Legal Help' (*Google*) https://support.google.com/legal/troubleshooter/1114905#ts=13778295%2C1115643 accessed June 2025.
4091. UDRP, 4(a)(iii).
4092. *Ibid.*
4093. *Ibid.*

However, the Apple App Store prohibits methods used to 'game the system'[4094] and abuse[4095] is covered through the policy that 'repeat offenders will be removed from the Apple Developer Program'.[4096] Apple also states that it 'may modify inappropriate keywords at any time or take other appropriate steps to prevent abuse'.[4097] Likewise, abuse[4098] is covered from the perspective that '[e]gregious violations and repeat behavior will result in removal from the Apple Developer Program'.[4099] Google Play requires blocking related to 'abusive users'.[4100]

5.5.3.3 *Digital Confusion*

Google Play warns that if the 'app uses another party's trademarks in a way that is likely to cause confusion, your app may be suspended'.[4101] The Apple App Store states to 'ensure your metadata, including app name and icons (small, large, Apple Watch app, alternate icons, etc.), are similar to avoid creating confusion'.[4102] While Google Play covers the app in general, Apple focuses on 'metadata, including app names and icons'.[4103] It should not cover specific elements, but rather the entire contents of the app.

5.5.3.4 *Digital Unfair Competition*

None of the mobile platforms directly state unfair competition,[4104] acts,[4105] or practices.[4106] The Apple App Store requires a 'unique app name'[4107] and that no

4094. Apple Inc, 'App Store Review Guidelines' (*Apple*) https://developer.apple.com/app-store/review/guidelines/ accessed June 2025.
4095. WIPO, 'WIPO Overview of WIPO Panel Views on Selected UDRP Questions, Third Edition' ('WIPO Jurisprudential Overview 3.0') (*WIPO*, 2017) https://www.wipo.int/amc/en/domains/search/overview3.0/ accessed June 2025.
4096. *Ibid.*
4097. *Ibid.*
4098. *Ibid.*
4099. *Ibid.*
4100. Apple Inc, 'App Store Review Guidelines' (*Apple*) https://developer.apple.com/app-store/review/guidelines/ accessed June 2025.
4101. Google, 'Intellectual Property' (*Google Play Console Help*) https://support.google.com/googleplay/android-developer/answer/9888072?hl=en&ref_topic=9876963 accessed June 2025.
4102. Apple Inc, 'App Store Review Guidelines' (*Apple*) https://developer.apple.com/app-store/review/guidelines/ accessed June 2025.
4103. *Ibid.*
4104. Anselm Kamperman Sanders, *Unfair Competition Law: The Protection of Intellectual and Industrial Creativity* (Oxford University Press, 1997) 8; Frauke Henning-Bodewig, *Unfair Competition Law European Union and Member States* (Kluwer Law International 2006) xv-xvi; Martin Senftleben, Michael Handler and Irene Calboli, 'Protection Against Unfair Competition Around the Globe' (2024) 19 Journal of Intellectual Property Law & Practice 79, 79-80 https://doi.org/10.1093/jiplp/jpad121; Paris Convention, Art. 10bis; EUTMR, Art. 9(2)(c); 15 U.S.C. § 1125(c)(2)(B).
4105. *Ibid.*
4106. *Ibid.*
4107. Apple Inc, 'App Store Review Guidelines' (*Apple*) https://developer.apple.com/app-store/review/guidelines/ accessed June 2025.

'misleading, false, or copycat representations, names ...'[4108] be used, while Google Play also prohibits misleading through impersonation[4109] and prohibits counterfeit goods.[4110] Mobile app platforms should directly incorporate unfair competition[4111] in mobile apps.

5.5.3.5 *Digital Terms, Policies, and Disclaimers*

The platforms do not directly or adequately address this area. While there are specific terms for both mobile app platforms, these should address all relevant issues. While Apple's trademark related policies are largely within one document,[4112] Google Play trademark-related policies or help pages are in various.[4113] Disclaimers[4114] are not adequately covered by either.

5.5.3.6 *Digital Jurisdictional and Territorial Considerations*

This element is simply addressed by Apple through a statement that laws can be different in different countries, and a summary of common errors that may apply broadly.[4115] This does show a direct attempt to base policies on common trademark principles as does the UDRP, generally. While the policy does not adequately address these by directly mentioning the principles that apply, it is the basis for a uniform policy to apply. Google Play says that the mobile app operator is responsible to comply with relevant laws globally[4116] and generalizes that '[l]egal standards vary greatly by

4108. *Ibid.*
4109. Google, 'Impersonation' (*Google Play Console Help*) https://support.google.com/googleplay/android-developer/answer/9888374 accessed June 2025.
4110. Google, 'Intellectual property' (*Google Play Console Help*) https://support.google.com/googleplay/android-developer/answer/9888072?hl=en&ref_topic=9876963 accessed June 2025.
4111. *Ibid.*
4112. Apple Inc, 'App Store Review Guidelines' (*Apple*) https://developer.apple.com/app-store/review/guidelines/ accessed June 2025.
4113. Google, 'Intellectual Property' (*Google Play Console Help*) https://support.google.com/googleplay/android-developer/answer/9888072?hl=en&ref_topic=9876963 accessed July 2024; Google, 'Impersonation' (*Google Play Console Help*) https://support.google.com/googleplay/android-developer/answer/9888374 accessed June 2025; Google, 'Removing Content from Google: Legal Help' (*Google*) https://support.google.com/legal/troubleshooter/1114905#ts=13778295%2C1115643 accessed June 2025.
4114. WIPO, 'WIPO Overview of WIPO Panel Views on Selected UDRP Questions, Third Edition' ('WIPO Jurisprudential Overview 3.0') (*WIPO*, 2017) https://www.wipo.int/amc/en/domains/search/overview3.0/ accessed June 2025; Alexander Peukert, 'The Coexistence of Trade Mark Laws and Rights on the Internet, and the Impact of Geolocation Technologies' (2016) 47 International Review of Intellectual Property and Competition Law 60, 81 https://doi.org/10.1007/s40319-015-0427-8; Leslie Fair, 'Full Disclosure' (*FTC Business Blog*, 23 September 2014) https://www.ftc.gov/business-guidance/blog/2014/09/full-disclosure accessed June 2025.
4115. Apple Inc, 'App Store Review Guidelines' (*Apple*) https://developer.apple.com/app-store/review/guidelines/ accessed June 2025.
4116. Google, 'Google Play Developer Distribution Agreement' (*Google Play*) https://play.google.com/about/developer-distribution-agreement.html accessed June 2025.

country/region …'[4117] and focuses on removing content illegal in a particulary country or internationally if violating its policies.[4118] Co-existence[4119] is not covered.

5.5.3.7 *Digital Justification*

Other than in the case where the user has permission of the mark holder, justification is not directly or adequately covered by either mobile app platform. This creates much uncertainty.

While specific terms exist for developers of apps on mobile app platforms, Apple App Store and Google Play, these are insufficient even where supplemented with some help pages in the case of Google Play. However, as was the case for all platforms, the level of discretion on how these terms will be applied may result in inconsistency. Likewise, decisions are not public causing legal uncertainty.

5.5.4 Solution: A Uniform Policy for Trademarks in Mobile App Platforms

As with e-commerce marketplace, search ad and social media platforms,[4120] it is recommended that mobile app platforms adopt a very similar approach. A uniform policy is proposed as there is much overlap between the platforms on issues that pertain to trademarks within mobile app services. This approach can likewise enhance consistency[4121] between platforms. Provisions which are relevant to mobile apps and not currently included can be covered to avoid legal uncertainty.

4117. Google, 'Removing Content from Google: Legal Help' (*Google*) https://support.google.com/legal/troubleshooter/1114905#ts=13778295%2C1115643 accessed June 2025.
4118. *Ibid.*
4119. EUIPO, '3.1 Coexistence Between the Marks Involved in the Opposition' (*EUIPO Trade mark Guidelines*) https://guidelines.euipo.europa.eu/2058843/2043906/trade-mark-guidelines/3-1-coexistence-between-the-marks-involved-in-the-opposition accessed January 2024;15 U.S. Code § 1052(d); Alexander Peukert, 'The Coexistence of Trade Mark Laws and Rights on the Internet, and the Impact of Geolocation Technologies' (2016) 47 International Review of Intellectual Property and Competition Law 60, 81 https://doi.org/10.1007/s40319-015-042 7-8; Tamara Nanayakkara, 'IP and Business: Trademark Coexistence' (*WIPO*, November 2006) https://www.wipo.int/wipo_magazine/en/2006/06/article_0007.html accessed June 2025.
4120. Rajeev Sachdev, 'Towards an Improved Framework for Trade-Mark Law and Regulation in Social Media Usernames: A Study of the Canadian, U.S., and U.K. Positions' (2016) 28 Intellectual Property Journal 379, 379-418; Daniel Doft, 'Facebook, Twitter, and the Wild West of IP Enforcement on Social Media: Weighing the Merits of a Uniform Dispute Resolution Policy' (2016) 49 The John Marshall Law Review 959; Thomas J Curtin, 'The Name Game: Cybersquatting and Trademark Infringement on Social Media Websites' (2010-2011) 19 Journal of Law and Policy 353; Erick J Heels, 'How to Twittersquat the Top 100 Brands' (*GiantPeople*, 8 January 2009) http://www.giantpeople.com/1298.html accessed 4 August 2025; Paul D McGrady, *McGrady on Social Media and the Metaverse* (Mathew Bender & Company, Inc. 2023) §12; John McElwaine and Christopher D Casavale, 'Tackling Bad Faith Registration of Domain Names in a Fast-Changing Landscape' (*WIPO Magazine*, December 2019) https://www.wipo.int/wipo_magazine/en/2019/06/article_0006.html accessed June 2025.
4121. Rajeev Sachdev, 'Towards an Improved Framework for Trade-Mark Law and Regulation in Social Media Usernames: A Study of the Canadian, U.S., and U.K. Positions' (2016) 28

The following is a sample uniform policy based on the mobile app platforms adopting it themselves and making their own decisions on complaints received.

Table 5.11 Uniform Mobile App Trademark Dispute Resolution Policy (UMATDRP)

Uniform Mobile App Trademark Dispute Resolution Policy (UMATDRP)	Adapted or directly from the UDRP[4122] and UDNDRP (Chapter 4). The name reflects specifically the platform type and subject matter.
(1) *Purpose.* This Uniform Mobile App Trademark Dispute Resolution Policy ('Policy') has been adopted by [Mobile App Platform] ('Platform' or 'We'), is incorporated by reference into the Terms of Use of Platform and your Mobile App Registration Agreement, and sets forth the terms and conditions in connection with a dispute between you and any party other than Platform over the utilisation of a trademark in Platform. Decisions under Paragraph 4 of this Policy will be made in accordance with the Policy. Guidelines to this policy are set forth in the document entitled: Guidelines to the UMATDRP.	Adapted or directly from the UDRP[4123] and UDNDRP (Chapter 4) and Apple App Store and Goole Play terms and policies.[4124] The policy refers to any disputed utilisation of a mark within the platforms. Guidelines should make clear that utilisation of a trademark includes in all areas of mobile apps including but not limited to app icons, app names, app advertising, notifications, designs, features, content, and all other areas relating to mobile apps.
(2) *Your Representations.* By registering a mobile app on Platform, you hereby represent and warrant to us that: (a) the statements that you made in your Mobile App Registration Agreement are complete and accurate; (b) to your knowledge, the mobile app will not infringe upon or otherwise violate the	Adapted or directly from the UDRP[4125] and UDNRDP (Chapter 4).

Intellectual Property Journal 379, 379-418; Paul D McGrady, *McGrady on Social Media and the Metaverse* (Mathew Bender & Company, Inc. 2023) §12.

4122. ICANN, 'Uniform Domain-Name Dispute-Resolution Policy' (*ICANN*, 25 February 2012) https://www.icann.org/resources/pages/policy-2012-02-25-en accessed June 2025.

4123. *Ibid.*

4124. Apple Inc, 'App Store Review Guidelines' (*Apple*) https://developer.apple.com/app-store/review/guidelines/ accessed June 2025; Google, 'Intellectual Property' (*Google Play Console Help*) https://support.google.com/googleplay/android-developer/answer/9888072?hl=en&ref_topic=9876963 accessed June 2025; Google, 'Impersonation' (*Google Play Console Help*) https://support.google.com/googleplay/android-developer/answer/9888374 accessed July 2024; Google, 'Removing Content from Google: Legal Help' (*Google*) https://support.google.com/legal/troubleshooter/1114905#ts=13778295%2C1115643 accessed July 2024.

4125. ICANN, 'Uniform Domain-Name Dispute-Resolution Policy' (*ICANN*, 25 February 2012) https://www.icann.org/resources/pages/policy-2012-02-25-en accessed June 2025.

rights of any third party; (c) you are not registering the mobile app for an unlawful purpose; and (d) you will not knowingly use Platform in violation of any applicable laws or regulations. It is your responsibility to determine whether your account and/or mobile app infringes or violates someone else's rights.	
(3) *Changes, Suspensions, and Cancellations.* We will make changes to, suspend, or cancel your account and/or mobile app on Platform under the following circumstances: (i) our receipt of written or appropriate electronic instructions from you or your authorized agent to take such action except that you may not transfer your account or mobile app to another holder: (a) during a pending administrative proceeding brought pursuant to Paragraph 4 or for a period of fifteen (15) business days after such proceeding is concluded; or (b) during a pending court proceeding or arbitration commenced regarding your account, mobile app or its content unless the court or party to whom the account is being transferred agrees, in writing, to be bound by the decision of the court or arbitrator. We reserve the right not to permit the transfer of your account or mobile app to another party in accordance with this subparagraph; (ii) our receipt of an order from a court or arbitral tribunal, in each case of competent jurisdiction, requiring such action; (iii) our decision requiring such action based on a complaint received under this or a later version of this Policy; and/or (iv) in accordance with the terms of your Mobile App Registration Agreement (such as but not limited to where you have engaged in abuse with respect to one or more trademarks) or other legal requirements.	Adapted or directly from the UDRP[4126] and UDNDRP (Chapter 4). Updated based on services. Added that 'abuse'[4127] can result in a change, suspension or cancellation and guidelines can be used to clarify when certain actions may take place.

4126. *Ibid.*

4127. WIPO, 'WIPO Overview of WIPO Panel Views on Selected UDRP Questions, Third Edition' ('WIPO Jurisprudential Overview 3.0') (*WIPO*, 2017) https://www.wipo.int/amc/en/domains/search/overview3.0/ accessed June 2025.

(4) *Mandatory Decision Process and Remedies*. This Paragraph sets forth the type of disputes for which you are required to submit to a Mandatory Decision Process. A decision on a complaint lodged under this Policy will be made by Platform.

(a) Applicable Disputes. You are required to submit to a decision by Platform in the event that a third party (a 'complainant') asserts to Platform, through a Trademark Complaint Form <URL for Form> that that your mobile app or its content:

(A) is identical or confusingly similar to trademarks in which a complainant has rights and which you are using on an unauthorised basis in the course of trade AND

(B) (i) is being used to engage in unfair competition in the course of trade with respect to a trademark OR (ii) is being used in bad faith or is being abused with respect to a trademark. For clarity, in the administrative proceeding, the complainant must prove element A AND one element from B (either i or ii) are present.

(b) Permitted use. Trademarks will be permitted if you demonstrate that you have rights or legitimate interests in respect of your mobile app or its content by showing one or more of these justifications: (i) you (as an individual, business, or other organization) have been commonly known by the term and are using

Adapted or directly from the UDRP,[4128] UDNDRP, Paris Convention, TRIPS, Dispute Resolution Service for.eu,[4129] EUTMR, Lanham Act 1946 15 U.S. Code §§ 1051 et seq. (as amended), the TDRA 2006 15 U.S. Code § 1125(c), Apple App Store and Google Play terms and policies.[4130]

Key UDRP aspects have been retained including relevant concepts from the Overview.[4131]

This uniform policy largely follows the UDNDRP (Chapter 4) but is adapted for mobile app platforms. Please see Chapter 4 (section 4.3.3) for further details and explanations of the adaptations under the model.

Interpretation of this Paragraph should be set out in the Guidelines.

4128. ICANN, 'Uniform Domain-Name Dispute-Resolution Policy' (*ICANN*, 25 February 2012) https://www.icann.org/resources/pages/policy-2012-02-25-en accessed June 2025.

4129. WIPO, 'WIPO Domain Name Dispute Resolution Service for .EU (and.ею and.ευ)' (*WIPO*) https://www.wipo.int/amc/en/domains/cctld/eu/index.html accessed July 2024.

4130. Apple Inc, 'App Store Review Guidelines' (*Apple*) https://developer.apple.com/app-store/review/guidelines/ accessed June 2025; Google, 'Intellectual Property' (*Google Play Console Help*) https://support.google.com/googleplay/android-developer/answer/9888072?hl=en&ref_topic=9876963 accessed June 2025; Google, 'Impersonation' (*Google Play Console Help*) https://support.google.com/googleplay/android-developer/answer/9888374 accessed June 2025; Google, 'Removing Content from Google: Legal Help' (*Google*) https://support.google.com/legal/troubleshooter/1114905#ts=13778295%2C1115643 accessed June 2025.

4131. ICANN, 'Uniform Domain-Name Dispute-Resolution Policy' (*ICANN*, 25 February 2012) https://www.icann.org/resources/pages/policy-2012-02-25-en accessed June 2025; WIPO, 'WIPO Overview of WIPO Panel Views on Selected UDRP Questions, Third Edition' ('WIPO Jurisprudential Overview 3.0') (*WIPO*, 2017) https://www.wipo.int/amc/en/domains/search/overview3.0/ accessed June 2025.

it legitimately, (ii) you are making genuine noncommercial legitimate fair use of the trademark, (iii) you are fairly utilising the trademark in marketing of authorized, replacement, compatible or used goods or services, (iv) you are utilising the trademark in an ordinary dictionary sense, (v) you are genuinely and noncommercially utilising the trademark under freedom of speech and expression or legitimate criticism, parody, or review of the company, good or service associated with the trademark, OR (vi) you are making fair and legitimate use of the trademark in comparative advertising. (c) Remedies. The remedies available to a complainant pursuant to any decision by Platform shall be limited to requiring the cancellation of, suspending, or making changes to your account and/or mobile app. (d) All Other Disputes. All other disputes between you and any party other than Platform regarding your mobile app in Platform that are not brought pursuant to this Policy will not be resolved through a decision under this Policy. Platform reserves the right to make a decision on any matter outside of this policy as set forth in our Terms of Use available at <terms> including any remedies or actions it, in its sole discretion, deems appropriate.	
(5) *Procedures.* (a) Initiation of Proceeding. Submitting a Trade mark Complaint Form initiates the process for a decision by Platform. (b) Consolidation. In the event of multiple disputes between you and a complainant, either you or the complainant may request to consolidate the disputes for a single decision. Platform may consolidate before it any or all	Adapted or directly from the UDRP[4132] and UDNDRP (Chapter 4).

4132. ICANN, 'Uniform Domain-Name Dispute-Resolution Policy' (*ICANN*, 25 February 2012) https://www.icann.org/resources/pages/policy-2012-02-25-en accessed June 2025.

such disputes in its sole discretion, provided that the disputes being consolidated are governed by this Policy or a later version of this Policy.

(c) Fees. No fees are charged to file a complaint under this Policy or to receive a decision by Platform.

(d) Availability of Court Proceedings. The Mandatory Decision Process requirements set forth in Paragraph 4 shall not prevent either you or the complainant from submitting the dispute to a court of competent jurisdiction for independent resolution before such Mandatory Decision Process is commenced or after it is concluded. If we decide that your accounts and/or mobile app should be cancelled, suspended, or changed, we will then implement the decision immediately unless we have received from you official documentation (such as a copy of a complaint, file-stamped by the clerk of the court) that you have commenced a lawsuit against the complainant in an appropriate jurisdiction. If we receive such documentation immediately following a decision, we will not implement the Panel's decision, and we will take no further action, until we receive: (i) evidence satisfactory to us of a resolution between the parties; (ii) evidence satisfactory to us that your lawsuit has been dismissed or withdrawn; or (iii) a copy of an order from such court dismissing your lawsuit or ordering that you do not have the right to continue the account and/or mobile app.

Because platforms currently expend their own resources to make decisions on complaints they receive, these resources may be redirected to an online panel decision under the assumption that this will not raise costs by unreasonable sums.
Platforms may wish to include an indemnification provision here.

(6) *Policy Modifications.* Platform reserves the right to modify this Policy at any time. Platform will post any revised Policy at <URL> at least thirty (30) calendar days before it becomes effective. Unless this Policy has already been invoked by the submission of a Trade mark Complaint Form, in which event the version of the Policy in effect at the time it was invoked will apply to you until the dispute is

Adapted or directly from UDRP[4133] and UDNDRP (Chapter 4).

4133. *Ibid.*

over, all such changes will be binding upon you with respect to any mobile app trademark dispute, whether the dispute arose before, on or after the effective date of our change. In the event that you object to a change in this Policy, your sole remedy is to cancel your Account with us, provided that you will not be entitled to a refund of any fees you paid to us. The revised Policy will apply to you until you cancel your Account.

The above draft solves various gaps. It can be adopted by any mobile app platform as a uniform policy.[4134] It not only includes the mobile app name but also content within and associated with apps. This approach will help to resolve potential inconsistencies[4135] with mobile app decisions relating to similar trademark complaints within mobile app platforms. It will reduce the discretion and time needed to make decisions by incorporating legal certainty.

The following is a sample uniform policy based on a panel approach as cases under the UDRP are decided.

Table 5.12 Uniform Mobile App Trademark Dispute Resolution Policy (UMATDRP)

Uniform Mobile App Trademark Dispute Resolution Policy (UMATDRP)	Adapted or directly from the UDRP[4136] and UDNDRP (Chapter 4). The name reflects specifically the platform type and subject matter.

4134. Rajeev Sachdev, 'Towards an Improved Framework for Trade-Mark Law and Regulation in Social Media Usernames: A Study of the Canadian, U.S., and U.K. Positions' (2016) 28 Intellectual Property Journal 379, 379-418; Daniel Doft, 'Facebook, Twitter, and the Wild West of IP Enforcement on Social Media: Weighing the Merits of a Uniform Dispute Resolution Policy' (2016) 49 The John Marshall Law Review 959; Thomas J Curtin, 'The Name Game: Cybersquatting and Trademark Infringement on Social Media Websites' (2010-2011) 19 Journal of Law and Policy 353; Erick J Heels, 'How to Twittersquat the Top 100 Brands' (*GiantPeople*, 8 January 2009) http://www.giantpeople.com/1298.html accessed 4 August 2025; Paul D McGrady, *McGrady on Social Media and the Metaverse* (Mathew Bender & Company, Inc. 2023) §12; John McElwaine and Christopher D Casavale, 'Tackling Bad Faith Registration of Domain Names in a Fast-Changing Landscape' (*WIPO Magazine*, December 2019) https://www.wipo.int/wipo_magazine/en/2019/06/article_0006.html accessed June 2025.

4135. Rajeev Sachdev, 'Towards an Improved Framework for Trade-Mark Law and Regulation in Social Media Usernames: A Study of the Canadian, U.S., and U.K. Positions' (2016) 28 Intellectual Property Journal 379, 379-418; Paul D McGrady, *McGrady on Social Media and the Metaverse* (Mathew Bender & Company, Inc. 2023) §12.

4136. ICANN, 'Uniform Domain-Name Dispute-Resolution Policy' (*ICANN*, 25 February 2012) https://www.icann.org/resources/pages/policy-2012-02-25-en accessed June 2025.

(1) *Purpose.* This Uniform Mobile App Trademark Dispute Resolution Policy ('Policy') has been adopted by [Mobile App Platform] ('Platform' or 'We'), is incorporated by reference into the Terms of Use of Platform and your Mobile App Registration Agreement, and sets forth the terms and conditions in connection with a dispute between you and any party other than Platform over the utilisation of a trademark in Platform. Decisions under Paragraph 4 of this Policy will be made in accordance with the Policy. Guidelines to this policy are set forth in the document entitled: Guidelines to the UMATDRP.	Adapted or directly from the UDRP[4137] and UDNDRP (Chapter 4) and Apple App Store and Google Play terms and policies.[4138] The policy refers to any disputed utilisation of a mark within the platforms. Guidelines should make clear that utilisation of a trademark includes in all areas of mobile apps including but not limited to app icons, app names, app advertising, notifications, designs, features, content, and all other areas relating to mobile apps.
(2) *Your Representations.* By registering a mobile app on Platform, you hereby represent and warrant to us that (a) the statements that you made in your Mobile App Registration Agreement are complete and accurate; (b) to your knowledge, the mobile app will not infringe upon or otherwise violate the rights of any third party; (c) you are not registering the mobile app for an unlawful purpose; and (d) you will not knowingly use Platform in violation of any applicable laws or regulations. It is your responsibility to determine whether your account and/or mobile app infringes or violates someone else's rights.	Adapted or directly from the UDRP[4139] and UDNRDP (Chapter 4).
(3) *Changes, Suspensions, and Cancellations.* We will make changes to, suspend, or cancel your account and/or mobile app on Platform under the following circumstances:	Adapted or directly from the UDRP[4140] and UDNDRP (Chapter 4). Updated based on services. Added that 'abuse'[4141] can result

4137. *Ibid.*
4138. Apple Inc, 'App Store Review Guidelines' (*Apple*) https://developer.apple.com/app-store/review/guidelines/ accessed June 2025; Google, 'Intellectual Property' (*Google Play Console Help*) https://support.google.com/googleplay/android-developer/answer/9888072?hl=en&ref_topic=9876963 accessed June 2025; Google, 'Impersonation' (*Google Play Console Help*) https://support.google.com/googleplay/android-developer/answer/9888374 accessed July 2024; Google, 'Removing Content from Google: Legal Help' (*Google*) https://support.google.com/legal/troubleshooter/1114905#ts=13778295%2C1115643 accessed June 2025.
4139. ICANN, 'Uniform Domain-Name Dispute-Resolution Policy' (*ICANN*, 25 February 2012) https://www.icann.org/resources/pages/policy-2012-02-25-en accessed June 2025.
4140. *Ibid.*
4141. WIPO, 'WIPO Overview of WIPO Panel Views on Selected UDRP Questions, Third Edition' ('WIPO Jurisprudential Overview 3.0') (*WIPO*, 2017) https://www.wipo.int/amc/en/domains/search/overview3.0/ accessed June 2025.

(i) our receipt of written or appropriate electronic instructions from you or your authorized agent to take such action except that you may not transfer your account or mobile app to another holder (a) during a pending administrative proceeding brought pursuant to Paragraph 4 or for a period of fifteen (15) business days after such proceeding is concluded; or (b) during a pending court proceeding or arbitration commenced regarding your account, mobile app or its content unless the court or party to whom the account is being transferred agrees, in writing, to be bound by the decision of the court or arbitrator. We reserve the right not to permit the transfer of your account or mobile app to another party in accordance with this subparagraph; (ii) our receipt of an order from a court or arbitral tribunal, in each case of competent jurisdiction, requiring such action; (iii) a panel decision requiring such action based on a complaint received under this or a later version of this Policy; and/or (iv) in accordance with the terms of your Mobile App Registration Agreement (such as but not limited to where you have engaged in abuse with respect to one or more trademarks) or other legal requirements.	in a change, suspension or cancellation and guidelines can be used to clarify when certain actions may take place.
(4) *Mandatory Administrative Proceeding and Remedies*. This Paragraph sets forth the type of disputes for which you are required to submit to a mandatory Panel Decision. A decision on a complaint lodged under this Policy will be made by an appointed Panel. a. Applicable Disputes. You are required to submit to a Panel Decision in the event that a third party (a 'complainant') asserts to Platform, through a Trademark Complaint Form <URL for Form> that that that your mobile app or its content:	Adapted or directly from the UDRP,[4142] UDNDRP (Chapter 4), Paris Convention, TRIPS, Dispute Resolution Service for.eu,[4143] EUTMR, Lanham Act 1946 15 U.S. Code §§ 1051 et seq. (as amended), the TDRA 2006 15 U.S. Code § 1125(c), Apple App Store and Google Play terms and policies.[4144]

4142. ICANN, 'Uniform Domain-Name Dispute-Resolution Policy' (*ICANN*, 25 February 2012) https://www.icann.org/resources/pages/policy-2012-02-25-en accessed June 2025.

4143. WIPO, 'WIPO Domain Name Dispute Resolution Service for .EU (and.ею and.ευ)' (*WIPO*) https://www.wipo.int/amc/en/domains/cctld/eu/index.html accessed July 2024.

4144. Apple Inc, 'App Store Review Guidelines' (*Apple*) https://developer.apple.com/app-store/review/guidelines/ accessed July 2024; Google, 'Intellectual Property' (*Google Play Console*

(A) is identical or confusingly similar to trademarks in which a complainant has rights and which you are using on an unauthorised basis in the course of trade AND

(B) (i) is being used to engage in unfair competition in the course of trade with respect to a trademark OR (ii) is being used in bad faith or is being abused with respect to a trademark. For clarity, in the administrative proceeding, the complainant must prove element A AND one element from B (either i or ii) are present.

(b) Permitted use. Trademarks will be permitted if you demonstrate that you have rights or legitimate interests in respect of your mobile app or its content by showing one or more of these justifications: (i) you (as an individual, business, or other organization) have been commonly known by the term and are using it legitimately (ii) you are making genuine noncommercial legitimate fair use of the trademark, (iii) you are fairly utilising the trademark in marketing of authorized, replacement, compatible or used goods or services, (iv) you are utilising the trademark in an ordinary dictionary sense, (v) you are genuinely and noncommercially utilising the trademark under freedom of speech and expression or legitimate criticism, parody, or review of the company, good or service associated with the trademark, OR (vi) you are making fair and legitimate use of the trademark in comparative advertising.

(c) Remedies. The remedies available to a complainant pursuant to any Panel Decision shall be limited to requiring the cancellation of, suspending, or making changes to your account and/or mobile app.

Key UDRP aspects have been retained including relevant concepts from the Overview.[4145] This uniform policy largely follows the UDNDRP (Chapter 4) but is adapted for mobile app platforms. Please see Chapter 4 (section 4.3.3) for further details and explanations of the adaptations under the model. Interpretation of this Paragraph should be set out in the Guidelines.

Help) https://support.google.com/googleplay/android-developer/answer/9888072?hl=en&ref_topic=9876963 accessed June 2025; Google, 'Impersonation' (*Google Play Console Help*) https://support.google.com/googleplay/android-developer/answer/9888374 accessed June 2025; Google, 'Removing Content from Google: Legal Help' (*Google*) https://support.google.com/legal/troubleshooter/1114905#ts=13778295%2C1115643 accessed June 2025.

4145. ICANN, 'Uniform Domain-Name Dispute-Resolution Policy' (*ICANN*, 25 February 2012) https://www.icann.org/resources/pages/policy-2012-02-25-en accessed June 2025; WIPO,

(d) All Other Disputes. All other disputes between you and any party other than Platform regarding your mobile app in Platform that are not brought pursuant to this Policy will not be resolved through a Panel Decision. Platform reserves the right to make a decision on any matter outside of this policy as set forth in our Terms of Use available at <terms> including any remedies or actions it, in its sole discretion, deems appropriate.

(5) *Procedures.*

(a) Initiation of Proceeding. Submitting a Trade mark Complaint Form initiates the process for a Panel Decision.

(b) Consolidation. In the event of multiple disputes between you and a complainant, either you or the complainant may petition to consolidate the disputes before a single Panel. This petition shall be made to the Panel appointed to hear a pending dispute between the parties. This Panel may consolidate before it any or all such disputes in its sole discretion, provided that the disputes being consolidated are governed by this Policy or a later version of this Policy.

(c) Fees. No fees are charged to file a complaint under this Policy or to receive a Panel Decision.

(d) Availability of Court Proceedings. The Panel Decision proceeding requirements set forth in Paragraph 4 shall not prevent either you or the complainant from submitting the dispute to a court of competent jurisdiction for independent resolution before such Panel Decision is commenced or after such proceeding is concluded. If a Panel decides that your accounts and/or mobile app should be cancelled, suspended, or changed,

Adapted or directly from the UDRP[4146] and UDNDRP.
Because platforms currently expend their own resources to make decisions on complaints they receive, these resources may be redirected to an online panel decision under the assumption that this will not raise costs by unreasonable sums.
Platforms may wish to include an indemnification provision here.

'WIPO Overview of WIPO Panel Views on Selected UDRP Questions, Third Edition' ('WIPO Jurisprudential Overview 3.0') (*WIPO*, 2017) https://www.wipo.int/amc/en/domains/search/overview3.0/ accessed June 2025.

4146. ICANN, 'Uniform Domain-Name Dispute-Resolution Policy' (ICANN, 25 February 2012) https://www.icann.org/resources/pages/policy-2012-02-25-en accessed June 2025.

we will then implement the decision immediately unless we have received from you official documentation (such as a copy of a complaint, file-stamped by the clerk of the court) that you have commenced a lawsuit against the complainant in an appropriate jurisdiction. If we receive such documentation immediately following a decision, we will not implement the Panel's decision, and we will take no further action, until we receive (i) evidence satisfactory to us of a resolution between the parties; (ii) evidence satisfactory to us that your lawsuit has been dismissed or withdrawn; or (iii) a copy of an order from such court dismissing your lawsuit or ordering that you do not have the right to continue the account and/or mobile app.	
(6) *Policy Modifications*. Platform reserves the right to modify this Policy at any time. Platform will post any revised Policy at <URL> at least thirty (30) calendar days before it becomes effective. Unless this Policy has already been invoked by the submission of a Trade mark Complaint Form, in which event the version of the Policy in effect at the time it was invoked will apply to you until the dispute is over, all such changes will be binding upon you with respect to any mobile app trademark dispute, whether the dispute arose before, on or after the effective date of our change. In the event that you object to a change in this Policy, your sole remedy is to cancel your Account with us, provided that you will not be entitled to a refund of any fees you paid to us. The revised Policy will apply to you until you cancel your Account.	Adapted or directly from UDRP[4147] and UDNDRP (Chapter 4).

5.6 MAJOR METAVERSE PLATFORM TRADEMARK TERMS AND POLICIES

Metaverse platforms largely have terms and conditions that prohibit using trademarks of others. This section overviews such policies after which gaps and problems are outlined. A policy is recommended based on the same.

4147. *Ibid.*

5.6.1 Roblox

Roblox may investigate any content within their service[4148] (in any 'place of use'[4149] within the service): 'If you are a trademark owner, or an agent of a trademark owner, and believe that any content on the Services infringes upon your registered trademark(s), please submit a trademark infringement notice ...'[4150]

They indicate that a registered mark is needed and that they do not act as a mediator for disputes 'between Users and the holders of trademark rights'.[4151] However, they indicate that they 'take intellectual property rights seriously'[4152] and when they receive a legitimate complaint, they 'will investigate and may remove content that engages in trademark infringement'.[4153] A registered trademark is required.[4154]

Roblox has specific policies under its Terms of Use and referencing User Generated Content (UGC), they indicate that they, without obligation 'may, in its sole discretion, suspend availability of or delete any UGC or other content on the Services at any time and for any period of time, including in perpetuity, without notice if such UGC or other content violates any laws or intellectual property rights or principles or any guidelines or policies associated with the Services'.[4155] Further, a 'copyright owner or an agent of a copyright or trademark owner ... may submit a notification pursuant to the reporting process'.[4156]

However, trademarks are discussed under the heading related to the Digital Millennium Copyright Act (DMCA) which is not designed for trademarks. Copyright is further mixed with trademark when they state: 'and use of such sound recording(s) and/or Musical Work(s) on the Services will not infringe upon the rights of any third party, including but not limited to trademark, copyright, or any other intellectual property rights ...'.[4157]

In the context of 'abuse',[4158] there is a repeat infringer reference: 'As referred to throughout the Roblox Terms, Roblox, in appropriate circumstances, may terminate the Accounts of Users (or Creators) who Roblox determines, in its sole discretion, are repeat infringers as contemplated by the DMCA.'[4159] However, likewise, the above is

4148. Roblox, 'Roblox Terms of Use' (*Roblox Legal Documents*) https://en.help.roblox.com/hc/en-us/articles/115004647846-Roblox-Terms-of-Use accessed June 2025.
4149. EUIPO, '3 Place of Use' (*EUIPO Trade mark guidelines* 2024) https://guidelines.euipo.europa.eu/2214311/1982069/trade-mark-guidelines/3-place-of-use accessed January 2024.
4150. Roblox, 'Roblox Terms of Use' (*Roblox Legal Documents*) https://en.help.roblox.com/hc/en-us/articles/115004647846-Roblox-Terms-of-Use accessed June 2025.
4151. *Ibid.*
4152. *Ibid.*
4153. *Ibid.*
4154. *Ibid.*
4155. *Ibid.*
4156. *Ibid.*
4157. *Ibid.*
4158. WIPO, 'WIPO Overview of WIPO Panel Views on Selected UDRP Questions, Third Edition' ('WIPO Jurisprudential Overview 3.0') (*WIPO*, 2017) https://www.wipo.int/amc/en/domains/search/overview3.0/ accessed June 2025.
4159. Roblox, 'Roblox Terms of Use' (*Roblox Legal Documents*) https://en.help.roblox.com/hc/en-us/articles/115004647846-Roblox-Terms-of-Use accessed June 2025.

stated within the DMCA section and appears to mix copyright and trademark matters.[4160] A more complete 'Repeat Infringer Policy'[4161] policy is also stated in the terms indicating that their 'policy is to: (i) remove or disable access to content that Roblox knows to be infringing on the intellectual property rights of third parties ... and, (ii) in appropriate circumstances, to suspend or terminate the Accounts of and block access to the Services by any User who repeatedly or egregiously infringes the copyrights or other intellectual property rights of third-parties'.[4162]

Roblox also requires a defence and indemnity in the context of intellectual property violations with respect to third parties: 'arising out of or in any way connected with: ... (c) Creator's violation of any third-party right, including any intellectual property ... or (d) any Dispute or issue between Creator and any third party'.[4163]

Under its Community Standards, there are intellectual Property standards: '[w]e expect you to respect the intellectual property rights of others, and will remove infringing content upon receiving a valid copyright or trademark takedown request from a rights holder. Examples of intellectual property infringement may include: ... [u]sing a brand's logo or designs for the content you create without their permission'.[4164] Further, 'Roblox may proactively delete or archive assets if we suspect that the content may be infringing on someone's intellectual property rights.'[4165]

Under its Advertising Standards, 'Advertisements may not violate the intellectual property of others ... Roblox will remove infringing content upon receiving a valid ... [t]rademark infringement removal request.'[4166] Additionally, 'Violations of our Community Standards or Advertiser Integrity requirements may result in removal of advertising content, ad campaign suspension, ad account suspension or Roblox account suspension ... also prevent violators or suspected affiliate accounts from creating new ad campaigns or ad accounts.'[4167]

Roblox has some supplementary terms, such as those for the 'European Union/European Economic Area and the United Kingdom',[4168] although generally not trademark-related.

5.6.2 Meta Horizon Worlds

Meta Horizon Worlds Terms of Service and Community Guidelines all point to Meta's policies. It is not permitted to 'violate ... these Terms, the Community Standards, or other terms and policies ... [t]hat is unlawful, misleading, discriminatory or fraudulent

4160. *Ibid.*
4161. *Ibid.*
4162. *Ibid.*
4163. *Ibid.*
4164. Roblox, 'Roblox Community Standards' (*Roblox Support*) https://en.help.roblox.com/hc/en-us/articles/203313410-Roblox-Community-Standards accessed June 2025.
4165. *Ibid.*
4166. Roblox, 'Advertising Standards' (Roblox Legal Documents) https://en.help.roblox.com/hc/en-us/articles/13722260778260 accessed June 2025.
4167. *Ibid.*
4168. Roblox, 'Roblox Terms of Use' (*Roblox Legal Documents*) https://en.help.roblox.com/hc/en-us/articles/115004647846-Roblox-Terms-of-Use accessed June 2025.

... [t]hat you do not own or have the necessary rights to share ... [t]hat infringes or violates someone else's rights, including their intellectual property rights (... trademark, or distributing or selling counterfeit or pirated goods), unless an exception or limitation applies under applicable law'.[4169]

Under its Supplemental Meta Platforms Technologies (MPT) Terms Of Service, there are additional prohibitions including that users 'may not use MPT Products to do or share anything that violates these Supplemental Terms, or other terms and policies that apply to your use of MPT Products ... [and are encouraged to] report content or conduct ... [w]e, at our sole discretion, may remove, delete or restrict access to content that we determine to violate such terms and policies, including content that infringes intellectual property rights'.[4170]

Policies pertaining to advertising were covered under the social media platform discussion in 5.4 above.

5.6.3 Epic Games

Epic Games Content standards dictate that 'User Contributions must not be illegal, fraudulent, deceptive ... infringing of intellectual property rights ...'[4171] Further that contributors 'represent and warrant that you own or otherwise control all of the rights to the User Contributions that you Post at the time of Posting; that the User Contributions are accurate and not fraudulent or deceptive; and that the User Contributions do not violate these Terms or the rights (intellectual property rights or otherwise) of any third party'.[4172] Further, they reserve the right but do not have a positive obligation 'to monitor and edit or remove ... also has the right to terminate ... access ... for any or no reason, including without limitation, any violation of these Terms ... may exercise these rights at any time, without notice or liability to you or any third party'.[4173]

Under its Community Rules, it says not to 'impersonate other players, streamers, celebrities, government officials, Epic employees, or anyone else. And don't take credit for another player or entity's creation ... [p]retending to be someone else in order to deceive or defraud others is not okay'.[4174] However, the Fortnite Island Creator Rules specifically mention 'companies'[4175] and 'brands'[4176] as well and indicates that creators must not 'impersonate other players, creators, streamers, celebrities, companies,

4169. Facebook, 'Terms of Service' https://www.facebook.com/terms.php/ accessed July 2024.
4170. Meta, 'Supplemental Meta Platforms Technologies Terms of Service' (*Meta*) https://www.meta.com/legal/supplemental-terms-of-service/ accessed June 2025.
4171. Epic Games, 'Terms of Service' (*Epic Games*) https://www.epicgames.com/site/en-US/tos accessed June 2025.
4172. *Ibid.*
4173. *Ibid.*
4174. Epic Games, 'Epic Games Community Rules' (*Epic Games*) https://www.epicgames.com/site/en-US/community-rules accessed June 2025.
4175. Fortnite, 'The Fortnite Island Creator Rules' (*Fortnite*) https://www.fortnite.com/news/fortnite-island-creator-rules accessed June 2025.
4176. *Ibid.*

brands, government officials, Epic employees, or anyone else … [p]retending to be someone else in order to deceive or defraud others is not okay'.[4177]

Under its Content Guidelines, specifically under 'Infringing or Unauthorized Content',[4178] it indicates that content that is created or published 'cannot infringe or violate someone else's rights, including their intellectual property rights … must own or have obtained the necessary rights to share and publish the content, and any such license must be broad enough to grant Epic a license to display the content'.[4179] For purposes of illustration, one gaming platform created by Epic Games is Fortnite which, like some other platforms it creates or owns, has its own additional rules. For example, under the Fortnite Island Creator Rules (with reference to its End User License Agreement (EULA), and its Unreal Editor for Fortnite (UEFN) calls for the respect of intellectual property ownership and a similar license to above.[4180]

Under the Fortnite End User License Agreement, Epic prohibits 'intellectual-property infringement activities through the Software or the Services'.[4181] It is not permitted 'to create, generate, or make available … any UGC to which you do not have the right to grant Epic such license in all of the elements … [y]ou are solely responsible for your UGC and represent and warrant that … you are the creator and owner of, and have all the necessary licenses and rights to use and authorize Epic to exploit the license granted above … will not infringe or violate any third-party rights, including … trademark …'[4182] They also require confirmation that 'Epic's use of … UGC will not violate any third-party contract or cause Epic to violate any applicable laws or regulations.'[4183] Epic confirms that users should ('please')[4184] not 'make objectionable content available on or through the Services … [and] may have to take it down'.[4185] Epic may also but does not have to 'edit or control any UGC'[4186] or may 'at any time screen, remove, delete, edit, block, or refuse to publish UGC that violates this Agreement or is otherwise objectionable as determined in Epic's sole discretion and without prior notice or any liability'.[4187]

Under its terms of use, 'Epic may also at its sole discretion limit access to the Services and/or update, transfer, suspend, or terminate the accounts of any users who infringe the intellectual property rights of others, whether or not there is any repeat infringement.'[4188] Likewise, under UEFN Supplemental Terms to the EULA, specifically

4177. *Ibid.*
4178. Epic Games, 'Epic Games: Content Guidelines' (*Epic Games*) https://www.epicgames.com/site/en-US/content-guidelines accessed June 2025.
4179. *Ibid.*
4180. Fortnite, 'The Fortnite Island Creator Rules' (*Fortnite*) https://www.fortnite.com/news/fortnite-island-creator-rules accessed June 2025.
4181. Fortnite, 'Fortnite End User License Agreement' (*Fortnite*) https://www.fortnite.com/eula accessed June 2025.
4182. *Ibid.*
4183. *Ibid.*
4184. *Ibid.*
4185. *Ibid.*
4186. *Ibid.*
4187. *Ibid.*
4188. Epic Games, 'Terms of Service' (*Epic Games*) https://www.epicgames.com/site/en-US/tos accessed June 2025.

under 'Alleged IP Infringement',[4189] 'Epic may also at its sole discretion limit access to UEFN or other Epic products or services and/or update, transfer, suspend, or terminate the accounts of any users who infringe the intellectual property rights of others, whether or not there is any repeat infringement.'[4190] There is a Report Infringement page which may be submitted.[4191]

4189. Fortnite, 'Unreal Editor for Fortnite Supplemental Terms to the EULA' (*Fortnite*) https://www.fortnite.com/unreal-editor-for-fortnite-supplemental-terms accessed June 2025.
4190. *Ibid.*
4191. *Ibid.*

5.6.4 Gaps and Problems with Current Metaverse Platform Trademark Terms and Policies

Table 5.13 Digital Trademark and Trade Practices Model, UDRP, and Metaverse Platform Terms and Policies

Digital Trademark and Trade Practices Model	*UDRP*	*Roblox*	*Meta Horizon Worlds*	*Epic Games*
Digital Use and Place of Use	Only some coverage. Any use of registered or unregistered marks in domain names which violate the policy.[4192]	Only some coverage. Use in Roblox.[4193] 'If you are a trademark owner, or an agent of a trademark owner, and believe that any content on the Services infringes upon your registered trademark(s), please submit a trademark infringement notice …'[4194] 'Note that for the purpose of a trademark infringement report you must be the owner of a registered trademark or their agent, pending trademark applications are not sufficient.'[4195]	Only some coverage. Use in Meta/Facebook. 'That you do not own or have the necessary rights to share.'[4196]	Only some coverage. Use in Epic Games sites When complaining about others using a mark, a trademark registration number is required.[4197]

Digital Trademark and Trade Practices Model	*UDRP*	*Roblox*	*Meta Horizon Worlds*	*Epic Games*
Digital Bad Faith and Abuse	'Registration and use of a domain name in bad faith'[4198] (abuse is covered in overview).[4199]	Only some coverage. As referred to throughout the Roblox Terms, 'in appropriate circumstances, may terminate the Accounts of Users (or Creators) who Roblox determines, in its sole discretion, are repeat infringers as contemplated by the DMCA'.[4200] 'Repeat Infringer Policy … .(i) remove or disable access to content that Roblox knows to be infringing on the intellectual property rights of third parties or that has been identified in a valid DMCA notice submitted by a valid copyright owner or their agent; and, (ii) in appropriate circumstances, to suspend or terminate the Accounts of and block access to the Services by any User who repeatedly or egregiously infringes the copyrights or other intellectual property rights of third-parties'.[4201]	Only some coverage. 'We may also disable or delete your account if you repeatedly infringe other people's intellectual property rights'.[4202] 'in our discretion, that you have clearly, seriously or repeatedly breached our Terms or Policies, including in particular the Community Standards, we may suspend or permanently disable your access … may permanently disable or delete your account. We may also disable or delete your account if you repeatedly infringe other people's intellectual property rights or where	Only some coverage. 'Epic may also at its sole discretion limit access to the Services and/or update, transfer, suspend, or terminate the accounts of any users who infringe the intellectual property rights of others, whether or not there is any repeat infringement.'[4203]

			we are required to do so for legal reasons.'[4204]	
Digital Confusion	'Confusing similarity' in domain names.[4205]	Generally or not directly covered. 'Using a brand's logo or designs for the content you create without their permission'.[4206] 'Roblox may, in its sole discretion, suspend availability of or delete any UGC or other content on the Services at any time and for any period of time, including in perpetuity, without notice if such UGC or other content violates any laws or intellectual property rights or principles or any guidelines or policies associated with the Services … Roblox is and shall be under no obligation of any kind to Creator for suspending any UGC in accordance with this Section.'[4207]	Generally or not directly covered. 'That infringes or violates someone else's rights, including their intellectual property rights (such as by infringing another's … trademark, …).'[4208]	Generally or not directly covered. 'that the User Contributions are accurate and not fraudulent or deceptive; and that the User Contributions do not violate these Terms or the rights (intellectual property rights or otherwise) of any third party'.[4209] 'Respect IP Ownership – The content you create, publish, or use cannot infringe or violate someone else's rights, including their intellectual property rights (such as by infringing their copyright or trademark). You must own or have obtained the necessary rights to share and publish

Digital Trademark and Trade Practices Model	*UDRP*	*Roblox*	*Meta Horizon Worlds*	*Epic Games*
				the content, and any such license must be broad enough to grant Epic a license consistent with the Fortnite EULA and the UEFN Supplemental Terms'.[4210]
Digital Unfair Competition	Only some coverage. The Overview states that '[a]lso noting the availability of trademark-like protection under certain national legal doctrines (e.g., unfair competition or passing-off) and considerations of parity, where acquired distinctiveness/secondary meaning is demonstrated in a particular UDRP case, unregistered rights have been found to support standing to proceed with a UDRP case including where the complainant is based in a civil law jurisdiction'.[4215]	Generally or not directly covered.	Only some coverage. 'distributing or selling counterfeit or pirated goods'.[4211] 'That is unlawful, misleading, discriminatory or fraudulent (or assists someone else in using our Products in such a way)'.[4212]	Only some coverage. 'User Contributions must not be illegal, fraudulent, deceptive … infringing of intellectual property rights …'[4213] 'Don't impersonate other players, creators, streamers, celebrities, companies, brands, government officials, Epic employees, or anyone else. Pretending to be someone else in order to deceive or defraud others is not okay/'[4214]

	Unfair advantage considerations may fall under bad faith and abuse (*see* Overview).[4216] 'Distinctiveness' and 'secondary meaning' is recognised in Overview along with a list of factors that may be considered.[4217] 'Secondary meaning'[4218] is covered in the Overview. Overview also states that 'the strength of the complainant's mark may be considered relevant in evaluating the second and third elements'[4219] of the UDRP.			
Digital Terms, Policies, and Disclaimers	Only some coverage. Is itself a uniform policy addressing covered domain names. Disclaimers have been treated briefly in Overview. In cases 'where the respondent appears to otherwise have a right or legitimate interest in a disputed domain name, a clear and sufficiently prominent disclaimer would lend support to circumstances suggesting its good faith'.[4220]	Generally or not directly covered (disclaimers). Trademark-related policies are contained in various documents.	Generally or not directly covered (disclaimers). Trademark-related policies are contained in various documents.	Generally or not directly covered (disclaimers). Trademark-related policies are contained in various documents.

Digital Trademark and Trade Practices Model	*UDRP*	*Roblox*	*Meta Horizon Worlds*	*Epic Games*
Digital Jurisdictional and Territorial Considerations	Only some coverage. Changes to a domain name may be made based on court or arbitral tribunal of competent jurisdiction.[4221] Overview states that 'rules and principles of law'[4222] may be considered (this is discretionary); however, 'in its own terms UDRP jurisprudence generally would not require resort to particular national laws'.[4223] For example, guidance indicates that where 'the parties share a common nationality and the import of a specific national law concept is particularly germane to an issue in dispute, panels have applied national law principles in assessing the UDRP elements'.[4224] Otherwise, the UDRP applies regardless of where domain is registered or used.	Generally or not directly covered.	Generally or not directly covered.	Generally or not directly covered.

Digital Justification	Only some coverage. Using marks for 'legitimate noncommercial or fair use'[4225] is recognised as a method to demonstrate 'rights and legitimate interests'.[4226] Fair use and freedom of speech are also covered in the Overview.[4227]	Only some coverage. With permission[4228]	Generally or not directly covered. General reference.[4229] 'unless an exception or limitation applies under applicable law'.[4230]	Only some coverage. 'You must own or have obtained the necessary rights to share and publish the content, and any such license must be broad enough to grant Epic a license to display the content.'[4231]

4192. ICANN, 'Uniform Domain-Name Dispute-Resolution Policy' (*ICANN*, 25 February 2012) https://www.icann.org/resources/pages/policy-2012-02-25-en accessed June 2025; WIPO, 'WIPO Overview of WIPO Panel Views on Selected UDRP Questions, Third Edition' ('WIPO Jurisprudential Overview 3.0') (*WIPO*, 2017) https://www.wipo.int/amc/en/domains/search/overview3.0/ accessed June 2025.
4193. Roblox, 'Roblox Terms of Use' (*Roblox Legal Documents*) https://en.help.roblox.com/hc/en-us/articles/115004647846-Roblox-Terms-of-Use accessed June 2025.
4194. *Ibid.*
4195. *Ibid.*
4196. Facebook, 'Terms of Service' (*Facebook*) https://www.facebook.com/terms.php/ accessed June 2025.
4197. Epic Games, 'Reporting Intellectual Property Infringement' (*Epic Games*) https://www.epicgames.com/site/en-US/infringement accessed June 2025.
4198. UDRP, 4(b).
4199. ICANN, 'Uniform Domain-Name Dispute-Resolution Policy' (*ICANN*, 25 February 2012) https://www.icann.org/resources/pages/policy-2012-02-25-en accessed June 2025; WIPO, 'WIPO Overview of WIPO Panel Views on Selected UDRP Questions, Third Edition' ('WIPO Jurisprudential Overview 3.0') (*WIPO*, 2017) https://www.wipo.int/amc/en/domains/search/overview3.0/ accessed June 2025.
4200. Roblox, 'Roblox Terms of Use' (*Roblox Legal Documents*) https://en.help.roblox.com/hc/en-us/articles/115004647846-Roblox-Terms-of-Use accessed June 2025.
4201. *Ibid.*
4202. Facebook, 'Terms of Service' (*Facebook*) https://www.facebook.com/terms.php/ accessed June 2025.
4203. Epic Games, 'Terms of Service' (*Epic Games*) https://www.epicgames.com/site/en-US/tos accessed June 2025.
4204. *Ibid.*
4205. ICANN, 'Uniform Domain-Name Dispute-Resolution Policy' (*ICANN*, 25 February 2012) https://www.icann.org/resources/pages/policy-2012-02-25-en accessed June 2025.

4206. Roblox, 'Roblox Community Standards' (*Roblox Support*) https://en.help.roblox.com/hc/en-us/articles/203313410-Roblox-Community-Standards accessed June 2025.
4207. Roblox, 'Roblox Terms of Use' (*Roblox Legal Documents*) https://en.help.roblox.com/hc/en-us/articles/115004647846-Roblox-Terms-of-Use accessed June 2025.
4208. Facebook, 'Terms of Service' https://www.facebook.com/terms.php/ accessed June 2025.
4209. Epic Games, 'Terms of Service' (*Epic Games*) https://www.epicgames.com/site/en-US/tos accessed June 2025.
4210. Fortnite, 'The Fortnite Island Creator Rules' (*Fortnite*) https://www.fortnite.com/news/fortnite-island-creator-rules accessed June 2025.
4211. Facebook, 'Terms of Service' (*Facebook*) https://www.facebook.com/terms.php/ accessed June 2025.
4212. *Ibid*.
4213. Epic Games, 'Terms of Service' (*Epic Games*) https://www.epicgames.com/site/en-US/tos accessed June 2025.
4214. Fortnite, 'The Fortnite Island Creator Rules' (*Fortnite*) https://www.fortnite.com/news/fortnite-island-creator-rules accessed June 2025.
4215. WIPO, 'WIPO Overview of WIPO Panel Views on Selected UDRP Questions, Third Edition' ('WIPO Jurisprudential Overview 3.0') (*WIPO*, 2017) https://www.wipo.int/amc/en/domains/search/overview3.0/ accessed June 2025.
4216. *Ibid*.
4217. *Ibid*.
4218. *Ibid*.
4219. *Ibid*.
4220. WIPO, 'WIPO Overview of WIPO Panel Views on Selected UDRP Questions, Third Edition' ('WIPO Jurisprudential Overview 3.0') (*WIPO*, 2017) https://www.wipo.int/amc/en/domains/search/overview3.0/ accessed June 2025.
4221. ICANN, 'Uniform Domain-Name Dispute-Resolution Policy' (*ICANN*, 25 February 2012) https://www.icann.org/resources/pages/policy-2012-02-25-en accessed June 2025.
4222. WIPO, 'WIPO Overview of WIPO Panel Views on Selected UDRP Questions, Third Edition' ('WIPO Jurisprudential Overview 3.0') (*WIPO*, 2017) https://www.wipo.int/amc/en/domains/search/overview3.0/ accessed June 2025.
4223. *Ibid*.
4224. *Ibid*.
4225. ICANN, 'Uniform Domain-Name Dispute-Resolution Policy' (*ICANN*, 25 February 2012) https://www.icann.org/resources/pages/policy-2012-02-25-en accessed June 2025; WIPO, 'WIPO Overview of WIPO Panel Views on Selected UDRP Questions, Third Edition' ('WIPO Jurisprudential Overview 3.0') (*WIPO*, 2017) https://www.wipo.int/amc/en/domains/search/overview3.0/ accessed June 2025.
4226. *Ibid*.
4227. WIPO, 'WIPO Overview of WIPO Panel Views on Selected UDRP Questions, Third Edition' ('WIPO Jurisprudential Overview 3.0') (*WIPO*, 2017) https://www.wipo.int/amc/en/domains/search/overview3.0/ accessed June 2025.

4228. Roblox, 'Roblox Terms of Use' (*Roblox Legal Documents*) https://en.help.roblox.com/hc/en-us/articles/115004647846-Roblox-Terms-of-Use accessed June 2025; Roblox, 'Roblox Community Standards' (*Roblox Support*) https://en.help.roblox.com/hc/en-us/articles/203313410-Roblox-Community-Standards accessed June 2025.
4229. Facebook, 'Terms of Service' https://www.facebook.com/terms.php/ accessed June 2025.
4230. *Ibid.*
4231. Epic Games, 'Epic Games: Content Guidelines' (*Epic Games*) https://www.epicgames.com/site/en-US/content-guidelines accessed June 2025.

5.6.4.1 *Digital Use and Place of Use*

None of the Metaverse platforms adequately discuss use[4232] that relates to commerce or a good or service.[4233] They cover utilising marks within their services. Place of use[4234] is not adequately recognised either. Roblox requires ownership of a registered trademark[4235] and Epic Games requires a registration number when complaining about the use of a mark by another party.[4236]

5.6.4.2 *Digital Bad Faith and Abuse*

None of the Metaverse platforms mention 'bad faith'.[4237] In terms of abuse, Roblox and Epic Games have a repeat infringer policies or references.[4238] Meta mentions repeat infringer but reserves the right to disable or delete regardless of whether repeat infringement was present.[4239]

5.6.4.3 *Digital Confusion*

None of the Metaverse platforms directly state confusion;[4240] however, all have a general infringement provision. Confusion should be directly and clearly incorporated.

4232. TRIPS, Art. 16; EUTMR, Art. 18; 15 U.S. Code § 1127; UK Trade Marks Act 1994, s. 46(1)(a); Canadian Trademarks Act R.S.C., 1985, c. T-13, s. 2.
4233. *Ibid.*
4234. Epic Games, 'Reporting Intellectual Property Infringement' (*Epic Games*) https://www.epicgames.com/site/en-US/infringement accessed June 2025.
4235. Roblox, 'Roblox Terms of Use' (*Roblox Legal Documents*) https://en.help.roblox.com/hc/en-us/articles/115004647846-Roblox-Terms-of-Use accessed June 2025.
4236. Epic Games, 'Reporting Intellectual Property Infringement' (*Epic Games*) https://www.epicgames.com/site/en-US/infringement accessed June 2025.
4237. *Ibid.*
4238. Roblox, 'Roblox Terms of Use' (*Roblox Legal Documents*) https://en.help.roblox.com/hc/en-us/articles/115004647846-Roblox-Terms-of-Use accessed June 2025; Roblox, 'Roblox Community Standards' (*Roblox Support*) https://en.help.roblox.com/hc/en-us/articles/203313410-Roblox-Community-Standards accessed June 2025; Epic Games, 'Terms of Service' (*Epic Games*) https://www.epicgames.com/site/en-US/tos accessed June 2025; Fortnite, 'Unreal Editor for Fortnite Supplemental Terms to the EULA' (*Fortnite*) https://www.fortnite.com/unreal-editor-for-fortnite-supplemental-terms accessed June 2025; Fortnite, 'The Fortnite Island Creator Rules' (*Fortnite*) https://www.fortnite.com/news/fortnite-island-creator-rules accessed June 2025.
4239. Facebook, 'Terms of Service' https://www.facebook.com/terms.php/ accessed July 2024.
4240. Paris Convention, Art. 6bis; TRIPS, Art. 16(1); EUTMR, Art. 8(1)(b) and Art. 9(2)(b); 15 U.S. Code § 1114;15 U.S. Code § 1125.

5.6.4.4 *Digital Unfair Competition*

Unfair competition,[4241] acts,[4242] or practices[4243] and related areas are not directly mentioned in these Metaverse platform policies. Meta Horizon Worlds prohibits 'distributing or selling counterfeit or pirated goods'[4244] or those which are 'misleading'[4245] or 'fraudulent',[4246] while Epic Games covers 'fraudulent or deceptive'[4247] as well as 'impersonation'[4248] and '[p]retending to be someone else in order to deceive or defraud others ...'.[4249] While some concepts are present, Metaverse platforms should consider relevant concepts under this head within their platforms and incorporate these fully and directly.

5.6.4.5 *Digital Terms, Policies, and Disclaimers*

While each has terms related to trademarks in various documents, these are limited in many ways, not consolidated, and should incorporate needed areas. Disclaimers[4250] are not mentioned or covered.

4241. Anselm Kamperman Sanders, *Unfair Competition Law: The Protection of Intellectual and Industrial Creativity* (Oxford University Press, 1997) 8; Frauke Henning-Bodewig, *Unfair Competition Law European Union and Member States* (Kluwer Law International 2006) xv-xvi; Martin Senftleben, Michael Handler and Irene Calboli, 'Protection Against Unfair Competition Around the Globe' (2024) 19 Journal of Intellectual Property Law & Practice 79, 79-80 https://doi.org/10.1093/jiplp/jpad121; Paris Convention, Art. 10bis; EUTMR, Art. 9(2)(c); 15 U.S.C. § 1125(c)(2)(B).
4242. *Ibid.*
4243. *Ibid.*
4244. Facebook, 'Terms of Service' https://www.facebook.com/terms.php/ accessed June 2025.
4245. *Ibid.*
4246. *Ibid.*
4247. Epic Games, 'Terms of Service' (*Epic Games*) https://www.epicgames.com/site/en-US/tos accessed June 2025.
4248. Fortnite, 'The Fortnite Island Creator Rules' (*Fortnite*) https://www.fortnite.com/news/fortnite-island-creator-rules accessed June 2025.
4249. *Ibid.*
4250. WIPO, 'WIPO Overview of WIPO Panel Views on Selected UDRP Questions, Third Edition' ('WIPO Jurisprudential Overview 3.0') (*WIPO*, 2017) https://www.wipo.int/amc/en/domains/search/overview3.0/ accessed June 2025; Alexander Peukert, 'The Coexistence of Trade Mark Laws and Rights on the Internet, and the Impact of Geolocation Technologies' (2016) 47 International Review of Intellectual Property and Competition Law 60, 81 https://doi.org/10.1007/s40319-015-0427-8; Leslie Fair, 'Full Disclosure' (*FTC Business Blog*, 23 September 2014) https://www.ftc.gov/business-guidance/blog/2014/09/full-disclosure accessed June 2025.

5.6.4.6 *Digital Jurisdictional and Territorial Considerations*

This element is not adequately covered by Metaverse platforms. They should consider the impact of this and how trademark issues will be resolved accordingly. Co-existence[4251] is not identified.

5.6.4.7 *Digital Justification*

Justification is covered on a very limited basis. For Roblox, getting permission[4252] appears to be the standard adopted. Meta Horizon Worlds makes a general reference and broadly refers to 'unless an exception or limitation applies under applicable law'.[4253] Epic Games says '[y]ou must own or have obtained the necessary rights to share and publish the content, and any such license must be broad enough to grant Epic a license to display the content'.[4254] Metaverse platforms should further incorporate specific justifications that may be availed of such as those based on common principles.[4255]

It appears that Metaverse platforms lack the detail and specificity in terms and policies for trademarks on their platforms. There appear to be glaring gaps that should be filled.

5.6.5 Solution: A Uniform Policy for Trademarks in Metaverse Platforms

As seen from the above, Metaverse platforms need to adopt policies that cover the necessary ground. Like other platforms, a uniform policy[4256] would benefit Metaverse

4251. EUIPO, '3.1 Coexistence Between the Marks Involved in the Opposition' (*EUIPO Trade mark Guidelines*) https://guidelines.euipo.europa.eu/2058843/2043906/trade-mark-guidelines/3-1-coexistence-between-the-marks-involved-in-the-opposition accessed January 2024;15 U.S. Code § 1052(d); Alexander Peukert, 'The Coexistence of Trade Mark Laws and Rights on the Internet, and the Impact of Geolocation Technologies' (2016) 47 International Review of Intellectual Property and Competition Law 60, 81 https://doi.org/10.1007/s40319-015-0427-8; Tamara Nanayakkara, 'IP and Business: Trademark Coexistence' (*WIPO*, November 2006) https://www.wipo.int/wipo_magazine/en/2006/06/article_0007.html accessed June 2025.
4252. Roblox, 'Roblox Terms of Use' (*Roblox Legal Documents*) https://en.help.roblox.com/hc/en-us/articles/115004647846-Roblox-Terms-of-Use accessed July 2024; Roblox, 'Roblox Community Standards' (*Roblox Support*) https://en.help.roblox.com/hc/en-us/articles/203313410-Roblox-Community-Standards accessed July 2024.
4253. Facebook, 'Terms of Service' (*Facebook*) https://www.facebook.com/terms.php/ accessed July 2024.
4254. Epic Games, 'Epic Games: Content Guidelines' (*Epic Games*) https://www.epicgames.com/site/en-US/content-guidelines accessed June 2025.
4255. ICANN, 'Uniform Domain-Name Dispute-Resolution Policy' (*ICANN*, 25 February 2012) https://www.icann.org/resources/pages/policy-2012-02-25-en accessed June 2025; WIPO, 'WIPO Overview of WIPO Panel Views on Selected UDRP Questions, Third Edition' ('WIPO Jurisprudential Overview 3.0') (*WIPO*, 2017) https://www.wipo.int/amc/en/domains/search/overview3.0/ accessed June 2025.
4256. ICANN, 'Uniform Domain-Name Dispute-Resolution Policy' (*ICANN*, 25 February 2012) https://www.icann.org/resources/pages/policy-2012-02-25-en accessed June 2025; Rajeev Sachdev, 'Towards an Improved Framework for Trade-Mark Law and Regulation in Social

platforms by allowing for enhanced consistency, more legal certainly, and reduced costs.

The text of the uniform policy for Metaverse platforms as recommended based upon the platform's own adoption and with making their own decisions is as follows.

Table 5.14 Uniform Metaverse Trademark Dispute Resolution Policy (UMTDRP)

Uniform Metaverse Trademark Dispute Resolution Policy (UMTDRP)	Adapted or directly from the UDRP[4257] and UDNDRP (Chapter 4). The name reflects specifically the platform type and subject matter.
(1) *Purpose.* This Uniform Metaverse Trademark Dispute Resolution Policy ('Policy') has been adopted by [Metaverse Platform] ('Platform' or 'We'), is incorporated by reference into the Terms of Use of Platform and your Metaverse Account or Creator Agreement, and sets forth the terms and conditions in connection with a dispute between you and any party other than Platform over the utilisation of a trademark in Platform. Decisions under Paragraph 4 of this Policy will be made in accordance with the Policy. Guidelines to this policy are set forth in the document entitled: Guidelines to the UMTDRP.	Adapted or directly from the UDRP[4258] and UDNDRP (Chapter 4) and Roblox, Meta Horizon World, and Epic Games terms and policies.[4259] The policy refers to any disputed utilisation of a mark within the platforms. Guidelines should make clear that utilisation of a trademark includes all areas of the Metaverse, including but not limited to avatars, characters, experiences, content, advertising, products, NFTs, services, displays, posts, discussions, or any other aspect in the Metaverse.

Media Usernames: A Study of the Canadian, U.S., and U.K. Positions' (2016) 28 Intellectual Property Journal 379, 379-418; Daniel Doft, 'Facebook, Twitter, and the Wild West of IP Enforcement on Social Media: Weighing the Merits of a Uniform Dispute Resolution Policy' (2016) 49 The John Marshall Law Review 959; Thomas J Curtin, 'The Name Game: Cybersquatting and Trademark Infringement on Social Media Websites' (2010-2011) 19 Journal of Law and Policy 353; Erick J Heels, 'How to Twittersquat the Top 100 Brands' (*GiantPeople*, 8 January 2009) http://www.giantpeople.com/1298.html accessed 4 August 2025; Paul D McGrady, *McGrady on Social Media: 2018* (Lexis Nexis 2018) §9; John McElwaine and Christopher D Casavale, 'Tackling Bad Faith Registration of Domain Names in a Fast-Changing Landscape' (*WIPO Magazine*, December 2019) https://www.wipo.int/wipo_magazine/en/2019/06/article_0006.html accessed June 2025; Edward C Anderson and Timothy S Cole, 'The UDRP: A Model for Dispute Resolution in E-Commerce' (2002) 6 Journal of Small & Emerging Business Law 235.

4257. ICANN, 'Uniform Domain-Name Dispute-Resolution Policy' (*ICANN*, 25 February 2012) https://www.icann.org/resources/pages/policy-2012-02-25-en accessed June 2025.

4258. *Ibid.*

4259. Roblox, 'Roblox Terms of Use' (*Roblox Legal Documents*) https://en.help.roblox.com/hc/en-us/articles/115004647846-Roblox-Terms-of-Use accessed June 2025; Facebook, 'Terms of Service' https://www.facebook.com/terms.php/ accessed June 2025; Epic Games, 'Terms of

(2) *Your Representations.* By registering an account or creating on Platform, you hereby represent and warrant to us that: (a) the statements that you made in your Metaverse Account or Creator Agreement are complete and accurate; (b) to your knowledge, your account, content and/or experience will not infringe upon or otherwise violate the rights of any third party; (c) you are not registering the account or creating for an unlawful purpose; and (d) you will not knowingly use Platform in violation of any applicable laws or regulations. It is your responsibility to determine whether your account, content and/or experience infringes or violates someone else's rights.	Adapted or directly from the UDRP[4260] and UDNRDP (Chapter 4).
(3) *Changes, Suspensions, and Cancellations.* We will make changes to, suspend, or cancel your account, content, and/or experience on Platform under the following circumstances: (i) our receipt of written or appropriate electronic instructions from you or your authorized agent to take such action except that you may not transfer your account or creations to another holder: (a) during a pending administrative proceeding brought pursuant to Paragraph 4 or for a period of fifteen (15) business days after such proceeding is concluded; or (b) during a pending court proceeding or arbitration commenced regarding your account, content, and/or experience or their content unless the court or party to whom the	Adapted or directly from the UDRP[4261] and UDNDRP (Chapter 4). Updated based on services. Added that 'abuse'[4262] can result

Service' (*Epic Games*) https://www.epicgames.com/site/en-US/tos accessed June 2025; Fortnite, 'Unreal Editor for Fortnite Supplemental Terms to the EULA' (*Fortnite*) https://www.fortnite.com/unreal-editor-for-fortnite-supplemental-terms accessed June 2025; Fortnite, 'Fortnite End User License Agreement' (*Fortnite*) https://www.fortnite.com/eula accessed June 2025; Fortnite, 'The Fortnite Island Creator Rules' (*Fortnite*) https://www.fortnite.com/news/fortnite-island-creator-rules accessed June 2025; Epic Games, 'Epic Games: Content Guidelines' (*Epic Games*) https://www.epicgames.com/site/en-US/content-guidelines# accessed June 2025; Epic Games, 'Epic Games Community Rules' (*Epic Games*) https://www.epicgames.com/site/en-US/community-rules accessed June 2025; Epic Games, 'Terms of Service' (*Epic Games*) https://www.epicgames.com/site/en-US/tos accessed June 2025.

4260. ICANN, 'Uniform Domain-Name Dispute-Resolution Policy' (*ICANN*, 25 February 2012) https://www.icann.org/resources/pages/policy-2012-02-25-en accessed June 2025.

4261. *Ibid.*

4262. WIPO, 'WIPO Overview of WIPO Panel Views on Selected UDRP Questions, Third Edition' ('WIPO Jurisprudential Overview 3.0') (*WIPO*, 2017) https://www.wipo.int/amc/en/domains/search/overview3.0/ accessed June 2025.

account is being transferred agrees, in writing, to be bound by the decision of the court or arbitrator. We reserve the right not to permit the transfer of your account or creations to another party in accordance with this subparagraph; (ii) our receipt of an order from a court or arbitral tribunal, in each case of competent jurisdiction, requiring such action; (iii) our decision requiring such action based on a complaint received under this or a later version of this Policy; and/or (iv) in accordance with the terms of your Metaverse Account or Creator Agreement (such as but not limited to where you have engaged in abuse with respect to one or more trademarks) or other legal requirements.	in a change, suspension or cancellation and guidelines can be used to clarify when certain actions may take place.
(4) *Mandatory Decision Process and Remedies*. This Paragraph sets forth the type of disputes for which you are required to submit to a Mandatory Decision Process. A decision on a complaint lodged under this Policy will be made by an appointed Panel: (a) Applicable Disputes. You are required to submit to a decision by in the event that a third party (a 'complainant') asserts to Platform, through a Trademark Complaint Form < URL for Form > that your account, content, and/or experience or their content:	Adapted or directly from the UDRP,[4263] UDNDRP (Chapter 4), Paris Convention, TRIPS, Dispute Resolution Service for.eu,[4264] EUTMR, Lanham Act 1946 15 U.S. Code §§ 1051 et seq. (as amended), the TDRA 2006 15 U.S. Code § 1125(c), Roblox, Meta Horizon World, Epic Games terms and policies.[4265]

4263. Paris Convention 1967, Art. 6bis; ICANN, 'Uniform Domain-Name Dispute-Resolution Policy' (*ICANN*, 25 February 2012) https://www.icann.org/resources/pages/policy-2012-02-25-en; 15 U.S. Code § 1125(d).

4264. WIPO, 'WIPO Domain Name Dispute Resolution Service for .EU (and.ею and.ευ)' (*WIPO*) https://www.wipo.int/amc/en/domains/cctld/eu/index.html accessed July 2024.

4265. Roblox, 'Roblox Terms of Use' (*Roblox Legal Documents*) https://en.help.roblox.com/hc/en-us/articles/115004647846-Roblox-Terms-of-Use accessed June 2025; Facebook, 'Terms of Service' https://www.facebook.com/terms.php/ accessed June 2025; Epic Games, 'Terms of Service' (*Epic Games*) https://www.epicgames.com/site/en-US/tos accessed June 2025; Fortnite, 'Unreal Editor for Fortnite Supplemental Terms to the EULA' (*Fortnite*) https://www.fortnite.com/unreal-editor-for-fortnite-supplemental-terms accessed June 2025; Fortnite, 'Fortnite End User License Agreement' (*Fortnite*) https://www.fortnite.com/eula accessed June 2025; Fortnite, 'The Fortnite Island Creator Rules' (*Fortnite*) https://www.fortnite.com/news/fortnite-island-creator-rules accessed June 2025; Epic Games, 'Epic Games: Content Guidelines' (*Epic Games*) https://www.epicgames.com/site/en-US/content-guidelines# accessed June 2025; Epic Games, 'Epic Games Community Rules' (*Epic Games*) https://www.epicgames.com/site/en-US/community-rules accessed June 2025; Epic Games, 'Terms of Service' (*Epic Games*) https://www.epicgames.com/site/en-US/tos accessed June 2025.

(A) is identical or confusingly similar to trademarks in which a complainant has rights and which you are using on an unauthorised basis in the course of trade AND (B) (i) is being used to engage in unfair competition in the course of trade with respect to a trademark OR (ii) is being used in bad faith or is being abused with respect to a trademark. For clarity, in the administrative proceeding, the complainant must prove element A AND one element from B (either i or ii) are present. Where abuse is found, a registrant or creator may be suspended for a period of one year in the first instance and a longer period or permanent ban in a single egregious circumstance or in further instances. (b) Permitted use. Trademarks will be permitted if you demonstrate that you have rights or legitimate interests in respect of the account, content, and/or experience or their content by showing one or more of these justifications: (i) you (as an individual, business, or other organization) have been commonly known by the term and are using it legitimately, (ii) you are making genuine noncommercial legitimate fair use of the trademark, (iii) you are fairly utilising the trademark in marketing of authorized, replacement, compatible or used goods or services, (iv) you are utilising the trademark in an ordinary dictionary sense, (v) you are genuinely and noncommercially utilising the trademark under freedom of speech and expression or legitimate criticism, parody, or review of the company, good or service associated with the trademark, OR (vi) you are making fair and legitimate use of the trademark in comparative advertising.	Key UDRP aspects have been retained including relevant concepts from the Overview.[4266] This uniform policy largely follows the UDNDRP (Chapter 4) but is adapted for Metaverse platforms. Please see Chapter 4 (section 4.3.3) for further details and explanations of the adaptations under the model. Interpretation of this Paragraph should be set out in the Guidance.

4266. ICANN, 'Uniform Domain-Name Dispute-Resolution Policy' (*ICANN*, 25 February 2012) https://www.icann.org/resources/pages/policy-2012-02-25-en accessed June 2025; WIPO, 'WIPO Overview of WIPO Panel Views on Selected UDRP Questions, Third Edition' ('WIPO Jurisprudential Overview 3.0') (*WIPO*, 2017) https://www.wipo.int/amc/en/domains/search/overview3.0/ accessed June 2025.

(c) Remedies. The remedies available to a complainant pursuant to any decision by Platform shall be limited to requiring the cancellation of, suspending, or making changes to your account, content, and/or experience. (d) All Other Disputes. All other disputes between you and any party other than Platform regarding your account, content, and/or experience in Platform that are not brought pursuant to this Policy will not be resolved through a Panel Decision. Platform reserves the right to make a decision on any matter outside of this policy as set forth in our Terms of Use available at <terms> including any remedies or actions it, in its sole discretion, deems appropriate.	
(5) *Procedures.* (a) Initiation of Proceeding. Submitting a Trade mark Complaint Form initiates the process for a decision by Platform. (b) Consolidation. In the event of multiple disputes between you and a complainant, either you or the complainant may request to consolidate the disputes for a single decision. This petition shall be made to the Panel appointed to hear a pending dispute between the parties. This Panel may consolidate before it any or all such disputes in its sole discretion, provided that the disputes being consolidated are governed by this Policy or a later version of this Policy. (c) Fees. No fees are charged to file a complaint under this Policy or to receive a decision by Platform. (d) Availability of Court Proceedings. The Mandatory Decision Process requirements set forth in Paragraph 4 shall not prevent either you or the complainant from submitting the dispute to a court of competent jurisdiction for independent resolution before	Adapted or directly from the UDRP[4267] and UDNDRP (Chapter 4). Because platforms currently expend their own resources to make decisions on complaints they receive, these resources may be redirected to an online panel decision under the assumption that this will not raise costs by unreasonable sums. Platforms may wish to include an indemnification provision here.

4267. ICANN, 'Uniform Domain-Name Dispute-Resolution Policy' (ICANN, 25 February 2012) https://www.icann.org/resources/pages/policy-2012-02-25-en accessed June 2025.

such Mandatory Decision Process is commenced or after it is concluded. If we decide that your account, content and/or experience should be cancelled, suspended, or changed, we will then implement the decision immediately unless we have received from you official documentation (such as a copy of a complaint, file-stamped by the clerk of the court) that you have commenced a lawsuit against the complainant in an appropriate jurisdiction. If we receive such documentation immediately following a decision, we will not implement the decision, and we will take no further action, until we receive: (i) evidence satisfactory to us of a resolution between the parties; (ii) evidence satisfactory to us that your lawsuit has been dismissed or withdrawn; or (iii) a copy of an order from such court dismissing your lawsuit or ordering that you do not have the right to continue the account, content, and/or experience.	
(6) *Policy Modifications*. Platform reserves the right to modify this Policy at any time. Platform will post any revised Policy at <URL> at least thirty (30) calendar days before it becomes effective. Unless this Policy has already been invoked by the submission of a Trade mark Complaint Form, in which event the version of the Policy in effect at the time it was invoked will apply to you until the dispute is over, all such changes will be binding upon you with respect to any account, content, and/or experience trademark dispute, whether the dispute arose before, on or after the effective date of our change. In the event that you object to a change in this Policy, your sole remedy is to cancel your Account with us, provided that you will not be entitled to a refund of any fees you paid to us. The revised Policy will apply to you until you cancel your Account.	Adapted or directly from UDRP[4268] and UDNDRP (Chapter 4).

This unform policy covers many areas related to the problems identified. It is anticipated, as in the case of other platforms that many Metaverse platforms could adopt this policy. This is expected to enhance the limited terms and policies of Metaverse platforms under this study and the gaps that these raise. Likewise, consistency may be encouraged, legal certainly can be enhanced, and costs may be reduced.

4268. *Ibid.*

The text of the uniform policy for Metaverse platforms as recommended based upon a panel approach is as follows.

Table 5.15 Uniform Metaverse Trademark Dispute Resolution Policy (UMTDRP)

Uniform Metaverse Trademark Dispute Resolution Policy (UMTDRP)	Adapted or directly from the UDRP[4269] and UDNDRP (Chapter 4). The name reflects specifically the platform type and subject matter.
(1) *Purpose.* This Uniform Metaverse Trademark Dispute Resolution Policy ('Policy') has been adopted by [Metaverse Platform] ('Platform' or 'We'), is incorporated by reference into the Terms of Use of Platform and your Metaverse Account or Creator Agreement, and sets forth the terms and conditions in connection with a dispute between you and any party other than Platform over the utilisation of a trademark in Platform. Decisions under Paragraph 4 of this Policy will be made in accordance with the Policy. Guidelines to this policy are set forth in the document entitled: Guidelines to the UMTDRP.	Adapted or directly from the UDRP[4270] and UDNDRP (Chapter 4) and Roblox, Meta Horizon World, and Epic Games terms and policies.[4271] The policy refers to any disputed utilisation of a mark within the platforms. Guidelines should make clear that utilisation of a trademark includes in all areas of the Metaverse including but not limited to avatars, characters, experiences, content, advertising, products, NFT's, services, displays, posts, discussions, or any other aspect in the Metaverse.

4269. *Ibid.*
4270. *Ibid.*
4271. Roblox, 'Roblox Terms of Use' (*Roblox Legal Documents*) https://en.help.roblox.com/hc/en-us/articles/115004647846-Roblox-Terms-of-Use accessed June 2025; Facebook, 'Terms of Service' https://www.facebook.com/terms.php/ accessed June 2025; Epic Games, 'Terms of Service' (*Epic Games*) https://www.epicgames.com/site/en-US/tos accessed June 0225; Fortnite, 'Unreal Editor for Fortnite Supplemental Terms to the EULA' (*Fortnite*) https://www.fortnite.com/unreal-editor-for-fortnite-supplemental-terms accessed June 2025; Fortnite, 'Fortnite End User License Agreement' (*Fortnite*) https://www.fortnite.com/eula accessed June 2025; Fortnite, 'The Fortnite Island Creator Rules' (*Fortnite*) https://www.fortnite.com/news/fortnite-island-creator-rules accessed June 2025; Epic Games, 'Epic Games: Content Guidelines' (*Epic Games*) https://www.epicgames.com/site/en-US/content-guidelines# accessed June 2025; Epic Games, 'Epic Games Community Rules' (*Epic Games*) https://www.epicgames.com/site/en-US/community-rules accessed June 2025; Epic Games, 'Terms of Service' (*Epic Games*) https://www.epicgames.com/site/en-US/tos accessed June 2025.

(2) *Your Representations*. By registering an account or creating on Platform, you hereby represent and warrant to us that: (a) the statements that you made in your Metaverse Account or Creator Agreement are complete and accurate; (b) to your knowledge, your account, content and/or experience will not infringe upon or otherwise violate the rights of any third party; (c) you are not registering the account or creating for an unlawful purpose; and (d) you will not knowingly use Platform in violation of any applicable laws or regulations. It is your responsibility to determine whether your account, content and/or experience infringes or violates someone else's rights.	Adapted or directly from the UDRP[4272] and UDNRDP (Chapter 4).
(3) *Changes, Suspensions, and Cancellations*. We will make changes to, suspend, or cancel your account, content, and/or experience on Platform under the following circumstances: (i) our receipt of written or appropriate electronic instructions from you or your authorised agent to take such action except that you may not transfer your account or creations to another holder: (a) during a pending administrative proceeding brought pursuant to Paragraph 4 or for a period of fifteen (15) business days after such proceeding is concluded; or (b) during a pending court proceeding or arbitration commenced regarding your account, content, and/or experience or their content unless the court or party to whom the account is being transferred agrees, in writing, to be bound by the decision of the court or arbitrator. We reserve the right not to permit the transfer of your account or creations to another party in accordance with this subparagraph; (ii) our receipt of an order from a court or arbitral tribunal, in each case of competent jurisdiction, requiring such action;	Adapted or directly from the UDRP[4273] and UDNDRP. Updated based on services. Added that 'abuse'[4274] can result

4272. ICANN, 'Uniform Domain-Name Dispute-Resolution Policy' (*ICANN*, 25 February 2012) https://www.icann.org/resources/pages/policy-2012-02-25-en accessed June 2025.
4273. *Ibid.*
4274. WIPO, 'WIPO Overview of WIPO Panel Views on Selected UDRP Questions, Third Edition' ('WIPO Jurisprudential Overview 3.0') (*WIPO*, 2017) https://www.wipo.int/amc/en/domains/search/overview3.0/ accessed June 2025.

(iii) a panel decision requiring such action based on a complaint received under this or a later version of this Policy; and/or (iv) in accordance with the terms of your Metaverse Account or Creator Agreement (such as but not limited to where you have engaged in abuse with respect to one or more trademarks) or other legal requirements.	in a change, suspension or cancellation and guidelines can be used to clarify when certain actions may take place.
(4) *Mandatory Administrative Proceeding and Remedies*. This Paragraph sets forth the type of disputes for which you are required to submit to a mandatory Panel Decision. A decision on a complaint lodged under this Policy will be made by an appointed Panel: (a) Applicable Disputes. You are required to submit to a Panel Decision in the event that a third party (a 'complainant') asserts to Platform, through a Trademark Complaint Form < URL for Form > that your account, content, and/or experience or their content: (A) is identical or confusingly similar to trademarks in which a complainant has rights and which you are using on an unauthorised basis in the course of trade AND (B) (i) is being used to engage in unfair competition in the course of trade with respect to a trademark OR (ii) is being used in bad faith or is being abused with respect to a trademark. For clarity, in the administrative proceeding, the complainant must prove element A AND one element from B (either i or ii) are present. Where abuse is found, a registrant or creator may be suspended for a period of one year in the first instance and a longer period or permanent ban in a single egregious circumstance or in further instances.	Adapted or directly from the UDRP,[4275] UDNDRP (Chapter 4), Paris Convention, TRIPS, Dispute Resolution Service for .eu,[4276] EUTMR, Lanham Act 1946 15 U.S. Code §§ 1051 et seq. (as amended), the TDRA 2006 15 U.S. Code § 1125(c), Roblox, Meta Horizon World, Epic Games terms and policies.[4277]

4275. ICANN, 'Uniform Domain-Name Dispute-Resolution Policy' (ICANN, 25 February 2012) https://www.icann.org/resources/pages/policy-2012-02-25-en accessed June 2025.
4276. WIPO, 'WIPO Domain Name Dispute Resolution Service for .EU (and.ею and.ευ)' (*WIPO*) https://www.wipo.int/amc/en/domains/cctld/eu/index.html accessed July 2024.
4277. Roblox, 'Roblox Terms of Use' (*Roblox Legal Documents*) https://en.help.roblox.com/hc/en-us/articles/115004647846-Roblox-Terms-of-Use accessed June 2025; Facebook, 'Terms of

(b) Permitted use. Trademarks will be permitted if you demonstrate that you have rights or legitimate interests in respect of the account, content, and/or experience or their content by showing one or more of these justifications: (i) you (as an individual, business, or other organization) have been commonly known by the term and are using it legitimately, (ii) you are making genuine noncommercial legitimate fair use of the trademark, (iii) you are fairly utilising the trademark in marketing of authorized, replacement, compatible or used goods or services, (iv) you are utilising the trademark in an ordinary dictionary sense, (v) you are genuinely and noncommercially utilising the trademark under freedom of speech and expression or legitimate criticism, parody, or review of the company, good or service associated with the trademark, OR (vi) you are making fair and legitimate use of the trademark in comparative advertising. (c) Remedies. The remedies available to a complainant pursuant to any Panel Decision shall be limited to requiring the cancellation of, suspending, or making changes to your account, content, and/or experience.	Key UDRP aspects have been retained including relevant concepts from the Overview.[4278] This uniform policy largely follows the UDNDRP (Chapter 4) but is adapted for Metaverse platforms. Please see Chapter 4 (section 4.3.3) for further details and explanations of the adaptations under the model. Interpretation of this Paragraph should be set out in the Guidance.

Service' https://www.facebook.com/terms.php/ accessed June 2025; Epic Games, 'Terms of Service' (*Epic Games*) https://www.epicgames.com/site/en-US/tos accessed June 2025; Fortnite, 'Unreal Editor for Fortnite Supplemental Terms to the EULA' (*Fortnite*) https://www.fortnite.com/unreal-editor-for-fortnite-supplemental-terms accessed June 2025; Fortnite, 'Fortnite End User License Agreement' (*Fortnite*) https://www.fortnite.com/eula accessed June 2025; Fortnite, 'The Fortnite Island Creator Rules' (*Fortnite*) https://www.fortnite.com/news/fortnite-island-creator-rules accessed June 2025; Epic Games, 'Epic Games: Content Guidelines' (*Epic Games*) https://www.epicgames.com/site/en-US/content-guidelines# accessed June 2025; Epic Games, 'Epic Games Community Rules' (*Epic Games*) https://www.epicgames.com/site/en-US/community-rules accessed June 2025; Epic Games, 'Terms of Service' (*Epic Games*) https://www.epicgames.com/site/en-US/tos accessed June 2025.

4278. ICANN, 'Uniform Domain-Name Dispute-Resolution Policy' (*ICANN*, 25 February 2012) https://www.icann.org/resources/pages/policy-2012-02-25-en accessed June 2025; WIPO, 'WIPO Overview of WIPO Panel Views on Selected UDRP Questions, Third Edition' ('WIPO Jurisprudential Overview 3.0') (*WIPO*, 2017) https://www.wipo.int/amc/en/domains/search/overview3.0/ accessed June 2025.

(d) All Other Disputes. All other disputes between you and any party other than Platform regarding your account, content, and/or experience in Platform that are not brought pursuant to this Policy will not be resolved through a Panel Decision. Platform reserves the right to make a decision on any matter outside of this policy as set forth in our Terms of Use available at <terms> including any remedies or actions it, in its sole discretion, deems appropriate.

(5) *Procedures.*

(a) Initiation of Proceeding. Submitting a Trademark Complaint Form initiates the process for a Panel Decision.

(b) Consolidation. In the event of multiple disputes between you and a complainant, either you or the complainant may petition to consolidate the disputes before a single Panel. This petition shall be made to the Panel appointed to hear a pending dispute between the parties. This Panel may consolidate before it any or all such disputes in its sole discretion, provided that the disputes being consolidated are governed by this Policy or a later version of this Policy.

(c) Fees. No fees are charged to file a complaint under this Policy or to receive a Panel Decision.

(d) Availability of Court Proceedings. The Panel Decision proceeding requirements set forth in Paragraph 4 shall not prevent either you or the complainant from submitting the dispute to a court of competent jurisdiction for independent resolution before such Panel Decision is commenced or after such proceeding is concluded. If a Panel decides that your account, content and/or experience should be cancelled, suspended, or changed, we will then implement the decision immediately unless we have received from you official documentation

Adapted or directly from the UDRP[4279] and UDNDRP (Chapter 4).

Because platforms currently expend their own resources to make decisions on complaints they receive, these resources may be redirected to an online panel decision under the assumption that this will not raise costs by unreasonable sums.

Platforms may wish to include an indemnification provision here.

4279. ICANN, 'Uniform Domain-Name Dispute-Resolution Policy' (*ICANN*, 25 February 2012) https://www.icann.org/resources/pages/policy-2012-02-25-en accessed June 2025.

(such as a copy of a complaint, file-stamped by the clerk of the court) that you have commenced a lawsuit against the complainant in an appropriate jurisdiction. If we receive such documentation immediately following a decision, we will not implement the Panel's decision, and we will take no further action, until we receive: (i) evidence satisfactory to us of a resolution between the parties; (ii) evidence satisfactory to us that your lawsuit has been dismissed or withdrawn; or (iii) a copy of an order from such court dismissing your lawsuit or ordering that you do not have the right to continue the account, content, and/or experience.	
(6) *Policy Modifications*. Platform reserves the right to modify this Policy at any time. Platform will post any revised Policy at <URL> at least thirty (30) calendar days before it becomes effective. Unless this Policy has already been invoked by the submission of a Trade mark Complaint Form, in which event the version of the Policy in effect at the time it was invoked will apply to you until the dispute is over, all such changes will be binding upon you with respect to any account, content, and/or experience trademark dispute, whether the dispute arose before, on or after the effective date of our change. In the event that you object to a change in this Policy, your sole remedy is to cancel your Account with us, provided that you will not be entitled to a refund of any fees you paid to us. The revised Policy will apply to you until you cancel your Account.	Adapted or directly from UDRP[4280] and UDNDRP (Chapter 4).

5.7 CONCLUSION

This chapter provided recommendations for platform trademark policies in light of the UDRP, recommendations for the UDRP, and the Digital Trademark and Trade Practices Model.

As was seen, there is great inconsistency among platforms of a specific type, and generally across various platform types, relating to trademark terms and policies. The initial tables in each section summarised the gaps vis-à-vis the Digital Trademark and Trade Practices Model. While there is some detailed coverage for some areas by some of the platforms, there are many areas for improvement and consistency. And while no

4280. *Ibid.*

two platforms, even two of the same kinds of platforms, are the same, and each may raise different issues, there are strong similarities relating to the issues that trademarks raise in all platform categories and platforms generally. Peculiarities between platforms can be adequately covered in Guidelines to the policies that can fill the necessary gaps. Further, while general terms and conditions may raise different issues, it is anticipated that uniform policies[4281] based on common trademark principles can effectively cover the needful from the perspective of trademarks.

As was seen in Chapter 4, an adapted policy, the UDNDRP was recommended for and based largely on the UDRP with supplemental elements and adjustments based on the Digital Trademark and Trade Practices Model. In this chapter, a uniform policy modelled against the UDNDRP was recommended for each platform under consideration. Such policies would serve the platforms well and fill or mitigate the gaps identified. Guidelines will help to interpret the uniform policies for each platform. As also mentioned in Chapter 4, the UDNDRP has benefits for small businesses and digital consumers, and these benefits extend to the adapted policies mentioned for platforms in this chapter. An additional benefit will be consistency across platforms for such small businesses, which provides for legal certainty and adoption of similar approaches to trademarks used in different platforms. For digital consumers, this may mean a more consistent experience across platforms.

While the main recommendation is that each platform individually adopt a uniform policy, or that a UDRP panel approach be adopted for like platforms, there are other options that come out of this book. For example, it is contemplated that the above uniform policies might be able to be consolidated into a single uniform policy applicable to all platforms under this study. This would mean an adjustment of some of the terms to incorporate all platforms, and guidance would need to be expanded to include interpretation and examples from the various platforms. In this way, a single policy may apply for ease of incorporation by all platforms. Guidelines will need to be detailed to cover any peculiarities or provide for examples across platforms, as needed, although this is achievable.

4281. ICANN, 'Uniform Domain-Name Dispute-Resolution Policy' (*ICANN*, 25 February 2012) https://www.icann.org/resources/pages/policy-2012-02-25-en accessed June 2025; WIPO, 'WIPO Overview of WIPO Panel Views on Selected UDRP Questions, Third Edition' ('WIPO Jurisprudential Overview 3.0') (*WIPO*, 2017) https://www.wipo.int/amc/en/domains/search/overview3.0/ accessed June 2025; Rajeev Sachdev, 'Towards an Improved Framework for Trade-Mark Law and Regulation in Social Media Usernames: A Study of the Canadian, U.S., and U.K. Positions' (2016) 28 Intellectual Property Journal 379, 379-418; Daniel Doft, 'Facebook, Twitter, and the Wild West of IP Enforcement on Social Media: Weighing the Merits of a Uniform Dispute Resolution Policy' (2016) 49 The John Marshall Law Review 959; Thomas J Curtin, 'The Name Game: Cybersquatting and Trademark Infringement on Social Media Websites' (2010-2011) 19 Journal of Law and Policy 353; Erick J Heels, 'How to Twittersquat the Top 100 Brands' (GiantPeople, 8 January 2009) http://www.giantpeople.com/1298.html accessed 4 August 2025; Paul D McGrady, McGrady on Social Media: 2018 (Lexis Nexis 2018) §9; John McElwaine and Christopher D Casavale, 'Tackling Bad Faith Registration of Domain Names in a Fast-Changing Landscape' (*WIPO Magazine*, December 2019) https://www.wipo.int/wipo_magazine/en/2019/06/article_0006.html accessed June 2025.

CHAPTER 6
Conclusion and Implementation

A summary of recommendations for the UDRP and platform policies is provided. This is followed by a brief guide to implementation of the recommended uniform policies.

6.1 SUMMARY OF RECOMMENDATIONS FOR THE UDRP AND PLATFORM POLICIES RELATING TO DIGITAL TRADEMARKS

Overall, recommendations were made for the UDRP and platform policies relating to digital trademarks, specifically in the following platforms: (1) e-commerce marketplace, (2) search advertising, (3) social media, (4) mobile application, and (5) Metaverse.

6.1.1 Key Problems and the Digital Trademark and Trade Practices Model

In Chapter 2, the key problems pertaining to digital trademarks, specifically in e-commerce marketplace, search advertising, social media, mobile app, and Metaverse platforms were identified and an adapted model was developed to inform trademark issues in these platforms.

The first problem is that 'use'[4282] and specifically where marks are used on the Internet are not adequately dealt with by policies/platforms.[4283] Assessing use[4284] of

4282. TRIPS, Art. 16; EUTMR, Art. 18; 15 U.S. Code § 1127; UK Trade Marks Act 1994, s. 46(1)(a); Canadian Trademarks Act R.S.C., 1985, c. T-13, s. 2.

4283. WIPO, 'WIPO Overview of WIPO Panel Views on Selected UDRP Questions, Third Edition' ('WIPO Jurisprudential Overview 3.0') (*WIPO*, 2017) https://www.wipo.int/amc/en/domains/search/overview3.0/ accessed June 2025.

4284. TRIPS, Art. 16; EUTMR, Art. 18; 15 U.S. Code § 1127; UK Trade Marks Act 1994, s. 46(1)(a); Canadian Trademarks Act R.S.C., 1985, c. T-13, s. 2.

trademarks and the place[4285] where these are used[4286] is problematic on the Internet because there are numerous places and the platforms and the context may impact a trademark assessment. Not all utilisation of marks is commercial or in the 'course of trade'[4287] and it is not always easy to assess whether it is.

Second, trademarks may easily and on large scale be utilised in bad faith[4288] and abused[4289] on the Internet and this is not adequately addressed by policies/platforms. While the UDRP addresses 'bad faith',[4290] it does so, in part, from the perspective of unfair acts.[4291] The ACPA requires 'bad faith'[4292] for a domain name to be transferred to a complainant.[4293] Certain ccTLD policies require or have 'bad faith'[4294] as an alternative grounds.[4295] While incorporated in the context of domain names, limited platform policies specifically consider 'bad faith'[4296] and many do not do this adequately. Further, persistent (or repeated)[4297] 'bad faith'[4298] in the form of abuse[4299] is dealt with on a limited basis by the UDRP and platforms.

4285. WIPO, 'WIPO Overview of WIPO Panel Views on Selected UDRP Questions, Third Edition' ('WIPO Jurisprudential Overview 3.0') (*WIPO*, 2017) https://www.wipo.int/amc/en/domains/search/overview3.0/ accessed June 2025.
4286. TRIPS, Art. 16; EUTMR, Art. 18; 15 U.S. Code § 1127; UK Trade Marks Act 1994, s. 46(1)(a); Canadian Trademarks Act R.S.C., 1985, c. T-13, s. 2.
4287. TRIPS, Art. 16.
4288. UDRP, 4(a)(iii).
4289. WIPO, 'WIPO Overview of WIPO Panel Views on Selected UDRP Questions, Third Edition' ('WIPO Jurisprudential Overview 3.0') (*WIPO*, 2017) https://www.wipo.int/amc/en/domains/search/overview3.0/ accessed June 2025.
4290. UDRP, 4(a)(iii).
4291. Anselm Kamperman Sanders, *Unfair Competition Law: The Protection of Intellectual and Industrial Creativity* (Oxford University Press, 1997) 8; Frauke Henning-Bodewig, *Unfair Competition Law European Union and Member States* (Kluwer Law International 2006) xv-xvi; Martin Senftleben, Michael Handler and Irene Calboli, 'Protection Against Unfair Competition Around the Globe' (2024) 19 Journal of Intellectual Property Law & Practice 79, 79-80 https://doi.org/10.1093/jiplp/jpad121; Paris Convention, Art. 10bis; EUTMR, Art. 9(2)(c); 15 U.S.C. § 1125(c)(2)(B).
4292. 15 U.S. Code § 1125(d).
4293. *Ibid.*
4294. WIPO, 'WIPO Domain Name Dispute Resolution Service for .EU (and.ею and.ευ)' (*WIPO*) https://www.wipo.int/amc/en/domains/cctld/eu/index.html accessed July 2024; Registry Services, 'UsTLD Dispute Resolution Policy' (*Registry Services*, LLC, 2021) https://www.about.us/documents/policies/usTLD_Dispute_Resolution_Policy_(usDRP).pdf accessed July 2024.
4295. WIPO, 'WIPO Domain Name Dispute Resolution Service for .EU (and.ею and.ευ)' (*WIPO*) https://www.wipo.int/amc/en/domains/cctld/eu/index.html accessed July 2024; Anne-Laure Covin and Edward J Fennesey, *Trademarks Throughout the World* (Thomson West 2007) §54:32.
4296. *Ibid.*
4297. WIPO, 'WIPO Overview of WIPO Panel Views on Selected UDRP Questions, Third Edition' ('WIPO Jurisprudential Overview 3.0') (*WIPO*, 2017) https://www.wipo.int/amc/en/domains/search/overview3.0/ accessed June 2025.
4298. ICANN, 'Uniform Domain-Name Dispute-Resolution Policy' (ICANN, 25 February 2012) https://www.icann.org/resources/pages/policy-2012-02-25-en; 15 U.S. Code § 1125(d).
4299. WIPO, 'WIPO Overview of WIPO Panel Views on Selected UDRP Questions, Third Edition' ('WIPO Jurisprudential Overview 3.0') (*WIPO*, 2017) https://www.wipo.int/amc/en/domains/search/overview3.0/ accessed June 2025.

Third, utilising marks may cause 'confusion'[4300] on the Internet and this is somewhat but not adequately addressed by policies/platforms. The standards or the factors that may be used to assess confusion,[4301] while offering some clarity for the UDRP, are unclear for most platforms.

Fourth, there may be unfair competition[4302] involving marks on the Internet and this is not adequately addressed by policies/platforms. Engaging in unfair acts, trade practices[4303] or competition[4304] (including dilution,[4305] taking unfair advantage,[4306] passing off,[4307] etc.) with respect to trademarks in domain names and platforms can be problematic, although is not adequately and clearly addressed. Counterfeiting[4308] appears to be focus that is addressed by most platforms. Relatedly, whether and the extent to which well-known,[4309] famous,[4310] strong,[4311] reputable marks[4312] will be afforded greater protection in platforms is unclear and this has only been dealt with in some instances.

Fifth, terms, domain and platform policies inadequately address marks on the Internet.[4313] While a uniform policy, the UDRP, exists for covered domain names, this

4300. Paris Convention, Art. 6bis; TRIPS, Art. 16(1); EUTMR, Art. 8(1)(b) and Art. 9(2)(b); 15 U.S. Code § 1114;15 U.S. Code § 1125.
4301. *Ibid.*
4302. *Ibid.*
4303. *Ibid.*
4304. *Ibid.*
4305. EUTMR, Art. 9(2)(c); 15 U.S.C. § 1125(c)(2)(B).
4306. EUTMR, Art. 9(2)(c).
4307. Martin Senftleben, Michael Handler and Irene Calboli, 'Protection Against Unfair Competition Around the Globe' (2024) 19 Journal of Intellectual Property Law & Practice 79.
4308. Amazon, 'Intellectual Property Policy for Sellers: FAQ about Trademarks' (*Amazon*) https://sellercentral.amazon.com/help/hub/reference/external/GZUQ6GBBXQVHQKF2 accessed July 2024; eBay, 'Forgeries, Replicas and Unauthorized Copies Policy' (*eBay NL*) https://www.ebay.nl/help/policies/prohibited-restricted-items/fake-items-policy?id=4276 accessed July 2024; Google, 'Counterfeit Goods' (*Google Advertising Policies Help*) https://support.google.com/adspolicy/answer/176017?hl=en&ref_topic=1626336&sjid=17722085019300892729-NA accessed July 2024.
4309. Paris Convention, Art. 6bis; TRIPS, Art. 16(2); EUTMR, Art. 8(2)(c).
4310. Stefan Martin, 'Well Known Marks and Parody: Dilution and Denigration? Unfair Advantage?' (*EUIPO*, 2017), https://euipo.europa.eu/knowledge/pluginfile.php/77920/mod_resource/content/8/Limits%20of%20trade%20marks%2C%20Parody%2018-5-2017.pdf accessed January 2024.
4311. Timothy D Greene and Jeff Wilkerson, 'Understanding Trademark Strength' (2013) 16 Stanford Technology Law Review 535-582, abstract.
4312. EUTMR, Arts 8(5) and 9(1)(c).
4313. UDRP; Rajeev Sachdev, 'Towards an Improved Framework for Trade-Mark Law and Regulation in Social Media Usernames: A Study of the Canadian, U.S., and U.K. Positions' (2016) 28 Intellectual Property Journal 379, 379-418; Daniel Doft, 'Facebook, Twitter, and the Wild West of IP Enforcement on Social Media: Weighing the Merits of a Uniform Dispute Resolution Policy' (2016) 49 The John Marshall Law Review 959; Thomas J Curtin, 'The Name Game: Cybersquatting and Trademark Infringement on Social Media Websites' (2010-2011) 19 Journal of Law and Policy 353; Erick J Heels, 'How to Twittersquat the Top 100 Brands' (*GiantPeople*, 8 January 2009) http://www.giantpeople.com/1298.html accessed 4 August 2025; Paul D McGrady, *McGrady on Social Media and the Metaverse* (Mathew Bender & Company, Inc. 2023) §12.

does not extend to platforms.[4314] Platform policies are not consistent, often unclear, and are not adequate. The effect and use of disclaimers[4315] are largely unclear for platforms.

Sixth, the Internet is global in nature and rules are mostly jurisdictional and this is not adequately addressed by policies/platforms.[4316] While treaties establish minimum standards,[4317] trademark rules are largely jurisdictional.[4318] This challenges the notion of the Internet and a complicated patchwork of rules, terms, and policies creates legal uncertainty.

Seventh, how defences and justifications may apply is unclear for marks on the Internet and this is not adequately addressed by policies/platforms.[4319] While the UDRP addresses justifications to some extent, it does so by first requiring a prima facie case to be established before shifting the burden.[4320] Some platforms clarify permissible justifications, while for others, this is largely unclear.

These problems lead to the development of an adapted model, the Digital Trademark and Trade Practices Model. The elements of the model include the following:

4314. Rajeev Sachdev, 'Towards an Improved Framework for Trade-Mark Law and Regulation in Social Media Usernames: A Study of the Canadian, U.S., and U.K. Positions' (2016) 28 Intellectual Property Journal 379, 379-418; Daniel Doft, 'Facebook, Twitter, and the Wild West of IP Enforcement on Social Media: Weighing the Merits of a Uniform Dispute Resolution Policy' (2016) 49 The John Marshall Law Review 959; Thomas J Curtin, 'The Name Game: Cybersquatting and Trademark Infringement on Social Media Websites' (2010-2011) 19 Journal of Law and Policy 353; Erick J Heels, 'How to Twittersquat the Top 100 Brands' (*GiantPeople*, 8 January 2009) http://www.giantpeople.com/1298.html accessed 4 August 2025; Paul D McGrady, *McGrady on Social Media and the Metaverse* (Mathew Bender & Company, Inc. 2023) §12.

4315. WIPO, 'WIPO Overview of WIPO Panel Views on Selected UDRP Questions, Third Edition' ('WIPO Jurisprudential Overview 3.0') (*WIPO*, 2017) https://www.wipo.int/amc/en/domains/search/overview3.0/ accessed June 2025; Alexander Peukert, 'The Coexistence of Trade Mark Laws and Rights on the Internet, and the Impact of Geolocation Technologies' (2016) 47 International Review of Intellectual Property and Competition Law 60, 81 https://doi.org/10.1007/s40319-015-0427-8; Leslie Fair, 'Full Disclosure' (*FTC Business Blog*, 23 September 2014) https://www.ftc.gov/business-guidance/blog/2014/09/full-disclosure accessed June 2025.

4316. Roger E Schecter and John R Thomas, *Principles of Trademark Law* (West Academic Publishing, 2021) 385; Alexander Peukert, 'The Coexistence of Trade Mark Laws and Rights on the Internet, and the Impact of Geolocation Technologies' (2016) 47 International Review of Intellectual Property and Competition Law 60, 81 https://doi.org/10.1007/s40319-015-0427-8.

4317. Paris Convention, TRIPS.

4318. Julien Chaisse, 'The Merging of Two Worlds: Cyber Law and Trade Law Normative Convergence on Internet Domain Names' (2019) 37 Boston University International Law Journal 281; Brendan J Witherell, 'Trademark Law: The Extraterritorial Application of the Lanham Act – The First Circuit Cuts the Fat from the Vanity Fair Test' (2006) 29 Western New England Law Review 193, 197.

4319. The Constitution of the United States of America, The Charter of Fundamental Rights of the European Union; Constitution Act, 1982, Canadian Charter of Rights and Freedoms; Paris Convention, Art. 6bis; TRIPS, Art. 16; 15 U.S. Code § 1127; EUTMR, Art. 18.

4320. ICANN, 'Uniform Domain-Name Dispute-Resolution Policy' (*ICANN*, 25 February 2012) https://www.icann.org/resources/pages/policy-2012-02-25-en accessed June 2025.

6.1.1.1 *Digital Use and Place of Use*[4321]

This element considers how a mark is used[4322] on the Internet, including whether in the 'course of trade'.[4323] It also considers the place,[4324] or specifically where the mark is used on the Internet because there are an increasing number of places where a mark can be used across platforms.

6.1.1.2 *Digital Bad Faith and Abuse*[4325]

This element considers the many ways where trademarks may be utilised in 'bad faith'[4326] and how to assess this as distinguished from unfair competition[4327] (separate element of the model below). The role of 'abuse'[4328] on the Internet is also considered, including repeated 'bad faith'.[4329]

6.1.1.3 *Digital Confusion*[4330]

This element considers how this key infringement standard may be assessed on the Internet, including the factors which may be used to make such an assessment.

4321. TRIPS, Art. 16; EUTMR, Art. 18; 15 U.S. Code § 1127; UK Trade Marks Act 1994, s. 46(1)(a); Canadian Trademarks Act R.S.C., 1985, c. T-13, s. 2.
4322. *Ibid.*
4323. TRIPS, Art. 16.
4324. WIPO, 'WIPO Overview of WIPO Panel Views on Selected UDRP Questions, Third Edition' ('WIPO Jurisprudential Overview 3.0') (*WIPO*, 2017) https://www.wipo.int/amc/en/domains/search/overview3.0/ accessed June 2025.
4325. ICANN, 'Uniform Domain-Name Dispute-Resolution Policy' (*ICANN*, 25 February 2012) https://www.icann.org/resources/pages/policy-2012-02-25-en accessed June 2025; WIPO, 'WIPO Overview of WIPO Panel Views on Selected UDRP Questions, Third Edition' ('WIPO Jurisprudential Overview 3.0') (*WIPO*, 2017) https://www.wipo.int/amc/en/domains/search/overview3.0/ accessed June 2025.
4326. UDRP, 4(a)(iii).
4327. *Ibid.*
4328. WIPO, 'WIPO Overview of WIPO Panel Views on Selected UDRP Questions, Third Edition' ('WIPO Jurisprudential Overview 3.0') (*WIPO*, 2017) https://www.wipo.int/amc/en/domains/search/overview3.0/ accessed June 2025.
4329. ICANN, 'Uniform Domain-Name Dispute-Resolution Policy' (ICANN, 25 February 2012) https://www.icann.org/resources/pages/policy-2012-02-25-en accessed June 2025; WIPO, 'WIPO Overview of WIPO Panel Views on Selected UDRP Questions, Third Edition' ('WIPO Jurisprudential Overview 3.0') (*WIPO*, 2017) https://www.wipo.int/amc/en/domains/search/overview3.0/ accessed June 2025.
4330. Paris Convention, Art. 6bis; TRIPS, Art. 16(1); EUTMR, Art. 8(1)(b) and Art. 9(2)(b); 15 U.S. Code § 1114;15 U.S. Code § 1125.

6.1.1.4 *Digital Unfair Competition*[4331]

This element considers the importance of incorporating or clarifying unfair competition,[4332] including unfair acts,[4333] unfair trade practices[4334] or unfair competition[4335] and any associated concepts as these apply to and may greatly impact digital trademarks.

6.1.1.5 *Digital Terms, Policies, and Disclaimers*[4336]

This element considers the role of terms and policies (UDRP, platform policies, etc.) on the Internet. The importance, role and impact of disclaimers[4337] is also considered.

6.1.1.6 *Digital Jurisdictional and Territorial Considerations*[4338]

This element considers the 'global nature of the Internet',[4339] the jurisdictional/territorial[4340] rules that may apply, and how this is applied to digital trademarks.

4331. Anselm Kamperman Sanders, *Unfair Competition Law: The Protection of Intellectual and Industrial Creativity* (Oxford University Press, 1997) 8; Frauke Henning-Bodewig, *Unfair Competition Law European Union and Member States* (Kluwer Law International 2006) xv-xvi; Martin Senftleben, Michael Handler and Irene Calboli, 'Protection Against Unfair Competition Around the Globe' (2024) 19 Journal of Intellectual Property Law & Practice 79, 79-80 https://doi.org/10.1093/jiplp/jpad121; Paris Convention, Art. 10bis; EUTMR, Art. 9(2)(c); 15 U.S.C. § 1125(c)(2)(B).
4332. *Ibid.*
4333. *Ibid.*
4334. *Ibid.*
4335. *Ibid.*
4336. WIPO, 'WIPO Overview of WIPO Panel Views on Selected UDRP Questions, Third Edition' ('WIPO Jurisprudential Overview 3.0') (*WIPO*, 2017) https://www.wipo.int/amc/en/domains/search/overview3.0/ accessed June 2025; Alexander Peukert, 'The Coexistence of Trade Mark Laws and Rights on the Internet, and the Impact of Geolocation Technologies' (2016) 47 International Review of Intellectual Property and Competition Law 60, 81 https://doi.org/10.1007/s40319-015-0427-8; Leslie Fair, 'Full Disclosure' (*FTC Business Blog*, 23 September 2014) https://www.ftc.gov/business-guidance/blog/2014/09/full-disclosure accessed June 2025.
4337. *Ibid.*
4338. Julien Chaisse, 'The Merging of Two Worlds: Cyber Law and Trade Law Normative Convergence on Internet Domain Names' (2019) 37 Boston University International Law Journal 281; Brendan J Witherell, 'Trademark Law: The Extraterritorial Application of the Lanham Act – The First Circuit Cuts the Fat from the Vanity Fair Test' (2006) 29 Western New England Law Review 193, 197; Alexander Peukert, 'The Coexistence of Trade Mark Laws and Rights on the Internet, and the Impact of Geolocation Technologies' (2016) 47 International Review of Intellectual Property and Competition Law 60, 81 https://doi.org/10.1007/s40319-015-0427-8.
4339. WIPO, 'WIPO Overview of WIPO Panel Views on Selected UDRP Questions, Third Edition' ('WIPO Jurisprudential Overview 3.0') (*WIPO*, 2017) https://www.wipo.int/amc/en/domains/search/overview3.0/ accessed June 2025.
4340. Julien Chaisse, 'The Merging of Two Worlds: Cyber Law and Trade Law Normative Convergence on Internet Domain Names' (2019) 37 Boston University International Law Journal 281; Brendan J Witherell, 'Trademark Law: The Extraterritorial Application of the Lanham Act –

6.1.1.7 *Digital Justification*[4341]

This element considers the various justifications and defences for digital trademarks.

6.1.2 How the Digital Trademark and Trade Practices Model Is Informed and Resulting Considerations for the UDRP and Platform Policies

Chapter 3 covered how the Digital Trademark and Trade Practices Model is informed by select theories and concepts, and select aspects of the EU and US (with some reference to other) legal frameworks, and what the resulting considerations are for the UDRP and platform policies.

The Digital Trademark and Trade Practices Model is greatly informed by various theories and concepts. For example, but certainly not limited to, use theory,[4342] place of use concept,[4343] bad faith concept,[4344] abuse concept,[4345] confusion theory and concepts,[4346] unfair competition theory,[4347] unfair trade

The First Circuit Cuts the Fat from the Vanity Fair Test' (2006) 29 Western New England Law Review 193, 197; Alexander Peukert, 'The Coexistence of Trade Mark Laws and Rights on the Internet, and the Impact of Geolocation Technologies' (2016) 47 International Review of Intellectual Property and Competition Law 60, 81 https://doi.org/10.1007/s40319-015-0427-8.

4341. ICANN, 'Uniform Domain-Name Dispute-Resolution Policy' (*ICANN*, 25 February 2012) https://www.icann.org/resources/pages/policy-2012-02-25-en accessed 8 August 2025.

4342. Graeme B Dinwoodie and Mark D Janis, 'Confusion Over Use: Contextualism in Trademark Law' (2007) 92 Iowa Law Review 1597 Articles by Maurer Faculty. Paper 361.; Stephen L Carter, 'Does It Matter Whether Intellectual Property Is Property?' https://digitalcommons.law.yale.edu/fss_papers/2259/ accessed 4 August 2025; William Fisher, 'Theories of Intellectual Property' (*Harvard Law*) https://cyber.harvard.edu/people/tfisher/iptheory.pdf accessed 4 August 2025; Shontavia J Johnson, 'Memetic Theory, Trademarks & The Viral Meme Mark' (2013) The John Marshall Law School Review of Intellectual Property Law, 13 John Marshall Review of Intellectual Property Law 96.

4343. EUIPO, '3 Place of Use' (*EUIPO Trade mark guidelines* 2024) https://guidelines.euipo.europa.eu/2214311/1982069/trade-mark-guidelines/3-place-of-use accessed January 2024.

4344. Paris Convention, Art. 6bis; EUTMR, Art. 59; TTAB, 'Fighting Bad Faith Trademark Filings in the United States' (The Honorable Karen S. Kuhlke Administrative Trademark Judge) https://www.jpo.go.jp/e/news/kokusai/tm5/document/bad_faith_seminar2/01.pdf accessed July 2024; UDRP, 4(a)(iii).

4345. WIPO, 'WIPO Overview of WIPO Panel Views on Selected UDRP Questions, Third Edition' ('WIPO Jurisprudential Overview 3.0') (*WIPO*, 2017) https://www.wipo.int/amc/en/domains/search/overview3.0/ accessed June 2025.

4346. Ilanah Fhima and Dev S Gangjee, 'Assessing Likelihood of Confusion', The Confusion Test in European Trade Mark Law (New York, 2019; online edn, Oxford Academic) 160-203 https://doi.org/10.1093/oso/9780199674336.003.0006; Graeme B Dinwoodie and Mark D Janis, 'Confusion Over Use: Contextualism in Trademark Law' (2007) 92 Iowa Law Review 1597; Mark P McKenna, 'A Consumer Decision-Making Theory of Trademark Law' 98 Virginia Law Review 67; William M Landes and Richard A Posner, 'Trademark Law: An Economic Perspective' (1987) 30 The Journal of Law and Economics 265 https://doi.org/10.1086/467138; Lisa L Ouellette, 'The Google Shortcut to Trademark Law' (2014) 102 California Law Review 351; Lisa L Ouellette, 'The Google Shortcut to Trademark Law' (2014) 102 California Law Review 351, 358.

4347. Anselm Kamperman Sanders, *Unfair Competition Law: The Protection of Intellectual and Industrial Creativity* (Oxford University Press, 1997); Christian Riffel, *Protection Against*

practices,[4348] passing off concept,[4349] marketing and branding theories,[4350] dilution theory, unfair advantage, free riding, misappropriation concepts,[4351] disclaimers,[4352] fair use,[4353] freedom of expression,[4354] free speech,[4355] and parody concepts[4356] all inform the model.

Further, select aspects of the legal frameworks in the EU and US and reference to others also inform the model. For example, but not limited to, the TRIPS Agreement, the Paris Convention, the EUTMR, the Lanham Act, the ACPA, the TDRA, the U.S. Constitution, the UDRP, and ccTLD policies inform the model.

Based on these, a number of considerations are raised for the UDRP and platforms including in all areas of the model.

Unfair Competition in the WTO TRIPS Agreement: The Scope and Prospects of Article 10bis of the Paris Convention for the Protection of Industrial Property (Brill 2016) 223-224.

4348. Anselm Kamperman Sanders, *Unfair Competition Law: The Protection of Intellectual and Industrial Creativity* (Oxford University Press 1997) 6-10; Frauke Henning-Bodewig, *Unfair Competition Law European Union and Member States* (Kluwer Law International 2006) xv-xvi.

4349. Ethan Horwitz and Benjamin Levi, 'Fifty Years of the Lanham Act: A Retrospective of Section 43(a)E' (1996) 7 Fordham Intellectual Property, Media and Entertainment Law Journal Article 6; David Bainbridge, *Intellectual Property* (Pearson Education Limited 2018) Chapter 30.

4350. Angsar Ohly, '"Buy Me Because I'm Cool": The "Marketing Approach" and the Overlap Between Design, Trade Mark and Unfair Competition Law' in Annette Kur, Marianne Levin and Jens Schovsbo (eds), The EU Design Approach: A Global Appraisal (Edward Elgar 2018) 108-141; Lisa P Ramsey, 'Brandjacking on Social Networks: Trademark Infringement by Impersonation of Markholders' (2010) 58 Buffalo Law Review 851, 856.

4351. Anselm Kamperman Sanders, 'Odol: The Introduction of a Watery Concept with Steeled Resilience' in Christopher Heath and Anselm Kamperman Sanders (eds), *Landmark Intellectual Property Cases and Their Legacy* (Wolters Kluwer 2011) 51-56; Graeme B Dinwoodie, 'Dilution as Unfair Competition: European Echoes' in Rochelle C Dreyfuss and Jane C Ginsburg (eds) *Intellectual Property at the Edge: The Contested Contours of IP* (Cambridge University Press 2014) 100; Frank I Schechter, 'The Rational Basis of Trademark Protection' (1927) 40 Harvard Law Review 813 https://doi.org/10.2307/1330367;15 U.S. Code § 1125(c); Keola R Whitaker, 'Trademark Dilution in a Global Age' (2006) 27 University of Pennsylvania Journal of International Economic Law 907.

4352. WIPO, 'WIPO Overview of WIPO Panel Views on Selected UDRP Questions, Third Edition' ('WIPO Jurisprudential Overview 3.0') (*WIPO*, 2017) https://www.wipo.int/amc/en/domains/search/overview3.0/ accessed June 2025; Alexander Peukert, 'The Coexistence of Trade Mark Laws and Rights on the Internet, and the Impact of Geolocation Technologies' (2016) 47 International Review of Intellectual Property and Competition Law 60, 81 https://doi.org/10.1007/s40319-015-0427-8; Leslie Fair, 'Full Disclosure' (*FTC Business Blog*, 23 September 2014) https://www.ftc.gov/business-guidance/blog/2014/09/full-disclosure accessed June 2025.

4353. EUTMR, Recital 21; 15 U.S. Code § 1115(b)(4); Canadian Trademarks Act R.S.C., 1985, c. T-13, s. 22.

4354. European Convention on Human Rights (ECHR), Art. 10; EU Charter of Fundamental Rights of the EU, Art. 11; Lisa P Ramsey, 'Free Speech and International Obligations to Protect Trademarks' 35 The Yale Journal of International Law 405, 406.

4355. The Constitution of the United States of America, Amendment I.

4356. The Constitution of the United States of America, The Charter of Fundamental Rights of the European Union; Constitution Act, 1982, Canadian Charter of Rights and Freedoms; Paris Convention, Art. 6bis; TRIPS, Art. 16; 15 U.S. Code § 1127; EUTMR, Art. 18.

6.1.3 Recommendations for the UDRP in Light of the Digital Trademark and Trade Practices Model

Chapter 4 covered recommendations for the UDRP in light of the Digital Trademarks and Trade Practices Model. The UDRP serves as a long-standing policy applicable to covered domain names. It provides an efficient, cost-effective, and streamlined way to resolve trademark concerns in domain names.[4357]

However, it should be updated based on the substantial changes to the Internet, the evolutions of trademarks and how these are utilised on the Internet. While a total upheaval was not recommended, several recommendations were made for the UDRP based on the model. For example, some recommendations are to directly state within the policy itself, some of the concepts mentioned in the Overview. It was recommended that, instead of three elements as currently required by the UDRP, it be adapted to require, first, 'confusing similarity'[4358] which is 'unauthorized'[4359] and in the 'course of trade'[4360] AND it should require either 'unfair competition'[4361] in the 'course of trade'[4362] OR 'bad faith or abuse'.[4363] Also, 'legitimate rights and interests'[4364] should

4357. Rajeev Sachdev, 'Towards an Improved Framework for Trade-Mark Law and Regulation in Social Media Usernames: A Study of the Canadian, U.S., and U.K. Positions' (2016) 28 Intellectual Property Journal 379, 379-418; Daniel Doft, 'Facebook, Twitter, and the Wild West of IP Enforcement on Social Media: Weighing the Merits of a Uniform Dispute Resolution Policy' (2016) 49 The John Marshall Law Review 959; Thomas J Curtin, 'The Name Game: Cybersquatting and Trademark Infringement on Social Media Websites' (2010-2011) 19 Journal of Law and Policy 353; Erick J Heels, 'How to Twittersquat the Top 100 Brands' (*GiantPeople*, 8 January 2009) http://www.giantpeople.com/1298.html accessed 4 August 2025; Paul D McGrady, McGrady on Social Media: 2018 (Lexis Nexis 2018) §9; John McElwaine and Christopher D Casavale, 'Tackling Bad Faith Registration of Domain Names in a Fast-Changing Landscape' (*WIPO Magazine*, December 2019) https://www.wipo.int/wipo_magazine/en/2019/06/article_0006.html accessed June 2025.

4358. ICANN, 'Uniform Domain-Name Dispute-Resolution Policy' (ICANN, 25 February 2012) https://www.icann.org/resources/pages/policy-2012-02-25-en accessed June 2025.

4359. WIPO, 'WIPO Overview of WIPO Panel Views on Selected UDRP Questions, Third Edition' ('WIPO Jurisprudential Overview 3.0') (*WIPO*, 2017) https://www.wipo.int/amc/en/domains/search/overview3.0/ accessed June 2025; *Banco Itau S.A. v. Laercio Teixeira* Case No. D2007-0912 https://www.wipo.int/amc/en/domains/decisions/html/2007/d2007-0912.html accessed July 2024.

4360. TRIPS, Art. 16.

4361. Anselm Kamperman Sanders, *Unfair Competition Law: The Protection of Intellectual and Industrial Creativity* (Oxford University Press, 1997) 8; Frauke Henning-Bodewig, *Unfair Competition Law European Union and Member States* (Kluwer Law International 2006) xv-xvi; Martin Senftleben, Michael Handler and Irene Calboli, 'Protection Against Unfair Competition Around the Globe' (2024) 19 Journal of Intellectual Property Law & Practice 79, 79-80 https://doi.org/10.1093/jiplp/jpad121; Paris Convention, Art. 10bis; EUTMR, Art. 9(2)(c); 15 U.S.C. § 1125(c)(2)(B).

4362. TRIPS, Art. 16.

4363. Paris Convention, Art. 6bis; EUTMR, Art. 59; TTAB, 'Fighting Bad Faith Trademark Filings in the United States' (The Honorable Karen S. Kuhlke Administrative Trademark Judge) https://www.jpo.go.jp/e/news/kokusai/tm5/document/bad_faith_seminar2/01.pdf accessed July 2024; UDRP, 4(a)(iii); WIPO, 'WIPO Overview of WIPO Panel Views on Selected UDRP Questions, Third Edition. ('WIPO Jurisprudential Overview 3.0') (*WIPO*, 2017) https://www.wipo.int/amc/en/domains/search/overview3.0/ accessed June 2025.

4364. UDRP, 4(A)(ii).

be factored in as permitted uses (justifications) rather than an element that a complainant should need to prove.

This resulted in the recommended amended UDRP called the Uniform Domain Name Dispute Resolution Policy (UDNDRP) as the current name does not reflect the limitation that this is only for covered domain names. The UDNDRP is largely based on the UDRP with considerations from the Digital Trademark and Trade Practices Model while still maintaining the template-like approach that the UDRP provides.

Further, guidelines should be established alongside this new recommended amended policy to illustrate factors and considerations for each of the key aspects of the policy, including, for example, factors that may be used to assess confusion,[4365] bad faith,[4366] unfair competition,[4367] fair use,[4368] etc.

Together, these will provide for enhanced legal certainty, clarified language, adoption of relevant principles within the policy language itself, alternative grounds where appropriate, and guidance as needed. This not only benefits various trademark holders including small businesses but also digital consumers.

6.1.4 Recommendations for Platform Trademark Policies

Chapter 5 covered recommendations for platform trademark policies in light of the UDRP, recommendations for the UDRP, and the Digital Trademark and Trade Practices model.

A review of the trademark-related policies and terms for major e-commerce marketplace, search ad, social media, mobile app and Metaverse platforms was conducted. These were considered in light of the UDRP and the model and gaps were identified. Many platform policies, while covering some of the needed elements, were found to be inconsistent, lacking in coverage or adequate coverage, containing policies and rules within various documents or links, and sometimes confusing or too general to effectively apply.

In light of the UDRP and the UDNDRP, various recommendations were made for platforms. A uniform policy, similar to the UDNDRP was recommended for each type of platform.[4369] This would help resolve or mitigate many of the problems identified.

4365. Paris Convention, Art. 6bis; TRIPS, Art. 16(1); EUTMR, Art. 8(1)(b) and Art. 9(2)(b); 15 U.S. Code § 1114;15 U.S. Code § 1125.
4366. UDRP, 4(A)(iii).
4367. *Ibid.*
4368. EUTMR, Recital 21; 15 U.S. Code § 1115(b)(4); Canadian Trademarks Act R.S.C., 1985, c. T-13, s. 22.
4369. Edward C Anderson and Timothy S Cole, 'The UDRP: A Model for Dispute Resolution in E-Commerce' (2002) 6 Journal of Small & Emerging Business Law 235; Rajeev Sachdev, 'Towards an Improved Framework for Trade-Mark Law and Regulation in Social Media Usernames: A Study of the Canadian, U.S., and U.K. Positions' (2016) 28 Intellectual Property Journal 379, 379-418; Daniel Doft, 'Facebook, Twitter, and the Wild West of IP Enforcement on Social Media: Weighing the Merits of a Uniform Dispute Resolution Policy' (2016) 49 The John Marshall Law Review 959; Thomas J Curtin, 'The Name Game: Cybersquatting and Trademark Infringement on Social Media Websites' (2010-2011) 19 Journal of Law and Policy 353; Erick J Heels, 'How to Twittersquat the Top 100 Brands' (GiantPeople, 8 January 2009) http://www.giantpeople.com/1298.html accessed 4 August 2025; Paul D McGrady, *McGrady*

Further, it could be adopted by individual platforms directly in replacement of their current trademark policies and they can then make their own decisions on complaints filed. Alternatively, platforms may agree to adopt a panel approach in line with how covered domain disputes are decided under the UDRP. These policies could even potentially be consolidated into one single policy applicable to all platforms.

As with the UDNDRP, implementation of the recommended platform policies will provide for uniform approaches, enhanced legal certainty, clarified language, adoption of relevant principles and relevant guidance. This not only benefits various trademark holders including small businesses but also digital consumers who can know what to expect across platforms.

Overall, it is hoped that platforms consider the outcomes of the problems identified and adopt the recommended policies drafted for this purpose.

6.2 GUIDE TO IMPLEMENTATION OF RECOMMENDED UNIFORM POLICIES

Given the above conclusions, it is important for the proper implementation of the recommendations. This section provides practical guidance for the implementation for both the proposed UDNDRP and the proposed platform policies.

6.2.1 Implementing the Proposed UDNDRP

It is recognised that an update to the UDRP continues to involve a deliberate process which entails various steps and can take some time.[4370] While this guide does not outline all of the detailed procedural steps to update the UDRP, if it is ultimately updated with the recommendations outlined in Chapter 4, the following serves as brief guidance for additional implementation that is recommended to take place.

6.2.1.1 Update Policy

The UDRP should be updated with the wording outlined in Chapter 4 and the name should be changed to UDNDRP. To achieve this, recommendations would need to be taken into consideration by ICANN. More specifically, these could be considered during the 'GNSO's Phase 2 Policy Development Process (PDP) on the Review of Rights Protection Mechanisms' or other processes.[4371]

---

on Social Media: 2018 (Lexis Nexis 2018) §9; John McElwaine and Christopher D Casavale, 'Tackling Bad Faith Registration of Domain Names in a Fast-Changing Landscape' (*WIPO Magazine*, December 2019) https://www.wipo.int/wipo_magazine/en/2019/06/article_0006.html accessed June 2025.

4370. ICANN, 'Revised Uniform Domain Name Dispute Resolution Policy (UDRP) Status Report' (ICANN, July 2022) https://gnso.icann.org/sites/default/files/file/field-file-attach/udrp-status-report-redlined-13jul22-en.pdf accessed July 2024.

4371. ICANN, 'GNSO Council Meetings' Motions 2024-11-13 – GNSO Council Meetings – Confluence accessed June 2025; ICANN, 'Revised Uniform Domain Name Dispute Resolution Policy (UDRP) Status Report' (ICANN, July 2022) https://gnso.icann.org/sites/default/files/file/

6.2.1.2 Guidelines Should Be Created

The Overview[4372] is a very helpful and welcomed document which sets forth valuable information for domain name registrants, trademark holders, and panellists alike. Using key information from this document, Guidelines to the UDNDRP should be developed to help interpret the new policy. Importantly, these guidelines should use common principles to address what is meant by specific terms in the policy. For example, common factors to assess 'confusing similarity'[4373] should be provided to include common trademark principles of a 'likelihood of confusion'[4374] test. They should document how the platform will interpret base principles of unfair competition,[4375] such as what is included in 'unfair competition',[4376] such as 'passing off'[4377] or 'free riding'.[4378] While these may be complex concepts, the key common ways in which 'unfair competition'[4379] does or may take place in the platform should be covered in line with the Paris Convention.

6.2.1.3 Panel Training and Calibration Sessions

Panels should be provided training on the policy, guidelines, and procedures. Calibration sessions[4380] should be required whereby appropriate methods of promoting consistency and application are fostered.

---

field-file-attach/udrp-status-report-redlined-13jul22-en.pdf accessed July 2025; ICANN IPC, 'Comment on the Initial Report of the WIPO-ICA UDRP Review Project Team' (*WIPO*, 2025) https://www.wipo.int/export/sites/www/amc/en/docs/commentsjune27-6.pdf accessed June 2025.

4372. WIPO, 'WIPO Overview of WIPO Panel Views on Selected UDRP Questions, Third Edition' ('WIPO Jurisprudential Overview 3.0') (*WIPO*, 2017) https://www.wipo.int/amc/en/domains/search/overview3.0/ accessed June 2025.
4373. UDRP, 4(a)(i).
4374. Paris Convention, Art. 6bis; TRIPS, Art. 16(1); EUTMR, Art. 8(1)(b) and Art. 9(2)(b); 15 U.S. Code § 1114;15 U.S. Code § 1125.
4375. Anselm Kamperman Sanders, *Unfair Competition Law: The Protection of Intellectual and Industrial Creativity* (Oxford University Press 1997) 6-10; Frauke Henning-Bodewig, *Unfair Competition Law European Union and Member States* (Kluwer Law International 2006) xv-xvi.
4376. *Ibid.*
4377. Ethan Horwitz and Benjamin Levi, 'Fifty Years of the Lanham Act: A Retrospective of Section 43(a)E' (1996) 7 Fordham Intellectual Property, Media and Entertainment Law Journal Article 6; David Bainbridge, *Intellectual Property* (Pearson Education Limited 2018) Chapter 30.
4378. Anselm Kamperman Sanders, 'Odol: The Introduction of a Watery Concept with Steeled Resilience' in Christopher Heath and Anselm Kamperman Sanders (eds), *Landmark Intellectual Property Cases and Their Legacy* (Wolters Kluwer 2011) 51-56; Graeme B Dinwoodie, 'Dilution as Unfair Competition: European Echoes' in Rochelle C Dreyfuss and Jane C Ginsburg (eds) *Intellectual Property at the Edge: The Contested Contours of IP* (Cambridge University Press 2014) 100; Frank I Schechter, 'The Rational Basis of Trademark Protection' (1927) 40 Harvard Law Review 813 https://doi.org/10.2307/1330367;15 U.S. Code § 1125(c); Keola R Whitaker, 'Trademark Dilution in a Global Age' (2006) 27 University of Pennsylvania Journal of International Economic Law 907.
4379. *Ibid.*
4380. Law Society of Ireland, 'Sport Dispute Solutions Ireland', (*Judicial Chair*, 2019) https://www.lawsociety.ie/globalassets/documents/news/archive/2019/judicial_chair_final.pdf accessed June 2025.

6.2.2 Implementing the Proposed Platform Policies

A commitment to adopt a uniform policy among platforms will breed the many benefits as described throughout this book. Yet, the effective implementation of a uniform policy requires a thoughtful approach by management and platform counsel and advisors. Below are approaches, to serve as a guide, by which the recommended uniform policies may be implemented. Two possible approaches were discussed in Chapter 5, the first, where platforms will continue to be the decision makers on complaints filed, and the second, where an external panel approach is adopted. Both are discussed in turn.

6.2.2.1 Uniform Trademark Dispute Resolution Policies (UEMTDRP, USATDRP, USMTDRP, UMATDRP, UMTDRP): Platform Decision Making Approach

6.2.2.1.1 Update Policy

Platforms should create an updated policy in accordance with the uniform policies recommended for their type of platform, as seen in Chapter 5. The platform should establish an effective date in accordance with current policies and contractual requirements, as to when this policy will go into effect.

6.2.2.1.2 Officially Incorporate into Terms and Consolidate into One Document

The uniform policy recommended for each platform includes wording to incorporate by reference into specific terms and contracts, such as an account, seller agreement, advertising agreement, etc. For example, the terms (or terms of use, or conditions of use, etc.) of a platform may incorporate the uniform policy directly into their terms. All policies that pertain to trademarks and trade practices should refer back to the policy or incorporate it within. Therefore, the uniform policy should be reflected in one single document.

6.2.2.1.3 Create Guidelines

Guidelines to the policy should be established by the platform for its users, including account holders, contributors, sellers, advertisers, etc. These guidelines should be created based on the discussion provided for the UDRP in the previous sub-section.

For e-commerce with country specific sites or platforms targeting specific jurisdictions, the guidance should make clear that local law, although unlikely needed, may be applied in relevant decisions. This will help avoid country specific rules but does not prohibit it from applying the same in relevant circumstances. Alternatively, the guidelines may state that the uniform policy shall be applied in ways relevant to the jurisdiction relating to the dispute. Nevertheless, it is anticipated that a platform can elicit specific actions that fall within common principles and use those as examples.

6.2.2.1.4 *Use in Conjunction with Not only Trademark Use in Platform but also Trademark and Brand Protection Services and Tools*

Some platforms provide services that may be relevant to trademark and brand holders. For example, the Amazon Brand Registry,[4381] eBay's VeRO[4382] and like services should be based on the same uniform policy applicable to the platform.

6.2.2.1.5 *Make Publicly Available*

The policy and guidelines should be publicly available; the latter preferably being linked from the Homepage or other conspicuous place of each of the platform sites to which it applies. The guidelines should be linked from the policy itself.

6.2.2.1.6 *Notification/Agreement*

It is important to ensure all relevant parties receive a link to the publicly available policy and associated guidelines and, if and as required, obtain their agreement. New users should also receive and agree to these when creating an account, advertising, listing, signing up, etc.

6.2.2.1.7 *Encourage Parties to Resolve Their Disputes*

Despite the policy, parties should still be encouraged to resolve their disputes.[4383] This should be set forth at relevant intervals such as in forms, guidance, and other places.

6.2.2.1.8 *Update Forms and Create Counter Form*

Trademark and trade practice-related forms should be updated to reflect the new policy and guidelines. Those filling these forms should be required to explain, in line with the policy, how they believe, for example, their trademark is being infringed. They should be encouraged to use the guidelines to help them prepare their reasoning. It may be best to create selection options, as some platforms do,[4384] whereby specific reasons may be selected (such as trademark infringement, or counterfeit product, etc.).[4385]

4381. Amazon, 'Let's Protect the Brand You Built' (*Amazon Brand Registry*) https://sell.amazon.com/brand-registry accessed June 2025; Amazon.nl, 'Amazon Brand Registry' (*Amazon.nl*) https://sell.amazon.nl/brand-registry accessed June 2025.
4382. eBay, 'Intellectual Property Policy' (*eBay*) https://www.ebay.nl/help/policies/listing-policies/selling-policies/vero-policy?id=4349 accessed June 2025.
4383. Apple, 'App Store Content Dispute' (*Apple*) https://www.apple.com/legal/intellectual-property/dispute-forms/app-store/ accessed June 2025.
4384. eBay, 'Verified Rights Owner Program' (*eBay*) https://www.ebay.com/sellercenter/ebay-for-business/verified-rights-owner-program#m17-1-tb2 accessed June 2025.
4385. *Ibid.*

A counter notice or form (as implemented by some platforms)[4386] should be created to allow a responding party to submit their justification. This should not prevent platforms from removing, pausing, or otherwise taking down content, such as in clear cut cases, even if temporarily.

6.2.2.1.9 Establish Employee and Decision Maker Training

All relevant employees should be familiar with the new policy and guidelines. However, decision makers who will be deciding on the result of complaints filed should be provided with specialised training.

6.2.2.1.10 Monitor Activity and Results

Platforms should monitor the number, types of complaints, and resulting decisions. This may allow the platform to consider further strategies to combat specific types of violations. Further, this information may be helpful to improve the guidelines to the policy.

6.2.2.1.11 Provide Publicly Available Information and Data

Platforms should consider what information they might disclose publicly. This can provide enhanced trust and showcase the benefits of implementation of the new policy. Platforms may provide analytics for transparency.[4387]

6.2.2.2 Uniform Trademark Dispute Resolution Policies (UEMTDRP, USATDRP, USMTDRP, UMATDRP, UMTDRP): Panel Approach

If adopting a panel approach, where a panel will decide on trademark matters pertinent to disputes within a platform (such as Amazon does for utility patents[4388] as well as the method that is used for the UDRP),[4389] the above implementation will largely be the same excepting the alternative language provided in the proposed policies in Chapter 5 would be needed. Additionally, the following measures should be considered:

4386. LinkedIn, 'LinkedIn's Trademark Policy' (*LinkedIn Help*) https://www.linkedin.com/help/linkedin/answer/a1337296?trk=d_microsites-frontend_legal_copyright-policy&lang=en accessed June 2025.
4387. Meta, 'Notice and Takedown' (*Meta Transparency Center*) https://transparency.meta.com/reports/intellectual-property/notice-and-takedown/facebook/ accessed June 2025.
4388. Amazon, 'Let's Protect the Brand You Built' (*Amazon Brand Registry*) https://sell.amazon.com/brand-registry accessed June 2025; Amazon.nl, 'Amazon Brand Registry' (*Amazon.nl*) https://sell.amazon.nl/brand-registry accessed June 2025.
4389. ICANN, 'Uniform Domain-Name Dispute-Resolution Policy' (ICANN, 25 February 2012) https://www.icann.org/resources/pages/policy-2012-02-25-en accessed June 2025.

6.2.2.2.1 *Establish Pool of Third-Party Panellists or a Contracted Service*

Platforms may establish a pool of panellists as does WIPO[4390] and other bodies who engage these panellists to make decisions on specific matters. The qualities of 'impartiality, sound judgment, and experience'[4391] form the basis on which these should be selected in line with WIPO selection principles. Appropriate levels of resources currently designated to handling complaints within platforms may be redirected towards panel services. It may be considered by platforms, whether to charge a fee to abusive[4392] actors within platforms, such as those who repeatedly abuse trademarks.[4393]

6.2.2.2.2 *Create Panel Guidance*

In order to promote consistency, it will be important not only to have guidelines to the policy but to also implement guidelines for panellists. For example, in given circumstances in line with policy and guidance, panellists should be given the tools and guidance needed to make uniform decisions.

6.2.2.2.3 *Outline Procedures or Requirements*

While it is not anticipated that rules pertinent to panel decisions making are necessary since, at least procedurally, platforms may create or update forms to lodge a complaint, and incorporate procedures associated with the process. Therefore, extensive procedural rules such as the UDRP Rules[4394] are likely not necessary. Platforms may find a simpler approach beneficial and procedural matters such as panel appointment, timelines, and other matters may be indicated on the forms or in the guidance. Forms should also be updated to reflect the panel decisions and any associated procedural matters.

6.2.2.2.4 *Panel Training and Calibration Sessions*

As indicated previously, panels should be given training on the policy, guidelines, and procedures. Further, calibration sessions[4395] will help to promote consistency.

4390. WIPO, 'WIPO Domain Name Panelists' (*WIPO*) https://www.wipo.int/amc/en/domains/panel.html accessed June 2025.
4391. *Ibid.*
4392. *Ibid.*
4393. *Ibid.*
4394. ICANN, 'Rules for Uniform Domain Name Dispute Resolution Policy (the "Rules")' (*ICANN*, 2013) https://www.icann.org/resources/pages/udrp-rules-2015-03-11-en accessed July 2024.
4395. Law Society of Ireland, 'Sport Dispute Solutions Ireland', (*Judicial Chair*, 2019) https://www.lawsociety.ie/globalassets/documents/news/archive/2019/judicial_chair_final.pdf accessed June 2025.

6.2.2.2.5 *Provide Public Information*

Platforms should consider providing public information on panel decisions to the extent feasible and where this does not implicate privacy considerations. At a minimum, reporting, in aggregate, and providing information on the types of activities that resulted in or did not result in a violation decisions should be provided.

Overall, the above present some key areas that platforms and their management and legal advisors will need to consider. A consolidated implementation of the policy, associated guidelines, and the appropriate steps surrounding an implementation will be key to its success.

Table of Selected Legislation, Treaties, Regulations and Directives

Table of Selected Cases and Proceedings

Index

A

B

C

F

G

H

I

J

www.ingramcontent.com/pod-product-compliance
Lightning Source LLC
Chambersburg PA
CBHW071235230926
51849CB00001B/114
9789403541693